INTO THE STORM

THE ASSASSINATION OF PRESIDENT KENNEDY VOLUME III

John M. Newman

Copyright © 2019 John M. Newman
All rights reserved.

ISBN: 9781722648978
Interior design by booknook.biz
Library of Congress Control Number: 2018914241

For Robert Francis Kennedy

If a free society cannot help the many who are poor,
it cannot save the few who are rich.

—John F. Kennedy, Inaugural Address
20 January 1961

ACKNOWLEDGEMENTS

I want to thank my longtime friend and research associate, John, "Jay," C. Harvey, Jr. Jay has been a tremendous help to me for more than twenty-seven years. Our work together began with ***Oswald and the CIA*** and has continued on every project since then. Jay has worked tirelessly with me on the volumes of this new series—they would not exist without his help.

I also want to acknowledge my friend and research associate Alan Dale. Alan became an important part of our team during the research that produced Volume I, ***Where Angels Tread Lightly***. His contributions to Volume II and the long overdue reissue of ***JFK and Vietnam*** were truly remarkable. Alan rendered valuable help, insights and editing—night and day—on every aspect of the present volume.

I want to recognize, once again, the support that Malcolm Blunt has given to me ever since the appearance of ***Oswald and the CIA***. During the course of Volume II and the present volume, Malcolm has been a constant source of crucial details on the internal structure of the CIA and, in general, of trenchant insights on numerous important matters. Malcolm's expertise extends also to the Kennedy presidency—a subject of increasing importance to me as the volumes of my present work continue to unfold. I am fortunate to be working with such an extraordinary researcher again. I want to thank Dan Hardway, once again, for his feedback as a reader of this manuscript and for sharing his essays and thoughts on the case in general with me. I continue to treasure his extensive experience and sharp observations. As researchers, we are all fortunate that Dan continues to apply himself to a wide array of issues important to the Kennedy presidency and case.

I am deeply appreciative of the constant support I have received from Bill Simpich. Bill's interests and knowledge in the Kennedy case span an astonishing breadth of time—from the Cold War to the present. He has been very generous with his time and

INTO THE STORM

a never-ending source of insightful observations. I am very fortunate to have access to such a brilliant researcher. Bill continues to be the indefatigable czar of breaking cryptonyms and pseudonyms—work that all researchers profit from. Thanks also to Rex Bradford, Larry Hancock and Carmine Savastano for their work on cryptonyms. The more I get to know Jerry Shinley, the more I am impressed with his insights and incisive analysis. We worked together on a number of occasions that produced important identifications for this volume.

For more than thirty-five years Peter Dale Scott's works have profoundly impacted mine. He continues to inspire me not only on the Kennedy presidency but also with his visionary works on a wide range of subjects. I want to acknowledge Rex Bradford's continuing great work on the Mary Ferrell Foundation website and all that he does for the research community. Rex's work with the new 2017-2018 releases has been superb and has made the MFF website the most valuable online resource anywhere. I want to thank Joe Backes for his help on matters large and small, including in my search for the elusive KGB mole in American intelligence during the Cold War. Continuing to the present day, this is a hunt that Pete Bagley invited "an alert journalist or historian in the future" to dig deeper for—and lay this *ghost* to rest.

I want to acknowledge the diligent work of my James Madison University intern, Celine Gomes, and her generous assistance for this manuscript. Research for this volume has also required access to materials kept at the National Archives, College Park, MD (NARA II), and I would like to acknowledge the valuable assistance of Gene Morris, Stanley Fanaris and Robert Thompson.

I want to thank the leading members of the Assassination Archives and Research Center (AARC), including Alan Dale, Dan Hardway, Dan Alcorn, Rex Bradford, David Wrone, Randy Robertson, Brenda Brodie, Tink Thompson, Gary Aguilar, David Talbot, Malcolm Blunt, Bill Simpich, Eric Hamburg and, especially our president, James H. Lesar. Jim's Freedom of Information Act requests have led to the release of many gigabytes of documents on Cuba (and other subjects relevant to the Kennedy assassination) without which several of the chapters in this volume (and Volume I) would not have been possible.

I want to acknowledge Debra Conway, Larry Hancock and the other members of the JFK Lancer team for all that they have done to promote the work of so many researchers.

I want to thank my wife and best friend, Sue Newman, who has tirelessly helped me with my research for nearly forty-four years. For this volume, once again, she has generously devoted time and effort as a reader and editor. I want to thank my children, Alexandra Kahler, Mary Singer, and John Newman III for their continuing support and understanding—and for giving me six beautiful grandchildren.

The mistakes in this book are mine.

PROLOGUE

Invasion D+2—17 April 1961

The news that 100 Cuban pilots were being trained in Czechoslovakia, the information that MIGs and other jet planes had already been shipped to Cuba and that these shipments were expected to continue, that thousands of tons of military equipment had arrived each month in Havana, were all matters of consternation. Cuba, it was realized, was swiftly becoming a major military arsenal for all of the activities of the Communist Bloc in the Western Hemisphere.

The alternative to the steps that were taken this past week would have been to sit and wait and hope that in the future some fortuitous event would occur to change the situation. This, it was decided, should not be done. The immediate failure of the rebels' activities in Cuba does not permit us, it seems to me, to return to the status quo with our policy toward Cuba being one of waiting and hoping for good luck. The events in the last few days makes this inconceivable.

Our long-range foreign policy objectives in Cuba are tied to survival far more than what is happening in Laos or the Congo or any other place in the world. Because of the proximity of that island our objective must be at the very least to prevent that island from becoming Mr. Khrushchev's arsenal. In our concern over the present situation, we must not lose sight of our objective.

It seems to me that this is the time to decide what our long-term policies are going to be and what will be the results of those policies. *The time has come for a showdown for in a year or two years the situation will be vastly worse. If we don't want Russia to set up missile bases in Cuba, we had better decide now what we are willing to do to stop it.*

—Attorney General Robert Kennedy, Memorandum to President Kennedy
17 April 1961

TABLE OF CONTENTS

Acknowledgement v
Prologue vii
Introduction 1

PART I: CUBAN CATACLYSM
Chapter One: Kennedys and King and The Race Issue—1960 9
Chapter Two: The New Frontier—Part I (Continued In Volume IV) 35
Chapter Three: Veciana and Phillips in Cuba—1959-1960 65
Chapter Four: The Aftershocks of The Bay of Pigs 93

PART II: THE STRENGTHENING STORM
Chapter Five: Berlin—1961 117
Chapter Six: Kennedys and King and The Race Issue—1961 147
Chapter Seven: Castro Assassination Plots—1961 179
Chapter Eight: KGB-CIA Spy Wars—1952-1961 197

PART III: SHIPWRECK
Chapter Nine: RFK and The Castro Assassination Plots—Part I 225
Chapter Ten: RFK and The Castro Assassination Plots—Part II 257
Chapter Eleven: Veciana: The Secret Years—1961-1962 281
Chapter Twelve: KGB-CIA Spy Wars—1962 317
Chapter Thirteen: RFK and The Castro Assassination Plots—Part III 341
Chapter Fourteen: Into The Storm: Operation Mongoose and Northwoods 367
Chapter Fifteen: Intermission 389

MISCELLANEOUS

Appendix: Gary Thomas Rowe ... 397
Acronyms ... 401
Bibliography ... 405
Index ... 411

INTRODUCTION

The present volume is the third in a series of volumes about the assassination of President John F. Kennedy. In the introduction to Volume II, I reported that this series will eventually comprise four or perhaps five volumes. However, the amount of work expended on the present volume may portend an eventual six-volume series. Only time will tell. My research methodology is responsible for this uncertainty. The first eighteen months of the Kennedy Administration came fully into the crosshairs of my investigation in the present volume. Several surprises encountered during that study required intensive research and analysis. New leads led to disturbing insights and several chapters that had not been anticipated.

The upshot is that tackling the Kennedy presidency from the inauguration through the 1962 Missile Crisis will eventually consume the better part of *two* volumes. A substantial amount of overlap between Volumes III and IV will be the inevitable result. The new threads of investigation in Volume III converge in a startling cliffhanger (see Chapter Fifteen)—raising new questions about the nature of the case and the contours of the investigation that lies ahead.

The arrangement of foci around the clusters of people, events and operations in Volume II produced a contextual narrative centered between two important mileposts in the life of Lee Harvey Oswald. Those mile markers were Oswald's defection to the USSR on 31 October 1959 and his queries about returning to America that began on 9 December 1960 (see Countdown to Darkness, Chapters One and Eighteen).

The events described in Volume III occurred between Oswald's decision to return to America and the day he and Marina arrived in Hoboken, New Jersey on 12 June 1962. A cascading series of Cold War crises are crowded into the space between those two mile markers. I will deal with Oswald's journey during that time period at the beginning of Volume IV. The harsh enormity of the trials facing the new president were staggering and only grew more difficult during those eighteen months of tribulation. The crises multiplied, and their solutions grew more difficult as the hour of maximum danger—the Cuban Missile Crisis—approached. The situation was the same as it had been when Kennedy described it during his Inaugural Address: "In each of the principal areas of crisis the tide of events has been running out and time has not been our friend."

Any standard—i.e., open-minded—examination of the events in Volumes III and IV is encumbered by a labyrinth of deceptive information. The inaccurate and false clutter must first be succinctly identified and processed, and then disposed of, before the task of assembling the true sequence of events can begin. The investigator must be alert for false information generated at different points in time. False information invented during the conduct of past intelligence and espionage operations has led many reputable investigators down old dark dead-end alleyways many years after the fact. False information interwoven or superimposed on the true sequence of past events—whether cleverly or clumsily—many years later by liars and charlatans with disparate agendas is an equally challenging and time-consuming problem.

These challenges to a successful investigation go well beyond the usual problems of lies and cover stories to protect sources and methods of American intelligence agencies. The handiwork of the KGB in the case of Yuri Nosenko was and *remains* an enormous impediment to the investigation of the Kennedy assassination. But it doesn't stop there. More than the guileful Russians were active in the games of deception that *still* interfere with our ability to make sense of this case. The handiwork of Cuban and American actors has also inflicted significant damage on our ability to navigate through the clutter of lies to uncover the true facts of history.

And so, in Volume III, I found myself struggling for months on end trying to peer through the fog created by Yuri Nosenko, Samuel Halpern, and Antonio Veciana. Their stories are fraught with deceptions and inaccuracies. And so, I have resorted to putting their accounts under an electron microscope. In the end, I arrived at an intermission—a dark zone between the events that took place leading up to the summer of 1962 and what they portended for the rest of the Kennedy presidency.

And I chose, as I did in Volumes I and II, to share my findings in Volume III without knowing how things will turn out in Volumes IV and V and, if necessary, beyond.

The Organization of Volume III

The first four chapters of Volume III describe Kennedy's victory in the 1960 election, the programs of his administration, and the chaos unleashed by his mistake to go along with the Eisenhower plan to overthrow Castro.

INTRODUCTION

In Chapter One, I retrace the unlikely set of circumstances that led to Senator Kennedy's surprising victory over Vice-President Nixon in the 1960 presidential election. In the end, the issue of race and the Kennedy-King connection was the wild card that determined the outcome of the election. The race issue festered throughout the Kennedy presidency—and beyond—and I will take a timeout in Chapter Six to examine the indelible tragedy of brutality and bravery in the summer of the Freedom Rides in 1961.

In Chapter Two, I will closely examine what President Kennedy called "The New Frontier." His bold dream included plans and policies directed at the problems facing America at home and abroad—in science and space, peace and war, ignorance and prejudice, and questions of poverty and surplus. Kennedy defined the choice facing America as being "between the public interest and private comfort," a formula foreshadowing the eventual showdown between his vision of the future and that of powerful Wall Street bankers and big business. Kennedy engaged in an intense effort to educate and prepare himself to chart the principal directions of policy. To do so, he established special "task forces." Seven were in put in place during the campaign and nineteen more by mid-December 1960—eleven in foreign policy and eight in domestic policy—and three more domestic policy task forces were added in January. By the inauguration, nearly all of the task forces had turned in their reports. After studying the reports, Kennedy sent them to those who would become his cabinet and agency chiefs after his inauguration, along with instructions to hammer out the new policies, programs, people and priorities.

In Chapter Three, we get our first taste of Antonio Veciana's intrusion into the Kennedy assassination controversy. I will offer a detailed examination of Veciana's claims about his alleged recruitment by the ubiquitous CIA propaganda sleuth David Phillips in mid-1959. Perhaps surprisingly, for some observers, not a single detail of this version of Veciana's recruitment ever happened. Strangely, this version was his sixth attempt to explain the date of his alleged recruitment. But I will examine it closely anyway to find clues for what *really* happened in Cuba in 1959 and how those clues can help us understand what happened later.

Chapter Four is a geostrategic analysis of the cataclysm caused by the disastrous failure of the Bay of Pigs invasion and its long-term consequences. The *aftershocks* included the Berlin and Cuban Missile Crises of 1961 and 1962. In the outcome produced by these crises, Khrushchev had to give up on the removal of a capitalist cancer in a communist sea (Berlin) and settle instead on gaining a communist cancer in a capitalist sea (Havana). Kennedy's November 1961 decision to overthrow the Castro regime precipitated Khrushchev's decision in the spring of 1962 to place nuclear-tipped missiles in Cuba. As these events played out in the larger East-West geopolitical chess match, neither Kennedy nor Khrushchev were able to control their subordinates. Both leaders faced increasing internal opposition from political-military-national security elites opposed to their external strategies *and* their internal attempts to improve their economies. In the end, neither leader survived. Ironically, President Kennedy's assassination in 1963 played a key role in the purge of Premier Khrushchev in 1964.

The next four chapters are best understood as a strengthening storm in both domestic and foreign policy. At home, the Kennedy brothers were tested by the race issue that erupted during the summer of 1961. Chapter Six reviews how the Kennedy Administration handled the harrowing Freedom Rides endured by black and white students as they tested desegregation laws while traveling through the southern United States. Chapters Five and Seven are devoted to the developing storm in the Cold War conflicts over Berlin and Cuba. Chapter Eight reviews the spy wars between the KGB and the CIA from the early 1950s forward, but are focused principally on KGB and CIA penetrations of each other and the role of Lee Harvey Oswald in the hunt for a KGB mole inside the CIA.

The core of Volume III—Chapters Nine through Fifteen—are best understood as a shipwreck. Having parried a series of crises in Berlin, Laos and Vietnam, the Kennedy Administration unwisely waded once again into another attempt to overthrow Castro—Operation Mongoose. It nearly ended in World War III. This is the point where the documentary record and later interpretations of the tumultuous events taking place during the Cold War—from the Bay of Pigs to the Cuban Missile Crisis—became hopelessly corrupted by post-Kennedy assassination myths.

Volume III attempts to tackle these myths head on and to expose the agendas of those who fabricated them. That job is enormous. But it is a necessary task in order to proceed. The work on these problems in Volume III leaves us in what can best be described as an intermission—a timeout to ponder what this separation of fact from fiction means for the work that still lies ahead.

This volume also contains an appendix that publishes portions of the FBI's "Summary of Results of the Department of Justice Task Force Investigation of Gary Thomas Rowe, Jr." Rowe was the FBI informant in the Alabama Ku Klux Klan referred to often in Chapter Six.

Major Working Hypotheses

The following working hypotheses pertain to the entire series of volumes in the present work. The substance and many of the details of Hypotheses Three and Four were presented in the 2008 edition of my previous work, **Oswald and the CIA**. If I discover a mistake or new information that requires adjustments of these working hypotheses, I will make them. As of this writing, these hypotheses remain unchanged and as they were in Volumes I and II:

INTRODUCTION

- Hypothesis One: At some point in 1962, regardless of how much earlier someone might have wanted President Kennedy to be assassinated, the contours of the plot that eventually emerged began to fall into place: an American Marxist, Lee Harvey Oswald would *appear* to have assassinated JFK and to have done so for Fidel Castro with the assistance of the KGB.
- Hypothesis Two: The plot was designed to make it *appear* that the Kennedy brothers' plan to overthrow Castro had been successfully turned around by Fidel, resulting in the assassination of President Kennedy.
- Hypothesis Three: Lee Harvey Oswald was sent by his agent handler to New Orleans in the summer of 1963 to build upon his pro-Castro Cuban legend that he had begun to establish in Dallas at the beginning of that year.
- Hypothesis Four: Oswald's CIA files were manipulated by CIA counterintelligence in the weeks before the assassination to support the design mentioned in Hypotheses One and Two. In this connection, Oswald (or an imposter) traveled to Mexico City (28 September-3 October 1963) and spent time in the Cuban Consulate and met with a Soviet diplomat, Valery Kostikov, who was known by U.S. intelligence to be the head of KGB assassinations (Department 13) for the Western Hemisphere.
- Hypothesis Five: An essential element of the plot was a psychological operation to raise the specter of WWIII and the death of forty million Americans. This threat of a nuclear holocaust was then used by President Johnson to terrify Chief Justice Earl Warren—and some of the other men who served on the Warren Commission—to such an extent that they believed there was no alternative to writing a report stating that Lee Harvey Oswald, acting alone, had assassinated the president.

Several further assumptions pertaining to the events covered in Volumes I and II may be found in the introductions to those volumes. Further assumptions pertaining to the events described in this volume will be discussed in the introduction to Volume IV.

PART I
CUBAN CATACLYSM

CHAPTER ONE

THE KENNEDYS, KING, AND THE RACE ISSUE—1960

Slavery was our original sin. For a very long time the race issue has been a dark shadow hanging over our republic and we are still cursed by it today. Fewer issues in our history cut as deeply into the fabric of American identity and moral purpose. In the twentieth century, the issue of civil rights for African Americans became inextricably intertwined with the Kennedy presidency—more so than in any other presidency except for that of President Lincoln.

By 1960, one century after emancipation, Southern white bigotry had succeeded in clawing back almost every step toward racial justice—save for slavery itself. The race issue had, by and large, settled down to the point that segregation was an accepted part of the American landscape. This embarrassing injustice had become fundamentally enmeshed in American electoral politics. Where African Americans were able to vote at all, for the most part their votes remained firmly in the electoral lockbox of the party of Lincoln—the Republican Party.

It was more or less an Act of Providence that a quick series of events took place late in the 1960 presidential campaign that changed the course of history.

Many white American lay public who lived through the 1960 election do not remember—most of them did not even understand it at the time—the role that race played in the outcome of that election. The Cuban crisis, the missile gap, and the Eisenhower recession dominated the news and rhetoric of the campaign. There has been a lot of talk—probably true—about the Chicago mob stealing ballot boxes to help put the state of Illinois in Kennedy's column. Obviously, in a very close election, such as it was in 1960, the margin of victory can be attributed to various circumstances.

INTO THE STORM

But the truth is that the *crucial role* of the 1960 African American vote has often been overlooked—especially as that event recedes into the past. Historians of the civil rights movement know differently.

Research shows that the margin of victory in Illinois was due to Kennedy's appeal to African American voters. The same was true in the states of New Jersey, South Carolina and Missouri. The Republican national chairman at the time, Thruston Morton, regarded the African-American vote as the single most crucial factor in the election.[1] Kennedy historian Arthur Schlesinger, Jr. recalls that the president, reflecting on his margin of victory after the election, knew how indebted he was to Martin Luther King, Jr. and African American voters:

> Had only whites gone to the polls in 1960, Nixon would have taken 52 per cent of the vote. In the electoral college Kennedy could not have carried Illinois and Michigan, not to mention Texas, South Carolina and possibly Louisiana. He needed to lose only the first two of those states to have lost the election.[2]

The Republican loss in Louisiana was close. Kennedy carried it by 50.4 per cent of the popular vote, while Republicans and segregationists split the balance.[3]

Nixon's handling of the race issue was byzantine. In the end, it was fatal. Initially, he insisted that the platform committee replace the moderate plank on civil rights with the more progressive Rockefeller position. Later, under the duress of the tightening election campaign in September and October, Nixon waffled between campaigning for Northern electoral votes or Southern electoral votes. As Theodore White's study of the 1960 election recalls:

> He [Nixon] later completely befuzzed his original position in Chicago and succeeded, in the end, in alienating Northern Negro *and* Southern white, *losing both along with the election*. This is one of Nixon's characteristic and fatal flaws—that he presents too often a split image.[4]
> [Emphasis added]

How Kennedy handled the race issue was equally—if not more—complicated. Ultimately, he profited from opportunities created by Southern bigotry and conflicting views among his own campaign staff on how to handle the sensitive race issue.

No study of the Kennedy presidency and his assassination would be complete without looking carefully at the consequences of how he won the 1960 election. That story permanently changed the role of race in American electoral politics. In retrospect, it

---

1. Middleton, Russell, "The Civil Rights Issue and Presidential Voting Among Southern Negroes and Whites," **Social Forces**, *40*: 209–215, March 1962.
2. Schlesinger, *A Thousand Days* (New York: Houghton Mifflin, 2002 ed.), p. 930.
3. Theodore White, **The Making of the President—1960** (New York: Harper, paper ed., 1961), pp. 204-205.
4. White, **The Making of the President—1960**, p. 204.

is clear that without the black vote in 1960 the assassination of Kennedy in 1963 would not have taken place—simply because there would not have been a President Kennedy.

Nevertheless, when looked at by itself, the unlikely path by which Kennedy came to occupy the White House is a heartwarming piece of American history. This chapter is devoted to that amazing story—how the black vote, for so long taken for granted by the Republican Party, delivered the presidency to John Kennedy in 1960. That improbable path was the result of the African American thirst for freedom and the exceptional role played in that dream by Martin Luther King, Jr.

The unique civil rights strategy of Dr. King and how it was shaped remains a little known but crucial part of American history to this day. It explains not only how Kennedy won the presidency but also the stony uphill path of race relations that took place during his presidency (also see Chapters Six). I begin Volume III with an examination of the most unusual and successful strategy for defeating social injustice in the annals of modern history.

Dr. King's Unique Civil Rights Strategy: *Coercive Nonviolence*

I have been teaching *America in the Sixties* for more than a quarter century, first for the University of Maryland Honors College [1994-2014][5] and since then for the Political Science Department at James Madison University. In the classroom, young students learning about the civil rights movement are as shocked today as they were when I began teaching this course in 1994. The brutality of the filmed footage does not lie.

It took several years in the classroom for it to dawn on me just how unusual Dr. King's strategy to defeat racial injustice was. He was highly educated, a skilled orator and a remarkable rhetorical genius. In 1948, King graduated at age 19 from Morehouse College with a B.A. in sociology. At Crozer Theological Seminary, where he was elected president of the student body, he graduated with a Bachelor of Divinity in 1951. King earned his Ph.D. in Systematic Theology from Boston University in 1955. At Crozer, his peers admired his oratorical techniques so much that they packed the chapel whenever he delivered the regular Thursday student sermon.[6]

---

[5] During that period, I also taught many classes for the University of Maryland, University College (UMUC). In 2002, I was the recipient of the ***Stanley J. Drazek Teaching Excellence Award***—the most prestigious award recognizing the highest teaching accomplishments by outstanding UMUC faculty members. My selection was largely the result of several letters of recommendation submitted by African American students regarding my teaching on Martin Luther King, Jr., and the civil rights movement in America. Among the academic awards I have received over the years, that award is the one I treasure the most.

[6] Taylor Branch, ***Parting the Waters: America in the King Years*** 1954-63 (New York: Simon & Schuster, 1988), p. 75.

INTO THE STORM

Behind the many years of King's practice in the pulpit, however, lurked a deep struggle over his long attachment to the Social Gospel. Prominent in early-20th-century North American Protestantism, the Social Gospel Movement applied Christian ethics to issues of social injustice such as race relations, poverty and economic inequality.

In popular wisdom, the shaping force in Dr. King's thinking was Mahatma Gandhi. However, it was the eminent American theologian Reinhold Niebuhr who fundamentally shaped King's religious views. King recalled:

> Niebuhr has extraordinary insight into human nature, *especially the behavior of nations and social groups.* He is keenly aware of the complexity of human motives and of the relation between *morality and power.* His theology is a persistent reminder of the reality of sin on every level of man's existence. These elements in Niebuhr's thinking helped me to recognize the illusions of a superficial optimism concerning human nature and the dangers of a false idealism. While I still believed in man's potential for good, Niebuhr made me realize his potential for evil as well. Moreover, Niebuhr helped me to recognize the complexity of man's *social involvement* and the glaring reality of *collective evil.*[7]
>
> [Emphasis added]

Niebuhr's **Moral Man and Immoral Society** was published in 1932, when King was just three years old. That work was the beginning of the end of classical liberalism in American theology because Niebuhr successfully attacked the Social Gospel's premise that the modern advance of reason could eliminate social evils. Niebuhr argued that there was no evidence that human beings became less predatory as they became better educated.[8]

Dr. King was in his last year at Crozer when he first read Reinhold Niebuhr. That experience fundamentally changed King's outlook on life. By that time, Hitler's evil agenda had transformed Niebuhr's theory of immoral society into the most fiercely debated topic in the world—especially among students of religion in America:

> If Niebuhr was correct ... any Social Gospel preacher was necessarily a charlatan, and the Negroes among them were spiritual profiteers, enjoying the immense rewards of the Negro pulpit while dispensing a false doctrine of hope. Such a prospect deeply disturbed King, who already felt guilty about his privileges compared with the other Negro students at Crozer.

---

[7] *The Papers of Martin Luther King, Jr.*, vol. IV, Senior editor Clayborne Carson, Volume editors: S. Carson, A. Clay, V. Shadron and K. Taylor, University of California Press, Berkeley - Los Angeles 2000, pp. 473-484.

[8] Reinhold Niebuhr, **Moral Man and Immoral Society** (New York: Charles Scribner's Sons, 1932), pp. 250-251.

After contact with the work of Niebuhr, King lost interest in the Social Gospel overnight. The trauma was such that King was never again so completely influenced by any school of thought—including Niebuhr's.[9]

George W. Davis, a pacifist and strong proponent of Gandhi on the Crozer faculty, introduced Dr. King to Frederick Fisher's *That Strange Little Brown Man of India, Gandhi*. Niebuhr's interest in Gandhi's methods was not lost on King:

> [Gandhi's methods] actually belong to a type of *coercion* which offers the largest opportunities for a harmonious relationship with the moral and rational factors in social life ... This means that non-violence is a particularly *strategic instrument* for an oppressed group which is hopelessly in the minority and has no possibility of developing sufficient power to set against its oppressors. [Emphasis added]

Niebuhr argued that when applied correctly to the cause of African Americans, Gandhi's methods could work against injustice and the selfish forces of the immoral society.[10]

In my view, Niebuhr actually invented a new type of strategic nonviolence. I will use the term *coercive nonviolence*. Niebuhr actually used the term "non-violent coercion to describe it:"

> *Non-violent coercion and resistance*, in short, is a type of coercion which offers the largest opportunities for a harmonious relationship with the moral and rational factors in social life. It does not destroy the process of a moral and rational adjustment of interest to interest completely during the course of resistance.[11] [Emphasis added]

Niebuhr sought to preserve cooperative rational and moral attitudes during coercive nonviolence to augment moral forces without destroying them.

Ironically, Martin Luther King is probably the last person that most observers would associate with coercion. But this active *strategic* formula is precisely what attracted King to Niebuhr. It was Niebuhr who first drew the crucial distinction between, on the one hand, the character of individual people and, on the other hand, the character of people acting in large social groups.

Niebuhr reasoned that while individuals could respond to the call of justice, nations and large social and economic groups would always be predacious. Furthermore, Niebuhr applied this paradigm directly to the race issue in America and ridiculed the view that moral suasion could ever bring fundamental economic and political rights to African Americans:

---

9 Branch, *Parting the Waters*, pp. 81-85.
10 Ibid, p. 86.
11 Niebuhr, *Moral Man and Immoral Society*, pp. 250-251.

INTO THE STORM

> The Negro schools, conducted under the auspices of white philanthropy, encourage individual Negroes to higher forms of self-realization; but they do not make a frontal attack upon the social injustices from which the Negro suffers. ... *they do not touch his political disfranchisement or his economic disinheritance. They hope to do so in the long run, because they have the usual faith in the power of education and moral suasion to soften the heart of the white man. This faith is filled with as many illusions as such expectations always are.*[12]

Niebuhr believed passionately that the white race would have to be *coerced* into accepting equal rights for African Americans:

> However large the number of individual white men who ... will identify themselves completely with the Negro cause, *the white race in America will not admit the Negro to equal rights if it is not forced to do so*. Upon that point one may speak with a dogmatism which all history justifies.[13]
> [Emphasis added]

This was the key to the triumph of the civil rights movement under Dr. King's leadership. He *successfully applied the strategy of coercive nonviolence during the tumultuous years of the Kennedy presidency*. The race issue in America during the Kennedy Administration cannot be understood apart from King's strategy and the Kennedys' reluctance to embrace it.

As time passed, King never attempted to dismiss the many characterizations of him as a Gandhian:

> King mentioned buying a half-dozen books about Gandhi in a single evening, but he never bothered to name or describe any of them. He almost never spoke of Gandhi personally, and his comments about Gandhism were never different than his thoughts about nonviolence in general. By contrast, he invoked Niebuhr in every one of his own major books, always with a sketch of **Moral Man and Immoral Society**.[14]

King devoted most of his remaining graduate studies to Niebuhr. While King said little about this in public, privately he described Niebuhr as the primary influence in his life, and Gandhian nonviolence as "merely a Niebuhrian stratagem of power."[15]

King passionately challenged the system of segregation everywhere, whether it was in schools, public parks, churches, lunch counters, or public libraries. He put it this way:

---

12 Ibid, p. 253.
13 Ibid.
14 King, *The Autobiography of Martin Luther King, Jr.*, pp. 138-139.
15 Ibid.

> Segregation had to be removed from our society. And Negroes had to *be prepared to suffer, sacrifice, and even die to gain their goals.* We could not rest until we had achieved the ideals of our democracy. I prayed much over our Southern situation, and I came to the conclusion that we were in for a season of suffering.[16] [Emphasis added]

For King, such suffering was the price *and* the opportunity arising from the practice of coercive nonviolence. It meant unflinchingly putting one's body on the line—a sacrifice that is not normal and does not come easily. In my view, the quintessential example of coercive nonviolence is found in the teachings and practice of Jesus of Nazareth. His advice to turn the other cheek (Matthew 5:39; Luke 6:29) was a key tenet of his social prophecy, and his suffering during the "Passion of Christ" was the ultimate example of willing redemptive suffering.

Fourteen Days that Changed the Course of History

In the remainder of this chapter, I will lay out what I believe was a *causal* chain of six race-related events that led to Kennedy's victory in the 1960 presidential election. Those six events took place during a crucial fourteen-day period, just before the election, in the following order:

>17 October: JFK scuttles a proposed meeting with Dr. King.
>
>19 October: King is arrested at student sit-ins in Atlanta, Georgia.
>
>26 October: Approximately 3:00 a.m.; King is transferred to the chain gangs in Reidsville Federal Penitentiary.
>
>26 October: Approximately 10:00 a.m.; Kennedy makes a sympathy telephone call to Coretta King.
>
>27 October: Robert Kennedy makes a call to Judge Mitchell to secure King's release from Reidsville prison.
>
>28 October: The "Blue Bomb" scheme is secretly launched; the pamphlets are distributed on Sunday, 6 November, two days before the election.

As Raymond Arsenault—a scholar of the civil rights movement—observed in 2006, the beginning of these six events "set the stage for one of the most fateful decisions in modern American political history."[17]

It is my contention that 1) *each one* of these events had to occur in order that the next event could take place; and, 2) if *any* of these six events had failed to take place,

---

16   Ibid.
17   Raymond Arsenault, **Freedom Riders** (New York: Oxford University Press, 2006), p. 90.

INTO THE STORM

John Kennedy would not have been elected president on 8 November 1960. There would have been no New Frontier; no Keynesian economics; no increased minimum wage; no depressed areas redevelopment; no proposals for Medicaid, Medicare and increased Social Security benefits; no Peace Corps; and no Alliance for Progress (see Chapter Two). On the other hand, it is likely that America would have gone to war not only in Vietnam but also in Cuba and Laos.

Kennedy's Providential Scuttling of a Meeting with King

Martin Luther King, Jr. first met John Kennedy in New York during June 1960. At the time, Senator Kennedy was seeking the Democratic nomination for president. King recalled:

> We talked for about an hour over the breakfast table. I was very frank about what I thought: that there was a need for a strong executive leadership and that we hadn't gotten this during the Eisenhower administration. If we didn't get it in the new administration, we would be set back even more.

King was impressed by the forthright and honest manner in which JFK discussed the race issue and with his willingness to learn more about civil rights.[18]

However, King felt that Kennedy did not grasp the depths of the problem at that time, as he did later:

> He knew that segregation was morally wrong, and he certainly intellectually committed himself to integration, but I could see that he didn't have the emotional involvement then. ... He had never really had the personal experience of knowing the deep groans and passionate yearnings of the Negro for freedom, because he just didn't know Negroes generally and he hadn't had any experience in the civil rights struggle.[19]

At that time, King concluded that Kennedy had no more than an intellectual commitment to the African American cause.

By the time of the 1960 Presidential campaign, Martin Luther King had emerged as a genuine hero of the increasingly violent African American struggle for equality. He had become the most visible spokesperson and leader of the civil rights movement. His star had taken off during the successful Montgomery Bus Boycott (December 1955-December 1956) that led the United States Supreme Court to strike down as unconstitutional the Alabama and Montgomery laws on segregated buses.

---
18 King, *The Autobiography of Martin Luther King, Jr.*, p. 143.
19 Ibid, p. 144.

THE KENNEDYS, KING, AND THE RACE ISSUE—1960

After Kennedy won the Democratic nomination, King became the target of three conflicting forces. They converged upon him at the time of the Student Nonviolent Coordinating Committee (SNCC) conference which opened on 14 October. The students wanted King to join their lunch counter sit-ins; Atlanta's African American leaders—including King's father—wanted him to endorse Nixon; and, within the Kennedy campaign organization, civil rights staffers Harris Wofford and Louis Martin wanted King to help Kennedy.[20]

At that time, King met with Kennedy again, on this occasion at his Georgetown apartment. King noticed that in the short time since their previous meeting Kennedy had been well advised and had learned a lot more about civil rights. King recalled:

> He was very much concerned then about the election and possibly losing. Some of his friends were concerned about this and felt he had to do something dramatic to convince the nation of his commitment to civil rights. Some of the advisors thought that he should come South and make a civil rights speech in the South which would really convince people. They wanted him to come under my auspices to speak for a board meeting or a dinner sponsored by SCLC (Southern Christian Leadership Conference).[21]

King received many phone calls from Kennedy campaign staffer Harris Wofford about a potential public venue. Wofford thought a meeting in Nashville might work. King signaled that the location was "Southern enough." However, due to the loud howling of Southern politicians, it turned out to be "too Southern" for Kennedy. King biographer Taylor Branch recounts:

> A hundred phone calls and many white lies later, Wofford called King again to offer Miami instead of Nashville, the next afternoon or evening. King was not very happy about the switch. Wofford repeated the Kennedy arguments that Miami was a "Deep South city," but he did not do so very forcefully. He said it was the best he could do. ... "I'll do it," King told Wofford. "But you should tell Mr. Kennedy that I will be obliged to issue a pro forma invitation to Mr. Nixon." Wofford's heart sank. "Do you really feel you have to do that?" he asked. "Yes," said King. "I don't think Mr. Nixon will accept, but I have to give him the chance."[22]

King had mentioned to Wofford that he was inclined to accept the Miami meeting because he would be able to skip a student sit-in in Atlanta planned for the same time. Wofford later recalled:

---

20   Branch, *Parting the Waters*, pp. 344-345.
21   King, *The Autobiography of Martin Luther King, Jr*, p. 144.
22   Branch, *Parting the Waters*, pp. 348-349.

> King didn't want to be arrested in Atlanta at that time. He really thought that it would be better not to have a racial crisis during the election campaign. He had wanted to be meeting with Kennedy somewhere in the South, and negotiations had gone on, but each time something went wrong.[23]

King's heart was with the students, but he was obviously under great pressure from his father—who disapproved of King's participation in the sit-ins. "You don't need to go!" King Senior exclaimed, "This is the students, not you."

As it turned out, Dr. King was *destined* to attend that particular Atlanta student sit-in. *The Nixon glitch in King's response ensured the latter's presence at the lunch counter on 19 October and his arrest that day set in motion the remaining causal chain of events leading to Kennedy's victory on election day.*

When Wofford relayed King's response to Kennedy afterward, the senator instantly replied, "The hell with that … I'm taking a much greater risk in the South than Nixon, but King wants to treat us as equals. Tell him it's off."[24]

Many of King's close friends urged him to declare his support for Kennedy. But King recalls that he spent "many troubled hours searching for the responsible and fair decision" on this suggestion and, in the end, he made it clear to Kennedy that he would not endorse candidates publicly.[25]

King's silent soul searching to resolve the issue of his public closeness to Kennedy took a lot more time than the senator's quick decision to scuttle the proposed meeting in Miami. But although neither of the two leaders suspected it then, Providence can—and sometimes does—have a funny way of turning a dark moment into a path that produces an unexpected golden opportunity.

The 19 October 1960 Arrest of Martin Luther King, Jr.

During the early part of October 1960, three Southern governors directly threatened Senator Kennedy that if he intervened in Southern affairs in support of Martin Luther King, then the South would abandon the Democratic ticket.[26] It was in that context that the students of SNCC descended on King's hometown of Atlanta to engage in protest activity.

As King and African American students steered the strategy of civil rights work toward coercive nonviolence, the emphasis shifted from the *slow legal processes* of

---

23 Wofford in Hampton and Fayer, ***Voices of Freedom*** (New York: Bantam Books, 1990), p. 68.
24 Branch, ***Parting the Waters***, pp. 348-349.
25 King, ***The Autobiography of Martin Luther King, Jr.***, p. 144.
26 White, ***The Making of the President—1960***, p. 322.

THE KENNEDYS, KING, AND THE RACE ISSUE—1960

courtroom proceedings to *swift direct action* in bus protests, economic boycotts, and mass gatherings. As Dr. King recounted:

> The most significant aspect of this student movement was that *the young people knocked some of the oldsters out of their state of apathy and complacency.* … One may wonder why the movement started with the lunch counters. The answer lay in the fact that the Negro had suffered indignities and injustices … of lunch counter segregation. He could not understand why he was welcomed with open arms at most counters in the store but was denied service at a certain counter because it happened to be selling food and drink. In a real sense the "sit-in" represented more than a demand for service; it represented a demand for respect.[27]
>
> [Emphasis added]

Historian and activist Howard Zinn agreed: "For the first time in our history, a major social movement, shaking the nation to its bone, is being led by youngsters."[28]

On 17 October, the students caught up with Dr. King in the kitchen of his home after he had returned from a speaking trip. As King munched on his mother's turnip greens they pleaded with him to join their sit-in and indicated they had to move in two days. Daddy King burst into the kitchen, told King Junior not to go to the protest, and then "scattered the students like bowling pins."[29]

The next day, 18 October, King Senior and the rest of the leadership of the Atlanta Baptist Ministers' Union endorsed the Nixon-Lodge ticket. An additional factor requiring them to support the Republicans that year was Kennedy's Catholic faith. They even took the unusual step of signing a declaration of Republican support.[30]

On 19 October, the Atlanta student movement leader Lonnie C. King called Dr. King and made one final plea: "You are the spiritual leader of the movement, and you were born in Atlanta, Georgia. And I think it might add tremendous impetus if you would go." King asked, "Where are you going to go tomorrow, L. C.?" "I'm going to be on the bridge down at Rich's," Lonnie replied. "Well, I'll meet you on the bridge tomorrow at ten o'clock," King volunteered.[31] *With this promise, King became a key player at a sharp inflection point in Western theological history—the choice between the pacifism of the social gospel and the activism of Niebuhrian coercive nonviolence.*

By this time, King understood that the 1960 student movement taking place all over the South was the most significant development in the whole civil rights struggle:

---

27   King, *The Autobiography of Martin Luther King, Jr.*, p. 139.
28   Howard Zinn, *SNCC—The New Abolitionists* (New York: Haymarket Books, 2013 edition), pp. 34-35.
29   White, *The Making of the President—1960*, p. 348.
30   Ibid, pp. 349-350.
31   Ibid, p. 350.

INTO THE STORM

> It was no overstatement to characterize these events as historic. Never before in the United States had so large a body of students spread a struggle over so great an area in pursuit of the goal of human dignity and freedom. The student movement finally refuted the idea that the Negro was content with segregation. The students had taken the struggle for justice into their own hands. Negro freedom fighters revealed to the nation and the world their determination and courage. *They were moving away from tactics which were suitable merely for gradual and long-term change. This was an era of offensive* on the part of oppressed people.[32]

It was on 19 October 1960 that, in such a rarified atmosphere, Martin Luther King was arrested, along with two hundred and eighty students, for refusing to leave lunch counters at a restaurant in Rich's Department Store in Atlanta, Georgia.

King was the first to be arrested and the first to speak in court that night in front of Judge James E. Webb, who set bond at $250, pending a trial. This was King's plea to Judge Webb:

> *If, by chance, Your Honor, we are guilty of violating the law, please be assured that we did it to bring the whole issue of racial injustice under the scrutiny of the conscience of Atlanta. I must honestly say that we firmly believe that segregation is evil, and that our Southland will never reach its full potential and moral maturity until this cancerous disease is removed. We do not seek to remove this unjust system for ourselves alone but for our white brothers as well. The festering sore of segregation debilitates the white man as well as the Negro. So, if our actions in any way served to bring this issue to the forefront of the conscience of the community, they were not undertaken in vain.*
>
> *And, sir, I know you have a legal obligation facing you at this hour. This judicial obligation may cause you to hand us over to another court rather than dismiss the charges. But, sir, I must say that I have a moral obligation facing me at this hour. This imperative drives me to say that if you find it necessary to set a bond, I cannot in all good conscience have anyone go buy my bail.* **I will choose jail rather than bail, even if it means remaining in jail a year or even ten years.** *Maybe it will take this type of self-suffering on the part of numerous Negroes to finally expose the moral defense of our white brothers who happen to be misguided and thusly awaken the dozing conscience of our community.*[33]
>
> [Emphasis added]

Judge Webb refused King's request to vacate the charges. King spent the first night of his life behind bars.

---

32   King, *The Autobiography of Martin Luther King, Jr.*, pp. 139-140.
33   Ibid, p. 145.

King's choice of phrase "jail rather than bail" had already become the civil rights staple "Jail. No Bail!" Many demonstrators and movement leaders had long agreed with Thurgood Marshall's pronouncement that only fools would refuse bail in a Southern jail. Yet, convincing demonstrators to do just that had become a cornerstone of the Congress of Racial Equality (CORE) policy. As early as August 1960, the CORE staff at the Miami "Second Interracial Action Institute," began experimenting with the "jail—no bail" tactic.[34] Charles Jones, a theological student at Johnson C. Smith University during the sit-in era, said young people believed that they could change the world. "We'd seen Martin Luther King, we'd seen Mahatma Gandhi," he said. "Jail, No Bail was about accepting the full responsibility at hand of putting your body out and saying bring it on."[35] That callout embodied the *essence* of coercive nonviolence. Jail time would become a rite of passage, a ribbon of distinction—even a cause for celebration and loud singing. As King eventually wrote to Harold DeWolf, "I came away more convinced than ever before that unearned suffering is redemptive."[36]

Of course, King's jail—no bail stand was exactly what CORE and SNCC militants had been advocating. But circumstances quickly conspired that undermined the simplicity of that no bail strategy. Even though Georgia dropped the charges related to the sit-in, *a cruel coincidence set in motion the next stage of a serendipitous alteration in the course of history.*

King's Transfer to Reidsville Penitentiary

Five days passed without calamity before matters escalated to crisis proportions. It all began on 25 October, when cries of betrayal went up after King's arrest for a lunch counter sit-in in Atlanta was rolled into a previous traffic misdemeanor in another county. King was then convicted for the traffic violation and sentenced to immediate punishment on a Georgia road chain gang. On top of that, bond was then denied for the minor traffic conviction! This blatant subversion of justice created a perfect storm at a key moment in the 1960 presidential election. Ironically, the actions of a judge in De Kalb, Georgia would ultimately help put John Kennedy in the White House.

Here is how that unlikely string of events began. During the vacating of the charges related to the sit-in, Georgia officials informed King's lawyers that they had just received a bench warrant ordering them to hold King in jail on other charges. As the students were being released, King was served with a warrant issued by a judge in neighboring

---

34 Arsenault, *Freedom Riders*, p. 89.
35 2/8/2011, Sommer Brokaw, "Jail, No Bail" Activists Mark 50th Anniversary," *The Charlotte Post*.
36 David Garrow, *Bearing the Cross* (New York: Open Road Media, 2015), p. 149.

INTO THE STORM

De Kalb County. In May 1959, King and his wife had driven a white writer, Lillian Smith, to Emory Hospital for cancer treatment. When county patrol officers spotted interracial groups of travelers, they frequently stopped them. A De Kalb County policeman had done so on this occasion.

Now, a year and a half later, King found himself in a De Kalb jail awaiting sentencing there for a trumped-up traffic violation. King recalled how it all started:

> On the night of 4 May 1960, police had stopped me in DeKalb County and discovered I still had an Alabama driver's license. Because of this, they gave me a ticket. I had gone to court, and I didn't even know it at the time, but the lawyer pleaded guilty for me and they had fined me something like $25 or $50 and placed me on probation for I guess six months. It was such a minor case; I didn't pay attention to it and never knew that the lawyer had pleaded guilty. He had just told me, "I've got everything worked out." He made me think it was clear and all I needed to do was pay.[37]

King's lawyers later discovered in court that De Kalb County had *never* arrested or fined anyone else on such a charge. Incredibly, there was *no statutory mandated time* for how long King would have to have been in Atlanta before changing his license. King had been singled out for the dispensation of justice De Kalb style.

When King appeared in Judge Mitchell's courtroom in the De Kalb County courthouse, nearly two hundred King supporters—including four presidents from the Atlanta University complex—crowded into the hearing. De Kalb County territory was terrifying to African Americans who knew that *county officials sanctioned Ku Klux Klan parades through the corridors of the courthouse.*[38]

The atmosphere felt more like a murder trial than a minor traffic case. Taylor Branch's biography of King recalled that the hearing was permeated by a sense of latent racial violence:

> Solicitor Jack Smith demanded a harsh penalty, saying that King had shown "no sign of penitence or remorse." After King's chief attorney, Donald Hollowell, presented character witnesses and cogent arguments, Mitchell banged the gavel, revoked King's probation, and ordered him to serve four months *at hard labor on a state road gang*, beginning immediately. [Emphasis added]

Hollowell asked that King be released on bond pending appeal of the traffic sentence—a routine request that should have been granted on the spot. But the fix was in. Judge Mitchell denied the motion and ordered the sheriff's deputies to take King away.[39]

---

37 King, *The Autobiography of Martin Luther King, Jr.*, pp. 146-147.
38 Branch, *Parting the Waters*, p. 358.
39 Ibid.

THE KENNEDYS, KING, AND THE RACE ISSUE—1960

King sat in the back of the courtroom as the spectators gasped in shock during this spectacle of kangaroo injustice. He recalled what happened next:

> So they took me back upstairs and put me in jail in the DeKalb County Jail. Then early in the morning, about three o'clock in the morning, they came and got me and took me to Reidsville. That was the state prison some two hundred and twenty miles from Atlanta. On the way, they dealt with me just like I was some hardened criminal. They had me chained all the way down to my legs, and they tied my legs to something in the floor so there would be no way for me to escape. They talked with themselves. It was a long ride. I didn't know where they were taking me; but finally, I assumed it must be to one of the state prisons after we had been gone so long. That kind of mental anguish is worse than dying, riding for mile after mile, hungry and thirsty, bound and helpless, waiting and not knowing what you're waiting for. And all over a traffic violation.[40]

Hollowell contacted the jail early Wednesday morning (26 October) to say that he was on the way with a writ of habeas corpus to secure King's release. He was told that it was too late for that. Hollowell learned that King had been transferred to the maximum-security prison at Reidsville, Georgia.

Hollowell was dumbfounded by this malicious maneuver. The news swept through Atlanta within the hour:

> Coretta King was nearly hysterical by the time she reached Harris Wofford. She had just received the one phone call King was allowed on arrival at the Reidsville state prison. They had yanked him out of jail in the middle of the night without warning, she said. No one had any idea what would happen next.

The African American community girded for the likelihood that King might never get out of Reidsville alive. As Branch pointed out, "The state road gang meant cutthroat inmates and casually dismissed murders. King had to be freed or he would be dead."[41] Wofford recalled later that the country had been galvanized, "not just by the arrest of King but by the fact that the judge then sentenced him to four months on a hard labor gang because he had had a previous arrest for driving with an out-of-state license."[42]

Events had conspired to create a most improbable spectacle. The heroic African American leader who had most imperiled the traditional privileged place of Southern whites was trapped deep in "cracker" territory and assigned to a chain gang. With good reason, King's six months pregnant wife, Coretta Scott, feared her husband would be lynched. The crisis stunned the Kennedy campaign. The senator now faced the

---

40 King *The Autobiography of Martin Luther King, Jr.*, p. 147.
41 Branch, *Parting the Waters*, pp. 359-361.
42 Wofford, *Voices of Freedom*, p. 68.

seemingly impossible task of balancing votes between Northern African Americans and Southern white bigots.[43] The Nixon campaign faced the same vexing problem. *How the two candidates decided to handle the crisis crucially impacted one of the closest U.S. presidential elections in history.*

The Two Phone Calls

The Reidsville crisis was another chapter in Kennedy's serendipitous and inexorable march to the White House. Had King's transfer to the Reidsville Penitentiary not taken place, two decisive phone calls by the Kennedy brothers—*the next causal link in the chain*—would not have taken place. In the short run, the more important of the two calls was made by Robert Kennedy. In the long run, the more dramatic call was made by John Kennedy.

The senator's call was the brainchild of campaign staffer Harris Wofford. In response to King's transfer to Reidsville, Wofford realized that a propitious moment had arrived for Kennedy to intervene in King's life. As Arsenault later correctly pointed out, frustrated by the senator's reluctance to take a more forthright stand on civil rights, Wofford "sensed that King's endangerment provided his candidate with a golden opportunity to make up for past mistakes."[44]

King had been placed in a frightening segregated cell-block where inmates who had attacked guards, psychotics, and other special cases, were housed. On top of that, De Kalb County Judge Mitchell had sentenced King to four months of the most dreaded duty at the penitentiary—work on a chain gang. King recalls how John and Robert Kennedy reacted to the sudden crisis in Georgia, starting with the senator:

> The first thing he did was call my wife. She was pregnant, and this was kind of a rough experience for her, so he called her and expressed his concern. He said that he would do whatever he could and that he would think this over with his brother and try to use his influence to get me released. In the meantime, Robert Kennedy called the judge to find out about the bond. I understand Robert Kennedy was really angry about it, when they let him know all of the facts in the situation. In that spirit of anger, he called the judge. I don't know what he said in that conversation with the judge, but it was later revealed his main point was "Why can't he be bonded out?" I was released the next day. It was about two weeks before the election.[45]

---

43 White, *The Making of the President—1960*, pp. 321-322.
44 Arsenault, *Freedom Riders*, p. 90.
45 King, *The Autobiography of Martin Luther King, Jr.*, pp. 147-148.

THE KENNEDYS, KING, AND THE RACE ISSUE—1960

It was RFK's call from Washington that made it impossible for Mitchell's to keep King in prison.

Dr. King was correct to say that RFK's call to Mitchell was made in anger, but during the call Bobby kept his renowned cool. Biographer Arthur Schlesinger, Jr. recalls how Robert Kennedy acknowledged his outrage to campaign aide John Seigenthaler during a plane trip:

> "Yes, it just burned me all the way up here on the plane. It grilled me. The more I thought about the injustice of it, the more I thought what a son of a bitch that judge was. I made it clear to him that it was not a political call; that I am a lawyer, one who believes in the right of all defendants to make bond and one who had seen the rights of defendants misused in various ways. ...and I wanted to make it clear that I opposed this. I felt it was disgraceful." The conversation, Kennedy added, was restrained and calm; he had not been angry nor the judge hostile.[46]

But, as fate turned out, it was the phone call by Senator Kennedy, not the one by his brother that actually created *the next karmic step* in the fourteen days that changed the course of history.

There was relevant background to how that bit of karma came about. Wofford later explained that John Kennedy had already been puzzling about how to get King out of Reidsville:

> We initially drafted a very strong statement that Kennedy liked, opposing what had happened to Dr. King and calling for his release. And then Governor [Ernest] Vandiver of Georgia called and said, "Look, I'll get the son of a gun out of jail if you won't issue a public statement. Believe me, I'll get him out." So Kennedy called me and said, "Look, we can't issue the statement." But then the governor dragged his feet. Whether he was going to do it, or not really going to do it, or how long it might take, nobody knew. Day after day the question was, "What would you do?"[47]

And that is where the call to Coretta King entered the chain of events.

In fact, when Robert Kennedy had telephoned his request to Judge Mitchell to arrange for King's release, he *already* knew about his brother's call to Coretta King. The previous evening (25 October), Wofford had reached his boss, Sargent Shriver, in Chicago. Shriver was married to Eunice Kennedy, the senator's favorite sister. Wofford recalled the sequence of events:

> The idea came to me, and was backed by others in the civil rights section of the campaign, that why shouldn't he just call Mrs. King? She

---

46   Arthur Schlesinger, Jr., ***RFK and his Times*** (New York: Houghton Mifflin, 2002 Ed.), pp. 217-218.
47   Wofford, ***Voices of Freedom***, p. 68.

was pregnant. She was very anxious. She had been on the phone to me telling me about how worried she was, and the thought came, why can't Kennedy at least just call her and say, "We're working at it, we're going to get him out. You have my sympathy." A personal, direct act. We then said, "How do we get this to him?"[48]

After reaching Shriver, Wofford quickly relayed the horrific details of King's precarious situation and mentioned his idea about a call to Mrs. King. "That's a wonderful idea," Shriver said. I'll get to O'Hare International Inn, where Kennedy is for another hour and a half, and I'll put the idea to him."[49] Having secured Coretta's home phone number from Wofford and put it in his pocket, Shriver located Kennedy at the O'Hare Inn as the senator was leaving for a day of barnstorming in Michigan.[50]

Shriver joined a huddle of campaign advisors around Kennedy in his bedroom. Astutely, Shriver waited for them to leave the bedroom, fearing that a general discussion of his idea would kill it.[51] The group soon left for their telephones and typewriters and Kennedy said that he was not feeling well and went into the bedroom to lie down. According to the account of Taylor Branch, Shriver alone followed him and gently repeated Wofford's proposition: "I think you ought to give her a call, Jack."[52]

Kennedy's immediate reaction to Wofford's suggestion was impulsive. Without consulting anyone, he placed a long-distance telephone call to Mrs. Martin Luther King, Jr.[53] *That call was the fourth causal link in the epic drama that placed John Kennedy in the White House.* It provided the spark that lit the prairie fire. Taylor Branch captured this part of that historic moment:

> Kennedy sat up wearily on the bed. "What the hell," he said. "That's a decent thing to do. Why not? Get her on the phone." Shriver quickly pulled the paper from his pocket and dialed the number. The phone rang in the King bedroom, where Coretta was dressing to keep an appointment ... When Coretta identified herself, Shriver said, "Just a minute, Mrs. King, for Senator Kennedy," and handed the phone to the candidate on the bed.[54]

Coretta King later remembered the call from Kennedy:

> "Hello, Mrs. King, this is Senator Kennedy, and I'm calling because I wanted to let you know I was thinking about you. How are you? I understand you are expecting your third child." I was amazed that he even

---

48   Ibid. p. 69.
49   Ibid.
50   White, *The Making of the President—1960*, p. 322.
51   Schlesinger, *RFK and his Times*, p. 217.
52   Branch, *Parting the Waters*, pp. 361-362.
53   White, *The Making of the President—1960*, p. 322.
54   Branch, *Parting the Waters*, p. 362.

said third child. Someone of course had to tell him, but anyway, it was a very personal touch. He said, "I'm thinking about you and your husband, and I know this must be very difficult for you. If there's anything I can do to be of help, I want you to please feel free to call on me."

Not knowing quite what to say, Coretta responded, "Well, I really appreciate this and if there is anything that you can do, I would deeply appreciate it."[55]

The call lasted only two minutes. Shriver, knowing he would be punished for his role in the coup that had just taken place, quickly sneaked out the back door of the suite before the aides arrived to whisk Senator Kennedy to the plane.

Wofford's prediction came true. The word about the senator's call spread swiftly through the channels of African American leadership, outward from Atlanta and on to the press. The news that Kennedy had intervened to protect the imprisoned civil rights leader had long legs—*lasting all the way to the finish line on the day of the election*.[56] King later acknowledged Senator Kennedy's key role in his release from Reidsville Prison *and his personal obligation* to the Kennedy brothers for their intervention. King later reflected on that unforgettable moment:

> He [Kennedy] did it because of his great concern and his humanitarian bent. I would like to feel that he made the call because he was concerned. He had come to know me as a person then. He had been in the debates and had done a good job when he talked about civil rights and what the Negro faces. Harris and others had really been talking with him about it. At the same time, I think he naturally had political considerations in mind. He was running for an office, and he needed to be elected, and I'm sure he felt the need for the Negro votes.[57]

Yet, King acknowledged that it had taken courage for Kennedy to take this action. King said he had always felt Nixon had "lost a real opportunity" to express his support at that critical moment:

> It indicated the direction that this man would take, if he became president. And I had known Nixon longer. He had been supposedly close to me, and he would call me frequently about things, seeking my advice. And yet, when this moment came, it was like he had never heard of me. So this is why *I really considered him a moral coward* and one who was unwilling to take a courageous step and take a risk. *And I am convinced that he lost the election because of that.*[58] [Emphasis added]

---

55 Coretta King, in *Voices of Freedom*, p. 68.
56 White, *The Making of the President—1960*, pp. 322-323.
57 King, *The Autobiography of Martin Luther King, Jr.*, p. 148.
58 Ibid.

INTO THE STORM

King was also impressed that his father, after so long endorsing Nixon, changed his mind and became a strong supporter of Kennedy.

Despite his father's endorsement of Kennedy, King himself never made an endorsement. He said he wanted to maintain a nonpartisan posture at all times. He explained, "I made a statement of thanks, and I expressed my gratitude for the call, but in the statement, I made it clear that I did not endorse any candidate and that this was not to be interpreted as an endorsement."[59]

On the campaign flight to Detroit, Press Secretary Pierre Salinger and the others quickly figured out that Shriver had pulled a fast one on them "at the urging of the pesky Wofford." Salinger was concerned enough to immediately alert Robert Kennedy who, with the genie unalterably out of the bottle, was clearly beside himself with rage.[60] JFK had already told his brother about the call. RFK's response was immediate: "You've lost the election. We had three southern governors tell us that if you support Khrushchev, Castro, or Martin Luther King, we're going to throw our votes to Nixon."[61]

Back at campaign headquarters in Washington, RFK made a fuming call to Sargent Shriver that he probably came to regret later:

> When Shriver disclosed the facts of the phone call from the Chicago airport, Kennedy tongue-lashed and belittled him in a tirade that permanently strained the family relationship between them. "*You bomb-throwers have lost the whole campaign*," he said. When he hung up on Shriver, he sent orders for Wofford and Martin to report to his office at once.[62]
> [Emphasis added]

Nowhere near finished, Bobby picked up with Louis Martin where he had left off with Shriver. Amid a "stream of curses delivered in an ominously quiet manner," Martin waited for an opening to defend himself. He said:

> Well, one reason we did it was that they took Dr. King out of Atlanta on an old traffic charge of driving without a license. Then they sentenced him to four months on the chain gang, denied bail, and took him off in the middle of the night to the state prison. All in one day. "How could they do that?" Kennedy asked doubtfully. "Who's the judge? You can't deny bail on a misdemeanor."

At length, RFK said, "Uh, goddammit," in a weary expletive that could have cut in many directions.[63]

---

59   Ibid, p. 150.
60   Branch, *Parting the Waters*, p. 364.
61   Wofford, *Voices of Freedom*, p. 68.
62   Branch, *Parting the Waters*, p. 364.
63   Ibid, pp. 364-365.

When Wofford arrived he, too, received a verbal beating. Kennedy reprimanded him for insubordination and putting Senator Kennedy into the middle of an explosive political controversy. In no uncertain terms, RFK directed Wofford and Martin to refrain from doing *anything else* controversial for the rest of the campaign. There would be no literature, no press conferences, no little schemes, nothing at all that made it into the newspapers. The abruptness with which he dismissed them underscored the thin ice upon which their campaign jobs remained.

King biographer Branch surveyed how the senator's call to Mrs. King was covered in the media. Senator Kennedy had encountered a reporter when he deplaned that night in New York who asked about his alleged telephone call to Coretta King. Kennedy had lied, saying he was concerned about a friend. The truth was that he had never met her and never would. Fortunately, the damage was minimal the next morning. JFK's sympathy call only appeared in a minor two-inch item on page 22 of the **New York Times**. Even better, the **Times** article mentioned that Vice President Nixon would have no comment on the King situation. Nixon's inaction further widened the gap that was opening for the Kennedy campaign with respect to the black vote. The rest of the news media gave even less attention to the story. Shriver, Wofford and Martin must have been relieved.

Although this good fortune presented an opportunity to publicize the phone call among African American media, Robert Kennedy's gag order dampened—for the moment—any enthusiasm for publicizing the senator's intervention on behalf of King. It would have been overkill anyway. That very morning Judge Mitchell changed his mind and signed an order to release King on $2,000 bond. Plenty of publicity followed the four chartered planes of lawyers and reporters who made their way to Reidsville to record King's release from prison.

Wofford and Martin had *a very good reason* to be ecstatic but, for the time being, also to lay low. By his own intervention with Judge Mitchell, *Robert Kennedy had broken his own ban against campaign involvement with the case.* The civil rights staffers in the Kennedy campaign were poised to exploit this change. It was only a matter of when to take the leap. *The situation was indeed ripe for the final step in the amazing fourteen-day sequence of race related events that changed history.*

The Blue Bomb

Despite Robert Kennedy's bare-knuckled scoldings, Wofford, Martin and Shriver still held their jobs inside the Kennedy campaign. Moreover, the previous week's events had not led to a public uproar from Southern politicians. Crucially, Wofford and Martin still had Shriver's full support for what they wanted to do—exploit the phenomenal "sea change" within the African American electorate due to the King case. In short, the Kennedy organization was now poised to achieve a decisive breakthrough.[64] *Incredibly, it was as though the Reidsville crisis had opened the final gate to an alternate dimension in space-time.* The path lay open to an opportunity that no one could have foreseen just two weeks earlier.

At the last minute, the Kennedy campaign civil rights team set about developing a stealth scheme designed to *flood African American voters with the Kennedy side of the King case* in a way that minimized the danger of a backlash among white voters. Taylor Branch later summarized their plot:

> [Their plan] was to print a pamphlet for mass distribution within the Negro churches of the nation *on the last Sunday before the presidential election.* They would run no newspaper ads, even in Negro papers, nor do anything else likely to filter into the white press. They would establish a "dummy committee" of preachers to protect the Kennedy campaign against being identified as the sponsor of the pamphlet. *They would include no statement from a Kennedy spokesman. ... It would not mention Robert Kennedy's call to the judge.*[65] [Emphasis added]

The pamphlet included remarks by Ralph Abernathy of the Southern Christian Leadership Conference (SCLC) and by Coretta King. It also included this moving comment by Daddy King:

> As a Baptist I was going to vote against John Kennedy because he was a Catholic, but if he had the courage to wipe the tears from my daughter-in-law's eyes then I have the courage to vote for him, Catholic or not. And I've got a whole suitcase full of votes that I'm taking up and putting in the lap of John Kennedy.[66]

The pamphlet title was "'No Comment' Nixon—Versus a Candidate with a Heart, Senator Kennedy."

The clock was running out. The plan was a daring gamble. In the short time left, everything else the civil rights office had scheduled for action before the election had to be cancelled. Shriver made the final decision to proceed. He ordered Wofford and Martin not to say anything about it to Robert Kennedy! Furthermore, Shriver said he would shoulder the responsibility *and* would finance the pamphlet himself, thereby hiding the plot from the campaign manager—RFK. No explicit endorsement of Kennedy from King was necessary—King's published statement of deep indebtedness to Senator Kennedy was good enough.

---

64   White, *The Making of the President—1960*, p. 323.
65   Branch, *Parting the Waters*, p. 368.
66   King, Sr., *Voices of Freedom*, p. 68.

THE KENNEDYS, KING, AND THE RACE ISSUE—1960

Because the pamphlet was printed on cheap blue paper it became known as the "blue bomb." Wofford directed the printing of approximately two million pamphlets at various locations across the country. Half a million were printed in Chicago alone. The pamphlets were shipped to their final locations by Greyhound bus.[67] Out of sight of the press and campaign professionals, the "blue bomb" spread quickly through the most effective private African American communications medium—the church. At their final destinations across the country, the pamphlets were praised from pulpits. This logistical miracle was kept secret from the Kennedy brothers until after the election.

The Blue Bomb plot was so secret that neither Shriver nor Wofford knew the secrets behind its distribution—Louis Martin only dimly understood the scheme:

> ...their main distribution network was drawn almost entirely from the Gardner Taylor faction of the National Baptist Convention, which was still in a death struggle with J. H. Jackson for control of the national church. The Kennedy "dummy committee" was located in Philadelphia, site of the riotous church schism in September. Its co-chairman was one of the preachers J. H. Jackson had expelled from the Convention and sent off to jail three years earlier, and the cover endorsement on the "blue bomb" was a quotation from Gardner Taylor himself.[68]

Everywhere in the African American community the church bells of the Kennedy intervention were ringing. On the Sunday before the election, all across the country the Blue Bomb pamphlets were distributed outside of African American churches after enthusiastic worship services were over. Taylor Branch described the stunning result this way:

> One cannot identify in the narrowness of American voting of 1960 any one particular episode or decision as being more important than any other in the final tallies: yet when one reflects that Illinois was carried by only 9,000 votes and that 250,000 Negroes are estimated to have voted for Kennedy; that Michigan was carried by 67,000 votes and that an estimated 250,000 Negroes voted for Kennedy; that South Carolina was carried by 10,000 votes and that an estimated 40,000 Negroes there voted for Kennedy, the candidate's instinctive decision must be ranked among the most crucial of the last few weeks.[69]

A dejected President Eisenhower was stunned by what he regarded as a "repudiation" of his eight years. He said Nixon had been too little concerned with Negro votes instead of too much. Eisenhower blamed the loss on "a couple of phone calls" by John and Robert Kennedy to Dr. King.[70]

---

67 White, *The Making of the President—1960*, p. 323.
68 Branch, *Parting the Waters*, pp. 372-373.
69 White, *The Making of the President—1960*, p. 323.
70 Branch, *Parting the Waters*, p. 374.

INTO THE STORM

The single most amazing statistic about Kennedy's victory was his 40 percent margin among African American voters. Whereas in 1956, their vote had split 60-40 for the Republican candidate, in 1960, their vote had split 70-30 for the Democratic candidate. This 30 percent shift produced Kennedy victory margins in the key states of Michigan, New Jersey, Pennsylvania, Illinois, and the Carolinas. Theodore White's detailed analysis of the 1960 results was incisive:

> Hard work (chiefly by the Civil Rights Section, led by the able Sargent Shriver and Harris Wofford) and the master stroke of intervention in the Martin Luther King arrest, not only reversed this Negro indifference to him [Kennedy], but gave him a larger share of the Negro vote than Stevenson had received in 1956 … In analyzing the Negro vote, almost all dissections agree that seven out of ten Negroes voted for Kennedy for president. In Detroit, Negro percentages ran at 8 to 1 or better; in the five Negro wards of Chicago's swollen South Side, the percentage ran approximately 4 to 1. And not only did the Northern Negro vote Democratic—so did the Southern Negro, in a complete reversal of form. In Memphis, Tennessee, Ward Thirty-five, a typical Negro ward, switched from 36 per cent Democratic in 1956 to 67 per cent Democratic in 1960; similar staggering switches occurred in South Carolina, in Georgia and in Texas.[71]

As Taylor Branch pointed out in 1988, in the 1960 election postmortem the King case "leaped to national attention as the overlooked master clue." Some reporters unearthed the story of the Blue Bomb. Others mentioned how the JFK and RFK phone calls—to Coretta King and Judge Mitchell, respectively—established the difference between the two candidates on civil rights: Kennedy's reaction to King's plight and Nixon's failure to do so.[72]

However, I believe that such knowledge as was apparent to interested observers in the aftermath of the 1960 campaign is now gathering dust in libraries. This extraordinary information is no longer extant in the minds of most Americans—now in their late 60s and older—who lived through those six critical events that changed the outcome of the 1960 election and, with it, the course of history.

Moreover, I am left pondering this strange forgotten dichotomy: The bad things that *did not happen, which would have taken place* because of the role that race played in the 1960 election, counterpoised against the good things that *did happen, which would not have taken place* without the role that race played in the 1960 election. The bad things that *would* have happened include the continuing avaricious plundering of the

---

71 White, *The Making of the President—1960*, pp. 354-355.
72 Branch, *Parting the Waters*, p. 375.

earth's resources by the sons of the Robber Barrons *and* war in the eastern and western hemispheres of our planet. The good things that *would not* have happened include the entire spectrum of the New Frontier—proposals for Medicaid, Medicare, increased Social Security benefits, minimum wage, low income housing, the Peace Corps, the Alliance for Progress, and peace instead of war.

I am also left marveling at this disquieting postscript. While JFK's call played the key role in the election, it was Robert Kennedy's call to Judge Mitchell that probably saved King's life. Furthermore, RFK's tight leash on Shriver, Wofford and Martin also played a key role in their development of the stealth aspect of the Blue Bomb scheme. In retrospect, the three key people responsible for the remarkable change in the course of world history that took place in 1960 were MLK, JFK *and* RFK. Within eight years, all three would be assassinated.

CHAPTER TWO

THE NEW FRONTIER—I

President John Kennedy's famous 20 January 1961 inaugural address did not mention his domestic vision of a New Frontier for America. That speech was almost entirely devoted to world affairs and did not mention his plans for solving the many vexing economic, political and social issues on the home front. But even with that limited scope, some of the more important fragments in his inaugural address on foreign aid and the Cold War were written by an economist:

> To those people in the huts and villages of half the globe struggling to break the bonds of mass misery, we pledge our best efforts to help them help themselves, for whatever period is required—*not because the communists may be doing it, not because we seek their votes, but because it is right.*
>
> So, let us begin anew—remembering on both sides that civility is not a sign of weakness, and sincerity is always subject to proof. *Let us never negotiate out of fear. But let us never fear to negotiate.*[73]

Those lines were suggested by John Kenneth Galbraith and Kennedy kept them in his address. At six feet eight, Galbraith was a giant and he was also a towering intellect in the field of economics—the heir to John Maynard Keynes.

Kennedy contacted Galbraith during the presidential campaign in the fall of 1960, and in January 1961 Galbraith notified Harvard that he would be leaving his post to join the Kennedy Administration as the American Ambassador to India. Before allowing him to leave for India, JFK kept Galbraith close to the flagpole as a senior advisor on economic and foreign policy.[74] Galbraith was one of the most important of Kennedy's "braintrusters" and played a key role in the president-elect's comprehensive

---
[73] John Kenneth Galbraith, *Ambassador's Journal* (New York: Paragon House, 1969 ed.), p. 16.
[74] Along with Council of Economic Advisers Chairman Walter Heller and incoming Treasury Secretary Douglas Dillon.

preparation for the panoply of issues he would be facing in designing the New Frontier program.

Kennedy's New Frontier dream included plans and policies directed at the problems facing America at home and abroad. His earliest and most concise articulation of what he meant by the term "New Frontier" was set forth in his 15 July 1960 acceptance speech at the Democratic National Convention in the Los Angeles Memorial Colosseum. In that acceptance speech, JFK referred to the westward expansion of the American pioneers as "the last frontier," a struggle "to conquer the enemies that threatened from without and within." He then cautioned his listeners that those problems had not all been solved and that the battles had not all been won. He declared, "we stand today on the edge of a New Frontier—the frontier of the 1960's—a frontier of unknown opportunities and perils—a frontier of unfulfilled hopes and threats."[75]

Kennedy contrasted his vision with those of Presidents Wilson and Roosevelt. Woodrow Wilson's New Freedom promised a new political and economic framework; Franklin Roosevelt's New Deal promised help and security to those in need. JFK said that he spoke not of promises but instead of "a set of challenges"—not what he intended to offer Americans, but what sacrifices he intended to ask of them. He wanted to appeal to their pride instead of their pocketbooks:

> But I tell you the New Frontier is here, whether we seek it or not. Beyond that frontier are the uncharted areas of science and space, unsolved problems of peace and war, unconquered pockets of ignorance and prejudice, unanswered questions of poverty and surplus. ... I believe the times demand new invention, innovation, imagination, decision. I am asking each of you to be pioneers on that New Frontier. ... For the harsh facts of the matter are that we stand on this frontier at a turning-point in history. We must prove all over again whether this nation—or any nation so conceived—can long endure—whether our society—with its freedom of choice, its breadth of opportunity, its range of alternatives—can compete with the single-minded advance of the communist system. ... Are we up to the task—are we equal to the challenge? Are we willing to match the Russian sacrifice of the present for the future—or must we sacrifice our future in order to enjoy the present? ... That is the question of the New Frontier.

Kennedy concluded by emphasizing that the real choice facing America was "between the public interest and private comfort," a remark that foreshadowed the eventual showdown between his vision of the future and that of many powerful Wall Street bankers and businessmen.

---

[75] 7/15/60, JFK acceptance speech at the Democratic National Convention.

THE NEW FRONTIER—I

Tumultuous events took place during the 188 days between the Democratic Convention speech and Kennedy's inaugural address (see Volume II of this series). Yet, in the short ten days between JFK's inauguration and his 2 February 1961 State of the Union speech, he said that he and the country were sailing into a storm more perilous than he had at first anticipated (see the excerpt in the Preamble to this volume).

Kennedy's Coup in the Eighty-Seventh Congress[76]

The election of 1960 was the first time in the twentieth century that the party taking over the presidency failed to gain in the Congress. The Democrats lost one seat in the senate and twenty-two in the House. In the Eighty-Seventh Congress the Democratic Party still had large paper majorities in both Houses—262-174 in the House and 65-35 in the senate. But the balance of power had swung significantly in the direction of the conservative coalition of Republicans and southern Democrats. Larger Democratic majorities were needed in both Houses to pass bills on housing, education, minimum wages, depressed areas, civil rights and medical care.

Crucially, no bill reported by a House committee could be considered on the House floor. No bill passed by both Houses in differing forms could proceed to a Senate-House conference committee, unless Howard Smith's (D-VA) Rules committee granted a "rule." Numerous "rules" were blocked while others were granted after long delays. Although the Democrats had an 8-4 edge in the committee, the conservatives—who had dominated the committee since 1937—effectively produced a 6-6 tie on any controversial issue. This guaranteed, as President Kennedy foresaw, that "Our whole program would be emasculated." In this dire situation, Kennedy did something extraordinary: With the help of Speaker Sam Rayburn, he engineered a coup in Congress. The president provoked a showdown with the conservative coalition over control of the House Rules Committee.

"The fight," as Sorensen recalled, "became vicious." Speaker Rayburn threatened to "purge" William Colmer (D-MS) from the committee because of his support of anti-Kennedy electors in Mississippi. Moderate southern leaders pleaded with Rayburn to compromise. The speaker offered a temporary addition to the committee of two Democrats and one Republican, making possible an 8-7 majority on most bills. The moderates agreed but a floor vote was required. Republican leader Charles Halleck announced that his party would oppose this change.

---

76   This section is mostly, but not exclusively, a recapitulation of a sequence of events described by Ted Sorensen in *Kennedy* (New York: Harper-Collins, 2009 Ed.), pp. 339-342.

An atmosphere of high suspense reigned as the vote was delayed until the day after the president's State of the Union Message, hoping that his speech would win fence-sitters. The proposal carried 217-212 but the meaning was clear. No bill could pass the House of Representatives without the votes of 40 to 60 southerners or Republicans, or a combination of the two. It also meant that the president could not afford any additional antagonists. He would be unable to bring the same degree of pressure to bear on every single confrontation that he had brought on the Rules Committee.

Kennedy's 1 January 1961 State of the Union Message

President Kennedy's first State of the Union speech was remarkable for its frank and deep alarm with respect to the numerous national security crises facing the U.S. in Asia, Africa and Latin America. It was even more significant for what it revealed about what the new president intended to do on the domestic front. The alarm bells had already begun ringing on Wall Street after JFK's inaugural address ten days earlier:

> The most striking thing about President Kennedy's inaugural address, it seems to us, is that it did not sound as though it came from the same dazzling man who not so long ago was promising to turn everything upside down in less than a hundred days. ... The president not only failed to elaborate on the New Frontier here at home, he spoke as though he had never heard of it. ... That [Democratic Convention] platform gave a long list of what it claimed to be "the rights of man"— and every item was a claim of some material thing upon the generosity of the state. Men should look to the state to provide them with jobs, homes, education, medical care; these are the inalienable rights for which, we are told, governments are instituted among men.

This *Wall Street Journal* (*WSJ*) editorial opinion piece warned its readers that Kennedy was not about to "abandon the liberalism of the campaign's New Frontier" with its "boldly experimental" foreign policy. "The words of an inaugural address," the editorial noted forebodingly, "are not necessarily the recipe by which an administration will act."[77]

From the *WSJ's* adverse perspective, the president's State of the Union address did not disappoint. Referring to Kennedy's staggering surprise at learning, during the previous ten days, about the depth of the peril facing America, a *WSJ* edition the next day said, "There were moments yesterday when we thought President Kennedy was trying to scare the nation out of its wits." The editorial incorrectly quoted the president as

---

77   1/23/61, *Wall Street Journal*, OPED, "President Kennedy."

saying, "I speak today in an hour of national peril and national emergency," when what he actually said was, "in an hour of national peril and national opportunity."

The editorial continued with this rant:

> The president's list [of crises] embraces not only the enduring problems of the struggles with communism—in Asia, in Africa, in Europe, in our own hemisphere—but almost every aspect of our life at home, from the state of the economy to juvenile delinquency and stream pollution. ... We would feel more reassured if we were sure that this administration, in its haste to deal with the things which are wrong, will not upset the things that are right.

An accompanying editorial on the same page piled on:

> In the domestic area his proposals for new spending include still more aid to distressed areas, more aid to housing under a new federal department, more aid to education, to medical research and medical care for old people ... Abroad, the president promises a "towering" foreign aid effort to patch up Asia, Africa and Latin America ... We do not know how the Congress will react to these spending promises. But even if a fraction of them are added to the Eisenhower budget, they will not only unbalance it but topple it over completely.[78]

These sarcastic, disparaging *WSJ* editorials—right out of the gate—made no attempt to conceal the depth of Wall Street's negative view of the new president. That aversion would deepen without relief for the remainder of Kennedy's life.

Far from attempting to scare America out of its wits, the president's address was an amazingly accurate prediction of what lay ahead and an attempt to turn peril into opportunity:

> I speak today in an hour of national peril and national opportunity. Before my term has ended, we shall have to test anew whether a nation organized and governed such as ours can endure. The outcome is by no means certain. The answers are by no means clear. All of us together—this administration, this Congress, this nation—must forge those answers. ... To state the facts frankly is not to despair the future nor indict the past. The prudent heir takes careful inventory of his legacies and gives a faithful accounting to those whom he owes an obligation of trust. And, while the occasion does not call for another recital of our blessings and assets, we have no greater asset than the willingness

---

78   1/31/61, *Wall Street Journal*, OPEDs, "One View of the Nation," and "No Reassurance Here." Embarrassed by the atrocious misquote, in a correction on 2/2/61 the *WSJ* apologized to the president.

of a free and determined people, through its elected officials, to face all problems frankly and meet all dangers free from panic or fear.[79]

Kennedy said that the state of the economy was disturbing:

> Business bankruptcies have reached their highest level since the Great Depression. Since 1951 farm income has been squeezed down by 25 percent. Save for a brief period in 1958, insured unemployment is at the highest peak in our history. Of some five and one-half million Americans who are without jobs, more than one million have been searching for work for more than four months. And during each month some 150,000 workers are exhausting their already meager jobless benefit rights.
>
> Nearly one-eighth of those who are without jobs live almost without hope in nearly one hundred especially depressed and troubled areas. The rest include new school graduates unable to use their talents, farmers forced to give up their part-time jobs which helped balance their family budgets, skilled and unskilled workers laid off in such important industries as metals, machinery, automobiles and apparel.

In an effort to begin remedying this situation, JFK announced his intent to propose measures to Congress to improve unemployment compensation, provide more food and other assistance for the families of the unemployed, to expand the services of the U.S. Employment Offices, to stimulate housing and construction, to raise the minimum wage, to offer tax incentives for sound plant investment, to offer federal grants for both higher and public school education, to further develop natural resources, and to encourage price stability. Kennedy also asked for measures to be undertaken in 1961 to provide health care for the aged under Social Security.

In foreign policy Kennedy urged seeking neutrality for Laos, and he objected to Cuba's domination by foreign and domestic tyrannies. He announced a new Alliance for Progress in Latin America, plans to expand the Food-for-Peace Program by using America's enormous agricultural surpluses to relieve hunger and help economic growth around the world. JFK also called for the formation of a National Peace Corps.

With respect to matters of defense, the **Wall Street Journal** editorials took no exception with Kennedy's plans to increase U.S. military strength to combat the "communist menace," but criticized his "hope" that he could ease Cold War tensions "simply by talking softly." They criticized the president for publicly censuring Chief of Naval Operations Arleigh Burke for "planning to speak harshly of the Soviets," and lamented, "and so every administration official is weighing the tone of his words."[80]

---

79   1/30/61, JFK annual message to the Congress on the State of the Union.
80   2/7/61, **Wall Street Journal**, OPED, "Twilight Diplomacy."

Preparing for the Presidency

As Kennedy took on the difficult task of picking the cabinet and sub-cabinet members of his administration, he simultaneously engaged in an intense effort to educate and prepare himself to chart the principal directions of policy. To do so, the president established special task forces that he considered as a service for himself. Schlesinger reports that in addition to seven task forces set up during the campaign, nineteen more were created by mid-December 1960—eleven in foreign policy and eight in domestic policy. Three more domestic policy task forces were added in January:

> Sorensen recruited what they regarded as the best talent in the country— Roosa, Samuelson, Robert Triffin and E. M. Bernstein on balance of payments; Galbraith, Rostow, Robert Nathan, Max Millikan, Harlan Cleveland on foreign economic policy; Berle and Lincoln Gordon on Latin America; Samuelson, Seymour Harris and Walter Heller on the domestic economy; James M. Landis on regulatory agencies; Paul Douglas on area redevelopment; Wilbur J. Cohen on social welfare; and many others.[81]

By the inauguration, twenty-four of the twenty-nine task forces had turned in their reports. Kennedy studied them and sent most of the reports to those who would become his cabinet or agency heads after 20 January 1961. The task forces gave the New Frontiersmen an opportunity to hammer out the new policies, programs, people and priorities.

JFK and the Dillon Dilemma

John Kenneth Galbraith had suggested Ford Motor Company President Robert McNamara for Treasury Secretary. McNamara declined the offer, nevertheless, he impressed Kennedy enough to be offered the position of Secretary of Defense.[82] Adlai Stevenson had wanted to become Secretary of State but had to settle instead for Ambassador to the UN. William Fulbright had actually been the president-elect's primary choice for Secretary of State but, when that fell through, JFK settled on Dean Rusk.[83]

But as the inauguration neared, the appointment of the Treasury Secretary was still unresolved and proved more difficult than the other major appointments. Besides McNamara, Yale Skull and Bones man Robert Lovett also turned down the job. Throughout the presidential campaign, JFK heard much about the twin problems

---

81 Schlesinger, *A Thousand Days* (New York: Houghton Mifflin, 2002 ed.) pp. 60-61
82 Galbraith, *Ambassador's Journal*, p. 1.
83 Ibid, p. 3 and p. 7.

of the balance of payments and the flight of gold from the U.S. After the election it became the dominant economic issue. Paul Nitze's national security task force reported to the president that everyone in the New York business community they had consulted had put the gold drain at the top of their list of issues. Nitze said that appointing a Secretary of the Treasury who was highly respected in the international financial world "would do more than anything else to consolidate confidence in the U.S. balance of payments position."[84]

Besides recommending Robert Lovett and John J. McCloy—Chairman of Chase Manhattan Bank and Chairman of the Council on Foreign Relations—for Treasury Secretary, Professor of Government at Columbia University Richard Neustadt also suggested the outgoing Under Secretary of State, Douglas Dillon. "Since Treasury is a major foreign policy post," Neustadt told Kennedy, "you would be advantaged further if your man had had a previous experience in State." Neustadt warned the president-elect that he would have to have to get assurances from Dillon before deciding on him.[85]

Dillon wanted the job, but as Eisenhower's Under Secretary of State for Economic Affairs, he might be accused of disloyalty if he turned around and supported President-elect Kennedy, whose campaign platform had disparaged the "high interest, tight money" policies of Eisenhower.[86] Schlesinger recalled that there had been a widespread feeling among Kennedy's supporters against the "Wall Street-acceptability thesis" and apprehension at the thought of appointing a Republican in such a commanding economic position. That opposition was present at Cambridge when Schlesinger, Galbraith and noted Keynesian economist Paul Samuelson met to come up with a candidate for the Treasury. They settled on four prospects: Averell Harriman, Senator Albert Gore, and Congressmen Henry Reuss and Richard Bolling. While all of them were well qualified, they lacked Wall Street's imprimatur.

A few days later, Galbraith and Schlesinger went to Washington to go over the Cambridge slate with Sargent Shriver, a democratic activist and husband of Eunice Kennedy. This threesome was an "informal committee" on personnel set up by the president-elect.[87] When the group dined with *Washington Post* editor and owner Philip Graham, they were distressed by his insistence that Douglas Dillon be appointed Secretary of the Treasury. They mistrusted Dillon on principle as an exponent of Republican economics and as a sub-cabinet official of a defeated administration.[88]

Schlesinger reported this conversation to Kennedy on 1 December 1960, and was surprised by his reaction: "Oh, I don't care about those things. All I want to know is:

---

84   Schlesinger, *A Thousand Days*, p. 133.
85   Ibid.
86   1/26/61, *TIME*, "The Dillon Dilemma."
87   Galbraith, *Ambassador's Journal*, p. 1.
88   Schlesinger, *A Thousand Days*, pp. 134-135.

is he able? —and will he go along with the program?" Dillon, too, had been surprised to get a phone call from Kennedy "kitchen cabinet" adviser Pierre Salinger in late November reporting that the president-elect wanted to speak with him that evening. Schlesinger recalled that Kennedy thought he had found someone the bankers would trust and would also support expansionist policies. And so, he ignored the protests of his informal personnel committee. However, JFK did relent to Bobby Kennedy's plea to get assurances from Dillon before moving forward. Asked point blank what he would do if he found himself at odds with presidential policy, Dillon responded that he would go quietly if he felt he had to resign. Schlesinger recalled that eventually "no two people became closer friends in the next years than Dillon and Bobby."[89]

But when Kennedy's selection of Dillon for Secretary of the Treasury was announced in mid-December, both Democrats and Republicans criticized the appointment. Dillon announced that he had cleared it with Eisenhower and Nixon, neither of whom objected so long as Dillon would pursue a sound fiscal policy. According to *Time* magazine there was more to the story than what Dillon had shared:

> But Doug Dillon had not told the whole story. He got no encouragement at all from Nixon, and Ike twice urged Dillon not to accept without a commitment in writing from Kennedy that he would have a free hand in setting Treasury policy. Dillon answered that he had such an agreement, although not in writing, but seemed to miss the presidential point. From the tone of his warning, it was clear that Dwight Eisenhower had not wanted Dillon to serve under Jack Kennedy and was mighty unhappy that his advice had been ignored.[90]

Time added that Eisenhower had reason to be madder than ever. At a Palm Beach press conference, Kennedy stated Dillon had been given no commitment at all. "A president," said Kennedy, "can't enter into treaties with cabinet members."[91]

Finding a Disciple of Growth to Chair the Council of Economic Advisers—Walter Wolfgang Heller

TIME praised Kennedy's choice of Dillon for Secretary of the Treasury, saying it promised to make the department "a fortress of moderation." But the magazine was more circumspect about the president's choice of Walter Heller for Chairman of the Council

---

89 Ibid, pp. 135-136.
90 1/26/61, *TIME*, "The Dillon Dilemma."
91 Ibid.

of Economic Advisers (CEA), because the Keynesian economist was one of the nation's most eloquent believers in government-planned growth of the economy:[92]

> Like Harvard University Economist John Kenneth Galbraith (***The Affluent Society***), Heller believes that a steady growth rate in the economy is a national necessity. Such growth, as he sees it, probably will require a "forced draft" of new capital investment. *The Federal Government (aided by state and local governments), rather than private enterprise, should be in charge of the increased investment*—concentrating on such fields as education, scientific research, health and other forms of "human capital." ... He hopes that foreign competition and an attack on domestic monopolies and labor featherbedding will help keep wages and prices in line. If they do not, "we should not shrink from selective controls" over such fields as consumer credit, mortgage rates and depreciation allowances—but not necessarily over prices and wages. He is for lower interest rates to spur the economy, and for a broader taxation base to pay for the new projects. On the budget: "You run a big surplus to fight inflation; you run a big deficit to fight recession." [Emphasis added]

Kennedy's first thought for the chairmanship of the CEA was Paul Samuelson, but Samuelson did not want to leave the Massachusetts Institute of Technology. With so many Harvard men among Kennedy's braintrusters, Heller's University of Minnesota alma mater (the same as Samuelson's) was a plus and JFK had been personally impressed by him during the election campaign.[93]

Heller suggested James Tobin for the second place on the CEA. A brilliant economic theorist from Yale, Tobin told Kennedy he was not qualified for the job: "I am afraid that I am only an ivory-tower economist." Kennedy replied, "That is the best kind. I am only an ivory-tower President." The deal was promptly consummated. Heller wanted Kermit Gordon of Williams College for the third member. Kennedy, unenthusiastic at first, finally agreed when Heller emphatically insisted that Gordon was the best man for the job. JFK advisor Clark Clifford proposed another Harvard economist, David Bell, for director of the Bureau of the Budget. JFK agreed: "He's a quiet fellow, but I like him, and I think I'll go through with him."[94]

The 2 February ***TIME*** magazine article also highlighted a few of Heller's more liberal views:

> On Tax Reform: Plug such unfair loopholes as percentage depletion allowances on oil and other minerals, rebates on stock dividends, and unbusinesslike expense-account deductions. Cut down the scope of

---

[92] 1/2/61, ***TIME***, "The New Administration—Disciple of Growth."
[93] Schlesinger, *A Thousand Days*, p. 137.
[94] Ibid, pp. 137-138.

THE NEW FRONTIER—I

income that can be classified as capital gains and is thus taxable at a lower rate…

On the Federal Debt: Congress should remove the federal debt limit (currently $293 billion) because it amounts to "fiscal hypocrisy" and leads to "financial brinksmanship"—frantic and artificial government efforts to stay within the debt limit in years when a revenue deficit is inevitable.

Under proper care and feeding, he believes, the U.S. economy can become "the most affluent economy the world has ever known"; by 1970 the gross national product will expand 50%, average family income will be up 30%.[95]

However, when Heller advised Kennedy to support the stand-by public works program then being proposed by Senator Joseph S. Clark on Capitol Hill, he encountered opposition in the White House and at the Treasury. At this time, the president and Ted Sorensen felt that plans for military and space spending put further domestic appropriations out of the question.[96] The economists writing for ***TIME*** and the ***Wall Street Journal*** could not have imagined that *in just three years* under JFK (including part of 1964), the gross national product would increase by 25 percent!

Kennedy aide Ted Sorensen described Heller as being knowledgeable without being doctrinaire, and liberal without being rigid:

Once he learned to adjust to Kennedy's methods, views and emphasis on the possible, Heller and his associates became the most highly influential and frequently consulted Council of Economic Advisers in history. In fact, both Heller and Science Adviser Jerome Wiesner, by learning to adapt their pedagogy to the president's preference for brevity and to accept philosophically his decisions contrary to their advice, greatly raised the stature of their offices.[97]

Sorenson remembers that during their first week in office he worked late one night with Dillon, Heller and Bell—on Kennedy's first budget, which required an increase in the deficit. When the president reluctantly accepted that conclusion the next morning, Sorenson observed, "The press will say, Mr. President, a spendthrift Democratic president insisted on this deficit over the protests of his Republican Secretary of the Treasury, but the truth is exactly the opposite!"[98]

The most important point about Kennedy's choice of Heller for the CEA chairmanship is that the president agreed with what Heller wanted to do even if he had

---

95   1/2/61, ***TIME***, "The New Administration—Disciple of Growth."
96   Schlesinger, *A Thousand Days*, p. 269.
97   Ibid, pp. 264-265.
98   Ted Sorensen, *Kennedy*, p. 272.

INTO THE STORM

to implement the strategy in stages. The OPED articles in the ***Wall Street Journal*** complained about this strategy right away. Presidential election chronicler Theodore White captured the essence of Kennedy's intention nicely:

> What he was interested in above all was movement—the United States, in its growth rate, must not lag behind other nations expanding at a rate greater than America's. He entered office with a Gross National Product of about $500 billion a year in 1960, and a growth rate of 2 1/2 percent annually in the previous administration.[99]

Kennedy understood that any national deficit should be no more than the gap between what was actually being produced and what could be produced *if the economy was working at full capacity*:

> In the past seven years, our rate of growth has slowed down disturbingly. In the past 3 1/2 years, the gap between what we can produce and what we do produce has threatened to become chronic. ... But realistic aims for 1961 are to reverse the downtrend in our economy, *to narrow the gap of unused potential*, to abate the waste and misery of unemployment, and at the same time to maintain reasonable stability of the price level. For 1962 and 1963 our programs must aim at expanding American productive capacity at a rate that shows the world the vigor and vitality of a free economy. ... The labor force is rising by 1.5 percent per year. Output per man rises annually by 2 percent as a result of new and better plants and equipment, modern technology, and improved human skills. *These increases in manpower and productivity provide the base for a potential annual growth of 3.5 percent in the nation's total output. This is not high enough. Our potential growth rate can and should be increased.* To do so, we propose to expand the nation's investments in physical and human resources, and in science and technology.[100] [Emphasis added]

In a nutshell, President Kennedy's plan was to use budgetary deficits and tax cuts to close the gap between full capacity and underachievement:

> The Federal Budget can and should be made an instrument of prosperity and stability, not a deterrent to recovery. This Administration is pledged to a Federal revenue system that balances the budget over the years of the economic cycle—yielding surpluses for debt retirement in times of high employment that more than offset the deficits which accompany—and indeed help overcome—low levels of economic activity in poor years.[101]

---

99 White, *The Making of the President 1964*, pp. 26-27.
100 2/2/61, President Kennedy's Special Message to the Congress: Program for Economic Recovery and Growth.
101 Ibid.

And just as important, the president was patient enough to time his proposals to create the least number of Republican antibodies as possible. By 1964, the gross national product had grown to $622 billion—a leap of 25 percent—and a growth rate of 5 percent a year. JFK's ability to understand this simple strategy for growth and his courage to apply it is what made him a great leader.

How the First Keynesian President Pulled His Punches

The *Wall Street Journal* was right about one thing: the manner in which President Kennedy intended to roll out his economic program. He intentionally moderated his proposals in order to get as many bills as possible through Congress in his first year. When Congress recessed in late 1961, 35 of the 55 bills proposed by Kennedy had been enacted.[102]

When JFK entered the White House, Wall Street was bracing for life under the first Keynesian president while Kennedy was bracing for life with an entrenched conservative power elite. Schlesinger described the problem this way:

> In the president's mind what was theoretically desirable had to be tempered by what was politically feasible. His campaign had emphasized discipline and sacrifice; his victory had been slim; his Congress was conservative; and, at least in the mind of the business community, his party had a reputation for fiscal irresponsibility.[103]

From the very beginning, Paul Samuelson, who chaired an interregnal task force, adjusted his recommendations to fit the mood of the president and Congress. While Samuelson believed in deficits and some social spending, for the time being he abstained from recommending investment in public works programs and mentioned a temporary tax cut only as an emergency weapon.[104]

For these reasons, in early 1961 Kennedy was opposed to increasing the deficit. Arthur Schlesinger made this observation about the president's cautious strategy:

> I have no doubt that his objections were political and not intellectual. He believed in 1961, as he had in 1952, in the general validity of compensatory fiscal policy; he was unquestionably the first Keynesian President. His problem throughout was not doctrine but politics.[105]

Kennedy complained to the eminent political commentator Walter Lippmann that, when asked, most economists avoided being pinned down on exactly how to stimulate

---

102 Theodore White, *The Making of the President 1964*, p. 26.
103 Schlesinger, *A Thousand Days*, p. 315.
104 Ibid, p. 628.
105 Ibid, p. 630.

growth. But the noted American economist Robert R. Nathan responded to JFK candidly:

> Nathan replied that the president could get his 5 per cent growth rate, but the price would be a deficit of $5 billion a year for the next ten years. The president said skeptically that would be great if only Nathan would organize the political support for such a policy. ... [But] the systematic creation of annual deficits, he said, was the one thing which the political situation, short of a depression, precluded his doing.

Kennedy told Schlesinger, "I don't want to be tagged as a big spender early in this administration. If I do, I won't get my programs through later on."[106]

This 24 December 1960 diary entry in John Kenneth Galbraith's *Ambassador's Journal* recalls Kennedy's concern as the inauguration approached:

> On the issue of economic recession and a tax cut, I urged that needed public expenditures be pressed first as an anti-recession measure. Therefore, if unemployment was still high, taxes could be reduced. I believe JFK agrees. He faces trouble with William McChesney Martin, Chairman of the Federal Reserve, and dislikes the prospect of a fight with him—which he thinks may be inevitable. Martin has been in office for a long time and, in his chosen sphere, obviously regards himself as superior to the president. It is the old notion that money gives a man position above politics and that banking, like the judiciary, is a separate power. I doubt, however, that in a showdown the president would be without resources. I would rather welcome this row were I in the White House.[107]

Kennedy knew that he needed the cooperation of the Federal Reserve for his plans to work. However, the outlook was uncertain as this 30 January 1961 entry in Galbraith's diary on the day of JFK's State of the Union speech makes clear:

> We talked of ways of getting the interest rates down. The Federal Reserve had submitted through Roosa [Robert V. Roosa—a brilliant young economist at the New York Federal Reserve Bank] some language which made no sense except that it seemed to urge that nothing be done. It had been billed as a great concession. The president telephoned Roosa, read it to him over the phone and asked him to explain. I think Bob had trouble; it sounded as though static was coming back over the phone."[108]

---

106 Ibid.
107 Galbraith, *Ambassador's Journal*, p. 8.
108 Ibid, p. 24.

THE NEW FRONTIER—I

The day before Kennedy's press conference on getting the economy moving (1 February), Galbraith joined Sorensen, Bundy and press secretary Pierre Salinger to help the president bone up on answers to potential questions he might encounter during the event. Galbraith's witty diary entry that day recounts this conversation he had with the president before the skull session:

> I did have a brief chat with the president in which he expressed great satisfaction that I was going to India. "Otherwise, you and Heller would have me expounding a far too radical position. *My policy is to be moderate and do much.*" I denied that I was a radical; only a realist. But I agreed that since I enjoyed stating moderate positions in abrasive form, I might be better in India.[109] [Emphasis added]

Clearly, Kennedy and Galbraith already had a certain chemistry that, with few exceptions,[110] most senior administration officials would not experience during the troubled waters that lay ahead.

Kennedy's 2 February 1961 Special Message to Congress[111]

Kennedy's 2 February 1961 7,500-word special message to Congress was a brilliant blueprint for recovery and economic growth.

Monetary Policy

At the top of nearly two dozen measures that Kennedy proposed to spur economic recovery was monetary policy and managing the deficit in the U.S. balance of payments. The president explained that monetary policy and debt management had to serve two apparently contradictory objectives: checking declines in the short-term rates that directly affect the balance of payments and lowering long-term interest rates to increase the flow of credit into the capital markets in order to promote domestic recovery and growth.

Those contradictory objectives could only be achieved concurrently, Kennedy said, if there was close cooperation between the Federal Reserve Board (FRB) and the Treasury. The White House believed it had secured the backing of the Federal Reserve "for the delicate trick of preventing a further drop in short-term interest rates while permitting long-term borrowing costs to decline." FRB officials acknowledged that

---

109   Ibid, p. 26.
110   Notably Robert Kennedy, Arthur Schlesinger and Ted Sorensen.
111   2/2/61, President Kennedy's Special Message to the Congress: Program for Economic Recovery and Growth.

"they shared the widespread view that such a rate pattern would be desirable," but said no decision had been made yet.[112]

In a disparagement of JFK's message to Congress the next day, a *Wall Street Journal* editorial alleged that these contradictory monetary objectives were paradoxes that inevitably result "once the view is accepted that the government's role in the economy is to manage everything."[113] Apparently, the author of that editorial was unable to understand that this particular contradiction resulted from *the government's failure to manage the economy*. The recessionary growth problem and the balance of payments problem—and the fact that solving both problems at once called for a delicate monetary strategy to handle the temporary contradiction between short-term and long-term interest rates—were the result of *Eisenhower's economic policies*.

As Galbraith later observed, not before or since had economists been so influential in public policy as during the Kennedy Administration—specifically Walter Heller, James Tobin and Kermit Gordon:

> Heller and his associates on the Council of Economic Advisors were scholars of high academic distinction and a strong practical orientation. Enjoying the confidence of the President, they dominated the making of economic and related political policy.[114]

In the White House in the first months after Kennedy's inauguration, and later from India and on frequent visits to Washington, Galbraith often played a key role in the discussions of economic policy. The country was fortunate to have brains in the White House and in the administration.

Housing[115]

The second measure on Kennedy's list to Congress addressed housing and community development. He said that housing and community development called for the revitalization of administrative machinery at the federal, state and local levels; expansion of long-term credit; reduction of mortgage interest rates; and Federal Housing Administration reduction of the maximum interest rates on FHA-insured loans from 5¾ to 5 ½ percent.

Not surprisingly, the 3 February negative *Wall Street Journal* editorial on JFK's economic growth plan included a disingenuous critique of the proposed housing measures. The editorial stated that no one doubted that the housing industry could build more houses, and then added this specious rebuke:

---

112 2/3/61, *Wall Street Journal*, White House Sees Backing by FRB on Rate Policy."
113 2/3/61, *Wall Street Journal*, OPED, "The Economic Proposals."
114 John Kenneth Galbraith, *A Journey Through Economic Time—A Firsthand View* (New York: Houghton Mifflin, 1994), pp. 169-170.
115 2/2/61, President Kennedy's Special Message to the Congress: Program for Economic Recovery and Growth.

> But it is something else to suppose that the government can determine what the home building potential should be and that, having determined it, the government then has a duty to see that this many houses get built willy-nilly. Quite apart from the political philosophy involved, it doesn't make much practical sense.[116]

Perhaps the editorial's author assumed that most of the newspaper readers would not bother to read the text of the president's message to Congress. There was *no haphazard specific number* of houses mentioned or implied in the president's proposal. The idea was to see more houses built because they were more affordable—for the wealthy, the middle class, and the poor in depressed areas. The only housing backlog was homes for the wealthy.

JFK ordered the FHA rate cut to be effective immediately. The cut reduced the monthly payments of home buyers who obtain new mortgages at or under the 5½ percent ceiling. This measure was also expected to exert a further downward pull on interest rates for conventional private mortgages not backed by the government.[117]

The fact that the interest rates for FHA-insured mortgages was something that Kennedy *could change without congressional approval* must have stuck in the craw of the editorial's author. JFK told his advisors that in the affluent sectors of American society major expenditures and innovations were resisted "by people who like it the way it used to be. Change is always pleasant to some people and unpleasant to others."[118]

A 24 February **TIME** article properly argued that cheaper houses were needed and that "not nearly enough effort" had been made for those who could not purchase homes "at the upper end of the price scale." Some builders were trying to build cheaper houses, the article said, and added that an expanding market was housing for "old people."[119]

Unemployment[120]

Three measures in Kennedy's special message to Congress concerned the problems associated with unemployment:

- Temporary unemployment insurance extension calls for Congress to enact a temporary program for extending the duration of benefits; and the establishment of a permanent unemployment compensation system which can do the job it was intended to do.

---

116 2/3/61, *Wall Street Journal*, OPED, "The Economic Proposals."
117 2/3/61, *Wall Street Journal*, "Kennedy Moves to Aid Economy."
118 Ted Sorensen, *Kennedy*, p. 405.
119 2/24/61 *TIME*, "Business: Housing Troubles?"
120 2/2/61, President Kennedy's Special Message to the Congress: Program for Economic Recovery and Growth.

- Expansion of the U.S. Employment Service requires expanded counseling and placement services for workers or job-seekers (a) in depressed areas; (b) in rural areas of chronic underemployment; (c) displaced by automation and technological change in factories and on farms; (d) in upper age brackets; and (e) recent graduates from college and high school.
- Under the Aid to Dependent Children program, needy children are eligible for assistance if their fathers are deceased, disabled, or family deserters. In logic and humanity, a child should also be eligible for assistance if his father is a needy unemployed worker. Congress should enact an interim amendment to the Aid to Dependent Children program to include the children of the needy unemployed.

Obviously, unemployed fathers should not have to desert their families so that their children would be eligible for assistance.

By February 1961, unemployment had reached a twenty-year high with 7.7 percent of the nation's 70 million workers jobless. Unemployment hit virtually every industry in every state. African Americans were the hardest hit—last hired and first fired—they comprised 10 percent of the population and 20 percent of the unemployed.[121]

On 16 February, Labor Secretary Arthur Goldberg asked the House Ways and Means Committee for quick approval of the president's proposal to give extra unemployment compensation payments to workers who had exhausted their benefits. The Kennedy proposal called for $950 million in government outlays, to begin on 1 April 1961, extending the 26 weeks of payments to 39 weeks. The measure was thought not only to be helpful to the jobless but also to spur the entire economy "by putting money quickly into the hands of people who can be expected to spend it in a hurry." Goldberg said the money would initially be taken from the Treasury and given to the states, who would reimburse the Treasury by 30 June 1966.[122]

On 23 February, the plan sailed through the House Ways and Means Committee, but without the president's plan on how to permanently finance the bill. The panel proposed instead to finance the new unemployment payments through a two-year rise in the federal unemployment tax rate from 3.1 percent to 3.5 percent.[123] On 22 March, Senate-House conferees cleared the way for final passage of the emergency unemployment compensation bill, removing the pay-as-you-go tax provision and sending Kennedy the bill almost exactly as he had requested.[124] He signed the bill into law on 27 March.

---

[121] 2/17/61, *TIME*, "The Economy: Unemployment's new face."
[122] 2/16/61, *Wall Street Journal*, "Goldberg Says Joblessness May Worsen, Asks Speedy Approval of Added Benefits."
[123] 2/23/61, *Wall Street Journal*, "What's New, Business and Finance."
[124] 3/22/61, *Wall Street Journal*, "Conferees Clear Extra Jobless Pay Bill; Final Passage is likely Today."

Of course, the ***Wall Street Journal*** lamented this plan to help the unemployed. In a 16 April editorial, the journal printed a derisive criticism of the president's program:
> …Alleviation of the suffering of those who are unemployed by no fault of their own … is not done by ill-considered, scatter-gun, inflationary "recovery" measures. It is not done by depressing (and denouncing) private business in order to expand the size and cost of government. It is not done by leading the whole people, including the unemployed, to believe that only Washington can solve their difficulties."[125]

This sort of mean-spirited lecture is another illustration of an eloquent maxim in Kennedy's inaugural address: "If a free society cannot help the many who are poor, it cannot save the few who are rich."

Minimum Wage[126]

The president urged Congress to pass a minimum wage bill that would immediately raise the minimum to $1.15 an hour and within two years to $1.25. He also asked that coverage be extended to several million workers not then covered in significant low-wage sectors of the labor market such as the retail trade and services. The new workers would begin with a minimum payment of $1.00, and then receive a gradual increase to the general $1.25 minimum. Kennedy offered these arguments for the increase:

> This will improve the incomes, level of living, morale, and efficiency of many of our lowest-paid workers and provide incentives for their more productive utilization. This can actually increase productivity and hold down unit costs, with no adverse effects on our competition in world markets and our balance of payments. More than four-fifths of those commodities affected by either export or import trends are produced by industries which would not be significantly affected by a moderate increase in the minimum wage.

He added that previous minimum wage increases had little effect on prices and that the prices charged for commodities produced in low-wage industries showed negligible change.

Key senate Democrats saw no problem getting the proposal though the senate, but the odds were not so good in the much more conservative House. A similar bill had failed in 1960 when, after a coalition of Republicans and southern Democrats proposed a watered-down version of the bill, Senate and House conferees were unable to reconcile their respective versions of the bill. JFK's bill was similar to the 1960 senate version and did not meet organized labor's goals and those of many employer groups.

---

125 4/17/61, *Wall Street Journal*, OPED, "Approaches to Unemployment."
126 2/2/61, President Kennedy's Special Message to the Congress: Program for Economic Recovery and Growth.

INTO THE STORM

The White House plan was to avoid a proposal that was too liberal to help its chances of passage in the House. Some observers felt that the retirement of conservative Representative Graham Arthur Braden, Chairman of the House Labor Committee, who for years had stalled and whittled down liberal minimum wage proposals, might increase the chances for passage.[127] White House officials hoped that the three-step increase would undercut any argument that a minimum wage rise would add to the recession by causing more unemployment.[128]

A 14 February *Wall Street Journal* editorial called the president's minimum wage proposal a "fraud" because he had stated the nation could not afford to have "an underpaid class." The editorial then goaded JFK for being "niggardly":

> Almost nobody bothers to ask why, if that underpaid class can thus be banished by the law, the government does not raise the minimum wage to $1.50 or $2.00 an hour. Why should the government be niggardly with its fiats?[129]

The answer, the writer admitted, was because that would be so high as to increase unemployment:

> The legislators, of course, understand this. The present figure of $1.25 was picked because, in the opinion of its supporters, it simply, more or less, confirms the realities. If they have guessed wrong, the law will throw some "underprivileged" people out of work entirely. If they have guessed right, then it is largely an unnecessary law.

"Either way," the editorial concluded, "the promises of the lawmakers aren't what they seem."

This miserly piece of editorial mischief misses the point entirely. The lawmakers, no less the president and the *Wall Street Journal*, understood very well why southern Democrats for years had *stalled and whittled down* minimum wage proposals: the employers of the poor underclass wouldn't pay a dime more than the law required. Furthermore, if an employer violated the law, only the worker—not the government—could, probably at certain risk, lodge a complaint. Under Kennedy's new proposal, the government could seek injunctions against violators on its own.[130]

In March, White House aides, worried by strong conservative opposition to the bill, began "putting the heat on recalcitrant Democrats" through phone calls and visits to the Capitol. Democratic sponsors were reportedly ready to compromise on the

---

127 2/1/61, *Wall Street Journal*, "Administration Minimum Wage Bill Likely Soon."
128 2/7/61, *Wall Street Journal*, "Kennedy Seeks to Raise Minimum Wage to $1.25 in 3 Years, Extend Coverage."
129 2/14/61, *Wall Street Journal*, OPED, "A Bit of Fraud." Use of the Fourteenth Century Middle English word "niggardly" technically is not a racial slur. Whether or not it is being used as a racial code word depends upon the context. In the context of "underclass" wages, African Americans were clearly at the top of the list of those suffering. In my view the remark was in poor taste.
130 2/7/61, *Wall Street Journal*, "Kennedy Seeks to Raise Minimum Wage to $1.25 in 3 Years, Extend Coverage."

floor by reducing "somewhat" the scope of the administration bill to "make it more generally acceptable."[131] On 24 March, the administration threw its full weight behind a new compromise bill to stave off a "more modest measure" backed by a conservative House coalition:

> The compromise reduces the number of people who would be newly covered by the minimum wage and limits their minimum to $1, dropping the "escalator clause" that would have raised their minimum to $1.25 by 1964. But this does not assure passage when the House starts voting either later today or tomorrow. Many liberal Democrats fear the odds still favor the competing measure which has widespread support among southern Democrats and Republicans.

Workers newly covered were also reduced from 4.3 million to 3.8 million. At a press conference, Kennedy said, "I find it difficult to understand how anybody could object to paying anybody who works in a business which makes over $1 million a year by 1963, $50 a week. I consider it to be a very minimum wage."[132]

On 4 May 1961, both Houses of Congress passed a compromise minimum wage bill raising the minimum to $1.15 per hour four months after the president signed it, and to $1.25 two years after that. For the 3.6 million newly covered workers—many working in retail enterprises—the starting minimum wage was set at $1 per hour four months after the bill was signed, to be increased to $1.15 three years later, and then to $1.25 a year after that. Fifteen southern Democratic votes were obtained by excluding the new coverage to laundry workers.[133] This exclusion fell heavily on African American women. Many were laundry workers for businesses or worked as maids for white families.

On 8 May, a predictably acerbic editorial attack on Kennedy's victory appeared in the ***Wall Street Journal***:

> With so much high-sounding talk about "conflict of interest" and the presumed need for higher ethical standards in government and business, maybe it's time for some down-to-earth thinking about the state of political morality in Washington D.C. ... Both the minimum wage and depressed areas laws are marvels of political hypocrisy. ... The basic concept of the minimum wage bill has been described this way: Extend coverage to as many workers as possible while incurring as few enemies as possible. By noting that the law covers 3.6 million workers

---

131   3/21/61, *Wall Street Journal*, "Administration Launches Effort to Save Minimum Wage Bill, Ponders Compromises."
132   3/24/61, *Wall Street Journal*, "Kennedy Supports New Minimum Wage Bill to Stave off More Conservative Measure."
133   5/24/61, *Wall Street Journal*, "Congress Votes Compromise Minimum Bill; House Margin Exceeds Expectations."

> not previously included, the politicians can trumpet their compassion for the "poor little people." That is a sham.[134]

The editorial charged that because the law excluded many workers and included others—like construction workers—whose pay was above the minimum wage; the new law was fraudulent. By this logic, previous minimum wage laws were also fraudulent. If the *Wall Street Journal* had been beating the drums for years to protect all American workers with a minimum wage law, then this editorial would not be the sham that it was. Its resort to the phrase "poor little people" was in very poor taste.

Depressed Areas and Surplus Food Distribution[135]

The distressed areas and surplus food distribution measures in Kennedy's special economic message to Congress went hand-in-hand. His very first executive order doubled the rations of surplus food that the federal government provided to four million needy people across the nation. According to Schlesinger, this was a response to JFK's memories of West Virginia and "the pitiful food rations doled out to the unemployed miners and their families."[136] His food distribution measure called for immediate steps to expand and improve the distribution of surplus food to needy families and the creation of pilot food-stamp programs as rapidly as possible for needy families in West Virginia, Pennsylvania, Eastern Kentucky, Northern Minnesota, Southern Illinois and the Detroit area. In addition, the president asked that the school lunch program be strengthened to "make the best possible nutrition available to every school-child, regardless of the economic condition of his family or local school district."

Depressed Areas[137]

A principal purpose of Kennedy's proposed Area Redevelopment Act was to create new jobs in chronic labor surplus areas by bringing in new private industries. His 2 February special economic message asked Congress to enact legislation for depressed areas that included these general measures: to provide for loans for private projects, technical assistance, loans and grants for public facilities, and programs for training and retraining workers in depressed areas. A senate banking subcommittee began some hearings on depressed areas legislation in February but suspended them pending receipt of a more exact administration policy.[138]

---

134 5/8/61, *Wall Street Journal*, OPED, "Ethics and Politics."
135 2/2/61, President Kennedy's Special Message to the Congress: Program for Economic Recovery and Growth.
136 Schlesinger, *A Thousand Days*, p. 166.
137 2/2/61, President Kennedy's Special Message to the Congress: Program for Economic Recovery and Growth.
138 2/22/61, *Wall Street Journal*, "Kennedy Asks Funds for Depressed Areas, Five Changes to Broaden Social Security."

On 3 March, the same senate banking subcommittee approved Kennedy's request for $400 million in four years for help to depressed areas, but liberal Democrats disapproved his request that the funds be administered by the Commerce Department and subject to control by congressional appropriations committees. Worried by the generally conservative nature of those committees, the senate liberals proposed to establish an independent agency to run the program using direct withdrawals from the treasury. The banking unit also removed a provision that would limit spending in the first year to $100 million.[139]

On 16 March, the Senate passed the $400 million depressed area aid bill by a surprisingly lopsided margin of 63 to 27. The Senate liberal Democratic bloc succeeded by a 49 to 44 margin in getting all program loans by direct withdrawals from the Treasury, whereas the House subcommittee bill stipulated that all funding had to go through the appropriations committees.[140] On 30 March, the full House passed the bill by a lopsided margin 250 to 157, after twice rejecting a watered-down Republican measure.[141]

A 28 April ***Wall Street Journal*** editorial slammed the depressed areas bill as an "untidy package" of "an impressive assortment of evils." No one, the editorial said, seriously expected the bill to "put so-called depressed areas on their feet." Moreover, the author bemoaned, the bill's financing should give even politicians "the horrors":

> Out of the $451 million to be dished out over four years, *$300 million will be dispensed without benefit of congressional review. The treasury will just sign for it—and then go out and borrow the money,* as though the government didn't have enough debt, deficits and inflationary potential. Apparently, Congress doesn't give a hoot any more about its once-prized power of the purse, at least when it conflicts with the vision of all those millions pouring into selected congressional districts.[142] [Emphasis added]

In spite of the ***Wall Street Journal's*** histrionic conjuring of *evils* and *horrors*, they owed President Kennedy and the House of Representative an apology for getting the story so wrong.

The author's inability to predict the correct outcome was undoubtedly the result of his zeal to stick it to the "politicians." When the House and Senate conferees met to iron out the principal, the only difference between the two versions of the bill—how to finance the program—they decided to stick with the House version. They chose financial control *by the appropriations committees, not withdrawals from the treasury.* That was the outcome that president Kennedy had asked for. He signed the bill into law on

---

139 3/3/61, ***Wall Street Journal***, "Senate Unit Approves Kennedy Depressed Area Plan, but Liberals Block Key Points."
140 3/16/61, ***Wall Street Journal***, "Senate Passes $400 Million Distress Area Aid Bill; House Unit Votes Similar Plan."
141 3/30/61, ***Wall Street Journal***, "House Passes Depressed Areas Bill, 250 to 167."
142 4/28/61, ***Wall Street Journal***, OPED, "Depressing Victory."

1 May, and William Blatt, the Pennsylvania Commissioner of Labor, was designated as the new Area Redevelopment Administrator under the Department of Commerce.[143]

Accelerating Procurement and Construction[144]

The president directed his cabinet and agency heads to submit by 17 February inventories of the following:

> (1) Ongoing public works projects which can be speeded up quickly, but for which additional appropriations might be needed, (2) needed natural resource conservation and development, light construction, maintenance, repair, and other work which likewise can be speeded up or started quickly, and (3) any additional construction or other projects which could be initiated at an early date. Excellent possibilities include programs to improve the roads, recreational facilities, and forests in the Project Work Inventories of the Forest Service, the National Park Service, and the Bureau of Land Management.

Kennedy noted that a particularly high priority should be assigned to projects located in areas of labor surplus.

Social Security and Medical Care for the Aged[145]

Improvements in the Old-Age, Survivors, and Disability Insurance Program: Raise the minimum monthly social security benefit for the retired worker from $33 per month to $43 per month; improve retirement protection by paying actuarially reduced benefits to men beginning at age 62; provide benefits for 170,000 additional people by liberalizing the Insured Status Requirement; increase the Aged Widow's Benefit from 75% to 85% of her Husband's Benefit Amount; and broaden disability insurance protection.

In his economic message, Kennedy had said that this program had to be undertaken in 1961, but some lawmakers said that it might not be acted on until 1962. This was because the president had endangered the chances for its passing by asking Congress to first pass five liberalizations of social security by 1 April 1961.[146] Kennedy modified the bill before he sent it to Congress on 9 February to meet some critics' objections.[147]

The heartless 13 February *Wall Street Journal* editorial about Kennedy's bill for medical care for the elderly will be mentioned below. In the end, the bill was shelved without ever coming up for a vote.

---

143   5/2 61, *Chicago Tribune*, "Kennedy Signs 394 Million Depressed Aid."
144   2/2/61, President Kennedy's Special Message to the Congress: Program for Economic Recovery and Growth.
145   Ibid.
146   2/7/61, *Wall Street Journal*, "Kennedy Medical Aid Bill Expected Soon; Congress May postpone Action Until 1962."
147   2/10/61, *Wall Street Journal*, "Kennedy Modifies Aged Health Plan to Meet Some Critics' Objections."

THE NEW FRONTIER—I

Additional Measures[148]

In addition to the above plans, JFK called for special tax incentives to increase business investment in physical plant and increase economic growth; investments in human resources; and investment in natural resources—including flood control, irrigation, navigation, watershed development, water pollution control, and above all, water desalinization. The president ordered the early payment of veterans' life insurance dividends.

Wages, Prices and the Payments Imbalance[149]

Finally, and most importantly, Kennedy called for measures to keep wages and prices stable. He was determined to do better than the 10 percent inflation that had taken place during Eisenhower's second term.

Kennedy faced a triple menace that had no modern precedent: a world-wide dollar threat, an economic recession, and a dangerous imbalance of payments that could be not remedied while American exports remained too high-priced for world markets.

John Kennedy was convinced that the new balance of payments problem made continued inflation intolerable. And so, he decided that there was no alternative to finding the elusive solution to the problem of constantly rising prices in a free and expanding economy. His entire economic program would go up in smoke unless the tradition of inflation could be broken. JFK understood clearly the inevitability that if prices rose as rapidly as income his plan for economic growth was doomed. As soon as the inflationary spiral picked up, the Federal Reserve Board would have to abandon low long-term interest rates.

The recipients of increases in social security, minimum wages, and welfare benefits would never be able to buy more with their larger checks than previously. His efforts to help people living on fixed incomes—pensioners, annuitants and others clearly in need—would suffer terribly, as he explained in his special economic message, from this "cruel tax upon the weak."

JFK succeeded in finding a way 1) to NOT countenance continued slack in the economy in order to postpone fighting inflation; 2) to NOT tighten long-term credit in order to fight it; and 3) to NOT avoid necessary spending in order to fight it.

During his presidency 1) prices remained stable to a degree unmatched in the tenure of his predecessor or by any other industrial country in the world during the same period; 2) wholesale industrial prices actually fell while production and income were rising; 3) the Wholesale Price Index fell to a point lower than when he took office; 4) the Consumer Price Index remained well below the "normal inflation" of 2-3 percent

---

148   2/2/61, President Kennedy's Special Message to the Congress: Program for Economic Recovery and Growth.
149   This section is my paraphrasing of a passage on wages, prices and imbalance of payment by Ted Sorensen in ***Kennedy***, pp. 434-436.

a year; and, 5) the record rises in national output, business profits and labor incomes was real, undiminished by any noticeable rise in prices.

It was an astonishing performance, and the *Wall Street Journal* editors hated him for it.

Reaction of Congress and Wall Street

Schlesinger characterized all of the above measures as a program of welfare but said that Kennedy continued to wrestle with the problem of obtaining a 5 per cent growth rate. Like Sorensen, Schlesinger felt that Kennedy's record with a conservative Congress was impressive:

> Congress proved responsive to the structural approach. Within six months it passed an area redevelopment bill, an omnibus housing bill, a farm bill, a rise in the minimum wage, the liberalization of social security, temporary unemployment benefits, benefits for dependent children of unemployed parents and a program to combat water pollution—a record of action on the domestic front unmatched in any single sitting since 1935.[150]

Initially, Republican reaction to Kennedy's 2 February economic message to Congress was rather mute. *TIME* reported this reaction from House Republican Minority Leader Charles Halleck: "We find no great quarrel with them, but we do not find them earthshaking."[151]

Not so for the *Wall Street Journal*. A 3 February editorial remarked that, in view of all of the president's task force reports, his 2 February recommendations were "rather modest proposals." However, the editorial warned that one could find in this message—"sometimes half hidden"—the view that one of the government's chief responsibilities is management of the economy, to ensure that it operates at its "full potential" and that the government "knows precisely what this potential is."[152] Another editorial on the same page called the unemployment proposal "massive." The writer scoffed at the minimum wage hike, grants to "so-called" depressed areas, federal aid to support local schools, and "other costly schemes" for giving everybody involved in the economy a boost:

> Well, if these plans are a sampling of what the president meant when [in his inaugural address] he called upon all Americans to ask what they

---

150   Schlesinger, *A Thousand Days*, pp. 628-629.
151   2/10/61, *TIME*, "The Economy: President Meets Recession."
152   2/3/61, *Wall Street Journal*, OPED, "The Economic Proposals."

could do for their country, then it is likely he will never find himself short of heroic volunteers.[153]

That snide derision of President Kennedy just two weeks into his presidency betrayed the depth of Wall Street's distaste for spending government money to help Americans in need.

Just ten days later, a ***Wall Street Journal*** editorial revealed rabid resentment toward Kennedy's request to provide help to children of the unemployed and health care for the ailing elderly under Social Security:

> When a man comes promising to do good for little children and to ease the sorrows of age, anyone who questions him is bound to sound a little like a skinflint who would take candy from babies and push his grandmother out in the cold. If you think not so, watch what is going to happen to those in Congress bold enough to raise questions about President Kennedy's proposals to meet the "urgent needs" of the nation's children and the "haunting fears" of old age that beset the rest of us. ... ...the promise itself is not all what it seems. ... ... [that] the government is going to improve medical care of all the people. *That promise, it seems to us, is pure deceit.*[154] [Emphasis added]

This editorial branded Kennedy's program of medical care for the aged "socialized medicine," and warned that "somebody had better ask questions about what is being built."

Kennedy and Business

Apart from the single statement in his special economic message to Congress that economic growth required the expansion of expenditures for business plants and equipment, Kennedy said nearly nothing specific about his plans for U.S. business. And he said nothing at all about his plans for business tax reform. The reason, as we shall see, was because those plans were the most radioactive part of his entire economic strategy. The president hoped to receive a number of important stimulative welfare bills on his desk to sign into law *before* revealing his plans for the wealthy and Wall Street. In the meantime, his Republican Secretary of the Treasury carried out his assignment to do what he could to win the confidence of the business community.

JFK's special assistant Arthur Schlesinger thought that Secretary Dillon's pursuit of business confidence practically went to the point of endorsing Eisenhower's balanced

---
153   2/3/61, *Wall Street Journal*, OPED, "Heroic Volunteers."
154   2/13/61, *Wall Street Journal*, OPED, "Questions on a Modest Proposal."

INTO THE STORM

budget principle. Schlesinger recalled Galbraith's congratulation to Dillon at the end of 1961 for his role in the "best ever" economic policy, and that the ambassador could not resist adding this quip:

> You have had a good performance because the budget was *not* balanced. Yet you keep saying that a balanced budget is the test. You have now promised a balanced budget for the next year although there is little chance that in the end it will be balanced. Therefore, though there is a very good chance you will have continued recovery and continued reduction in unemployment, improvement in balance of payments and stable prices, it will still be possible to say that you have failed. You are so bent on your discredit that you plan for it. I am reminded of a courtesan whose conquests have made her the cynosure of all men and the envy of all women and who at any critical moment in the conversation insists on the absolute importance of chastity.[155]

But Dillon's activities served the president's purpose for a while. The secretary's courting of business confidence for the administration, however, was unrequited.

Schlesinger acknowledges that Kennedy's initial appointments to the regulatory agencies were not reassuring to the business community.[156] Businessmen drew a distinctly negative message from these appointments:

> (They) expressed the theory that these agencies should respond to the public interest rather than to the industries regulated. This naturally outraged businessmen who, in earlier years, had grown used to regarding regulatory agencies as adjuncts of their own trade associations.[157]

On the other hand, business applauded the president's choice of Luther Hodges as Secretary of Commerce. The former governor of North Carolina had been a businessman himself, and he was, from the generation before, the radical New Frontiersmen. Still, Hodges declared he would never say that "this country should do this or that simply because business wants it."[158]

Kennedy's announcement that Harvard Law Professor Stanley S. Surrey was his choice for the Treasury Department's Assistant Secretary in charge of tax policy did not help matters with businessmen. A strong advocate for tough treatment of several types of business income getting special tax advantages, Surrey's posting sent the business community into orbit:

---

155 Schlesinger, *A Thousand Days*, pp. 630-631.
156 William L. Cary as chairman of the Securities and Exchange Commission; Newton Minow as chairman of the Federal Communications Commission; McCulloch as chairman of the National Labor Relations Board; Frank Joseph Swidler as chairman of the Federal Power Commission; and Paul R. Dixon as chairman of the Federal Trade Commission.
157 Ibid, p. 632.
158 Ibid, p. 633.

It provoked a storm of protests from mining companies, building and loan associations and other groups that feared higher taxes would result. A number of influential senators and representatives also protested the planned appointment, and for some days Mr. Kennedy debated whether to go ahead.[159]

In the end, Kennedy decided to dig in his heels and ignore the protests. Apparently, he was hoping that Surrey's announcement of a business tax incentive plan in late-March would mute the business protests.[160]

In an effort to send a positive signal to the business community, the treasury offered tax credits as an incentive for businesses to modernize their plants and equipment and in that manner to spur investment. Surprisingly, businessmen flinched at this offer. They would have preferred liberalized depreciation allowances. In any event, they were unable to believe that Democrats would ever do very much for business.[161]

But JFK's plans to end tax credits for dividends and to limit tax credits for business expenses surfaced in April[162] and sparked a rebellion in May,[163] putting his business tax reform plans on life support. At the end of June, Dillon's consent to a flat credit for new plant outlays appeared to breathe a bit of life back into the situation.[164] In mid-July, the House Ways and Means Committee defeated the president's tax dividend plan, but approved his tax credit plan to spur capital spending.[165] At the end of July, when the Berlin crisis raised the specter of a tax hike, Kennedy's tax credit was back on life support again.[166] With time running out for the passage of anything, the president abandoned bringing his business tax bill to a vote for 1961.[167]

Schlesinger recollected with disappointment that the summer "miscarriage" of Kennedy's business tax reform bill set the tone for Kennedy's relations with business for the remainder of his presidency. In 1963, Robert Kennedy shared his disillusionment with an interviewer:

---

[159] 2/1/61, *Wall Street Journal*, "Kennedy to Ignore Protests, Name Surrey Treasury's Number One Tax Policy-Maker."

[160] 3/24/61, *Wall Street Journal*, "Kennedy Nominee Bids to Spur Investment Now with Promise of Retroactive Tax Plan."

[161] Schlesinger, *A Thousand Days*, pp. 630-631.

[162] 4/3/61, *Wall Street Journal*, "Kennedy to Ask Easing of Depreciation Rules, End of Dividend Credit"; and 4/5/61, *Wall Street Journal*, OPED, "The First Reform."

[163] 5/5/61, *Wall Street Journal*, "President's Tax Plan is Greeted Skeptically by Democrats, Republicans in House Unit"; 5/10/61, *Wall Street Journal*, "House Republican Hits Kennedy Tax Plan; Democrats See Move to Stir Business Ire"; 5/12/61, *Wall Street Journal*, "Business Attacks Kennedy Plan to Tighten Dividend Taxation; Labor Backs Proposal"; 5/19/61, *Wall Street Journal*, OPED, "Crossed Tac Purposes"; 5/22/61, *Wall Street Journal*, "Business Criticism of Plans to Withhold Dividends Expected at Hearings This Week."

[164] 6/27/61, *Wall Street Journal*, "Tax Plan to Spur Business Outlays Wins Growing Support in Congress."

[165] 7/14/61, *Wall Street Journal*, "Dividend Tax Plan Defeated in Part by House Panel"; 7/18/61, *Wall Street Journal*, "House Unit Votes Tax Plan to Spur Capital Spending."

[166] 7/22/61, *Wall Street Journal*, "Kennedy Aim to Balance '63 Budget May Kill Business Tax Credit Plan."

[167] 8/23/61, *Wall Street Journal*, "Kennedy Abandons Effort to Bring Tax Plan to Vote This Year; Measure May be Revived in '62."

> The business community always has greater mistrust of any Democratic administration than of a Republican administration. It is an ideological reflex—obsolete, in my opinion—but that's one of the facts of life, so I don't know that businessmen, the big ones, anyway, no matter what we do, will ever be in love with us.

Nevertheless, in 1961 the president had hoped that the hostility from the business community might be overcome. At the same time, Schlesinger observed in his memoir of the president, "he had no great respect for the ideas of businessmen, and the respect declined the further their ideas moved away from their experience.[168]

---

[168] Schlesinger, *A Thousand Days*, pp. 631-633.

CHAPTER THREE

WHEN FICTION IS STRANGER THAN TRUTH: VECIANA AND PHILLIPS IN CUBA—1959–1960

Antonio Veciana Blanch was born on 18 October 1928 in Havana, Cuba. In 1960, he was a public accountant working as an assistant manager at Banco Financiero, the bank owned by Cuban sugar magnate and CIA asset Julio Lobo. Veciana was also president of the Cuban Certified Public Accountants Association. The Veciana story is ubiquitous among researchers of the Kennedy assassination, but views vary considerably about which events did or did not take place in his life. The lengthy and byzantine history of Veciana's activities with the U.S. Military and the CIA is dominated by his claim that he had a meeting with Dave Phillips—who was using the pseudonym Maurice Bishop—in Dallas, Texas, in September 1963; and, further, that a man Veciana later recognized as Lee Harvey Oswald was also present at that meeting. For nearly four decades, that single assertion has sucked the oxygen out of attention to the less sensational but necessary research into the rest of Veciana's story and the documentary record surrounding it, such as it is.

Veciana's accounts have radically changed over the four decades leading up to the appearance of his 2017 book *Trained to Kill*. His first account on 2 March 1976 was given to Gaeton Fonzi, an investigator then working for Senator Schweiker of the Select Committee on Intelligence Activities (SSCIA). That interview occurred while he was incarcerated for cocaine trafficking, an offense for which he still claims he was innocent. Three months after his parole, Veciana was interviewed by journalist Dick Russell. Veciana gave his third account in a 25-26 March 1978 deposition to the House Select Committee on Assassinations (HSCA). The fourth phase of his story took place during the numerous lengthy sessions he had with Gaeton Fonzi during the fifteen years between the HSCA's final report (2 January 1979) and the 1993 appearance of Fonzi's book, *The Last Investigation.*

Gaeton Fonzi passed away on 30 August 2012. Two years later, on 26 September 2014, Veciana gave his fifth account at the Assassination Archives Research Center (AARC) symposium in Bethesda, Maryland. At the time, Veciana was already at an advanced stage of preparation for his book, *Trained to Kill.* In that work, he offered his sixth and final version of the events that took place between 1959 and 1961.

There are many minor differences among Antonio Veciana's versions of the Bishop-Phillips saga. But there are also significant structural and existential changes to his story. Among these, the two most important are the date that Phillips first approached Veciana in Cuba, *and* the true identity of the person using the name Maurice Bishop. The vast majority of the relevant intelligence documents in the available record were not released until late in this epic tale—not until the mid-1990s as a result of the JFK Assassination Records Collection Act of 1992. As such, they were not available to Veciana until then. In the late 1970s, the HSCA did get access to significant amounts of pertinent classified records. However, many CIA records were not shared with the committee. The committee and its researchers were bound by secrecy oaths not to publicly reveal classified information gained during their investigation.

Minor differences in Veciana's various accounts may, in some cases, be excused as resulting from confusion or faulty memory. However, there is no getting around this unwelcome problem: major structural and existential changes to Veciana's story indicate deception—if not in one place, then inescapably in another. The principal task facing researchers today is to decide which accounts are true—or partly true—and which are not. If we are to rescue *any* pieces of this puzzle that were true, we must first strip away many pieces that were false.

This job is made more difficult by the accounts of American and Cuban intelligence officers whose experiences bear upon this mission, most notably CIA staff officer David Phillips and Cuban intelligence chief Fabian Escalante. Escalante's Washington-based officers from the Cuban Interest Section were naturally researching the new records as they poured out in 1994.[169] And as far as I can determine, in his 1995 book, *The Secret*

---

169 In December 2004, I met with Cuban intelligence chief Fabian Escalante for an extended private discussion during a joint conference of 25 select Cubans and Americans in Nassau, the Bahamas. It was clear to me that Fabian was fully up to speed on the documents released in the U.S. as a result of the JFK Assassination Records Collection Act.

War, Fabian Escalante was the *only* author who immediately discovered the most glaring problem with Veciana's chronology—the date Phillips allegedly recruited Veciana in Cuba. In 1995, Escalante made the *forced readjustment* of that date from mid-1960 to mid-1959, *two decades before* Veciana followed suit in 2014!

The release of CIA documents left Veciana with a difficult choice. He realized that he had to give up the entire story of his recruitment by Phillips in Cuba *or* adjust the date to the time when Phillips *really was in Cuba*. Veciana decided to preserve his Phillips story and therefore was *forced* to change the date of the recruitment. Why he waited until 2014 to do that raises problems that I will address in future volumes. Veciana's unfortunate decision ended up causing more problems than it solved. I will mention them later in this chapter. In Chapter Eleven, I will show what happens when Veciana's Cuban story is moved forward in time into his *original* chronology—*back where it belongs*—when Phillips was *not* in Cuba.

I hope the reader will not be disappointed that I will *not* start my examination of Veciana's history with his alleged meeting with Oswald and Phillips in Dallas during September 1963. For reasons that will become obvious, I will get to that shiny object in Volume V. In this chapter, I will only mention the claim about 1963 in connection with a caper Veciana pulled off with his best friend Zabala in 1976.

And so, in this chapter, I will begin my examination of Veciana by taking the reader back to the point in time where he now claims he was recruited in Cuba by a man he knew as Maurice Bishop. In Veciana's final two accounts at the 2014 AARC conference and in his 2017 book, **Trained to Kill**, he forcefully and *unequivocally* contended that Maurice Bishop *was* Dave Phillips. For this reason, in this chapter I will be using the name Phillips instead of Bishop. When I mean the true Phillips, I will use the appellation "Phillips"; when I mean Bishop, I will—for the most part—use the appellation "*notional* Phillips." Only in instances where clarity demands it will I use the pseudonym Bishop.

The 38-Year-Long Wrong Date—Mid-1960—for Phillips' First Approach to Veciana in Cuba

When did Phillips first approach Veciana in Cuba? Veciana's *six* accounts of that event have left us—with only the slightest permutations—with three different periods of time. While the dates of those six accounts moved *forward in time*, the date of their first encounter in Cuba moved *backward in time*. The start of those three time periods are first, mid-1960; then, the end of 1959; and, finally, mid-September 1959.

INTO THE STORM

In the table below, I have assembled the dates given by Veciana to congressional investigations and in his book, as well as the dates given by other American and Cuba investigators and researchers:[170]

DATE OF FIRST MEETING	DATE OF SOURCE	CLAIMS, EVENTS AND SOURCE DETAILS
Mid-1960	3/2/76	Veciana to Schweiker investigation, interview by Fonzi, p.1.
1960	6/1976	Dick Russell interview of Veciana for *New Times* magazine.
Mid-1960	4/26/78	Veciana HSCA deposition, pp. 5-8, 65.
8/1/1960	1993	Fonzi, *The Last Investigation*, p. 445
1960	1994	*The Plot to Kill Kennedy and Castro*, Claudia Furiati, p. 36; and 1960 again on p. 145, in interview with Fabian Escalante.
	1994	Appearance of large volume of CIA records on Phillips' activities and movements due to the passage of **October 1992 JFK Records Collection Act.**
1959	1995	*The Secret War*, Fabian Escalante, p. 95, "recruited in 1959," and trained "in the final months of 1959…"
1960	2003	*The Man Who Knew Too Much*, (1992 Ed.) Dick Russell, p. 295, and p. 419 [Interview was in June 1976].
Late 1959	2004	*The Cuba Project*, Fabian Escalante, p. 93.
	8/30/2012	**Death of Gaeton Fonzi.**
1960	2013	Fonzi, *The Last Investigation*, (2013) pp. 128-129.
1960	2013	Summers, *Not in Your Lifetime,* (2013) p. 302.
Late 1959	9/26/2014	AARC Symposium; links to the time of Veciana's two interviews with Che Guevara [Problem: The two Guevara interviews did not happen until approximately February 1960: "some months after" Che was named head of the Banco Nacional in November 1959," (see *Trained to Kill*, p. 82).
Mid-Sept 1959	2017	"Just a few days after Jack Ruby departed Cuba," *Trained to Kill*, p. 40, [Note: Ruby departed Cuba on 9/13/59].

---

170 Besides Veciana's versions given to the SSCIA and HSCA, his 2014 version to the AARC conference, and his 2017 autobiography, this table addresses only those authors who personally spoke with Veciana. For obvious reasons, the one exception is Cuban intelligence chief, Fabien Escalante.

Fonzi's 2013 edition of *The Last Investigation* (published just after his death) shows no awareness that Veciana's identification of Bishop as Phillips *destroyed*—as Escalante had discovered—*any* possibility that Veciana's first meeting with Phillips could have taken place in mid-1960.

Swiss Cheese

For thirty-eight years, Veciana's accounts to the SSCIA, HSCA, Gaeton Fonzi, Tony Summers, and Dick Russell about his recruitment by the *notional* Phillips had more holes than Swiss cheese. For example, Phillips was a contract "NOC"—a non-official-cover CIA asset in Havana *without diplomatic protection*. His duties concerned Agency propaganda activities and, if he observed anything significant in the course of that work, to report it to the Havana station. Nothing more. His work *precluded* recruiting anti-Castro Cubans. Phillips' participation in recruiting Cuban dissidents would have endangered his life and the lives of his wife and children—not to mention CIA operations against Castro in Cuba.

Even if all of that was *not* true, Veciana's thirty-eight-year claim of being recruited in Cuba by the notional Phillips in mid-1960 was *impossible* for an even more compelling reason: the real Dave Phillips was nowhere near Cuba! Even the most *cursory examination* of the declassified CIA records on Phillips reveals that he was *not* in Cuba in mid-1960. He was at CIA headquarters in Langley, Virginia, up to his eyeballs setting up the propaganda and psychological warfare operations for Eisenhower's covert program to overthrow Castro.

It is equally impossible that—given Phillips' valuable work on the Eisenhower plan to overthrow Castro—that he would have been sent back into Cuba covertly on a dangerous mission to recruit and train a single anti-Castro asset. As I will demonstrate in this chapter, in mid-1960, Phillips' work for the CIA was well-known to Cuban intelligence. *If*, for any reason, Phillips *had* made a trip to Cuba in the second half of 1960, he would have been executed.

The reason why it took researchers so long to catch up with Escalante about the chronological impossibly of Veciana's original scenario is a problem I will leave to others to ponder. In this chapter, I am concerned with why it took Veciana so long to abandon his mid-1960 scenario. One obvious reason it took him so long is because he invented his *notional* Phillips story twenty years *before* the public release of Phillips' CIA records. When Veciana fabricated his mid-1960 recruitment by the CIA in Cuba, *he knew nothing about Phillips history during that period.* But the point is that when the records were released and Veciana found himself stuck with an impossible scenario—*he still waited almost twenty more years* to follow Escalante's lead and adjust the recruitment date back to mid-1959. Why?

The Death of Gaeton Fonzi, the Backward Movement in Time of the Recruitment, and Veciana's Increasing Certainty that Bishop Was Phillips

We do not know for certain *exactly* when Veciana first figured out that his mid-1960 scenario was unworkable. What we do know is that he did not publicly endorse a 1959 scenario until after Gaeton Fonzi's death in 2012. Similarly, Veciana did not give a full-throated claim that Bishop was Phillips until then. *Those two existential changes in Veciana's story happened at the same time.*

Thus, the backward movement in time for the *notional* Phillips' initial approach to Veciana was a fundamental structural alteration that bears crucially on the existential change of the name Veciana used for the man he now claims recruited him. Between the publication of the HSCA's final report in early 1979 and the publication of Fonzi's **The Last Investigation** in 1993, Fonzi asked Veciana—over and over again—if Bishop was David Phillips. Eventually, after more than a decade of unfaltering denials that he knew who Bishop was, Veciana began to begrudgingly concede that Bishop *might* have been Phillips. Two years after the death of Gaeton Fonzi, at the AARC symposium in Bethesda, Maryland, Veciana surprised the many researchers attending the conference by declaring *unequivocally* that Phillips had been Bishop.

To do that, however, Veciana had to face the complicated task of *recasting the entire saga* of Phillips' initial approach to, assessment of, and training for Veciana into a time period when Phillips was *actually* in Havana. And so, at the 2014 AARC symposium, Veciana replaced his mid-1960 start date scenario with a start date at the end of 1959. In his 2017 book, **Trained to Kill**, Veciana repeated his claim that Bishop was Phillips *and* pushed the first encounter with his *notional* Phillips *even further* back in time—to mid-September 1959. Veciana anchored his recruitment by the *notional* Phillips to a known firm event: "David Phillips came to meet me for the first time just a few days after Jack Ruby departed Cuba."[171] When viewed against the chronological backdrop of what was happening to Phillips at that time, Veciana's decision to anchor his recruitment on Ruby's departure would result in a Keystone Cops comedy. I will get to that problem shortly.

---

171   Antonio Veciana *Trained to Kill—The Inside Story of CIA Plots Against Castro, Kennedy, and Che* (Skyhorse: New York, 2017), p. 40.

VECIANA AND PHILLIPS IN CUBA—1959-1960

Out of Place and Out of Context

And so, after thirty-eight years, Veciana made the difficult choice to abandon his original chronology about his recruitment and handling by his alleged CIA case officer, the *notional* David Phillips. But when Veciana *finally* faced the music, that major chronological *makeover* turned out to be about as easy as placing a square peg into a round hole. Back in the summer and fall of 1959, Phillips and his family were in *great danger*. When Veciana superimposed his notional Phillips scenario on the situation in 1959, the result was an unmitigated mess. The activities that Veciana claimed the notional Phillips undertook were out of place and out of context.

As Phillips situation became increasingly precarious, the CIA decided to pull Phillips out of Cuba and Phillips and his wife decided to leave the CIA for good. In his memoir, ***The Night Watch***, Phillips recalled:

> In the final days of 1959, I realized how *precarious* my situation had become, and how *I would surely be jailed* should Castro's new intelligence service discover I was an intelligence officer working for the CIA. I had spotted another American, also a businessman in Havana, whom I suspected was cooperating with CIA. I wasn't certain at the time, and there was obviously no need for me to know. I was *shocked* when he was arrested by Cuban authorities and, without ceremony or trial, *executed*.[172]
> [Emphasis added]

Phillips and his family left Cuba sometime in February 1960, narrowly escaping Castro's clutches. Phillips would never set foot on the island again.

In the sections below, I will undertake an examination of Veciana's story about the birth of his work for the *notional* Phillips in Cuba during the last half of 1959. To do that, I will juxtapose that story on the extensive CIA documentary record about Phillips' activities in Cuba during the same period. I will set the established record beside *each episode* of Veciana's narrative—from the moment of the *notional* Phillips' alleged recruitment in mid-September 1959 to the end of his alleged training program on or about 21 November 1959. I will use Veciana's description of events in ***Trained to Kill*** to assist measuring the approximate time benchmarks in this nine-and-a-half-week story about the *notional* Phillips. I will use those benchmarks to compare Veciana's scenario of the *notional* Phillips to the known events in the CIA documentary record about the *true* Phillips.

The documentary record of Phillips' work for the CIA in Cuba during the last half of 1959 is *robust*. That record does *not reflect any* of the episodes of Veciana's *notional* Phillips narrative for that period. At the same time, Veciana's *first appearance* in the

---
172 Phillips, *The Night Watch: Twenty Five Years of Peculiar Service* (New York: Atheneum, 1977), p. 79.

INTO THE STORM

CIA's records from Havana did *not occur* until 9 December 1960—ten months *after* Phillips' departure from Cuba. On that occasion, Veciana approached the Havana Chief of Station, James Noel, and asked him for CIA assistance in a plot to kill Castro and his top associates. Noel refused.[173] I will examine that event in Chapter Eleven. The point is that *not a single CIA record exists for either Veciana or his account of Phillips' activities in Cuba during 1959*.

Below, I will proceed to a detailed comparison of the CIA record with Veciana's *notional* narrative about Phillips in the second half of 1959. Veciana's final (2017) sequence of events covers slightly more than nine and a half weeks of activity in Cuba during 1959. As I mentioned above, Veciana anchors his *notional* narrative about Phillips in Cuba "a few days after" Jack Ruby left the island in 1959.[174] Cuban immigration records show that Ruby's departure occurred on 11 September 1959, and that he arrived in Miami the next day. Therefore, the sections below on Veciana's *notional* Phillips' cover a period that lasted from approximately 15 September until 21 November 1959.[175]

In Volumes I and II of my current multi-volume series, I described how CIA operations at headquarters and the Havana station were jeopardized by security threats resulting from the *real* Phillips' dire situation in Cuba during the final six months of 1959. Phillips' nightmares began when, on orders from headquarters, he became entangled in the Cuban cattlemen's conspiracy to kill Castro. That bad dream was further compounded by another major breach of security. Phillips' *hazardous situation in Havana* was so bad that it not only undermines the plausibility of Veciana's original accounts but also leaves one wondering by what logic *any* of Veciana's claims can be trusted.

I return once again to Phillips' involvement in the 1959 Cuban cattlemen's conspiracy to kill Castro.

The Cattleman's Conspiracy and the Implausibility of Veciana's 1959 Scenario

Toward the end of July 1959, the CIA Station in Havana instructed Dave Phillips to contact Michael P. ("Jack") Malone, vice president of the Czarnikow Rionda firm, which controlled four of the major sugar companies in Cuba. He was also the manager of Robert Kleberg's (King Ranch) $5.7 million 40,000-acre cattle ranch in Camaguey

---

173 12/9/60, HAVA 7133 to DIR; RIF 104-10181-10434.
174 Veciana, ***Trained to Kill***, p. 39.
175 Thomas Hunt, "Jack Ruby's 1959 Visit to Havana," ***Informer: The Journal of American Mafia History***, October 2009; see also, http://mafiahistory.us/a001/f_ruby.html.

Province, Cuba. In a 6 August 1959 memo, Phillips wrote down what happened as a result of that instruction.[176]

On 29 July, Phillips met Malone in his room at the Hotel Nacional in Havana. Malone said he had talked with several people at CIA HQS about his association with a group of Cuban cattlemen anxious to do something about Castro's Agrarian Reform Program. CIA HQS had told Malone that Phillips would be able to act as an advisor in a public relations program. The cattlemen had approached Malone in the hope that he and the interests he represented would contribute to a fund being generated to prepare "a plan of action."

Malone told Phillips that Caines Milanes was the president of the National Association of Cattlemen of Cuba (NACC). Phillips was driven to meet Caines at a large home in Miramar that belonged to a prominent Cuban rancher, Gustavo de Los Reyes. Phillips had been assured that he and Malone would only be meeting with Caines and one other associate. However, an attorney for the Cuban Cattleman's Association and others also joined the meeting. In his detailed account about the meeting afterward, Phillips said that in view of being in this "sudden crowd" he was inclined to be "as discreet as possible."

Caines, who dominated the two-hour meeting, headed a group working inside of Cuba in support of a plot hatched by Dominican Republic dictator Raphael Trujillo (discussed in detail in Volume I). Caines was to become the new vice president of Cuba if the plot succeeded in overthrowing Castro. When Caines challenged Phillips to offer a plan, Phillips responded with the idea of buying a newspaper and using it to make "daily editorial attacks against the drastic aspects of the Agrarian Reform Program ... and growing communist activity in Cuba." Phillips recalled that the cattlemen "liked the idea" and talked about which newspaper to buy.

Phillips soon discovered that this group of Cubans was less interested in publicity work than in *direct militant action to overthrow the Castro government*. They spoke about what would happen if *there was an invasion of Cuba from the Dominican Republic* and if *Castro were assassinated*. Phillips wrote afterward:

> *Things really became conspiratorial.* Malone was an enthusiastic supporter of the most militant ideas. Generally, he exuded a "give 'em hell" attitude. *I felt it was time to leave.* I promised to report back to the group two days later with a plan of some kind. But I made it clear that I would have to consult with my home office. [Emphasis added]

Phillips suspected, correctly, that there may have been an informant in the group.

---

176 8/6/59, CIA memorandum by Michael H. Choaden, Subject: Meeting with Cuban Group RE Public Relations Campaign. RIF 104-10267-10168.

INTO THE STORM

The danger of meeting with Caines' group was much greater than Phillips had imagined. July 1959 was the moment, as Castro told Herb Matthews in 1963, that the Cuban communists "had men who were truly revolutionary, loyal, honest and trained. I needed them."[177] July 1959 was also the moment that Castro decided to lower the boom on the Cuban cattlemen.

After Phillips extricated himself from that scary 31 July meeting, he spent the next several days composing a very disturbing 4-page, 15-paragraph memorandum for the record about his frightening experience with the Cuban cattlemen. Dated 6 August 1959, that memo was just five weeks before Antonio Veciana's book **Trained to Kill** claims that he was first approached by the *notional* Phillips in Havana."[178] As that moment neared, there was a great deal of angst at the Havana station and at CIA HQS over the potential danger facing Phillips, his family, and CIA operations in Cuba.

In his autobiography, Phillips recalled that he was sorry for accepting such a "downright dangerous" mission. As a result, he and his wife decided to leave Cuba *and* the CIA behind and to investigate a long-standing job offer in New York.[179] On 11 August, the CIA summoned Phillips to HQS to analyze the security implications arising from his involvement with the cattleman's conspiracy.[180] Phillips left on 13 August, en route through New York, to discuss a CIA propaganda film deal. He arrived in Washington on 17 August.[181]

The next day, 18 August 1959, the Havana station sent a priority cable to HQS with the alarming news that the conversation with Caines' group had been taped by a government tape recorder. The station warned HQS that a "*distinct possibility [exists] that government may have some knowledge of Choaden [Phillips] through direct recording or by later mention of his name by others.*" The cable added that Cuba's counterespionage capabilities had been upgraded and that the Cuban police had rounded up the cattlemen along with 3,000 other people.[182] Caines Milanes and his group were in prison.[183] They would be interrogated, charged with crimes, and tried.

On 19 August, the chief of the CIA's Office of Security, Robert Bannerman, immediately became actively involved in Phillips' case.[184] On 21 August, Phillips attended an

---

177 Herb Matthews **Return to Cuba** (pamphlet) as cited in Hugh Thomas, **Cuba—The Pursuit of Freedom** (New York: Harper & Row, 1971), p. 1233.
178 Veciana, **Trained to Kill**, p. 40.
179 David Phillips, **The Night Watch**, p. 82.
180 Ibid., p. 82.
181 8/13/59, HAVA 2545 to DIR; 104-10267-10167.
182 8/18/59, HAVA 2573 to DIR; RIF 104-10267-10166.
183 Hugh Thomas, **Cuba—The Pursuit of Freedom** (New York: Harper & Row, 1971), p. 1238.
184 9/30/59 Fred Hall memo to Deputy Director of Security (Investigations and Support) re C-11937, #40696 (David Phillips): refs cables including 8/22/59 info copy to Chief, CI Staff (Angleton): "It is understood by this office that consideration has been given to the possibility of information having been secured by the Cuban authorities which might impair subject's (Phillips') future usefulness." Marginalia: "Mr. Bannerman had an interest in this case as of 19 August 1959."

VECIANA AND PHILLIPS IN CUBA—1959-1960

urgent meeting at HQS headed by Henry Hecksher (using file pseudo Lawrence R. Charron) to discuss this security compromise and what to do about it.[185] That same day (21 August), the Havana station sent word to HQS saying that they had not obtained information about whether or not Cuban intelligence had Phillips in their cross hairs. The station added that they needed Phillips' services and asked HQS for his views about returning to Cuba.[186]

On 22 August, Phillips and senior officers from the CIA's Western Hemisphere Division (WHD), the Cuban desk, WH/3/Caribbean, were joined by officers from the Agency's Psychological and Paramilitary (PP) Staff for a meeting to decide on a final plan.[187] After careful consideration and further phone calls at HQS, the decision was made to send Phillips back to Havana with the story that had been worked out the previous day. Further contact with any cattlemen by Phillips was ruled out, and he was told *to begin planning for his permanent departure from Cuba.*[188]

On 25 August, Phillips arrived safely back in Havana.[189] Within a week, however, more disturbing news caused CIA HQS to launch a second security investigation regarding Phillips' situation in Havana. Phillips' work for the CIA had been discovered by Malone's lawyer and by Carlos Todd of the **Havana Times**. On 31 August, HQS ordered the station to conduct an immediate investigation of the risks this posed to CIA personnel and operations in Cuba.[190]

That *second* dire security situation in Havana was the context during which Veciana's final version of events claims that the *notional* Phillips decided to recruit and train Antonio Veciana for use in CIA operations in Cuba. Back in Havana, on 15 September 1959 Henry Hecksher completed the station investigation of the threat posed to CIA operations by Phillips' presence in Havana. The lengthy report was dispatched to HQS on 18 September. Hecksher concluded that Phillips' security situation was the "*major concern at the present time.*"[191]

Now, here we have come to the cornerstone event of this examination of Veciana's *notional* narrative about the date Phillips recruited him in Havana against the backdrop of Phillips' *true* situation there. That situation was a *security nightmare*. The day that the Havana security review of the *real* Phillips' was written—15 September 1959—was an exact match for the day that Veciana's *notional* Phillips first approached him in Havana!

As I discussed above, Veciana's *notional* Phillips recruited him at the time of an *easily* verifiable date: the departure from Cuba of Jack Ruby, Oswald's killer. Veciana

---

185   8/21/59, Charron MFR, "Conversation with Choaden" (Phillips), 21 August 1959.
186   8/22/59, HAVA 2588 to DIR; 104-10128-10335.
187   8/22/59, DIR 41198 to HAVA. 104-10177-10088.
188   David Phillips, *The Night Watch*, p. 82.
189   8/27/59, HAVA 2603 to DIR; RIF 104-10267-10161.
190   8/31/59, DIR 42454 to HAVA; RIF 104-10178-10281; see also 104-10128-10330.
191   9/18/59, HAVA Dispatch to DIR; 104-1026710158.

INTO THE STORM

says he *now* views this timing as curious but probably only coincidental. To repeat, Veciana alleges that the *notional* Phillips "came to meet me for the first time just *a few days after Jack Ruby departed Cuba.*" For the time being, I will use 15 September as the date for the alleged recruitment. But I cannot help but wonder why it took Veciana more than forty years to remember Ruby's departure as the trigger event. *Nowhere* in any of his previous accounts did Veciana mention Ruby's departure from Cuba.

On that day, according to **Trained to Kill**, Veciana's *notional* Phillips walked into the reception area of Julio Lobo's Banco Financiero in Havana. Such a dramatic scene for the *notional* Phillips involved a role that the *real* Phillips—who was himself an actor—could *not*, in his *wildest* dreams, have *ever* imagined playing. To be *seen* merely walking into the lobby of Lobo's bank would have been a huge *risk* for the *real* Phillips in September 1959. The entrances to Lobo's bank would almost certainly have been under surveillance by Cuban intelligence.

Lobo was the wealthiest sugar magnate in Cuba and a source of information for the CIA—*known to Cuban intelligence*—on anti-Castro Cuban organizations. By the fall of 1959, Cuban intelligence understood not only that Lobo was close to the CIA but *also* that the sugar king was *bankrolling* several anti-Castro counterrevolutionary groups in Cuba *and* Miami.

In a futile attempt to mask the CIA's relationship with Lobo, the station had arranged for an embassy cut-out for Lobo to use for communications. But the station had also made it clear that if at any time Lobo should have something of particular interest to the CIA, he could contact CIA Station Chief James Noel directly. According to CIA documents, Julio Lobo was one of the best known and most *closely surveilled* figures in *all of* Cuba. In June 1959, Lobo went to the U.S. to contact officials to secure American approval for his plans to help counterrevolutionary Cuban groups *overthrow Castro*. Much later, in the immediate aftermath of Veciana's December 1960 appeal to the station in Havana for visas (discussed in Chapter Eleven), Lobo would vouch for Veciana's bona fides.[192]

The visit by Veciana's *notional* Phillips to Lobo's bank in mid-September 1959 would have taken place at the very moment the Havana station and CIA HQS were struggling to ensure that *the work of the real Phillips* for the CIA would not come to the attention of Cuban intelligence. Lobo's bank and counterrevolutionary associates—*including* Veciana—had been under tight surveillance for quite some time. Only a *few* months later, Che Guevara summoned Veciana to two meetings in which he attempted—*unsuccessfully*—to *recruit* Veciana to *penetrate* and report on Lobo's anti-Castro activities.[193]

---

192 12/13/60, DIR 16224 to HAVA; RIF 104-10181-10207.
193 In his work **The Sugar King of Havana**, John Rathbone reported that Lobo had been a personal source for the Director of Central Intelligence, Allen Dulles for a number of years before 1960. Julio Lobo was eventually assigned the CIA cryptonym **AMEMBER-1**. While we are not certain when that crypt was assigned, the infor-

According to **Trained to Kill**, Veciana's *notional* Phillips told the receptionist his name was Maurice Bishop and asked to speak with him. Veciana, who was working as an assistant manager at the bank, told the receptionist to send him right up.[194] The reception room of Lobo's Banco Financiero was the *last* place the *real* Phillips would want to have been seen on 15 September 1959. And if being seen in that place appears to be exceedingly poor tradecraft, what Veciana claims happened next, was *even worse*.

The *Notional* Phillips Recruits Veciana over Lunch and Drinks at the Famous La Floradita Restaurant

Veciana's *notional* Phillips invited him to lunch to listen to a proposition. Veciana said he couldn't oblige just then, but the two agreed to meet for lunch the next day at 1 p.m. at the famous *La Floridita* restaurant. The iconic bar and restaurant were just a few blocks from the bank, *a short walk along old Havana's busy main thoroughfare, Obispo Street*.

According to **Trained to Kill**, the *notional* Phillips was already there when Veciana arrived and *spotted him at the bar, nursing a martini*. The *notional* Phillips asked the bartender to get Veciana a drink. Veciana ordered a daiquiri and the two men took their drinks to a table. During the lunch the *notional* Phillips asked Veciana if he was willing to cooperate with "*us*" to organize a resistance against Castro's government. Veciana said he replied, "Yes, I'll do it."[195]

There is clearly something out of place in this scene. The *real* Dave Phillips was in the middle of not one but *two* unnerving investigations about his precarious security situation in Cuba. I find implausible the spectacle of the *true* David Phillips, entering from one of Havana's busiest streets, the capitol's *most* famous restaurant-bar—frequented by Ernest Hemingway and American diplomats—to meet for lunch and drinks with the bank manager of a known CIA asset like Julio Lobo.

The *real* Phillips—who did not have the protection afforded by State Department cover—had been dismayed to find out that there were more than two anti-Castro Cubans in his *secret meeting* with the Cuban cattlemen. They had *all* been rounded up and were in prison at the *very* moment that Veciana claims Phillips casually recruited

---

mation Lobo was passing to Dulles would continue for many years as a CIA Foreign Intelligence operation centered around Lobo to collect economic information on the Cuban sugar industry. Among the remaining large companies with sugar holdings in Cuba during the period 1957-1959 was the United Fruit Company. That particular company and the information provided by Lobo on the Cuban sugar business were acutely important to Secretary of State John Foster Dulles and his brother, Allen Dulles. The Dulles brothers had been on the United Fruit payroll for nearly four decades. During 1958-1959, in a *blatant* conflict of interest, the Dulles brothers and their Wall Street law firm, Cromwell and Sullivan, occupied *several* seats on the board of directors of United Fruit.

194 Veciana, **Trained to Kill**, p. 40.
195 Ibid, pp. 44-45.

INTO THE STORM

him over drinks at the *La Floridita*. At the cattleman's secret meeting, the participants had been compromised by a hidden government tape recorder. But here, in the *La Floridita* restaurant, watchful eyes of Cuban intelligence agents would have been on the lookout for indiscretions by the Americans. Had Phillips and Veciana really been there, their every move would have been noted and reported to the authorities. It is not out of the question that a hidden microphone would have been under their table recording their conversation.[196]

Like the scene in the bank, this *public meeting* in the bar-restaurant smacked of trade craft as *careless and risky* as what we expect to see in a James Bond movie. I am confident that there was no way in *hell* that the *real* Phillips—especially during the security investigations he found himself the subject of—would have allowed himself to be seen in a prominent public place with anyone connected to the resistance against Castro—period.

Phillips Arranges Certain Tests for Veciana

At the end of lunch at the *La Floridita*, the *notional* Phillips in **Trained to Kill** said that there were *certain tests* Veciana would need to undergo before continuing with the plan to organize resistance against Castro. One week later (that would have been approximately 22 September), Veciana's *notional* Phillips *telephoned* Veciana at Lobo's bank and arranged to *drive him* to an apartment building close to the U.S. Embassy. Here, I would hasten to point out that the phones to Lobo's bank would certainly have been monitored by Cuban intelligence.

A man using the name Joe Melton was waiting for them in an apartment on the sixth floor. Veciana's *notional* Phillips read the newspaper while Melton administered a polygraph to Veciana. The meeting ended uneventfully.[197] Here, I should point out that Joe Melton was not a *notional* character. That name was a pseudonym for James Joseph O'Mailia, a paid CIA contract agent working for the CIA Station in Havana. I will have more to say about O'Mailia's activities later in this chapter.

---

196 The *La Floradita* had not always been a spot crawling with Cuban intelligence agents. In his previous assignment in 1955-1956 during Batista's reign, the *La Floradita* was Phillips' favorite restaurant for lunch in Havana. Phillips recalled:
> I was enjoying one of the frozen (daiquiri) cocktails with a friend when I remarked, "This place really has atmosphere. That man at the other end of the bar looks just like Ernest Hemingway." He replied, "That man *is* Ernest Hemingway." As we watched, Hemingway downed a dozen daiquiris—yes, twelve—and, when he departed, he carried a quart-sized ice cream container filled with the delicious mixture of rum and lime juice for the ride back to his villa. Later, I learned that he was a friend of the Havana Chief of Station—whether personal or professional I do not know."
> —Phillips, **The Night Watch**, p. 65.

197 Veciana, *Trained to Kill*, pp. 47-52.

VECIANA AND PHILLIPS IN CUBA—1959-1960

Another week passed before Veciana's *notional* Phillips *phoned* Veciana at the bank again—around 29 September. Phillips *drove* Veciana to a ranch-style home in Miramar where a Spanish speaking American man using the name John Smith administered a truth drug to Veciana and interrogated him about life style habits and activities and his views on other topics. Again, according to Veciana, this meeting ended uneventfully, and the *notional* Phillips *drove* him back to the bank and, again, said he'd be in touch. Seeing the *real* Phillips nonchalantly driving Veciana all over Havana is about as likely as a germ at a Lysol convention. It's a wonder Veciana didn't describe Phillips' car as an Aston Martin with automatically revolving license plates.

The day after Veciana's alleged Miramar interrogation, approximately 30 September, concern was percolating in the ongoing CIA security and counterintelligence investigations about the situation of the *real* Phillips in Havana. Earlier in the year, in April 1959, the HQS Cuban desk had requested a Provisional Operational Approval (POA) *and* also an Operational Approval (OA) to use Phillips in developmental propaganda activities in the television field in Havana. That assignment was to be under the supervision of the CIA station and assigned the project cryptonym **AMOURETTE-X**.[198]

On 14 May 1959, the CIA's Central Cover Division approved the Agency's use of the *real* Phillips for that purpose. On 30 September 1959, however, a week after Joe Melton's polygraph of Veciana (at which the *notional* Phillips was allegedly present), the **AMOURETTE-X** project ran into *strong headwinds* in the CIA's Office of Security. The Deputy Director of Security for Investigations and Support, Fred H. Hall, sent a memo about the real Phillips' security problems through Office of Security Chief Robert Bannerman to the Counterintelligence OA Chief, Thomas Carroll, Jr.[199]

Hall drew Carroll's attention to the April request for Phillips' use in project **AMOURETTE-X**. Hall *questioned* whether *Phillips* should be *used* in the project. Hall drew attention to the 22 August 1959 HQS cable about the cattlemen's conspiracy *and* questioned the wisdom of sending Phillips *back* to Cuba. Hall reminded the Counterintelligence POA office that an information copy of that 22 August cable had been sent to Counterintelligence Chief James Angleton. Hall added his office understood that *information gained by Cuban intelligence might impair Phillips' future usefulness.*

Hall admonished Carroll to send a *demand* to the Cuban desk for the details about Phillips' case. Sent on 12 October 1959, Carroll's memo said that he was *unable to give further consideration* to authorizing an OA for Phillips. In addition to the details about the cattleman's conspiracy, Hall wanted access to Henry Hecksher's major security review of the compromise of Phillips' work for the Havana station.[200]

---

198 4/1/59, WH/3/Caribbean Request for Approval RE David Phillips; RIF104-10178-10286.
199 9/30/59, DDS/IS memorandum through COS to CI/OA RE C-11937, #40696 (Phillips); RIF 104-10128-10328.
200 10/12/59, Chief CI/OA request for HAVA, HKHA-5479; RIF 104-10178-10277.

INTO THE STORM

Meanwhile, as these gears were grinding in the Agency's security and counterintelligence components, not surprisingly the activities of the *notional* Phillips with Veciana in Havana continued as *carefree* as the recruitment lunch at the *La Floridita*. According to Veciana's *notional* 1959 narrative, the next day, on 13 October 1959, the *notional* Phillips picked him up and *casually drove him* to the Hotel Riviera for a meeting. It was supposed to be a two-hour discussion of the results of the tests administered by Melton and Smith, but it lasted more than *six* hours.

The two men went over Veciana's test questions in minute detail. The *notional* Phillips had concerns about Veciana: He was too compassionate; religion and family could blind him; and nationalism was a dangerous devotion. Veciana claims that the *notional* Phillips *cautioned* him that he would need to learn how to lie, steal, and, if it came down to it, to *kill*.[201]

Replacing Phillips with Emilio Americo Rodriguez

On 12 November 1959, the Counter Intelligence OA office finally gave the green light for using the *real* Phillips in project **AMOURETTE-X**. Ironically, however, Phillips' *usefulness* for the CIA station in Havana was *over*. HQS and the Havana station both understood they would have to find a replacement to carry on the important work Phillips had been shouldering for the CIA station. Filling Phillips' shoes would take time.

In Volume II, I discussed the CIA's incredible luck in late 1959, when Emilio Americo Rodriguez stopped by CIA HQS in Langley, Virginia, to offer his services to the Agency in any capacity. His surprise visit probably took place sometime during the third week of November.[202] Afterward, HQS reported to the Havana station that "Arnaldo Berenguer" had accepted an offer to work in Cuba as a CIA contract agent provided that he received a minimum gross income of *$12,000 a year*. On 19 November 1959, a station cable replied that they contemplated using *Berenguer* as a cut-out for psychological and paramilitary operations under the **AMOURETTE-X** project. The station said that in view of the *anticipated departure of Phillips in two or three months*, Berenguer would *also* be used as a cut-out to take over Phillips' provincial press operations.[203]

A December 1959 CIA Personal Data Sheet on Emilio Rodriguez said that he was interested in working for an American company either at home or abroad with a starting base salary of $12,000 a year.[204] From these documents alone—although

---

201 Veciana, **Trained to Kill**, pp. 56-59.
202 1/28/60, Agency Interview Sheet, 104-10180-10207. NB: In volume II, I thought Emilio's visit in Washington was in December 1959. My research for this volume has revealed that the visit actually took place in the latter part of November 1959.
203 11/19/59, HAVA 2919, REF DIR 02454; RIF 104-10178-10274.
204 12/00/59, Personal Data Sheet, RIF 104-10180-10156; see also 1/28/60, Agency Interview Sheet, 104-10180-

there are many more that support them—we can surmise that Arnaldo Berenguer was a pseudonym for Emilio Rodriguez. In volume II, I proposed that Emilio later blossomed into one of the principal CIA agents for the stay-behind nets after the break in relations between the U.S. and Cuba in January 1961. The July 2017 NARA release of JFK records confirmed this prediction,[205] as well as my prediction that Emilio's CIA cryptonym was **AMIRE-1**,[206] *and* that he used, among his many pseudonyms, the name "Eugenio."[207]

Joe Melton's Training Program for Veciana

While the CIA was laying the groundwork for Emilio Rodriguez to take over Dave Phillips' propaganda operations in Cuba, the final chapter in Veciana's 1959 *notional* Phillips scenario was unfolding. According to ***Trained to Kill***, on approximately 30 October, the *notional* Phillips directed Veciana to return to the building where he had been polygraphed by Joe Melton and to come up to an office in a suite occupied by the "Cuban Mining Company." Veciana got the name wrong but it *was* a mining company—the Moa Bay Mining Company.[208] Veciana also noticed that *a Berlitz Language School was on the first floor*. He went up to the sixth floor and rang the bell. The *notional* Phillips and Melton ushered him into a small vestibule inside and closed the door.[209]

The three weeks that Veciana claims were necessary for the nightly training sessions on psychological warfare and sabotage operations administered by Joe Melton would have ended on approximately 21 November 1959. According to ***Trained to Kill***, the *notional* Phillips attended some of these evening training sessions. After this training was completed, Veciana's meetings with the *notional* Phillips became virtually nonexistent, he says, because they began communicating via secret writing:

> …they communicated only when absolutely necessary, and then mostly through messages written in invisible ink, hidden in letters sent to an intermediary's address in the name of Caridad Rodríguez. Anyone reading any of them would have been impressed at how dutiful and loving Caridad and her cousin Adolfina, who lived in the United States, continued to be with each other, and how lovely their handwriting was. As I ironed them, though, the heat brought out Bishop's hidden message.

10207; and 2/9/60, Biographic Sketch, 104-10180-10154.
205 1961 CIA stay-behind network diagram; RIF 104-10180-10133.
206 4/13/61, CARA 5827; RIF 104-10180-10167.
207 5/17/61, WAVE 6247; RIF 104-10180-10164.
208 The HSCA learned that the name of the company on the door was the "Moa Bay Mining Company." See 8/25/78, HSCA request to the CIA for information on Joe Melton, RIF 104-10406-10260.
209 Veciana, ***Trained to Kill***, pp. 60-61.

> After I read them, I destroyed the letters. *That became our only means of communication barely six months after I first met him.*[210] [Emphasis added]

That method of communication contradicts what Veciana had said *before* 2014 in *all* of his previous accounts. In his various depositions and previous interviews, Veciana *never* mentioned secret writing—not once in *all the years* of his conversations with Gaeton Fonzi. And the true Phillips' handwriting was *not* lovely.

Veciana's 2017 claims about using secret writing are contradicted by his 1978 HSCA deposition. In that testimony, Veciana described a *very different* method by which he and the *notional* Phillips communicated during the post-Cuba period—1960 to 1969. Veciana was asked by the HSCA *how* Bishop was able to get in touch with him. Veciana explained how their arrangement worked: The *notional* Phillips always knew how to locate him *through a person familiar with his whereabouts.*[211]

The committee tried three times to get Veciana to provide the name of that person, but he *refused* and succeeded in getting them to withdraw the question. In his earlier 2 March 1976 interview with Gaeton Fonzi for the Schweiker Subcommittee, Veciana had said that this person was a woman and that the arrangement was that the *notional* Phillips *only* contacted him through her.[212]

In a 1978 interview with Anthony Summers, Veciana explained his arrangement with "Bishop" in more explicit terms:

> He explained that, *in line with intelligence tradecraft,* "Bishop" had *always* initiated their clandestine meetings, *either by telephoning direct, or through a third person* who always knew where to reach Veciana.[213] [Emphasis added]

What happened to the secret writing? While secret writing is one of the techniques used in intelligence tradecraft, it *only* entered *Veciana's vocabulary* in 2017. One element in this part of Veciana's scenario was partly true: there was a woman who functioned as the cut-out between Veciana and someone he called Maurice Bishop.

Delores Cao: The Cut-Out Between Bishop and Veciana

In this section, I will drop the usage of the adjective "notional" for the name Phillips for two reasons. One reason is the special role Delores Cao played as the intermediary between Veciana and the man he called Bishop *and* the circumstances under which Cao remembered that the man's name *was*, in fact, "Bishop." The other reason is Cao's

---

210 Ibid, pp. 69-70.
211 4/26/78, Veciana HSCA deposition, pp. 7-8 and 16-17; RIF 104-10406-10260.
212 3/2/76, Gaeton Fonzi interview of Antonio Veciana for SSCIA; RIF 157-10004-10158.
213 Anthony Summers, **Conspiracy** (New York: Paragon House, 1989), p. 514

recollection that when she had worked as Veciana's secretary in Cuba, he had started taking *language courses* in the evening *and* the implications of that memory for who the "Bishop" in Cuba might have been. The investigative work of Tony Summers has given us important new evidence about Cao's recollections. For reasons of clarity, this evidence is best understood by using the name "Bishop" instead of the *notional* Phillips.

In one of his 1978 interviews with Veciana, Tony Summers succeeded in doing what the SSCIA and the HSCA had been unable to do. Summers got Veciana to cough up the name and location of the woman "Bishop" used to contact Veciana. On 15 November 1978, Summers explained to Fonzi how he pulled it off:

> Summers said he managed to squeeze the name of the woman out of Veciana by goading him, telling him that everything was just a lot of balderdash and that he hadn't given out one iota of information that could be confirmed. Summers said he told Veciana he didn't believe the woman even existed.[214]

Provoked by this, Veciana said her name was Mrs. Delores Cao and that her address was P.O. Box 7474, Barrio Obrero Station, Puerto Rico.

Summers located Cao and interviewed her in Puerto Rico during 1978. In his 2013 edition of **Not in Your Lifetime**, Summers said Mrs. Cao had "acted as a cutout between Veciana and Bishop."[215] In the interview, Summers learned that before Bishop and Veciana both left Cuba, Delores had been Veciana's secretary at Julio Lobo's Banco Financiero in Havana. Cao told Summers that when Veciana became a leading anti-Castro activist, she had "agreed to act as a sort of human answering machine and take messages for him."[216]

Summers decided to employ the following strategy to test Mrs. Cao's familiarity with the name Bishop:

> During the interview, the author [Summers] ran through a large number of names of people who might have called—all of them entirely imaginary except the name "Bishop." She promptly responded that, of all the names mentioned, the one name she remembered was Bishop.[217]

That was a prudent strategy—*providing* that Veciana had not mentioned the name "Bishop" to Cao *before* Summers interviewed her. The importance of this point cannot be overemphasized because Summers interviewed Cao in 1978—many years after she had last spoken with Veciana. And, we know for a fact that Veciana *did* speak with Cao *right before* Summers interviewed her.

---

214   11/15/78, Gaeton Fonzi, HSCA Outside Contact Report on Tony Summers; RIF 180-10103-10395. Veciana said that she was married to Sergio Arias. Her nickname was "Lolli" and, in the early 60s, and that she was a pretty girl of 25 or 30 years old. She was fervently anti-Castro and had some contact with Victor Espinosa.
215   Anthony Summers, *Not in Your Lifetime* (New York: Open Road, 2013 Edition) p. 304.
216   Ibid, p. 440.
217   Ibid.

INTO THE STORM

Gaeton Fonzi kept in touch with Summers after the publication of his 1980 book, **Conspiracy**. When Summers eventually went to Puerto Rico, he found that the address Veciana had furnished for Delores was no longer where she lived. He was able to track her down and interview her, and afterward he returned to Miami to tell Fonzi about what she had said. Fonzi's 2013 edition of *The Last Investigation* reveals a noteworthy remark Mrs. Cao made to Summers: "*until Veciana had called her to ask if she would talk with me, she hadn't been in touch with him for years.*"[218] [Emphasis added] Therefore, Veciana *could* have steered Delores into using the name Bishop *before* Summers arrived to interview her.

In both of the 2013 editions of their books, Summers and Fonzi refer to Delores Cao by the pseudonym "Fabiola." However, her true name had been released twenty years earlier—in 1993—in Fonzi's HSCA Outside Contact Report with Summers.[219] Summers reported that he found Delores was a grandmother in her 60s, working as an administrative assistant in a social service office, and living comfortably with her husband in a suburb of San Juan, Puerto Rico.

Cao told Summers that Veciana had never mentioned any connection with U.S. intelligence activities. Cao knew Veciana disagreed with Castro's policies but did not know exactly when he became actively involved in anti-Castro activities.[220] In the 2013 edition of his book, *The Last Investigation*, Fonzi reported this *crucial* detail from Summers' report about his interview with Cao:

> She did remember a time when he [Veciana] *started taking "language courses" in the evening.* (That coincided with the period *when Bishop put Veciana through intelligence training with "Mr. Melton,"* in the building which housed the Berlitz Language School, *one of David Phillips' "public relations" clients.*)[221] [Emphasis added; parentheses by Fonzi in original]

The importance of this single recollection by Mrs. Cao needs to be emphasized. Language instruction was the cover Veciana created for his presence in the Edeficio LaRampa building. Similarly, the importance of Fonzi's parenthetical comment that the timing of Veciana's language studies coincided with Melton's training sessions cannot be overemphasized. I will return to that point below and in Chapter Eleven.

Before further discussion of Fonzi's chronological comment about *when* Veciana's Berlitz cover began, more needs to be said about other intelligence operatives who might have needed to enter that building without arousing suspicion. Veciana *was not the only person* who needed that cover. It was a critical requirement for *whoever* might have been Veciana's case officer in Havana. Of course, Veciana *now* claims that Phillips

---

218 Gaeton Fonzi, *The Last Investigation* (New York: Skyhorse, 2013 Edition) p. 318.
219 11/15/78, Gaeton Fonzi, HSCA Outside Contact Report on Tony Summers; RIF 180-10103-10395.
220 Mrs. Cao did not recall that anyone besides Veciana was involved with his "scheme," but she did recall an "incident" when Veciana tried to destabilize Cuba's monetary system. At one point, she said, "he asked her to hide a half-million dollars for a while." Gaeton Fonzi, *The Last Investigation* (2013 Edition), p. 318.
221 Ibid.

VECIANA AND PHILLIPS IN CUBA—1959-1960

was his case officer. Although Veciana was not forthright with Fonzi about that decisive detail, Fonzi suspected that it was true. And so, this passage in Fonzi's **The Last Investigation** should not surprise us:

> Phillips admitted that after he hung up his shingle as a public relations counselor, "No one rushed the door in any event, nor did I solicit clients." He noted, though, that *he did eventually wind up with at least one client with which he briefly worked a trade for French lessons: the Berlitz Language School.*[222]

I located the first sentence from the above passage by Fonzi without difficulty in Phillips' memoir **The Night Watch**.[223] I have been unable thus far to locate the source for the second—very important—sentence in **The Night Watch**, **Trained to Kill**, or elsewhere. Both sentences appear in Veciana's **Trained to Kill**[224]; however, they are in a direct quote attributed to Fonzi's **The Last Investigation**.

I have no reason to doubt that Fonzi did have a source other than **The Night Watch** for a statement by Phillips that he *briefly worked a trade for French lessons* with Drexel Gibson's Berlitz Language School. That source was most likely Veciana himself, in an interview with Fonzi.

The inference that we can draw from Phillips' alleged trade with Gibson is that it was a device for creating a cover. Doing so was a major requirement for anyone working in Cuba against Castro without diplomatic protection.[225]

The reason I am drilling down on this point is because I believe *whoever* Veciana's case officer was would also have needed the same plausible cover for regular access to the Edeficio LaRampa. Therefore, Fonzi's *linkage* of Veciana's evening language classes to his *intelligence training with Mr. Melton*—a language professor at Villanueva University—crucially gives us a CIA candidate *other than Phillips*.

Whoever that person was, the cover attributed to Phillips could have been a cover jointly worked out by Veciana and his CIA handler. Delores Cao has given us the Veciana half of that arrangement. Veciana himself gave Fonzi the other half but attributed it falsely to Bishop/Phillips.

All of this leads directly to a question that has never—before the publication of this volume—been asked: If Phillips was not Veciana's CIA case officer in Cuba, then who was? And if that question is worth investigating, what about this question: Did Veciana have handlers in Cuba who were not working for the CIA?

---

222 Ibid, p. 265.
223 Phillips, **The Night Watch**, p. 77.
224 Veciana, **Trained to Kill**, p. 61.
225 See for example, Phillips' worries about his public relations cover in **The Night Watch**, p. 82.

INTO THE STORM

James Joseph O'Mailia, Jr. and Joe Melton

During his 26 April 1978 HSCA deposition, Veciana was asked if he recalled "Mr. Melton's" first name. Veciana replied, "I don't know if this is correct, but I think it was Joe."[226] In his 2017 book, *Trained to Kill*, Veciana said the name was "Dick Melton."[227] As I have indicated above, many details have changed in the six versions of the Bishop story proffered by Veciana over the past forty-one years. On 25 August 1978, the HSCA requested the CIA to grant access to the following records:

> ...all files and index references pertaining to the following individual, and in addition to the standard search of indices by name, it is requested that a search be made for persons closely fitting the enclosed biographical profile, even though those persons may have no similarity in name to MELTON: FNU "Melton" AKA Joe Melton.[228]

That HSCA profile included the following five characteristics:

- A white American male
- Living in Havana
- During the period 1959-1961
- Engaged in anti-Castro propaganda, clandestine paramilitary and explosives training
- Gave instruction in psychological warfare, and infiltration activities.

The HSCA request also noted that, on various occasions, such training occurred in an office in the Edeficio LaRampa building located in the El Verdado section of Havana. The building "also housed offices for the Moa Bay Mining Company and, in addition, a Berlitz language school."

By 29 August 1978, the following CIA components had conducted records checks on the name "Mr. Melton AKA Joe Melton":

- Policy Coordination Staff/Liaison and Oversight Control (PCS/LOC),
- Directorate of Administration/Office of Personnel (DA/OP),
- Directorate of Operations Information Management Staff/Operations Group (DO/IMS/OG)

On 1 September the Office of Legislative Counsel (OLC) sent HSCA Chief Counsel Robert Blakey this terse response: "Agency records contain no information on the person named in HSCA request letter of 25 August 1978."[229]

---

226 4/26/78, HSCA deposition of Antonio Veciana; RIF 180-10118-10145.
227 Veciana, *Trained to Kill*, p. 61.
228 8/25/78, HSCA Chief Counsel Blakey to CIA (Breckinridge); RIF 180-10141-10150.
229 9/5/78, Marvin Smith (C/OG) to Donald Greg (PCS/LOC), HSCA Request on Melton; RIF 1993.07.10.11:41:32:090240.

VECIANA AND PHILLIPS IN CUBA—1959-1960

Four months earlier, on 25 April 1978, the HSCA had deposed David Philips. They had asked him if he had ever worked in Havana with a person named Melton. He replied, "That may have been the name of the man at the Berlitz School, but I am not—I can't recall for sure." When asked a second time, this was Phillips' disorganized response:

> I am not sure. If Melton was the man who ran the Berlitz school, I did not, unless there was one of those casual things of he was one of the friendly Americans who passed you information, and to that degree I might very well have because we became fairly friendly, but I don't recall that he was, had any—that we asked him to provide cover or he ran a group. I don't recall that.[230]

This testimony suggests that the name Melton rang a bell for Phillips. But, strangely, he placed Melton in the right building—the Edificio LaRampa—but in the wrong office. Drexel Gibson, not Joe Melton, ran the Berlitz School on the ground floor.

Drexel Gibson was among the hundreds of thousands of Cubans and Americans arrested on 19 April 1961 as Castro's forces were finishing off the exile invasion force at the Bay of Pigs. Also arrested that day was James Joseph O'Mailia, an American professor teaching English at the University of Villanueva. O'Mailia was released three months later and, along with 87 other Americans, was flown to the U.S. on a U.S. State Department plane. Upon disembarking, the reporters waiting for the plane honed in on O'Mailia for an interview. His comments about the arrests and releases in Cuba appeared in newspapers across America. The *UPI* story included this statement: "The professor said that at least two other Americans were still in Cubana prison when he was freed. He identified them as Charles McAvoy and Drexel Gibson, former director of the Berlitz School in Havana."[231]

It is not out of the question that James Joseph O'Mailia might have sometimes been addressed by a version of his middle name—Joe. O'Mailia also told *UPI* that he had been arrested "on suspicion" by the Cuban secret police, and that he was "glad to be back in the good old USA." And well he should have been. He had been a paid CIA agent in Havana since 1959. His cryptonym was **AMCRACKLE-1**, and his files pseudonym was Gordon M. Biniaris (I will discuss how we know this in the next section below). By the spring of 1959 O'Mailia was the principal CIA Station "cut-out" directing *many* of the proliferating anti-Castro groups being groomed for action against Castro by the CIA. The only CIA station officer (using the files pseudonym "Gebaide") who had contact with these groups *severed his contact* with Cubans for security reasons, and O'Mailia had so many responsibilities that his contract was amended to pay him $700 a month beginning 1 May 1960.[232]

---

230 4/25/78, HSCA deposition of David Phillips; RIF 180-10110-10016.
231 7/00/61, Statement of James Joseph O'Mailia to *UPI* and other reporters after landing at Miami Airport.
232 4/29/60, HAVA 4382; RIF 104-10271-10008.

INTO THE STORM

O'Mailia's operational profile included the following characteristics:
- A white American male
- Living in Havana
- During the period 1959-1961
- Engaged in anti-Castro propaganda and psychological warfare activities (with **AMPALM-1**)
- Engaged in clandestine paramilitary and explosives activities (with **AMPALM-4**)
- Engaged in infiltration and exfiltration activities with support from the CIA station

That is nearly an exact match for the profile of Joe Melton that the HSCA provided to the CIA. I know of no better candidate for this identification. Clearly, the CIA *should* have provided O'Mailia's profile to the HSCA as a candidate for Joe Melton.

James Joseph O'Mailia, Jr., was born on 20 November 1915 in Midland, Pennsylvania. At the time, his father, James, was 17 and his mother, Margaret, was 19. He had three sisters, Mary, Catherine, and Margaret (who passed away before her first birthday). The family moved to Sparrows Point, Maryland in 1920. When James was 5, his mother died in 1921—she was just 25 years old. The family moved to Lackawanna, New York, in 1930.

In 1945 O'Mailia graduated from Canisius College, a small private Jesuit school in Buffalo, New York. On 10 March 1942, he enlisted in the U.S. Army. He was released in November 1945. After that, he traveled to Lima, Peru, where he received a degree from Universidad de San Marcos and met his wife-to-be Yolanda de los Santos.

At the time the CIA was created in 1947, O'Mailia made three trips to Miami from Cuba—on 16 May, 22 August, and 18 December. Missing travel records make it impossible to determine the length of his stays in Miami and when he returned to Havana and/or Lima. Yolanda was not on any of the passenger manifests for the three trips from Havana to Miami. James and Yolanda eventually moved to Havana in 1952 and were married on 9 May. O'Mailia became the principal at Saint George's School in Havana, and later began teaching English at Universidad de Villanueva.

We know from his activities as **AMCRACKLE-1** for the Havana station that O'Mailia became a paid agent for the CIA in Havana no later than 10 November 1959—at the time Veciana claims he was trained by Melton (O'Mailia).[233] However, O'Mailia's frequent trips to Miami before then—11 April 55, 26 August 55, 21 December 56, 14 November 57, 24 February 58, 20 May 59, and 9 August 59—suggest that his operational use for the Agency might have begun much earlier. The incomplete nature of O'Mailia's travel records may be due to the use of other CIA operational pseudonyms backstopped by false passports, driver's licenses and other documentation.

---

233 11/10/59, HAVA 2870; RIF 104-10162-10443.

Establishing O'Mailia's CIA Cryptonym and Files Pseudonym

For two weeks in late January 2017, during research for this volume on the identity of the man that Veciana knew as Joe Melton, I was fortunate to work with two expert researchers on this problem. They are Jerry Shinley and Bill Simpich. Jerry had astutely identified O'Mailia's CIA files pseudonym—Gordon M. Biniaris—from two 1969 CIA documents about Reinol Gonzalez y Gonzalez' wife, Mrs. Teresita Gonzalez. Her husband (cryptonym **AMCALL-1**) had been the leader of the Catholic-based People's Revolutionary Movement (MRP) in Cuba until his October 1961 arrest at the farm of Cesar Odio. O'Mailia had been Gonzalez' case officer.

A 13 June 1969 cable was sent from the chief of the Western Hemisphere Cuban Operations Group (WH/COG), Dave Phillips, to Miami CIA station inquiring about Mrs. Gonzalez.[234] She was receiving $150 monthly payments while her husband remained imprisoned in Cuba. She had attached a note to her May 1969 payment receipt requesting that *Mr. James O'Mailia* telephone her. Phillips' office wanted to know why she would assume that O'Mailia could "be contacted through the [CIA] local payment office."

On 18 June, the station responded that Mrs. Gonzales "did not assume that she could contact *Gordon M. Biniaris* through the CIA local payment office"; rather, she merely wished to pass along recent information about her husband to him.[235] Shinley was able to show that the use of the Biniaris pseudonym in the response to Mrs. Gonzales' request for a call from O'Mailia proves that the Biniaris pseudo belonged to O'Mailia. From there, I was able to establish the case for linking the **AMCRACKLE-1** cryptonym to O'Mailia (see Volume II[236]). This identification is supported by the following combination:

- HAVA wants Biniaris assistance given to **AMCALL-1** (8/2/60, HAVA 5522, 104-10217-10390)[237]
- **AMCALL-1** loyal service to **AMCRACKLE**; 11/3/61, WAVE 8995, 104-10271-10023)[238]

---

234 6/13/69, DIR 11816, Memo, C/WH/COG, Phillips, to WH/Miami; RIF 104-10217-10114.
235 6/18/69, WH/MIAMI 4307 to DIR; RIF 104-10217-10115.
236 Newman, ***Countdown to Darkness***, see pp. 65-66, 412, ad 414; in addition, see the work of Bill Simpich and Juan Giusti on Reinol Gonzalez y Gonzalez—cryptonym **AMCALL-1**—in the Mary Ferrell cryptonym project.
237 8/2/60, HAVA 5522; RIF 104-10217-10390. "**AMOURETTE-9** opposed to this development, but Station feels **AMCALL-1** should receive encouragement and assistance this undertaking through Gordon M. Biniaris in name of **AMWAIL**."
238 11/3/61, WAVE 8995; RIF 104-10271-10023. **AMCALL-1** was a paid agent of the CIA. This cable discusses **AMCALL-1's** 1961 arrest and imprisonment in Cuba. "Former head of UTC and internal coordinator of MRP gave loyal service (to) **AMCRACKLE** and (Cuban) station (Project **AMCALL**)."

Reinol Gonzalez y Gonzalez (**AMCALL-1**), was head of the People's Revolutionary Movement (MRP) in Cuba until his arrest in October 1961 for his participation in Veciana's bazooka assassination attempt on Castro (Operation Liborio). Veciana was the head of MRP sabotage at the time.

Veciana's Account of When the *Notional* Phillips Left Cuba for Good

In his 2017 book, **Trained to Kill**, Veciana describes a six-month period for his relationship with the *notional* Phillips in Cuba. It began in mid-September 1959 and ended in mid-March 1960: "In March 1960, he left Cuba for good."[239]

That date is more or less consistent with the accounts in **The Night Watch** and CIA documents. However, Veciana appeared to be oblivious to that information when—many years earlier—he served up this whopper to Gaeton Fonzi:

> Bishop left Cuba *before the Bay of Pigs invasion in April 1961*, and Veciana says they had not met for some months prior to it. After the Bay of Pigs fiasco, Bishop *returned to Cuba* (probably with a Belgian passport) and Veciana recalls that *he and Bishop had long discussions about what had happened*. He says *Bishop told him that Kennedy's refusal to provide air support was the crucial factor in the failure of the operation*. Bishop obviously felt a terrible frustration about that because, according to Veciana, it was then that "*Bishop decided that the only thing left to be done was to have an attempt on Castro's life.*"[240] [Emphasis added]

In **Trained to Kill**, Veciana says *nothing* about JFK's role in the Bay of Pigs fiasco and, of course, nothing at all about the *notional* Phillips being in Cuba up to that event and returning to Cuba afterward. Obviously, Phillips did *not* return to Cuba after the Bay of Pigs. Phillips left Cuba for god around February 1960 (see above).

And so, Veciana's *original* Cuban chronology of his time with the *notional* Phillips—mid-1960 to October 1961—is mere fantasy. But jettisoning Veciana's unworkable mid-1959 chronology is only the first—relatively easy—task at hand. However, we should not be too quick to throw out *all* of the events that Veciana has placed into that implausible time period. Many of them may fit perfectly into the time period Veciana *originally* used for his recruitment in Cuba.

---

239 Veciana, *Trained to Kill*, p. 70.
240 Fonzi, *The Last Investigation*, p. 130.

VECIANA AND PHILLIPS IN CUBA—1959–1960

Returning to Veciana's Original Cuban Chronology: Mid-1960 to October 1961

In 2017, Veciana moved his *notional* Phillips Cuban chronology back to mid-September 1959. That alteration allowed Veciana to *adjust* his Phillips myth to a period when Phillips really *had* been in Cuba. A recruitment by Phillips in Cuba was necessary to substantiate Veciana's claim that he met Phillips with Oswald in Dallas in 1963. As we will see in Chapter Eleven, Veciana devised a stunt to begin laying the groundwork for establishing his bona fides as a "CIA agent" just six months after Gaeton Fonzi first interviewed him for the Church Committee in March 1976.

However, the genesis of Veciana's work for the American government did not begin until the middle of 1960—*not* the middle of 1959. The Cuban episode of that secret work ended with the failure of Operation Liborio in October 1961. I will address Veciana's role in that operation in Chapter Eleven. The distraction caused by the backward movement in time of Veciana's 1959 engrossing *notional* Phillips' spy saga has left us looking in the wrong place for the hidden episodes in Veciana's long campaign to bring down Castro. We *should* be looking in the very span of time in which Veciana originally placed his work for Phillips! For example, the training by "Joe Melton" (true name James O'Mailia) *did* take place when Veciana originally said it did—in the fall of 1960! The fact that the real Phillips had nothing to do with those training sessions helps us pry open the lid of the crypt in which the secret years of Veciana's life have long been buried.

Some of Veciana's activities in the four months prior to the Bay of Pigs may have been loosely connected to the CIA. His activities afterward might also have been connected to the U.S. military. Bill Simpich has extensively investigated Operation Patty that took place in October 1961. Veciana was associated with some of the participants in this operation. Simpich argues that Patty looks more like a plan orchestrated by the Office of Naval Intelligence (ONI).[241] A prime mover in this scheme was Spanish-speaking ONI Navy Lieutenant Commander Harold "Hal" Feeney (AKA Finney), the Base Intelligence Officer at the Guantanamo Bay Naval Facility.[242] I will deal with those activities in Chapter eleven.

Once we focus our search for Veciana's secret activities in the right place, we encounter a history *far more dramatic* than his 1959 tale of secret writing and intrigue, driving all over Havana with Phillips, meeting with him in Julio Lobo's bank, and drinking daiquiris with him in the *La Floradita* on Obispo Street. In the fall of 1960, while

---

241 September-November 2018, personal communication with Bill Simpich.
242 2/10/62, Passavoy (Colonel Wendell G. Johnson) MFR No. 200, U.S. Navy Officer Harold Finney (or Feeney) Visits Dr. Miro 7 February; RIF 104-10233-10432. See also 4/2/62, JMWAVE dispatch UFGA-3694, Possible Use of FPO Shipment of Weapons to Guantanamo Bay Naval Facility; RIF 104-10163-10235.

INTO THE STORM

O'Mailia was training Veciana in the Edeficio LaRampa in Havana, great pains were being taken by the CIA at HQS and in Havana to prepare for the impending break in relations between Havana and Washington.

The brave CIA officers selected to remain in Havana without diplomatic protection to manage the stay-behind nets—Emilio Rodriguez, Tony Sforza, and James O'Mailia—would all be gone within ninety days after the Bay of Pigs disaster. *Only* Veciana's cover would hold up after that, but only until October 1961. October 1961 was the moment that the White House finally returned to the problem of disposing of Castro with the implementation of Operation Mongoose. That was also the point at which Harvey took over the CIA-Mafia plot to kill Castro. Against the backdrop of all that, Veciana's Operation Liborio failed in October 1961, and, having narrowly escaped arrest in Cuba, he stepped off a small boat in Miami and launched Alpha-66.

CHAPTER FOUR

THE SEISMIC AFTERSHOCKS FROM THE CUBAN CATACLYSM

In the early stages of the Cold War, Moscow and Washington were focused on consolidation of their respective "spheres of influence." For example, the U.S. suppressed dissent in Guatemala (1954) and the USSR suppressed dissent in Hungary (1956). Cold War historians that have chronicled the Kennedy-era crises—caused by competition between the United States and the Soviet Union for influence in Latin America and the decolonizing states of Africa and Asia—typically focused on the Berlin Crisis of 1961 and the Cuban Missile Crisis of 1962.

As important as these two crises were, the devastation wrought by the disaster at the Bay of Pigs was the *true Cold War fault line* of the early 1960s. The Berlin and Cuban Missile Crises of 1961-1962 were substantial *aftershocks* of the April 1961 Cuban cataclysm at the Bay of Pigs. That event was the seminal geopolitical boundary of the Kennedy Administration. In geological terms, it was comparable to a comet colliding with the earth and causing the end of one geologic era and the beginning of a new one. Like the flora and fauna of geological transitions, the old geopolitical landscape gave way to a new emergent landscape.

The disaster at the Bay of Pigs led to Soviet Premier Khrushchev's decision to test President Kennedy's resolve with respect to Western access to Berlin. In Chapter Five, I will describe how the Bay of Pigs failure led directly to Khrushchev's plan to publicly feign a cooperative posture toward Kennedy while luring the president into a summit meeting and ambushing him with an ultimatum on Berlin. In the outcome of the crisis that followed, Khrushchev had to give up on the removal of a capitalist cancer in a communist sea (Berlin) and settle instead on gaining a communist cancer in a capitalist sea (Havana).

President Kennedy's November 1961 decision to overthrow the Castro regime precipitated Khrushchev's decision in the spring of 1962 to place nuclear-tipped missiles in Cuba. How these Cold War episodes played out in the larger East-West geopolitical chess match—that also included Laos and Vietnam—is summarized in the opening to Chapter Five.

Of particular note, for most of the chapters in the present volume, a coincidentally parallel paradigm in Washington and Moscow was taking place during these chaotic Cold War years. Neither Kennedy nor Khrushchev were able to control their subordinates. Both leaders faced increasing internal opposition from political-military-national security elites opposed to their external strategies *and* their internal attempts to improve their economies. In the end, neither leader survived. Ironically, President Kennedy's assassination in 1963 played a key role in the purge of Premier Khrushchev in 1964.

The Time Has Come for a Showdown

In the wake of the disastrous Bay of Pigs fiasco, Robert Kennedy's 19 April 1961 call for a showdown with Castro (see the Prologue) specifically—and correctly—predicted that the Soviet Union would be able to "set up missile bases in Cuba."[243] Undersecretary of State Chester Bowles described the cabinet meeting the next day (20 April) "as grim as any meeting I can remember in all my experience in government":

> Reactions around the table were almost savage, as everyone appeared to be jumping on everyone else. ...*The angriest response of all came from Bob Kennedy*... ...The discussion rambled in circles with no real coherent thought. Finally, after three quarters of an hour, the president got up and walked toward his office. I was so distressed at what I felt was a dangerous mood that I walked after him, stopped him, and told him I would like an opportunity to come into his office and talk the whole thing out. Lyndon Johnson, Bob McNamara, and Bobby Kennedy joined us. Bobby continued his tough, savage comments, most of them directed against the Department of State for reasons which are difficult

---

243   4/19/61, *FRUS*, Vol. X, Cuba, Document 157, Memorandum from the Attorney General (Kennedy) to President Kennedy.

THE SEISMIC AFTERSHOCKS FROM THE CUBAN CATACLYSM

>for me to understand. *When I took exception to some of the more extreme things he said by suggesting that the way to get out of our present jam was not to simply double up on everything we had done, he turned on me savagely.*[244] [Emphasis added]

The president was "shattered," Bowles recalled in his memoir.[245]

Kennedy convened another cabinet meeting on Cuba on 22 April, an expanded session attended by thirty-five people.[246] Undersecretary Bowles remembers that on that occasion the atmosphere was as "emotional" as it had been during the previous meeting:

>Again, Bob Kennedy was present, and took the lead... ...slamming into anyone who suggested that we go slowly and try to move calmly and not repeat previous mistakes. ...I stressed that while we were in a bad situation, it would be a mistake for us to assume that it could not disintegrate further... ...[and] *create additional sympathy for Castro in his David and Goliath struggle with the United States. ...These comments were brushed aside brutally by the various fire eaters who were present.*[247] [Emphasis added]

Defense Secretary McNamara later told the Church Committee:

>We were hysterical about Castro at the time of the Bay of Pigs and thereafter, and there was pressure from President Kennedy and the attorney general. I don't believe we contemplated assassination. We did, however, contemplate overthrow.[248]

Apparently, McNamara was unaware that *at that very moment* the CIA was plotting with the Mafia to assassinate Castro.[249]

A lingering question is whether Attorney General Robert Kennedy had learned from the FBI about the ongoing CIA-Mafia plot to kill Castro. In Chapter Thirteen, I will discuss that question in detail, and only briefly introduce it here. After investigating that question, the Church Committee came to this conclusion:

>By May 1961, however, the attorney general and Hoover were aware that the CIA had earlier used Giancana in an operation against Cuba, and FBI files contained two memoranda which, *if simultaneously viewed*, would have left one to conclude that the CIA operation had involved assassination.[250] [Emphasis added]

---

244 4/20/61, *FRUS*, Vol. X, Cuba, Document 158, Bowles Notes on Cabinet Meeting.
245 Chester Bowles, ***Promises to Keep*** (New York: Harper & Row, 1971), pp. 329-330.
246 4/20/61, *FRUS*, Vol. X, Cuba, Document 167, Record of the 478th Meeting of the National Security Council.
247 4/20/61, *FRUS*, Vol. X, Cuba, Document 166, Bowles Notes on Cuban Crisis.
248 7/11/75, McNamara deposition, SSCIA, *Interim Report*, pp. 157-158.
249 Ibid.
250 11/20 75, SSCIA, *Interim Report*, p. 129. The two memoranda referred to were the 10/18/60 memorandum linking Giancana to a Castro assassination plot—but not mentioning the CIA—and the 5/22/61 memorandum linking Giancana to a CIA operation against Cuba involving "dirty business," but without using the word "assassination."

INTO THE STORM

The committee's Interim Report states they uncovered a chain of events which would have enabled Hoover to have "assembled the entire picture" and reported it to the president. However, there was no documentary evidence that anyone in the FBI had linked a Giancana assassination operation to the CIA by May 1961. The documentary record indicates that not until May 1962 was RFK told that the CIA-Giancana operation had involved an assassination attempt against Castro.[251]

By the end of April 1961, the president's attention was fixed on Laos and Berlin. Looming large over both problems was the potential use of nuclear weapons—*an option that the Joint Chiefs would repeatedly advise the president to take if necessary.*

On 18 April, the day after the Cuban exile brigade landed on the beachhead at the Bay of Pigs, Khrushchev sent a warning to Kennedy that if the conflict continued "a new conflagration may flare up in another area"—a transparent reference to West Berlin.[252] Kennedy's failure in Cuba was a windfall for Khrushchev, who interpreted it as a sign of weakness, validating his view that he could manipulate the young president on Berlin. As will become apparent in Chapter Five, the Vienna Summit was not only on, but had also become a deadly Soviet snare.

The Reverberating Aftershocks of the New Fault Line in Cuba

The Thespian tragedy of the Eisenhower-inspired Cuban debacle gripped the incoming Kennedy Administration in a full Nelson hold for its first ninety days. The outcome left the foreign policy foundations of the New Frontier in smoldering ruins. The sheer depth of the cataclysm created the irresistible temptation for Premier Khrushchev to abandon his courting of the American president and led to the alteration of Soviet strategy in Southeast Asia and Berlin. The cataclysm in Cuba created a new Cold War fault line and its abrupt aftershocks were the ensuing crises in Laos and Berlin.

The immediate lesson for President Kennedy and his brother was the necessity to clean house at the Pentagon and CIA. Unfortunately for the Kennedy brothers, the lessons of the Bay of Pigs did not include avoiding the Cuban snake pit in the future. From their perspective, cleaning house in Washington was not enough; they decided to clean house in Cuba too. In retrospect, the Kennedy Administration should have done a better job of cleaning house close to the flagpole in Washington *and* let the light of truth about Castro's dictatorship shine in Cuba instead of carelessly playing into his hands with endless new aggressive schemes to overthrow him.

---

251   Ibid, p. 132.
252   Ibid.

THE SEISMIC AFTERSHOCKS FROM THE CUBAN CATACLYSM

I will address the epic events of the struggle for power in Washington and between Kennedy and Khrushchev in the present and remaining volumes of this series. In the remainder of this chapter, I will describe the three major aftershocks of the new Cold War fault line and the concentric tremors each of them produced. I will identify and discuss these three major Cold War disturbances:

- November 1961: The new plan (Mongoose) by the Kennedy brothers to overthrow the Castro regime.
- May 1962: Khrushchev's decision to deploy offensive nuclear weapons in Cuba.
- October 1962: The Cuban Missile Crisis.

The outward radiating seismic activity along this fault line was centered around three principal foci—Laos, Berlin, and Vietnam. The activity taking place in these areas was triggered by adjustments of Soviet Cold War strategy and the resulting American responses. The long-term Kennedy strategy was to resolve—to the extent possible—these three developing Cold War hot spots *before* returning to their plan to overthrow the Castro regime.

The Calls for Nuclear War Over Laos

Meanwhile, tempers had not yet settled down after the disaster in Cuba when the final decision on intervention in Laos had to be made. I discussed the Laos issue in Volume II (Chapter Twenty-One) and in more detail in ***JFK and Vietnam*** (2017 edition, Chapter One). Here, I will recapitulate some of that history to highlight the bellicosity of the Joint Chiefs of Staff (JCS), especially Chief of Naval Operations (CNO) Admiral Arleigh Burke and the JCS deputy chairman, Air Force Chief of Staff General Curtis Lemay. They pressured the president to go to war in Laos and, if necessary, to *use nuclear weapons.*

The end of April 1961 was a moment of "prolonged crisis meetings" on Laos.[253] In his memoir, Deputy Undersecretary of State for Political Affairs U. Alexis Johnson recalled, "The president was under great pressure." Kennedy was concerned that the capitol, Vientiane, would fall in hours, and feeling that a peace conference would be pointless if the Pathet Lao captured all of the key areas in southern Laos.[254]

In the crucial meeting on 27 April, CNO Arleigh Burke sat in for Joint Chiefs of Staff Chairman General Lyman Lemnitzer who was in Laos awaiting the American invasion. In a bizarre briefing, Burke argued that the U.S. would *either lose Southeast Asia without a war or be forced to fight a long one and use nuclear weapons.* The CNO urged the

---
253 *PP*, Gravel ed., vol. 2, p. 42.
254 U. Alexis Johnson, ***Right Hand of Power***, pp. 322-23.

president to implement Southeast Asian Treaty Organization (SEATO) Plan 5—the deployment of a 500,000-man SEATO force (mostly U.S.) to Laos and South Vietnam, to defend Southeast Asia from a base centered on the Mekong River. Burke then startled those present by saying that "this was not enough." He believed more troops were needed but pointed out that strategic reserves were too low to deploy enough men to win without *resorting to nuclear warfare.*

The Army Chief of Staff, General George Decker, and the Marine Corps Commandant, General David Shoup, exposed the unfeasibility of the plan. They interjected that due to limitations of U.S. airlift and Laotian airfields, only 1,000 men per day could be put on the ground in Laos. This was insufficient to defend the capitol and the forces themselves would be vulnerable.[255] The remarks of the chiefs made it hard, Presidential Advisor Arthur Schlesinger, Jr. recalled, "to make out what the chiefs were trying to say."[256] Secretary of Defense McNamara turned the discussion into a free-for-all with the comment that perhaps it was too late to intervene because these U.S. forces might be "driven out."[257]

The problem was the seeming incoherence of the Joint Chiefs' position, which evoked an image, as Alexis Johnson recalled, of a small, beleaguered band of American troops stuck on an airstrip in Laos while the president contemplated *using nuclear weapons against China* to rescue them.[258] The JCS, writes Charles Stevenson, a scholar who interviewed most of those who attended the meeting, "were not really concerned" about a war with China; but, he adds:

> Their plans in case of Chinese intervention, however, were quite frightening. These called for the seizure of Hainan Island, which was defended by three Chinese divisions, deployment of 250,000 U.S. troops to South Vietnam, followed by operations across North Vietnam into Laos to block Chinese intrusions. If these U.S. forces were in danger of being overrun, the chiefs expected to *use nuclear weapons.*[259] [Emphasis added]

---

255 *USN and the Vietnam Conflict*, p. 69. Sustainment was equally vexing: of the 3,279 STONS (short tons) required daily during the first three days of the operation, only 1,766 could be transported, and only 778 of the daily required 1,053 for the next five days.
256 Schlesinger, *A Thousand Days*, p. 315.
257 *USN and the Vietnam Conflict*, pp. 69-71. The reactions of others listening to the chiefs' proposals were similarly confused, especially those of the State Department. Under Secretary of State Chester Bowles, sitting in for Secretary of State Dean Rusk, argued that SEATO Plan 5 would trigger a Chinese intervention, but Deputy Under Secretary of State for Political Affairs U. Alexis Johnson, contended the best way to avoid war was "to be seen as ready to use force." See U. Alexis Johnson, *Right Hand of Power*, p. 324. Completing this merry-go-round of disparate recommendations made to the president in this meeting, Deputy Special Assistant to the President for National Security Affairs Walt Rostow said he still favored a limited troop deployment to Thailand as a show of force, a view supported by Ambassador-at-Large Averell Harriman and JCS Chairman General Lemnitzer, who were both in Laos at that time. See *Congressional History*, vol. 2, p. 26; and Schlesinger, *A Thousand Days*, p. 316.
258 U. Alexis Johnson, *Right Hand of Power*, p. 323.
259 Stevenson, *The End of Nowhere*, pp. 301-2, n. 60. This extraordinary plan Stevenson attributes to a confidential source. However, it is not unlike the position that General LeMay argued for the following day (see below).

THE SEISMIC AFTERSHOCKS FROM THE CUBAN CATACLYSM

Deputy Special Assistant to the President for National Security Affairs Walt Rostow later said of the chiefs' advice, "I never saw a worse performance by our military." He told Schlesinger it was the worst White House meeting of the entire Kennedy Administration.[260]

What happened next was an unusual move by Vice President Johnson. He attempted to create an opportunity for the chiefs to regroup and more clearly state their views. LBJ proposed that each of them separately put their ideas into writing.[261] Kennedy agreed, and the group reconvened on 29 April. The president, to provide for the contingency that a decision to go to war would be made, broadened participation to include eight senators and seven congressmen.

All of the administration participants except for the president then met in a brainstorming session. They foresaw dire consequences to the loss of Laos. McNamara said, "We would have to attack the DRV [North Vietnam] if we gave up Laos." Rusk argued that if a cease-fire was "not brought about quickly" it would be necessary to implement SEATO Plan 5. Admiral Burke stated flatly that the loss of Laos would require the deployment of U.S. forces to Thailand and Vietnam, and that the U.S. "would have to throw in enough to win—*perhaps the 'works.'*" "The thing to do now," he said, was "to land and hold as much as we can and make clear we were not going to be pushed out of Southeast Asia." Marine Corps Commandant Shoup stated that bombing with B-26s before landing the troops would make it "possible to obtain a cease-fire and get the panhandle of [southern] Laos." Army Chief of Staff General Decker stated, "We [under Eisenhower] should have [gone in] last August [1960]." He now urged that troops be put in Thailand and Vietnam to see if this would pressure the communists into a cease-fire in Laos.[262] The only one of the chiefs not present, the Chairman, General Lemnitzer—in Laos at the time— "endorsed the case" for a "limited commitment."[263]

McNamara worried that U.S. forces would be vulnerable to sabotage, attack by guerrillas, and Chinese air strikes. But Burke, LeMay, and even Rusk felt intervention was still feasible. In the end, McNamara said, "The situation was worsening by the hour and that if we were going to commit ourselves, then we must do so sooner rather than later." Rusk wanted to put troops in Vientiane and seize the Laotian panhandle as well. Shoup wanted to bomb the Pathet Lao, land troops, *and then* secure a cease-fire and the Laotian panhandle. Burke wanted to take Vientiane airport initially, and then land

---

260 Rostow interview with Richard Neustadt, April 11, 1964, p. 46; Schlesinger, *A Thousand Days*, p. 315.
261 Schlesinger, *A Thousand Days*, p. 315.
262 Army Chief of Staff General Decker's comment that a conventional war was unwinnable, and "if we go in" it would mean bombing Hanoi and China and perhaps using nuclear weapons, has led some observers to surmise that the Joint Chiefs were not in favor of intervention. This interpretation is obviously misinformed, as the minutes of this meeting make abundantly clear. Lemnitzer, Burke, Shoup, and LeMay all clearly favored intervention, and so did Decker.
263 Schlesinger, *A Thousand Days*, p. 316. Schlesinger says the "military" did not want to put troops in unless "they could send at least 140,000 men armed with tactical nuclear weapons."

INTO THE STORM

and hold as much as possible. Decker wanted to put troops in Thailand and Vietnam and then invade Laos if a cease-fire was not obtained. LeMay wanted SEATO Plan 5, air strikes, *and war with China as well*, saying, "We should go to work on China itself and let Chiang [President of Taiwan] take Hainan Island."

The issue of whether intervention would trigger a Chinese response found the brainstorming group evenly divided. The lengthy discussion on this point boiled down to this: McNamara, Burke, Decker, and Bowles, in varying degrees, all felt U.S. intervention could very easily trigger a Chinese response and the consequent need to *resort to nuclear weapons*. Rusk, Bohlen, and LeMay felt U.S. intervention would not trigger a Chinese response, although LeMay, as noted above, wanted to "go to work on China" anyway.

On the general question of intervention in Southeast Asia, the record of this extraordinary brainstorming session shows that Kennedy's principal civilian and military advisors:

- were sharply divided on what form this intervention should take and on whether it would trigger a Chinese response;
- differed somewhat on the significance of the loss of Laos;
- and were nearly unanimous in advocating U.S. intervention in Laos.

Despite the consensus among most of Kennedy's top advisors that intervention was necessary, there was no such consensus on the president's most basic questions: What form should it take? What would the Chinese reaction be? And, where would it lead in the end?

The administration participants in the brainstorming session then went into the NSC meeting joined by fifteen members of Congress.[264] Originally scheduled to look only at a Vietnam report, the agenda was broadened to include a discussion of Laos.[265] Surprisingly, this Laos discussion has to date escaped historical scrutiny: it has almost never been commented on in works covering this period.[266] This is unfortunate, for that day the NSC examined issues of great national importance. There *is* a surviving draft record of this meeting, located in the Vice-Presidential Security Files of the Lyndon Baines Johnson Library. This record states that the council examined "considerations involved in the various alternative courses of action" in Laos.[267]

Kennedy authorized *preparations* to move two brigades and associated combat support elements into position for a unilateral U.S. intervention in Laos under a SEATO

---

[264] Robert Kennedy, McNamara, Gilpatric, Burke, Rusk, Bowles, and Steeves did, while Decker, LeMay, and Shoup did not. McGarr, Nolting, and Young were added.
[265] This was not unexpected, for on the 28th Burris informed Vice President Johnson that Laos was expected to be added to the agenda. See Burris memo to LBJ, 28 April 1961, LBJ Library, VP Security File, Box 4.
[266] The only reference for this 29 April meeting is *FRUS*, Volume I, Vietnam, Document 40, Editorial Note; but it says that no record of this discussion has been found.
[267] "Draft Record of Actions" of the 480th NSC meeting, 29 April 1961, LBJ Library, VP Security File, Box 4.

cover. The campaign plan appeared to include ground offensives along multiple axes, one from Thailand and the other from Vietnam. From the foregoing, it is obvious that Kennedy had indeed agreed to *threaten* intervention in Laos. But Kennedy's plan, says his aide, Theodore Sorensen, "combined bluff with real determination in proportions he made known to *no one.*"[268] Apparently, Kennedy kept even his closest advisors in the dark about his ultimate intentions in Laos.

By the time the 1 May NSC meeting finally convened, the "realities of Laos," as Rusk called them, had produced an overwhelming sentiment among Kennedy's advisors for intervention there.[269] A force of 10,000 men was ready for action, and the views of the Joint Chiefs were again delivered to the president in writing. Whereas on 27 April the chiefs had appeared confused about going into Laos, they now left no doubt about their unity. National Security Advisor McGeorge Bundy wrote in a note to Kennedy that "it's not at all clear why they are now unanimous."[270] Sorensen says there were still "splits" in the chiefs' written responses, but the majority "appeared to favor the landing of American troops in Thailand, South Vietnam and the government-held portions of the Laotian panhandle."[271]

The fifteen congressional leaders also attended this meeting. On his feet in front of a map, Admiral Burke addressed the entire group. Burke ardently advocated fighting in Laos regardless of the difficulties or the possibilities of escalation and the *use of nuclear weapons.* He asked:

> If we do not fight in Laos, will we fight in Thailand where the situation will be the same sometime in the future as it is now in Laos? Will we fight in Vietnam? Where will we fight? Where do we hold? Where do we draw the line?[272]

Kennedy Kills U.S. Intervention in Laos

Chastened by the Bay of Pigs, however, Kennedy was now far more skeptical of the chiefs' recommendations. According to Sorensen, Kennedy "began asking questions he had not asked before about military operations in Laos." The chiefs were no more successful in explaining their proposals than they had been four days earlier and

---

268 Sorensen, **Kennedy**, p. 646.
269 One notable opponent was Senator Mansfield, who wrote a lengthy letter to Kennedy on May 1 arguing against intervention. Mansfield warned Kennedy the U.S. public reaction to a neutral government in Laos would be mild compared to a pro-U.S. government "kept in power with American blood and treasure." See Mansfield letter to Kennedy, May 1, 1961, **Declassified Documents**, 1978, 208C.
270 Bundy note to JFK, JFK Library, POF, Country File, Laos, Box 121.
271 Sorensen, **Kennedy**, pp. 644-45.
272 *USN and the Vietnam Conflict*, pp. 71-72.

INTO THE STORM

proceeded to crumble under Kennedy's detailed questioning. He raised the most basic military issues about their campaign plan, and their answers seem incomprehensible in retrospect.

"How many airstrips were in Laos?" the president asked. Only *two* was the answer. And these were only usable during daylight and good weather and were always vulnerable to attack. If the communists attacked us and "we didn't use nuclear weapons," Kennedy asked, "would we have to retreat or surrender in the face of an all-out Chinese intervention?" The answer was affirmative. "If we put more forces in Laos," he asked, "would that *weaken our reserves for action in Berlin* or elsewhere?" The answer was again in the affirmative.[273]

Kennedy sat in "stunned silence" as he heard that the dispatch of even 10,000 men to Southeast Asia would denude American strategic reserves.[274] I would hasten to point out here that *this would also have been the case if JFK had dispatched 10,000 men to Cuba*—where they would still be mired in the mountainous jungles. The meeting was "unforgettable for all present," says Rostow. There was no order or consensus. "It was chaos."[275]

The president then asked for the views of those present and encountered virtually unanimous opposition to sending in U.S. forces. Only one person in the room spoke out in support of Admiral Burke's proposal: Vice President Johnson.[276] "He said he thought I had something," Burke recalls of LBJ that day, "but that was because he spoke first, perhaps. ... I've been grateful to him ever since ... I lost that battle, and I lost it completely."[277]

Kennedy decided to defer "final decisions" pending "further developments in the cease-fire negotiations." That was little more than a placebo, a tactic Kennedy often used to avoid flatly turning down a proposal from the chiefs. He would send them away with instructions to do a study and get back to him.

Those present, including Burke, knew what the Navy history of the war would later conclude: "The decision not to intervene had, in effect, been made."[278] Burke remembers thinking afterward "a lot of people are going to die in this country sometime in the future if this thing is allowed to go by." And Burke did not give up:

> ... I went back [that same day]. I wrote a memorandum to the president, and you just don't send a memorandum over to the president: You take it over. And I got thrown out. ... the president said, "This is settled."

---

[273] Ibid, p. 645.
[274] Stevenson, *The End of Nowhere*, p. 135.
[275] Rostow, interview with Richard Neustadt, 11 April 1964.
[276] Stevenson, *The End of Nowhere*, p. 152. Here Stevenson's source was an interview with Admiral Burke. Burke makes that same claim in his oral history, interview with Joseph O'Connor, 20 January 1967, JFK Library, Oral History Collection.
[277] Burke, interview with Joseph O'Connor, 20 January 1967, pp. 35-36.
[278] *USN and the Vietnam Conflict*, p. 72.

THE SEISMIC AFTERSHOCKS FROM THE CUBAN CATACLYSM

That same night, Burke cabled the news to the Commander-in-Chief Pacific (CINCPAC), Admiral Felt: "I am afraid that we may not execute [in Laos]."[279]

And so, the first casualty of the Cuban cataclysm in April 1961 was the recommendation to intervene in Laos—come what may. Kennedy killed that idea two weeks later. Moreover, four days after the invasion at the Bay of Pigs, retired Army Chief of Staff Maxwell Taylor, who had been forced out of the government for criticizing the Eisenhower administration's emphasis on strategic weapons, received a call from the president. Kennedy said he was in "deep trouble," and asked Taylor to come to the White House to talk about it. Taylor later wrote of his experience the following day:

> I was ushered into the Oval Room and there met Kennedy, Vice President Johnson, and McGeorge Bundy along with a few other officials who drifted in and out. I sensed an air which I had known in my military past—that of a command post which had been overrun. There were some glazed eyes, subdued voices, and slow speech that I remembered observing in commanders routed at the Battle of the Bulge or recovering from the shock of their first action.[280]

This passage dramatically illustrates the painful aftermath of the Cuban blunder. It was an experience that Kennedy would never forget. He looked upon the Cuban failure as a lesson well learned—he could not trust the leadership at the Pentagon and the CIA. The alienation between the president and his subordinates could not be repaired. On 3 May he told Schlesinger:

> "If it hadn't been for Cuba, we might be about to intervene in Laos." Waving a sheaf of cables from Lemnitzer, he added, "I might have taken this advice seriously."[281]

Sorensen later had a nearly identical experience with Kennedy:

> "Thank God the Bay of Pigs happened when it did," he would say to me in September. ... "Otherwise we'd be in Laos by now—and that would be a hundred times worse."[282]

Kennedy was "appalled," Schlesinger said, "at the sketchy nature of American military planning for Laos—the lack of detail and the unanswered questions."[283]

Kennedy's growing antipathy toward the Joint Chiefs was matched by their growing irritation with him. General LeMay was particularly unhappy. As Robert Futrell, in *The United States Air Force in Southeast Asia*, explains:

---

279 Ibid.
280 Maxwell Taylor, *Swords and Plowshares*, (Boston: De Capo Press, 1990). p. 180.
281 Schlesinger, *A Thousand Days*, p. 316.
282 Sorensen, *Kennedy*, p. 644.
283 Schlesinger, *A Thousand Days*, p. 315.

> Part of the difficulties in dealing with a possible use of force, General LeMay believed, was due to President Kennedy's procedural habits and tendencies. The president seemed to depend on ad hoc committees in lieu of the Joint Chiefs, leading to vetoes, stalling, lengthy discussions, and too many people "in the act and making decisions in areas where they weren't competent." This approach to policy, LeMay believed, failed to recognize that "going to war is a very serious business and once you make [the] decision that you're going to do that, then you ought to be prepared to do just that."[284]

Lemnitzer similarly "deplored the tendency of the U.S. government to waste time in quibbling over policy."[285]

This picture of a president pitted against his military advisors is an unpleasant one. A commander-in-chief must have confidence in the generals under him and rely on their professional judgments if the national security mechanism is to perform correctly or at all. Unfortunately, Schlesinger recalled, that was not the case during the Kennedy presidency:

> After the Bay of Pigs, the Kennedys began to question the Chiefs' professional competence. They also resented their [the chiefs'] public relations tactics. The new president was not one for men in uniform with pointers reading aloud sentences off flip charts he could read much faster for himself.[286]

The Pentagon's advice with respect to the use of nuclear weapons in Laos was just as inept as their advice had been for the invasion at the Bay of Pigs. The chiefs' advice would remain useless even as the president began a wide-ranging purge of his administration.

As these complicated Cold War events played out in Laos and Berlin, the growing U.S. lead in strategic nuclear forces became an increasingly important factor that both sides had to deal with carefully. How to manage these concurrent crises without being forced to use America's nuclear advantage was the key component of Kennedy's strategy. Predictably, however, the president's generals wanted to use those forces before the Soviet Union could catch up.

The Net Evaluation Subcommittee

On 20 July 1961, the CIA was settling Tony Sforza (**AMRYE-1**) and Emilio Rodriguez (**AMIRE-1**)—who had just escaped Castro's clutches in Cuba—into their new foreign

---

284 *Air Force History*, p. 65.
285 Ibid, p. 69.
286 Schlesinger, *Robert Kennedy and His Times*, p. 449.

THE SEISMIC AFTERSHOCKS FROM THE CUBAN CATACLYSM

intelligence (FI) jobs at the CIA's JMWAVE station in Miami (See Volume II, Chapter Four). Within twelve months, they would learn from their Cuban informants that the Soviet Union was placing offensive nuclear missiles in Cuba.

Meanwhile, on that same day (20 July 1961) at a meeting in the White House, the Net Evaluation Subcommittee of the National Security Council (NSC) presented President Kennedy with an extraordinary plan to launch *a surprise nuclear attack on the Soviet Union.*

The Pentagon chiefs and DCI Dulles told the president that the window of maximum opportunity for a disarming counterforce strike against the USSR's nuclear capability would occur in late 1963. The timing of the president's first Net Evaluation briefing is interesting. It is possible that such briefings had not been given to President Eisenhower; at that time, with the missile race in its infancy, it was thought that the Soviet Union was in the lead. President Kennedy's first briefing came just three months after the Bay of Pigs fiasco *and* during the looming crisis over Berlin when the credibility of the U.S. nuclear deterrent was in question.

At a morning meeting of the Berlin Steering Group the previous day, 19 July 1961, the president asked whether a proposed U.S. military build-up would increase the credibility of the U.S. nuclear deterrent and McNamara replied that it would. At the NSC meeting that afternoon, Kennedy emphasized his own view that the proposed U.S. preparations would not be adequate without an effective allied response, especially from the Germans and the French.[287]

A few days earlier, in July 1961, the U.S. intelligence community produced a Special National Intelligence Estimate (SNIE) on possible Soviet reactions to U.S. options with respect to Berlin.[288] The SNIE made this prediction:

> The Soviet leaders are confident of the prospects for advancing their cause by means short of all-out war. We continue to believe that, so long as they remain vulnerable to U.S. strategic power, they will not willingly enter into a situation which, by their calculations, the risks of general war are substantial.

While that judgment turned out to be prescient, it was not uniformly accepted in the Kennedy Administration at the time.

Kennedy's advisors were split over how to proceed in Berlin. Former Ambassador Dean Acheson had been brought in by the president to ensure that he had access to the hardline arguments about how to deal with Khrushchev in the crisis. Most of

---

[287] 7/19/61, **FRUS**, 1961-1963, Volume XIV, Berlin Crisis, 1961-1962, Document 77, Memorandum of Minutes of the National Security Council Meeting.
[288] 7/11/61, SNIE 2-2-61, "Soviet and other Reactions to Possible U.S. Courses of action with Respect to Berlin, cia.gov/library.

Kennedy's closest advisors preferred—as he did—negotiation to demonstrate that the West favored a reduction in tension over West Berlin while protecting Western access rights.

During an argument at a 29 June NSC meeting, many of those present were troubled by Acheson's apparent indifference about the risk of nuclear war.[289] In his report to the NSC meeting, Acheson had argued that the entire position of the U.S. hung in the balance. Acheson wanted the president to declare a national emergency and order a rapid buildup in American *nuclear as well as conventional forces.*

Those events were the context for the 20 July 1961 meeting of the NSC, at which General Thomas Francis Hickey, Staff Director of the NSC's Net Evaluation Subcommittee, was on hand to brief President Kennedy. Hickey, along with JCS Chairman Lemnitzer and DCI Dulles—with other members of the subcommittee attending—presented plans for "a surprise nuclear attack [against the USSR] in late 1963, preceded by a period of heightened tensions." On 4 June 1993, the LBJ Library declassified the notes, taken by Vice President Johnson's military aide Colonel Howard Burris, at the 20 July 1961 presentation.[290] The Burris memorandum to LBJ was first published by Dr. James Galbraith of the University of Texas at Austin, in *The American Prospect* in 1994.[291]

Presidential Special Advisor Arthur Schlesinger, Jr. derisively described the meeting and Kennedy's disgusted reaction:

> In the spring of 1961 Kennedy received the Net Evaluation, an annual doomsday briefing analyzing the chances of nuclear war. An Air Force general presented it, said Roswell Gilpatric, the deputy secretary of defense, "as though it were for a kindergarten class. . . . Finally, Kennedy got up and walked right out in the middle of it, and that was the end of it.[292]

According Burris' memo, "The president directed that no member in attendance at the meeting disclose even the subject of the meeting." National Security Advisor McGeorge Bundy described the president's adverse reaction to the proposed surprise strike: "He expressed his own reaction to Dean Rusk as they walked out of the cabinet room to the Oval Office for a private meeting on other subjects. "And we call ourselves the human race."[293]

The timing of the chiefs' proposal was not lost on the president. Kennedy was facing Soviet ultimatums on Berlin at a time when conventional U.S. military forces,

---

289 Michael Beschloss, *The Crisis Years—Kennedy and Khrushchev, 1960-1963* (New York: Harper Collins, 1991), p. 243.
290 7/20/61, Notes on National Security Council Meeting by Colonel Burris. LBJ Library.
291 James Galbraith, "Did the U.S. Military Plan a Nuclear First Strike for 1963?" *The American Prospect*, Fall 1994, pp. 88-96.
292 Schlesinger, *Robert Kennedy and His Times*, p. 449.
293 McGeorge Bundy, *Danger and Survival*, p. 354.

THE SEISMIC AFTERSHOCKS FROM THE CUBAN CATACLYSM

by themselves, could not prevent the loss of West Berlin to East Germany. All present at the meeting understood that without the American nuclear deterrent, Berlin could not be saved. But the crisis over Berlin wasn't *all* that Kennedy had on his mind during that bizarre Net Evaluation presentation. *Twice*, the president obliquely broached something that those present could not yet have been aware of. Burris' memo captured what else might have been on Kennedy's mind:

> In recalling General Hickey's opening statement that these [net evaluation] studies have been made since 1957, the president asked for an appraisal of the *trend* in the effectiveness of the attack. General Lemnitzer replied that he would also discuss this [later personally] with the president. [Emphasis added]

Because Kennedy had already been told that the best window of opportunity for such a nuclear attack against the USSR would occur in late 1963, this question about the *predicted trend line* betrays his interest about a time *other* than late 1963. And Kennedy's next comment revealed what that period was:

> Since the basic assumption of this year's presentation was an attack in late 1963, *the president asked about probable effects in the winter of 1962.* Mr. Dulles observed that the attack would be much less effective since there would be considerably fewer missiles involved.[294] [Emphasis added]

Only the president knew what he was thinking about: *how would the Cold War landscape look in late 1962?* And, with the benefit of hindsight, we now know what the Kennedys had in mind. Their intention—after dealing with the flash points in Berlin, Laos, and Vietnam—was to reactivate the plan to overthrow Castro. The question was: *what would Khrushchev be able to do about it?*

That question aside, at the time of the Net Evaluation proposal, the prospect of an imminent nuclear nightmare was real. As James Galbraith—the first observer to notice the importance of the 20 July 1961 NSC meeting—explained: The Net Evaluation briefing took place in the context "of an increasing nuclear edge based on a runaway lead in land-based missiles" facing the president in the perilous "nuclear-tinged crisis that erupted over Berlin in July of 1961."[295]

By the summer of 1961, the Berlin Crisis had evolved into the most dangerous flashpoint for a nuclear conflict since the onset of the Cold War. President Kennedy was walking a tightrope—trying to strike an effective balance between intimidating the Soviets while giving them a way out of their dilemma.[296] Acute arguments among his

---

294 7/20/61, Notes on National Security Council Meeting by Colonel Burris. LBJ Library.
295 James Galbraith, "Did the U.S. Military Plan a Nuclear First Strike for 1963?" *The American Prospect*, Fall 1994, p. 90.
296 See Robert Dallek, *An Unfinished Life, John F. Kennedy, 1917-1963* (New York: Little, Brown and Company, 2003), p. 418.

INTO THE STORM

advisors were boiling over. Schlesinger recalled that the president was "fighting his way through the thicket of debate to his own conclusions." At that point, Cuba and Laos were side issues, "But Berlin threatened a war which might destroy civilization, and he thought about little else that summer."[297]

The moment to delineate his position to the public arrived just five days after the Net Evaluation presentation. On 25 July, Kennedy delivered this warning in a televised address to the nation:

> But above all it [West Berlin] has now become—as never before—*the great testing place of Western courage and will*, a focal point where our solemn commitments, stretching back over the years since 1945, and Soviet ambitions now meet in basic confrontation.[298] ...Now, in the thermonuclear age, *any misjudgment on either side about the intentions of the other could rain more devastation in several hours than has been wrought in all the wars of human history.*[299] [Emphasis added]

One wonders if the chiefs' recommendation to conduct a surprise counterforce strike against the USSR was on the president's mind when he added that warning to his speech.

One point that Kennedy made crystal clear in his televised address was that the U.S. would make a stand to preserve the freedom of West Berlin—come what may. I will closely examine the 1961 Berlin Crisis in the following chapter of this volume.

The Emerging Crisis in Vietnam

Between the Bay of Pigs and the end of 1961 three trends were on the rise in South Vietnam: the success of the communist insurgency; the American commitment to stop it; and the resultant discord in Washington over how to do that. Although President Kennedy refused to send U.S. combat troops to South Vietnam, he approved NSAM-52, a decision that committed U.S. policy to preventing communist domination in South Vietnam and that dispatched 400 U.S. Special Forces advisors.

As I mentioned above, in addition to the aftershocks in Laos and Berlin, the deepening vortex of the new Cold War fault line included numerous tremors in Vietnam. Khrushchev seized upon the opportunity created by the Bay of Pigs upheaval to initiate a more aggressive strategy to draw the Americans into Southeast Asia (see the introduction to Chapter Five). Begun during the runup to the Bay of Pigs invasion, the Soviet

---

297 Schlesinger, *A Thousand Days* (New York: Mariner Books, 2002), p. 391.
298 7/25/61, ***The American Presidency Project***, JFK Radio and Television Report to the American People on the Berlin Crisis.
299 Ibid.

THE SEISMIC AFTERSHOCKS FROM THE CUBAN CATACLYSM

airlifts of North Vietnamese forces into Laos quickly created the communist "pocket of Tchepone" in southern Laos.[300]

While the situation in Laos continued to deteriorate and the crisis in Berlin mushroomed, a new Viet Cong offensive erupted in South Vietnam. In early May, the president had killed the planned U.S. invasion of Laos. That left open the crucial communist infiltration routes to South Vietnam and led to the doubling of the rate of communist infiltration.[301] *The aftershock in Laos thus triggered a new one in Vietnam.*

For the remainder of 1961, the non-stop tremors in South Vietnam led to calls for the dispatch of American combat troops to counter the rapid expansion of Viet Cong forces. As early as the end of May 1961, Kennedy had quashed the scheming of Military Assistance Advisory Group (MAAG) Chief General McGarr, Colonel Trafficante, Vice President Johnson and President Diem in Vietnam to finagle the dispatch of U.S. combat troops to Vietnam (see Chapters Four and Five of *JFK and Vietnam*, 2017 Edition).

After the April 1961 Bay of Pigs catastrophe, Kennedy's patience with the CIA and the JCS had been worn down to a frazzled hair. To counter the increasing pressure to send combat troops to Vietnam, Kennedy turned to someone outside the policy apparatus—someone he thought he could trust—General Maxwell D. Taylor. Taylor recollected:

> My active involvement in Vietnam matters began about mid-June [1961] while I was still working on the Cuba report. I would fix the specific moment as a chance encounter with the president outside the door of his White House office. He was holding in his hands President Diem's letter of 9 June which he passed to me and asked how he should answer it. My effort to provide him an answer was the beginning of an involvement in the Vietnam problem to which I was to commit a large part of my life during the next eight years.[302]

Taylor, along with Rostow, would dominate Vietnam policy for the next five months. Taylor's reign, culminating with a trip to Vietnam in mid-October, would, as it turned out, only add fuel to the momentum, already strong among Kennedy's advisors, for intervention in Vietnam.

General Taylor's first major recommendation to the president on Vietnam policy was a 27 July memo framing U.S. policy options in South-east Asia in this goldilocks manner: 1) disengage as gracefully as possible; 2) find a pretext and, using U.S. force, attack Hanoi; or 3) build up indigenous strength to the extent possible, while

---

300 7/18/61, *FRUS*, Volume I, Vietnam, Document 98, Memorandum of a Conversation.

301 During his June talks with Kennedy, Thuan said 2,800 communist troops had entered Vietnam over the previous four months; see State Department Memorandum of Conversation, 14 June 1961, JFK Library, NSF, Country File, Box 193. A 12 July CIA field report indicated that, in June alone, 1,500 troops had infiltrated into South Vietnam.

302 Maxwell Taylor, *Swords and Plowshares*, p. 221.

INTO THE STORM

preparing to intervene with U.S. forces if "the situation gets out of hand."[303] Obviously, *only* the third alternative was acceptable.

Although few people recognized it then or afterward, Taylor's Cuba report would have far-reaching and profound effects on Vietnam policy.[304] As a result of that report, on 28 June Kennedy approved three NSAMs that Taylor played a major role in crafting—NSAMs 55, 56, and 57. Taken together, these three documents reaffirmed Kennedy's desire to get moving with the development of counterinsurgency and paramilitary capabilities and, at the same time, to reorganize agency and departmental responsibilities using the lessons learned from the defeat in Cuba.

The first of three national security memoranda, NSAM-55[305] had the distinction of Kennedy's personal signature—most NSAMs were signed by his national security advisor, McGeorge Bundy. This NSAM also had the additional unique feature of being addressed only to Chairman of the Joint Chiefs of Staff General Lemnitzer. Kennedy was angry with Lemnitzer for being poorly informed about the military dimensions of the Cuban operation and, by the time he signed NSAM-55, Kennedy was certain this same weakness had marked Lemnitzer's proposals for the invasion of Laos. Titled "Relations of the Joint Chiefs of Staff (JCS) to the President in Cold War Operations," NSAM-55 reflected Kennedy's dour frame of mind. There is no way to describe this NSAM other than an incensed presidential finger-wagging lecture to JCS Chief Lemnitzer.

Kennedy began with a detailed scolding about giving advice and responding to requests and added that he expected the chiefs' advice "to come to me direct and unfiltered." The rest of this NSAM was a didactic sermon on how the chiefs should present their views in government councils, when to do so, how to do their homework to speak with unity, how to broaden themselves to "be more than military men," and so on. The crux of NSAM-55, however, was this: Kennedy charged the Joint Chiefs with responsibility for "defense of the nation in the Cold War" and "dynamic and imaginative leadership . . . of military and paramilitary aspects of Cold War programs."

This mandate was big news, since cold war paramilitary operations had been—up to that moment—predominantly the responsibility of the CIA. On this point, NSAM-55 was more than a memo to Lemnitzer, whom Kennedy would replace with Taylor the following year. It was the opening shot in Kennedy's campaign to curtail the CIA's control over covert paramilitary operations—eventually leading to what became known as "Operation Switchback."[306]

---

303 Taylor/Rostow memo to JFK, 27 July 1961, JFK Library, NSF, Regional Security, SEA, Box 223/231.
304 The most notable exception is Fletcher Prouty, an Air Force Colonel at the time working in the Pentagon. See his book ***The Secret Team*** (Englewood Cliffs, NJ: Prentice-Hall, 1973), pp. 114-21.
305 JFK Library, NSF, Box 330.
306 After the failure of the Bay of Pigs invasion, President Kennedy ordered the transfer of covert paramilitary operations from the CIA to the Pentagon, beginning with unconventional warfare against communists in Southeast

THE SEISMIC AFTERSHOCKS FROM THE CUBAN CATACLYSM

NSAM-56 and NSAM-57 flowed from the requirements generated by NSAM-55. NSAM-56[307] was addressed only to the Secretary of Defense and titled "Evaluation of Paramilitary Requirements." It called for an inventory of paramilitary assets in the U.S. Armed Forces, a determination of the requirements for indigenous paramilitary forces in various areas of the world, and then set the goal— "a plan to meet the deficit"—in each case. Within the Department of Defense, the task of compiling this inventory was given to Lansdale.[308]

NSAM-57, addressed to State, Defense and the CIA, was titled "Responsibility for Paramilitary Operations." This NSAM was important because it spelled out the ramifications and precise definitions lacking in NSAM-55. Anytime a covert paramilitary operation required large numbers of people, equipment, or military experience "peculiar to the Armed Services," primary responsibility would rest in the Defense Department, with the CIA in a supporting role.[309]

The consequence of these presidential directives was the first significant chink in the CIA's covert armor since its creation. Walter Bedell Smith, Eisenhower's Under Secretary of State, in his remarks to the 13th meeting of Taylor's Paramilitary Study Group, described this change in these words: "It's time to take the bucket of slop and put another cover on it."[310] What this sarcastic remark meant, of course, was that some of the CIA's larger covert operations should be transferred to the Defense Department.

The myriad aftershocks from the Cuban cataclysm widened the gap between the president and his advisors over intervention in Vietnam during the fall of 1961. The advocates of intervention pleaded for an *understanding* that "the president would at some future time have a willingness to decide to intervene if the situation seemed to him to require it." As the Berlin crisis approached its climax in the fall of 1961, the repetitive tremors from the runaway insurgency in South Vietnam reverberated in Washington.

Asia. Operation SWITCHBACK ordered the transfer of clandestine operations from the CIA to the Military Assistance Command, Vietnam (MACV). However, the assassinations of Presidents Ngo Dinh Diem and Kennedy in November 1963 delayed this transfer of responsibility. On 24 January 1964, the U.S. military formally created the Special Operations Group (SOG) to plan and conduct clandestine operations in Southeast Asia. The SOG later became the Studies and Observation Group, retaining the same acronym (SOG), to disguise its mission as an academic study.

307 Ibid.
308 The result of his work was three papers, issued in Deputy Secretary of Defense Gilpatric's name, which were sent directly to Taylor's office in the White House. The three papers were: "Defense Resources for Unconditional Warfare"; Unconventional Warfare Resources—Southeast Asia; and "Indigenous Paramilitary Forces." See Edward Claflin, *JFK Wants to Know* (New York: William Morrow, 1991), p. 69.
309 JFK Library, NSF, Box 330. NSAM-57 decreed that all paramilitary operations had to be presented to the Strategic Resources Group, which would assign the operation to the "department or individual best qualified" to carry it out. The Defense Department would normally run overt paramilitary operations. Only paramilitary operations "wholly covert or disavowable" could be assigned to the CIA, and then only if they were within the "normal capabilities" of the agency.
310 *Declassified Documents*, 1978, 442A.

INTO THE STORM

On 4 August, Kennedy issued NSAM-65, providing U.S. equipment and training assistance for an increase in the South Vietnamese Army from 170,000 to 200,000 soldiers.[311] However, South Vietnam's battlefield losses were fast canceling out the force increase being carried out with the new American aid program.[312] By May, 43 percent of the 6,000 new recruits in 1961 were already battlefield losses.[313] The size of Viet Cong forces was fast approaching the point where the South Vietnamese Army would be unable to cope with them.

A 20 September report listed four battalion-sized Viet Cong attacks in northern South Vietnam during the previous three days.[314] It was the first time the Viet Cong had attacked in the northern I Corps area in such magnitude. At a 22 September Vietnam Task Force briefing, the size of Viet Cong forces adjacent to Laos was estimated at over 7,000, more than double their size at the beginning of the year.[315] A 25 September report estimated total VC strength around Saigon at 17,000[316]; that was an increase from 7,000 reported at the beginning of 1961.[317] Given the ten-to-one ratio required in counterinsurgency operations, the South Vietnamese Army, which was still trying to expand to 170,000, was stretched to its very limit. In fact, total regular South Vietnamese strength stood at just 142,000 men—about 28,000 less than required to fend off an insurgent force of 17,000 guerrillas.[318]

In October, NSAM-80 dispatched the first Air Force Jungle Jim unit to participate in the war. In issuing NSAMs 52, 65 and 80, the president again resisted recommendations by his military and civilian advisors to send in U.S. combat troops to Vietnam.

The sharp deterioration in the battlefield situation in Vietnam pushed the policy apparatus inexorably toward intervention. A pivotal event was the trip of Brigadier General William Craig, of the Pentagon Joint Staff, to Vietnam in early September. Craig bluntly stated that SEATO Plan 5 had to be immediately implemented and warned that the future of the U.S. in Southeast Asia was at stake.[319] "It may be too late," he said, unless the U.S. acted immediately. On 15 September, Rostow sent a memo to Kennedy explaining the highlights of Craig's report, and added that Hanoi believed "that the end of Stage 2—in Mao's theory of warfare—had arrived; that is, the end of guerrilla

---

311   NSAM-65, *PP*, DOD ed., Book 11, pp. 241-44.
312   Robert Johnson memo to Rostow, 20 June 1961, JFK Library, NSF, Country File, Vietnam, Box 193.
313   The May figures were close to another set of 1961 figures submitted by Sterling Cottrell on 9 June 1961 (JFK Library, NSF, Country File, Vietnam, Box 193), which yielded the following 1961 monthly totals for killed and captured GVN forces: Jan-468; Feb-311; Mar-338; Apr-431; May-562. For those interested, the monthly average here is 422, but the figures were growing the last four months in a row.
314   MAAG report, JFK Library, NSF, Country File, Vietnam, Box 194.
315   Robert Johnson memo to Rostow, 22 September 1961, JFK Library, NSF, Country File, Vietnam, Box 194.
316   CHMAAG, Saigon, to CINCPAC, 25 September 1961, message, *Declassified Documents*, RC, 74C.
317   "Southeast Asia" report, 4 October 1961, JFK Library, NSF, Regional Security, SEA, Box 231A.
318   Rostow memo to Kennedy, 31 July 1961, JFK Library, NSF, Country File, Vietnam, Box 193.
319   Report, General Craig, 15 September 1961, JFK Library, NSF, Regional Security, SEA, Box 231A.

warfare and the beginning of open warfare."[320] In 1962, Craig's hawkish proclivities would be on display again during Operation Mongoose.

Unexpectedly, on 30 September, Diem transformed the context of the debate on Vietnam policy by asking for a bilateral defense treaty with the U.S.[321] This opportunity was not lost on Rostow, who told the president that the U.S. had to move "quite radically" to avoid total defeat in Vietnam. "The sense of this town," he told Kennedy, "is that, with Southern Laos open, Diem simply cannot cope." On 5 October, U. Alexis Johnson and others advised that there would be an "unfavorable outcome" in Vietnam without a major change in U.S. policy.[322]

What had taken place during the aftershocks of the April 1961 Cuban cataclysm was the education of John Kennedy. The failure in Cuba, the haranguing by Khrushchev in Vienna, and the tumult of the Berlin crisis had all been episodes of that frustrating learning process.

The developing crisis in Vietnam served only to magnify the widening gulf between Kennedy and his advisors, and to add to his impatience with them. He could not afford to procrastinate any longer on his plans to make major personnel changes in his government. These changes, many of which took Washington by surprise, followed an event that surprised and shocked the president: a report written by General Maxwell Taylor.

The Taylor Trip, the Thanksgiving Day Massacre, and NSAM-111

Kennedy was fed up with the bureaucratic entropy among his advisors over intervention in Vietnam *and* anxious to get moving on Cuba again. The president decided to use General Taylor to clear the thorny Vietnam issue off his desk. In mid-October 1961, Kennedy sent Taylor to Vietnam with express orders (privately) to return with a recommendation against sending U.S. combat troops to Vietnam. At the same time, JFK planted a false story in the *New York Times* saying that the JCS and Taylor opposed sending U.S. combat troops to Vietnam. (See *JFK and Vietnam*, 2017 Edition, Chapter Seven.)

When Taylor returned on 2 November with a recommendation *to send* U.S. combat forces to Vietnam under the cover of a flood relief task force, Kennedy was livid. In the end, Taylor *too*—knowing that Kennedy would be opposed to combat troops—had

---
320   Rostow memo to JFK, 15 September 1961, JFK Library, NSF, Regional Security, SEA, Box 231A.
321   Saigon cable to State No. 421, 1 October 1961, *Declassified Documents*, RC, 788F.
322   10/5/61, *FRUS*, Volume I, Vietnam, Document 144, Memorandum for the Record by Deputy Assistant Secretary of Defense for International Security Affairs (Bundy).

thrown in his lot with the interventionists. Combined with the intense lobbying from the president's other advisors to respond in a like manner to this crisis, Taylor's proposals left the president more isolated than ever before and under great pressure to intervene in Vietnam.

By the time Taylor returned, Washington was already in an uproar over the report he would make the next day. Kennedy was so shocked by Taylor's recommendation to send 8,000 combat troops to Vietnam that he recalled copies of the final report.[323] Not even Walter McConaughy, the Assistant Secretary of State for Far Eastern Affairs, was permitted to read it. Only those with access to the "eyes only" cables—Taylor, Rostow, McNamara, Rusk, and a handful of others—knew the truth.[324] The fact that Taylor had recommended combat troops was supposedly a very closely held secret.

Kennedy reacted to the Taylor report by planting misleading stories again. They stated flatly that Kennedy was opposed to sending combat troops to Vietnam and strongly implied that Taylor had not recommended doing so. Those stories, David Halberstam noted, enhanced Taylor's reputation "and again gave the impression that he was different and better than other generals."[325]

A crucial NSC meeting took place on 15 November 1961 and featured a caustic and revealing exchange between General Lemnitzer and President Kennedy. It began with the president resisting arguments by Rusk and McNamara in favor of intervention:

> The president asked the Secretary of Defense if he would take action if SEATO did not exist and McNamara replied in the affirmative. The president asked for justification and Lemnitzer replied that the world would be divided in the area of Southeast Asia on the sea, in the air and in communications. He said communist conquest would deal a severe blow to freedom and extend communism to a great portion of the world. The president asked how he could justify the proposed courses of action in Vietnam while at the same time ignoring Cuba. General Lemnitzer hastened to add that the JCS feel that even at this point the United States should go into Cuba.[326]

This passage is a dramatic illustration of the fact that, for Kennedy, Saigon was no Berlin. It illuminates the degree to which the president had become isolated from the interventionists demanding a similar commitment to Vietnam. It is also a stark reminder of the lingering mutual animosity and grudges that sprang from the debacle in Cuba. I will return to this confrontation in Chapter Fifteen.

---

323   David Halberstam, David, *The Best and the Brightest*, (New York: Fawcett, 1973), p. 169.
324   *PP*, Gravel ed., vol. 2, p. 102.
325   Halberstam, *The Best and the Brightest*, p. 177.
326   Notes on National Security Council Meeting, 15 November 1961, LBJ Library, VP Security File, Box 4.

THE SEISMIC AFTERSHOCKS FROM THE CUBAN CATACLYSM

There were more discussions, more memos, more pleas, and when Rusk and McNamara saw the writing on the wall, they made a joint effort to at least get a complete presidential commitment to Vietnam. This effort, too, was to no avail, and the final version of NSAM-111, issued on 22 November, contained no U.S. combat troops for Vietnam, and no ultimate American guarantees to save Vietnam from communism. In their place, Kennedy approved a significant increase in American advisors and equipment. There Kennedy drew the line. He would not go beyond it at any time during the remainder of his presidency. The main lesson of this climactic event is this: *Kennedy turned down combat troops, not when the decision was clouded by ambiguities and contradictions in the reports from the battlefield, but when the battle was unequivocally desperate, when all concerned agreed that Vietnam's fate hung in the balance, and when his principal advisors told him that vital U.S. interests in the region and the world were at stake.*

What does this tell us, if anything, about Kennedy's resolve and his aims in the larger U.S.-Soviet geostrategic struggle? What were his reasons for rejecting the proposals of his most senior advisors? Kennedy's stand in Berlin unquestionably demonstrated that he did not lack resolve, as his stand in the Cuban Missile Crisis the following year would again make abundantly clear.

By the end of November 1961, Kennedy finally got around to the unsavory business of putting people out to pasture. The personnel changes of 26 November became widely known as the "Thanksgiving Day Massacre." Their roots went back at least as far as the fallout from the Bay of Pigs fiasco earlier in the year. The final reorganization carried out at the State Department and Central Intelligence Agency between 26 and 29 November occurred in the wake of Kennedy's major decision on Vietnam, NSAM-111. The underlying dynamic of the "massacre" was the lack of compliance in the government with Kennedy's decisions. Sorensen goes so far as to argue that Kennedy was discouraged with the State Department right from the beginning. It was never clear to the president, he states, who was in charge, "and why his own policy line seemed consistently to be altered or evaded."[327] The battle over Vietnam policy in the fall of 1961 was the final catalyst that spurred these changes.

On 27 November, a historic meeting took place in the White House.[328] Soon after the president entered the room, he suddenly unloaded his frustration over the lack of support for his Vietnam policy. The rest of the meeting was short and electrifying. "When policy is decided on," Kennedy declared, "people on the spot must support it or *get out.*" Coming after the "massacre" of the previous day, the effect of this comment could not have been lost on those present who still had jobs. The president was

---

327 Sorensen, *Kennedy*, p. 287.
328 11/27/61, *FRUS*, Volume I, Vietnam, Document 285, Notes of a Meeting, the White House. Lemnitzer's notes indicate the president skipped the early part of the meeting. Lemnitzer's notes are all that remain of the meeting, a meeting that the president's log indicates was off the record.

not finished; he ordered that there be "whole-hearted support" for his decisions and demanded to know who at the Defense Department would personally be responsible for carrying out his Vietnam program. McNamara, prepared, answered the question. "Myself and L," he replied, the "L" referring to Lemnitzer. McNamara was just being kind to Lemnitzer, who would be replaced soon by Taylor as Chairman of the JCS.

Kennedy's final decision—NSAM-111—ruled out U.S intervention. It was the major Vietnam decision of his presidency, drawing, as it did, a line in the sand that he would never cross. For the last twenty-seven years, one of the principal theses of my work that has remained unchanged is this: President Kennedy would *never* have placed American combat troops in Vietnam as Johnson later did. Kennedy did, nevertheless, make a commitment short of that, giving in to the urgency of the situation and to the pressure from his advisors. NSAM-111 unleashed a flood of advisors, helicopters and other aircraft, and military equipment into Vietnam in the hope that American technology and know-how might somehow work a miracle.

Kennedy had cleaned house in Washington and had firmly taken charge, and the policy that emerged was his alone. Although he would not accept the recommendations for combat troops—an act of moral courage—neither would he, *for the time being*, accept defeat. Here was where the president became more personally entangled in the agony that his decision helped to prolong, and where his purpose became blurred by his own need to retain political power. Nevertheless, he was free, for the time being, of the Vietnam problem.

The Kennedy brothers turned their attention once again to the problem of Fidel Castro.

CHAPTER FIVE

BERLIN 1961—THE MOST DANGEROUS PLACE ON EARTH

In Chapter Four I discussed the seismic after effects from the Bay of Pigs disaster and how they shook the U.S. national security apparatus to its foundations. I described how the president wrestled with the men who had deceived him. Yet something sinister beyond his control had been unleashed: The April 1961 Cuban cataclysm sowed the seeds of deep animosity toward President Kennedy among disparate American circles and it festered for the rest of the year. That hostility would only deepen further in 1962, and I believe it played a role in the tragedy that took place in Dallas on 22 November 1963. My intent in this chapter is to open the door to another unnoticed but important accelerant of the incipient sentiment that President Kennedy had to be brought down. That role was inadvertently played by Soviet Premier Nikita Khrushchev.

Let me be clear about my views on this point: Khrushchev was *not* a part of the plot to assassinate President Kennedy—as was alleged by those who originally designed the cover-up of the conspiracy; *and* by those authors today who, one would hope, inadvertently, keep spinning that old canard, oblivious to the cover they are providing to the real perpetrators of the assassination. Premier Khrushchev did *not* want JFK killed—far from it. Khrushchev knew he would do much worse with a Lyndon Johnson or a Barry Goldwater in the White House.

Khrushchev did, albeit indirectly, contribute to the tragedy in Dallas by shaping the key events that helped bring it about. Ironically, it was those same events and the death of JFK that led to Khrushchev's overthrow on 14 October 1964. In 1960, Khrushchev had moved quickly to arm Castro's regime to the teeth, ensuring that the only way it could be overthrown was by a full-scale U.S. military intervention. Kennedy understood that short of a resort to nuclear war with the Soviet Union, *the price for the invasion of Cuba was West Berlin.* Khrushchev's ultimate goal was to eliminate the "thorn," the "ulcer," of West Berlin.

Kennedy's decision *not to invade Cuba*, while unpopular in America at the time, *left U.S. military forces available* to the president—forces that would have to be quickly and significantly increased—*to call Khrushchev's Berlin bluff* just four months hence. That is, in fact, what happened. Following the creation of the Berlin Wall (August-September 1961), a dangerous standoff between U.S. and Soviet tanks took place in Berlin at Check Point Charlie. Through a private channel, Kennedy signaled Khrushchev that he would go easy on Berlin in the future if the Soviet tanks withdrew first. The premier agreed. Privately, Kennedy told his aides, "It's not a very nice solution, but a wall is better than a war."[329]

But that was only the *first* episode in Khrushchev's strategy to push the West out of Berlin. The game was far from over. The Soviet premier was also attempting to draw the Americans into a "containing" position in Southeast Asia. The idea was to tie up U.S. military power there and also to put pressure on the Chinese Communist leadership to purge Mao Zedong and end the Sino-Soviet dispute. Not until the Berlin Crisis *appeared* to be in remission at the end of 1961 did Kennedy accept the bait in Vietnam—exactly in the manner Khrushchev wanted him to. The Soviet leader did not seek an immediate overwhelming use of American forces in Vietnam; rather, Moscow's long-term strategy was a slowly deepening vortex in Southeast Asia that would eventually bring about a Sino-American conflict there and resurrect the Sino-Soviet alliance.

In that context—and providing that a nuclear holocaust had not erupted—West Berlin would easily fall into communist hands. On 29 July 1961, KGB Chief Aleksandr Shelepin delivered an "array of proposals" to Khrushchev to help the premier achieve his objective in Berlin:

> To create a situation in various areas of the world that would favor dispersion of attention and forces by the United States and their satellites and would *tie them down during the settlement of the question of a German peace treaty and West Berlin.*[330] [Emphasis added]

As we will see, Khrushchev took this suggestion to heart. He would be willing to negotiate over Laos, Cuba, or the Congo, so long as he came away with Berlin.

---

329 Beschloss, *The Crisis Years*, p. 278.
330 Vladislav Zubok and Constantine Pleshakov, *Inside the Kremlin's Cold War—From Stalin to Khrushchev* (Cambridge: Harvard University Press, 1996), p. 253.

BERLIN 1961—THE MOST DANGEROUS PLACE ON EARTH

The second episode of Khrushchev's crisis strategy occurred in 1962, with a dangerous stunt that precipitated the Cuban Missile Crisis. Kennedy humiliated the Soviet premier by forcing him to remove his missiles from Cuba. The president's astute handling of the crisis, however popular it was with Americans and Europeans, enraged the same circles in the U.S. that were furious with the president for his handling of the Bay of Pigs crisis in 1961.

In the months following the Missile Crisis, Kennedy and Defense Secretary McNamara began secretly planning to withdraw the American advisors from Vietnam. I believe that during this period—in mid to late 1962—a plot to assassinate President Kennedy was hatched. And that was something Khrushchev had not foreseen. His grand scheme went up in smoke as the result of the Kennedy assassination in November 1963. JFK's death quickly led to a U.S. congressional blank check for massive direct American military intervention in Vietnam. Khrushchev's fall from power in Moscow took place exactly sixty-eight days after the passage of the Gulf of Tonkin Resolution in Washington on 7 August 1964.[331] That meant that Moscow would need land access through China to Vietnam to sustain North Vietnam, and that the price of Chinese cooperation was Khrushchev's removal.

In this manner, Khrushchev's manufacturing of crises to push the West out of Berlin succeeded only in his own overthrow in the aftermath of the assassination of President Kennedy. The removing of the "ulcer" of West Berlin had been a principal Soviet objective since the end of World War II in 1945. That goal came to its inevitable and ignominious end with the demolition of the Berlin Wall on 9 November 1989, and to the revolutions during that year in which all of the socialist regimes in Eastern Europe—except Romania—were peacefully toppled. The dissolution of the USSR took place on Christmas Day, 1991.

The European Chessboard—1945-1960

At the end of World War II, Germany was partitioned into Soviet, American, British and French zones of occupation. Although the city of Berlin remained deep inside the Soviet zone, it was also split, with the Soviets taking the eastern part of the city. Western Belin was split into three parts occupied by the allies. Stalin's attempt to blockade West Berlin in 1948 had been thwarted by a massive Allied airlift. In 1949, the three Western zones became the Federal Republic of Germany (West Germany) and the Soviet zone in the east became the German Democratic Republic (East Germany). During the next

---

331 Richard C. Thornton, "Soviet Strategy and the Vietnam War," *Asian Affairs*, No. 4, March-April 1974, pp. 205-228.

decade, over three million East Germans fled to West Germany through West Berlin, and by 1961 more than 1,000 skilled laborers, professionals and intellectuals were fleeing East Germany every day. This exodus exposed the Soviet Bloc for what it was: A dictatorship—not of the proletariat—but of the Communist Party of the Soviet Union.

During the Cold War, Europe had become the chessboard upon which the geo-strategic competition between Moscow and Washington played itself out. With the only substantial land army on the continent, France occupied the Western sub-center squares on the chessboard. France was the key to America's NATO strategy to contain Soviet influence. As a result, Washington repeatedly turned its back on African and Asian nations in deference to Paris' foolish attempt to maintain control of its colonial empire in North Africa and Indochina. This occurred at a time when independence from colonial rule had become the dominant trend in the world. Eisenhower did this to newly independent Congo in 1960, turning a blind eye to Belgium's naked attempt to break up the territorial integrity of that mineral rich African nation.

The center squares on the Cold War European chessboard were occupied by East and West Germany. As the game unfolded, the city of Berlin became much more than an "ulcer." It became a perpetual point of infernal danger. Berlin, a lonely pawn at the center of the board, anchored the Cold War in the dangerous reciprocal hostility that would grip the world for three decades. In 1958, Khrushchev had demanded a German peace treaty to permanently legitimize the division of Germany. That demand remained when the Paris Summit Conference exploded in May 1960. And it would become the focal point in Khrushchev's secret scheme for testing the newly elected forty-four-year-old American president.[332]

The March 1961 CIA Survey of Berlin-Related Clandestine Operations

In March 1961, about one month after Kennedy's inauguration, the CIA Berlin Operations Base (BOB) Deputy Chief—and also head of Soviet operations—David E. Murphy, visited CIA HQS in Washington. He took part in a survey being prepared in the Agency's Eastern European (EE) Division on possible clandestine activities to support the U.S. mission in Berlin. After he arrived at the base in the summer of 1954, Murphy was briefed by BOB Chief Bill Harvey on the highly sensitive intelligence operation to tap into Soviet underground communications by building a quarter-mile tunnel into

---

332 David E. Murphy, Sergei Kondrashev and George Bailey, ***Battleground Berlin—CIA vs KGB in the Cold War*** (New Haven: Yale University Press, 1997), pp. 361-362.

the Soviet sector of Berlin.[333] The ubiquitous Henry Hecksher[334] had, as BOB's Chief of Operations, supervised the effort to recruit German post office officials who knew the telecommunications wiring for all of Berlin.[335]

Murphy enlisted in the Army during WWII and was sent to California to learn French but due to a clerical error ended up learning Russian instead. While working for the Army in post-war South Korea, he was recruited by the newly created CIA. His Russian language skills were valuable to BOB. Murphy took over the base after Harvey's return to HQS in 1959.

When Murphy arrived at CIA HQS in 1961 to help with the East European Division (EED) Berlin survey, the Bay of Pigs landing was just a month away. In Washington almost no one was aware, except for DDP Bissell, that his two top operations men for the invasion, Jake Esterline (chief of the Cuban branch) and Jack Hawkins (chief of the paramilitary desk) wanted to resign because they were certain the plan was doomed. Ironically, neither Esterline nor Hawkins understood that DCI Allen Dulles and several of the Pentagon chiefs intended that the invasion would fail. The president had declared that under no circumstances would he authorize the use of U.S. military forces in Cuba. However, Dulles and several of the chiefs were certain that once the Cuban exiles were being cut down on the beachhead Kennedy would have no choice but to send in the Air Force and Marines.

In March, however, the unabated exodus of refugees fleeing to the West through Berlin seemed more likely than Cuba to develop into a crisis. The EE survey of potential clandestine operations in Berlin had been requested by Henry Kissinger, who was in Washington from Harvard to advise the administration on the Berlin problem. The survey's underlying assumption was that Moscow intended to integrate East Berlin into East Germany and "make the Western position in West Berlin so tenuous that the West will eventually see no alternative but to withdraw from Berlin and recognize East Germany as a sovereign state."[336]

The March 1961 Berlin survey offered suggestions similar to those contained in the September 1960 EE "Long Range Plan for Berlin." Those suggestions had been based on BOB's recommendations. The recommendations included a larger presence in Berlin—culturally and militarily—that would increase international interest in the city's continuing freedom and would also counter communist propaganda. Those goals were realistic. But the March 1961 survey contained something that was extremely

---

333 Murphy, Kondrashev and Bailey, *Battleground Berlin*, p. 209.
334 Hecksher's activities are covered in detail in Volumes I and II of the present series. See especially John Newman, *Countdown to Darkness—The Assassination of President Kennedy, Volume II* (Amazon: Create Space, 2017), see Chapters Nine and Twenty-One.
335 Bayard Stockton, *Flawed Patriot—The Rise and Fall of CIA Legend Bill Harvey* (Washington D.C.: Potomac Books, 2006), p. 76.
336 Ibid, p. 355.

INTO THE STORM

unrealistic. The final section concerned fomenting an "insurrection" in East Germany. Murphy and his colleagues in EE knew this was not feasible. Apparently, one or more senior policy makers—probably at the State Department—wanted suggestions aimed at increasing East Germany's "instability."

The CIA had no illusions that it was possible to cause a popular uprising against a Soviet-supported communist regime in Central Europe through the use of externally mounted clandestine operations. In Chapter Twenty of ***Countdown to Darkness***, I laid out the evidence that shows senior CIA officers and those close to invasion planning knew full well that a Cuban uprising in 1961 was a myth. Yet, even so, DDP Bissell and DCI Dulles lied to Kennedy by telling him a Cuban uprising would succeed.[337] The point here is that the efficiency of the East German police state was *far better* than Cuba's secret police and perhaps even better than the KGB.[338] The Berlin survey team's reaction to the idea of fomenting an insurrection in East Germany was decidedly negative:

> As for possible insurrection, the reaction was firm and to the point.
> Having raised the issue as a question, the Eastern European Division drafters stated flatly that "insurrection is not a feasible clandestine operation except in a situation in which open military action between the Soviet Union and the West is actually imminent."[339]

As I will note in a section below, former Secretary of State Dean Acheson would propose this *same* idea (insurrection in East Germany) to President Kennedy in June 1961, just one week after William Harvey and EE dismissed it out of hand.

---

337   Newman, *Countdown to Darkness*, see pp. 348-353. In his research for Volume III of the CIA ***Official History of the Bay of Pigs Operations***, Jack Pfeiffer discovered that a "strange" note had "appeared" at the 15 November 1960 WH/4 staff meeting with this important news:
>   Our [CIA's] original concept is now seen to be unachievable in the face of the controls Castro has instituted. *There will not be the internal unrest earlier believed possible*, nor will the defenses permit the type [of] strike first planned.

See Pfeiffer Volume III, p. 149. Although Pfeiffer discussed this document, it has not been released. I filed a FOIA request for it in United States District Court for the District of Columbia on 12 October 2016. The CIA indicated that they would take action by 24 May 2017, but they missed that deadline and revised the completed date to 19 December 2017. On 28 May 2018, the CIA indicated that they did not locate "any records responsive to your request" regarding the strange note. The Agency stated that I had "the legal right to appeal the finding of no records responsive to your request." On 11 August 2018, I filed such an appeal. On 17 August 2018, the Agency acknowledged that they had received my appeal. As of this writing, that is where matters stand.

338   John O Koehler. ***Stasi: The Untold Story of The East German Secret Police*** (Boulder: Westview Press, 1999), pp. 8-9: "The Gestapo had 40,000 officials watching a country of 80 million, while the [East German] Stasi employed 102,000 to control only 17 million." To ensure that the people would become and remain submissive, East German communist leaders saturated their realm with more spies than had any other totalitarian government in recent history. The Soviet Union's KGB employed about 480,000 full-time agents to oversee a nation of 280 million, which means there was one agent per 5,830 citizens. Using Wiesenthal's figures for the Nazi Gestapo, there was one officer for 2,000 people. The ratio for the Stasi was one secret policeman per 166 East Germans. When the regular informers are added, these ratios become much higher: In the Stasi's case, there would have been at least one spy watching every 66 citizens! When one adds in the estimated numbers of part-time snoops, the result is nothing short of monstrous: one informer per 6.5 citizens. It would not have been unreasonable to assume that at least one Stasi informer was present in any party of ten or twelve dinner guests.

339   Murphy, Kondrashev and Bailey, ***Battleground Berlin***, p. 357.

The Path to the Vienna Summit

After the failure of the May 1960 Paris Summit, Khrushchev began to support the Democratic Party in the fall 1960 U.S. presidential election. Never before had a Soviet Premier taken such an intense interest in a U.S. presidential campaign. In late November, the President-Elect sent campaign advisers Walt Rostow and Jerome Wiesner to Moscow to meet with Soviet disarmament experts. Deputy Foreign Minister Vasili Kuznetsov asked the Americans, "What can we do to help the new administration?" Rostow and Wiesner presented Kuznetsov a list of items drafted with the input of U.S. Ambassador Llewellyn Thompson:

> The RB-47 pilots[340] should be freed "without Kennedy's having to ask for them or bargain for them." *Pressure on Berlin should be relaxed.* During test ban talks, the Soviets must be "very generous" about on-site inspections.

Rostow told Kuznetsov there could be no summit with Kennedy unless it was "well prepared and concerned with very concrete business."[341] On 15 December, Soviet Ambassador to the U.S. Mikhail Menshikov spoke off the record to Harrison Salisbury of the *New York Times* to deliver this anxious message:

> "Time is of the essence." The two leaders must meet "before those who would not like to see agreement have had a chance to act and prevent it. ... There is more to be gained by one solid day spent in private and informal talk between Khrushchev and Kennedy than all the meetings of underlings taken together."

As presidential historian Michael Beschloss observed, this was the first time a Soviet leader "badgered" a U.S. president for a summit meeting before his inauguration.[342]

As the Kennedy inauguration approached, Khrushchev pivoted his policy abruptly toward détente by releasing the American RB-47 pilots and approving other measures to improve Soviet-American diplomacy. At his first press conference on 25 January 1961, President Kennedy said the U.S. government was "gratified" by this decision and "considers that this action of the Soviet government removes a serious obstacle to improvement of Soviet–American relations."[343] Kennedy and Khrushchev began using back-channel communications through Robert Kennedy on the U.S. side and, on the

---

340 On 1 July, the Soviet Union shot down a U.S. Air Force RB-47 airplane, which was on a proposed mission from the United Kingdom near the northern borders of Norway and the Soviet Union and over the Barents Sea, and rescued two of the six crew members. The two survivors were Captain John B. McKone and Captain Freeman Bruce Olmstead. The U.S. disputed the Soviet claim that the American airplane had entered Soviet airspace.
341 Beschloss, *The Crisis Years*, p. 41.
342 Ibid, p. 42.
343 1/25/61, Kennedy press conference.

Soviet side, through GRU Colonel Georgi Bolshakov, who was working undercover in Washington as a press secretary at the Soviet Embassy.[344]

There was much more to Khrushchev's courting of Kennedy than unassuming congeniality. The Premier was facing pushback from hardline Soviet leaders over his proposal to reduce the Soviet armed forces by 1.2 million men and his heated dispute with Beijing. Khrushchev needed a quick rapprochement with the U.S. to continue this course, and he had calculated Kennedy would be easier to manipulate than Mao Zedong. Khrushchev wanted a summit as soon as possible, before Kennedy's policies on Berlin, a test ban, and the arms race were cast in concrete.[345]

The U.S. Ambassador to the USSR, Llewellyn Thompson, lobbied JFK to meet Khrushchev and, for his part, President Kennedy was interested in meeting with him. So, on 27 February 1961 Kennedy sent a letter to Khrushchev proposing a summit take place in Vienna, Austria. The premier approved. In early March the two leaders agreed to meet during May in Vienna.

By this time, Khrushchev had already learned from his KGB chief, Aleksandr Shelepin, that the U.S. was preparing for "an economic blockade of and military intervention against Cuba."[346] On 18 April, the day after the Cuban exile brigade landed on the beachhead at the Bay of Pigs, Khrushchev sent a warning to Kennedy that if the conflict continued "a new conflagration may flare up in another area"—a transparent reference to West Berlin.[347] Kennedy's failure in Cuba was a bonus for Khrushchev, who interpreted it as a sign of weakness, validating his view that he could manipulate Kennedy on Berlin. The Vienna Summit was not only on, but also was a Soviet snare.

Khrushchev's May 1961 Secret War Council on Berlin[348]

Khrushchev had been secretly plotting since March 1961 to close Berlin's sector borders and build a wall in the city.[349] But Kennedy's colossal loss at the Bay of Pigs barely ninety days into his presidency played heavily into Khrushchev's hands. The Soviet leader then decided to play for more and test the president straight away on Western access to Berlin. While publicly feigning a cooperative posture toward JFK, Khrushchev's plan was to lure the president into a summit meeting and ambush him with an ultimatum on Berlin.

---

344 Zubok and Pleshakov, *Inside the Kremlin's Cold War*, p. 240
345 Beschloss, *The Crisis Years*, pp. 44-45.
346 Zubok and Pleshakov, *Inside the Kremlin's Cold War*, p. 241.
347 Ibid.
348 This section is taken from the excellent account in Frederick Kempe, *Berlin 1961—Kennedy, Khrushchev, and the Most Dangerous Place on Earth* (New York: G.P. Putnam's Sons, 2011), pp. 205-208. Kempe's account is based on a stenographic record of the meeting from the AVP-RF—the Russian Ministry of Foreign Affairs Archives.
349 Murphy, Kondrashev and Bailey, *Battleground Berlin*, pp. 361-362.

BERLIN 1961—THE MOST DANGEROUS PLACE ON EARTH

On 26 May 1961, Khrushchev convened a meeting of the Communist Party Presidium for a secret war council. The meeting's agenda concerned what he planned to do to Kennedy at the Vienna summit. The premier said he relished the opportunity for a summit with that "son of a bitch" Kennedy to bring "the German question" to a head. Only the First Deputy Premier of the Soviet Council of Ministers, Anastas Mikoyan, dared to differ with Khrushchev:

> Mikoyan argued that Khrushchev underestimated the American willingness and ability to engage in conventional war over Berlin. ... Khrushchev told those gathered that the United States was the most dangerous of all countries to the Soviets. ... Khrushchev told his comrades that he was prepared to risk war and that he also knew how best to avoid it. He said America's European allies and world public opinion would restrain Kennedy from responding with nuclear weapons to any change in Berlin's status. He said de Gaulle and Macmillan would never support an American lurch toward war because they understood that the Soviets' primary nuclear targets, given the range of Moscow's missiles, would be in Europe.

"They are intelligent people, and they understand this," Khrushchev said, and then he revealed exactly what his plan was.

The Soviet leader informed those present that after issuing a six-month ultimatum to Kennedy in Vienna, he would sign a peace treaty unilaterally with the East German government, to whom he would then turn over all of the access routes to West Berlin:

> "We do not encroach on West Berlin, we do not declare a blockade," he said, thus providing no pretext for military action. "We show that we are ready to permit air traffic but on the condition that Western planes land at airports in the GDR [not in West Berlin]. We do not demand a withdrawal of troops. However, we consider them illegal, though we won't use any strong-arm methods for their removal. We will not cut off delivery of foodstuffs and will not sever any other lifelines.

Khrushchev concluded, therefore, that this scenario would not "unleash a war." Only Mikoyan persisted in warning the premier that the probability of war was higher than he estimated:

> Khrushchev shot back that Kennedy so feared war that he would not react militarily. *He told the Presidium they perhaps would have to compromise in Laos, Cuba, or the Congo, where the conventional balance was less clear, but around Berlin the Kremlin's superiority was unquestionable.* Mikoyan countered that Khrushchev was backing Kennedy into a dangerous position where he would have no option but to respond militarily. Mikoyan suggested that Khrushchev continue to allow air traffic to arrive in

West Berlin, which might make his Berlin solution more palatable to Kennedy. [Emphasis added]

Khrushchev steamrolled over Mikoyan. He replied that not only would he be willing to shut down the air corridor but would also shoot down any Allied plane that tried to land in West Berlin.

Khrushchev ended his overbearing performance with a discussion of whether he should follow protocol and exchange gifts with Kennedy in Vienna. Foreign Ministry officials suggested he give President Kennedy twelve cans of the finest black caviar and phonographic records of Soviet and Russian music. Among other gifts, his aides had a silver coffee service in mind for Mrs. Kennedy. When the officials asked for Khrushchev's approval, he responded, "One can exchange presents even before a war."

The Ambush of JFK at the Vienna Summit

Khrushchev was shrewd to spring his test of the new president at the Vienna summit. The Pentagon and the CIA were not the only executive agencies in disarray after the Cuban fiasco. In his biography *A Thousand Days*, Arthur Schlesinger, Jr., described the feeble state of American diplomacy during the first six months of the Kennedy Administration:

> The frustrations of the summer over Berlin brought the president's *discontent with his Department of State to a climax.* One muddle after another—the Department's acquiescence in the Bay of Pigs, the fecklessness of its recommendations after the disaster, the ordeal of trying to change its attitude toward Laos, the maddening delay over the answer to Khrushchev's aide-mémoire[350] and the banality of the result, *the apparent impossibility of developing a negotiating position for Berlin*—left Kennedy with little doubt that the State Department was not yet an instrumentality fully and promptly responsive to presidential purpose.[351]
> [Emphasis added]

Thus, it was not only Kennedy's youth but also the feebleness of otherwise experienced American diplomats at this critical juncture that gave the wily Soviet premier the element of surprise at the 3-4 June 1961 summit in Vienna.

The 3 June discussion in the American ambassador's office was a preliminary sparring match by both leaders. Schlesinger summed it up this way: "Khrushchev had not given way before Kennedy's reasonableness, nor Kennedy before Khrushchev's

---

350 A formal document Khrushchev presented to Kennedy to make his ultimatum more "formal." Kennedy's officials were not prepared for this tactic.
351 Schlesinger, *A Thousand Days* (New York: Mariner Books, 2002), p. 406.

intransigence."[352] But Khrushchev had held back. He planned to take the gloves off in the afternoon session the next day at the Soviet Embassy. When the discussion turned to Berlin during the 4 June morning meeting,[353] Khrushchev taunted Kennedy with this belligerent boast: "Berlin is the most dangerous place in the world. The USSR wants to perform an operation on this soft spot to eliminate this thorn, this ulcer." Khrushchev then confronted President Kennedy with this bombshell: the USSR planned to sign a peace treaty with the GDR [East Germany], unilaterally, if necessary, after which "all rights of [Western] access to Berlin will expire because the state of war will cease to exist."

At this, Kennedy pushed back forcefully, saying Berlin was a primary and vital concern to the United States:

> [Kennedy declared] if we abandoned West Berlin, it would mean the abandonment of Western Europe, which America had deemed essential to its security in two wars. ... America, Kennedy said, *would not accept an ultimatum.* [Emphasis added]

As the argument went on endlessly, Khrushchev dug in his heels and became ever harsher. Although the conversation was civil at first, it had turned into a scuffle by lunchtime.

After the luncheon, the discussion turned into a brawl.[354] It began as Kennedy tried to tone down the rhetoric in a final effort to avoid a crisis. He asked to talk with Khrushchev alone, accompanied only by interpreters:

> The president began by expressing hope that in the interest of relations between their two countries the chairman would not present him with a crisis so deeply involving the American national interest as Berlin. Of course, any decision Khrushchev wanted to make about the Democratic Republic was his own.

Kennedy worried that no one could predict where the conflict would end and pleaded that "all decisions had to be carefully considered."

Khrushchev then attacked JFK unrelentingly:

> The United States, he said, wanted to humiliate the Soviet Union. If the president insisted on occupation rights after a treaty and if East German borders were violated, whether by land, sea or air, force would be met by force. The United States should prepare itself for this, and

---

352 Schlesinger, *A Thousand Days* (New York: Mariner Books, 2002), p. 361.
353 6/4/61, ***FRUS***, ***Foreign Relations of the United States***, 1961-1963, Volume XIV, Berlin Crisis, 1961-1962, Document 32, Memorandum of Conversation—morning discussion.
354 6/4/61, ***FRUS***, Volume XIV, Berlin Crisis, 1961-1962, Document 33, Memorandum of Conversation—afternoon discussion.

> the Soviet Union would do the same. "I want peace," said Khrushchev, "but, if you want war, that is your problem."

Kennedy shot back: "It is you, and not I, who wants to force a change." But the premier gave the president no quarter:

> Khrushchev said again that it was up to the United States to decide on peace or war. The Soviet Union had no choice but to accept the challenge. It must, and it would, respond. The treaty decision was irrevocable. He would sign in December.

As they parted Kennedy remarked, "It will be a cold winter."

The Berlin Crisis had obviously reached a new and very dangerous stage. Khrushchev's ultimatum to Kennedy moved Washington into high gear. Although the Soviet premier's bullying had failed to win any concessions from the president, at this point the Americans still had no idea that Khrushchev's original plan—the Berlin Wall—was coming. Khrushchev planned to restrict that secret to only a few people until the very last moment.

Kennedy's secret, which he confided to almost no one, was his fear that Khrushchev *would* move against Berlin. Beschloss argues, correctly in my view, that Khrushchev understood JFK's disquiet:

> ...it took the chairman and his analysts little effort to notice the diamond in the chandelier. They almost certainly concluded that Kennedy was so uncertain about the American commitment to the divided city that he was willing to brook the humiliation of the Bay of Pigs rather than face a new Berlin crisis now.

With few cards in his hand to play against the West, Khrushchev "could now conclude that Berlin might serve nicely."[355]

Khrushchev and Berlin—Wedded at the Hip

At the 20th anniversary celebration of Hitler's invasion of the Soviet Union on 21 June 1961, Khrushchev was feted for his leadership of the Berlin Crisis—even though he knew the summit had been a failure.[356] The Soviet premier wore his wartime lieutenant general's uniform while those participating watched a documentary film about Khrushchev's life as a military and political champion. Soviet cosmonaut Yuri Gagarin extolled Khrushchev as "the pioneer explorer of the cosmic age." The event was televised:

---

355   Beschloss, *The Crisis Years*, p. 150.
356   Ibid, p. 238.

> The Soviet leader received another Order of Lenin and a third golden hammer-and-sickle medal for "guiding the creation and development of the rocket industry ... which opened a new era in the conquest of space." Khrushchev decorated seven thousand others who had contributed to the flight. To consolidate personal alliances and neutralize rivals, he gave Orders of Lenin to his Politburo ally Leonid Brezhnev and to a potential rival at the [upcoming] October Party Congress, Frol Kozlov.

As former **Wall Street Journal** reporter and editor Frederick Kempe has observed, Khrushchev was a calculating politician protecting his flanks before acting on Berlin.[357]

Unsuccessful at the Vienna summit, Khrushchev's pompous demonstration at this anniversary celebration was an act. He condemned the Western refusal to compromise on Berlin. Yet Khrushchev knew that he had refused to compromise while Kennedy had signaled he was ready to negotiate. The premier also knew that the USSR could not keep pace with American military development. His declaration that the USSR's military strength would grow so much that the West would suffer complete failure was no more than an empty boast.

As Soviet military heroes and commanders lavished praise upon Khrushchev, he pretended to double down on Berlin:

> The historic truth is that during the assault on Berlin there was not a single American, British, or French armed soldier around it, except for the prisoners of war whom we freed. Thus, he said, the Allies' claims to special rights in Berlin so long after surrender are entirely unfounded.

As the crowd cheered, Defense Minister Rodion Malinovsky said the U.S. "gigantic military apparatus" and "aggressive blocks" ringing the Soviet Union had to be resisted.[358]

Khrushchev's Berlin battle cry was little more than a propaganda stunt in advance of the October Party Congress. He did not want war. He needed a compromise on Berlin and, more than ever, he needed the American president in order to make it work.

The Washington Reaction to the Vienna Summit

Kennedy had suspected that he would have to face more mischief from Khrushchev over Berlin. The president understood that the costs of unilateral U.S. intervention in Cuba for the cause of freedom throughout the hemisphere far outweighed Castro's continued presence. But Kennedy advisor Theodore Sorensen suggested that there

---

357 Kempe, *Berlin 1961*, pp. 277-278.
358 Ibid, pp. 278-279.

was another imperative at work in Kennedy's ardent refusal to send American forces into Cuba. The president envisaged this scenario taking place:

> American conventional forces ... were still below strength, and while an estimated half of our available Army combat divisions were tied down resisting guerrillas in the Cuban mountains, *the communists could have been on the move in Berlin* or elsewhere in the world.[359] [Emphasis added]

And so, those forces were not tied down in Cuba, the Congo, or Laos when Khrushchev sprung his Berlin bluff on Kennedy at the summit. The president was fully aware, however, that—short of using nuclear weapons—U.S. force levels were inadequate to deal with the developing Berlin crisis.

Thus, Kennedy responded to Khrushchev's ultimatum by ordering his administration to undertake a comprehensive review of the situation and make recommendations on the political and military measures to convince the Soviet Union that he meant business in Berlin. To help him lead this effort the president sought out President Truman's Secretary of State, Dean Acheson. Dean Acheson had turned down the president-elect's offer to be ambassador to NATO; the only appointment he would have accepted was his previous one—Secretary of State. That changed when the administration had begun to consider its Berlin policy well before the president went to the Vienna Summit. When Kennedy asked Acheson to advise him on Berlin, Acheson's secretary noted that he was "buoyed up by it all and looks better and younger than I have seen him in years."[360]

On 9 February 1961, Kennedy announced that Acheson would be coming to Washington to lead special studies on the problems of NATO, Germany, and balancing the use of conventional and nuclear weapons in future contingencies. Arthur Schlesinger recalled that although the president knew Acheson was a hardliner, he nevertheless considered him "one of the most intelligent and experienced men around and did not see why he should not avail himself of hardline views before making his own judgments."[361]

I will describe the recommendations of the Acheson report for the Berlin Crisis shortly, but I want to mention here a controversial hardline suggestion that the CIA had been opposed to since March. Acheson believed that the Soviets might be deterred if they could be convinced that the crisis would result in "greater instability—rather than stability" in Eastern Europe:

> The U.S. should try to convince the USSR that it would and could, in event of a Berlin crisis, stir up dissidence in East Germany and Eastern Europe. ... We can only convince the Soviets that this is our intention

---
359 Sorensen, *Kennedy* (New York: Harper Collins, 2009 edition), p. 297.
360 Beschloss, *The Crisis Years*, p. 242.
361 Schlesinger, *A Thousand Days* (New York: Mariner Books, 2002), p. 380.

> if that is, in fact, the case. As in the military field, bogus preparations will be of little value. ... The scale of civil disorder which we set out to stimulate should correspond, progressively, to the intensity of the crisis.

A full-scale revolt, the secretary counseled, should only be triggered if the crisis reaches the point of "a hair's breadth from general war."[362]

In a previous section of this chapter, I mentioned the March 1961 Berlin survey, and that its final section contained the unrealistic suggestion for fomenting an "insurrection" in East Germany. On that occasion, Dave Murphy from Berlin Operations Base (BOB) attended a meeting of East European Division (EED) officers. Given the high efficiency of the East German police state,[363] the group had concluded that it was not possible to incite a popular uprising in East Germany.[364]

In a meeting at CIA HQS on 22 June 1961, former BOB chief Bill Harvey[365] harshly criticized the concept of mounting clandestine operations in the east:

> It is unrealistic to believe that we could infiltrate into the East Zone a sleeper net of sufficient size, reliability, and skill to ... play a significant part in organizing resistance groups as well as remain in a state of readiness until called up in connection with military operations. Our abilities are not equal to this task when balanced against the defensive capability of the [East German] Ministry of State Security.

There was virtually unanimous agreement with Harvey's statement within the EED.[366]

Meanwhile, according to the CIA chronology of the 1961 Berlin Crisis, on 25 June, the U.S. Navy's Director of Submarine Warfare, Rear Admiral Joseph Gallatin, reported that American Polaris class submarines with their nuclear tipped missiles were "trained on the USSR."[367] The chronology did not specify whether or not Gallatin's report was public. At that time, it probably was not. It was, however, a revealing indication of just how serious the Berlin Crisis had become.

The 29 June 1961 NSC Meeting

On 29 June 1961, President Kennedy called the National Security Council (NSC) to the Cabinet Room to consider Acheson's report on Berlin. Secretary of State Rusk began the discussion with a summary account of the current state of the department's

---

362 6/28/61, *FRUS*, 1961-1963, Volume XIV, Berlin Crisis, 1961-1962, Document 49, Report by Dean Acheson.
363 John O Koehler. *Stasi: The Untold Story of The East German Secret Police* (Boulder: Westview Press, 1999), pp. 8-9.
364 Murphy, Kondrashev and Bailey, *Battleground Berlin*, p. 357.
365 At the time, Bill Harvey was working in a CIA signals intelligence support component—Foreign Intelligence, Staff D (FI/D).
366 Murphy, Kondrashev and Bailey, *Battleground Berlin*, p. 366.
367 CIA Berlin Chronology, 1961; cia.gov/library.

INTO THE STORM

work on Khrushchev's 4 June aide-mémoire, and on other pressing matters relevant to Berlin planning. Rusk then asked Secretary Acheson to discuss his report. Acheson began by arguing that Khrushchev's purpose in starting this crisis over Berlin was to weaken NATO, buttress the East German regime, and legalize the Oder-Neisse Line with Poland.[368] The Soviet leader had confronted the U.S. with a test that could not be backed down from, Acheson averred, because Khrushchev would take willingness to negotiate as a sign of weakness.[369]

Kennedy said, wryly, that he thought it difficult to sustain a strong political posture, while, at the same time, being prepared with the right answer if Khrushchev proposed another summit that summer. This was Acheson's humorous reply:

> In reply to a summit proposal, for example, the president could readily suggest that conversations be undertaken first at a lower level. Mr. Acheson believed that there were plenty of "elderly unemployed" people like himself who could be sent to interminable meetings.

Acheson added that the U.S. could converse indefinitely without negotiating at all, and that he could easily do this himself "for three months on end."[370]

In his report, Acheson had argued that the entire position of the U.S. hung in the balance. "Until this conflict of wills is resolved," he declared, "an attempt to solve the Berlin issue by negotiation is worse than a waste of time and energy." Acheson said it was necessary to shift Khrushchev's thinking and leave him with no doubt that the president's hardline response to any move on Berlin would be so tough that Khrushchev would not take the risk:

> [Acheson] wanted the president to declare a national emergency and order a rapid buildup in American nuclear as well as conventional forces. He said American forces in Germany outside Berlin should be reinforced immediately by two or three divisions, to a total of six. The underlying message: If anyone was to back down over Berlin, it would have to be the Soviets.

As I mentioned previously, the Acheson report also included a plan to deter the Soviets from provoking a Berlin crisis by stirring up dissident groups to destabilize Eastern Europe.[371]

Some of those present in the NSC meeting were troubled by Acheson's apparent indifference about the risk of nuclear war. They preferred negotiation to demonstrate that the West favored a reduction in tension over West Berlin while protecting Western

---

368 The Soviet Union had recognized this boundary as the East German frontier.
369 6/29/61, **FRUS**, 1961-1963, Volume XIV, Berlin Crisis, 1961-1962, Document 52, Memorandum for the Record, NSC Meeting.
370 Ibid.
371 Kempe, **Berlin 1961**, pp. 281-282.

access rights.[372] The president said very little during the meeting, except that he did not think the American people were prepared for the ambitious course Acheson proposed and, furthermore, that the allies would be even less enthusiastic.[373] Uncharacteristically, the Chief of Naval Operations, Admiral Arleigh Burke, voiced his opposition[374] to the scale of the action proposed by Acheson and his opposition to an airlift unconnected with a probe. Acheson responded that the military force had to be large enough to convince the Soviets that if the fighting continued, nuclear weapons would be used.[375]

The upshot of the meeting was a decision *not* to make any substantive decisions based on that first discussion. The president directed his security advisor, McGeorge Bundy, to prepare a list of departmental assignments for proposals that could be tabled for further discussion and decisions in two weeks.[376] The day after the NSC meeting, 30 June 1961, Bundy's list became National Security Action Memorandum 58.[377] Defense Secretary McNamara was directed to submit recommendations on the magnitude of a permanent increase in the size of the U.S. military forces. He was also directed to create a capability for:

- A garrison and civilian Quadripartite Berlin Airlift (QBAL) by 15 October
- Naval harassment and blockade of Bloc shipping by 15 November
- Large scale non-nuclear ground action within four months of such time after 15 October as it may be ordered—with tactical air support, as necessary—assuming appropriate use of forces in Europe and assuming reinforcement from the U.S. as necessary to permit the use of two, four, six, and twelve divisions in Europe
- Keeping SAC (Strategic Air Command) in a state of maximum readiness for flexible use over a prolonged period of crisis

---

372 Beschloss, *The Crisis Years*, p. 243.
373 Kempe, *Berlin 1961*, p. 282.
374 Burke had been in the Pentagon cabal that attempted to manipulate the president into sending U.S. forces into Cuba to support the exile invasion. Burke had personally—and unsuccessfully—confronted Kennedy in the oval office while the exile forces were still fighting on the beachhead at the Bay of Pigs. Burke didn't get the message. Two weeks later, after Kennedy refused to send U.S. forces into Laos, Burke again personally confronted Kennedy in the White House over that decision. Kennedy threw him out of his office. See John Newman, *JFK and Vietnam*, Second Edition (Amazon: Create Space, 2017), p. 28. Apparently, Burke finally got the message. By the time of the 29 June 1961 NSC meeting, Burke was just hoping to hold on to his job. He was in no mood to stick his neck out again.
375 6/29/61, *FRUS*, 1961-1963, Volume XIV, Berlin Crisis, 1961-1962, Document 52, Memorandum for the Record, NSC Meeting.
376 Ibid.
377 6/30/61, *FRUS*, 1961-1963, Volume XIV, Berlin Crisis, 1961-1962, Document 53, National Security Action Memorandum No. 58.

Secretary of State Rusk and DCI Dulles were directed to submit joint recommendations for preparations to create a capability for inciting progressively increasing instability in East Germany and Eastern Europe to be activated, if necessary, after 15 October.[378]

This last directive was given to a mismatched pair of agency chiefs. As I mentioned before, with respect to proposals to use clandestine operations to incite insurrection in the East, the CIA had been at odds with the State Department hawks since at least March 1961.

The Schism in Washington on Berlin Policy

Kennedy saw his administration breaking into two camps on the Berlin predicament. Frederick Kempe summarized the divide in this way: "The first [group] was becoming known as the Hard-Liners on Berlin and the other had been disparagingly labeled by the hawks in the room as the SLOBs, or the Soft-Liners on Berlin." The hard-liners included Acheson and other lesser lights at the State Department, the chiefs at the Pentagon, and Vice President Johnson. The SLOBS were a "formidable group" personally closer to Kennedy. They included U.S. Ambassador to the USSR, Llewellyn Thompson; Kennedy's adviser on Soviet affairs, Charles Bohlen; White House aide Arthur Schlesinger; White House consultant and Harvard professor Henry Kissinger; special counsel Ted Sorensen; Kennedy security advisor McGeorge Bundy; and Secretary of Defense Robert McNamara. After the NSC meeting, Schlesinger began to organize a plan to provide a "thinking man's alternative" to Acheson.[379]

An aside for a few observations is in order here. The 1961 Berlin Crisis leadership alignment in the Kennedy Administration was not lost on the chiefs at the Pentagon. In the ten weeks before the Bay of Pigs fiasco, their boss, Secretary McNamara, was more inclined to take their advice, but less so afterward. In a 1964 interview with Schlesinger, McNamara explained it this way: "I think I learned a lesson I had learned many times before, and that was never to rely on the advice anybody gives me on anything."[380] The divide at the Pentagon deepened during the 1961 Berlin Crisis and it would become permanent after Kennedy increased the American advisory role in the Vietnam War at the end of 1961.

Notably absent from the two groups listed by Kempe was the CIA leadership. Disgraced by their Cuban performance, their advice was not welcome in the White House. Another telling absence from the group close to Kennedy was Secretary of State Rusk. In my book *JFK and Vietnam* (2017 edition), I concluded that the president did

---
378 Ibid.
379 Kempe, *Berlin 1961*, p. 283.
380 4/4/64, Robert McNamara Oral History Interview by Arthur Schlesinger, Jr., JFK Library, JFKOH-RSM-01.

not trust Rusk enough to include him in the plan to withdraw the American advisors from Vietnam.

In any event, that same week in early July 1961, **Newsweek** published classified information on the Pentagon's contingency plans for Berlin, including the mobilization of American military forces. Khrushchev used this news to justify the recension of his plan to reduce the Soviet Army by 1.2 million men and increase his defense budget by $3.4 billion. According to Kempe, Kennedy was "livid" over the **Newsweek** leak and so upset that he ordered the FBI to find the source.[381] Beschloss expressed another view: "Like the transcripts of the Vienna talks, the president or his aides may have themselves authorized the leak—in this case, to send a stiff alarm to Khrushchev."[382] In his study of Kennedy, Robert Dallek agrees that the president probably leaked the story "to send Khrushchev an unmistakable message."[383]

Khrushchev got the message. In a Moscow speech, he scoffed at "reports" of Western mobilization plans. But he was anything but untroubled. At the end of the first week in July, aware that Britain was the weakest supporter of a tough line on Berlin, Khrushchev pulled a sobering prank on Sir Frank Roberts, the British Ambassador to the USSR. Both were attending a performance by Dame Margot Fonteyn at the Bolshoi Theater.

Khrushchev summoned Roberts to his box and warned that resistance to his German peace treaty was pointless. If the Western powers sent a new division to Germany, he warned, the Soviet Union would respond "a hundredfold."[384] The Soviet leader blustered that it would only take six hydrogen bombs to destroy Britain and that nine would take care of France. Khrushchev then asked Roberts, "Why should two hundred million people die for two million Berliners?"[385]

The Decision to Build the Berlin Wall

One thing JFK agreed with Acheson about was *not* to agree to another summer summit with Khrushchev. JFK had had enough. He would never meet with Khrushchev again. With East Germany's refugee problem spiraling out of control, Khrushchev could no longer wait for an answer on a meeting with Kennedy. East German refugees who got to West Berlin faced the risk of being arrested for desertion if they travelled by bus or

---

381   Ibid, pp. 305-306.
382   Beschloss, *The Crisis Years*, p. 244.
383   Robert Dallek, *An Unfinished Life, John F. Kennedy, 1917-1963* (New York: Little, Brown and Company, 2003) (paperback), p. 421.
384   Kempe, *Berlin 1961*, p. 306. See also, 7/6/61, "British Envoy Tells Khrushchev Soviet Policy on Berlin is Illegal," *New York Herald Tribune*.
385   Beschloss, *The Crisis Years*, p. 244.

train to West Germany. However, they were able to fly unmolested to West Germany from airports in West Berlin.

The Soviet Presidium met on 29 June and considered the request of East German leader Walter Ulbricht to do something about the "border-crosser" problem. Soviet Ambassador Pervukhin argued that once a peace treaty had been signed, control of Western access to West Berlin would be in East German hands.

> …the goal would be to have all external air traffic from West Berlin channeled through the East Berlin airport at Schönefeld, effectively giving the East control of who was permitted to leave by air. Refugees from the GDR would be marooned in West Berlin.

Unable to leave West Berlin by any means, East Germans would be stuck in West Berlin indefinitely, and the half-city would be unable to cope with a permanent influx. This, Pervukhin felt, would solve the refugee problem and so weaken West Berlin "that it would fall into the East's lap."[386]

Physically closing Berlin's sector borders posed technical problems and the risk of military conflict. But Ulbricht had given Khrushchev an ominous warning:

> …the situation in the GDR was growing visibly worse. The growing flood of refugees was increasingly disorganizing the entire life of the Republic. Soon it must lead to an explosion. If something was not done, then East Germany's collapse was "inevitable."[387]

Khrushchev did not need to be warned. For some time, he had concluded that the refugee problem was urgent.

Berlin was an open city. For Ulbricht and the East German leadership, the open status of the city caused two severe problems, Khrushchev recalled in a book about his recollections, **Khrushchev Remembers**.[388] First, there was the problem of the people crossing from East Berlin into West Berlin:

> The GDR had to cope with an enemy who was economically very powerful and therefore very appealing to the GDR's own citizens. … An East German with adequate professional qualifications had no difficulty finding a job if he moved to West Germany. The resulting drain of workers was creating a simply disastrous situation in the GDR, which was already suffering from a shortage of manual labor, not to mention specialized labor.

The second problem was the result of West Berliner's easy access to East Berlin:

---

386   Taylor, *The Berlin Wall, The Berlin Wall: August 13, 1961 - November 9, 1989* (New York: Harper Collins, 2007), pp. 138-139.
387   Ibid.
388   Edward Crankshaw **Khrushchev Remembers** (New York: Little, Brown and Company: 1970), pp. 454-455.

Residents of West Berlin could cross freely into East Berlin, where they took advantage of all sorts of communal services like barbershops and so on. Because prices were much lower in East Berlin, West Berliners were also buying up all sorts of products which were in wide demand—products like meat, animal oil, and other items, and the GDR was losing millions of marks.

Khrushchev told his son Sergei that in early July 1961 he asked his German commander-in-chief, General Ivan Yakubovski, to do a study on the feasibility of closing the border between the Western and Eastern sectors of Berlin. The two men studied special maps of Berlin at Khrushchev's Dacha in the Crimea.[389]

In July 1961, fear that the West Berlin safety hatch might disappear caused the refugee outflow to balloon to even more disastrous proportions—*one thousand people every day*.[390] It was during those July days at his Dacha that Khrushchev made up his mind to build the Berlin Wall. He concluded that "If the GDR was to be saved, something had to happen quickly." The wall project was codenamed "Rose." Super-secret handwritten progress reports were hand-carried to Ambassador Pervukhin by a single designated courier, and then forwarded on to Moscow via courier. No telephone or radio transmissions were permitted.[391]

The U.S. remained focused like a laser on the crisis of *Western access* to Berlin. At the Soviet Embassy in Berlin, however, Pervukhin had a much sharper focus on the crisis of the *exploding refugee flow*, and the predicament of pursuing a peace treaty while that flow intensified.[392] In that difference of focus there was a seed for a trade—and the potential abatement of the Berlin Crisis.

The 13 July 1961 NSC Meeting

In support of the 13 July NSC meeting, two days earlier the intelligence community gathered at CIA HQS for final coordination of a Special National Intelligence Estimate (SNIE) on possible Soviet reactions to U.S. options with respect to Berlin.[393] The SNIE offered this prediction:

> The Soviet leaders are confident of the prospects for advancing their cause by means short of all-out war. We continue to believe that, so long

---

389 Taylor, **The Berlin Wall**, pp. 138-139.
390 8/15/61, Special National Intelligence Estimate (SNIE) 12-4-61, "Stability of East Germany in the Berlin Crisis," cia.gov/library.
391 Taylor, **The Berlin Wall**, pp. 140-142.
392 Murphy, Kondrashev and Bailey, **Battleground Berlin**, p. 367.
393 7/11/61, SNIE 2-2-61, "Soviet and other Reactions to Possible U.S. Courses of action with Respect to Berlin, cia.gov/library.

as they remain vulnerable to U.S. strategic power, they will not willingly enter into a situation which, by their calculations, the risks of general war are substantial.

The Army intelligence representative at the coordination meeting took a footnote to add this fragment to the second sentence: "and will endeavor to draw back from such situations [i.e. general war] should they evolve."

In a paragraph devoted to "measures aimed at the Satellites," the SNIE stated that the Soviets probably believed the West had only a limited capability to stir up dissidence in East Germany. The SNIE predicted that overt Western actions to stimulate dissidence would probably produce a stiffening of Soviet resolve. Yet the SNIE then added this analysis:

If, however, private Western warning and clandestine activities convinced Moscow that a Berlin crisis could provoke a *covertly supported* wave of disorders in the Satellites, then the Soviets might be inclined to proceed more cautiously in their moves against Berlin. [Emphasis added]

In their 1997 book, **Battleground Berlin**, Dave Murphy and co-authors Sergei Kondrashev and George Baily criticized this finding, and argued that "this naïve faith in 'sending the Soviets a signal' was misplaced in the Berlin situation."[394] Two SNIEs released in August 1961 would also pour cold water on the prospects for clandestine incitement of uprisings in Central Europe.[395]

The record of the discussion at the 13 July NSC meeting indicates Secretary Rusk began the discussion by pointing out that "the Khrushchev timetable is not under our control."[396] When the subject of a declaration of national emergency arose, Rusk warned that to do it "at this time would have a dangerous sound of mobilization."

In his 1986 Department of Defense oral history, Secretary McNamara explained why he felt it had been important to call up the reserves:

In the case of Berlin, I favored calling up the reserves for two reasons: (1) we needed to make clear to the Soviets our determination and will to apply force if necessary to prevent them from taking over West Berlin, which was their objective, and (2) if we were going to apply force, we needed to have that additional force available.[397]

At the 13 July 1961 NSC meeting, the president asked Acheson what he thought about calling up the reserves. Acheson replied that if they left the call-up of reserves until "the end," Khrushchev's judgment about the shape of the crisis would not be affected.

---

394   Murphy, Kondrashev and Bailey, **Battleground Berlin**, p. 367.
395   8/15/61, SNIE 12-4-61, "Stability of East Germany in the Berlin Crisis," cia.gov/library; 8/24/61, SNIE 11-10-61, "Soviet Tactics in the Berlin Crisis," *FRUS*, 1961-1963, Volume XIV, Berlin Crisis, 1961-1962, Document 113.
396   7/13/61, *FRUS*, 1961-1963, volume XIV, Berlin Crisis, 1961-1962, Document 66, Memorandum for the Record, NSC Meeting. See also Document 67, Notes on the National Security Council Meeting, made by General Lemnitzer.
397   4/3/86, McNamara DOD Oral History, Part II—p. 19, LBJ Library.

Secretary Rusk agreed that reserve training should not be left until too late. Acheson proposed that it begin in August.[398]

During further discussion, Acheson pressed vigorously—with Vice President Johnson's backing—for the president to support a full program of "decisive action." Others present pushed back. They argued that taking such action at that time might jeopardize the foreign aid bill then awaiting congressional authorization and appropriation. Rusk commented that it would be "a great victory for Khrushchev" if he could weaken the foreign aid program with only a memorandum and a few speeches. Acheson urged the president to move forward with a full Berlin program and to make a speech to the nation "the week after next."

Once again, as it was at the 29 June NSC meeting, no clear decision was reached on these matters. The bucket was kicked down the road for "further discussion at the next meeting." At the 18 July meeting of the Interdepartmental Coordination Group on Germany and Berlin, Kennedy's team debated the merits of a rapid, spectacular build-up versus a slower build-up. Once again, the pros and cons of declaring a national emergency, modernizing U.S. conventional forces, and troop deployments were discussed.[399]

Later that day, the president attended a meeting of his senior military advisors on Berlin.[400] Kennedy said he wanted to postpone the declaration of a state of emergency until American reserve forces had been mobilized. The chiefs agreed and said it could be postponed until at least 1 September. When Kennedy asked if the additional U.S. combat-ready divisions could be used effectively without further strengthening of Allied forces, General Lemnitzer replied, "No." He added that the expected increases in Allied forces would provide NATO with a better capability for non-nuclear ground action.

The 19 July 1961 NSC Meeting

The president met with the Berlin Steering Group on the morning of 19 July in his study on the second floor of the Executive Mansion.[401] Secretary McNamara described the military program and stated it was not necessary to declare a national emergency before mobilization. He added that congressional authorization could be obtained for the reserve call-up without such a declaration. Kennedy asked whether the proposed

---

398 7/13/61, *FRUS*, 1961-1963, volume XIV, Berlin Crisis, 1961-1962, Document 66, Memorandum for the Record, NSC Meeting. See also Document 67, Notes on the National Security Council Meeting, made by General Lemnitzer.
399 7/18/61, *FRUS*, 1961-1963, Volume XIV, Berlin Crisis, 1961-1962, Document 74, Memorandum of a Conversation.
400 7/18/61, *FRUS*, 1961-1963, Volume XIV, Berlin Crisis, 1961-1962, Document 75, Memorandum of a Meeting on Berlin.
401 7/19/61, *FRUS*, 1961-1963, Volume XIV, Berlin Crisis, 1961-1962, Document 77, Memorandum of Minutes of the National Security Council Meeting.

military build-up would increase the credibility of the U.S. nuclear deterrent. McNamara replied that it would.

At the NSC meeting that afternoon, the president again emphasized his own view that the proposed U.S. preparations would not be adequate without an effective allied response, especially from the Germans and the French.

And then, as Kempe has observed, the Acheson plan died a quiet death after an exchange between its author and Defense Secretary McNamara.[402] Acheson wanted a declaration of national emergency and a call-up of the reserves not later than September. Secretary McNamara opposed a fixed target date, on the grounds that it would be wrong to accept a rigid time-table in advance. After some prodding by the president, it was clear that the current preparations would rapidly create a force in being, in the continental U.S., of six Army and two Marine divisions that could be deployed to Europe in the event of a rapidly developing crisis. Acheson acquiesced, and the president's decisions developing from these matters were recorded by McGeorge Bundy in National Security Action Memorandum No. 62.[403]

By the summer of 1961, the Berlin Crisis had evolved into the most dangerous flashpoint for a nuclear conflict since the onset of the Cold War. Robert Dallek concisely summed up the moment:

> It tested Kennedy's ability to strike an effective balance between intimidating the Soviets and giving them a way out of their dilemma. How could Moscow halt the migration from East to West, which threatened the collapse of East Germany, without altering existing U.S. treaty rights of unfettered access to Berlin and pushing Washington toward war?[404]

Schlesinger recalled that the president was "fighting his way through the thicket of debate to his own conclusions." Cuba and Laos were side issues, "But Berlin threatened a war which might destroy civilization, and he thought about little else that summer."[405]

President Kennedy's 25 July 1961 Television Address

Several of the president's aides helped him draft his television address. One of his principal concerns was the perception that he lacked the will to fight an all-out war. Robert Kennedy learned from his Soviet military intelligence source in the Soviet Embassy that the ambassador, Mikhail Menshikov, had privately told Khrushchev that Kennedy

---

402 Kempe, *Berlin 1961*, p. 311.
403 7/19/61, *FRUS*, 1961-1963, Volume XIV, Berlin Crisis, 1961-1962, Document 77, Memorandum of Minutes of the National Security Council Meeting.
404 Robert Dallek, *An Unfinished Life, John F. Kennedy, 1917-1963* (New York: Little, Brown and Company, 2003), p. 418.
405 Schlesinger, *A Thousand Days* (New York: Mariner Books, 2002), p. 391.

"didn't amount to very much, didn't have much courage." RFK dismissed this slight. But U.S. press reports, probably leaked by Pentagon sources to pressure JFK about Menshikov's opinion, were unhelpful to the president's Berlin strategy. Acheson didn't help much either. Sore because Kennedy had made it clear he would not be strictly following Acheson's advice, the former secretary told the Berlin working group, "Gentlemen, you might as well face it. This nation is without leadership." McGeorge Bundy believed it was essential for the president to overcome this perception of weakness.[406]

Kennedy's maneuvering to avoid the intrinsic risks of hardline nuclear missile-rattling *and* a negotiations-at-all-costs stance exposed him to criticism from both sides.[407] The president complained to Schlesinger that Acheson was lopsidedly focused on military solutions and tasked Schlesinger with writing a paper to bring balance to bear on Berlin planning. After working with State Department counselor Abram Chayes and Harvard professor Henry Kissinger, Schlesinger delivered a memo to Kennedy just two hours later, as he was leaving for a weekend in Hyannis Port with Rusk, McNamara and General Taylor. The memo proposed that the president direct Rusk to explore negotiations and order Acheson to inject "the missing political dimension" to his argument.[408]

Speaking from the Oval Office on 25 July 1961, Kennedy addressed the nation on radio and television. His speech turned out to be a skillful model of how to give something to both sides of the Berlin debate in his administration. But it was much more than that. His address was a warning to America and the world that the immediate threat to world freedom was in West Berlin:

> For West Berlin, lying exposed 110 miles inside East Germany, surrounded by Soviet troops and close to Soviet supply lines, has many roles. It is more than a showcase of liberty, a symbol, an island of freedom in a communist sea. It is more than a link with the free world, a beacon of hope behind the Iron Curtain, an escape hatch for refugees. West Berlin is all that. But above all it has now become—as never before—the great testing place of Western courage and will, a focal point where our solemn commitments, stretching back over the years since 1945, and Soviet ambitions now meet in basic confrontation.[409]

Kennedy said the U.S. was not looking for war and that he recognized the "Soviet Union's historical concerns about their security in central and eastern Europe."

The president stated he was willing to renew talks. But he warned, "We cannot and will not permit the communists to drive us out of Berlin, either gradually or by force."

---

406 Ibid. p. 423.
407 Taylor, *The Berlin Wall*, pp. 131-132.
408 Robert Dallek, *An Unfinished Life, John F. Kennedy, 1917-1963* (New York: Little, Brown and Company, 2003), p. 421.
409 7/25/61, *The American Presidency Project*, JFK Radio and Television Report to the American People on the Berlin Crisis.

Kennedy announced that he would immediately ask Congress for an additional $3.25 billion for new military spending—$1.8 billion for non-nuclear weapons, ammunition, and equipment, and $200 million for civil defense.[410]

The Berlin Wall

On Monday, 31 July 1961, the leader of East Germany, Walter Ulbricht, attended a meeting in Moscow. He suggested to Khrushchev that the air corridors between West Berlin and the West should be blocked to stanch the huge flow of refugees flying out every day. Khrushchev, saying that it might provoke war, refused. Once again, Ulbricht pleaded that the Berlin sector border be closed. Khrushchev told him to wait until the Warsaw Pact leadership conference, scheduled to meet on 2 September.[411]

At the Warsaw Pact meeting, Ulbricht cautioned Khrushchev that if the drain of valuable East German workers and professionals was not stopped, East Germany would not be able to meet its production commitments to the Soviet bloc. Ulbricht warned that unrest was everywhere and added, "An uprising like the one that nearly toppled his government in 1953 could succeed this time." The refugee problem, he declared, must be solved "here and now."[412]

Khrushchev said he would agree to a border closing only if Ulbricht could promise that East Germany's security forces could preserve order and that its economy could survive. Ulbricht rushed to East Berlin to seek the necessary assurances from his security chief, Erich Honecker, and other top leaders. On 5 September, Ulbricht returned to Moscow to give Khrushchev the news. The next day, Khrushchev disclosed his consent first to the Soviet Ambassador to East Germany, Mikhail Pervukhin, who ordered his aide, Yuli Kvitsinsky, to relay this news to Ulbricht: "We have a yes from Moscow," Pervukhin said.[413] All communication had to be transmitted orally until just before construction of the wall began.

On 12 August, Ulbricht signed the order to close the border crossings to the West and erect a wall in Berlin. In the darkness at midnight, police and army units—including units of the East German Army—began laying concertina wire and erecting barricades at the main crossing points. By morning, the border to West Berlin was sealed. Then, 32,000 combat and engineer troops were brought in to begin building the Berlin Wall, while the Soviet Army stood watch close to the city to discourage

---

410   CIA Berlin Chronology, 1961; cia.gov/library. General LeMay's 12 July appeal for retention of the B-52 and B-58 production levels and for an increase in B-70 program funding was not reflected in these appropriations figures.
411   Beschloss, *The Crisis Years*, p. 266.
412   Ibid.
413   Kempe, *Berlin 1961*, p. 293.

Western interference. Within a few weeks these improvised obstacles would become a formidable heavily fortified, guarded, and booby-trapped cement barrier.[414]

Publicly, Kennedy's reaction was low key as his administration mulled over what a fully coordinated response should be. The lack of a quick forceful response disappointed West Berlin's mayor, Willy Brandt, who believed that Kennedy had "thrown us in the frying pan." American reporters were saying that the border closure had shocked and depressed Kennedy. However, the president was actually relieved by the news of the wall and, privately, did not hide this reaction from his closest advisors. Frederick Kempe has explained how different the truth was from the press reports:

> He considered the border closure a potentially positive turning point that could help lead to the end of the Berlin Crisis … "Why would Khrushchev put up a wall if he really intended to seize West Berlin?" Kennedy said to his friend and aide Kenny O'Donnell. "There wouldn't be any need of a wall if he planned to occupy the whole city. This is his way out of his predicament. It's not a very nice solution, but a wall is a hell of a lot better than a war."

Besides, the optics for the communists were terrible—they were building a prison around West Berlin to lock in its people. As Kempe observed, "Nothing could have been more damning."[415]

Moreover, Khrushchev's Berlin Wall strategy played into Kennedy's hands. A reasoned but forceful American response was called for. It was an opportunity for the president to display resolve and statesmanship. On 30 August, President Kennedy responded forcefully. He ordered 148,000 Guardsmen and Reservists to active duty. Kennedy was now able to undertake an impressive mobilization of American military power with the full backing of Congress, without looking like a warmonger.

JFK's initial reactions came swiftly. On 18 August 1961, he ordered a battle group of 1,500 men to Berlin to reinforce the garrison. The next day, a plane carrying Vice President Johnson and General Clay landed in Berlin to assure West Berlin that the U.S. was willing to fight for the city's survival. On 20 August, the American battle group arrived in Berlin after having moved over the autobahn. After that, the U.S. and the USSR engaged in a tit-for-tat escalation of the crisis.[416]

On 22 August, the Western air corridors to Berlin were threatened by Soviet diplomatic demarches, and the access to East Berlin was cut to a single crossing point, Check Point Charlie. On 23 August, all people in West Berlin were warned by the East German communists to stay 100 meters from the Wall. The Allies immediately deployed

---

414 Taylor, *The Berlin Wall*, p. xix.
415 Kempe, *Berlin 1961*, p. 379.
416 CIA Berlin Chronology, 1961; cia.gov/library.

1000 troops, backed by 10 tanks, at the Wall in defiance of the 100-meter rule.[417] On 30 August, Robert Kennedy remarked that the Soviets "feel strongly that if they can break our will in Berlin then we will never be able to be good for anything else and they will have won the battle in 1961."[418]

The Soviets reacted by deploying tanks in all towns close to the border, and on 31 August, the Soviet Union announced resumption of nuclear tests and exploded its first nuclear devices on 1 September. On 5 September, President Kennedy announced resumption of U.S. tests, and the U.S. conducted its first test on 15 September. On 23 September the U.S. 7th Army was placed on a "combat ready" alert. On 25 September, President Kennedy, in an address to the UN General Assembly, reaffirmed U.S. determination to defend the Allied position in West Berlin.[419]

Tank Confrontation at Check Point Charlie

On 25 October 1961, U.S. tanks moved to the border of East Berlin, while General Clay decided to "test" Western access to the east sector that was guaranteed by the Potsdam Agreements of 2 August 1945.[420] Throughout the day, several official American civilian vehicles were escorted on short tours of East Berlin. After initial East German harassment, the vehicles were allowed to proceed unmolested. That evening, unidentified tanks were spotted … in a bombed-out lot in the Eastern sector of the city. The next morning, a CIA man under diplomatic cover was sent to check out the situation:

He strolled up to one of the groups of parked tanks. When a soldier popped up out of the turret, he asked him in German how to get to Karlshorst. The man stared at him in blank incomprehension. The American asked the same question in Russian. He was treated to a friendly grin and a stream of travel instructions.[421]

For the first time in years, an armored Soviet military unit had entered the city limits of East Berlin. The unit was comprised of thirty-three Soviet-manned tanks, accompanied by troops.[422]

The show of strength by Khrushchev and Kennedy in Berlin rapidly escalated. Both sides ended up with ten tanks, with engines running, facing each other at Check Point Charlie. The American tanks with bulldozer blades were conspicuously shown,

---

417 Ibid.
418 Kempe, *Berlin 1961*, p. 363.
419 Ibid.
420 Crankshaw, *Khrushchev Remembers*, p. 459.
421 Taylor, *The Berlin Wall*, p. 280.
422 CIA Berlin Chronology, 1961; cia.gov/library.

and American helicopters buzzed over the check point ignoring East German and Soviet protests.[423]

For many years, General Clay's view—that the Russians unleashed the Check Point Charlie confrontation in order to humiliate America—was generally accepted. However, the unearthing of new documentary evidence suggests Clay's view was incorrect and that what had taken place was that Ulbricht's aggressive anti-Western stance had trapped Khrushchev into a situation he did not want to be in. Taylor argues, correctly in my view, that Khrushchev's decision to put Soviet armor in East Berlin was "an attempt to claw back control of the crisis from the East Germans."[424]

The escalation had, for the first time during the Cold War, produced the dangerous spectacle of American and Russian tanks, facing each other at point blank range, and ready to fire if either side made any untoward move. The stand-off continued through the "chilly" night and lasted for sixteen hours. Moreover, the stand-off in Berlin was a possible point of ignition for a potential Armageddon:

> During the Check Point Charlie confrontation, four [U.S.] missile-firing atomic submarines of the Polaris class were submerged in the North Sea, Malinovsky reminded his colleagues—each with sixteen warheads aimed at targets in the Soviet Union.[425]

As the crisis in Berlin approached a hair's breadth from erupting into a violent tank battle, something unseen was also taking place during the dark hours of that night.

At Check Point Charlie the Soviet guard post was communicating, through General Anatoly Gribkov at the Soviet Army High Command, with Khrushchev. At the same time, the U.S. guard post was communicating, through the HQ of the US Military Mission in Berlin, with the White House. Frederick Taylor's study of the Berlin Crisis, ***The Berlin Wall***, captured a fascinating conversation that took place during the darkness in Berlin:

> Clay recalls that when he spoke with Kennedy that evening, the president asked if he was nervous. "Nervous? No, we're not nervous here," Clay answered. "If anybody's nervous, Mr. President, it will probably be people in Washington." That snarky remark failed to annoy the president who had his feet up on his desk during the entire call to Berlin. "Well," he told Clay, "there may be a lot of nervous people around here, but I'm not one of them."[426]

Unknown to Clay at the time was the fact that RFK had contacted his GRU friend Bolshakov as soon as the tank confrontation created the possibility that one wrong

---
423 Taylor, ***The Berlin Wall***, p. 282.
424 Ibid, pp. 282-283.
425 Ibid.
426 Ibid, p. 284.

move might end up in a war. Within hours, Kennedy and Khrushchev were messaging through RFK and Bolshakov. What exactly was said remains classified, but we know the gist: Kennedy offered to go easy over Berlin in the future in return for the Soviets removing their tanks first.

We also know that the following morning Khrushchev spoke to Marshal Konev in Berlin. According to Khrushchev's memoirs, Konev told him that at Check Point Charlie the barrels of their cannons "remained trained on each other across the border." Khrushchev described what happened then:

> I proposed that we turn our tanks around, pull them back from the border, and have them take their places in the side streets. Then we would wait and see what happened next. I assured my comrades that as soon as we pulled back our tanks, the Americans would pull back theirs. ...
> I said I thought that the Americans would pull back their tanks within twenty minutes after we had removed ours. This was how long it would take for their tank commander to report our move and to get orders from higher up of what to do. Konev ordered our tanks to pull back from the border. He reported that, just as I expected, it did take only twenty minutes for the Americans to respond.[427]

And that choreographed scene was how the Berlin Crisis of 1961 ended.

From the time Khrushchev ordered the erection of the Berlin Wall he knew that "starting a war over Berlin was stupid. There was no reason to do so."[428] The establishment of border control in East Germany did not infringe on Western access to West Berlin. Kennedy's 13 August statement about the Wall had been right: "It's not a very nice solution, but a wall is a hell of a lot better than a war."

---

427 Crankshaw, *Khrushchev Remembers*, p. 460.
428 Ibid, p. 458.

CHAPTER SIX

THE KENNEDYS, KING AND THE RACE ISSUE—1961

Federal law said that there should be no segregation in interstate travel. The Supreme Court had decided that. But still state laws in the southern states and local ordinances ordered segregation of the races on buses. Why didn't the federal government enforce its law? We decided it was because of politics. If we were right in assuming that the federal government did not enforce federal law because of its fear of reprisals from the South, then what we had to do was to *make it more dangerous politically for the federal government not to enforce federal law.* And how would we do that? We decided the way to do it was to have an interracial group ride through the South. This was not civil disobedience, really, because we would be doing merely what the Supreme Court said we had a right to do. The whites in the group would sit in the back of the bus, the blacks would sit in the front of the bus and would refuse to move when ordered. At every rest stop, the whites would go into the waiting room for blacks, and the blacks into the waiting room for whites, and would seek to use all the facilities, refusing to leave. We felt that *we could then count upon the racists of the South to create a crisis,* so that the federal government would be compelled to enforce federal law. That was the rationale for the Freedom Ride.

—James L. Farmer, National Director of the Congress of Racial Equality (CORE); initiator and organizer of the Freedom Rides. Oral history in ***Voices of Freedom***.[429]

* * * * * * *

---

[429] James Farmer in Hampton and Fayer, ***Voices of Freedom*** (New York: Bantam Books, 1990), p. 75.

INTO THE STORM

The Freedom Riders challenged the non-enforcement of the U.S. Supreme Court's decisions *Morgan v. Virginia* (1946) and *Boynton v. Virginia* (1960). Those decisions had ruled that segregated public buses were unconstitutional. Furthermore, in 1955 the Interstate Commerce Commission (ICC) issued the *Sarah Keyes v. Carolina Coach Company* ruling that denounced the *separate but equal* doctrine of the 1896 *Plessy v. Ferguson* Supreme Court decision. By the time John Kennedy was elected in 1960, none of these decisions had been enforced in the South, where Jim Crow laws remained in effect.

Chapter Two of this volume discusses how the Kennedy New Frontier pushed forward even as it was assailed in every category. Nowhere was the New Frontier assaulted more than on the thorny issue of civil rights. For example, Kennedy's desperately needed proposal for a new federal Department of Urban Affairs was a bold attempt to address the urban squalor in which African Americans were living. The idea was speciously rebuked by the **Wall Street Journal** as an impractical "willy-nilly" government attempt to build "haphazard" numbers of houses.[430] Kennedy historian Arthur Schlesinger, Jr., described the reaction of Congress this way:

> The president's attempts to persuade Congress to authorize a Department of Urban Affairs failed in 1961 and 1962, in part because of the expectation that he would give the new cabinet post to his Housing Administrator, Dr. Robert C. Weaver, eminently qualified in every way save, in the view of some, by the color of his skin.[431]

Put more bluntly, there was no way the alliance between Republicans and Southern Democrats was going to approve any cabinet appointment of an African American.

The African American challenge to racial segregation had been underway for some time and it was appropriate that this challenge was cresting at the moment the black vote put John Kennedy in the White House. In Montgomery, Alabama bus segregation laws had been successfully challenged in 1955. The segregated seating arrangements on buses was a sore point with whites whose racial prejudice would not allow them the indignity of having to sit next to a black person.

The same was true when segregated seating at lunch counters was challenged by black college students. The lunch counter was even more sensitive than bus seats. Ingrained bigotry made it unthinkable to break bread at the same eating space as a black person. The arrests of these students—and Dr. King—during the 1960 election was only the first round in this disturbing new chapter about the staunch defense of Southern racial privileges. With Kennedy in the White House, African Americans were about to take the lunch counter challenge to a whole new level in bus terminals by

---

430 2/3/61, *Wall Street Journal*, OPED, "The Economic Proposals."
431 Schlesinger, *A Thousand Days*, p. 660.

including waiting rooms and, heaven forbid, restrooms—that inviolable place where humans urinate and defecate.

In all of these encounters, on buses, at lunch counters, in waiting rooms and rest rooms, it was the concept of *place* that underpinned the entire politico-socio-psychological paradigm of racism. It was vitally important that African Americans be kept in their *place*. Just as it was in the story of the naked emperor, when the sacred barrier of *place* was violated in any one instance, the entire system was threatened.

This threat was so important that after taking office President Kennedy warned African American leaders about the difficulties that lay ahead for the passage of a civil rights bill:

> "If we go into a long fight in Congress," Kennedy told Martin Luther King, "it will bottleneck everything else"—including measures of vital importance to black Americans, like the increased minimum wage and federal aid to education— "and still get no [civil rights] bill."[432]

What the president did not understand at the time, however, was that brave young African Americans were unwilling to wait for a civil rights bill. The march of history was moving forward quickly—one way or another. And, like it or not, the White House, Congress, and the Southern governors were all going to get dragged into the chaos of progress on the race issue. It would be nothing less than a baptism by fire.

American State-Sponsored Terrorism

The busloads of Freedom Riders that ran the gauntlet of brutal white terrorism in Alabama and elsewhere in 1961-1963 faced a *special kind* of terrorism. Before I get to that, a word about the taxonomy of terrorism is in order.

In our universities, and by now the vast array of academic works on terrorism, a principal distinction is made between the more specific field of *state-sponsored terrorism* and the more generic field of *international terrorism*. The latter term has been used for many decades, but more recently it also subsumes the newer field of *transnational terrorism*, which has become the description of this newer and more dominant form of violence.

In American academe, use of the more traditional term *state-sponsored terrorism* has largely—although not exclusively—been used to refer to terrorism emanating from non-Western state actors, typically Middle Eastern nation states. However, American state-sponsored terrorism has a long history. It was used to suppress Native Americans internally, and other populations externally, such as occurred in the

---

[432] Schlesinger, *Robert Kennedy and His Times*, p. 288.

INTO THE STORM

Philippine-American War (1899-1902) and, more recently, against the Castro regime in Cuba.

Domestic terrorism is another recognized field of terrorism. It is more commonly used to refer to violence perpetrated by internal domestic groups—rather than the government—to suppress other domestic racial and ethnic groups. The violent activities by American white supremacist groups—especially the Ku Klux Klan (KKK)—against African Americans carried out since the American Civil War has received its fair share of academic attention. However, terrorist activities against African Americans actively supported by municipal and state governments and the United States Federal Government—much like terrorism earlier perpetrated against Native Americans—is not a subject in which the American public has been well schooled.

In this chapter, I will endeavor to demonstrate the culpability of our local, state and national government agencies in the terrorism inflicted on African Americans—not in the 1800s, but during the Kennedy Administration in 1961 and 1962. The terrorism inflicted upon African Americans and sympathetic white Americans who supported them during this period is state sponsored terrorism. In particular, local police and FBI authorities in Alabama—as well as FBI HQS in Washington—were complicit in wanton, brutal criminal violence against African Americans who dared to exercise their constitutional and legal rights in that state. Legally, our institutions of government were accessories *before and after* the fact in this sordid episode of American history. Fully cognizant of the plans to brutalize African Americans, these agencies of government did *nothing to warn* the Freedom Riders about the specific threats they faced and *nothing to stop* the attacks they knew were coming.

As the Freedom Riders travelled through Alabama, the FBI had an informant in the Ku Klux Klan—Gary Thomas Rowe in Klan unit "Klavern Palace 13"—reporting to FBI handlers about a two-part police-Klan agreement to terrorize the Freedom Riders.[433] An initial assault by the KKK Anniston Klavern would block the Riders' access to bus terminals in Anniston, Alabama and would then be followed by a mop-up thrashing in Birmingham.[434] The FBI Special Agent in Charge (SAC) of the FBI's Birmingham office reported the details of the police-Klan agreement to FBI headquarters in Washington several times *before* the attacks took place, beginning on 5 May 1961.[435] Beyond conspiring like this, when the police were present during Klan and mob administered terrorism, they often did nothing to stop the violence and even displayed approval of the beatings.

Arthur Schlesinger recalled that J. Edgar Hoover had the racist instincts of a white man who had grown up in Washington when it was still a southern city:

---

[433] See Appendix One for an FBI Summary Report on Rowe's activities as an FBI informant in the Alabama KKK.
[434] Raymond Arsenault, *Freedom Riders* (New York: Oxford University Press, 2006), p. 138.
[435] Taylor Branch, *Parting the Waters: America in the King Years* 1954-63 (New York: Simon & Schuster, 1988), p. 420.

In 1946 he had complained to Attorney General Tom Clark that the Bureau was expending too much manpower "investigating murders, lynchings and assaults, particularly in the Southern states." The result, he said, was only to enrage "vociferous minority groups" when the Bureau failed to produce immediate results. In 1948, Joseph Rauh asked Clark to have the FBI look into the attempted murder of Walter Reuther. Clark, after conferring with the director, brought back the irrelevant but revealing reply: "Fellows, Edgar says no. He says he's not going to send the FBI in every time some nigger woman gets raped."[436]

In 1957, Hoover gave the Eisenhower cabinet a briefing on racial tensions: Southerners simply did not accept "mixed education" as the means "whereby the races can best be served. And behind this stalks *the specter of racial intermarriages.*" The pro-segregationist White Citizens Councils were nonviolent; their membership included "some of the leading citizens in the South." The Ku Klux Klan was "pretty much defunct." As for the "crusade for integration," its leaders were threatening violence, and its organizations were major targets for communist infiltration. [Emphasis added]

For policy reasons as well as his prejudice, Schlesinger argued, Hoover withdrew the FBI from civil rights investigations, and internally "he preserved it as a lily-white agency.[437]

Hoover's failure to investigate the conspiracies against the Freedom Riders in Alabama in 1961 was only the tip of the iceberg where his crimes against African Americans during the 1960s are concerned. Hoover's activities against black leaders and entertainers—under his counterintelligence program (COINTELPRO)—were an appalling betrayal of the mission of the Justice Department. Small wonder that African Americans—and any ethically centered American—want Hoover's name removed from the FBI building in Washington D. C. For a number of reasons, Hoover's ignominious legacy has left a dark stain on our republic.

I will return to the state-sponsored aspects of the terrorism inflicted on the Freedom Riders in the sections of this chapter below. Suffice it to say, senior officers in the FBI and Department of Justice were never investigated or deposed to establish their level of complicity and/or criminal liability in these terrorist activities.

---

[436] Schlesinger, *Robert Kennedy and His Times*, p. 291.
[437] Ibid, pp. 291-292.

INTO THE STORM

Attack at Anniston Terminal (14 May 1961)

The first freedom ride began on 4 May 1961. Led by CORE Director James Farmer, thirteen riders departed Washington D.C. in two buses—a Greyhound and a Trailways. The riders were a mixture of CORE and Student Nonviolent Coordinating Committee (SNCC) members. Comprised blacks and whites, this group of brave people were the original ark of the Freedom Ride movement. The African Americans riders included Ben Cox, James Farmer, John Lewis, Joe Perkins, Charles Person, and Hank Thomas; the white riders included James Peck, Frances and Walter Bergman, Al Bigelow, Ed Blankenheim, Genevieve Hughes, and Jim Zwerg.

Farmer's plan called for whites to sit in the back of the bus and blacks to sit in the front of the bus, and they would refuse to move when ordered. At every rest stop, the whites would go into the waiting room for blacks, and the blacks into the waiting room for whites, and would seek to use all the facilities, refusing to leave.[438] Other than the beating of John Lewis, Al Bigelow, and Genevieve Hughes in Rock Hill, South Carolina, relatively "minor" incidents occurred until the buses crossed the state line into Alabama. It is fair to say that today we would not consider any of these incidents as minor.

Two weeks before the buses left Washington, a Birmingham police detective, "Red" Self, arranged the first of several meetings between Birmingham Police Sergeant Tom Cook and Gary Rowe, a member of the most violent Klan unit in Alabama. During the initial meeting, at which Cook described the details of the two-part plot to divert the Freedom Riders in Anniston and destroy their movement in Birmingham, neither Self nor Cook were aware that Rowe had been an FBI informant since 1960.[439] Cook revealed that members of the Birmingham Police Department and Alabama Highway Patrol would cooperate in the conspiracy.[440]

According to Raymond Arsenault's study of the Freedom Rides, Cook explained that Rowe and his Klan associates would get fifteen minutes to beat the Riders into submission:

> You can beat 'em, bomb 'em, maim 'em, kill 'em. I don't give a shit.
> There will be absolutely no arrests. You can assure every Klansman in the county that no one will be arrested in Alabama for that fifteen minutes.

Rowe, who also worked for Birmingham public safety commissioner Bull Connor, dutifully reported the details of these meetings to his FBI handlers. On 3 May, FBI headquarters ordered its Birmingham field office to be careful what they said to Connor and Cook because of the latter's contacts with Rowe. FBI HQS had learned from Rowe that Connor had been secretly meeting with Bobby Shelton, the Imperial Wizard of

---

438 James Farmer, *Voices of Freedom* (New York: Bantam Books, 1990), p. 75.
439 See Appendix One.
440 Arsenault, *Freedom Riders*, p. 136.

THE KENNEDYS, KING AND THE RACE ISSUE—1961

the Alabama Knights, Knights of the Ku Klux Klan, Inc.[441] Hoover wanted to conceal the extent of his knowledge about the cooperation of the Alabama authorities with the KKK against the Freedom Riders.

When the day finally arrived—on Mother's Day, 14 May 1961—there was no sign of any police as the Greyhound bus arrived at the Anniston bus terminal. The Freedom Riders could only look on forebodingly when they were immediately surrounded by an angry large mob of white men wielding clubs, iron pipes, knives and bricks. Initially, eighteen-year-old Klansman Roger Couch lay on the pavement in front of the bus blocking it from leaving, while the rest of the mob menacingly screamed "Dirty communists" and "Sieg heil!"[442] This was anything but befitting the slogan "Welcome to Alabama the Beautiful."[443]

The mob pulverized the bus exterior and slashed its tires. They ordered the Freedom Riders to come out and tried to force open the door. Inside the bus, two Alabama state investigators emerged from under cover to brace their bodies against the door's pull lever.[444] By the time the Anniston police arrived at the terminal, the bus looked like it had just come from a demolition derby. Unlike the pipe-wielding white mob around them, the policemen who mingled among them were calm. Swaggering through the crowd with billy clubs in hand, the officers casually examined the broken windows and slashed tires. They showed no interest in arresting any of the perpetrators.[445] The police were actually laughing and supporting the mob instead of interfering with them.[446]

The passengers in the bus screamed desperately at the driver to escape from the mayhem in the terminal. The driver agreed and began backing up. *As if on cue*, the police officers ceased their friendly banter with the crowd and suddenly cleared a path and motioned for the bus to exit the parking lot.[447] The Greyhound was soon speeding down Highway 78 on its way to Birmingham with two hundred men in fifty cars in hot pursuit.

Inevitably, the slashed tires went flat. The driver pulled off the highway, shut down the engine, and ran away into the countryside. The mob once again surrounded the bus. *This time, however, the mob held the bus doors shut.* They broke one of the windows and hurled a firebomb into the vehicle. It filled with smoke as the canister burst into flames.[448] Those riders who could, began slithering out through the broken holes of

---

441 Ibid, pp. 136-137.
442 Ibid, p. 143.
443 "Welcome to Alabama the Beautiful" was the sign posted on highways at entrances to the Alabama state line.
444 Taylor Branch, **Parting the Waters**, p. 417.
445 Arsenault, **Freedom Riders**, p. 143.
446 James Farmer, **Lay Bare the Heart** (Fort Worth: Texas Christian University Press: 1985), p. 202.
447 Arsenault, **Freedom Riders**, p. 143.
448 Farmer, **Lay Bare the Heart**, pp. 202-203.

INTO THE STORM

glass in the windows.[449] They were all lucky to get out alive. Several members of the mob pressed against the door screaming, "Burn them alive" and "Fry the goddamn niggers."[450]

According to James Farmer, one of the Freedom Riders on that bus, Albert Bigelow, was a former World War II navy combat veteran who was schooled in making decisions under fire. Bigelow took charge and was a true hero on the bus that day. He saved several lives by getting the bus emergency door open.[451] Hank Thomas was the first Rider to tumble out. As he crawled away from the door, a white man ran up to him and struck him in the head with a baseball bat. Thomas fell to the ground and was barely conscious as the rest of the Riders spilled out onto the grass.[452] Suddenly, a policeman among the mob fired his revolver into the air. Again, *as if on cue*, the mob pulled away from the bus, allowing the remaining Freedom Riders to stumble out, choking as they fell to the ground, "writhing and gasping for air."[453] The Greyhound bus burned to the ground.

The leader of the Greyhound group, Joe Perkins, placed an emergency call to Fred Shuttlesworth in Birmingham asking for immediate help to get the injured Riders to medical assistance. Shuttlesworth eventually arrived with the rescue group from his church and transported the Freedom Riders to a hospital where they received treatment for severe smoke inhalation.[454] Arsenault described the scene in the hospital:

> While the Riders waited for Shuttlesworth's deacons to make their way across the back roads of the Alabama hill country, the Anniston hospital superintendent grew impatient and reminded Perkins that the interracial group would not be allowed to spend the night in the hospital.[455]

As the rescue mission pulled into the hospital parking lot, the police had to hold back a jeering crowd. After being treated, the exhausted Riders were mercifully driven away to safety.

With time to reflect on the day's events, the true extent of their predicament dawned on the Riders:

> With the apparent *connivance of law enforcement officials*, the organized defenders of white supremacy in Alabama had decided to smash the Freedom Ride with violence, in effect, announcing to the world that they had no intention of letting the law, the U.S. Constitution, or

---

449   Taylor Branch, ***Parting the Waters***, p. 418.
450   Arsenault, ***Freedom Riders***, p. 145.
451   Farmer, ***Lay Bare the Heart***, p. 203.
452   Arsenault, ***Freedom Riders***, p. 145.
453   Farmer, ***Lay Bare the Heart***, p. 203.
454   Ibid.
455   Arsenault, ***Freedom Riders***, p. 148.

anything else interfere with the preservation of racial segregation in their sovereign state.[456] [Emphasis added]

This gloomy realization was not lost on the White House. A photograph of the flames leaping out of a window of the abandoned Greyhound bus appeared in both the national and international wires for distribution around the world.[457] One can imagine the expressions of angst on the Kennedy brothers as they gazed at the burning bus on the front page of the *Washington Post*.

Meanwhile, for the Riders on the Trailways bus the ordeal began soon after they left Atlanta. It happened before the bus crossed the state line into Alabama. In his oral history for *Voices of Freedom*, James Farmer said that a group of young white bullies boarded the bus with their weapons in sight—pieces of chain, brass knuckles, blackjacks, and pistols.[458] They were Alabama Klansmen and they lost no time in threatening the Riders: "You niggers will be taken care of once you get in Alabama," one Klansman sneered.[459]

The Riders sensed that something special had been planned for their arrival in Anniston. The situation was quietly ominous when the bus pulled into its berth. Peck and other Riders looked around suspiciously as they stepped off the bus. There was a creepy feeling in the waiting room through which they walked to get to the all-white lunch counter. All of the white folk simply looked away. After purchasing some sandwiches, the Riders thought better of testing the lunch counter situation and decided to return to the bus. When they sat back down, the driver slinked off the bus and huddled for a strategy session with Anniston police officers and the Klansmen.[460] Arsenault reconstructed the ultimatum that the driver then delivered to the Riders:

> Later, while waiting nervously to leave, they [the Riders] heard an ambulance siren but didn't think much of it until the bus driver, John Olan Patterson, who had been talking to several Anniston police officers, vaulted up the steps. Flanked by eight "hoodlums," as Peck later called them, Patterson gave them the news about the Greyhound riot. "We have received word that a bus has been burned to the ground and passengers are being carried to the hospital by the carloads," he declared, with no hint of compassion or regret. "A mob is waiting for our bus and will do the same to us unless we get these niggers off the front seats." His bus wasn't going anywhere until the black Freedom Riders retreated to the back of the bus where they belonged.[461]

---

456 Ibid.
457 Taylor Branch, *Parting the Waters*, pp. 418-419.
458 Farmer, *Lay Bare the Heart*, p. 202.
459 Arsenault, *Freedom Riders*, p. 149.
460 Taylor Branch, *Parting the Waters*, p. 419.
461 Ibid.

INTO THE STORM

Farmer recalls that when none of the Riders moved, the Klansmen got up and began beating the black Riders seated in the front of the bus.[462]

According to Arsenault's recapitulation, one of the Klansmen ordered, "Niggers get back. You ain't up north. You're in Alabama, and niggers ain't nothing here." A Klansman punched Person in the face while a second Klansman punched the Rider sitting next to Person. The Klansmen then dragged the students into the aisle and repeatedly pummeled them with their fists while callously kicking them. Arsenault described what happened next:

> At this point Peck and Walter Bergman rushed forward from the back to object. As soon as Peck reached the front, one of the attackers turned on him, striking a blow that sent the frail, middle-aged activist reeling across two rows of seats. Within seconds Bergman, the oldest of the Freedom Riders at sixty-one, suffered a similar blow, falling to the floor with a thud. As blood spurted from their faces, both men tried to shield themselves from further attack, but the Klansmen, enraged by the white Riders' attempt to protect their "nigger" collaborators, proceeded to pound them into a bloody mass. While a pair of Klansmen lifted Peck's head, others punched him in the face until he lost consciousness.[463]

While Peck's face was dismantled, another frenzied Klansman continued viciously stomping Dr. Bergman's head.[464] Realizing that the defenseless Bergman was about to die, one of the other Klansmen halted the beating by counseling, "Don't kill him."[465]

As Doctor Bergman's wife Francis described it, "They used my husband's head for a football." He later suffered a cerebral hemorrhage and was permanently confined to a wheelchair. His stroke later was a direct result of the beating he had suffered that day. Jim Peck was left lying unconscious in a pool of his own blood.[466]

At length, the Klansmen picked up the "pile of bleeding and bruised humanity" and bodily flung them into the back of the bus:

> Content with their brutal handiwork, the Klansmen then sat down in the middle of the bus to block any further attempts to violate the color line. At this point a black woman riding as a regular passenger begged to be let off the bus, but the Klansmen forced her to stay. "Shut up, you black bitch," one of them snarled. "Ain't nobody but whites sitting up here. And them nigger lovers . . . can just sit back there with their nigger friends."[467]

---

462 Farmer, *Lay Bare the Heart*, p. 202.
463 Arsenault, *Freedom Riders*, pp. 149-150.
464 Taylor Branch, *Parting the Waters*, p. 419.
465 Ibid.
466 Farmer, *Lay Bare the Heart*, p. 202.
467 Arsenault, *Freedom Riders*, p. 150.

THE KENNEDYS, KING AND THE RACE ISSUE—1961

The blood-splattered Trailways bus left Anniston for Birmingham. The Riders had no idea that their brutal beating in Anniston was only an hors d'oeuvres.

Mother's Day Mayhem in Birmingham

With the ghoulish beatings in the Anniston terminal over for the moment, the driver, John Patterson, returned to the Trailways bus with a police officer. Both men checked to make sure the blacks were in their proper *place*—the back of the bus. With a grin on his face, the policeman told the Klansmen, "Don't worry about no lawsuits. I ain't seen a thing." He signaled to Patterson that it was time to leave Anniston and then exited the bus. Patterson drove west on the back roads to avoid a mob waiting on the main road to Birmingham. While the Freedom Riders were relieved, they did not know that the driver and the Klansmen riding with them had *instructions* to save them for the "welcoming party" gathering in downtown Birmingham.[468]

As soon as the Trailways bus pulled into its Birmingham berth, the eight Klansmen quietly vanished into the terminal crowd to avoid detection. As the designated segregation testers for Birmingham, Person and Peck—whose faces and clothes were still caked in blood—stepped off the bus first. They surveyed the situation, searching for the best escape routes.[469] There were no apparent signs of an imminent attack. It was Mother's Day. And so, there were only a few bystanders in the terminal—*except for a small group of news reporters who had been tipped off that "something big" would happen at the Trailways terminal*. Despite the clandestine nature of the imminent terror operation, the organizers could not resist the temptation to let the outside world catch a glimpse of Alabama manhood in action.

Arsenault gave a detailed description of the scene at that moment in the terminal. In Hollywood speak it would have been described as a *dressed set*:

> …*the Klansmen and their police allies* were all in place, armed and ready to do what had to be done to protect the Southern way of life. Police dispatchers, *following the agreed-upon plan*, had cleared the "target" area. For the next fifteen minutes there would be no police presence in or near the Trailways station. The only exceptions were *two plainclothes detectives who were in the crowd to monitor the situation and to make sure that the Klansmen left the station before the police arrived.* [Emphasis added]

---

[468] Ibid, p. 150.
[469] Taylor Branch, ***Parting the Waters***, p. 421.

INTO THE STORM

Klansmen were hiding in the waiting room, in the rest rooms, and in the parking area.[470] It was a meticulously concocted and orchestrated covert scheme—no detail had been overlooked—a textbook example of domestic *and* state sponsored terrorism.

Battered, bleeding, and barely able to walk, Peck glanced at Person to gauge his intent. "Let's go," Person said. Then he headed for the white waiting room. Peck, Bergman and other Riders followed, unsure of what would happen next.[471] Birmingham Public Safety Commissioner "Bull" Connor, who had the power to call off the conspiracy, had no intention of doing so:

> He had been waiting too long for an opportunity to confront the Yankee agitators on his own turf. It was time to let Earl Warren, the Kennedys, the communists, and all the other meddling South haters know that the loyal sons of Alabama were ready to fight and die for white supremacy and states' rights. It was time for the blood to flow.[472]

At 4:15p.m., the bloodthirsty commissioner got exactly what he wanted. The Riders filed off onto the unloading platform to retrieve their luggage. Then, all hell broke loose.

The Klansmen burst into action, descending on the Riders with baseball bats, lead pipes and bicycle chains. Schlesinger later described that heartbreaking scene:

> "Everybody who got off the bus," Rowe wrote later, "was clubbed, kicked or beaten. …When people looked up, I couldn't see their faces for blood. …*I observed several FBI men taking movies of the beatings.*" No Klansman was arrested. It was Mother's Day, Eugene (Bull) Connor, the Birmingham police commissioner, later explained, and he had let most of his force off to perform filial duties.[473] [Emphasis added]

The perpetrators felt so safe about what they were doing that they even made movies of the carnage for trophies.

As the Klansmen moved toward Person to beat him, Peck made a futile attempt to intervene. The Klansmen shoved Person toward the black waiting room as others shouted, "Hit him." A detailed account of the terrible thrashing meted out to Person by the Klansmen was preserved by Taylor Branch:

> …a Klansman obliged with a fist to Person's face. Person rose with a bloodied mouth, only to be hit again. This time he fell back into the arms of a Klansman, who held him to receive a third blow, after which he fell to his knees. Peck moved to help him up and was flattened by a rain of five or six punches. Then about *a dozen Klansmen surrounded the two men* and pummeled them with kicks, pipes, and objects that

---

470 Arsenault, *Freedom Riders*, pp. 151-153.
471 Taylor Branch, *Parting the Waters*, p. 421.
472 Arsenault, *Freedom Riders*, p. 154.
473 Schlesinger, *Robert Kennedy and His Times*, p. 295.

looked to one horrified bystander, [reporter] Howard K. Smith, like heavy key rings. *FBI informant Rowe contributed lustily to the beatings.*[474] [Emphasis added]

This beating began in a corridor. It turned into a confused free-for-all with "fists and arms flying everywhere." Person luckily escaped into the street. Peck was not so lucky. The Klansmen continued to pound Peck into an unconscious pulp and left him lying in a pool of blood on the floor.[475]

At this point, the other Freedom Riders entering behind Peck attempted to retreat but they were hemmed in by Klansmen. Taylor Branch provided these details of the scene:

> When reporter Simeon Booker looked into the terminal a few seconds later, he saw a bloodied Walter Bergman on his hands and knees crawling desperately among the legs of the men beating him, groping for a door. Recoiling, Booker held a newspaper up in front of his face, punched a small hole in the middle of it for vision, and edged his way around the exterior of the building.[476]

This delirious disorder then degenerated into something akin to a scene from George Romero's movie *Night of the Living Dead*:

> Several white men attacked Ike Reynolds, kicking and stomping him before *heaving his semiconscious body into a curbside trash bin*. In the confusion, the mob also attacked a number of bystanders misidentified as Freedom Riders. *One of the victims was actually a Klansman* named L. B. Earle, who had the misfortune of coming out of the men's room at the wrong time. Attacked by fellow Klansmen who failed to recognize him, Earle suffered several deep head gashes and ended up in the hospital. Another victim of the mob, a twenty-nine-year-old black laborer named George Webb, was assaulted after he entered the baggage room with his fiancée, Mary Spicer, one of the regular passengers on the freedom bus from Atlanta. ...Dozens of others looked on, some yelling, "Kill the nigger." During the allotted fifteen minutes, *the violence had spread to the sidewalks and streets* surrounding the Trailways station, making it difficult to get the word to all of the Klansmen and NSRP [National States Rights Party] members involved in the riot.[477] [Emphasis added]

---

474 Taylor Branch, **Parting the Waters**, p. 421.
475 Arsenault, **Freedom Riders**, p. 155.
476 Taylor Branch, **Parting the Waters**, pp. 421-422.
477 Arsenault, **Freedom Riders**, p. 157.

INTO THE STORM

Eventually, the blood lust was interrupted by the plainclothes detective on hand, Red Self. He tapped Rowe by the shoulder and ordered him to leave. "*I'm ready to give the signal for the police to move in,*" he said.[478] [Emphasis added]

Peck was taken to Jefferson Hillman Hospital, where emergency surgery was necessary to patch-up several deep lacerations in his head. Fifty-three stitches were required, many of them to close a four-inch horseshoe-shaped gash on his forehead. Press reporters gathered around his bed to ask about the attacks and his plans for the future. "The going is getting rougher," he acknowledged, "but I'll be on that bus tomorrow headed for Montgomery."[479]

Meanwhile, at a late-night meeting with Rowe, Self said he felt the shedding of a *little* blood was a *small price* to pay for what they had accomplished:

> After *weeks of anticipation and careful planning,* they had done exactly what they set out to do. *Carried out in broad daylight,* the assault on the Freedom Riders had turned a bus station into a war zone, and the Klansmen involved had come away with only minor injuries and *little likelihood of criminal prosecution.*[480] [Emphasis added]

A late-night meeting was also held in Fred Shuttlesworth's Bethel Baptist Church. He defiantly cried out, "When white men and black men are beaten up together, the day is coming when they will walk together."[481]

From Shuttlesworth's home, Booker eventually succeeded in reaching John Seigenthaler, the special assistant to Attorney General Robert Kennedy. His reaction spoke volumes. When Seigenthaler suggested that Booker and the other reporters *downplay the story,* Booker replied that the story was too big. He added, "White reporters were milling around everywhere and some of them had been assaulted."[482]

The news from Birmingham hit the White House like a missile. Obviously, James Farmer's letters to John and Robert Kennedy announcing the Freedom Rides before they departed[483] had either not made it to their desks or had not been taken seriously. The FBI warning from Birmingham was more controversial. We know that on 5 May the Birmingham field office sent a wire to FBI Director J. Edgar Hoover summarizing Rowe's assessment about Shelton's plans to terrorize the Riders. What happened after that is not as clear-cut.

According to Arsenault, Hoover "forwarded some, *though apparently not all,* of this information to Attorney General Kennedy, Deputy Attorney General Byron White, and

---

478 Ibid, p. 156.
479 Taylor Branch, *Parting the Waters*, p. 423.
480 Arsenault, *Freedom Riders*, p. 158.
481 Taylor Branch, *Parting the Waters*, p. 423.
482 Ibid.
483 Arsenault, *Freedom Riders*, p. 110.

other Justice Department officials four days later."[484] [Emphasis added] The question is this: Did Hoover pass on the Rowe warning to the Attorney General?

There is no doubt that Attorney General Robert Kennedy was the point man on civil rights issues within the administration. Kennedy historian Arthur Schlesinger described how RFK handled communications with JFK concerning civil rights:

> "I kept [the President] advised," Robert Kennedy said later, "but I think it was just understood by us, which has always been understood, that I have my area of responsibility; and I'd do it. . . . If I had a problem about alternative steps, I'd call him. . . . But I wouldn't call him just to be gabby about what was going on in the south."[485]

Of specific relevance to what Bobby might have passed on to the president about the Birmingham FBI warning, Schlesinger recalled that RFK said, "I never knew they were traveling down there before the bus was burned in Anniston."[486]

Arsenault agreed that there was merit in RFK's claim of being surprised by the events in Alabama:

> The FBI, the agency that should have kept him informed about such matters, had detailed advance information on the Klan plot to disrupt the Freedom Ride, but *no one in the bureau saw fit to relay this information to anyone in the Justice Department. Although Robert Kennedy never knew the full extent of the FBI's advance knowledge of the Alabama plot, he and other Justice Department officials suspected that the FBI was partly responsible for the crisis.*[487] [Emphasis added]

Schlesinger recalls President Kennedy's initial reaction to the Birmingham mayhem was one of "dismay." But it was also tinged with exasperation:

> In the White House, John Kennedy, preparing for meetings with de Gaulle and Khrushchev in Europe, thought the Riders an unnecessary burden. "Tell them to call it off," he said to Harris Wofford. "Stop them." "I don't think anybody's going to stop them right now," Wofford said.[488] In Washington, the president's desire to pursue a strategy of "suasion" instead of "undue militancy"—while revealing—was no longer relevant to the events taking place on the ground in Alabama, which was a long way from Paris and Vienna.

Arsenault is correct in observing that if the Freedom Riders had understood the president's view, "their anxiety level" would have been much higher:

---

484 Ibid, p. 137.
485 Schlesinger, *Robert Kennedy and His Times*, p. 288.
486 Ibid, p. 295.
487 Arsenault, *Freedom Riders*, p. 164.
488 Schlesinger, *Robert Kennedy and His Times*, p. 295.

INTO THE STORM

>In mid-May 1961, though, *the political calculus of the administration allowed little room for interracial provocateurs,* however well-meaning they might be. To the Kennedy brothers, taking the civil rights movement into the streets, where uncontrolled conflict was inevitable, was *an embarrassing luxury that the United States could not afford in the context of the Cold War.* The president was first and foremost a Cold Warrior, and his focus on world affairs was never more intense than during the troubled spring following the Bay of Pigs fiasco.[489] [Emphasis added]

President Kennedy had just learned that Soviet Premier Nikita Khrushchev had agreed to a summit meeting in Vienna in June. Kennedy was consumed with the impending crisis over Berlin:

>…he did not appreciate the crisis that CORE had deliberately precipitated in Alabama. From the administration's perspective, *the timing of the confrontation in Alabama couldn't have been much worse*, as the president told Wofford in no uncertain terms after reading the Monday morning headlines.[490] [Emphasis added]

"Can't you get your goddamned friends off those buses?" Kennedy exploded. "Stop them."[491] President Kennedy was angry at being blindsided by the crisis in Alabama and why nobody had told him what was coming.

Robert Kennedy asked John Seigenthaler to go to Birmingham to see what could be done. "What sort of help do they need?" Seigenthaler asked. "I think they primarily need somebody along just to hold their hand and let them know that we care," said Kennedy. Seigenthaler left immediately for the airport.[492] Upon arrival, he found the beleaguered group, heads bloody and bandaged, still in the bus terminal. Simeon Booker, a black newspaperman, told Seigenthaler he didn't believe they would ever get out of Birmingham.

The administration's initial strategy attempted to *downplay the significance* of what had happened in Anniston and Birmingham. *That attempt immediately went up in smoke* when the first sensational radio reports of the attacks on the Freedom Riders were broadcast—including Howard K. Smith's gripping account—over the CBS radio network. By Sunday evening, millions of Americans were aware of the riveting story from Alabama. Early on Monday, front-page stories about the bloodshed in Anniston and Birmingham appeared in hundreds of newspapers—including the **New York Times** and **Washington Post**. Later that day, the stories were featured on several prominent

---

489   Arsenault, **Freedom Riders**, p. 164.
490   Ibid.
491   Robert Dallek, **An Unfinished Life** (New York: Little, Brown and Company, 2003), p. 384.
492   Taylor Branch, **Parting the Waters**, p. 428.

THE KENNEDYS, KING AND THE RACE ISSUE—1961

television news broadcasts. Clearly, the power of television brought a new dimension to political activism in America.

On Monday morning, Robert Kennedy called Booker. Booker said that the Riders were trapped by gangs of Klansmen still marauding through downtown Birmingham. Kennedy and Shuttlesworth discussed getting police protection for the bus ride to Montgomery but they soon found Governor John Patterson unwilling to cooperate. In this situation, the Freedom Riders decided to force the issue and headed to the bus terminal to catch the three o'clock Greyhound to Montgomery. With Patterson still refusing to cooperate, it became clear that the Freedom Riders would not be leaving Birmingham by bus. By five o'clock, they had reached a consensus to attempt leaving by plane.

It worked. At 10:38 p.m., an Eastern Airlines plane carrying Seigenthaler, fourteen Freedom Riders and four journalists lifted off from Birmingham and landed an hour later in New Orleans.

But the problem in Birmingham was far from over. When President Kennedy returned from a trip to Canada, a new influx of Freedom Riders had arrived in Birmingham and had been immediately jailed. They refused to eat in the jail and demanded to ride the bus to the state capitol, Montgomery. But Greyhound officials refused to transport Freedom Riders without guaranteed police protection, a guarantee Governor Patterson refused to give. Moreover, he was hiding to avoid being caught in a trap:

> If Patterson declared that he would protect the Freedom Riders as interstate travelers, then Alabama voters might say that he had knuckled under to the federal government, sacrificed Alabama's segregation laws, and accepted the unmanly role of nursemaid to the hated group of interracial troublemakers. If, on the other hand, Patterson declared he could not or would not protect the Freedom Riders, he would be admitting limits to state sovereignty and all but inviting the federal government to assume police power in his state. To Patterson, either course was political suicide.[493] The resulting stalemate was intolerable to President Kennedy, who began examining the use of American Army troops to protect the Freedom Riders traveling by bus.

Facing an upcoming summit with Premier Khrushchev already weakened by the Bay of Pigs failure, the president wanted to avoid being forced into the use of troops against Americans under these circumstances. So, Robert Kennedy asked Byron White to review the possibility of protecting the Riders by cobbling together a conglomerate force of civilian officers instead. To do this, White contacted the Marshal Service, the U.S. Border Patrol, the Treasury Department's Bureau of Alcohol, Tobacco and Firearms,

---

493 Ibid, p. 433.

INTO THE STORM

and the Bureau of Prisons to protect the Freedom Riders on the road between Birmingham and Montgomery.

Preparations along these lines were advertised to Governor Patterson to pressure him to protect the Riders to avoid federal intervention. The Justice Department soon learned about a *miracle cure* by commissioner Bull Connor:

> His men were dragging the limp, protesting Freedom Riders out of their cells into unmarked police cars. Connor himself assured federal officials that no harm would come to them, saying that he was taking two reporters along as witnesses. ... He was going to "escort" them personally through the state, under cover of darkness, and dump them into Tennessee. His plan, relayed instantly through the Justice Department and down to Seigenthaler, was received as an unorthodox and illegal but thoroughly effective remedy for the nightmarish stalemate.[494]

Connor's caravan halted at Ardmore, a small Tennessee border town. There, the seven Freedom Riders and their luggage were left on the side of the road.

The Freedom Fiders, however, would get the last laugh. First, they searched for a shelter. Soon they found a "Negro home" in the countryside, owned by an elderly black couple. From there, they contacted SNCC leader Diane Nash who, after collecting them, drove them back to Birmingham![495]

After the Riders reached Shuttlesworth's house, he fed them sandwiches and took them to the Greyhound terminal to catch the five o'clock bus to Montgomery. Police officers hauled Shuttlesworth away to jail, but their riot units had difficulty trying to restrain three thousand angry whites from mistreating the Riders. The Riders sang "We Shall Overcome" and other songs into the evening as the frustrated mob occasionally threw rocks over the heads of policemen and through the windows of the terminal.[496]

Washington immediately reentered a crisis mode. An irate Robert Kennedy threatened federal intervention and rushed Seigenthaler to confront Patterson at the state capitol in Montgomery. At length, the governor gave his word to the president on the phone that he would assign the men and equipment to give full protection to the riders in Alabama. Meanwhile, in Birmingham, Greyhound driver Joe Caverno refused to drive the bus for what were now nineteen Freedom Riders.

A day later, after Robert Kennedy did some arm twisting of the Greyhound superintendent in Birmingham, Caverno returned to the bus along with the president of the local bus drivers' union and the chief Greyhound dispatcher. Then this scene took place:

---

[494] Ibid, pp. 436-437.
[495] Ibid, pp. 437-438.
[496] Ibid, p. 441.

Without warning, policemen herded the startled Freedom Riders behind the three of them onto the bus, and, as reporters dashed to their cars to follow, the [proverbial] St. Petersburg Express raced through downtown Birmingham, escorted by police cars with sirens wailing. The highway patrol picked them up at the city line, and the entire convoy—shadowed by FBI observers, plainclothes state detectives, and a highway patrol airplane, plus the trailing reporters—headed for Montgomery at speeds nearing ninety miles per hour.[497]

Thus, at 8:30 a.m. on 20 May, the Freedom Ride was back in business. Diane Nash immediately called James Farmer. In view of how badly his CORE group of Freedom Riders had been "chewed up," she asked permission to send in fresh SNCC reinforcements to help carry on the Ride. Warning Nash that "it may be suicide," Farmer reluctantly agreed and said he would join her in Montgomery after the funeral of his father. Farmer also called his office in New York and ordered his staff to contact the New Orleans CORE chapter to rustle up a new contingent of young CORE members to join the SNCC group.[498]

Siege at Montgomery

As the final leg of the Alabama chapter of the Freedom Rides approached, once again the conspirators eavesdropped on all of the telephone communications of the Freedom Riders—including with the White House. They made no serious attempt to hide some of the juicier intercepts from their eavesdropping on the Kennedy brothers. When Bobby had berated the Birmingham Greyhound superintendent, George Cruit— "I think you had better be getting in touch with Mr. Greyhound or whoever Greyhound is"—that sentence promptly appeared in newspapers all across the South. Patterson's motive was to buttress the argument that the attorney general was working surreptitiously with the Riders and had been the mastermind behind the entire Freedom Ride all along.[499]

Around 10:00 a.m. on the morning of 20 May, the Freedom Rider convoy entered Montgomery County. The pilot of the patrol plane confirmed that the bus was only fourteen miles away from the state capitol. At the Montgomery city line, the Riders discovered that their police escort was limited to a lone patrolman on a motorcycle.[500] The Special Agent in Charge (SAC) of the Montgomery FBI office sent a warning

---

497 Ibid. p. 444.
498 Farmer, *Lay Bare the Heart*, pp. 203-204.
499 Taylor Branch, *Parting the Waters*, p. 443.
500 Arsenault, *Freedom Riders*, p. 211.

INTO THE STORM

to headquarters in Washington. The warning was relayed to Burke Marshall at the Justice Department. The Montgomery SAC said he did not believe "a word" of Police Commissioner Sullivan's promise to protect the Freedom Riders when they arrived in the capitol. Washington responded that Sullivan was to be reminded of Governor Patterson's assurances. When the SAC complied, Sullivan's slippery reply was that "plenty" of Montgomery policemen were at the Greyhound terminal. A notorious hardline segregationist, Sullivan knew, and of course did not say, that the policemen would soon disappear.[501]

Seigenthaler and the Freedom Riders expected to find the terminal full of police. But, as the bus eased into its bay at 10:23 a.m., and there were no policemen in sight. As they stepped onto the platform, there was an unsettling quiet, much like what they had experienced in Birmingham the previous Sunday. John Lewis, one of the original thirteen Freedom Riders, recalled, "when we arrived at the bus station, it was eerie. Just a strange feeling. It was so quiet, so peaceful, nothing."[502]

Once again, a fully organized conspiracy had been arranged to strike a blow for segregation. Lookouts in parked cars had been in position in the streets around the terminal since Friday evening. There were more than two hundred protesters in the immediate area, including many of Alabama's most notorious Klansmen:

> The ringleader of the "welcoming" party was Claude Henley, a local car salesman and former highway patrolman who had served on Montgomery's volunteer reserve police force since 1956. A close friend of Captain Drue Lackey, the commander of the city's patrol division, Henley had been promised that the police would not interfere with his plan to teach the Freedom Riders a lesson.

Commissioner Sullivan and Lackey had been aware of Henley's plot long before the Riders arrived.[503]

Lewis and several other Riders were met by a group of reporters. No sooner had Lewis warned a colleague that "things didn't look right" than a group of white men armed with lead pipes and baseball bats rushed them. Norman Ritter, a writer for **Life** magazine, attempted to protect the Riders with outstretched arms. He was pushed aside, and several attackers smashed television cameras and sound equipment and then began beating the Freedom Riders. Many Riders joined hands on the loading platform but were quickly broken up by the swelling mob. John Lewis recalled:

> One cameraman, I believe from NBC, had one of these heavy old pieces of camera equipment on his shoulder. This member of the mob took the equipment, bashed this guy, knocked him down, bashed his face

---

[501] Taylor Branch, *Parting the Waters*, p. 444.
[502] John Lewis in Hampton and Fayer, *Voices of Freedom*, p. 86.
[503] Arsenault, *Freedom Riders*, p. 212.

in. So, they beat up all of the reporters, then they turned on the black male members and white male members of the group. I was beaten—I think I was hit with a sort of crate thing that holds soda bottles—and left lying unconscious there, in the streets of Montgomery.[504]

According to Arsenault, "hundreds of men, women, and children emerged from alleys, side streets, and office buildings … all at once … They carried every makeshift weapon imaginable."[505]

Many of the Riders either jumped or were pushed over a railing into a parking lot below, landing on the hoods and roofs of cars. For a few seconds, they were fortunate to have a chance to escape. Soon however, they realized that whites who had been hiding were closing in on them, egged on by a woman in a yellow dress who kept yelling "Get those niggers!"[506]

Meanwhile, Seigenthaler was circling the block looking for a parking place when he realized that a full-scale riot was in progress—whites were smashing and tossing luggage into the street as Freedom Riders were running for their lives. Seigenthaler attempted to stop a fifteen-year-old boy from beating a female Rider. Then, he was attacked:

> Suddenly, two rough-looking men dressed in overalls blocked his path to the car door, demanding to know who "the hell" he was. Seigenthaler replied that he was a federal agent and that they had better not challenge his authority. Before he could say any more, a third man struck him in the back of the head with a pipe. Unconscious, he fell to the pavement, where he was kicked in the ribs by other members of the mob.[507]

Seigenthaler was pushed under the car where he remained motionless until discovered by a policeman twenty-five minutes later.

Watching the carnage from a window of the Federal Building, the Assistant Attorney General for Civil Rights, John Doar, described the disaster over the telephone to Burke Marshall:

> "Oh, there are fists, punching!" he cried. "A bunch of men led by a guy with a bleeding face [they] are beating them. There are no cops. It's terrible! It's terrible! There's not a cop in sight. People are yelling, 'There those niggers are! Get 'em, get 'em!' It's awful.'"[508]

---

504 John Lewis, *Voices of Freedom*, pp. 86-87.
505 Arsenault, *Freedom Riders*, p. 212.
506 Taylor Branch, *Parting the Waters*, p. 446.
507 Arsenault, *Freedom Riders*, pp. 213-214.
508 Taylor Branch, *Parting the Waters*, p. 447.

INTO THE STORM

"I saw whites and negroes beaten unmercifully while law officers calmly directed traffic," **Birmingham News** reporter Tom Lankford recalled. "Saturday was hell in Montgomery."[509]

Seigenthaler was beginning to regain consciousness when a police lieutenant discovered him under his car:

> "Looks like you got some trouble, buddy," he said. "Yeah, I did," said Seigenthaler, waking to pain. "What happened?" "Well, we had a riot." "Don't you think you better call Mr. Kennedy?" "Which Mr. Kennedy?" "The Attorney General of the United States." The lieutenant frowned. "Who the hell are you?" he asked. "I'm his administrative assistant," groaned Seigenthaler, in a manner that convinced the lieutenant he was talking with a bona-fide big shot.

The lieutenant brought help. Later, Seigenthaler woke up in the X-ray room of a hospital. A doctor who was talking on the telephone with Byron White in Washington.[510]

The worst violence took place on the loading platform, where Jim Zwerg was the first Rider to be assaulted. As the only white male Rider, the Klansmen selected him for special treatment:

> Klansmen kicked Zwerg in the back before smashing him in the head with his own suitcase. Dazed and bleeding, Zwerg struggled to get up, but one of the Klansmen promptly pinned the defenseless student's arms back while others punched him repeatedly in the face. To Lucretia Collins, who witnessed the beating from the backseat of a departing taxicab, the savagery of Zwerg's attackers was sickening. "Some men held him while white women clawed his face with their nails," she recalled. "And they held up their little children—children who couldn't have been more than a couple years old—to claw his face. I had to turn my head because I just couldn't watch it." Eventually Zwerg's eyes rolled back and his body sagged into unconsciousness. After tossing him over a railing, his attackers went looking for other targets.[511]

Turning to the black Freedom Riders huddled near the railing, a group of the Klansmen mercilessly beat several of them into unconsciousness. At length, the sound of gunfire was heard. The shots actually came from the gun of Floyd Mann, the director of the Alabama Highway Patrol, who was protecting three unconscious Freedom Riders from further injury.

Mann was uncertain about Sullivan's commitment to protect the Riders and had posted a unit of highway patrolmen near the terminal. He had arrived five minutes

---

509 Arsenault, **Freedom Riders**, p. 216.
510 Taylor Branch, **Parting the Waters**, p. 449.
511 Arsenault, **Freedom Riders**, p. 214.

THE KENNEDYS, KING AND THE RACE ISSUE—1961

after the melee began and wandered into the frenzied scene at the loading platform. A local black man named Miles Davis was being attacked while attempting to rescue a Rider and Mann pulled his pistol to fire two warning shots. He shouted, "I'll shoot the next man who hits him. Stand back! There'll be no killing here today." Eventually Mann succeeded in clearing Klansmen off the loading platform.[512]

When Sullivan learned that Mann was on the loading platform, he immediately took charge, only to be upstaged by the arrival of several state and county officials—including Alabama Attorney General MacDonald Gallion. Walking over to Lewis, who was still lying half-conscious on the pavement, Gallion asked a deputy sheriff to read an injunction to the semi-conscious John Lewis: The Freedom Riders had been declared outlaws in the state of Alabama.

No one other than Mann was interested in helping the injured Riders—especially the white Rider Zwerg. He was barely conscious and bleeding profusely, but the police refused to call an ambulance. Eventually Mann ordered one of his patrolmen to transport Zwerg to St. Jude's Catholic Hospital. By this time, all of the Freedom Riders had left the terminal and most of them had found refuge. When Reverend Solomon S. Seay heard about the Riders' plight, he offered his home as a safe house, and by early afternoon the Riders began to gather there.[513]

Order was not restored around the terminal until Mann used the Highway Patrol to impose it. Members of the press suspected that Sullivan was responsible for letting the Klan brutalize the Freedom Riders, but they focused their stories instead on the attack of John Seigenthaler and the rumor that Sullivan had initially refused to call an ambulance for the special assistant to the attorney general. Seigenthaler had a fractured skull and several broken ribs, but the doctor said he would make a full recovery.

Late on Saturday, RFK joined Byron White, Burke Marshall, and ten other Justice officials for an emergency conclave. After updating the president, RFK sent his staff lawyers to activate the makeshift army they had been preparing for. Marshall and Doar were ordered to prepare a federal injunction prohibiting the Klan and the National States Rights Party (NSRP) from interfering with interstate transit. Then, RFK called Seigenthaler's hospital room in Montgomery:

> "How are you doing?" he asked. "This is a terrible headache," Seigenthaler replied. "Well, we're sending the marshals there." "I'm sorry to hear that," said Seigenthaler, who knew this meant trouble, and he signed off with a weak joke, advising Kennedy never to run for governor of Alabama.[514]

---

512 Ibid, p. 215.
513 Ibid, pp. 216-218.
514 Taylor Branch, *Parting the Waters*, p. 451.

INTO THE STORM

Joking aside, the situation in Alabama was nowhere near under control. Governor Patterson was declaring publicly that the state had already restored order. He denounced Kennedy's decision to send in unsolicited federal marshals and complained that they would only cause an escalation of the Freedom Riders' activities. The timing was *awkward*: Federal forces would have arrived too late to stop the first riot *and* just in time to be blamed if and when a second one erupted.

The news that Martin Luther King was coming to Montgomery to lead a rally at Ralph Abernathy's First Baptist Church created a great deal more cause for concern. King would have to be protected. Both RFK and Marshall tried and failed to persuade King to stay away from Alabama. King's arrival under armed federal guard would send Governor Patterson into orbit.[515]

The Kennedy brothers suspected that Patterson had been behind the senseless escalation of violence. JFK and RFK would never trust Governor Patterson again. The lesson had been learned. Time and options were running out and something dramatic was necessary to end the crisis. With the Kennedy-Khrushchev summit in Vienna less than two weeks away, the president was anxious not to let the moral authority of America be ruined by mobs of racist vigilantes. On 20 May 1961, JFK delivered a public statement implicitly criticizing Alabama officials *and* the Freedom Riders:

> The situation which has developed in Alabama is a source of the deepest concern to me as it must be to the vast majority of the citizens of Alabama and all America. I have instructed the Justice Department to take all necessary steps based on their investigation and information. I call upon the Governor and other responsible state officials in Alabama as well as the Mayors of Birmingham and Montgomery to exercise their lawful authority to prevent any further outbreaks of violence. I would also hope that any person, whether a citizen of Alabama, or a visitor there, would refrain from any action which would in any way tend to provoke further outbreaks. I hope that state and local officials will meet their responsibilities. The United States Government intends to meet its.[516]

On Sunday morning (21 May), newspapers across the nation carried the president's statement along with detailed accounts of the riot and graphic pictures of the injured Freedom Riders and newsmen.[517]

Behind the scenes, however, the Freedom Riders project was being transformed overnight into a full-fledged national movement. By Saturday afternoon (20 May), the

---

515 Ibid, pp 451-452.
516 5/20/61, *The Presidency Project—the Papers of John F. Kennedy*, "Statement by the President Concerning Interference With the "Freedom Riders" in Alabama."
517 Arsenault, *Freedom Riders*, p. 223-224.

principal leaders of the Southern Christian Leadership Conference (SCLC),[518] SNCC and CORE had all signed up to make the pilgrimage to Montgomery.

Kennedy, too, had called King in Chicago in an effort to convince him to stay away from Montgomery, but again King refused to change his plans. King's plane was scheduled to arrive in Montgomery around noon on Sunday (21 May). White had posted fifty marshals at the airport to ensure no one would get hurt. They quietly escorted King to a brief private meeting with other leaders at a nearby black church before accompanying him to Abernathy's downtown parsonage.[519]

Later in the afternoon a group of marshals returned to the airport to provide an escort for Shuttlesworth and Farmer to join the Freedom Riders who were hiding in the basement library at First Baptist where they were under siege.[520] The support of so many African American leaders was welcome, but Diane Nash was certain that the presence of King was absolutely crucial to demonstrate that her Nashville students were not alone at this crucial juncture.[521]

While King and the other leaders finalized plans for the mass meeting later that night, the marshals did not tell the reporters and state agents outside of the church why they were there. At the state capitol, however, everyone understood that the marshals were guarding King:

> …to Governor Patterson it was an act of sneaky, cowardly treachery on the part of Attorney General Kennedy. Patterson also realized his sudden political opportunity. Having had little to gain when pitted against the lowly, mostly Negro Freedom Riders, whose stature rose in every clash with white Alabama, Patterson seized the new underdog role in a battle against the federal government itself. He summoned Byron White to the capitol for what amounted to a public council of war.[522]

Byron White had not arrived at Maxwell Air Force Base until eight o'clock that evening. He and his staff set up a command post in a nearby Quonset hut to process the hundreds of newly deputized marshals. Burke Marshall later described the rag tag nature of the marshals:

> … "the border patrol were the only ones that could shoot. . . . Most of them," he admitted, "were the product of senatorial patronage, middle-aged, fat, lethargic people with no law enforcement experience. Many of them came from the South and really thought they were being

---

518 Founded on 10 January 1957, the Southern Christian Leadership Conference's first president was Martin Luther King, Jr.
519 Ibid, pp. 226-229.
520 Farmer, *Lay Bare the Heart*, p. 204.
521 Arsenault, *Freedom Riders*, p. 225.
522 Taylor Branch, *Parting the Waters*, p. 453.

> asked to protect black people whom they considered communists, or worse. We weren't sure which side they would be on."[523]

At the "war council" in front of the Alabama cabinet and a host of reporters, Governor Patterson berated White: "We don't need your marshals. We don't want them, and we didn't ask for them. And still the federal government sends them here to help put down a disturbance which it helped create." White calmly responded that they had a common mission—preserving public order. Patterson countered that the Freedom Rides were inspired by communists and dismissed White after forty-five minutes. Patterson then announced on the radio that King and his supporters would meet in Abernathy's church that night.[524]

People had begun arriving at the First Baptist church around five o'clock, even though the mass meeting was scheduled to begin at eight. Outside, a dozen marshals stood watch over the few white protesters that were there. This was deceptive as carloads of whites had been arriving in Montgomery all day long. A few FBI agents and plainclothes state detectives were on hand at the church. More importantly, no city policemen, highway patrolmen, or National Guardsmen were present. As Arsenault observed, this was a formula for mob violence:

> Throughout the day local radio stations had broadcast "the news that Negroes would hold a mass meeting that night at the First Baptist Church," virtually ensuring that a large crowd of white protesters would eventually descend upon the church.

As dusk descended on Montgomery, the crowd outside the church grew to more than two thousand protesters, many carrying confederate flags. The Justice Department plan was weak: unless the situation blew up, they would wait for Patterson to call for more marshals.[525] That was something that Patterson would never do.

Farmer recalls the moment that he and Shuttlesworth finally arrived at the church:

> Several blocks before the church, the streets were clogged with crowds of men waving small Confederate flags and shouting rebel yells. We were forced to stop, and the mob rocked the car back and forth, their intentions clear. Fred shoved the automatic gear shift into reverse, heavy-footed the accelerator, and we zoomed backward. Screeching to a halt, he made a U-turn on two wheels with tires whining and tried another approach to the church.

Shuttlesworth and Farmer were advised to take an indirect route through a graveyard to the back of the church in the hope that the mob might not be at that entrance yet. However, they found that it was too late:

---

523 Arsenault, *Freedom Riders*, p. 227.
524 Taylor Branch, *Parting the Waters*, pp. 453-454.
525 Arsenault, *Freedom Riders*, p. 230.

> The mob was already there, blocking even that entrance to the church. "Can you get me into that church, Fred?" I asked. "Wrong question, Jim," replied Fred Shuttlesworth. "The only question to ask is: how will I get you in?" "Jim, we've got no choice. We have got to go right through them," said Fred. Without waiting for a response, he proceeded to walk right into the mob. Fred Shuttlesworth was a small man, short and thin, but never before in my life had I seen such physical courage. He walked right into the mob, elbowing the hysterical white men aside, saying, "Out of the way. Let me through. Step aside." Incredibly, the members of the mob obeyed. I walked behind Fred, trying to hide in his shadow.[526]

Inside the church, Farmer and Shuttlesworth were escorted up to the sanctuary, where they were greeted by King, Abernathy, and Nash, and a congregation growing increasingly concerned about what was happening outside.[527]

"We've got to go out and see what's happening," King announced. Runners brought Walker and Abernathy to dissuade him, but King insisted. "Let's go," he told them. "Leadership must do this." The preachers stepped outside. As they slowly walked around the church, they circled around King:

> The jeers and the occasional thuds of thrown missiles carried clearly through the early evening air, and soon there rose above them the cry of someone who recognized King. "Nigger King!" it rang out. "Come over here!" King moved slowly toward the challenge, but rocks began to land around him. Then a metal cylinder skidded to a stop at King's feet. ... The entourage pulled King in retreat during a frantic debate about whether the cylinder had been a bomb or a tear gas cannister, and if tear gas, where it had come from since there were no police in sight, and whether the police might be in collusion with the mob.[528]

Back in the church, King spoke positively to assuage the fears of those inside. He reassured them that the marshals had everything under control.[529] The congregation began singing "Leaning on the Everlasting Arms." Fifteen hundred people—the vast majority black—were crowded inside the church by eight o'clock. Reverend Seay opened the program with a recapitulation of the ordeals of the Freedom Ride.

In Washington, the Attorney General's office had become a command post with a permanent open line to White's command post at Maxwell Air Force Base. Wyatt Walker placed an emergency call to the attorney general. He told RFK forebodingly

---

526   Farmer, *Lay Bare the Heart*, pp. 204-205.
527   Arsenault, *Freedom Riders*, p. 232.
528   Taylor Branch, *Parting the Waters*, pp. 455-456.
529   Arsenault, *Freedom Riders*, p. 232.

INTO THE STORM

that only immediate federal action could save their lives. Kennedy reassured him that everything possible was being done and asked to speak with King.[530] King began listing the many signs of grave danger when Kennedy interrupted to emphasize that the marshals were coming. King replied emphatically that if they didn't arrive immediately "we're going to have a bloody confrontation" because the mob was already at the church door. Then, after hearing the news that the reinforcements had been sighted, King thanked Bobby: "You were right. They're here."[531]

However, the impact of the additional marshals was minimal, and the mob began closing in and shouting, "Let's clean the niggers out of here!" As the church grounds were deluged by rocks, bricks, and Molotov cocktails, the outnumbered marshals radioed this alarming news to White, who immediately relayed it to Robert Kennedy. The attorney general quickly approved the deployment of the four hundred marshals at Maxwell Field. King called Robert Kennedy to ask when the new contingent of marshals would arrive. Kennedy, who could only say it would be soon, changed the subject:

> Wasn't it time to call off or at least postpone the Freedom Ride? he asked. Would the Freedom Riders agree to some sort of "cooling-off period" that would give federal and state authorities the opportunity to work out a solution? ... King explained that he could not speak for the Freedom Riders; he would, however, broach the idea with Jim Farmer and Diane Nash.

The arrival of the fresh contingent of marshals ended the conversation. King thanked Kennedy and promised to call back. That would not happen until three *long* hours later—1:10 a.m. Montgomery time.[532]

In the meantime, King briefed the other leaders about the attorney general's suggestion for a cooling off period. Farmer later recalled that episode:

> "No, Martin," I replied. "I won't stop it now. If I do, we'll just get words and promises." "But, Jim," King said in his slow southern drawl, "don't you think that maybe the Freedom Ride has already made its point and now should be called off, as the attorney general suggests?"

Farmer asked King to wait while he checked with Diane Nash. Farmer recalled the outcome:

> I walked a few steps away, called Diane Nash over, told her the substance of the attorney general's request, and of my conversation with Dr. King. Diane shook her head. "No," she said. "The Nashville Student Movement wants to go on. We can't stop it now, right after we've been clobbered." I walked back to King and said, "My objective is not just

---

530 Taylor Branch, *Parting the Waters*, pp. 456-460.
531 Ibid, p. 460.
532 Arsenault, *Freedom Riders*, pp. 232-233.

to make a point, but to bring about a real change in the situation. ... *Please tell the attorney general that we have been cooling off for 350 years. If we cool off any more, we will be in a deep freeze.* The Freedom Ride will go on."[533] [Emphasis added]

At this point, the situation around Abernathy's First Baptist Church was doing anything but cooling off.

In fact, the Freedom Riders had successfully applied Dr. King's coercive nonviolence strategy to the situation in Alabama. Governor Patterson had used up all of the ugly schemes in his racist toolkit. The Riders had maneuvered him into a choice he could no longer avoid: on the one hand, he could allow and protect their legal right to integrate the interstate transportation system that ran through his state; or, on the other hand, he could watch Washington do it for him. While the first choice was a dose of castor oil, Patterson saw the second choice as political suicide. The Freedom Riders could smell victory. Time was on their side. They could sense that the fear in the state capitol was stronger than the fear in the Kennedy White House. Diane Nash and James Farmer decided to double down, and King was not about to stand in their way.

And so, a new contingent of marshals fell into formation in front of the church and proceeded to lob a massive volley of tear gas that momentarily cleared the rioters from the church grounds. And, predictably, the standoff remained. The giant cloud of tear gas drifted back into the church sanctuary, producing a frantic effort to rapidly close the windows. This, in turn, produced a sudden absence of ventilation and an acrid sauna for the fifteen hundred frightened people inside.[534] This also allowed an aroused frontline phalanx of protesters to pound on the front door of the church again. The rescue had turned into a debacle.[535]

Farmer later recalled the ebb and flow of this fiasco:

> During the rest of that night we were under siege in the church. The mob was still screaming outside. At one point, they pounded on the basement door. Some of the men in the church had propped a chair against the door handle and backed chairs up to the door to impede the progress of would-be intruders. It was not long before the door was kicked open and the barriers knocked away. Angry white faces surged inside.[536]

---

[533] Farmer, *Lay Bare the Heart*, pp. 205-206.
[534] Taylor Branch, *Parting the Waters*, pp. 460-461.
[535] Arsenault, *Freedom Riders*, p. 235.
[536] Farmer, *Lay Bare the Heart*, p. 206.

INTO THE STORM

The marshals had also heard cries that the mob had gained entry to the church through the back door of the basement. The marshals ran through the clogged corridors in time to push the rioters back outside with nightsticks and shoulders.[537]

Meanwhile, the violence in the streets around First Baptist continued to escalate. Marshals were attacked by brick-throwing rioters; some of marshals took refuge in their vehicles. Guns began firing randomly into black homes nearby the church. A Molotov cocktail nearly set the church roof on fire.[538]

Robert Kennedy ordered Army units placed on alert at Fort Benning, Georgia.[539] Byron White told Robert Kennedy that the marshals could not hold out. The attorney general had heard enough—he decided to ask the president to sign a proclamation authorizing the immediate deployment of the soldiers from Fort Benning. As it turned out, however, someone besides the attorney general had also heard enough. Dramatic news immediately came from Governor Patterson's office.[540] Unbeknownst to Kennedy and White, Patterson had some help from a telephone operator:

> *Patterson, who had been eavesdropping on the phone communications between Washington and White's office at Maxwell Field, decided to act. At ten o'clock, he placed the city of Montgomery under what he called "qualified martial rule."*[541]

The first fifteen white-helmeted soldiers of the Alabama National Guard marched double-time with bayoneted rifles. Another hundred came up shortly. The Guardsmen took positions around the front of the church as policemen chased the rioters out of the area.... near the church, Police Commissioner Sullivan made his first appearance of the night. White teenagers pelted his car with bricks.[542]

By that time, the police, with Commissioner Sullivan making a show of his authority, had cleared the immediate area of rioters. Nearby, a greatly relieved McShane, with White's approval, offered to place his marshals under the command of the National Guard. Accepting McShane's offer, the colonel in charge of the Guardsmen promptly ordered the marshals to leave the scene. As the overall commander of the Guard, Adjutant General Henry Graham announced a few minutes later that the sovereign state of Alabama had everything under control and needed no further help from federal authorities.[543]

The worst of the bedlam was over by 10 p.m. Sporadic violence continued for several hours. Inside the church, King began to deliver his main address sometime after ten o'clock. His speech contained the standard themes of love, and injustice, but he

---

537 Taylor Branch, *Parting the Waters*, p. 461.
538 Arsenault, *Freedom Riders*, p. 237.
539 Taylor Branch, *Parting the Waters*, p. 461.
540 Ibid, p. 462.
541 Arsenault, *Freedom Riders*, pp. 236-237.
542 Taylor Branch, *Parting the Waters*, p. 462.
543 Arsenault, *Freedom Riders*, p. 237.

felt compelled to reprimand Governor Patterson for his treatment of the Freedom Riders. Outside the church, the National Guard, aided by the Montgomery police and Mann's highway patrolmen, dispersed the remaining mobs in the streets.[544]

A defiant Governor Patterson called Robert Kennedy to suggest that the president was responsible if harm should come to King:

> "Now you got what you wanted," he said heatedly. "You got yourself a fight. And you've got the National Guard called out, and martial law. And that's what you wanted." ... During their raging argument, Kennedy managed to ask whether the Negroes would be allowed to leave the stifling church building now that Patterson had everything under control. The governor replied that the National Guard could guarantee the safety of all the Negroes except for King. They could not guarantee King's safety. "I don't believe that, John," said Kennedy. "Have General Graham call me. I want him to say it to me. I want to hear a general of the United States Army say he can't protect Martin Luther King."[545]

Patterson screamed that Kennedy was missing the point— "You are destroying us politically," he said. "John, it's more important that these people in the church survive physically than for us to survive politically," Kennedy replied.[546]

Despite some uncertainty about their safety, most of those inside the church moved to the exits. However, National Guardsmen with drawn bayonets blocked the exits. Only King was allowed outside to negotiate with General Graham. King found him in no mood to move quickly.[547]

The first groups left the church at four thirty in the morning—in National Guard trucks.[548] By morning, however, there was quiet outside. Farmer recalled:

> Martial law had been declared and steel-helmeted Alabama National Guardsmen patrolled the streets in Jeeps, with rifles in hand. Occasional gunfire could be heard. A curfew was enforced, and we proceeded, with permission and under guard, to the various homes to which we had been assigned to freshen up.[549]

To the relief of both federal and state officials, the story that appeared in the newspapers later that morning gave the impression that, while the situation had been terrible, cooperation had prevented it from becoming much worse. An unfortunate confrontation had been averted in the interest of reestablishing civil order. This spin allowed the Kennedy Administration to maintain its public neutrality on the Freedom

---

544 Taylor Branch, *Parting the Waters*, pp. 462-463.
545 Ibid, pp. 464-465.
546 Ibid, p. 465.
547 Arsenault, *Freedom Riders*, p. 239.
548 Taylor Branch, *Parting the Waters*, p. 465.
549 Farmer, *Lay Bare the Heart*, p. 206.

INTO THE STORM

Rides—as Arsenault later observed, "sanctioning the legality but not the advisability of forcing the issue of desegregated transit."[550]

The students who had been the backbone of the Freedom Rides were of no mind to give up on King's strategy of coercive nonviolence. Moreover, they expected—and even demanded—King to continue what he had started. Farmer recalls this discussion the night after the crisis in Montgomery had passed:

> The next evening, we all met at the YMCA to take stock of the situation and plan our next steps. The SNCC and CORE youngsters were of one mind: the Freedom Ride would go on to Jackson and New Orleans. They asked King if he would go with them to Jackson. "No, I can't go. You see, I'm on probation from my arrest in Atlanta." The answer was not satisfactory to the youngsters. They scoffed at the matter of probation. "I'm on probation too," said one. "So am I," shouted another. "Me, too," someone else yelled.[551]

The students continued to pressure King: "What's your real reason? Why can't you go? You're the leader of this nonviolent movement. How can you stay home?"

The meeting broke up when many of the students stormed out of the room, scornfully referring to King as "de Lawd." They looked at Farmer for a cue as Doris Castle said:

> I motioned them to silence and they said nothing. I don't know what was going through Martin's mind at that time, but I know what was in mine. I was frankly terrified with the knowledge that the trip to Jackson might be the last trip any of us would ever take. I was not ready for that.[552]

Only the eyes and words of the teenager Doris Castle persuaded Farmer to get on the bus at the last minute.[553]

---

550 Arsenault, *Freedom Riders*, pp. 242-244.
551 Farmer, *Lay Bare the Heart*, pp. 206-207.
552 Ibid, p. 207.
553 Ibid, p. 202.

CHAPTER SEVEN

CASTRO ASSASSINATION PLOTS—1961

Many myths grew out of the CIA's long and unsuccessful program to assassinate Fidel Castro. In this chapter I will examine one of the most controversial myths in the history of the Agency's anti-Castro activities. This particular myth is associated with the provocative term "assassination capabilities" program. That term was sometimes used interchangeably with the phrase "Executive Action" program and accompanied by the CIA cryptonym **ZR/RIFLE**. The origin of an "assassination capabilities program" in the CIA became inexorably involved in one of the long-standing debates surrounding the assassination of President Kennedy: Did the Kennedy brothers collude in a CIA-Mafia plot to assassinate Fidel Castro?

According to the myth I am discussing, President Kennedy ordered the creation of an "assassination capabilities program" in the CIA shortly after his inauguration in January 1961. The president's order was allegedly promulgated in anticipation of the Bay of Pigs invasion. However, the origin of that false myth *began* as a desperate device by the then CIA Deputy Director of Plans (DDP) Richard Bissell to save *his* plan for the doomed invasion *and* his hope to succeed Allen Dulles as the Director of Central Intelligence (DCI).

This demonstrably false myth eventually *ended up* being the *cornerstone* of the controversial contention that the Kennedy brothers were behind a CIA plot to murder Castro. That argument, in turn, became *a key component in the coverup* of the Kennedy assassination.

Concealing the conspiracy to assassinate the President of the United States was just as challenging—if not more so—than the murder itself. Getting away with a crime of this magnitude presented the perpetrators with a broad set of requirements. The concealment of such an *ambitious conspiracy* required the creation of several *false conspiracies*. The purpose of these "false conspiracies" was to sow distraction, confusion, and mirages among overt and covert audiences. Both truth and fiction had to be carefully arranged in a *hierarchy of conspiracies*—without which the coverup would not endure the test of time.

Unraveling this arrangement is my task in this volume and the remainder of my multi-volume work on the Kennedy assassination. To do that, I need to establish some conventional terms of reference and offer the reader the following taxonomy for the coverup of President Kennedy's assassination.

The JFK Assassination—A Taxonomy of the Coverup

The coverup of the president's murder was carefully prepared well before the event itself. In the days immediately following the shooting in Dealey Plaza, both overt and covert components of the coverup were put into play. Overt is what the public sees; covert is what people with appropriate security clearances see. The overt component created a calming public spectacle by framing Oswald as a crazy lone nut with communist sympathies but no *direct* connection to a larger conspiracy. The covert component created a threatening top-secret crisis by framing Oswald as a witting agent of an international communist conspiracy.

The overt component was a messy but straight-forward *public* exhibition of fabricated evidence in Dealey Plaza. The covert component was an intricate secret "*need-to-know*" exhibition of fabricated evidence in Oswald's top-secret government files. The fabricated top-secret evidence was weaponized to create a frightening impression of an impending crisis: The U.S. was facing a possible nuclear war with the USSR because the FBI and CIA had failed to connect the dots in their secret files on Oswald. In this manner, our national security institutions were incentivized to cooperate in the unfolding coverup.

The symbiotic relationship of these false conspiracies in the overt and covert components of the coverup was an ingenious fit. The calming effect of the lone nut non-conspiratorial overt scenario—*itself part of the true conspiracy*—was the antidote for the false conspiratorial crisis scenario unfolding inside of the government. The key to the long-term success of the coverup was the continuing survival of the covert component of the plan. As long as the covert communist conspiratorial scenario remained viable, the feasibility of the overt lone nut (apparently) non-conspiratorial component became less important over time.

CASTRO ASSASSINATION PLOTS—1961

The importance of *the role that these discrete conspiracies played in the hierarchy of false conspiracies* cannot be overemphasized. In the long run, it didn't matter how many holes were poked in the Dealey Plaza scenario. The coverup of the *true conspiracy*—the Wizard of Oz cabal behind the curtain—was dependent on a continuing staunch defense of the covertly engineered false conspiracy: especially the RFK-Mafia myth. The permanence of that covert false conspiracy permitted the dismissal of the less important fabricated evidence in Dealey Plaza as a *benign* conspiracy to save America.

How that plan was accomplished is the subject of this chapter and Chapters Nine, Ten, and Fifteen. In a nutshell, this was the plan: An international communist conspiracy to assassinate President Kennedy was the result of the Kennedy brothers' collusion in a plan to assassinate Fidel Castro. The key element in the plan was this ominous false scenario: Robert Kennedy got his brother killed and almost started World War III. A secret RFK-Mafia plot to assassinate Castro was turned around by Fidel and—with an assist by the KGB—used to assassinate President Kennedy instead.

The alleged involvement of the Kennedy brothers' collusion in Castro assassination plotting is the indispensable and inseparable foundation for the false international communist conspiracy scenario. To prevent the deaths of forty million Americans in a thermonuclear war, the *apparent* Castro-Kremlin role in the Kennedy assassination *had* to be suppressed by Chief Justice Earl Warren at the secret level. Today, this permits the CIA to characterize that suppression by the Warren Commission as a *benign* but necessary conspiracy to save us all.

Therefore, as these complicated components of the hierarchy of false conspiracies evolved over the last fifty years, it is not at all surprising that the Kennedy brothers' alleged participation in Castro assassination plotting has become *even more important* than the issue of whether the manufactured evidence in Dealey Plaza points to a conspiracy.

So, in recent years, a peculiar new paradigm of *benign* conspiracy has emerged. That paradigm goes something like this: *If* the Kennedy assassination was a conspiracy, *then* the Kennedy brothers were themselves to blame. And so, today, many mainstream observers, researchers, and authors have become inescapably attracted to the view that a Kennedy involvement in Castro assassination plots is the reason that President Kennedy was assassinated.

However, the Kennedy collusion subterfuge brought an element of risk with it. Baking Kennedy collusion into Castro assassination plotting left this otherwise cunning coverup with an Achilles heel: The demonstrably false RFK narrative had to be left in the open. Take it away and the role of both brothers vanishes with it, the nakedness of the emperor is exposed, and the light of truth illuminates one of the worst disasters ever to befall the American republic.

And so, I will proceed to the task at hand. I want to begin by taking the reader back to the starting point—the moment when it became tactically necessary to lay the creation of the CIA's Executive Action program at the feet of President Kennedy.

Bissell's Allegation that the President Ordered the Creation of an Executive Action Capability in the CIA

There is a large collection of CIA documents in the NARA RIF (National Archives and Records Administration Record Identification Form) system referred to simply as "DDP (Deputy Director of Plans) Files." They are copies of documents that, at one point or another, came to be filed in the covert directorate (DDP) of the CIA. In volume II (Chapter Sixteen), I mentioned a particularly significant seven-page document from this collection that bears the title "Highly Sensitive Activities."[554] That document has no date and no signature or component revealing the author or office responsible for its creation. However, the Church Committee obtained a nine-page version of this document and concluded that it was from the CIA Inspector General's (IG) office.[555] A comparison to the IG *Report on Plots to Assassinate Fidel Castro* confirms—in structure and content—that this "Highly Sensitive Activities" document was a partial early draft of the IG Report.[556] However, by the time the IG Report was finally published, the extraordinary opening section of this draft was missing.

The opening section of the early IG draft is entitled "Project **ZR/RIFLE**." The *second sentence* of the first paragraph informs us—*as does the final IG Report*—that the **ZR/RIFLE** cryptonym referred to the CIA's "Executive Action Program"—a highly sensitive stand-by program for assassinations. However, the *first sentence* of that paragraph informs us about something that did *not* make it into the IG Report:

> *Early in the Kennedy Administration, the "White House" urged* [DDP] *Richard Bissell to create an Executive Action capability; i.e., a general stand-by capability to carry out assassinations.* [Emphasis added]

This sentence captured my interest the moment I laid eyes on it. The quotation marks used in this sentence reflect a crucial and unexplained uncertainty about the use of the term "White House." Based upon several other declassified documents that I was familiar with, I realized straight away that the first sentence of this memo was a deliberate deception. Such deceits about CIA operations—especially a highly sensitive program for assassinations—are not spun for amusement.

---

554   00/00/00, CIA blind memorandum, "Highly Sensitive Activities," RIF 104-10310-10259.
555   See 6/9/75, Richard Bissell SSCIA Testimony, p. 48; RIF 157-10011 10020.
556   5/23/67, CIA IG Report, RIF 104-10213-10101.

It would take more than a decade to unravel the truth about who was behind the false claim in that first sentence (see inset above). As I will shortly demonstrate, the originator of the claim that the Kennedy "White House" urged Bissell to create an Executive Action capability was Bissell himself. Crucially, the first sentence of the early draft was missing when the IG Report was finally published, and had been replaced with this:

> *We cannot overemphasize* the extent to which responsible Agency officers felt themselves subject to *the Kennedy Administration's severe pressures* to do something about Castro and his regime. *The fruitless and, in retrospect, often unrealistic plotting should be viewed in that light.*[557] [Emphasis added]

In their final report, the IG drafters did not include *what they knew* about Bissell's desperate campaign to convince William Harvey that the president ordered the creation of a stand-by assassination capability. While the IG's handling of this sensitive subject managed to keep the lid on Bissell's pressures ploy in 1967, the Church Committee removed it for good in 1975.

What I will refer to in this volume as Bissell's *White House pressures ploy* began in early 1961, when he presented it as a fact to William Harvey. Bissell told Harvey that the president had twice directed him to establish an assassination capabilities program in the CIA. Harvey was a former FBI agent. Later, he had worked for the CIA as Chief of the Berlin Operations Base (BOB). Early in the Kennedy Administration, Harvey was chief of the super-secret CIA component—Staff D—that broke into foreign embassies to steal cipher codes for the National Security Agency (NSA).

Curiously, at the time DDP Bissell approached Harvey about White House pressure to create an Executive Action capability, Bissell knew that such a capability already existed in Staff D!

We cannot be certain whether Bissell's memory about a presidential directive for an assassination program had begun to conveniently lapse by the time of the IG Report. That might explain why Bissell's claim had been deleted from the final IG Report. Either way, we can be certain that by the time of Bissell's first deposition with the Church Committee in 1975, his memory about the president's alleged orders had gone up in smoke. At that moment, however, someone else had seized upon that false story. Someone else appropriated that story as the cornerstone of a much larger false narrative about the Kennedy brothers. That false narrative has survived to the present day. That someone was Samuel Halpern. I will shortly get to his interest in Bissell's White House pressures ploy.

---

557 Ibid, p. 4.

INTO THE STORM

When Did the ZR/RIFLE Program Really Begin?

The CIA plan to use the Mafia to assassinate Castro was put into motion in August of 1960, when DDP Bissell asked the Security Office to locate an asset to perform a "gangster-type operation."[558] Moreover, as I pointed out in Volume II, the first use of the CIA cryptonym **ZR/RIFLE** for Executive Action did not take place during the Kennedy presidency. **The ZR/RIFLE** documentary trail began on 13 October 1960—more than three weeks before Kennedy's victory in the presidential election on 8 November. In mid-October 1960, Bissell decided to activate the Executive Action program inside of William Harvey's Staff D.[559]

Here, I will briefly summarize the evolution of the Agency's campaign to assassinate Castro. CIA Director of Security Sheffield Edwards, with Bissell present, briefed DCI Allen Dulles and his deputy, General Charles Cabell, on their plan to use the syndicate to assassinate Castro. The discussion was circumspect, and Edwards was careful to avoid the use of any "bad words."[560] All present for this dark tryst in the director's office knew and observed the unwritten rules for how authorization was obtained for highly sensitive covert operations. Harvey said he was certain that the way the deniability system worked was that no one would sully the president with "the complete, dirty-handed details" of the assassination plans.[561] In his deposition to the Church Committee, Harvey's Executive Assistant, Sam Halpern, offered this explanation:

> I wouldn't expect the president to sign a piece of paper directing an assassination for any reason. ... I don't think you are going to find a piece of paper for everything this Agency (CIA) or any other agency has done.
> *There are lots of things that get done by word of mouth.*[562] [Emphasis added]

Halpern added that the knowledge of, and the directive for, any assassination was accomplished by word of mouth—it was "all oral." As we will see in Chapters Nine and Fifteen, Halpern made opportunistic use of the "no documentation" device. That stratagem came in handy for Halpern's pet theory about an alleged RFK assassination plot against Castro.

---

558   Church Committee Index card, RE the 23 May 1975 testimony of former CIA Director William Colby; see also, 5/21/75 William Colby SSCIA Testimony, pp. 21-22; RIF 157-0011-10024.
559   Ibid. We know from Harvey's now infamous handwritten notes that he met with Sydney Gottlieb (Bissell's Special Assistant) and Arnold Silver (Harvey's deputy)—before Kennedy's inauguration—to discuss his ideas on how to create a successful, secure Executive Action capability. See Undated CIA "Table of Contents," from the Russell Holmes Work Files, RIF 104-10431-10050. There are eleven items listed in the Table of Contents that are also attached. Item 10 is titled, "Nine pages of notes in draft regarding **ZR/RIFLE** Project." We know from a 6/25/75 deposition William Harvey gave to the Church Committee that the last two pages are Harvey's handwriting, and that the handwriting for the first seven pages belongs to Harvey's Operations Chief, Arnold Silver. See pp. 9-10 and 51-56, RIF 157-10002-10105.
560   The CIA IG Report, pp. 17-18, RIF 1994.03.08.14:54:36:690005.
561   6/25/75, William Harvey deposition to the Church Committee, p. 80, RIF 157-10002-10106.
562   6/18/75, Sam Halpern deposition to the Church Committee, pp. 54-55, RIF 157-10002-10087.

CASTRO ASSASSINATION PLOTS—1961

According to CIA asset Robert Maheu, from the beginning, Chicago mob boss Sam Giancana played a key role in the evolving assassination plot. Giancana's part was to find someone inside Castro's entourage to slip poison pills into his food.[563] At first, the CIA had envisaged a typical gangland-style killing in which Castro would be "gunned down." Giancana refused. He pointed out that no one would sign up to do that because the chance of survival and escape would be negligible. So, Giancana argued that a lethal pill in Castro's food or drink would work best.

According to an 18 October 1960 FBI report from Director Hoover to DDP Bissell, Giancana had bragged in front of one of his girlfriends and her sister that he had taken care of the matter. According to an FBI informant close to Giancana, the latter had revealed to Phyllis McGuire and her sister Christine Teeter that Castro was to be killed very shortly:

> When doubt was expressed regarding this statement Giancana reportedly assured those present that Castro's assassination would occur in November. Moreover, he allegedly indicated that he has already met with the assassin-to-be on three occasions, the last meeting taking place on a boat docked at the Fontainbleau Hotel in Miami Beach, Florida. Reportedly, Giancana claimed that everything has been perfected for the killing of Castro and that the "assassin" had arranged with a girl, not further described, to drop a "pill" in some drink or food of Castro's.[564]

Christine's husband, John Teeter, quickly reported the incident to the FBI. While Hoover relayed this indiscretion to Bissell, at this point the FBI director had no idea that the CIA was behind Giancana's plot. Dulles and Bissell were content to leave it that way, and the FBI would not find out about the Agency's involvement until the McGuire wiretap incident in Las Vegas went viral in the spring of 1962.[565] Like ships passing in the night, the FBI was as blind to the CIA-Mafia plot as the CIA was to the Giancana-Campbell-JFK triangle.

The CIA-Mafia plot to assassinate Castro by poisoning was to be carried out by June Cobb's boss in Havana, Juan Orta Cordova. Santo Trafficante ("Joe, the courier") often travelled to and from Cuba and had been in touch with Juan Orta, the then Director General of the Office of Prime Minister Castro. Orta had become increasingly disaffected with Castro's extreme measures and the communization of Cuba. As the plot evolved in the fall of 1960, the alienation between Orta and Castro reached the breaking point.

---

563 7/29/75 Maheu deposition to the Church Committee, pp. 18-19, and 34, RIF 157-10011-10047.
564 10/18/60 Hoover Memorandum to CIA Director, Attn: Deputy Director of Plans, RIF 104-10102-10105.
565 3/6/67 FBI Memorandum to the Attorney General, Subject: Central Intelligence Agency's Intentions to Send Hoodlums to Cuba to Assassinate Castro, RIF 124-10278-10288.

INTO THE STORM

According to the 1967 CIA IG Report, the gangsters incorrectly interpreted this positively. They thought this meant Orta would be especially motivated to accept the task. Orta, they told the CIA, had been receiving kickbacks from their gambling interests, but had lost that source of income, and was therefore in need of money.[566] However, Orta lost his position in Castro's office on 26 January 1961—six days after Kennedy's inauguration. Nonetheless, planning for Orta's use in the assassination operation was still ongoing in Miami and Washington. When the mob finally did get the pills to Orta in February 1961, he returned them within two weeks. Orta eventually sought asylum in the Venezuelan Embassy.

With Orta out of the picture, Santo Trafficante soon approached his long-time associate Antonio Varona to handle the job of poisoning Castro. As fate would have it, the CIA plan called for Varona to become the new president of Cuba after the invasion. Already involved in a scheme to help the mob restore its former gambling, prostitution, and narcotics activities in a post-Castro Cuba, Varona was happy to oblige Trafficante.[567]

In late February 1961, as JFK listened to his advisors describing their plans for the Bay of Pigs invasion, Varona sent word to the head of his new Rescate Movement in Cuba, Alberto Cruz Caso, asking him to send someone trustworthy to Miami. Cruz selected Varona's old friend Rodolfo Leon Curbelo.[568] On 12 March 1961, the CIA provided Trafficante with the poison capsules. Subsequently, just under five weeks before the Bay of Pigs, Varona gave the capsules to Curbelo, along with instructions for using the Rescate team in Havana to carry out the plot.

Curbelo returned to Havana and delivered the capsules to Cruz Caso and Maria Leopoldina Grau Alsina (the niece of former Cuban President Ramon Grau San Martin; CIA cryptonym: **AMCOG-2**). These two put a plan in motion to assassinate Castro at a restaurant that he frequented. They were told to wait until Varona gave the "green light" to carry out the plot. However, as fate would have it, Varona and the rest of the exile leadership were placed in seclusion for the security of the Bay of Pigs invasion. Varona *would therefore be unable to give the green light,* and the poison pills would not be placed in Castro's food.[569] There was great irony for Bissell in how these events played out in Cuba and I will return to them shortly.

---

566 5/23/67, CIA IG Report, pp. 24-25; RIF 104-10057-10270.
567 5/23/67, CIA IG Report, pp. 29-32.
568 Escalante, Fabian, ***The Secret War: CIA Covert Operations Against Cuba, 1959-62*** (New York: Ocean Press, 1995), pp. 84-86.
569 *Alleged Assassination Plots Involving Foreign Leaders*, United States Senate, Interim Report of the Select Committee to Study Governmental Operations (Washington DC: US Government Printing Office, 1975), p. 82. Hereafter referred to as SSCIA Interim Report. Escalante, *The Secret War*, p. 85.

Bissell's False Story about Whose Idea it Was to Hire the Mob for the Job in the First Place

The present chapter is focused principally on Bissell's false claim that the president ordered the creation of the Executive Action program. Bissell had a habit of making false claims. Another example was his claim about whose idea it was to hire the mob for the job to kill Castro. In Chapter Fourteen of Volume II, I laid out a very detailed recapitulation of how Bissell attempted to conceal the fact that the idea to hire the mob for the job was *his*. I will repeat a short version of that subject here.

Bissell testified to the Church Committee that the idea of using the mob originated with Western Hemisphere Division Chief J.C. King. Bissell insisted that he, Bissell, only asked the Security Director, Sheffield Edwards, to locate *someone* who could assassinate Castro. However, Bissell's version of that chain of events is contradicted by J. C. King. The 1967 CIA Inspector General's (IG) Report states that King said he did not know about the plot until mid-1962.[570]

In his deposition to the Church Committee, former DCI William Colby (1973-1976) told the committee that CIA documents indicated that in August 1960 *Bissell asked Edwards* to locate an asset to perform a "gangster-type operation."[571] Bissell's version of events is also contradicted by the first internal CIA investigation of the mob plot conducted in 1966 by then Security Director Howard Osborn:

> In August 1960, *Mr. Richard M. Bissell approached* [Director of Security] *Colonel Sheffield Edwards* to determine if the Office of Security had assets that may assist in a sensitive mission requiring gangster-type action. *The mission target was the liquidation of Fidel Castro.* Because of its extreme sensitivity, only a small group was made privy to the project. The DCI [Allen Dulles] was briefed and gave his approval.[572] [Emphasis added]

The 1967 CIA Inspector General's Report agrees with the Osborn memorandum about whose idea it was to hire the mob:

> *Richard Bissell, Deputy Director for Plans, asked Sheffield Edwards*, Director of Security, if Edwards could establish contact with the U.S. gambling syndicate that was active in Cuba. The objective clearly was the assassination of Castro although Edwards claims that there was a studied avoidance of the term in his conversation with Bissell.[573] [Emphasis added]

---

570 5/23/67, CIA IG Report, p. 14; RIF 104-10057-10270.
571 Church Committee Index card, RE the 23 May 1975 testimony of former CIA Director William Colby.
572 6/24/66, Howard J. Osborne, Director of Security, Memorandum for the Deputy Director of Central Intelligence. RIF 104-10122-10218.
573 5/23/67, CIA IG Report, p. 14; RIF 104-10213-10101.

When Bissell wrote his memoir in 1996, he changed his story. J. C. King was no longer said to be the originator of the idea; instead, Bissell blamed it on Edwards. Bissell wrote that the idea did not originate with him as "some authors and historians claimed it did."[574] The problem with that statement is that it is at odds with both of the internal CIA studies—the Office of Security (Osborn) report that handled the operation and the Inspector General's Report that looked into the matter.

Authors and historians did not invent that story. Bissell invented it to conceal his own role in getting the CIA-mob plot moving. But that subterfuge was only the beginning of Bissell's deceptions.

With the complicated context in the above two sections in mind, I now return to Bissell's White House pressures ploy.

Bissell's Amnesia About President Kennedy's Alleged Order to Create an Executive Action Program

On 25 June 1975, William Harvey was deposed by the Church Committee. Harvey testified that in February 1961—a few weeks after the inauguration of President Kennedy—he received the following request from DDP Richard Bissell:

> *I have been charged by the White House with the development of an Executive Action capability.* Will you please survey it and see what you can do about it and tell me what you can do about it.[575] [Emphasis added]

Harvey testified that at that time (early 1961) Bissell told him *on more than one occasion* that the White House urged him to create an Executive Action capability in the CIA:

> In the first instance, which would have been, as best I can reconstruct, late January or early February, although my memory is somewhat later than that, in 1961, it was that on either more than one or on two occasions, the White House had been quite insistent that—to him [Bissell]—that *the Agency develop a capability for Executive Action.*[576] [Emphasis added]

There seems to be no more than a normal questioning of memory by Harvey—he was not pleading any significant, let alone total, absence of memory. In my view, given the number of occasions that Bissell brought up the subject *and* the magnitude of

---

574   Richard Bissell, **Reflections of a Cold Warrior** (New Haven: Yale University Press, 1996), p. 157.
575   6/25/75, William Harvey SSCIA Testimony, p. 44; RIF 157-10002-10105. Two months earlier, in an interview in his home with David Belin of the Church Committee, Harvey said the date of Bissell's comment was a year later—in February 1962! See, 4/10/75, David Belin Interview with William K. Harvey, pp. 37-44; RIF 157-10005-10169. It is not surprising that Harvey, a notorious drunk, had a foggy memory. Fortunately, by the time of his first deposition he had familiarized himself with the record and was sufficiently sober to get his story straight.
576   Ibid, p. 77.

importance associated with such a high-level charge from the Kennedys, there seems to be no compelling reason to doubt Harvey's sworn testimony.

The problem with all of this is Harvey's good memory and Bissell's bad memory about the same events—with the president's role hanging in the balance. On 9 June 1975, just two weeks before Harvey's testimony, Bissell had been deposed by the Church Committee. During his testimony, this bizarre exchange took place:

> Senator Baker: Now this memo [IG Report] ... alleges the "White House" laid a requirement on you for an assassination capability and that it was in connection with the Castro situation. ... Is that true or untrue?
>
> Mr. Bissell: *As far as I know* that is true, sir.
>
> Senator Baker: Who in the White House?
>
> Mr. Bissell: *I don't know*, this could have been Bundy?
>
> Senator Baker: Well, was it?
>
> Mr. Bissell: *I don't remember.*
>
> Senator Baker: Was it someone in the White House?
>
> Mr. Bissell: It obviously must have been, but *I don't remember of* [sic] *my own memory.*

At this point in Bissell's deposition, committee Chairman Church became suspicious:

> The Chairman [Senator Church]: May I just take up here? When was this? When were you asked to develop this assassination capability which became known as **ZR/RIFLE**?
>
> Mr. Bissell: Mr. Chairman, I would have to go back to the text that the senator has just read [from the IG Report] for the date.
>
> Senator Baker: I'm sorry. I did not hear you.
>
> Mr. Bissell: I said I'd have to take the date from that [IG Report].
>
> The Chairman [Senator Church]: In early 1961, after Kennedy had become president?
>
> Mr. Bissell: Yes.
>
> The Chairman: And to the best of your recollection, it was McGeorge Bundy who asked you to do this?
>
> Mr. Bissell: I can't say to the best of my recollection on this because *I don't remember receiving the request.*

In disbelief, Senator Church bored in on Bissell's strange lapse of memory:

> The Chairman: You don't remember receiving the request?
>
> Mr. Bissell: *I don't remember it,* although I think in that document [IG Report] it is quoted from Mr. Harvey who in turn quotes me as saying at the time I had received the request. In fact, I think what this document

says, if I remember my reading of it correctly, it says I told Harvey that I had twice been requested by the White House.

The Chairman: *Well, if you had been twice requested by the White House to develop a capability to assassinate, isn't it strange that you wouldn't remember?*

Mr. Bissell: *Well perhaps it is, but that is the case.* I remember—please understand, I remember talking to Mr. Harvey about this and assigning him the task. *I don't remember a specific request from the White House.* … What I am saying now is I remember assigning Harvey the task of undertaking the **ZR/RIFLE** project in just the [mat]ter stated here. *I do not have any recollection of a specific conversation with anybody in the White House as to the origin of that request.* I did read in the document [IG Report] that Harvey quoted me at the time as saying I have been asked to do this by the White House. I have no reason to believe that Harvey's quote is wrong. *If* I said it at the time, presumably it's true. I'm not denying it in any sense. *But I do not remember specific conversations.*[577]

[Emphasis added]

On *six* separate occasions in as many minutes, Bissell claimed that he had no memory of receiving any request from the Kennedy White House about establishing a capability for assassination.

Close examination of Bissell's unforgettable performance that day suggests that a principal concern was to *avoid perjuring himself.* That, in turn, corroborates Harvey's description of events: that Bissell *had* told Harvey—*before* the Bay of Pigs—that he had twice been pressured by the White House to create an Executive Action capability. Moreover, Bissell's six-fold denial of any memory about these White House pressures suggests that they probably never happened.

And so, we are left with a high probability that Bissell lied to Harvey about pressures from the White House—*just as Bissell had earlier concocted a false story about who first proposed hiring the Mafia to assassinate Castro.* The committee suspected that Bissell's amnesia during his first deposition about the alleged White House order required further investigation. The key parties involved in this controversy—Harvey, Bissell, and the president's national security advisor, McGeorge Bundy—had to be deposed multiple times; and they also found it necessary to confer with each other. Only after all of that was the committee finally able to establish *who said what to whom.*

When Bissell appeared before the committee on 17 and 22 July 1975, he *retracted* his claim that President Kennedy told him to create an Executive Action project: "His testimony, given in light of information obtained since his earlier appearances, was

---

577 6/9/75, Richard Bissell SSCIA Testimony, pp. 48-51; RIF 157-10011-10020.

that *there was no White House urging* for the creation of the Executive Action project."[578] In Chapter Thirteen, I will revisit the tortured path by which the committee finally extracted the truth from Bissell about his White House pressures tale. At the end of several weeks of depositions to sort out the facts, the committee's investigation established that *an Executive Action capability had neither been requested by the president nor discussed with him.*

What Was the Motive for Bissell's Deception?

This question needs to be answered and I believe it *can* be answered with confidence. By the time Kennedy was in the White House, Bissell was desperate for a miracle. Here, from Bissell's perspective, are some of the reasons why:

- Bissell was personally responsible for the Bay of Pigs plan—a plan in tatters and that appeared to be doomed by early 1961.
- Bissell was desperate for a Hail Mary option to save the plan and his political future.
- The *only* option that might have had a chance to save the day appeared to be the assassination of Fidel Castro.
- The *only* active scheme to kill Castro was the Mafia plot that Bissell himself had been shepherding since August 1960.
- Besides the Security Office, the *only other* action element in the Agency for that plot was Harvey's super-secret Staff D.

Presumably, Bissell calculated that if Harvey was convinced that the new president was secretly serious about assassinating Castro, then the gun-toting king of luncheon martinis might be motivated to help make it happen.

Many years later in a 1998 interview, CIA officer Sam Halpern finally grasped how crucially important the assassination of Castro would have been for Bissell's imperiled Bay of Pigs invasion. Without an assassination, the chances of a successful invasion were nil:

> I think Bissell really thought he had a deal going on an assassination plot of some kind. It makes *no sense* that all these things [problems with the plan] wouldn't bother him ... *that whole story—makes no sense at all without an assassination plot in the background.*[579] [Emphasis added]

---

578 SSCIA Interim Report (*Alleged Assassination Plots Involving Foreign Leaders*), p. 184.
579 4/7/98, CIA Study of Intelligence, Sam Halpern Interview by Brian Latell and Michael Warner, pp. 5-6; RIF 104-10324-10000.

As I mentioned above, it was Bissell's idea in the first place to use the Mafia to assassinate Castro.

Bissell still had hopes for Castro's assassination on his mind as the bitter end approached. In his memoir, he offered this recollection:

> No doubt as I moved forward with plans for the brigade [invasion], *I hoped the Mafia would achieve success.* My philosophy during my last two or three years in the Agency was very definitely that *the end justified the means, and I was not going to be held back.* Shortly after I left the CIA, however, I came to believe that it had been a great mistake to involve the Mafia in an assassination attempt. ...These were people who were not subject to any kind of security control by the Agency, and they posed a great risk.[580] [Emphasis added]

And so, Bissell refused to call off the invasion—even though the plan's task force chief (Jacob Esterline) and the paramilitary chief (Jack Hawkins) had both pleaded with him to do so *and* tendered their resignations.

For Bissell, *much more than his position as the DDP* was riding on the success or failure of the Bay of Pigs invasion. In early 1961, Under Secretary of State Chester Bowles wanted Bissell to accept the position of Under Secretary of State for Political Affairs. Bissell got an appointment with Secretary of State Rusk to talk about it, and Rusk said he would be delighted if Bissell served in that position. Afterward, Bissell spoke with the president. Kennedy told Bissell it would be best if he remained in his job as the CIA Deputy Director of Plans.[581] Kennedy had let it be known that Bissell would be replacing Dulles as DCI in July 1961.[582] It was "no great secret," Bissell wrote in his memoir, that JFK "viewed me as Dulles' successor."[583]

The Cruel Irony of Bissell's Personal Defeat

Clearly, nothing less than Bissell's future chance to become the Director of Central Intelligence was at stake. This single fact explains a lot about Bissell's flawed judgement. In his mind at the time, Castro's assassination *before* the exile landing was the only card left in the deck and the only person able to play that card appeared to be Harvey. Having accepted that the ends justified the means, Bissell lied to Harvey. Bissell fabricated his story about a presidential order at the first possible opportunity—immediately

---

580 Richard Bissell, **Reflections of a Cold Warrior**, p. 157.
581 Ibid, p. 192.
582 David Talbot, **The Devil's Chessboard—Allen Dulles, the CIA, and the Rise of America's Secret Government** (New York: Harper Collins, 1015), p. 400.
583 Richard Bissell, **Reflections of a Cold Warrior**, p. 192.

after Kennedy's inauguration. Did Bissell hope that a scenario without Castro might improve the odds that JFK would approve U.S. intervention to save the lives of the doomed brigade on the beachhead? We will never know the answer to that question.

There is great irony in how events played out in Cuba. I believe it is safe to say that Bissell did not know the exact details of the gangster plot after the Orta plan fell through. If Bissell *had* known, he would *never* have allowed Varona to be put in a situation that would prevent him from signaling the restaurant in Havana where the assassination was to take place. Bissell had *not* foreseen this, Varona did *not* give the green light, and the poison pills were *not* placed in Castro's food.[584]

So, Bissell's plot to assassinate Castro crashed and burned. The brigade exiles who were not massacred on the beachhead ended up in prison. As Dulles had cleverly planned (see Volume II, pp. 402-403), Bissell was left holding the bag. Bissell would *not* become the DCI. He would not even keep his job as the DDP. Bissell's friendship with John Kennedy was ruined. Bissell's career came to an ignominious end.

Bissell had not felt constrained to avoid telling lies and manipulating others. His lie about whose idea it was to use the Mafia to assassinate Castro and his lie that JFK had ordered an assassination capability were only two examples of his lack of moral character. Even when the Bay of Pigs invasion was still in its planning stage between the outgoing and incoming administrations, Bissell's questionable ethics led him to lie to his friend, John Kennedy. In November 1960, DCI Dulles took Bissell to Florida to brief the president-elect on the Cuban operation. At that meeting, knowing that the so-called inevitable uprising of Cubans against Castro concomitant with the invasion would not happen, Bissell told Kennedy that it would.

None of Bissell's lies resulted from a dislike, let alone a hatred, for John Kennedy. But his selfish interests had long term consequences that he could not have foreseen. His last lie was his worst lie. Bissell could never have imagined that his whopper about a presidential order to establish an Executive Action capability would ultimately fall into the hands of a CIA staff officer who held nothing but hatred for the Kennedy brothers. Bissell could never have imagined that his last lie would be used to deprecate his former friend John Kennedy in perpetuity. Bissell could never have imagined that the CIA would carry on his Mafia plot to assassinate Castro, lie to Attorney General Robert Kennedy that it had been terminated, and then continue the operation *against* the AG's orders and behind his back.

And, finally, Bissell could never have imagined that Sam Halpern would lie to the Agency and to the world that RFK had waged a secret Mafia campaign to assassinate Castro. All of these unforeseen events would come to pass. Did Bissell ever wonder, had

---

584   SSCIA Interim Report, p. 82. Escalante, *The Secret War*, p. 85.

it not been for his idea to use the mob to kill Castro, that this tragic outcome might have been avoided?

Epilogue: Senator Church's Challenge to Bissell about an Executive Action Capability Already Being in Place

Here, I will shift the reader's focus forward fourteen years hence. At that point, all of the plots and all of the lies described above were investigated and published by the Church Committee. As we refocus on that crucial period of time, we need to be mindful of the opportunistic CIA staff officer, Samuel Halpern, into whose hands those revelations would fall.

Senator Church was skeptical about the White House pressures yarn foisted on Harvey by Bissell. As a result, during Bissell's 9 June 1975 deposition, Church steered the former DDP into this sand trap:

> The Chairman: Now even if we were to accept that testimony ... that there must have been a conversation with someone in the White House who asked you to create a capability to assassinate, when that request was made *you had personal knowledge that you had the capability but [also] that attempts were underway.*
> Mr. Bissell: Had been underway, *yes, sir.*
> The Chairman: *Had been underway.*
> Mr. Bissell: *Correct.*
> The Chairman: And were underway.
> Mr. Bissell: *Yes. Yes, sir.*

Having exacted that admission from Bissell three times, Senator Church delivered the coup-de-grâce:

> The Chairman: You knew that you not only had the capability, but attempts had been underway and were underway at the moment. *Didn't you tell that to the White House?*
> Mr. Bissell: *I do not have a recollection of so doing,* and you must remember that I had a great deal of doubt as to the effectiveness of that capability.
> The Chairman: Well, that is something else again. ...*It just seems to me so strange* that if the White House did in fact say to you, "Mr. Bissell, develop a capability for assassination which we may or may not exercise at some future date," and you didn't say, "Well, we already have it." After all, you must be aware of the assassination attempts that are presently underway. *I can't understand why you would keep that matter concealed in the face of a direct request by the White House to develop a capability.* ...To the best

of your recollection, then, you did not disclose the ongoing attempts in your conversation with the White House when you were requested to develop a capability?

Mr. Bissell: That is correct.[585] [Emphasis added]

Senator Church obviously knew the truth—the CIA began to engineer an assassination capability directed at Castro in the summer of 1960, during the party nominating conventions for the presidential election.

Moreover, that truth also meant that ultimately there could be no certainty about concealing the extensive history of the **ZR/RIFLE** program from the incoming Kennedy Administration. The large numbers of CIA and FBI personnel who had been involved in the CIA-Mob plot to assassinate Castro—not to mention the large number of other law enforcement personnel and social circles surrounding Giancana—made it inevitable that the Kennedy brothers would eventually discover what had been going on. And when Attorney General Robert Kennedy finally found out, he was infuriated.

Postscript: RFK Was "Johnny at the rathole on everything"

In the beginning of this chapter, I mentioned that the Church Committee had to go to great lengths to get the truth out of Bissell—that the president had *not* ordered the creation of an Executive Action program and that *no one* had asked him to do so. I also mentioned that Sam Halpern had no inkling about Bissell's White House pressures ploy until the committee's investigation uncovered it. In Chapters Nine, Ten, and Thirteen, I will trace the history of Halpern's campaign to build upon Bissell's ruse—*without once mentioning Bissell's confession that it had never happened*—by incorporating it into a thirty-year campaign to defame RFK.

After the Bay of Pigs, Halpern would sardonically state, Robert Kennedy was *Johnny at the rathole on everything*.[586] The converse was true. As we will see, on all things Cuban, Sam Halpern was actually *Johnny at the rathole*.

---

585   6/9/75, Richard Bissell SSCIA Testimony, pp. 52-53; RIF 157-10011-10020.
586   4/7/98, CIA Center for the Study of Intelligence, Sam Halpern Interview by Brian Latell and Michael Warner, p. 22; RIF 104-10324-10000.

CHAPTER EIGHT

KGB-CIA SPY WARS 1952-1961

In my 1995 work ***Oswald and the CIA***, I examined the possibility that CIA Counterintelligence Chief James Jesus Angleton *might* have orchestrated the dispatch of Oswald to the USSR as a provocation—a "dangle"—to help surface a KGB mole in the CIA. I now believe the case for a false Oswald defection is much stronger than I realized in 1995. I recently discovered—and reported in Volume II (***Countdown to Darkness***, Chapter One)—that America's most accomplished intelligence sleuth, Tennent "Pete" Bagley, concluded that Oswald was a *witting* false defector. I will return to that revelation at the end of Chapter Twelve.

Oswald's 1959 defection in Moscow ignited an intense new chapter in the battle between American and Soviet counterintelligence components. In the midst of the moles, mysteries, and ghosts of those KGB-CIA spy wars we find a small but critical pawn on the Cold War chessboard: Lee Harvey Oswald. The espionage and counterintelligence games taking place from 1952 to 1964 are the *essential* backdrop that enables us to understand Oswald's journey during that intense time.

The implications of Oswald's false defection fundamentally affect our understanding of Oswald's behavior: his service in Japan; his reason for leaving the Marines; his 31 October 1959 defection in Moscow; his 1962 re-defection to the U.S.; his 1963 attempt to defect again to the USSR; and his presence in Dealey Plaza on the President Kennedy was assassinated.

In this chapter, I will explore the origins of the espionage games in which the young Oswald became ensnared. In Chapter Twelve, I will examine the activation of an extraordinary disinformation provocation against the CIA. That operation was the

INTO THE STORM

brainchild of Major General Oleg Mikhailovich Gribanov, the chief of Counterintelligence in the KGB Second Chief Directorate. Gribanov assigned a minor officer from his Department 14—responsible for mounting penetrations of foreign intelligence services—to Geneva, Switzerland. That man would *forever* play a central role in the investigation of the assassination of President Kennedy: At the end of May 1962, Yuri Nosenko volunteered to spy for the CIA.

Even to this day, the Nosenko saga remains an enigma. It is still nurtured by devoted descendants of that distant epic duel of Cold War espionage. Unscrambling the nonsense with which Nosenko infected the CIA is impossible without a *clear* understanding of the origins of the espionage games that erupted after Oswald's defection in October 1959.

KGB-CIA Spy Wars: Key Source Materials

In addition to gleaning scraps of information from disparate sources, in this chapter I will be working primarily from the following five important sources:

- William Hood's 1983 book, **Mole**
- The Dave Murphy, Sergey Kondrashev, George Bailey 1997 book, **Battleground Berlin**
- Pete Bagley's 2007 book, **Spy Wars**
- Pete Bagley's 2013 book, **Spymaster**
- Pete Bagley's 2014 essay, **Ghosts of the Spy Wars**

In doing research for their landmark book **Battleground Berlin**, authors David Murphy, Sergey Kondrashev and George Bailey consulted extensively with Major General Valentin Vladimirovich Zvezdenkov, the KGB officer primarily responsible for the KGB aspects of the Popov case both in Karlshorst, Germany and in Moscow.

Bill Hood was a career CIA staff officer and one of the four men in the CIA's Vienna station that handled the GRU (Soviet military intelligence) defector Pyotr Popov from 1952 to 1957. The CIA initially declined to approve Hood's 1983 Popov biography, but eventually agreed to the publication—if pseudonyms were substituted for the true names of the CIA officers involved.

The remaining authors in the above list did not have to work under this restriction. And so, I had to resort to a close comparison of the events described in all their accounts to decipher who the men behind the pseudonyms in **Mole** were. My reason for going to this trouble is straightforward: Hood's 1983 biography on Popov is the most detailed work ever written on this extraordinary Russian peasant. The CIA's Vienna Popov team made extensive notes, tape recordings, and transcriptions, and then analyzed those materials for use in detailed reports about every word Popov uttered.

All of this found its way into Hood's book and allows us to be transported back in time and become passive participants in the Popov drama. The intense fear, anxiety, and exhaustion of their harrowing experience in this consequential chapter of espionage and counterintelligence operations in the Cold War is nothing less than spell binding. Of course, what Hood contributed in 1983 is attenuated by the works of Murphy, Kondrashev and Bagley during the three decades that followed.

In order to reduce confusion for the reader, in this chapter I will (mostly) use the true names of the CIA officers involved—even in direct quotes where their pseudonyms were used by Hood. In the countless hours spent discussing and writing cables in the Popov case in Austria, not once was his name mentioned. He was simply **ATTIC**, a cryptonym, and, as the operation progressed, his cryptonym was changed every few months. Popov's case officers and other field personnel were also assigned pseudonyms, that, like the cryptonyms for agents, were used in every cable, dispatch, and record kept in the field.[587]

It was not difficult to link the true names of the CIA's Popov team to the pseudonyms in Hood's *Mole*. The first step was to find Bagley. This fragment from his *Spy Wars* was the cornerstone: "Popov's death held special meaning for me. For three years after he first came to us in Vienna in late 1952, I had supported the operation as one of the four officers most intimately involved."[588] It is easy to spot Bagley and the remaining members of the team. For those readers who wish to acquire and closely examine Hood's Popov biography, these identifications will be helpful:

- Peter Todd is William Hood; Hood was also known as "Captain Olsen"; [Hood is Ted Peterson in Bagley's *Spy Wars*]
- Gregory Domnin is George Kisevalter; Popov knew him only as Colonel Grossman
- Amos Booth is Tennent "Pete" Bagley

Before proceeding it is worth reflecting on the striking context of the world of espionage. This concerns the strict security practices observed by the CIA and KGB in their spy wars and the heavy toll it inevitably exacted on the defectors, moles and agent handlers. Hood described it best:

> At no time in their marriage did Popov as much as hint at his political disaffection. Nor could he discuss his GRU work with her [his wife]. Soviet intelligence officers are strictly enjoined from mentioning any aspect of their operational work to their families. There was no one to whom Popov could speak freely but Domnin, the case officer he met clandestinely. In the six years they worked together, Popov never

---

587 William Hood, *Mole—The True Story of the First Russian Spy to Become and American Counterspy* (London: Endeavor Press, 1982), pp. 90-91.
588 Tennent Bagley, *Spy Wars—Moles, Mysteries, and Deadly Games* (New Haven: Yale University Press, 2007), p. 9.

learned George Kisevalter's [Gregory Domnin] name. The strain showed. Popov was tired, and it was clear to Roberts and Bagley [Amos Booth] that Popov was drinking too much.[589]

Like most people and all of the spies I know anything about, Popov was an imperfect man. He drank too much. He was forgetful. ... Given the opportunity, he ran breathtaking—in retrospect, almost insane—risks. Although he loved his wife and children, he was hopelessly devoted to a randomly acquired mistress. But for six years he trundled bales of top-secret information out of the secret centers of Soviet power. In the process he shattered the Soviet military intelligence service, caused the transfer of the KGB chief (a four-star general and one of the most powerful men in the USSR), and saved the United States half a billion dollars in military research.[590]

Popov was also the defector who warned the CIA about a KGB mole in the Agency; a mole who betrayed the technical details of the CIA's super-secret U-2 spy plane. Ironically, the hunt for Popov's mole eventually destroyed the Agency's components working against the KGB.

The vicarious experience of reliving the Cold War KGB-CIA spy wars today is obviously less exhausting than it was for those who lived through it—but it is daunting nonetheless.

The Defection of Pyotr Popov

The confrontation between the KGB and the CIA that Popov's defection kindled reveals how tense the situation in Berlin had become—and how essential the Berlin Operations Base (BOB) and the KGB unit in Berlin were to their respective sides in the Cold War.

Two bombshell events in the drama of the Popov defection took place fifteen months apart during his GRU assignments in East Germany. In January 1957, the chief of KGB operations against the U.S. Embassy in Moscow, Vladislav Kovshuk, was dispatched to the Soviet Embassy in Washington. During this trip he learned that Popov had defected in place to the CIA. The source of this bombshell was very sensitive: a KGB mole that had penetrated the CIA.[591] Then, in April 1958, Popov delivered his

---

589 Hood, *Mole*, pp. 108-109.
590 Ibid, p. 8.
591 See Bagley, *Spymaster* pp. 207-208; see also Bagley, *Spy Wars*, pp. 65-67; see also Tennent Bagley, "Ghosts of the Spy Wars, A Personal Reminder to Interested Parties," *Journal of Intelligence and Counterintelligence*, Volume 28, No. 1, Spring 2017; see also Sandra Grimes and Jeanne Vertefeuille, *Circle of Treason* (Annapolis: Naval Institute Press, 2012), pp. 26-54.

own bombshell to Kisevalter: he had overheard a drunken GRU colonel boast that a KGB mole in the CIA had provided the complete technical details of the CIA's secret U-2 operations.[592]

These two events imperiled one of the most valuable Soviet moles in the Cold War. The counterintelligence chiefs in the KGB and the CIA locked horns as both took action to neutralize the successful penetration by the other side. In the spring of 1958, CIA Counterintelligence Chief James Angleton put into motion a plan to trap the KGB mole. Eventually, Angleton's plan led to the false defection of Lee Harvey Oswald. He was a former Marine who had tracked the U-2 flights from Atsugi, Japan as they headed out to photograph the missile impact areas in the Soviet Far East.

At the same time, Major General Gribanov put a complicated deception plan in motion that would enable the KGB to isolate and arrest Popov without endangering the KGB mole in the CIA. When this spy wars battle was over, Angleton had not uncovered the KGB mole in the CIA, and much of the Agency's operations against the USSR lay in smoldering ruins. Popov was eventually trapped, tried, and executed. The KGB won this battle, but not the war. At the end of the Cold War, the Soviet Union ended up as a carcass.

So, I will take the reader back to the moment when the Popov case began. In 1952, Popov was assigned to the Soviet intelligence *rezidentura* in Vienna, Austria. Popov had dropped a note into an American diplomat's car. The note offered to trade information for money:

> I am a Russian officer attached to the Soviet Group of Forces Headquarters in Baden bei Wien. If you are interested in buying a copy of the new table of organization for a Soviet armored division, meet me on the corner of Dorotheergasse and Stallburgasse at 8:30 P.M., November 12. If you are not there I will return at the same time on November 13. The price is 3,000 Austrian schillings."[593] [Approximately $125]

The authors of **Battleground Berlin** initially thought Popov needed the money to pay for an abortion for his mistress, Lyuba Bielic.[594] The Vienna CIA Station Chief, "Joel Roberts," decided to test the bona fides of the Russian major and Bagley chose a low-security safehouse suitable for a walk-in candidate.

"Alex Koenig," the Russian speaking station officer who had met Popov at the designated corner, handled the first interview. Popov said he was embarrassed to admit that after drinking too much he had been "rolled by a bar-girl" who had stolen all of

---

592 John Newman, *Oswald and the CIA* (New York: Skyhorse, 2008 ed.), p. 87. See also Mark Reibling, **Wedge: The Secret War Between the FBI and CIA** (New York: Knopf, 1994), p. 155; and Nigel West, **Historical Dictionary of Cold War Counterintelligence** (Lanham MD: Scarecrow Press, 2007), p. 350.
593 Hood, *Mole*, pp. 19-20.
594 Murphy, Kondrashev and George Bailey, **Battleground Berlin**, p. 268. The authors do not give their source for this detail and I have been unable to confirm it in any other principal sources I consulted for this chapter.

INTO THE STORM

his cash. Some of the money was official funds and if he did not replace the funds soon, he would be court-martialed. Popov asked for 3,000 shillings as he handed Alex a brand-new table of organization for a Soviet armored division—the first reorganization since WWII—that included Soviet strategy for coping with tactical nuclear weapons.[595] He was quickly recruited by the CIA station as a defector-in-place and assigned the code-name **ATTIC**.[596]

Roberts' cable to CIA HQS afterward presented a cautiously favorable evaluation of Popov's document and urgently requested that a Russian-speaking case officer be sent to Vienna in time for the next meeting. Within twenty-four hours a HQS cable responded that in addition to the Russian-speaking case officer, George Kisevalter (Gregory Domnin), a specialist on Soviet intelligence, Brooks Newby, would be immediately dispatched to Vienna.[597] The case officer, George Kisevalter, was from the CIA's East European Division, and would remain Popov's case officer for the six and a half years before Popov's arrest by the KGB.[598]

George Kisevalter handled the next meeting with Popov. The meeting began as both men showed each other fake identification cards. "Take a good look—it's just as phony as yours," Popov said. He then produced his authentic identification document issued by the GRU Chief Intelligence Directorate of the Soviet General Staff with the name, photograph, and serial number of the bearer, Major Pyotr Semyonovich Popov. This session was mostly routine questioning. Be with the Mafia to arrange the assassination of Fidel in "the early spring of 1962."[599] Before it was over Popov, had identified twenty-four GRU officers along with their pseudonyms and operational assignments.

Good stuff. Kisevalter gave Popov his three thousand shillings. Kisevalter and Bagley realized that Popov's information was solid but not sensational and considered this normal for the early hours from a defector. However, Roberts and Bagley were also convinced that Popov's information was detailed enough to make it unlikely that the GRU would have released so much information merely to build Popov's bona fides with the CIA. A HQS cable was less certain, and asked why Popov was risking his life to provide this information.[600] They would soon find out the fateful answer to that question: Popov was more than willing to take risks.

---

[595] Hood, *Mole*, pp. 40-41.
[596] Tom Mangold, *Cold Warrior*, p. 250.
[597] Hood, *Mole*, pp. 43-45.
[598] Murphy, Kondrashev and Bailey, *Battleground Berlin*, p. 268.
[599] Hersh, *The Dark Side of Camelot*, p. 286.
[600] Hood, *Mole*, pp. 66-69.

The Girlfriend

At the end of the second session Kisevalter asked Popov to explain the jam he was in. This was his reply:

> It was a dumb thing, but I got involved with a woman. ... She's someone I recruited, a Serb. My wife hadn't gotten here yet. Things just took their course. ... When my wife and daughter got here I was broke. They needed things, Lyuba needed things. I just didn't have money enough to go around. She's not a bad agent, but I wanted to give her more money and my boss caught it. He's a bastard and he hates me.[601]

Kisevalter asked Popov if he was in love with his agent. "Look, I love my wife," he said, "I love my daughter. They're what's important. I don't know what I feel about Lyuba."

Asked for her full name, Popov said it was Lyuba Bielic. Then, this rather testy exchange took place:

> "Are you still seeing her?" "Of course, she's my best agent. She knows every Yugoslav in Vienna. I meet her every week." "That's not what I mean," Kisevalter said. "Are you seeing her on the side?" "Sure. Every chance I get." "You know what kind of risks you're taking?" Kisevalter warned. "One whiff of this and your ass will be back in Moscow."[602]

The next morning, Kisevalter's chastisement of Popov proved to be prescient.

Just before Joel Roberts was due to arrive for a briefing, Bill Hood (Peter Todd) burst into Bagley's office. After running station traces on Lyuba Bielic, he found that there was only one piece of paper in the file. There was no doubt she was Popov's mistress but there was also disturbing news:

> Late one night in August a district police station in the Soviet sector of Vienna had received an excited telephone call. A drunken Russian officer was shouting and kicking at the door of an apartment on Am Werd Strasse. Fraulein Bielic, a stateless Yugoslav refugee, did not have a telephone. It was her alarmed neighbors who made the call.

First Secretary Maximenkov was responsible for Yugoslav operations in Vienna. When the Austrian police arrived, the drunk officer had apologized and Lyuba Bielic declined to make a complaint. The precinct police report, however, landed on Bill Hood's desk a week later.[603]

The problem was that the incident had occurred in the Soviet sector and had involved a Soviet officer. Because Bielic was a GRU agent, if Soviet intelligence received the precinct report, Popov's girlfriend might well be questioned about the details of her

---
601   Ibid, pp. 79-81.
602   Ibid, pp. 81-82.
603   Ibid, p. 84.

extracurricular activities. Popov, however, was not worried enough to take Kisevalter's advice to end the affair. He kept up the relationship even when living with his family, and later he recommended her as an agent for the GRU's base on the Baltic.[604]

Thirteen days passed before the next meeting with Popov. His CIA debriefing team had prepared for a full session in order to meet the mounting requirements coming from HQS. But Popov had come under increasing pressure from his boss, Ivan Yegerov, to make three new recruitments. Popov told his disappointed case officer that he could not stay for a session that evening but added that he had "brought a little something" to make up for missing the previous opportunity:

> He reached into his pocket and pulled out three carefully folded sheets of onionskin paper. "When I was in Baden bei Wien ... Orlov, the Baden finance officer—a tight little bastard—asked me to bring the payroll sheets to Vienna for the boss. ... The payroll listed every GRU officer, technician, clerical worker, and driver working in the Vienna rezidentura and in the Baden offices and gave their rank, date of grade, pay, and allowances. It even showed how many rubles they had converted into schillings in the GRU finance office.

Not bad. As time went by, Popov would meet Kisevalter up to three times each month. It was crucial that the periodicity being set by Popov had to be based on the times he might have available and the most secure opportunities for disappearing from the Soviet community without drawing too much attention.[605]

In the summer of 1953, Joel Roberts left Austria for a headquarters assignment, and his replacement arrived just before Popov returned from six weeks of home leave in the USSR. "Mike Andenko" had been sent to fill the Russian language gap created by the reassignment of Brooks Newby to HQS. Andenko had also worked on the Popov case at HQS. "Five tense days" passed before Popov called to arrange a meeting:

> Hours were spent in Bagley's office as Kisevalter manfully attempted to rationalize Popov's drinking, his continuing relationship with Lyuba Bielic, and to explain away the difficulty Popov was having meeting Colonel Yegerov's demands for new recruits. Repeatedly Kisevalter tried to convince Bagley that the station should provide Popov with a stable of agents he could ostensibly recruit for the GRU rezidency.

This idea had originated with Popov. Kisevalter searched through the station's files for an agent prospect to turn over to Popov. As tempting as this proposal was for Popov and Kisevalter, Bagley—as the station operations chief—refused to go along with it.[606]

604　Bagley, "Ghosts of the Spy Wars," p. 18.
605　Hood, *Mole*, pp. 92-94.
606　Ibid, pp. 113-114.

The need for an independent view of Popov had become a high priority for the Vienna station. By pure happenstance, another parallel defection provided just such a window.

The Defection of Peter Deryabin

On 15 February 1954, KGB Major Peter Sergeyevich Deryabin defected to the CIA in Vienna.[607] Bill Hood burst through the door of Pete Bagley's office with the big news. Deryabin was quickly rushed into the CIA station where a nervous young case officer, "Fred Gordon," began the initial interview of Deryabin. As Gordon began taking notes, the KGB major broke into a broad grin and said, "Aha, Captain Olson, I've been wondering when we would meet."[608] In his book *Mole*, Hood uses the name Olson, but we know from Bagley's *Spy Wars* it was Ted Petersen:

> Fifteen minutes into the preliminary questioning, Ted bolted out of the room. "He knows I'm Captain Peterson!" Ted had used that pseudonym when meeting Sergey Feoktistov, a Soviet economic official, whom we too casually assumed was in our employ. Ted was taking notes in a characteristic *left-handed* manner, which Deryabin observed with a growing smile. Tongue in cheek, he asked if Ted knew a Captain Petersen. "If you should happen to see him, you might mention that his agent Feoktistov is actually working for us."[609] [Emphasis added]

As Hood recalled, the wily Deryabin had established his bona fides in one sentence. Deryabin was showing off and making it crystal clear that he knew "the pseudonym of the only case officer in Austria who spoke Russian and took notes with his pen cradled between the first and second fingers of his *right hand*."[610]

The *right* hand or the *left* hand? The hand Peterson used to write with is probably less important than the way he held his pen—cradled between the first and second fingers. In any event, as Bagley later observed, Deryabin's unexpected remark to Peterson "blew Feoktistov out of our stable and proved that Deryabin was for real and that we had an important defector in our hands."[611]

Deryabin later took Bagley aside to explain that he had tried to communicate with Gordon through Sergey Feoktistov, the Russian manager of a Soviet-controlled factory.

---

607 Bagley, *Spy Wars*, p. 37.
608 Hood, *Mole*, p. 136.
609 Bagley, *Spy Wars*, p. 38.
610 Hood, *Mole*, pp. 136-137. Obviously, it cannot be both his right hand and his left hand.
611 Bagley, *Spy Wars*, p. 38.

Gordon misunderstood the situation, and the opportunity was lost for the station to contact Deryabin to see if a defection-in-place might be arranged.[612]

The station was fortunate indeed to have Deryabin. His presence in Vienna was another unusual happenstance. He was so trusted in Moscow that he had been promoted to the KGB's elite Guard Directorate, whose mission was the security of the Kremlin and the top communist dignitaries. Bagley knew of no other member of the elite Guard Directorate who had ever been posted abroad— "they knew too much."[613]

The preliminary questioning of Deryabin convinced the Vienna station that Deryabin was probably the most valuable intelligence defector since WWII. His detailed data on the KGB's Vienna organization and his inside knowledge of Kremlin intrigues was unique. More interrogation would have to come later. All hands were on deck to handle the immediate critical problem: how to get Deryabin safely out of Vienna during the "most barefaced KGB surveillance the station had ever detected" in the Austrian capitol.[614]

With air travel out of the question, the decision was quickly made to smuggle Deryabin out on the famous "Mozart Express"—a U.S. military train ride through ninety-miles of the Soviet occupation zone to Salzburg in the American zone. A used hot-water tank was engineered so that Deryabin could be hidden inside and placed with the other machinery in the cargo car for the excruciating ride.[615] Bagley recalls that Bill Hood accompanied him in a passenger compartment. To keep their minds off of the danger they were facing they played the most intense game of chess in their lives.[616]

Afterward at the safehouse in Salzburg, Hood asked Deryabin about GRU personnel and if any of them were peasants. Deryabin recalled a "Petro" Popov who was working on recruiting Yugoslavian agents: "He was an amiable fellow, well liked and an enthusiastic fisherman."[617] Deryabin and Bagley were taken to the American military airfield near Munich, Germany, and both were placed on an unmarked plane that was waiting to take them to Washington.[618]

Popov's Stony Path into Soviet Illegals Operations

George Kisevalter held five more meetings with Popov before his home leave to the USSR in July 1954. During his three-week visit to the Kaliningrad rest center, Popov

---

612   Hood, *Mole*, p. 138.
613   Ibid.
614   Bagley, *Spy Wars*, p. p. 38; Hood, *Mole*, p. 142.
615   Hood, *Mole*, p. 142; Bagley, *Spy Wars*, p. 38.
616   Bagley, *Spy Wars*, p. 38.
617   Hood, *Mole*, p. 148.
618   Bagley, *Spy Wars*, p. 39; Hood, *Mole*, p. 148.

had managed to gather high-level intelligence on Soviet guided missiles and nuclear submarines—the first data the CIA had been able to disseminate on these naval craft. But his return to Vienna had been delayed due to an order by Khrushchev to reduce Yugoslav operations. This move led to a concomitant cutback in the GRU staff in Vienna, and Popov's slot was the first to be cut. At the same time, however, a new position had opened in the Vienna rezidency of the GRU's Operational Directorate, so Popov and his family were still able, although belatedly, to return to Vienna.[619]

In November 1954, Popov stumbled onto an opportunity that was to shape the remainder of his intelligence career. Within two years it would land him in the catbird seat—the GRU illegals section in Berlin. Soviet "illegals" were agents posted abroad with false documentation. That catbird seat, however, brought with it risks that Popov had not foreseen. While hunting for prospective recruitments in Vienna, Popov spotted a morose mid-level Viennese policeman in a bar. After several beers, Popov listened sympathetically as the man divulged how difficult it was to support his family on a policeman's wages. Popov encouraged further discourse on this subject, knowing he had found an excellent prospect for a recruitment.[620]

The next morning, Popov shared his good news with Colonel Alexei Kriatov, chief of the GRU illegals support section in Vienna. Among the details that came spilling out of his Viennese drinking partner, was the fact that this particular policeman was pure gold for Soviet illegals operations. Popov's drinking partner oversaw a district police bureau that issued identification cards, birth certificates, resident permits and more to Austrian citizens. Moreover, these documents were stored in his office. Kriatov was impressed:

> This was exactly the material required by Soviet agents who would be sent abroad documented as Austrians. If the policeman could be recruited, the GRU would have its own source of documentation. ... No longer would he have to go to the KGB, cap in hand, and put up with their humiliating questions every time he wanted to document a spy.

The recruitment was made. Before the end of the Soviet occupation in June 1955, Kriatov had acquired dozens of passports and many other documents *along with* the crucial rubber stamps, seals, and copies of the signatures. Coming as it did on the eve of the extensive post-occupation reorganization of Soviet intelligence in Central Europe, Popov's destiny would be crucially influenced by the hand of Colonel Kriatov.[621]

In the fall of 1955, Popov was recalled to Moscow. He remained there until early 1956, when he was reassigned to the GRU tactical intelligence unit in Schwerin, East

---

619 Hood, *Mole*, pp. 153-157
620 Ibid, p. 158.
621 Ibid, pp. 158-160.

INTO THE STORM

Germany, where CIA reestablished contact with him via a courier.[622] The CIA had learned about Popov's planned return to Moscow *long before* it happened. A decision was made that communicating with Popov in the Soviet capitol would be too risky. However, because this meant the loss of the Agency's best inside source on Soviet military matters, a plan was approved to scout out and create potential dead drops for Popov's possible use.[623] But, at that point, the CIA did not have a station in Moscow. And so, in the spring of 1954 a one-man station was established. Edward Ellis Smith was sent to find the potential dead drops while working undercover as the American Embassy security officer—without the knowledge of Ambassador Charles Bohlen![624] Smith's assignment to Moscow would open a can of worms like none other. I will return to how that unfolded in Chapter Twelve.

In June 1955, Pete Bagley was finally reassigned to CIA HQS in Washington:
> After my more than four years in Vienna… good fortune placed me in a spot… assigned by William Hood, who had become operations chief of the Middle-Europe (later to be renamed Eastern European) Division, my new job was to head the counterintelligence section of the Poland Branch.

In early 1958, Bagley would be reassigned to the CIA station in Bern, Switzerland and would still be there to accept Yuri Nosenko's defection in place in 1962.[625] I will get to the entertaining Bagley-Nosenko spy duel in Chapter Twelve.

In the meantime, in December 1956, "Paul Hopkins" had come to visit Bagley in his Washington office. Hopkins was checking for operational leads from underground traffic intercepted in William Harvey's Berlin tunnel. Hopkins gave Bagley a routine intercept from the tunnel of a phone call in Schwerin, East Germany. The call discussed Pyotr Popov's expected arrival the following morning. Bagley sent a flash Eyes Only cable to alert William Harvey, chief of the Berlin Operations Base (BOB), and the Agency immediately reassigned George Kisevalter to Berlin hoping that contact with Popov might be reestablished.[626]

What the CIA did not know about Popov's work at Schwerin was that it would be short-lived. When Colonel Kriatov discovered that Popov had been assigned to Schwerin, he ordered that Popov be transferred to the GRU illegals section in

---

622 Bagley, *Spy Wars*, p. 71.
623 Hood, *Mole*, p. 163.
624 Smith, Richard Harris, "The First Moscow Station: An Espionage Footnote to Cold War History," *Journal of Intelligence and Counterintelligence*, 1989, Volume 3, Number 3, pp. 340-343.
625 Bagley, *Spy Wars*, pp. 44-47.
626 Hopkins had replaced Bill Hood [AKA Peter Todd] in Austria a few months before the occupation ended. As chief of the Soviet section, he worked closely with George Kisevalter [AKA Gregory Domnin] in the closing weeks of Popov's Vienna assignment. See Hood, *Mole*, p. 171.

Karlshorst, East Berlin.[627] Furthermore, the CIA Berlin station had no idea that Popov, overly eager to make contact, had made a crucial mistake.

Popov had spotted two British military officers, Lieutenant Colonel Kirkland and Captain Wickham, dining in a crowded restaurant in Schwerin. Kirkland stepped out of the restaurant to find the men's room and Popov, after a moment, followed him in and closed the door. Popov gave Kirkland an envelope and whispered in broken German a request that it be delivered to "Colonel Grossman" [Kisevalter] at the Berlin CIA station as soon as possible.[628]

The following morning, Kirkland took the envelope to the British foreign intelligence (MI-6) chief who ordered that the contents be examined. The message inside was in Russian and, by chance, the MI-6 Russian translator was on leave. So, the message was sent to another office that had a case officer with limited Russian capability for translation. In that room, that stars were not aligned in Popov's favor. The translator had been at work an hour when a British case officer who shared *that office* happened to enter the room. It was George Blake, one of the infamous KGB moles that had penetrated MI-6. Blake asked how things were going. "It looks as if Bill Harvey's got a good GRU case, somewhere out in the zone," the translator replied. Blake was careful not to say anything else and not to appear curious. With the translation complete, the letter was hand-carried to Bill Harvey at BOB.[629]

It is certain that Blake found a way to get this devastating news to his KGB case officer immediately. Soviet intelligence in Berlin still did not know the identity of the GRU mole whose message had fallen into their hands. But Hood realized how serious Popov's Schwerin letter drop was:

> Soviet counterintelligence would unhesitatingly have made a maximum effort to run down such a lead. Given Russian competence in counterespionage, Blake's report alone could have been enough to undo Popov.[630]

Blake's discovery in Berlin took place only days before a far more devastating event for Popov's future occurred in Washington. In January 1957, the chief of KGB operations against the U.S. Embassy in Moscow, Vladislav Kovshuk, was dispatched to the Soviet Embassy in Washington using the pseudonym "Komarov." On this trip he learned about Popov's defection from a KGB mole who had penetrated the CIA.[631] The combination of the news from Blake *and* Kovshuk left no doubt in Moscow that Popov was working for the CIA in East Germany. I will return to the 1957 Kovshuk trip to Washington below.

---

627 Hood, *Mole*, p. 184.
628 Ibid, pp. 175-176.
629 Ibid, p. 178.
630 Ibid, p. 171 and p. 270.
631 Bagley, *Spymaster* pp. 207-208; see also Bagley, *Spy Wars*, pp. 65-67; see also Bagley, "Ghosts of the Spy Wars," p. 4, fn. 7; and also Grimes and Vertefeuille, *Circle of Treason*, pp. 26-54.

INTO THE STORM

Although Popov's transfer to the GRU Strategic Intelligence Operational Group (Opergruppa) in Karlshorst had been approved in April 1957, he did not arrive in Karlshorst for his job in the illegals section until late June.[632] Harvey and Murphy began planning for regular communications with Popov. They planned to do this through an elderly BOB support agent who made courier runs about once a month until December 1956. Popov began by providing BOB details about the illegals he handled and furnishing a complete description of the GRU Opergruppa's organizational structure and its personnel and offices in Karlshorst. He also sent BOB valuable information on the agent nets run by the intelligence unit (RU) at the Group of Soviet Forces Germany (GSFG) as well as the first solid details of the contents of Khrushchev's famous 25 February 1956 secret speech.[633] Once again, very nice work by Popov.

In a March 1957 meeting at the CIA station in West Berlin, Popov unloaded an important piece of secret intelligence information that led to further severe consequences for his security. During a visit to GSFG, Marshall Georgy Zhukov had given a sensitive presentation to senior troop commanders about GSFG combat readiness and new Soviet weapons developments. Popov had attended the meeting. On 29 March 1957, he gave the text of Zhukov's speech to the CIA Berlin station. Regrettably, Popov's amazing ability to provide such significant secret intelligence often involved significant risks—not to mention the dangerous risks he was taking in his personal life.

The CIA distributed Zhukov's speech under tight controls and very limited distribution, but that distribution included London. And that was a problem. Still unaware of the extent to which they had been penetrated, British intelligence naturally shared this important speech with their Special Intelligence Service (SIS) in Berlin. There it was almost certainly read by George Blake, who was responsible for Soviet operations. Because everything of interest that crossed Blake's desk went to the KGB, the Zhukov report would have been included.[634] It was yet another opportunity for the KGB to discover Popov's treason.

By the time Kisevalter arrived from Washington, he was anxious to set up personal meetings to help stiffen Popov's resolve. As the authors of **Battleground Berlin** noted, "Kisevalter had become Popov's friend, father figure, confidante, and advisor—no one else could have managed the case as well."[635] The first meeting took place weeks before Popov's transfer to Karlshorst became effective. Popov was brimming to share the news about his new job. He explained that the GRU was making an organization in East Germany. Lieutenant General Feodor Federenko, the deputy chief of the GRU in Moscow, was being transferred to Karlshorst, East Berlin, to direct all GRU operations

---

632   Bagley, *Spy Wars*, p. 71.
633   Murphy, Kondrashev and Bailey, **Battleground Berlin**, p. 273.
634   Ibid, pp. 271-272.
635   Ibid, p. 270.

based in East Germany. Federenko planned to establish a new strategic operations group with a staff of ninety GRU case officers—the "Opergruppa." Popov then offered Kisevalter this important news:

> It's as if a section of the GRU headquarters were transferred from Moscow to Karlshorst. ... When Kriatov heard I was in Schwerin, he told Federenko what I had done for him in Vienna and asked for my transfer to the illegals section in Karlshorst.[636]

Soviet military and foreign intelligence relied heavily on "illegals"—Soviet bloc intelligence officers falsely documented as foreign citizens—who were sent abroad to conduct intelligence operations. The illegals section, or Third Department, had grown into the largest department at KGB Karlshorst.[637] Aside from penetration agents, Soviet illegals were the most important counterintelligence targets. Popov had hit the jackpot. But Kisevalter was justifiably upset with his Russian agent for carrying on with Lyuba and handing "a devastatingly revealing letter to a stranger" in Schwerin.

Popov acknowledged Kisevalter's disappointment about the letter and said he had come to the meeting with a present to make up for his mistake. Popov had been the duty officer one night in Schwerin and had copied five pages of charts for each of the five Soviet trans-border intelligence bases in Berlin. Popov explained that he had hidden them inside his jacket as he proudly handed them to his case officer. Although happy to have the documents, Kisevalter felt this action also had been too risky. He instructed Popov not to come into West Berlin again until he had been transferred to Karlshorst in East Berlin. But the dangers associated with Popov's new illegals assignment soon changed Kisevalter's mind.

In KGB Karlshorst, Popov would be handling the Soviet illegals as they transited East Berlin en route to the West. As I mentioned above, Popov had been responsible for the recruitment of the East Berlin policeman. The policed provided Colonel Kriatov with the passports and other documents, along with the stamps and seals, to create the false documentation to backstop the false identities used by the illegals operating in Western countries. At the time, these illegals were provided to Popov by GRU Colonel Dmitry Polyakov.[638] In 1959, Gribanov would send Polyakov to the U.S. as a false defector as part of a new KGB deception program (discussed below).

The first illegal agent Polyakov escorted to Berlin for Popov to handle was Margarita Tairova. Worried about the woman after meeting her, Popov called Kisevalter for an emergency meeting to discuss his mission. The Tairova assignment was fraught with sand traps that would invite more suspicion about Popov's work for the CIA. Standing

---
636 Ibid, pp. 183-184.
637 Murphy, Kondrashev and Bailey, **Battleground Berlin**, p. 267.
638 Grimes and Vertefeuille, **Circle of Treason**, pp. 26-54.

alone, the Tairova affair would provide the fourth opportunity for the KGB to arrest and execute Popov without endangering their mole in the CIA.

Gribanov, and the Poisonous Woman from Moscow

All Popov could report to Kisevalter was that he had been assigned to escort and dispatch Margarita Tairova to New York City to join her husband, also an illegal. Popov explained:

> The final step in Tairova's settling down in New York would be her meeting with her husband. According to Popov, the meeting was prearranged. Ostensibly it would be a casual encounter, but romance would blossom, and they would "marry" as soon as plausible. Although the Tairovas had been man and wife for almost ten years, the new marriage license would be a useful document to support their legend.[639]

Listening to Popov's report, the dark dimensions of the looming threat dawned on Kisevalter:

> It had been the most difficult meeting Kisevalter could remember. Now that Popov had given the details on Tairova, the FBI would have no choice but to tail her from the moment she arrived in New York until she met her husband. If the jittery woman spotted the surveillance, Popov would be in jeopardy.[640]

When the news of the Tairova operation reached BOB chief Bill Harvey, he had to draft an urgent cable that he did *not* want to send to Washington:

> When he released the cable on his desk and Popov's latest report reached Washington, CIA would have to pass it to the FBI. Harvey knew this could mean trouble. J. Edgar Hoover ran his own show and nobody, not even a president, could tell him how to do it.[641]

As Hood recalled, the FBI surveillance was poor from the start and the couple noticed it. "Had the Tairova surveillance not been blown," Hood concluded, "the FBI might have uncovered a GRU agent as important as Abel [the KGB *rezident* in New York]."[642]

In my view, however, if the performance of the FBI was poor, the performance of the Tairova's was so sloppy it suggests that they intended to be seen. Something else was going on. There was a lot more to the Tairova affair than the botched surveillance of the FBI's "bucket brigade." After more than a month, they suddenly pulled the plug

---

639   Hood, *Mole*, p. 199.
640   Ibid, p. 203.
641   Ibid, p. 206.
642   Ibid, p. 231.

and vanished into thin air. The couple had *never made any discernible counter-surveillance moves*. Marguerite Tairova made no attempt to follow Moscow's plan to build her cover as a beautician.

I think Bagley got it right when he surmised that Polyakov "had never been a genuine illegals support officer"[643] when he unloaded Mrs. Tairova on Popov:

> It was possible that the KGB (using Polyakov) had dispatched Tairova—through Popov in full or partial awareness of Popov's treason, with one or both of two purposes: to test Popov (seeing whether a KGB mole in the New York Field Office of the FBI would confirm that the Americans knew in advance of her arrival) and/or to create a collateral excuse to arrest Popov in a way that would hide a mole who actually betrayed him.

In my view, it was not either/or; rather it was both/and.

The point is that if Tairova had actually spotted surveillance, or simply said that she had, Popov would be at the top of the list as the person that betrayed her mission. What she actually said about it afterward was that "she was followed all the way from Berlin," and that was a lie.[644] If what she said was true, why did she stay in America for another six weeks? Why did the Tairovas not bolt straight away?

At the time, Popov was in the USSR on home leave and had not seen any threatening signs about his security. However, Zvezdenkov told the authors of **Battleground Berlin** that the KGB "was very concerned about the number of GRU illegals, including the Tairovas, whom Popov might have compromised and was fearful that Popov had reported extensively on GRU personnel stationed abroad."[645] Both Polyakov and Zvezdenkov worked for Gribanov's deception department (Department 14) in 1957. The woman they sent from Moscow was a deception—a poison pill—to throw the CIA off the trail of the KGB mole in the CIA.

The Failure of Angleton's Hunt for Popov's Mole

We are uncertain of how many details about Popov's treason the KGB mole in the CIA was able to convey to Kovshuk. We *do* know that fifteen months after Kovshuk's discovery of Popov's April 1958 defection, the CIA learned from Popov himself about the KGB mole in the CIA.[646] As discussed above, Popov had overheard a drunken

---

643 Bagley, *Spy Wars*, p. 171.
644 Ibid, p. 297.
645 Murphy, Kondrashev and Bailey, **Battleground Berlin**, p. 274.
646 Newman, *Oswald and the CIA*, p. 87. See also Reibling, **Wedge**, p. 155; and West, **Historical Dictionary of Cold War Counterintelligence**, p. 350.

INTO THE STORM

GRU officer state that the mole had betrayed the *full* technical details of the CIA's super-secret U-2 spy plane.

The U-2 could fly at 80,000 feet—above the ability of Soviet radar to pinpoint its location to shoot it down. The primary mission of the U-2, as it flew over Soviet territory, was to collect data on the USSR's ballistic missile developments. At the time, the U.S. and USSR were in a race to develop nuclear tipped intercontinental ballistic missiles.

Popov's revelation about the KGB mole in the CIA led Counterintelligence Chief Angleton to design a trave[647] to trap the mole. Angleton's plan began in October 1959, with the false defection of Lee Harvey Oswald in Moscow. Oswald had served as a Marine radar specialist in Atsugi, Japan, tracking the U-2 flights flying over Russian territory. The idea behind this scheme was that the KGB would be anxious to obtain more information about Oswald.

In Chapters One and Eighteen of Volume II (***Countdown to Darkness***), I wrote extensively about how Angleton worked with the CIA Security Office to design an intricate trap to catch the mole. In addition, at several public events during 2017 and 2018 I gave very detailed presentations on the way this plan was implemented.[648]

Here, I will only briefly mention how the plan was designed to operate inside the Agency. Angleton hoped that dangling Oswald as U-2 flypaper in Moscow would entice the KGB to contact its mole inside the CIA for more information. It was hoped that the mole—unable to find any information because the CIA Security Office had captured and sequestered all incoming Oswald documents—might be exposed by making inquiries about Oswald. There was no question that the Soviet Union was extremely disturbed by the CIA's U-2 overflights of its territory and was very interested in acquiring information on how to shoot down the aircraft.

The mole trap was set, yet the bait was *not* taken. That did *not* mean, however, that the KGB had no interest in what Oswald *might* know about the U-2 program. *On the contrary*, as we found out after the fall of the Soviet Union, the KGB's interest *had* been significant enough to covertly debrief Oswald *often*, watch him *very* closely, *bug* his apartment in Minsk, *open* his mail, and *use his coworkers* as informants at the radio factory where he *worked*.

Despite all this interest in Oswald, the KGB was *not sufficiently* aroused to risk exposing their mole. The failure of Angleton's plan had disturbing consequences that only heightened Angleton's angst. Popov's mole was *extremely* valuable. Angleton concluded that the KGB's decision *not* to take the bait could only mean that the mole had already betrayed—or would be able to do so in the future—far more sensitive secrets to the

---

[647] A trave is a word for an inescapable frame to confine an unruly horse or ox for shoeing—and a suitable counterintelligence term for neutralizing a mole.

[648] These events took place at James Madison University, at JFK Lancer in Dallas, and in San Francisco. All of them are available for viewing on my website at jfkjmn.com.

KGB. As a result, the Oswald gambit intensified what had already become the hardest fought battle in the history of KGB-CIA spy wars.

Angleton kept looking for the elusive KGB mole for another fifteen years. That search would tear asunder the Agency's operations against the Soviet Union.

The Arrest and Execution of Popov

When Popov returned to Berlin in January 1958, neither he nor Kisevalter and Harvey understood the storm clouds that were gathering in Moscow. That was three months *before* Popov mentioned the KGB mole to Kisevalter in April 1958. Unbeknownst to Kisevalter and Popov, at that moment Gribanov was planning to unleash a series of deceptive events to set a trave for Popov. *None* of these events were related to the mole in the CIA—they were designed for use as an *excuse* to arrest Popov.

During May and June 1958, Popov went on home leave again to the Soviet Union. In July, after he returned to Berlin, an old friend of his, Ivan Markovich Stakh, put in a surprise appearance at Popov's birthday party. At the time, Stakh was an officer in the KGB First Chief Directorate (CFD). He and Popov had been classmates at the Military Diplomatic Academy in Moscow. They had become friends during long train rides between Moscow and their homes in Kalinin. Mulling over Stakh's presence at that party in their book **Battleground Berlin**, Murphy and Kondrashev wondered, "Was this meeting coincidence, or had it been planned by KGB?"[649]

The KGB's "concern" over the blown Tairova operation in New York was suddenly revived in November 1958. So was Popov's affair with Lyuba Bielic. On 8 November, Popov called BOB for an emergency meeting. He was irate at having received a message from Moscow with questions about his Yugoslav girlfriend, Lyuba Bielic. Popov had no idea that she had turned against communism after the Soviet suppression of the Hungarian revolt. She testified against the Austrian Communist Party's role in election frauds and, unfortunately, in August 1958, she informed the Viennese police about her relationship with Popov. And so, the ensuing flap brought Lyuba's relationship with Popov back to official scrutiny again. Moscow directed Popov to write a letter of self-criticism. He minimized the periodicity of his letters to Lyuba and claimed operational justification for them.[650]

At first, Popov's work in the Opergruppa seemed to be proceeding normally. But that lasted for only one week. On the night of 15-16 November, Popov was the duty officer. This gave him access to all of the unit's files. Murphy and Kondrashev later

---

[649] Murphy, Kondrashev and Bailey, **Battleground Berlin**, p. 275.
[650] Ibid, p. 276.

INTO THE STORM

surmised this might have been a *trap*. The next morning, 16 November, a troubling cable arrived from GRU Headquarters. The cable directed Popov to hand-deliver to Moscow the file on the American student that he had—with help from BOB—recruited to pad his recruitment quota. Zvezdenkov later told Murphy and Kondrashev that by the time of the GRU directive to Popov, "the GRU had been advised by the KGB of the necessity of removing Popov from Berlin."[651] Zvezdenkov was still covering for the mole in the CIA that had never been discovered. While Kondrashev was willing to tell Bagley that much—he, too, never mentioned the name of the mole. Nothing more was heard from Popov. The CIA station in Berlin would never see him again.

For nearly all of 1958, Gribanov had been playing for time. He had been carrying out his deception plan to *protect the KGB mole in the CIA*. Gribanov's series of deceptive events were designed so that the KGB could safely dispose of Popov. Crucially, those events provided excuses for arresting Popov on grounds unrelated to the KGB mole in the CIA. The 12 March 1958 sudden flight of the Tairovas to the USSR, the July 1958 surprise birthday party appearance of Popov's old friend Ivan Stakh in Berlin, and the sudden resurfacing of the Lyuba Bielic affair in early November 1958, were not disparate occurrences. They were controlled preparations.

With Popov in Gribanov's trave—and thus unable to escape to the West—Soviet Premier Nikita Khrushchev was free to do as he pleased. *Heads rolled* in Soviet intelligence over the Popov affair. Khrushchev demoted KGB Chief Ivan Serov, sending him to become head of the GRU. At the same time, Khrushchev promoted Aleksandr Shelepin to become the new chief of the KGB. *But*, in sending Serov to the GRU, Khrushchev planned to use him to shake up the GRU and then *fire him too*.

The 9 December 1958 firing of KGB Chief Ivan Serov tells us today that the decision to arrest Popov had finally been made at KGB HQS. At the time, it was still *nearly a month before Popov was lured to Moscow by a ruse*.[652] Popov was arrested as soon as he arrived in Moscow. The KGB had figured out Popov's defection no later than January 1957. The decision not to arrest him for a whole year was driven principally by the highly sensitive source in the CIA that had betrayed Popov and confirmed the less specific but obvious lead provided by MI-6 mole Blake in Berlin around the same time. In my view, it is likely that either the same mole that provided the technical details of the U-2 program to the KGB—or another KGB mole at CIA HQS or in Berlin—had learned about Popov's discovery of the leak almost immediately.

Once Popov was in Moscow at the end of December 1958, the KGB was in no hurry to torture and execute him. Popov was quietly arrested. His contrition in the initial interrogation enabled the KGB to double him back against the CIA in Moscow for

---

651 Ibid, pp. 276-277.
652 Ibid, pp. 4-5.

several months. This gave the KGB the time to organize the safe return to the USSR of the GRU illegals[653] that Popov might have compromised.[654] Over the course of the next ten months, Popov met five times—under KGB control—with a Moscow CIA station officer, Russell Langelle. Gribanov's officers Zvezdenkov and Sumin scripted the theater that took place in these meetings and the CIA willingly carried on with the playacting to protect Popov.[655]

At an 18 September 1959 meeting with Langelle in a restaurant men's room, Popov passed a *real* message he had prepared without KGB's knowledge:

> In this message Popov explained that he had been arrested in February and that he had attempted to minimize the extent of his CIA work, picturing himself a "victim of your [CIA's] aggression." Popov also confirmed CIA's suspicions that the meetings held with him since February had been under KGB control.[656]

That was the end of the line. On 6-7 January 1960, Popov was tried before the Military Collegium Court of the Supreme Soviet.

The KGB claimed, as the story went, to have recommended against the death penalty. Not surprisingly, probably on orders from Khrushchev himself, Popov was found guilty and sentenced to death. He was executed by firing squad in June 1960.[657] But as Hood pointed out (see above), *Popov's comprehensive provision of top-secret intelligence shattered the Soviet military intelligence service, caused the transfer of the KGB chief, and saved the United States half a billion dollars in military research.*

The "Shelepin Plan"

Meanwhile, in Moscow, by 1959 the new KGB Chairman Aleksandr Shelepin had reorganized the KGB into *two* entities—an *outer* and an *inner* KGB:

> The "inner" KGB was to be where the deceptions were planned, orchestrated, and assessed. It was limited to a small number of trusted officers, under the direct supervision of the Politburo, who planned, orchestrated, controlled, and analyzed these operations.[658]

---

653 Soviet military and foreign intelligence relied heavily on "*illegals*." They were Soviet bloc intelligence officers *falsely documented* as foreign citizens who were sent abroad to conduct intelligence operations. The illegals were also the most important counterintelligence targets.
654 Murphy, Kondrashev and Bailey, **Battleground Berlin**, p. 279.
655 Bagley, **Spy Wars**, p. 74.
656 Murphy, Kondrashev and Bailey, **Battleground Berlin**, pp. 279-280.
657 Ibid, p. 281
658 Edward Jay Epstein, **Deception—The Once and Future Cold War** (New York: EJE Publications, 2014), pp. 67-68.

INTO THE STORM

The "Shelepin Plan," also known as the *active measures* service, originated from a five-page memorandum authored by Ivan Agayants, the head of KGB disinformation operations, proposing world-wide coordination of clandestine political action.[659]

Agayants' intelligence career had an auspicious beginning. His first supervisor was the "mastermind of cunning deception operations," Artur Kristianovich Artuzov, whose successful feats included the false anti-Soviet resistance organizations during the 1920s. At the end of WWII, Agayants became the first post-war KGB rezident in Paris. His deception operations there were famous and included credit for the defeat of the proposed European Defense Community.[660]

In 1959, KGB Chairman Aleksandr Shelepin wanted the KGB to improve its support for Soviet foreign policy objectives. Shelepin adopted Agayants' proposal, and the Communist Party Central Committee ordered this mission to be centralized and carried out by a new independent KGB department. Designated as Department D, Agayants was selected as the chief.[661]

Gribanov's "Boomerang" and the Penkovsky and Polyakov Defections

In 1957, KGB agent Vladislav Kovshuk learned from a Soviet mole inside the CIA that a GRU Colonel, Pyotr Popov, was passing Soviet secrets to the CIA. The political and strategic damage caused by his defection was so widespread that the investigation was taken over by the chief of Soviet counterintelligence—KGB Major General Oleg Gribanov.[662] Kondrashev recalled that no sooner had Agayants set up his deception department (D) in the First Chief Directorate (FCD) than Gribanov set up his own deception unit in the Second Chief Directorate (SCD), naming it Department 14. Kondrashev told Bagley that Gribanov "was always out to beat the FCD at its own game."[663] The Department 14 mission was "mounting complicated counterintelligence operations and operational *games* to penetrate foreign intelligence services."[664] Indeed, such operations were very much like the deep game of penetration and deception that has always been the great Russian pastime—chess.

In his 2013 biography of Kondrashev, ***Spymaster***, Bagley said Kondrashev had revealed that an earlier contact of Polyakov had caused SCD chief Gribanov to choose him for this assignment. Gribanov, Kondrashev explained, had made the choice after

---

659 Bagley, *Spymaster* pp. 166-168.
660 Ibid.
661 Ibid, p. 168.
662 Bagley, "Ghosts of the Spy Wars," p. 4.
663 Ibid, pp. 196-197.
664 Ibid, p. 5.

a "thorough analysis" by one of his officers, whom Kondrashev chose not to name. Bagley surmised that this early contact had been the GRU illegals agent, Margarita Tairova, whom Polyakov had fed to Popov in Berlin in 1957.[665]

> During another conversation with Bagley, Kondrashev provided more context: Kondrashev identified Valentin V. Zvezdenkov as the first chief of Oleg Gribanov's new (1959) Department 14 for operational deception. Just before then, Zvezdenkov had assisted Gribanov in investigating Pyotr Popov, the CIA's spy inside the GRU, and then had interrogated him. Popov confessed having made the GRU an open book for the CIA by identifying more than 650 of its officers, giving leads to hundreds of GRU agents, and describing its secret procedures. Now Gribanov could *re-use all this information* by sending a GRU officer into the hands of American Intelligence to *tie them up, lead them astray, and expose their work.*[666]

In that way, Gribanov resolved to turn disaster into opportunity by weaponizing Popov's betrayal for use against the Americans. Gribanov appropriately named his operation "Boomerang" and assigned it to Department 14. Gribanov selected another GRU Colonel, Dmitry Polyakov, for his first attempt to penetrate U.S. intelligence. Polyakov was sent to New York City in October 1959, where he worked undercover as a military official in the United Nations Soviet delegation. The plan called for Polyakov to establish his bona fides with American intelligence by reusing and adding to Popov's information.

Gribanov ended up delaying the launch of Boomerang for two years because of another defection—by the most celebrated Western spy during the Cold War. In April 1961, GRU Colonel Oleg Penkovsky arranged through Greville Wynne, a British businessman visiting Moscow, to meet with U.S. and U.K. intelligence officers in London. The defection took place soon afterward in late April. George Kisevalter and Joe Bulik of the CIA along with two MI-6 officers met Penkovsky in the Mount Royal Hotel near Hyde Park.[667]

After the end of the Cold War in 1991, former KGB officers disclosed that they had learned about Penkovsky's defection *right away* in the spring of 1961. The leak almost certainly came from a valuable mole in Britain's MI-6. As a result, Gribanov was forced to weigh the effects of the Penkovsky affair before moving ahead with Boomerang and the planned false defection of Polyakov.[668] To protect the mole who gave away Penkovsky, Gribanov had no alternative but to risk letting Penkovsky share more

---

665 Bagley, **Spymaster** (New York: Skyhorse, 2013), p. 215.
666 Ibid, pp. 215-216.
667 Bagley, **Spy Wars**, pp. 21-22.
668 Bagley, "Ghosts of the Spy Wars", pp. 4-6.

INTO THE STORM

genuine Soviet secrets with his Western handlers. Penkovsky met repeatedly with the joint handling team during a July-August trip to London and again during a September-October trip to Paris.[669]

More insurance was added to the protection for the KGB mole in MI-6 after Penkovsky returned to Moscow in late October 1961. Gribanov allowed him to pass important secret documents for *another year* to American and British Embassy officials in Moscow.[670] However, Penkovsky applied five more times for further official trips abroad that were sponsored and backed by the GRU; but they were all turned down at the last minute—by the KGB for trivial matters that had long since been settled.[671] Penkovsky was not arrested until a false surveillance scenario for the arrest had been concocted, and Gribanov was satisfied that he had Penkovsky cornered "like a bear in its den."[672] Penkovsky sensed the impending danger. In August 1962, he wrote that he had "grown used to the degree of surveillance and control over my movements," and that "there is some reason for this KGB activity."[673] Penkovsky was arrested during the Cuban Missile Crisis in October 1962. He was tried and executed in 1963.

Meanwhile, by April 1962, with Penkovsky securely confined to Moscow, Gribanov had felt it safe to finally launch operation Boomerang. Later that year, Polyakov was "recruited" by the FBI in New York and given the codename "Tophat." By that time, however, it had become necessary for Polyakov to return to Russia. He remained there until 1966.[674] During subsequent assignments abroad, Polyakov—for his own reasons—decided to become *a triple agent*. Once again, Gribanov soon learned about this turn of events. His first false defector had turned against his KGB masters. And, *once again*, Gribanov had to wait for years before concocting a false "discovering" of Polyakov's treachery to protect the source of the tipoff. Eventually, in 1986, Polyakov was secretly tried and shot.

---

669   Ibid, p. 22.
670   Ibid, p. 9.
671   Bagley, ***Spy Wars***, p. 22. As Bagley explained: Penkovsky "was given to understand that this was merely a provisional situation, pending the KGB's clarification of doubts about the true fate of his father, a White Russian officer killed in 1919 during the Russian Civil War. For some unknown reason this old question, long ago laid to rest, had been revived.
672   Bagley, "Ghosts of the Spy Wars", p. 9.
673   Oleg Penkovsky, ***The Penkovsky Papers*** (New York: Doubleday, 1965), p. 372.
674   Ibid, pp. 4-8. Polyakov reappeared in 1966, when he was posted as the Soviet military attaché in Rangoon, Burma. The CIA handler in Burma initially assessed Polyakov as a KGB plant, but after the passage of time, a dramatic improvement in his reporting developed, and it appeared certain that Polyakov was genuinely cooperating. In May 1980, he was abruptly recalled to Moscow where he was tried in secret and executed for being a CIA spy. Pete Bagley learned from Kondrashev that Polyakov had been sent as a false defector but, after some time and for his own reasons, he decided to switch sides. Kondrashev explained that Polyakov was executed "Because they found out he was giving you more than he was supposed to." However, Kondrashev did not reveal to Bagley the source who knew "exactly how much Polyakov was reporting to the CIA." As Bagley surmised, "It had to be someone inside CIA's Soviet operations staff. ... The whole gamut of Polyakov's reporting could have been known only by his CIA handlers and those dealing with his raw reports."

After the Cold War, Kondrashev revealed to Bagley that Polyakov had gone off script and revealed much more to the CIA than he was supposed to. From that tip, Pete Bagley surmised that Gribanov's source had to have been a mole *inside CIA's Soviet operations*.[675] In his 2009 autobiography **Spymaster**, Oleg Kalugin, who had served as the chief of foreign counterintelligence (K branch) of the First Chief Directorate (FCD), supported Bagley's surmise about Polyakov. Kalugin recalled a meeting in the 1970s with one of his top agents in Paris:

> ...we talked at length about *information he had picked up from CIA sources* that the Americans had a high-level spy in the KGB or Soviet military intelligence (GRU). I got the distinct impression from the Frenchman that the mole was in the GRU, and years later I would be proven right when *our sources in the CIA and the FBI* gave us information that led to the arrest of GRU General Nikolai Polyakov. The GRU man had been spying for the Americans for fifteen years, passing on key information on Soviet military strategy.[676] [Emphasis added]

The name of the mole who identified Polyakov as a triple agent has never been revealed. Nor has the name of the KGB mole in the CIA who gave up Popov. They would, as Bagley described them, become more *ghosts of the spy wars*. They might have been the same person.

The Defection of Anatoliy Golitsyn

On 15 December 1961, KGB Major Anatoliy Golitsyn defected with his wife and daughter to the CIA from his post as the vice counsel in Helsinki, Finland. Born in 1926 near Poltava, Ukraine, Golitsyn joined the communist youth movement (Komsomol) in Moscow in 1941. In 1945, while studying at the officers' artillery school in Odessa, Golitsyn became a member of the Communist Party of the Soviet Union (CPSU). During that same year Golitsyn entered military counterintelligence, and he graduated from the Moscow School of Military Counterespionage in 1946. He then entered the Soviet intelligence service.

After several years in Vienna, Golitsyn returned to Moscow and attended the KGB Academy and graduated with a law degree in 1959. This was the moment that KGB Chief Shelepin created the super-secret "inner" KGB for the purpose of coordinating world-wide strategic deception in support of Soviet foreign policy objectives. Already

---

675 Ibid, p. 8.
676 Oleg Kalugin, *Spymaster* (New York: Basic Books, 2009), p. 192.

INTO THE STORM

disillusioned with the Soviet system, the Shelepin Plan precipitated Golitsyn's decision to break with the regime:

> Having reached his decision, he began systematically to elicit and commit to memory information that he thought would be relevant and valuable to the West. ... He felt that the necessity of warning the West of the new dimensions of the threat that it was facing justified him abandoning his country and facing the personal sacrifices involved.[677]

At the time, Golitsyn was the vice counsel and attaché at the Soviet Embassy in Helsinki, Finland. On 22 December 1961, he walked into the American Embassy in Helsinki in the midst of a blinding snowstorm. Golitsyn told the Marine guard on duty that he was a Soviet Embassy official and asked to see the CIA station chief by name.[678]

Golitsyn provided information about many famous Soviet agents including Donald Maclean, Guy Burgess and John Vassall. His defection led to the process that definitively proved that the head of counterespionage operations for Britain's MI-6, Kim Philby, was a Soviet mole. But Golitsyn's most important gift to Western intelligence was his warning about the new Soviet efforts in the field of *dezinformatsiya*, Russian for disinformation:

> The term means a systematic effort to disseminate false information and to distort or withhold information so as to misrepresent the real situation in, and policies of, the communist world and thereby to confuse, deceive, and influence the noncommunist world, to jeopardize its policies and to induce Western adversaries to contribute unwittingly to the achievement of communist objectives.[679]

Golitsyn stated that although this new strategic capability had been in effect since 1958, its existence had been either ignored or discounted in the West.

In his book ***New Lies for Old***, Golitsyn described the dark dimensions of the Soviet disinformation threat:

> The special role of disinformation is enhanced by the aggressive and ambitious character of the communist external policy. ... It is the combination of aggressiveness with disinformation that gives communist policy its conspiratorial charter. This combination is not a matter of speculation but an existing and constant reality in communist activity that cannot be arbitrarily ignored by Western governments and scholars without affecting the accuracy and realism of their assessments of the communist world. ... Communist disinformation operations are controlled at the highest level of government. They

---

677   Anatoliy Golitsyn, *New Lies for Old* (San Pedro California: GSG & Associates, 1984), p. xv.
678   Epstein, *Deception*, p. 54.
679   Golitsyn, *New Lies for Old*, pp. 4-5.

> serve to support the interests of long-range policy, and their forms, patterns and objectives are therefore determined by the nature of the policy in any given period.

In short, Golitsyn warned, the scope and scale of communist disinformation activity was "virtually unlimited."[680]

Golitsyn was also able to assist the CIA in its most challenging endeavor—distinguishing the difference between genuine and false Soviet defectors. The CIA approved Golitsyn's immediate evacuation from Helsinki. The Soviet Russia Division wanted to use him to identify other potential defectors in the Soviet diplomatic corps.[681] Upon his arrival at the CIA, Golitsyn rang alarm bells by revealing that the KGB had discovered Popov's treason in 1957. This lead would ultimately help Bagley to realize that the head of the KGB's unit working against the American Embassy in Moscow, Vladislav Kovshuk, had travelled to Washington to meet with the Soviet mole in the CIA who reported Popov's defection.[682]

Anatoliy Golitsyn's defection took place in between two tantalizing job offers to General Sergey Kondrashev, the then acting KGB chief in Vienna. Within weeks of the second offer from Gribanov, his subordinate, Yuri Nosenko, defected in Geneva, Switzerland. CIA staff officer Bagley was on hand to accept Nosenko's defection. Within a year, Bagley concluded that the KGB might have sent Nosenko to CIA to divert them from Golitsyn's leads.[683]

After the Cold War, a close friendship developed between Kondrashev and Bagley. Startling revelations emerged from their relationship that would cast light on the defections of Popov and Nosenko and how Lee Harvey Oswald became entangled in the hardest fought counterintelligence battle of the Cold War. I will have much more to say about these matters in Chapter Twelve.

---

680 Ibid, pp. 7-8.
681 Epstein, *Deception*, p. 55.
682 Bagley, *Spy Wars*, pp. 26, 64, and 14; see also Bagley, "Ghosts of the Spy Wars," pp.14 and 33.
683 Bagley, *Spy Wars*, pp. 23-26.

CHAPTER NINE

RFK AND THE CASTRO ASSASSINATION PLOTS— PART I

For more than thirty years, Halpern continued to spread slanderous stories, painting JFK and RFK as the masterminds of the CIA's assassination intrigues.
Robert F. Kennedy, Jr., **American Values**[684]

This chapter picks up where Chapter Seven left off. That chapter explored an imaginary event: the alleged repeated demands by President Kennedy—right after his inauguration—for the creation of an assassination capability in the Central Intelligence Agency. I discussed how Sam Halpern *piled onto* the false JFK Executive Action directive. That lie did not originate with Halpern; rather, it was the brainchild of DDP Bissell. Halpern, however, *owned* the RFK-Mafia plot—lock, stock and barrel. Moreover, Halpern expropriated Bissell's JFK fabrication for use as the cornerstone of his RFK myth.

This chapter is the first of a *three-chapter series* (including Chapters Ten and Thirteen) that will focus on a false and deeply disturbing story furtively implanted into American consciousness. Over the past five decades, deceptive new information has

---

[684] Robert F. Kennedy Jr., *American Values—Lessons I Learned from My Family* (New York: Harper Collins Publishers, 2018), p. 131.

INTO THE STORM

been gradually woven into the fabric of an already disturbing nightmare—the assassination of President Kennedy.

At the secret level, the interleaving of this disturbing data began at least as early as the 1967 CIA Inspector General's Report. Since then, fragmentary details have seeped into a much broader spectrum of the body politic, surfacing in interviews, books, and documentaries about the Kennedy presidency. The hodge-podge fictional narrative history that emerged was this: a Robert Kennedy plot to use the Mafia to assassinate Fidel Castro in 1962 that was turned around and ended up killing his brother and nearly starting World War III.[685]

The tethering of Bobby Kennedy to that make-believe Mafia plot was the handiwork of CIA staff officer Sam Halpern. The *history* of the preposterous lie that RFK was behind a CIA-Mafia plot to kill Castro is one of the least understood and most successful deception campaigns ever conducted by a CIA staff officer. The Association of Former Intelligence Officers (AFIO) were awe struck with Halpern's performance—so much so that AFIO singled out the *blaming of RFK* for this "covert" Mafia scheme as the shining example of Halpern's lifetime of accomplishments.

In this chapter and Chapters Ten and Thirteen, I will subject Halpern's RFK-Mafia myth to an examination at a level of resolution never before attempted.

Examining Halpern's RFK Narrative—A Methodological Approach

Given the historical significance of Halpern's RFK story and the present popularity of the Castro-killed-Kennedy paradigm, nothing less than a rigorous examination is called for. The methodology I will employ is analogous to what most people have experienced when watching time-lapsed photography. The slow movement of objects through time are observable through the *horizontal merging* ("splicing") of frames separated by longer units of time.

A similar effect can be achieved with information arranged through *vertically merging* transparent overlays of the data. By selecting information for the overlays from different sources, a more complete picture of the subject becomes visible. In U.S. Army Intelligence we use this approach to obtain an accurate picture of the battlefield. One overlay would be information about the disposition of friendly forces; another overlay would be information about the disposition of enemy forces; and

---

[685] 11/22/63, Hoover memorandum RE 4:01 p.m. telephone call to Robert Kennedy, see Newman, *Oswald and the CIA* (2008 Edition), p. 642; 11/29/63 LBJ-Russell Telephone Conversation, see Beschloss, *Taking Charge—The Johnson White House Tapes, 1963-1964*, pp. 66-72; 12/8/72, "Johnson Feared War After Slaying of JFK—Warren," *Washington Star News*.

other overlays would be information about geography, weather, illumination, and other factors that can affect the outcome of a conflict. We call this the *Intelligence Preparation of the Battlefield* (IPB).

To examine Halpern's theories about Robert Kennedy's activities in 1962, I will employ a methodology similar to the IPB. Three transparent overlays of information will be superimposed together. In this chapter, I will discuss the first overlay. The information in it will present a chronological illustration of Halpern's RFK-Mafia façade. The complicated nature of Halpern's fabrications will require careful analysis and explanation. The audit trail of every piece of oral evidence must be carefully tracked from the moment of creation to its resting place in Halpern's epic RFK-Mafia story.

In Chapter Ten, I will add the second overlay. Mercifully, it is more straightforward than the first. The second overlay is a thorough arrangement of information from contemporary CIA cables and internal memoranda from 1962 describing Bobby Kennedy's routine requests for CIA assistance. When this layer of evidence is superimposed over Halpern's RFK history, the results are startling.

Finally, in Chapter Thirteen I will add a third revealing overlay and superimpose it over the first two. That overlay sets forth the *true CIA-Mafia plot* to assassinate Castro and the secret transfer of that plot in 1962 from the CIA Security Office to Halpern's boss, William Harvey. The superimposition of this third overlay reveals how the CIA kept RFK in the dark about the transfer of the plot to Harvey *and* how Sam Halpern conflated Bobby's routine requests described in the second overlay (Chapter Ten) into the threads of a single epic.

Samuel Lieb Halpern

Samuel Lieb Halpern was born on 23 February 1922, in Brooklyn, New York. His father, Henoch, was 26 and his mother, Edis, was 24; he had a brother, Nathan, and a sister, Helen. In 1942, he graduated Phi Beta Kappa in History from City College of New York. Halpern married Kathryn Louise Detreux on 5 June 1948, in the District of Columbia. They had two children during their marriage, Michael and Anne Louise. Halpern died from dementia on 7 March 2005, at the age of 83.[686]

During World War II, Halpern's graduate studies at Columbia University and George Washington University soon fell victim to a fascination with intelligence work. In 1943, he was assigned to the Research and Analysis Branch in the Far East Division of the Office of Strategic Services (OSS), and was posted to India, Ceylon, and Burma. In October 1945, the Secret Intelligence and Counterintelligence branches of the OSS

---

[686] 3/12/2005, *Washington Post* obituary on Samuel Halpern.

were reorganized into the Strategic Services Unit (SSU). In January 1946, the SSU was subsumed into the Central Intelligence Group (CIG). Finally, in 1947, the SSU and CIG were transferred into the newly created Central Intelligence Agency (CIA).

Halpern spent several years in the CIA's Tokyo Station before his 1961 transfer to the Agency's Cuban operation in the post-Bay of Pigs wasteland at CIA headquarters. In October, Halpern was assigned as the deputy chief on the Cuba Desk (WH/4) by DDP Bissell.[687] In early 1962, Halpern became a special assistant (and later, executive assistant) to William Harvey, the chief of the new Cuban component Task Force W (TFW). TFW handled the CIA's part of the Kennedys' Operation Mongoose, headed by Attorney General Robert Kennedy and General Edward Lansdale.

Halpern retired in 1974. He served on the Board of Directors of the Association of Former Intelligence Officers (AFIO—created by David Atlee Phillips) from 1984 until his death in 2005. His AFIO obituary lauded his CIA career and his *uncanny recall* with this memorial:

> Many of us had his number on speed-dial as questions arose needing his precision and uncanny recall of who said what, when, and why. His dedication to the work of and mission of OSS and CIA (and later, AFIO), and his willingness in his retirement years to assist so many organizations, authors, researchers, journalists—a rare trait by one who closely guarded thousands of secrets of the clandestine services—leaves an immense gap in our institutional memory.

For the purposes of the critique of Halpern in this chapter and Chapters Ten and Thirteen, it is especially noteworthy that the author of his AFIO obit singled out—*above all else*—this particular legacy of Halpern's generosity:

> Halpern corrected many misperceptions about the role CIA officers played in covert actions, showing that most were done at the behest of the White House (e.g., *that Robert Kennedy put the CIA under pressure to arrange the assassination of Castro*).

Sooner or later this incongruous tribute to Sam Halpern's legacy will become an embarrassing lapel pin for AFIO. Ironically, Halpern's RFK assassination pressures accolade is the *worst* example of his legendary encyclopedic recall. His shiny RFK bauble *was not only* a correction of a misperception, it was *also* a terrible lie. That raises these questions: Did Halpern know it was a lie and, if so, when did he figure out that it was? And, if he did so, then what did he do about it?

---

[687] Weber, ***Spymasters: Ten CIA Officers in their Own Words*** (Lanham MD: Rowman & Littlefield Publishers, 1999), p. 122.

RFK AND THE CASTRO ASSASSINATION PLOTS—PART I

The Historical Sources for Halpern's Alleged RFK-Mafia Plot to Assassinate Castro

The history of Halpern's RFK-Mafia Castro assassination plot is scattered among a variety of accounts that took place over a period of more than three decades. From what I have thus far been able to reconstruct, those accounts include the following:

- Halpern's 1967 discussions with Scott Breckinridge during the latter's participation in the CIA Inspector General's investigation of the Agency's assassination plots against Castro.[688]
- Halpern's discussions with former DCI Richard Helms prior to Helms' 13 June 1975 Church Committee deposition—those discussions may possibly have taken place much earlier.[689]
- Helms' 13 June 1975 Church Committee deposition; the DCI's assistant *Walter Elder mistakenly thought Helms' testimony independently confirmed Halpern's RFK claims.*[690]
- Halpern's 18 June 1975 Church Committee deposition.[691]
- Halpern's 30 October 1987 long interview with Ralph E. Weber, former member of the AFIO Board of Directors and former CIA and NSA Scholar in Residence; and Halpern's later 1995 interview with Weber for his 1997 book.[692]
- Halpern's 15 January 1988 interview with Deputy Chief of the CIA History Staff Mary McAuliffe.[693]
- Halpern's interviews with Seymour Hersh for his book, ***The Dark Side of Camelot***.[694]
- Halpern's 7 April 1998 interview with CIA officers Brian Latell and Michael Warner.[695]

The central character in Halpern's RFK-Mafia myth was CIA staff officer Charles Ford. Halpern claims that Ford was Robert Kennedy's "personal case officer" for contacts with the Mafia. In Chapter Ten, I will discuss Ford's 18 September 1975 seminal sworn interview with the Church Committee in detail. In this chapter, it will be necessary to occasionally refer to Ford.

---

688 5/23/67, CIA Inspector General's (IG) **Report on Plots to Assassinate Fidel Castro**; RIF 104-10213-10101.
689 6/13/75, Helms SSCIA deposition, pp. 129-130; RIF 157-10014-10075.
690 Ibid. See also 8/26/75, Walter Elder memo for Special Assistant to DDO; RIF 104-10310-10198.
691 6/18/75, Halpern SSCIA deposition; RIF 157-10002-10087.
692 Weber, **Spymasters: Ten CIA Officers in their Own Words** (Lanham MD: Rowman & Littlefield Publishers, 1999).
693 1/15/78, Halpern interview with Mary McAuliffe; 104-10324-10003.
694 Hersh, Seymour, **The Dark Side of Camelot** (New York: Little, Brown and Company, 1997 ed.).
695 4/7/98, CIA Center for the Study of Intelligence, Sam Halpern Interview by Brian Latell and Michael Warner, pp. 23-24; RIF 104-10324-10000.

INTO THE STORM

Halpern's 1967 Tale to Breckinridge about the RFK-Mafia Plot

Before delving into Halpern's interviews with CIA Deputy Inspector General (IG) Scott Breckinridge for the IG *Report on Plots to Assassinate Fidel Castro*, I need to mention the circumstances under which the details of those interviews were made public. Those details provided the first *known* occurrence of Sam Halpern's story about an RFK-Mafia plot to assassinate Fidel Castro. Although the interviews took place during the spring of 1967, they were *not* memorialized until Breckinridge's 1993 book, *CIA and the Cold War*.[696] That long delay raises this question: Given Breckinridge's role as a principal author of the IG Report, why did Halpern's account fail to make it into the report? As I suggested in Chapter Seven, Bissell's convenient lapse of memory about his allegation that JFK ordered the creation of an Executive Action program might have contributed to the absence of Halpern's claims in the final IG Report.

Many important events transpired during the twenty-six years between those 1967 Halpern interviews and the appearance of the Breckinridge book. Three years *after* the publication of *CIA and the Cold War*, Seymour Hersh interviewed Breckinridge in preparation for his 1997 book, *The Dark Side of Camelot*. Hersh was *very* interested in what Breckinridge had to say about Halpern's account of RFK's alleged Mafia plot to assassinate Castro. I will postpone a detailed discussion of Hersh's intrusion into these matters until Chapter Thirteen.

Here, I want to mention the *chronological scope* of RFK's alleged plotting that Halpern provided to Hersh. During his mid-1990s interviews with Hersh, Halpern anchored the start of RFK's alleged *eighteen-month-long* campaign to kill Castro in "the early spring of 1962"; and Halpern placed the end of that campaign with the death of JFK in November 1963.[697] The importance of this *changing* time horizon will become more apparent as the chapters devoted to Halpern's foul fiction unfold.

Breckinridge's handling of Halpern's RFK tale in 1993 is noteworthy. I will constrain my discussion about this to Breckinridge's published recollections resulting from his 1967 interviews with Halpern. Those conversations with Halpern took place during a two-month period (mid-March to mid-May) during the 1967 investigation for the IG Report. In his 1993 book, Breckinridge described Halpern's RFK-Mafia thesis in what he [Breckinridge] referred to as a "footnote on the Cuban affair, as told to me initially and in part by Xog, added to later *by Sam H., a senior officer in CIA'S Cuba task force much of that time.*"[698] Xog was an obvious pseudonym for Halpern's colleague, Goshen Zogbey, and Sam H. was an obvious reference to Samuel Halpern.

---

696 Breckinridge, *CIA and the Cold War* (Westport, Connecticut: Praeger, 1993).
697 Hersh, *The Dark Side of Camelot*, p. 286.
698 Breckinridge, *CIA and the Cold War*, pp. 94-95.

RFK AND THE CASTRO ASSASSINATION PLOTS—PART I

Breckinridge's 1993 account recalled how Bill Harvey was assigned to organize and energize the Cuban program and how he was subjected to "intense pressure from the attorney general [RFK] to do more." Breckinridge offered this recollection:

> Among the initiatives emanating from Mongoose [in 1962] was one arising from a *theory* entertained by the attorney general that the criminal syndicate, the Mafia, must have channels into Cuba to protect such remaining assets as they might have there. *CIA was directed to provide an operations officer to meet with Mafia figures identified by Kennedy under circumstances over which CIA had no control.*[699] [Emphasis added]

The operations officer being alluded to in the above alleged RFK-Mafia plot was *obviously* Charles Ford (RFK's alleged case officer)—although Hersh would later describe Breckinridge's identification of Ford as *cryptic*.[700] In Chapter Ten, I will describe how this apparent dramatic use of Ford resulted from nothing more than routine RFK referrals of requests to the CIA for assistance to anti-Castro Cubans.

Meanwhile, Breckinridge's Cuban "footnote" also included a memorable description about how Bobby Kennedy's *unprofessional* activities made life uneasy and difficult for the CIA officers who got caught up in them:

> *It was not at all easy or comfortable* for CIA operations officers to carry out unprofessionally conceived clandestine activities run by a young man who spoke for the president as few, if any, could. The attorney general's initiative in involving the syndicate is interesting… …*For some it will suggest the genesis of CIA's decision to approach the syndicate again in its plan against Castro during the Kennedy Administration.*[701] [Emphasis added]

This recollection and interpretation are significant for two reasons. One reason concerns how Breckinridge's description of the *unease and discomfort* endured by CIA officers at the hands of Bobby Kennedy metastasized in the hands of Halpern. It grew aggressively into an *exaggerated tale* in Hersh's 1997 book and Halpern's 1998 CIA interview with Latell and Warner (mentioned below and discussed in detail in Chapter Thirteen). According to those later accounts, the CIA operations officers of Task Force W suffered *humiliation* under the pressures of an overzealous attorney general.

The other reason Breckinridge's book is important concerns his false accusation that RFK was behind the *CIA's decision to approach the syndicate again*. No matter what Breckinridge did or did not know at the time, that indictment was just about the most perverse subversion of the truth in the then twenty-five-year-old canard (fifty-six years today) about the RFK-Mafia plot. In Chapters Ten and Thirteen, the facts will show indisputably that in May 1962, when the CIA Security Office discovered how angry

---

699 Ibid, p. 95.
700 Hersh, *The Dark Side of Camelot*, p. 287.
701 Breckinridge, *CIA and the Cold War*, p. 95.

Robert Kennedy was upon learning about the CIA-Mafia plot to assassinate Castro, its officers lied to the attorney general. They told RFK that *they had put a stop to the operation*. The truth was that the Security Office had passed the operation on to Bill Harvey. Afterward, it was, as Helms admitted in 1975, a Harvey hip pocket plot.[702] It was *not* a back channel RFK operation. In a nutshell, *the very operation that Robert Kennedy had forbade was secretly continued behind his back, and then, later, blamed on him!*

In 1967, Breckinridge said Halpern's RFK-Mafia scenario suggested, "for some" people, the use of assassination. Under oath in his 1975 deposition to the Church Committee, however, Halpern denied that the alleged RFK-Mafia plot involved assassination. That denial illustrates Halpern's perfidy. Not under oath in his later interviews, Halpern alleged that RFK *did* intend assassination to be the purpose of his plot. Then, as now, lying in not a crime, but perjury is.

I will return to these events in Chapter Ten and close this section of the present chapter with this observation: The primary source of Breckinridge's misinformation about RFK was Sam Halpern. It was in play no later than the spring of 1967. It might have been invented even earlier.

Halpern's 1975 Briefing of DDP Helms for His Church Committee Deposition

The second episode of Sam Halpern's story about an RFK-Mafia plot to assassinate Fidel Castro occurred seven years after Halpern's interviews with Breckinridge. It took place during the period between the spring of 1974 and the summer of 1975. I have identified two sources for that episode. The first source was Halpern's recollection—proffered during a 1987 interview with CIA biographer Ralph Weber—about a briefing he gave to former DCI Richard Helms. At that time in June 1975, Helms was preparing for his deposition before the Church Committee. (In late 1961, Helms had succeeded Bissell as the DDP.)

The second source was Helms testimony during his Church Committee deposition about the remarks made to him by Halpern about the RFK-Mafia matter during their "chat." I will discuss Helms' recollection of that chat in a section below. Here, I will deal with Halpern's recollection of that event.

I will begin with the reason why Helms was called to testify before the Church Committee. On 20 September 1974, a dramatic expose by Seymour Hersh appeared under a page-one banner headline in the ***New York Times***: "CIA is Linked to Strikes that Beset Allende in Chile." On 22 December 1974, an even more sensational expose

---

702   SSCIA Interim Report, p. 151; see also 6/13/75 Helms SSCIA deposition, pp. 57-58; RIF 157-10014-10075.

appeared under another front-page banner headline in the *New York Times*: "Huge CIA Operation Reported in U.S. Against Anti-War Forces, Other Dissidents in Nixon Years." The Hersh revelations about the CIA's role in the overthrow of Chilean President Salvador Allende and in illegal domestic spying operations in the U.S. precipitated congressional investigations into the so-called "family jewels" of the Agency.

Thus, a direct result of Hersh's two 1974 articles was the formation of the Rockefeller Commission and the Senate Select Committee to Study Governmental Operations with Respect to Intelligence Activities (SSCIA), commonly known as the Church Committee, for its chairman, the Democratic senator from Idaho, Frank Church. The large number of senior CIA officers who were hauled before the Church Committee led to the formation of a makeshift "Review Staff" in the Agency to deal with the work caused by this sudden unwelcome limelight. This temporary staff was created by Walter Elder, the assistant to DCI William Colby. Scott Breckinridge was assigned to the Review Staff and was joined by Seymour Bolten, a CIA staff officer who was called out of retirement to help.[703]

Bolten persuaded Halpern—who described Bolten as his "sidekick"—to join the staff:

> ...he finally convinced me to come on back to the Agency to help out, pulling together the stuff, because they kind of felt *I knew where the poop was*. ... and so, I was there in January of 1975 and stayed on until about March, I think, maybe April 1975.[704] [Emphasis added]

Among the key CIA witnesses were former DCI Dick Helms and former Counterintelligence Chief Tom Karamessines. In the Weber interview, Halpern described how he ended up briefing Helms:

> Helms was being called back so many times for the various committees, that he was almost like a yo-yo from Teheran as ambassador. ... And on one of his trips, *he asked me to brief him*, and Tom Karamessines, as matter of fact, about the background of the Cuban Missile Crisis and some of the activities during the Cuban Missile Crisis. The whole Operation Mongoose thing. *Particularly Mongoose which was very hot at that particular point. And a few other details.*[705] [Emphasis added]

Halpern explained that the "brass" was not supposed to remember *details* and that his role was to supply that kind of "*poop*":

> So, I talked to Dick and talked to Tom and gave them as much as I could. And I just guessed that somewhere along the way in their private discussion or private testimony the stuff that wasn't the public stuff,

---

703 10/30/87, Ralph E. Weber Interview with Sam Halpern, p. 88; RIF 104-10324-10002.
704 Ibid.
705 Ibid, p. 77.

> before you get in front of the public television and what have you, Dick must have said, or Tom must have said, "*and if you want any more detail get a hold of Sam.*" ... And sure enough, I got the call. I didn't care. I got nothing to hide. I'm proud of what I did all these years. And so, if they don't like it, that's tough. ... *And that's how I think I got picked.*[706]
> [Emphasis added]

Halpern's recollection on this point is accurate and he *wasn't* guessing. He had read Helms' transcript. Halpern was called to testify before the Church Committee because Helms, during one of his depositions, *had* suggested it.

We know that Halpern relished all of this attention and exposure. He told Ralph Weber about the social gatherings that occurred as the Review Staff prepared for the media frenzy surrounding the depositions of CIA officers. Halpern basked in the adulation he had received at committee dinner parties:

> Anyway, at this dinner party *I was the target of the night, obviously, and everybody zeroed in on me*, before dinner and after dinner and everything else. ... and *I said*, "You are going to be surprised at the fact that you are not going to find very much paper around." ... And the guy said, "Don't you guys ever put anything in writing?" *I said*, "We can, but if we can avoid it, no." ... *And the whole purpose was to try to get me, I suppose, to tell them how to find things and what to look for.*[707]

So, just as he did for the guests at that dinner party, Halpern told Helms *what to look for*. As events turned out—probably at the direction of Committee Chairman Frank Church—Halpern was called to testify after Helms.

Halpern on the Paperwork Paucity Problem

Before moving on, I want to very briefly expand upon a point Halpern made at the above committee staff dinner party. I will call it the *paperwork paucity problem*. At the party, his remarks about the deliberate lack of supporting "paper" for certain events were devoid of any innuendo about assassinations. But, on occasions when assassination *was* the topic of conversation, Halpern *frequently invoked* the paperwork paucity problem. He did so in his Church Committee deposition[708]; he used this explanation in his interview

---

706 Ibid.
707 Ibid, p. 78.
708 See, for example, 6/18/75, Halpern SSCIA deposition, pp. 54-55; RIF 157-10002-10087.

with Ralph Weber[709]; he did so again in his interview with Latell and Warner[710]; and, of course, he made *special* use of this device in his interviews for Seymour Hersh.[711]

But here, I want to alert the reader to the fact that Halpern found the paperwork paucity problem *particularly* useful when it came time to explain the lack of supporting documentation *for his own* RFK-Mafia myth. In Chapters Ten and Thirteen, I will discuss the *abundant Church Committee and CIA paperwork* that debunks Halpern's Kennedy mythology. Moreover, I will show conclusively that Halpern and Sy Hersh *ignored* that documentation when they concocted another malicious lie about Robert Kennedy. They blamed the *disappearance* of reports Ford allegedly made about his contacts with the Mafia on "instructions" from Bobby. In Chapter Ten, I will show that Ford's Cuban contact reports *were preserved in CIA records*—and also how they thoroughly discredit Halpern's RFK-Mafia fiction.

Here, I want to return the reader's attention to Richard Helms. He becomes increasingly important as the four crucial chapters of the present volume unfold (Seven, Nine, Ten, and Thirteen). They form a multifaceted expository treatment of Halpern's RFK myth, alongside the CIA's assassination plotting against Fidel Castro. As we delve deeper into the labyrinthine activities of William Harvey and his aspiring self-possessed assistant Sam Halpern, we notice the shadowy figure of Richard Helms looming ever larger.

Halpern's 1975 Deposition about McCone's Bombshell and "His Man on Cuba"

One of the more stimulating moments in Sam Halpern's 18 June 1975 Church Committee deposition concerned the moment that the new DCI, John McCone, informed his subordinates about who would henceforth be running Cuban operations in the CIA. As I have already indicated, the officer was Helms:

> Mr. Schwarz: Now did Mr. Helms enter the picture in the latter part of December 1961?
>
> Mr. Halpern: That is correct.
>
> Mr. Schwarz: Describe how he came into the picture.
>
> Mr. Halpern: To my knowledge [Zogbey] described to me a meeting he had attended at the director's morning staff meeting—this is Mr. McCone's morning staff meeting—in which Mr. McCone almost in terms of a *bombshell* for the group at the meeting stated that Mr. Helms

---

709   10/30/87, Ralph E. Weber Interview with Sam Halpern, p. 101, RIF 104-10324-10002.
710   4/7/98, CIA Center for the Study of Intelligence, Sam Halpern Interview by Brian Latell and Michael Warner, p. 24, RIF 104-10324-10000.
711   Hersh, ***The Dark Side of Camelot***, p. 449.

would henceforth be—the words were, *his man on Cuba*. This was something that nobody in the room apparently had any inkling of, and particularly Mr. Helms, nor [Mr. Zogbey].

The Chairman: May I ask you to repeat that? I am sorry, I just didn't catch it.

Mr. Halpern: At a meeting sometime in December 1961, which was the morning staff meeting that the Director held, and [Mr. Zogbey] was present.

Mr. Schwarz: But you were not?

Mr. Halpern: I was not, I got this from [Mr. Zogbey]—the Director, Mr. McCone, announced that *Mr. Helms would be his man on Cuba*. Mr. Helms would then be the Chief of Operations for the Deputy Director of Plans, and Mr. Bissell was in the room as the DDP. Mr. Helms had no inkling of this before the meeting, and so stated to [Mr. Zogbey] and even asked [Zogbey] if he had had any inkling before the meeting. [Mr. Zogbey] told me that he had none whatsoever.[712] [Emphasis added]

It was an unusual management style to announce such an important decision unknown to those present—all of whom were directly affected by the news.

McCone's take-charge style during that December meeting was no doubt partly or mostly the result of the impression left on him by the president's remarks at McCone's White House swearing in ceremony on 29 November as the new DCI. The firing of Allen Dulles and his deputy, Charles Cabell, was the direct consequence of the Cuban cataclysm (see Chapter Four), but McCone's ceremony was also timed to coincide with the purge at State connected to Vietnam policy. President Kennedy limited his remarks to a few sentences, and the last one was an unmistakable warning: "We want to welcome you here and to say that you are now living on the bull's-eye, and I welcome you to that spot."[713] That threat no doubt impressed McCone and also resonated throughout the rest of the agency.[714]

It did not take Helms long to take a close look at just who was left in the Cuban shop—after the Bay of Pigs debacle—to handle the difficult mission that lay ahead. That subject, too, came up in Halpern's Church Committee deposition:

Mr. Schwarz: Did Mr. Helms then come and visit your new organization and tell you to make some changes?

Mr. Halpern: Yes. He came to [Mr. Zogbey's] office and looked at the list of officers, male and female, who were still working in the branch.

---

712   6/18/75, Halpern SSCIA deposition, pp. 12-14; RIF 157-10002-10087.
713   Kennedy remarks at the swearing in of John McCone, Central Intelligence Agency, November 29, 1961, **Public Papers**, 1961, p. 490.
714   Newman, *JFK and Vietnam* (2017 Edition), p. 143.

RFK AND THE CASTRO ASSASSINATION PLOTS—PART I

> Most of them were the remnants of the people from the old Bay of Pigs operation who had not yet been reassigned. And when Mr. Helms found that we were also responsible for the rest of the islands of the Caribbean at that time, he immediately decided to call George King [sic],[715] who was the Chief of the Western Hemisphere Division and directed that henceforth Cuba would be a separate activity, and no longer part of the WH Division.
>
> Mr. Schwarz: Now, after that change was made there was another organizational change made, which was the bringing in of Mr. Harvey as the man full time in charge?
>
> Mr. Halpern: That is correct. And that happened about sometime the latter part of January, the beginning of February. I think the announcement within the Agency was that Mr. Harvey was in charge of a new task force that wasn't actually made until about the first of March 1962.[716]

Much can be said—as I will in the chapters that follow—about William Harvey's work as head of the new CIA Cuban component, Task Force W (TFW). And that is also true for Harvey's dubious working relationships with Robert Kennedy and General Lansdale as the new Kennedy program to topple the Castro regime, Operation Mongoose, was launched.

But looming above it all was the new DDP heir apparent, Richard Helms. While his activities take up little space—with few exceptions—in books about the Cuban-American debacle, Helms' role was—in this and other matters—important enough to rate no less than seven depositions before the Church Committee. One of those Helms depositions, taken on 13 June 1975, is sometimes cited as evidence for Halpern's alleged RFK-Mafia plot. *Helms' deposition contained no such evidence.* I now turn to that testimony.

Helms' Crucial 13 June 1975 Church Committee Deposition

It was no coincidence that Halpern was called to testify after only *one particular* deposition out of the seven Helms appearances before the committee. It is that deposition to which I now turn—Helms' 13 June 1975 testimony at which he was asked about Robert Kennedy and the Mafia. On this occasion, Helms also mentioned—without being prompted—that he had discussed Bobby's alleged Mafia case officer, Charles Ford, with Halpern. Helms' testimony about RFK and Halpern was the reason Church would summon Halpern to testify *just* five days later.

---

715 This must be a reference to Colonel J. C. King, the then chief of the Western Hemisphere Division (WHD). Note: John Caldwell was a pseudonym for J. C. King.
716 6/18/75, Halpern SSCIA deposition, pp. 12-14; RIF 157-10002-10087.

Based on how the committee questioned Helms about the RFK-Mafia matter, committee staffers had obviously interviewed Helms before his deposition began:

> Mr. Smothers: *Isn't it true, Mr. Ambassador [Helms], that Mr. [Robert] Kennedy had himself indicated that he desired contact with a Mafia source?* Hadn't he put out a search for Mafia people that might be of help?
>
> Mr. Helms: Well, at one time that's correct, *he suggested* we might have a look at underworld figures and so on. *I'm not sure* exactly in what part of Mongoose or subsequent operations *this came up*, but I believe at one time in connection with the Cuban Task Force there was a case officer actually assigned pursuant to the suggestion to check in New York, Chicago, places like that and see if there were any underworld figures who had ties to Cuba.[717] [Emphasis added]

The reader should note that Smothers did not ask Helms if he had been told this *personally* by RFK or, if not, *who* had told him Bobby wanted contact with a Mafia case officer.

As the deposition continued, Helms was reluctant to be more specific about crucial details of RFK's alleged underworld request:

> Mr. Smothers: So pursuant to Mr. Kennedy's request, a CIA case officer actually began a search for the underworld, the Mafia contacts?
>
> Mr. Helms: Underworld contacts, *I'm not sure* they were Mafia or not.

This exchange shows that Helms was only *vaguely* familiarity with the alleged RFK-Mafia story. If Helms had known about an RFK plot to use the Mafia in 1962, his recollection on such an unusual and controversial affair would still have been sharp. But it was *not* sharp. So much so, that, at this point, Helms was forced to punt the ball to Halpern:

> Mr. Helms: *Some of these facts, I think if you want to run them down, his recollection is much better than mine, you might try Mr. Halpern* or some of the people who were intimately involved in the day to day work of this task force who are still alive. I mean, Harvey is one, but maybe someone from the staff to talk to…
>
> Senator Baker: Which Halpern is this?
>
> Mr. Helms: *It's Samuel Halpern. It's not anybody who's known to you. He's now retired from the agency, but he was involved in these activities.*
>
> Mr. Schwarz: Is he the case officer who was assigned on the Mafia case, is that what you're saying?
>
> Mr. Helms: No, he was not. He was in the operation, *but he recalls this.*
>
> Mr. Schwarz: He recalls the name that you just said?
>
> Mr. Helms: Yes.
>
> Mr. Schwarz: What was the name of the case officer?

---

717   6/13/75 Helms SSCIA deposition, p. 128; RIF 157-10014-10075.

RFK AND THE CASTRO ASSASSINATION PLOTS—PART I

Helms' answers to Baker and Schwarz gave away the identity of the Agency officer from whom he had learned what little he knew about RFK's alleged Mafia case officer. But Helms had *no idea who* that alleged case officer was:

> Mr. Helms: *I don't know. As a matter of fact, the reason I don't know is that he [Halpern] was giving me, when we chatted about this for a moment, he [Halpern] was laughing and gave the nickname that the case officer was given, and I don't remember what his real name was.*[718] [Emphasis added]

Somewhat flummoxed by his inability to provide information about the alleged Mafia case officer, Helms gave away another gem. He said he couldn't remember "the time span" when "this matter [the chat with Halpern] came up." To have revealed how close his "chat" with Halpern had been to this deposition might have been even more embarrassing.

The most important takeaway from these crucial moments of Helms' deposition is this: The sum total of Helms' knowledge about the RFK-Mafia story came from a recent short chat with Sam Halpern, *not* a request from Robert Kennedy in 1962!

There is nothing in the above passage or the rest of Helms' deposition where he mentions that he heard *one word* from Bobby Kennedy about a request for a personal Mafia case officer, the name of the case officer, or the nickname for the case officer. In my view, Helms had no recollection of a 1962 RFK request for a Mafia case officer—because Bobby made no such request. On the other hand, as I will discuss in detail in Chapter Thirteen, Helms *did know about* the crucial details of the *true CIA-Mafia plot* that were unknown to Halpern. The RFK-Mafia plot was a fiction fabricated by Halpern.

So, what led to the belief among a few Church Committee staff members—including Andy Postal and Mike Madigan—that Helms testified that "*he recalls the attorney general asking him to try to find a case officer*" to contact the Mafia?[719] In Chapter Ten, I will show how not one but two memos by DCI assistant Walter Elder—circulating just before the sworn testimony of Charles Ford—led to that erroneous belief. I believe it is likely that Elder had not read the transcript of the above Helms' 13 June 1975 deposition. In addition, it is not impossible that committee staff members attending those evening dinner soirees had picked up misleading scuttlebutt from Halpern about what Helms might say.

Before moving on, it would be useful to spend a moment on the changing of the guard in the CIA's Cuban operations at the end of Kennedy's first year in office.

---

718   Ibid, pp. 129-130.
719   8/26/75, Walter Elder memo for Special Assistant to DDO; RIF 104-10310-10198.

INTO THE STORM

The Ascendancy of Richard Helms in the CIA

The transition from 1961 to 1962 ushered in a sea change in the lineup of players on the Cuban problem at the CIA. DCI Allen Dulles, DDCI Charles Cabell, DDP Richard Bissell, and WH/4 Chief Jacob Esterline had been or would soon be removed, along with an exodus of many officers who had held supervisory positions in the runup to the Bay of Pigs fiasco. Their replacements included DCI John McCone, DDCI General Marshall Carter, DDP Richard Helms, Task Force W Chief William Harvey and his deputy, Bruce Cheever. Initially, Goshen Zogbey was the new chief of WH/4; Zogbey and Halpern soon became assistants to Harvey.

In this round of musical chairs at headquarters, only Richard Helms would survive from the old guard. His presence on Cuban matters was the most interesting aspect of the new lineup. Thomas Parrott[720] remarked that "everyone was depressed" after the Bay of Pigs "except for those who were elated."[721] That quip applied to no one better than Helms, who had triumphed over Bissell, whose temporary delay in leaving the Cuban mission—at President Kennedy's insistence—amounted to slow torture. The president had offered Bissell the chance to take over the new directorate of science and technology, but Bissell declined.

The painfully slow Bissell-Helms transition was marked by a significant twist of fate. In mid-October 1961, Bissell told Harvey that he had received a chewing out in the Cabinet Room by Robert Kennedy for "sitting on his ass" and doing nothing to get rid of Castro and his regime. At the time, Bissell had no explicit authority as he waited for Helms to take his place. What we can take away from Bissell's complaint is that he might have become disgruntled with the attorney general—whether such a chewing out in the Cabinet Room had taken place or not.

In his work, ***The Very Best Men***, Evan Thomas speculated about Bissell's response to the alleged Cabinet Room dressing down:

> *Bissell responded by reactivating the assassination machinery.* A few days after his tongue-lashing, Bissell went to William Harvey and told him to take over the Mafia contacts from Sheff Edwards. Since Harvey was already the head of **ZR/RIFLE**, Bissell's "stand-by executive action capability," it made sense to consolidate.[722] [Emphasis added]

Four months later, the official announcement of Harvey's assumption of the Cuba mission took place. It was merely a formality that had to await the official transition from

---

720 The CIA officer who was formerly the secretary for the Special Group and had since been assigned by President Kennedy as Assistant to the President's Military Representative (Maxwell Taylor); see ***FRUS***, Volume X, Cuba 1961-1962, p. 663.
721 Evan Thomas, ***The Very Best Men***, p. 268.
722 Ibid, p. 271.

RFK AND THE CASTRO ASSASSINATION PLOTS—PART I

Bissell to Helms as the DDP. Evan Thomas suggests that this slow transfer of leadership to Helms left Bissell with time on his hands and an opportunity that he took advantage of. To impress upon the attorney general the old maxim that one should be careful about what one asks for, Bissell left Helms with a live hand grenade—an assassination plot against Castro on steroids.

So, as the new DDP, Helms inherited a secret hot seat atop a Cuban tinderbox. Bissell was aware that the pressure from the White House to get moving on Cuba was taking place in a strange vacuum. *No one* had briefed the Kennedy brothers during the ten months since the inauguration about the fact that there *was* a live CIA-Mafia plot to assassinate Castro!

Helms was a prudent and shrewd bureaucrat. His successful rise in the CIA's covert operations directorate was the result of a risk-averse strategy. His cautious avoidance of participation in Bay of Pigs planning had now been completely vindicated. Dick Drain, who had been the officer in charge of operations in the Cuban task force (WH/4) during the runup to the invasion, offered his perspective for Jack B. Pfeiffer's CIA **Official History of the Bay of Pigs Operation**. Drain's detailed and colorful recollection deserves to be quoted in full:

> Helms was COPS [Chief of Operations]. Either on his own volition, which I suspect or on order—which I doubt—Dick Helms completely divorced himself from this thing. I mean absolutely! The one time that I heard from Helms during this entire project was ... a telephone call from Dick Helms' long-time secretary. "Mr. Helms would like to speak to you." ... three times he said to me in different parts of the conversation ... "As you know I have nothing to do with this project." I said, "Well Mr. Helms, I don't want to be fatuous about this, but I wish to Christ that you did have because we could use your expertise." He said "Hahaha ... yes, well thank you very much," and that was the end of that. He avoided the thing like the plague. One of the reasons may have been that, of course, life went on; and if Bissell was getting increasingly immersed in this one thing, somebody had to watch the whole worldwide store ... which of course Helms was damned good at. A less attractive suggestion is that *Helms figured that there was a high likelihood that this thing would screw up, and he didn't want to have the tar baby around him.* I don't know.[723] [Emphasis added]

Pfeiffer also interviewed Bissell about Helms' non-participation in Bay of Pigs planning. In responding to Pfeiffer's question about this, Bissell gave this rather opaque description:

---

723   Jack B. Pfeiffer, CIA *Official History of the Bay of Pigs Operation, Volume III*, pp. 40-41; 104-10301-10004.

> I think that he [Helms] saw most all of the cable traffic and I think he was pretty well informed as to what was going on, very well informed; but he was really out of the line of command on this operation. There was something of a tacit agreement between us, that he would be devoting himself to a lot of the other ongoing business of the DDP office, because this was taking a great deal of my time. ... Let me say this was probably not that explicit. I would make an observation here and I don't want you to infer anything really beyond what it says, it was not particularly easy—I did not find it particularly easy—to discuss things clearly and derive a clear understanding with Dick [Helms] about the division of labor between us when he was my Deputy. ... it really was our habit during the whole time that we were in those positions that the division of labor between us was more tacit than explicit.[724]

So, ironically, in the end, Helms wound up being the one receiving the most pressure from the White House about getting rid of Castro. But Helms was unable to anticipate much about that in November 1961, as the moment of his succession to Bissell approached.

The inheritance of the CIA-Mafia assassination plot would land the careful career bureaucrat in a precarious position. Evan Thomas described Helms' quandary:

> He felt that he could not simply shut it down, or he would not be carrying out RFK's insistent demands. Yet, *he could not discuss assassination directly with the president or his brother without violating the code of plausible deniability.* Helms personally disapproved of assassination as a tool. But as head of the clandestine service, *he did nothing.* He didn't really expect it to work; indeed, he hoped, in a way, that the whole business would quietly disappear.[725] [Emphasis added]

Helms' resort to the code of plausible deniability to protect the president from responsibility was not a unique practice. At the same time, Helms *still* had the option of arranging a way for the president to know the truth. While we cannot be certain, it is possible that JFK's track record on Cuba, Laos and Vietnam led Helms to decide it was best to keep the Kennedy brothers in the dark.

That was how matters stood in November 1961, but not for long. In Chapters Ten and Thirteen I will discuss the sensitive and startling May 1962 CIA briefing of Bobby Kennedy about the ongoing CIA-Mafia assassination plot. In that briefing, the Agency would lie to the attorney general, telling him the operation had been dropped. The truth was that it had—at that moment—evolved into a Harvey hip pocket plot.[726]

---

724   Ibid, pp. 41-42.
725   Evan Thomas, ***The Very Best Men***, pp. 271-272.
726   SSCIA Interim Report, p. 151; see also 6/13/75 Helms SSCIA deposition, pp. 57-58; RIF 157-10014-10075.

Besides Inspector General Houston, Security Office Director Edwards, and Harvey, *no one else* knew the truth until Harvey let Helms in on the secret. Helms and Harvey agreed to *not* inform the president.[727]

So, from May 1962 onward, the president, the attorney general, and DCI McCone would remain in the dark—*as did Sam Halpern*—about the continuing CIA-Mafia plot. Ironically, Mr. "Encyclopedia" in all things Cuban was remarkably uninformed about the most critical information bearing directly upon his trademark expertise: Robert Kennedy's alleged collusion with the Mafia. Halpern ended up accusing RFK of running an operation he had forbidden, and that Halpern's boss was carrying out *behind the attorney general's back.*

Senator Church's Characterization of Helms' Deposition

The reader will recall (as I stated above and will discuss at length in Chapter Ten) the two memoranda by Walter Elder circulating among the Church Committee staff. Those memos erroneously reported an RFK request to Helms for a Mafia case officer. Helms' supposed recollection of that request under oath was the only independent attestation of Halpern's RFK myth. However, the transcript of Helms' deposition— quoted above—dealt a fatal blow to that myth. Helms appears to have been happy to leave Halpern and his RFK-Mafia story under the bus.

The coup-de-grâce was applied three months later—when Charles Ford testified under oath. Ford's testimony left no doubt that he had no part whatsoever in Halpern's RFK-Mafia scheme. In Chapter Ten, I will add the details of Ford's Church Committee sworn interview and written report about his activities in 1962 to the CIA documentary record about RFK's activities in 1962.

In Chapter Thirteen, I will show the important implications of Halpern's close examination of the Church Committee's November 1975 Interim Report, *Alleged Assassination Plots Involving Foreign Leaders*. That was the moment that Halpern discovered that his boss, Bill Harvey, had been carrying out what he was accusing RFK of doing— working with the Mafia to assassinate Castro!

There is much more to attend to in this chapter before taking up Halpern's eureka moment in the wake of the committee's Interim Report. Here, I want to take the reader to a private prediction that Senator Church shared with his committee colleagues as

---

727 6/13/75, Helms SSCIA Deposition, pp. 90-91: Senator Hart of Michigan: "There is a note in the Inspector General's file there, phase II, that 'Harvey added that when he briefed Helms on Roselli he obtained Helms' approval not to brief the director.'" RIF 157-10014-10075. Also see 7/11/75, Harvey SSCIA Deposition, p. 66, RIF 157-10011-10053.

they waited for Sam Halpern to enter the chamber. Helms' crucial remarks on the alleged RFK-Mafia plot just days earlier were foremost on Church's mind.

At 10:20 a.m. on the morning of 18 June 1975, Church Committee Chairman Frank Church, along with his colleagues Senators Hart (Michigan), Hart (Colorado), Huddleston, Morgan, Goldwater and Schweiker were sitting together in Room S. 407 of the Capitol Building in Washington D. C.

The senators were in the midst of a lengthy procedural discussion prior to the arrival of the witness for that day, William Harvey's former executive assistant, Sam Halpern. Frank Church had attended Helms' deposition a few days earlier and made some important remarks about it. Church told those present that he expected *Halpern's testimony would conflict with the recent testimony of DDP Richard Helms*:

> The particular reason we asked him [Halpern] to come in was because in *Mr. Helms' testimony last week* he [Halpern] was referred to by name as being the *source of a story* that the Attorney General [Robert Kennedy] *had told the Special Group, or rather told the people working Cuba, to use the Mafia*. The implication, I think, in Helms' testimony was *to use the Mafia for the purpose of assassinations*.[728] [Emphasis added]

Church was anticipating that Halpern's testimony might have a "little bit different flavor" than had come across in Helms' testimony. As we will see, Church's call was right on the money.

There are two reasons to pay close attention to Church's characterization of Helms' earlier deposition:

- First, Church's remarks indicated that Helms had *not been the source* of the allegation about an RFK-Mafia plot, as Walter Elder would report afterward [see Chapter Ten].
- Second, Church provided valuable information about the date of the Helms deposition in question—specifying that *the testimony had occurred "last week."*

Therefore, from Church's characterization of Helms' (13 June) testimony *alone*, we see that Helms did *not* testify that Robert Kennedy asked him to provide a Mafia case officer. From Helms' deposition we know that he *did* testify that Halpern was the source of that allegation, effectively putting the monkey where it belonged—on Halpern's back.

But, the second point is also noteworthy. As far as I can determine, Helms' comments during his 13 June 1975 deposition about Halpern's RFK-Mafia myth have gone unnoticed in secondary literature up to the present. That is odd because Church's comment about the date makes it possible to easily locate the date of that deposition. Observers who failed to find and use Helms' crucial comments about Halpern's RFK

---

728 6/18/75, Halpern SSCIA deposition, p. 3; RIF 157-10002-10087.

charade are apparently satisfied with explanations by CIA officers unfamiliar with that deposition.

Senator Church wanted to make sure that his colleagues understood the important implications of Helms' testimony five days earlier—*before* Halpern entered the chamber for his deposition. It is fascinating that the committee's questioners were careful *not to reveal* to Halpern—when he took his turn in the witness chair—what they had just learned about him (Halpern) from Helms' testimony five days earlier.

Halpern's 18 June 1975 Pre-Deposition Meeting with Committee Staff Members

Church Committee staff members often met with and interviewed witnesses before they were sworn in for their depositions. That procedure was followed in the case of Sam Halpern. Normally, staff pre-deposition interviews of the witnesses took place a number of days before their depositions to give the staff and the committee lawyers time to prepare their questions. That did *not* happen in Halpern's case. And, as discussed above, what Halpern was *not* asked during his deposition was more important than what he *was* asked.

Halpern had no inkling that he would be deposed by the committee on the same day that his pre-deposition took place. All he expected to happen that day was a meeting with A. O. Schwarz Jr. and other staff members for an interview. Halpern told Weber:

> I'd been called to talk to Schwarz on the staff first [thing] in the morning, a crack of dawn kind of thing. And I got down there. And this was in the old, oh, what the hell is the building... ...but any way they had taken over the auditorium in that building and they were [in] a secured area. They had safes and what have you, all over the place and they had taken the seats out.[729]

Halpern said he had been talking to "Schwarz and some of his cohorts" for about two hours when something unexpected happened:

> ... then suddenly out of the clear blue sky he says, "Well let's walk over to the Capitol Building. The Committee is going into session and they want to talk to you." And I said, "Just like that?" He said, "Yeah, you got nothing to hide, do you?" And I said, "No, I got nothing to hide." He said, "Yeah, I was thinking you might as well go and talk to them directly."[730]

---

729   10/30/87, Ralph E. Weber Interview with Sam Halpern, pp. 79-80; RIF 104-10324-10002.
730   Ibid.

Halpern was not impressed by the fact that he had not been given a chance to speak with a lawyer. He said that it wasn't that he cared about it except for this:

> But it was a lousy way to do business, and it wasn't according to the rules at the time, because I had the rule book, procedures, and what have you. ... And they were supposed to give me a notice for that... But I didn't want to stop the proceedings.[731]

Halpern remained behind with the group while Schwarz went on ahead to join Church and his colleagues on the fourth floor of the capitol building where, as described above, they were talking about Halpern and Helms.[732] Eventually, Halpern was ushered into the room. He recalled that moment this way: "I was told to stand up, and sworn in, and we went to town."[733]

Halpern's testimony that day contained an exchange that included an extraordinary revelation about an *alleged order from Robert Kennedy to William Harvey to make use of the Mafia's assets on the island of Cuba.* According to Halpern's testimony, that order would have taken place in early 1962. I will discuss Halpern's testimony about RFK's directive that Harvey use the Mafia in a section below.

The committee also questioned Halpern about an important meeting in the fall of 1961 with DDP Bissell. Here, I will turn to what Halpern told the committee about that meeting. Then I will examine what Bissell told the committee he remembered about it.

Halpern's 1975 Deposition and Bissell's Mid-October 1961 Instructions to "Get Rid of Castro"

On 18 June 1975, Sam Halpern was deposed before the Church Committee.[734] This time, however, Halpern was not among CIA friends as he had been during the 1967 IG investigation. In front of the Church Committee, the word "assassination" was eschewed, in favor of the phrase "get rid of Castro." Halpern explained that, during that 1961 meeting, both the president and the attorney general had "chewed out" Bissell for "sitting on his ass" instead of "getting rid of Castro."

At the outset of Halpern's deposition, he described a subsequent meeting he attended that took place after Bissell's formative meeting with the Kennedy brothers in the White House. Halpern testified that his branch chief, Goshen Zogbey, was also present at the subsequent meeting with Bissell. It was during that meeting that Bissell

---

731 Ibid, p. 80.
732 See 6/18/75, Halpern SSCIA deposition, p. 3; RIF 157-10002-10087.
733 10/30/87, Ralph E. Weber Interview with Sam Halpern, p. 80; RIF 104-10324-10002.
734 6/18/75, Halpern SSCIA deposition, p. 8; RIF 157-10002-10087.

issued "instructions" to Halpern and Zogbey to formulate a plan for an operation to "get rid of Castro and the Castro regime."

> Mr. Schwarz: Did you have in the fall of 1961 a meeting at which you were given instructions by Mr. Bissell?
> Mr. Halpern: Yes, sir.
> Mr. Schwarz: Who else was present at that meeting?
> Mr. Halpern: [A Mr. Goshen Zogbey].[735] He was my branch chief.
> Mr. Schwarz: Approximately when in the fall of 1961 did that meeting take place?
> Mr. Halpern: *About the middle of October 1961.*

The line of questioning that followed clearly shows what the committee was *really* fishing for:

> Mr. Schwarz: What instructions were you given by Mr. Bissell at that meeting?
> Mr. Halpern: Mr. Bissell said he had recently—and he didn't specify the date or the time—he had recently been chewed out in the Cabinet room by both the president and the attorney general for, as he put it, sitting on his ass and not doing anything about getting rid of Castro and the Castro regime. *His orders to [Mr. Zogbey] and to me were to plan for an operation to accomplish that end.*
> Mr. Schwarz: Was any content put into the term "get rid of," or was that the term that was used, and only that term?
> Mr. Halpern: To the best of my recollection, that was it. There was no limitation of any kind. Nothing was forbidden, and nothing was withheld. And *the objective was to get rid of Castro and his regime.*[736] [Emphasis added]

The question came up again later in Halpern's deposition:

> Mr. Smothers: Was it your understanding that these plans were to extend to assassination?
> Mr. Halpern: That *word* was not used, sir. But no holds were barred, and we had no limitations.
> Mr. Smothers: Did Mr. Bissell ever convey to you the idea that that included killing Castro?
> Mr. Halpern: *The subject never came up per se.*[737]

---

[735] NB: I was able to establish the name of Halpern's branch chief from other CIA documents. See, for example, 4/7/98, CIA Center for the Study of Intelligence, Sam Halpern Interview by Brian Latell and Michael Warner, p. 8; RIF 104-10324-10000.
[736] 6/18/75, Halpern SSCIA deposition, pp. 8-9; RIF 157-10002-10087.
[737] Ibid, p. 37.

Halpern's off-the-mark answer about the absence of the word assassination was an unsubtle way of avoiding perjury while inferring that assassination might have been intended.

In a 1988 interview during which Halpern was not under oath, he was more succinct: "It didn't mean assassinate him, per se, just meant change the government. But if it meant assassination, fine, too."[738] In fact, Senator Church told the committee that his interpretation of Helms' earlier testimony was that the *"implication"* of Halpern's story was *"to use the Mafia for the purpose of assassinations."*[739]

In Chapter Seven, I discussed Halpern's embrace of DDP Bissell's claim—made to William Harvey—that he had been pressured during two meetings in the White House to create an executive action capability in the CIA. The reader will recall that Halpern had not heard about that story until early 1975. When he saw the **ZR/RIFLE** documents at that time, he immediately accepted the authenticity of Bissell's claim.[740]

As discussed in Chapter Seven, on six occasions under oath before the Church Committee, Bissell said he was unable to remember the meeting or who in the White House the request had come from. I turn now to Bissell's loss of memory on the witness stand before the Church Committee.

Bissell's 22 July 1975 Deposition and His Amnesia About Attending the mid-October 1961 White House Meeting

On 22 July 1975, a month after Halpern's Church Committee deposition, former DDP Bissell was deposed by the committee. Like Bissell's early 1961 White House pressures ploy, his story about the October 1961 Kennedy order fell apart once he was on the stand:

Mr. Schwarz: Do you recall having a meeting with him [Halpern] in the fall of 1961 about the subject of Cuba?

Mr. Bissell: *I don't specifically know.*

Then, after Schwarz read Halpern's 18 June testimony to Bissell, he put this question to him:

Mr. Schwarz: Now, in substance, did you have such a conversation with Mr. Halpern?

Mr. Bissell: I *assume* the testimony is correct. *I don't remember the meeting.*

---

738   1/15/88, Halpern interview with Mary S. McAuliffe, p. 18; RIF 104-10324-10003.
739   Ibid, p. 3.
740   10/30/87. Ralph E. Weber Interview with Sam Halpern, p. 99; RIF 104-10324-10002.

RFK AND THE CASTRO ASSASSINATION PLOTS—PART I

> Mr. Schwarz: All right. And did you have some conversation with the president and the attorney general in which they told you in effect, in substance, to get off your ass about Cuba?
>
> Mr. Bissell: Yes, I think I have—*again, I cannot place that precisely,* but there were several occasions between the Bay of Pigs failure and the date of my conversation with Mr. Halpern, *several occasions when that could have been the course of the conversation.*[741] [Emphasis added]

Indeed, Bissell was correct to point out that there had been many opportunities for Robert Kennedy to chew him out for failing to overthrow Castro.

In White House meetings in the wake of the Bay of Pigs failure, Bobby Kennedy chewed out just about anyone who had anything to say. By 19 January 1962, Robert Kennedy was still riding herd on U.S. government agencies:

> The big bird is on your shoulders, you members of the group. There is no question but that you must see that absolutely nothing stands in the way. We must do this job now. We cannot stand by and *sit on our asses*. We must get going now. This is not a three or four-year project but an immediate one that must show results now.[742] [Emphasis added]

The point, however, is that all of these ass-chewings by the attorney general were not evidence of Bissell's claim (to Halpern) that the all-important chewing out took place during a mid-October 1961 meeting.

In his deposition, Bissell denied three times remembering having been present in such a meeting with the Kennedy brothers. There is no record of that White House meeting in the State Department Foreign Relations series. There is no indication of such a meeting in the NARA JFK records collection—other than Halpern's hearsay. There is no independent record in the memoirs of those who knew the president. Citing the Church Committee's Interim Report, Arthur Schlesinger, Jr. mentioned the possibility of such a meeting but added that Bissell had no memory of it.

As promised, I now turn to the most extraordinary moment in Halpern's 18 June deposition with the committee.

Halpern's 18 June 1975 Church Committee Deposition and RFK's Order to Use the Mafia

To repeat, one week before Halpern's deposition the committee had learned from Helms that he had *not* personally heard about RFK's alleged Mafia case officer request

---

741 7/22/75 Bissell SSCIA deposition, pp. 36-38; RIF 157-10011-10017.
742 1/19/62, Lansdale Minutes of Meeting in Robert Kennedy's office; RIF 178-10002-10479.

INTO THE STORM

from RFK; rather, *Helms had learned about it during a "chat" with Halpern*. Thus, although Halpern had prepped Helms before the latter's testimony, Halpern was unaware (at that time) about how things had turned out in Helms' deposition.

Therefore, despite what the committee had learned from Helms a week earlier, their line of questioning purposely did *not* draw Halpern out about Robert Kennedy's alleged request for a Mafia case officer. Instead, Senator Church's plan was to skirt around the edges of Halpern's "different flavor"—as compared to Helms' testimony five days earlier—about RFK's "search for Mafia people that might be of help."[743] To carry out this strategy, the committee lawyers constrained their questions to Halpern *exclusively* about remarks made to him by William Harvey. Those remarks concerned *Harvey's use of the Mafia* to collect information on assets inside of Cuba:

> Mr. Schwarz: Did Mr. Harvey at any time discuss with you any plans or attempts to assassinate Mr. Castro?
>
> Mr. Halpern: No, sir.
>
> Mr. Schwarz: Did Mr. Harvey at any time discuss with you the use of the Mafia for any purpose?
>
> Mr. Halpern: Not by that name, no, sir.
>
> Mr. Schwarz: *Did Mr. Harvey discuss with you the use of underworld figures for any purpose?*
>
> Mr. Halpern: *Yes sir—underworld not by name or figures, but in general, underworld in general.*
>
> Mr. Schwarz: Now, if he didn't discuss them in terms of assassination efforts in what context did he discuss the Mafia with you? I use the word Mafia, you use your word underworld.
>
> Mr. Halpern: Fine. *The underworld would be used in terms of the charge from the attorney general to make use of any and all assets on the island of Cuba. And the attorney general made it clear* that there obviously were existing assets left over from the days when the underworld was very strong in Cuba. And we were supposed to try to *contact anybody in the underworld* as well as anybody else *who had any possibility of providing any kind of assets inside Cuba.*
>
> Mr. Schwarz: Now, that is something the attorney general said to you or someone else told you the attorney general said it?
>
> Mr. Halpern: *Someone else told me.*
>
> Mr. Schwarz: But *you don't associate in your mind the underworld as far as you understood it with any effort to assassinate Castro is that right?*
>
> Mr. Halpern: *No, sir.*[744] [Emphasis added]

---

743   6/18/75 Halpern SSCIA deposition, pp. 15-16; RIF 157-10002-10087.
744   Ibid.

The committee's plan paid off. Halpern's statement about his discussion with Harvey was revealing. It was the only account among any of the committee's depositions of CIA officers that mentioned orders from Bobby Kennedy to Harvey to make use of the Mafia. Although Schwarz failed to ask who told Harvey about "the charge from the attorney general," he did get Harvey to admit he had *not* heard it personally from Robert Kennedy.

The Church Committee interviewed William Harvey once and then deposed him three times. Harvey's 25 June deposition was exactly *one week after* Halpern's 18 June deposition. The committee did not take advantage of that occasion to ask Harvey to confirm Halpern's testimony about Bobby's alleged orders that Harvey contact the underworld and ask them to survey their "assets on the island of Cuba." Moreover, at no time during any of the committee's interview and depositions of Harvey did they ask him about using the underworld for any purpose.

To repeat, the committee got Halpern to state under oath that he had learned from Harvey about RFK's order to use the Mafia to collect information from their assets in Cuba. And although Halpern denied associating that order with an *effort to assassinate Castro*, we know that, on the basis of Helms' 13 June testimony, Senator Church believed that RFK's request for a mafia case officer was *"for the purpose of assassinations."*[745] But the committee kept close to the vest what they had learned from Helms about the RFK-Mafia case officer story.

As we will see, in nearly all of his interviews during the years *after* his Church Committee deposition, Halpern would link assassination to his tale of RFK's use of a Charles Ford channel to the Mafia. The reader will recall that Deputy Inspector General Breckinridge's 1967 interview with Halpern suggested that RFK had reactivated the CIA-Mafia plot to assassinate Castro. That bogus allegation occurred eight years *before* Halpern's 1975 sworn deposition.

Halpern's testimony about RFK's alleged order to Harvey to use the Mafia is not supported by any Church Committee or CIA records that have been released. But Halpern's allegation in this regard was an important buttress for his RFK-Mafia fiction. In Chapter Thirteen I will deal with this subject in the context of the *true* CIA-Mafia plot to assassinate Castro.

Halpern's 1987 and 1995 Interviews with Ralph Weber

Ralph E. Weber was a history professor at Marquette University. His service in the U.S. Navy during WWII later led to research on codes and ciphers. Weber also authored

---

[745] Ibid, p. 3.

a book on a select number of senior officers of the CIA. On 11 November 1995, he interviewed Sam Halpern. Minor extracts of that interview appeared in Weber's 1999 book, *Spymasters: Ten CIA Officers in their Own Words*.[746] Weber became a board member of David Atlee Phillips' Association of Former Intelligence Officers (AFIO) and was a CIA and NSA Scholar in Residence. The published portions of Weber's 1995 interview with Halpern were disappointing and included barely two pages on the Kennedy years.

What little Weber chose to share in his book about Halpern's opinion of the Kennedy brothers was this unflattering scurrilous diatribe:

> The brothers were gadflies. When it came to Cuba, they were persons with a fixation. In my humble opinion, they couldn't care less about the United States of America and what it stood for. They were interested in one thing only, and that was clearing the blemish on the Kennedy escutcheon [coat of arms].[747]

Other than that insult, the only other Halpern observation about the Kennedys in Weber's book was this disparaging dig:

> In 1961 and 1962, the Kennedys wanted things done literally by mirrors... ... and nothing we did pleased them. And when we did have some success—I believe we blew up some small power plant or a generator—we got chewed out because the story about the explosion and damage made headlines in Cuba and in Florida, where it hit the front pages. Bobby Kennedy screamed at us and said, "I thought you guys did things in a secret way! What's the matter with you guys? Why all the publicity?" And we had to tell him in no uncertain terms that when you're going to blow something up, it's going to make noise, people are going to see it, it's going to be on television, and it's going to be in the newspapers. That's the kind of stupidity we were getting from the White House, from the president and his brother the attorney general.[748]

Other than revealing Halpern's hatred for the Kennedys, Weber's book tells us nothing at all about Halpern's work in the CIA during the Kennedy years.

Surprisingly, *eight years earlier* on 30 October 1987, Weber had conducted a far more important and lengthier interview with Halpern. That interview *did* reflect events that had taken place during the Kennedy years and the Church Committee investigation. Fortunately for history, a complete transcript of that 200-page interview was gathering dust in a file at the CIA until it was released in the late 1990s.[749] Astonishingly, hardly

---

746 Weber, *Spymasters: Ten CIA Officers in their Own Words* (Lanham MD: Rowman & Littlefield Publishers, 1999).
747 Weber, *Spymasters*, p. 123.
748 Ibid, pp. 123-124.
749 10/30/87, Ralph E. Weber Interview with Sam Halpern, p. 88; RIF 104-10324-10002.

RFK AND THE CASTRO ASSASSINATION PLOTS—PART I

anything from that interview found its way into Weber's 1995 book or, for that matter, in any other publication.

During the 1987 interview, Halpern embraced Bissell's fabrication of a January 1961 White House order to establish an executive action capability in the CIA. Halpern told Weber that was when Bissell got ahold of Bill Harvey and **ZR/RIFLE** was created.[750] The reader will recall from Chapter Seven (and Chapters Fifteen and Nineteen of Volume II—*Countdown to Darkness*) that the CIA's executive assassination program was created in the summer of 1960, long before the inauguration of President Kennedy. Bissell's fabrication of the January 1961 White House pressures ploy was a last-minute Hail Mary. Faced with the looming failure at the Bay of Pigs, he was hoping that if he could get Harvey to assassinate Castro it might somehow alter the outcome.

Halpern, of course, liked Bissell's White House pressures ruse and used it to bolster his RFK-Mafia scenario. Halpern was *Johnny at the rathole* (his words for RFK) at every possible inflection point on the path to building that adverse RFK legend. The approaching Helms Church Committee deposition in the spring of 1975 was another one of those opportunities that Halpern could not resist.

A temporary staff was created by Walter Elder, the assistant to DCI William Colby, to help prepare the large number of senior CIA officers who were hauled before the committee. Scott Breckinridge was assigned to that staff and was joined by Halpern's "sidekick," Seymour Bolten, a CIA staff officer called out of retirement to help run the day-to-day operations of the staff.[751] Halpern told Weber he was persuaded by Bolten to join the staff. Halpern then waxed eloquent about how he ended up briefing Helms, about how he was the center of attention at staff social events, and about how he was called to be a witness for the committee.[752]

Perhaps the most significant point in Weber's interview of Halpern occurred when Weber mentioned the word "assassination." In the discourse that followed Halpern's consciousness wandered between *two* assassination attempts. The one he mentioned first was one he *had* been involved in and *had* talked about many times—the 1963 CIA plot to assassinate Castro using Rolando Cubela [**AMLASH-1**]. The other assassination attempt, he said, "wasn't in my area." He explained that it was also "one of the one's against Castro." But he added, cryptically, "*I did not know about the use of the Mafia by Bill Harvey.*"[753]

That ignorance, Halpern said unhappily, had been due to Harvey's characteristic *tight secrecy*. Halpern could only draw comfort from the fact that he "*wasn't the only one*" who didn't personally know what Harvey had been doing *mucking around with Roselli and*

---

750   Ibid, p. 99.
751   Ibid, p. 88.
752   Ibid, pp. 77-78.
753   Ibid, p. 98.

the Mafia.[754] "Even though I was his executive," Halpern grumbled, "*I had no idea and I know his deputy had no idea at all.*"[755]

This interview occurred in 1987, twelve years *after* Halpern's Church Committee deposition and twenty years after his interviews with Breckinridge for the IG Report. The above portion of this Weber interview helps us—for the *first* time in Halpern's long RFK charade—begin to how he was struggling with Harvey's direction of the CIA-Mafia plot to assassinate Castro.

One can barely imagine what went through Halpern's mind the first time he realized the implications of that extraordinary discovery—that his own boss had been in charge of the super-secret CIA-Mafia assassination plot against Castro during the exact same period that he [Halpern] had been accusing Robert Kennedy of running just such an operation. I will return to Halpern's conundrum about Harvey in Chapter Thirteen.

The 15 January 1988 Mary McAuliffe Interview of Halpern

On 1 January 1988, seventy-five days after the Weber interview, the Deputy Chief of the CIA History Staff, Mary S. McAuliffe interviewed Halpern.[756] The disturbing realization about Harvey's use of Roselli was *still* on Halpern's mind. I will reserve until Chapter Thirteen my analysis of Halpern's remarks to McAuliffe about that problem. There, McAuliffe's revelations about Halpern's RFK-Ford fiction will be viewed astride Ford's sworn testimony for the Church Committee.

Unlike his silence with Weber on the RFK-Mafia myth, Halpern *did* expand on his narrative about that myth with McAuliffe. Halpern claimed Task Force W was "under the gun" of Bobby Kennedy's pressure to get rid of Castro and "do it fast." RFK, he told Weber, was constantly on the phone giving orders to "case officers on the Task Force," and they had to assign a case officer "whose sole job was to carry out Bobby's wishes vis-a-vis the underworld." Charles Ford's "sole job in life" was to go to the underworld people Bobby sent him to "all across the United States."[757] Halpern told McAuliffe that Bobby did not go through regular channels and that neither DCI McCone nor DDP Helms knew what was going on.

In 1998, Halpern told Brian Latell and Michael Warner the same tale—with a few more embellishments. I will get to that in Chapter Thirteen. In that chapter, I will

---

754   Ibid, pp. 98-99.
755   Ibid, p. 101.
756   1/15/78, Halpern interview with Mary McAuliffe; 104-10324-10003.
757   Ibid, pp. 16-18.

RFK AND THE CASTRO ASSASSINATION PLOTS—PART I

argue that by the mid-1990s, Halpern's memory became confused because he was suffering from dementia.

I am ready to now turn to the second overlay—the true activities that Robert Kennedy and Charles Ford were involved in together in 1962. For that story we do not encounter Halpern's paperwork paucity problem. On the contrary, we have a rich CIA documentary record to work from.

CHAPTER TEN

RFK AND THE CASTRO ASSASSINATION PLOTS— PART II

This volume chronicles the history of the false allegations about attempts by the Kennedy brothers to assassinate Fidel Castro. These false narratives were embellished in the decades after the Kennedy assassination because of their value in underpinning a central characteristic of the conspiracy: linking Castro, with an assist from the KGB, to the murder in Dealey Plaza.

One of these myths began *before* the Bay of Pigs and its architect was CIA Deputy Director of Plans (DDP) Richard Bissell. At the time, of course, it had nothing at all to do with the death of President Kennedy. Rather, it was a desperate attempt by Bissell to stimulate a plot by the chief of the Agency's Staff D, William Harvey, to assassinate Castro. Later, that legend proved useful to the larger Castro-did-it narrative (discussed in Chapter Seven) that was hatched in the runup to the president's murder and nourished afterward—all the way up to the present day.

Bissell's allegation that it was the Kennedys who ordered the creation of an assassination capability in the CIA [**ZR/RIFLE**] was the subject of Chapter Seven. The disturbing nature of Bissell's act of self-preservation pales in comparison with the machinations of Sam Halpern, whose self-aggrandizing RFK-Mafia myth became—and remains—such an important feature in the coverup of President Kennedy's assassination.

The history of Halpern's RFK handiwork is detailed in three Chapters of the present volume, beginning with the previous chapter, continuing with the present chapter, and ending with Chapter Thirteen at the end of this volume. By now, the reader is aware of my firm belief that the CIA documentary evidence and sworn depositions of the knowledgeable Agency officers overwhelmingly discredits Halpern's intricate forty-year-long framing of Robert Kennedy.

No matter how Halpern's deception began—whether by accident or design—it *did* eventually become part of a witting obstruction of justice. That is a crime. Whether we speak of the crime of murder or we speak of the crime of aiding the obstruction of justice afterward, we are speaking of criminal activity. No sane individuals engaged in criminal activity would knowingly leave their fingerprints behind to be discovered by investigators later. This is especially true for a shrewd, well-connected perpetrator.

As such, laying out the facts to make the case for Halpern's duplicity—let alone prove it beyond a reasonable doubt—requires rigorous investigation and analysis. I have attempted to do just that in this book by employing what I know about finding and exposing the intent of any opposition force. To prepare the case, I am placing a series of three overlays onto my metaphorical sand table to expose the plot to frame Bobby Kennedy.

In Chapter Nine, I placed the first overlay onto the sand table to illustrate the history—up to a crucial inflection point—of Halpern's allegation about RFK's complicity in a plot to use the Mafia to assassinate Castro. I followed that history up to and beyond the point at which Halpern discovered the complicity of his boss, William Harvey, in a CIA-Mafia plot to assassinate Castro.

In this chapter, I will place the second overlay on top of the first. This transparency lays out the CIA documentary record of RFK's routine referrals of requests for assistance to anti-Castro Cubans in the crucial time zone of 1962. I will also examine the Church Committee's sworn interview of Charles Ford. Halpern claimed that RFK used Ford to maintain contact with the Mafia as part of a plot to assassinate Castro. However, Ford's sworn interview with the committee destroyed that claim.

Finally, in Chapter Thirteen, I will superimpose the third and final overlay over the first two. That transparency exposes actions of CIA officers who organized and directed the *true CIA-Mafia plot* to assassinate Castro. We will be able to observe the final evolution of Halpern's framing of RFK after his discovery—in the Church Committee's 1975 Interim Report—of the surreptitious transfer of the *real* CIA-Mafia assassination plot from the Security Office to Bill Harvey in 1962.

The Inventory of CIA Records Resulting from RFK's Referrals to the CIA and the Activities of Charles Ford

CIA Task Force W (TFW) Special Assistant Charles Ford was assigned to look into two routine RFK referrals to the Agency of requests for assistance to anti-Castro Cubans.

RFK AND THE CASTRO ASSASSINATION PLOTS—PART II

In both instances, that assignment *did produce a hefty written record* of what Ford learned *and shared* with *all* of the relevant CIA officers. Ford's activities were *not* the result of a *secret* back channel operation run by Robert Kennedy.

The Agency officers in the know included top CIA decision-makers such as the Director of Central Intelligence (DCI), Deputy Director of Central Intelligence (DDCI) and the chief of TFW; senior officers of the CIA Office of Security and their subordinates working in the Security Analysis Group (SAG), Physical Security Division (PSD), and other security components; senior officers in the CIA Directorate of Administration; other officers in TFW, including those working in the security, paramilitary, propaganda components, and Harvey's Special Assistant Sam Halpern; and officers working at the CIA JMWAVE Station in Miami.

That documentary record includes, but is not limited to, the following CIA and Church Committee documents:

- 3/30/62, C. S. Gikas memo for Chief, SD/2, Subject: Ford, Charles D., #38497; RIF 104-10310-10061.
- 4/2/62, Joseph F. Langan, Chief, TFW/Security, memo to Deputy Director of Security (Personnel & Support); RIF 104-10310-10061.
- 8/1/62, P.O. Box Action Request, Chief, Investigative Division, Office of Security; RIF 104-10310-10061.
- 8/1/62, Victor R. White, office of the Deputy Director of Security (Investigations and Support), to Chief, Task Force W; RIF 104-10310-10061.
- 8/30/62, John F. Blake, Chief of Support, Task Force W, Memorandum for Deputy Director of Security (Investigations and Support); RIF 104-10310-10061.
- 9/28/62, Charles D. Ford, TFW/Special Assistant, MFR, Subject: Contacts with Ernesto Betancourt, et al, at the Request of the Attorney General; RIF 140-10171-10345.
- 9/29/62, CIA Director 39547, drafter: Charles D. Ford, TFW/SA, Operational Immediate to JMWAVE, RE "At request **GPFOCUS** (Robert Kennedy) 24 September, IDEN (Charles Ford) met Ernesto Betancourt; 104-10171-10351.
- 10/3/1962, William Harvey Memorandum for the Deputy Director of Central Intelligence (DDCI), through the Deputy Director of Plans (Richard Helms), subject: Ernesto Betancourt and the Ejercito Libertador de Cuba (ELC); RIF 104-10171-10345.
- 10/3/1962, William Harvey attachment, Draft Memorandum to the Attorney General From DDCI—first version; RIF 104-10171-10345.
- 10/4/1962, William Harvey attachment, Draft Memorandum to the Attorney General for the DDCI's signature—second version; RIF 104-10171-10345.
- 9/4/75, Robert Gambino Memorandum for the Review Staff, Subject: Senate Select Committee Request (Charles Ford); RIF 104-10310-10061.

- 9/19/1975, Charles D. Ford Memorandum, Subject: (18 September) Interview by Senate Committee Investigators (Andy Postal, Gordon Rhea, Rhett Dawson, Fred Baron, Robert Kelley—under oath, second meeting); RIF 104-10310-10119.

The above robust CIA documentary record demolishes Halpern's fictitious narrative about RFK and the Mafia. And the above record also annihilates the false charge—discussed below—by Halpern and Hersh that *"Ford, obviously following instructions from Kennedy, relayed nothing to his nominal superiors in Task Force W.* "*We never got a single solitary piece of [written] information.*" [Emphasis added]

Robert Kennedy's 30 March 1962 Referral to the CIA of the Cuban Exile Prisoners Project

At the end of March 1962, CIA Office of Security files described a short-fused situation that had taken place after a lawyer in New York City contacted Attorney General Robert Kennedy with this proposal:

> [The New York attorney] offered his services to help some of the Cuban prisoners [captured during the Bay of Pigs invasion] who were currently scheduled for trial in Cuba. Mullane advised that the attorney general referred the matter to the Agency with instructions to follow through.[758]

By 30 March, the referral from Robert Kennedy had made its way to the CIA's Western Hemisphere (WH) security officer, Jerry Mullane. He contacted the appropriate branch (SD/2) in the Office of Security and verbally requested approval for the issuance of an Alias CIA Identification Card for Charles Ford.

On the same day, an officer in SD/2, C. S. Gikas, gave a verbal security approval for the issue of the card (#3429) to Charles Ford under the alias Charles D. Fiscalini. *The Fiscalini alias was not assigned to Ford—as Halpern alleges—pursuant to a request from Bobby Kennedy for a CIA case officer for contacts with the Mafia.*

On 2 April 1962, the Chief of Task Force W (TFW) Security, Joseph F. Langan, confirmed the expedited issue of Ford's credential for the Fiscalini alias to the CIA's Deputy Director of Security:

> This credential is required to permit Subject [Ford] to contact within the United States, as an official representative of this Agency, individuals to whom CIA interest but not the true identity of Subject must be disclosed. The cooperation of Mr. Gikas ... of your office, in expediting issuance of this credential is greatly appreciated.[759]

---

758 3/30/62, C. S. Gikas memo for Chief, SD/2, Subject: Ford, Charles D., #38497; RIF 104-10310-10061.
759 4/2/62, Joseph F. Langan, Chief, TFW/Security, memo to Deputy Director of Security (Personnel & Support); RIF 104-10310-10061.

RFK AND THE CASTRO ASSASSINATION PLOTS—PART II

On 30 July 1962, TFW requested that a letter drop for Ford be created in New York City.[760] On 1 August, the New York "letter drop" for Ford was created under the alias C. D. Fiscalini.[761] That same day, the Security Office notified TFW about the creation of Ford's letter drop.[762]

Decades later, Sam Halpern invented a story in which he played the starring role in creating the alias Charles Fiscalini for Ford in September 1962. According to Halpern, Ford used this alias to contact the Mafia on behalf of Bobby Kennedy. That was not true. As discussed above, the Fiscalini alias was created for Ford in March 1962, in preparation for investigating an offer from a New York lawyer to Robert Kennedy to help with the exile prisoners in Cuba. That alias was *not* created for an operation that occurred in September 1962. That operation—discussed below—resulted from the attorney general's call to DDCI Carter for help to Ernesto Betancourt and a proposed uprising by the Ejercito Libertador de Cuba (ELC). I will get to that operation in the next section of this chapter.

Pursuant to a Church Committee request for information on Charles Ford, on 4 September 1975, the director of the CIA's Office of Security, Robert W. Gambino, forwarded a memorandum to the CIA's ad hoc Review Staff for the Church and Rockefeller Committees. The memo concerned a March 1962 request for assistance in a matter about Cuba exile prisoners:

> A memorandum contained in the files, dated *30 March 1962*, indicates Mr. Ford was issued alias documentation under the name of "Charles D. Fiscalini." Cited memorandum further indicates that Mr. Ford was then assigned to "Task Force W," and was to travel to New York on *31 March 1962* to meet with an unidentified attorney who had contacted Mr. Robert Kennedy, the then attorney general, concerning assistance for Cuban prisoners.[763] [Emphasis added]

Ford's sworn interview with the Church Committee on 18 September 1975 indicates that he had been assigned to the Economic Action Group in the DDP since 1960 and was assigned to Task Force W in September 1961.[764]

In his 18 September 1975 Church Committee interview—two weeks after the Gambino memo—Ford revealed the remaining details of how the New York attorney story turned out. The interview was attended by Church Committee staff members Andy Postal, Gordon Rhea, Rhett Dawson, Fred Baron and Robert Kelley. According to Ford:

---

760 8/30/62, John F. Blake, Chief of Support, Task Force W, memorandum for Deputy Director of Security (Investigations and Support); RIF 104-10310-10061.
761 8/1/62, P.O. Box Action Request, Chief, Investigative Division, Office of Security; RIF 104-10310-10061.
762 8/1/62, Victor R. White, office of the Deputy Director of Security (Investigations and Support), to Chief, Task Force W; RIF 104-10310-10061.
763 9/4/75, Robert Gambino memorandum for the Review Staff, Subject: Senate Select Committee Request (Charles Ford); RIF 104-10310-10061.
764 9/19/75, Charles D. Ford, memorandum, Subject: Interview by Senate Committee Investigators; RIF 104-10310-10119.

> The circumstances involved a contact by a New York lawyer, through the Department of Justice, concerning a client who had access to Cuba and wanted to visit Castro to put in a special word on behalf of Bay of Pigs prisoners. I identified the individual concerned (I still can't remember his name) as the manager of the Teresa Hotel in New York. ... I identified a man I met at a second meeting in New York named "Bubbles" Abdallah. ... I explained to the [DOJ] investigators that *I had no further contact with these people* after I discovered that Abdallah was wanted, or under indictment—I forget which—by Texas authorities for smuggling drugs from Mexico.[765] [Emphasis added]

From the above CIA documents, it is obvious that RFK's Cuban prisoners request and the Fiscalini alias assigned to Ford had nothing to do with a request for an Agency case officer to handle contacts with the Mafia or underworld mobsters.

RFK and the 30 September 1962 Abortive ELC Uprising in Santiago de Cuba Province

The immediate context for the events described in this section was the unfolding Cuban Missile Crisis. On 19 September 1962, the United States Intelligence Board (USIB) approved a secret Special National Intelligence Estimate (SNIE-85-3-62) stating that "intelligence indicates the ongoing deployment of Soviet nuclear missiles to Cuba."[766] A few days later, in late September 1962, the Assistant Administrator of the Economic Branch of the Organization of American States (OAS), Ernesto Betancourt, personally met with Robert Kennedy with a request for American help. Considered a moderate anti-Castro Cuban, Betancourt was advocating support for the Ejercito Libertador de Cuba (ELC), a group planning an uprising in Santiago Province at the end of the month.

The ELC was a military organization whose members included former soldiers of Batista's Regular Constitutional Army *and* Castro's Rebel Army that fought against Batista. In 1962, this moderate coalition was the kind of anti-Castro group that interested President Kennedy and his soon-to-be chairman of the joint chiefs, General Maxwell Taylor. The ELC's principal leaders were former Rebel Army officers who had fought under Huber Matos.[767]

---

765 Ibid.
766 9/19/62, *CIA National Intelligence Estimate, The Military Buildup in Cuba*; see Laurence Chang and Peter Kornbluh, **The Cuban Missile Crisis, 1962** (News York: New Press, 1992), p. 356.
767 7/5/62, Robert F. Maroney, TFW/Security, MFR, "Ernesto Francisco Betancourt"; RIF 104-10171-10378.

RFK AND THE CASTRO ASSASSINATION PLOTS—PART II

Contrary to the claims of Sam Halpern and Sy Hersh, that, on RFK's instructions, Ford left no records for his TFW superiors about the results of his work for the attorney general, Ford *did* create and leave such a record—as the footnotes to the following events prove. On 24 September 1962, Attorney General Robert Kennedy telephoned then Deputy Director of Central Intelligence (DDCI) General Marshall S. Carter. Kennedy asked the CIA to send someone to speak with him about a planned sabotage action in Cuba by "some unidentified Cubans."[768] The DDCI passed this request on to TFW Chief William Harvey who assigned TFW Special Assistant (TFW/SA) Charles Ford to speak to the attorney general. At 5:20 p.m. that afternoon, when Ford met with RFK, the attorney general voiced interest in Betancourt and the ELC and mentioned their plans to carry out sabotage activities and a "general uprising" in Santiago Province before the end of the month:[769]

> The attorney general said that Betancourt wants to work outside the framework of the U.S. Government and, in particular, does not want to work with the CIA. The attorney general further said that he had explained to Betancourt the danger of a premature uprising. The attorney general went on to say, however, that Betancourt's group and its plans might fall within the framework of decisions reached by the Special Group about a month ago.[770]

RFK asked that someone appearing to be other than a CIA officer get in touch with Betancourt to *look over the plan and perhaps provide technical advice.*

At noon the next day (25 September), Robert Kennedy *phoned Charles Ford directly* to inform him that some of Betancourt's men were in Washington but had to leave for Florida that afternoon. At 12:45 p.m. that day, Ford interviewed Betancourt using the alias "Don Barton" (an alias once used by Dave Phillips[771]!) and claimed no specific organizational affiliation.[772] This important detail is worth mentioning because the alias was *not* Fiscalini. Halpern claimed that Ford's Fiscalini alias was created for an RFK assignment that flowed through the DDCI and TFW Chief *and* with which Ford could not be connected to the CIA. The creation of the Fiscalini alias where it doesn't belong—in this late September 1962 ELC operation—is one of the numerous

---

768 9/28/62, Charles Ford MFR, "Contacts with Ernesto Betancourt, et al, at the Request of the Attorney General"; RIF 104-10171-10345.
769 9/19/62, Charles Ford SSCIA sworn interview, p. 1; RIF 104-10310-10119.
770 9/28/62, Charles D. Ford, TFW/Special Assistant, MFR, Subject: Contacts with Ernesto Betancourt, et al, at the Request of the Attorney General; RIF 140-10171-10345.
771 00/00, CIA Station Asset Report on **AMCORE-2** (Conte Aguero), "Knows previous contacts Michael C. Choaden (Phillips) as Donald Barton"; RIF 104-10244-10018.
772 9/29/62, DIR 39547 and 39548 to JMWAVE; 104-10171-10351. NB: This cable was written by TFW/SA Ford and authenticated by TFW/EXEC Halpern, a significant fact that helps establish what Halpern knew about Ford's work for RFK at this time.

inconsistencies in Halpern's manufactured RFK-Mafia medley. To repeat, the "Fiscalini" alias was created for the exile prisoners' operation in March 1962.

Betancourt told Ford that five Cubans from the ELC were waiting to be contacted in a Falls Church, Virginia house. One of these men was Eduardo Perez Gonzalez [AKA Eddie Bayo of the infamous 1963 Bayo-Pawley operation; CIA cryptonym **AMDENIM-11**]. A former CIA asset, he had returned from Cuba the previous week with, ostensibly, significant information and a proposition requiring an answer by 28 September. Betancourt explained that his ELC associates were disinclined to deal with the CIA because in the past it had resulted in nothing getting accomplished.[773]

Four hours later at 4:45 p.m., Ford and Betancourt met with three Cubans claiming to be leaders of the ELC operations section—Captain Eduardo Perez Gonzalez, Captain Dunney Perez Alamo, and Manuel Toyos. The principal spokesman, Perez Gonzalez, made this immodest announcement:

> An uprising involving as many as *fifteen thousand persons* is scheduled for 30 September and will occur with or without U.S. assistance. However, help is wanted—primarily arms and ammunition—and …it will be necessary to hold a meeting no later than 28 September at the Guantanamo Naval Base. Once there, Perez Gonzalez is to activate an existing courier link to the internal leaders in Santiago who will then travel to Guantanamo to discuss all of the details of the planned uprising. [Emphasis added]

Ford told the group it would be next to impossible to arrange effective logistical support on two days' notice, but he promised to relay the information to the proper authorities right away.[774]

On 26 September, *Ford briefed Task Force W Chief Harvey*, who in turn informed DDP Helms about the details of the previous day's meeting. On Harvey's instructions, *Ford telephoned*[775] *the following assessment to the attorney general*:

> …that in the frank opinion of the CIA, there is little likelihood of there being fifteen thousand persons ready to carry out even a partially successful revolt; that CIA does not believe such a revolt will take place, and that *in the unlikely event that it does occur, it will be ruthlessly and totally suppressed*.[776] [Emphasis added]

---

773 9/29/62, DIR 39547 to WAVE; RIF 104-10171-10351.
774 Ibid.
775 NB: In his various interviews over the years, Halpern made much ado about the phone calls between Charles Ford and Robert Kennedy. Therefore, what documentary evidence exists about such calls needs to be carefully considered.
776 9/28/62, Charles D. Ford, TFW/Special Assistant, MFR, Subject: Contacts with Ernesto Betancourt, et al, at the Request of the Attorney General; RIF 140-10171-10345.

RFK AND THE CASTRO ASSASSINATION PLOTS—PART II

After listening to Ford's report, *Bobby Kennedy told Ford* that the 28 September meeting would be pointless in terms of helping a revolt and that Betancourt might have been "taken in" by the ELC. However, *RFK directed Ford* to "keep in touch with Betancourt and do whatever we can to help the group."

Shortly after noon that day (26 September), Ford announced this U.S. government response to Betancourt:

> …that "higher authority" had been consulted as promised; that the answer to the proposed meeting on the 28th is negative; that the uprising on the 30th would be a grave mistake resulting in needless loss, and that the development of a working relationship with the ELC is desired.[777]

Both sides salvaged what remained and made arrangements to meet on 2 October to discuss the possibility of future collaboration.

In the meantime, on 28 September, an impatient Eduardo Perez—on his own—contacted a CIA representative in Miami. On 29 September, TFW/SA Charles Ford sent a comprehensive Operational Immediate cable to the CIA JMWAVE Station.[778] This important cable was authenticated by Sam Halpern and released by William Harvey. Their signatures are on the bottom. It is noteworthy that *nowhere* in all of Halpern's interviews did he mention this ELC operation and *all of the communications about it between RFK and Ford*—and the many other CIA officers involved at CIA HQS and JMWAVE. In view of Halpern's alleged "uncanny recall," *this omission is striking.*

The presence of Halpern's signature is conclusive evidence *proving how much he knew about the details of Robert Kennedy's role in this ELC operation.* I will superimpose this key point on Halpern's tedious RFK-Mafia story in the next section of this chapter. Ford's cable began by relaying this background to JMWAVE:

> At request **GPFOCUS** (Robert Kennedy) 24 September, IDEN (Ford) met Ernesto Betancourt, **ZRMETAL** (Washington) front man for ELC on 25 September. Because **GPFOCUS** said Betancourt did not want contact **KUBARK** (CIA), IDEN *used name Don Barton* and claimed no specific organizational affiliation. …It is not known whether these [ELC] men aware **GPFOCUS** interest. [Emphasis added]

Ford's cable then added this update:

> Late afternoon 28 September **GPFOCUS** (Robert Kennedy) phoned IDEN (Ford) and …strongly suggested arranging **YOACRE** (Guantanamo Base) meeting "to see what the plan is." [Researchers NB: Yet another Ford phone call to RFK—*unrelated to any Mafia back*

---

777 Ibid.
778 9/29/62, DIR 39547 to WAVE; RIF 104-10171-10351.

> *channel*—that apparently slipped Halpern's mind.] IDEN immediately phoned Betancourt who said would contact **AMDENIM-11** (Eduardo Perez) in Miami to convey decision **YOACRE** meeting feasible but only for discussion with no implied prior **ODYOKE** (U.S.) commitment. ... Complicating factor this case in addition **GPFOCUS** interest are prior interest in ELC by **GPIDEAL** (President Kennedy) and **GPPHOTO** (JCS Chairman General Maxwell Taylor). ...Please advise **AMDENIM-11** debriefing results soonest.

Harvey later (3 and 4 October) drafted two responses to Robert Kennedy for the DDCI to sign, but, apparently, neither draft was sent.[779] According to Harvey, Perez' CIA debriefings on 28, 29, and 30 September revealed "numerous inaccuracies" in his stories and contradictions with what he said in Washington on 25 September. Harvey's overall assessment was frank: "As you know, we looked into Betancourt and the ELC earlier and concluded, as we still do, that the ELC represents nothing extraordinary."[780]

In Washington, Perez Gonzalez had regaled Betancourt and RFK with a story about a *brave swimming* exfiltration from Guantanamo to Cuba he had done on 1 September. HQS discovered the truth from the Guantanamo Naval Base and reported it to JMWAVE on 30 September:

> **ODOATH** (Navy) **YOACRE** (Guantanamo) says **AMDENIM-11** (Perez Gonzalez) and Roberto Cobas Alvarez AKA Maceo ...approached Captain William Gentry, Marine Corps security and intel officer **YOACRE**, with request exfiltrate **YOACRE** to **PBRUMEN** (Cuba) ...**YOACRE** commander approved exfiltration for night 1 September [hoping to] get missile and troop buildup from operation. Plan called for **BPRUMEN**S swim from **YOACRE** but rough seas and *failing courage* of **AMDENIM-11** and Cobas forced cancellation operation.[781] [Emphasis added]

On 1 October, JMWAVE responded to HQS with this desultory description of Perez Gonzalez, who reported the revolt would occur on the night of 30 September regardless of whether help arrived:

> **AMDENIM-11** (Perez Gonzalez) certain we can expect assassination attempt on **AMTHUG-1** (Fidel Castro), **AMLOUT-1** (Raul Castro), and **AMQUACK-1** (Che Guevara) which will trigger revolt. Following two days of debriefing during which **AMDENIM-11** became increasingly exasperated at not being believed and not being allowed [to] go **YOACRE** (Guantanamo), he revealed having had contact with

---

779   10/3/62, TFW/Chief Harvey to DDCI General Carter, Subject: Ernesto Betancourt and the Ejercito Libertador de Cuba; RIF 104-10171-10345.
780   10/3 and 10/4/62, Harvey draft Memoranda to Robert Kennedy for DDCI signature; RIF 104-10171-10345.
781   9/30/62, DIR 39555; RIF 104-10171-10349.

RFK AND THE CASTRO ASSASSINATION PLOTS—PART II

> **GPFOCUS** (Robert Kennedy) 25 September... ...added his nephew Enrique Perez Perez is member of office of security [sic] at **GPIDEAL** (President Kennedy) residence.

The JMWAVE cable concluded that in view of the many inconsistencies in Perez Gonzalez' story the conclusion was unavoidable that the revolt described by Gonzalez would "not take place within the foreseeable future."[782]

Perez Gonzalez' claim about a triple assassination accompanied by a fifteen-thousand-person uprising was no more than an empty boast intended to help secure U.S. government support. And the CIA knew it. Crucially, *RFK did not send Ford to meet with the ELC officers to seek their help in an assassination attempt against Castro.*

Merging the Sam Halpern Overlay with the Robert Kennedy Overlay

The presence of Halpern's signature on Ford's 29 September 1962 cable to JMWAVE is solid proof that *Halpern was familiar with all of the salient details of RFK's interaction with Charles Ford and the latter's work for Bobby*—discussed immediately above—during the week-long abortive ELC operation. *Of course,* Bobby did *not* instruct Ford to hide his work from his TFW superiors. Halpern's thorough familiarity with the *true* RFK-Ford relationship during this abortive ELC operation collides in a colossal way with his *false* RFK-Mafia plot—like the comet that wiped out the dinosaurs sixty-six million years ago.

In Chapter Nine, I highlighted a critically important portion of Halpern's 15 January 1988 interview with Mary S. McAuliffe. I will repeat it here. Halpern was on a tear about his favorite subject—the extent of Bobby Kennedy's *exclusive* use of Charles Ford as a case officer for *continuous* contact with the Mafia to assassinate Castro:

> I remember we had to have a case officer *whose sole job* was to carry out Bobby's wishes vis-à-vis the underworld—let me call it the gangster world. The case officer was given an Italian-sounding name [Fiscalini]. ...And *his sole job* in life was to go to the various people that Bobby sent him to, all underworld types, all across the United States. ...So, we assigned *one guy full time*...[783] [Emphasis added]

In Halpern's unrelenting account to McAuliffe, the *exclusivity* of RFK's use of Ford *only* for continuing contacts with the Mafia stands out like a sore thumb. Halpern also insisted that in carrying out RFK's instructions "Helms didn't know about this" and

---

782   10/1/62, WAVE 9243; RIF 104-10171-10348.
783   1/15/88, Halpern interview with Mary S. McAuliffe, pp. 16-17; RIF 104-10324-10003.

Ford "wasn't going to bother" Bill Harvey "with all those details."⁷⁸⁴ Obviously, the above ELC operation discredits this nonsense.

Halpern's parameters of RFK's use of Ford are off by more than a Mississippi mile. Charles Ford *did* meet with Bobby Kennedy and the two men *did* often make phone calls to each other during their participation in the CIA's anti-Castro activities. Moreover, as discussed above, immediately after his meeting with the ELC Operations Section, Ford *did* brief Task Force W Chief Harvey who in turn informed DDP Helms about the details of that meeting. Not only was Harvey fully informed about the operation's details, but he was also the drafter of the two responses to Robert Kennedy for DDCI General Carter.⁷⁸⁵ Crucially, *none of the Cubans that Ford maintained contact with during these operations were Mafia gangsters.*

And so, Halpern's moniker as the CIA's most celebrated example of *uncanny recall* crashes and burns under the close scrutiny of his extensive knowledge about RFK's ELC operation. Given Halpern's authenticating signature on Ford's detailed cable about the ELC operation,⁷⁸⁶ how can his above claims to Mary McAuliffe about the *exclusive* gangster limitations to RFK's use of Ford be true? They cannot be true. Given Halpern's signature on the cable, how can his claims about *Harvey's and Helms' ignorance of Ford's operations* be true? They cannot be true. Given Ford's SSCIA sworn statement (discussed below) that *he often worked for Halpern*, how can that be reconciled with the exclusive use of Ford by RFK? It cannot be reconciled.

Moreover, given Halpern's authentication of Ford's use of the Barton alias during the ELC operation, how can we reconcile that with Halpern's claim that the Fiscalini alias was created for that operation? It cannot be reconciled. There is no record of any meeting—as Halpern alleges—between Halpern, Cheever and Harvey *followed* by the assignment of the Fiscalini alias to Ford. The birth of the Charles "Rocky" Fiscalini alias occurred six months *before* the ELC operation. The alias was created for what began as the exile prisoners project in late March-early April 1962. That early spring operation was triggered by a request from Attorney General Robert Kennedy in a phone call to the CIA. That operation was unconnected to Halpern and his colleagues in TFW.

Finally, in the exile prisoners' project, RFK had no role in the case *after* his phone call to the CIA. Bobby had no contact with Ford in *any* of the events that took place after the call. Those events included Ford's contact with the lawyer, the hotel manager, and "Bubbles"; Ford's discovery that Bubbles was wanted by Texas authorities; and Ford's termination of any further investigation of the matter. Thus, the exiles prisoners' project cannot be reconciled with any of these Halpern claims:

---

784 Ibid.
785 10/3/62, TFW/Chief Harvey to DDCI General Carter, Subject: Ernesto Betancourt and the Ejercito Libertador de Cuba; RIF 104-10171-10345.
786 9/29/62, DIR 39547 to WAVE; RIF 104-10171-10351.

- Ford was exclusively assigned as a case officer for RFK.
- Ford worked exclusively and personally for RFK "full time."
- Ford worked exclusively on gangster operations for RFK.

Bobby Kennedy's referral of the exile prisoners' project to the CIA and Ford's management of that project is another example that is inconsistent with Halpern's allegations about Robert Kennedy's exclusive use of Ford for contacts with the Mafia.

Similarly, the above discussed ELC project cannot be reconciled with Halpern's RFK-Mafia allegations for these reasons:
- Charles Ford did not use the alias Charles "Rocky" Fiscalini for contacts with Betancourt and his ELC associates.
- None of the period memoranda by the principal CIA officers involved in the ELC matter—including DDCI General Carter and TFW Chief William Harvey—mention anything about contacting Mafia or underworld types.
- The Church Committee interview with Charles Ford (see below) denies any involvement with Mafia or underworld figures—let alone instructions from Bobby Kennedy to engage in such activity.
- Ernesto Betancourt and his ELC contacts were not members of the Mafia or the underworld.
- The ELC had nothing to do with prostitution, gambling, or drug running in Cuba.

The time has come to examine Ford's sworn interview for the Church Committee in detail. To do that, it is first necessary to look at the events that took place during the build-up for that seminal interview. Specifically, we need to examine the memoranda generated by the CIA Review Staff in anticipation of their interview with Ford.

The Major Mistake in Church Committee Documents in Anticipation of Ford's Deposition

From Chapter Nine, the reader will recall that on 18 June 1975 Senator Church and his colleagues were discussing the witness for that day, Sam Halpern. Just before Halpern arrived for his deposition, Frank Church, who had attended former DDP Helms' deposition five days earlier, said Helms testified that Halpern was the source of a story that Attorney General Robert Kennedy *"had told the Special Group, or rather told the people working Cuba, to use the Mafia."* Church added, *"The implication, I think, in Helms' testimony was to use the Mafia for the purpose of assassinations.*[787] [Emphasis added]

---

787 6/18/75, Halpern SSCIA deposition, p. 3; RIF 157-10002-10087.

INTO THE STORM

Crucially, the transcript of Helms' 18 June 1975 deposition clearly corroborates key aspects of Church's characterization of Helms' testimony. The committee asked Helms if the attorney general had indicated he wanted contact with "a Mafia source" and Helms replied that it would be best for the committee to ask Halpern about that.[788] Helms mentioned he had learned details about this matter during a "chat" with Halpern.[789]

A close examination of Helms' transcript reveals that *what he knew* about the alleged RFK request for a Mafia contact *had come from Halpern.* Yet—as the reader will also recall from Chapter Nine—when the committee had Halpern in the witness seat, they did not ask him about his RFK-Mafia story.

The committee's decision to keep Helms' disclosures close to the vest may have contributed to a major mistake made by the committee's Review staff. The staff director, Walter Elder (who was also the executive assistant to DCI William Colby at that time), authored two short cover memos about RFK's alleged intention to use a case officer to contact the Mafia. In the first memo, Elder incorrectly stated that Helms *had* testified that *RFK had asked him* (Helms) to provide a case officer for the underworld.[790] That was *not* true.

Let us carefully review Elder's two memoranda. On 26 August 1975, Elder wrote this memorandum for the CIA Deputy Director of Operations, Enno Henry Knoche:

> Andy Postal and Mike Madigan, SSC (Senate Select Committee) staff members, state that Mr. Helms has testified that he recalls the attorney general's *asking him to try to find a case officer* who could be used as a contact with underworld figures in New York and Chicago. Helms cited an Italian name which they are trying to recapture. They do remember Helms saying that Sam Halpern would know the name.[791]
> [Emphasis added]

Just two days later, 28 August 1975, Elder sent a *different* version of this information to the Church Committee Review Staff:

> Mike Madigan, SSC staff, reports that Mr. Helms and Mr. Halpern have testified that *in response to a request* by Attorney General Robert Kennedy, the Agency assigned an officer to establish contacts with the underworld to look for possible assets for use against Castro. Sam Halpern says the officer was Charles Ford who used the name, Rocky Fiscalini.
> [Emphasis added]

---

788 6/13/75 Helms SSCIA deposition, p. 129; RIF 157-10014-10075.
789 Ibid, pp. 129-130.
790 8/26/75 and 8/28/75, Walter Elder memos for the Special Assistant to the DDO, and the CIA Task Force, respectively; RIF 104-10310-10198.
791 Ibid.

Elder added that Madigan wanted to interview Ford.[792] A few weeks later, a group of five Church Committee staff investigators interviewed Ford.

The two versions of the story as told by Walter Elder just two days apart bear directly on the audit trail of Robert Kennedy's alleged instructions to procure a case officer for the Mafia. To repeat, the first version stated unequivocally that Helms said under oath that *he was asked personally* by RFK to assign a case officer to the attorney general to establish contacts with the "underworld." The truth was that neither Helms nor Halpern had so testified. In addition, the second version did *not specify who* RFK made that request to. The truth was that RFK had not made such a request. So, why did Helms think that he had made such a request at all?

In my view, it is obvious that Elder had *not* read Helms' 13 June 1975 deposition. The same was probably the case for the source of the first memo, Review Staff officer Mike Madigan. We will not easily find out *when* Madigan came to believe RFK made a personal request to Helms. However, one clue *might* be the Review Staff dinner soiree that Halpern had attended. What if, in front of Madigan on that occasion, Halpern had represented that he had knowledge of a personal RFK request to Helms for an underworld case officer? That possibility—and that is all that it is—would put a different light on Madigan's report to Elder.

Unfortunately, the path by which these two incorrect Elder memos happened to come into being is less important than their ultimate effect. This major mistake added false but powerful evidence that would lead observers many years later to conclude that the RFK-Mafia story was an historical fact. It was not.

Charles Ford's 18 September 1975 Sworn Interview for the Church Committee

I begin this section with a frustrating—even suspicious—state of affairs with respect to Church Committee records. Charles Ford was interviewed *twice* by the Church Committee in September 1975. In the second interview, Ford referred to the first interview *five* times. Yet, no transcript of his first interview has survived. Moreover, save for the second interview, there is not a single surviving document—from the Church Committee or anywhere—that so much as mentioned the first interview. There is no question as to the singular importance of Charles Ford to Halpern's claims about a Bobby Kennedy plot to assassinate Castro. The disappearance of Ford's first sworn statement to the committee is either an incredible coincidence or a scandalous mystery.

---

792 8/28/75, Cover sheet for 9/19/75 MFR by Charles Ford, Subject: "Interview by Senate Committee Investigators"; RIF 157-10303-10001.

INTO THE STORM

On Thursday, 18 September 1975, Ford was interviewed for the second time by investigators from the Senate Committee. That interview had been scheduled as a formal deposition by the committee's senators. It turned into an "interview" because they were busy with televised public hearings and were therefore unavailable to depose him. Nevertheless, in this interview with committee staff, Ford was under oath.[793]

The primary questioning was handled by Andy Postal and Gordon Rhea, the same investigators with whom Ford spoke during his initial interview. As the second interview began, Ford was asked to generally describe his work with the CIA:

> I told them that I joined [the CIA] in 1949; that I was and am now a member of the Office of Training; that in 1960 or thereabouts I had a short tour of duty with the Economic Action Group in the DDP, and that I went directly from that assignment to WH/4 [in TFW] in September of 1961.

Ford was also asked about the organization of Task Force W and how many echelons there were between he and DDP Helms:

> I told them that I reported to Bill Harvey; that my title was Special Assistant; that Mr. Harvey reported to Mr. Helms; *that I frequently received assignments and reported to Sam Halpern*; and that occasionally I undertook tasks for Bruce Cheever, Harvey's deputy, although these tasks were concerned with the workings of Task Force W and did not involve contact with the Cubans. [Emphasis added]

I will mention this crucial sentence in Ford's sworn statement again at the end of this chapter. The committee staff also asked Ford about job titles:

> I was asked if there were any Special Assistants other than me in Task Force W and I replied that Mr. Zogby C/WH/4 [Chief, Western Hemisphere, Branch 4] *prior to Mr. Harvey's arrival* on the scene, had been retained as a member of Task Force W in a SA status. [Emphasis added]

The questions and answers then moved on to Ford's numerous major activities while assigned to the Agency's Cuban operations. Ford described the exile prisoners project and the abortive Betancourt/ELC operation—both previously discussed at length in this chapter. There is no need here to repeat Ford's participation in those 1962 operations other than to remind the reader that neither of them had anything to do with Halpern's alleged RFK-Mafia myth.

With respect to his first assignment in WH/4, Ford reported this:

> My first assignment was the handling of a Cuban agent, one we were using to build a nucleus of an organization for eventual operations

---

[793] 9/19/75, Charles D. Ford, memorandum, Subject: Interview by Senate Committee Investigators; RIF 104-10310-10119.

> into Cuba. I identified this man as Mr. Rojas. Mr. Rhea, having heard my description of this activity at our earlier session, did not pursue this matter any further.

I will give Halpern a pass on that Sergio Rojas Santamarina assignment because it appears to have taken place in late 1961—technically before Halpern's RFK-Ford case officer saga began.

Since the staff did not pursue the Rojas assignment in this interview, it is unfortunate that the first Ford interview disappeared. Rojas was a former (under Batista) Cuban ambassador to England. On 31 October 1961, the CIA liaison to the FBI, Jane Roman, denied that the Agency was involved in anti-Castro propaganda activities being conducted by Rojas and his associates throughout Latin America.[794] However, on 21 December 1961, the CIA advised the FBI that it *was* financing Rojas. At that time, he was involved in dropping anti-Castro leaflets from aircraft over Cuba. An FBI memorandum the next day revealed that a leaflet drop on 21 October 1961 *was* a CIA operation in which Rojas and former Castro followers Frank Sturgis (AKA Fiorini, a soldier of fortune and CIA source) and former rebel air force commander Pedro Diaz Lanz were involved.[795] The planes were flown from an island in the Bahamas.

Apparently, the Rojas operation was sensitive and Ford's handling of him might have been under an alias. In the operations discussed earlier in this chapter, Ford used the names Fiscalini and Barton. On 9 February 1962, a blind CIA memorandum was based on information from Sturgis about Rojas' involvement in the bombing of electrical and oil targets in Cuba. The source of the memo was Bernard Barker (a paid CIA informant in Miami). Barely legible marginalia on that memorandum indicated the memo was filed under what *might* have been the name Barton, an alias later used by Ford in the fall 1962 ELC operation.[796]

Once again, the committee staff investigators asked Ford when he was first assigned the Fiscalini alias. And, once again, Ford explained—as he had in the first interview—that the alias had been assigned at the end of March 1962 in conjunction with the exile prisoners project (discussed above). That date poses problems for Halpern's story. He claimed that the Fiscalini alias was assigned in conjunction with an operation with a unique transmission signature—RFK to DDCI Carter; Carter to Harvey; and Harvey to Halpern. In the extant CIA documentary record, that particular transmission footprint only occurred once—in late September 1962 at the time of the abortive ELC operation. As I have already pointed out, although Halpern signed the key CIA HQS

---

[794] 10/31/61, FBI memorandum, Anti-Fidel Castro Activities; RIF 124-90139-10057.
[795] 12/22/61, FBI memorandum, Anti-Fidel Castro Activities; RIF 124-10289-10328.
[796] 2/9/62, CIA blind memorandum RE information obtained from Frank Fiorini (true name Frank Sturgis); RIF 104-10048-10243.

cable describing the ELC operation, he never mentioned it in any of his interviews. Halpern never mentioned the exile prisoners project either.

The committee staff also wanted to know who assigned the Fiscalini alias to Ford. Halpern claimed he was the one who came up with that alias. Ford, however, could not recall who had assigned that alias. He could only remember that the alias documents came from the security office.

In this interview, the story of Ford's contact with a Canadian citizen named "Joe" was discussed. Ford recalled one meeting and a telephone call:

> I explained to the investigators that my interest lay in the fact that Joe claimed he could speak with Che Guevara and that I had attempted to get Joe to serve as a means of communication between us and Che, which Joe refused to do. As for the telephone call, I told them that when Joe returned from his trip to Cuba, he called to say that big things were going on in Cuba and we should meet right away.

At the time, the CIA was consumed with the Cuban Missile Crisis and Ford told Joe he could not see him. That was the last time Ford heard from Joe. Ford did not mention Robert Kennedy in association with the Canadian contact and CIA records contain no evidence that the attorney general had any role in this matter.

The committee staff asked Ford about visits he had made to New Orleans—a visit that he had mentioned in the original interview:

> I explained that these two trips were for the purpose of attempting to find ways of establishing channels of communication between the exiled Cubans in New Orleans and their friends in Cuba. I indicated that I had come up with a very fine prospect, a Cuban, and that *I had turned him over to one of our FI* [foreign intelligence] *case officers.* [Emphasis added]

Ford did not include any role for Bobby Kennedy in this operation. It was obviously an internal matter handled by Harvey's TFW Foreign Intelligence section.

Later in the interview, the committee staff also brought up the subject of RFK again—asking Ford if he remembered a meeting of the attorney general and Cuban exile leaders in the summer of 1962. Ford replied that such a meeting would not have been unusual but that he had no knowledge of such a meeting.

The constant interest of the committee staff in Bobby Kennedy moved Ford to make this observation at the end of the interview:

> This is probably the appropriate point to underline *my conviction that the main, if not the only, point of concern to the investigators is whether I was directed to sally forth and initiate contact with members of the underworld in the U.S., and who directed me to do so.* Their interest is *even more pointedly focused on* whether I had anything to do with the *Roselli, Giancana et al,* "operations." Once again, I explained that my job was broader than

this by a long shot, and that *I was never directed to take the initiative in establishing contacts with the underworld.* I said that several, probably no more than five or six, of the people with whom I dealt were somewhat "shady" characters, in some cases with recorded run-ins with law enforcement agencies.

This statement is a powerful rebuff of Halpern's thesis that Bobby Kennedy used Charles Ford in a Mafia plot to assassinate Castro. But Ford was not finished. He wanted to make it crystal clear that he had *not* been a party to such a plot. Moreover, Ford told the committee staff that he "*had never heard of or engaged in conversations with Agency officers about any plan, the direct and only aspect of which was the assassination of Fidel Castro.*" [Emphasis added] The committee's *pointed focus* on Roselli and Giancana is extremely important because it dovetails with Halpern's various RFK-Mafia allegations about meetings in Chicago and Miami. I will return to this subject in Chapter Thirteen.

Halpern's claim that Ford worked *exclusively for Robert Kennedy* was also completely discredited by Ford's sworn statement to the committee staff. On this point, I return again to what Ford told the committee staff about his assignments and chain of command:

> I told them that I reported to Bill Harvey; that my title was Special Assistant; that Mr. Harvey reported to Mr. Helms; *that I frequently received assignments and reported to Sam Halpern*; and that I occasionally undertook tasks for Bruce Cheever, Harvey's deputy, although these tasks were concerned with the workings of Task Force W and did not involve contact with the Cubans.

The CIA documentary record supports Ford's sworn testimony and completely flies in the face of Halpern's RFK-Mafia story—a myth that he never proffered under oath. In his many long discourses about RFK's exclusive use of Ford, Halpern never mentioned the *many* times that Ford worked for him (Halpern)—let alone that he *ever* worked for him at all.

The October 1975 CIA Request for the Church Committee Interview of Charles Ford

Pursuant to a Church Committee information request approximately one month after Ford's interview with the committee, the CIA's Latin American Division (LAD) interviewed Ford regarding his use of the Charles D. Fiscalini alias. The LAD wanted "to determine if Ford could recall specific individuals he contacted under this alias." The Agency also reviewed "pertinent files" to reconstruct Ford's use of that alias. On 16 October 1975, the LAD provided a memorandum to the CIA Review Staff with this result:

In 1962, Mr. Ford met with sponsors of Mario Oscar Garcia Antiga AKA Mario Garcia Kohly, Sr., (and on one occasion with Kohly) in which he used the alias "Rocky Fiscalini." Kohly was a Cuban exile and has been characterized as a gifted charlatan and confidence man who was talented in impressing people with access to high level U.S. government circles. Some of Kohly's associates had dubious reputations and others were solid, well-meaning U.S. citizens who desired to assist Kohly in his efforts to overthrow Fidel Castro. In October 1963, Kohly was arrested by the United States Secret Service on charges of counterfeiting Cuban currency. Subsequently, Kohly was indicted, convicted and sentenced to one year's imprisonment on 16 July 1964. This Agency had no operational relationship with Kohly.[797]

Six days later, 21 October 1975, CIA Review Staff Chief Seymour Bolten sent a response about Ford's use of the Rocky Fiscalini alias to the Church Committee. Bolten's reply was identical, word-for-word, with the above LAD memorandum.[798]

The Bolten memo said that no mention of the Kohly matter by RFK had been located by the LAD in CIA records. On all occasions that the attorney general made a request for CIA investigation of Cuban exiles, such requests were recorded in the relevant CIA documents.

Crucially—for Halpern's RFK-Mafia myth—the LAD memorandum concluded that they had been unable to document that Ford "used the alias 'Rocky Siscalini' [Fiscalini] alias *to establish contact with the underworld for possible use against Fidel Castro.*" LAD could not document such a use of the alias by Ford because—as he testified to the Church Committee–he was "never directed" to establish "contacts with the underworld."[799]

Halpern and Hersh Blame RFK for Ordering the Destruction of Ford's Reports on His Cuban Contacts

In Chapter Nine, I mentioned that Halpern found it normal that a paucity of paperwork existed about CIA assassination plots. I also briefly interjected that Halpern found the paperwork paucity problem *very* useful when it came time to explain the lack of supporting documentation *for his own* RFK-Mafia myth. I promised that this chapter and Chapter Thirteen would address the abundant Church Committee and CIA paperwork that debunks that myth.

---

797 10/16/75, Raymond A. Warren, Chief Latin American Division, Memo for the Review Staff, subject: SSC Request; RIF 104-10310-10062.
798 10/21/75, Seymour R. Bolten, Chief, Review Staff, memorandum to William G. Miller, SSCIA Staff Director; RIF 104-10310-10038.
799 9/19/75, Charles D. Ford, memorandum, Subject: Interview by Senate Committee Investigators; RIF 104-10310-10119.

RFK AND THE CASTRO ASSASSINATION PLOTS—PART II

Here, I want to briefly discuss how Halpern and Sy Hersh ignored that rich documentation when they concocted another malicious lie about Robert Kennedy. They blamed the *disappearance* of reports Ford allegedly made about his contacts with Cubans on "instructions" from Bobby. But the truth is that Ford's Cuban contact reports *were* preserved in CIA records. Furthermore, those reports thoroughly discredit Halpern's RFK-Mafia myth. For that reason, Halpern *and* Hersh had to ignore the declassified record.

The following excerpt from Hersh's ***The Dark Side of Camelot*** captures how a CIA officer renowned for his *uncanny memory* and a celebrated investigative reporter combined forces to do a hatchet job on Bobby Kennedy, based entirely on hot air:

> Ford arranged to have two trips a month for the attorney general and would dictate *reports* for Kennedy upon his return. "I know," Halpern said, "he went to places like Chicago, San Francisco, Miami—wherever Bobby sent him—including one trip to Canada." *Ford, obviously following instructions from Kennedy, relayed nothing to his nominal superiors in Task Force W.* "We never got a single solitary piece of [written] information," Halpern said. *Charlie Ford's reports*, if they still exist, presumably are among the millions of pages of Robert F. Kennedy papers that *have yet to be released* by the John F. Kennedy Library.[800] [Emphasis added; brackets are in the original]

Hersh *unsuccessfully* investigated Halpern's theory that Ford's written reports to RFK remain classified at the JFK Library. All Hersh came up with was this: "Few of [Robert] Kennedy's working papers from his days as attorney general have been made available."[801]

These allegations by Halpern and Hersh are *outrageously false*. *Of course*, Ford relayed reports *to his nominal superiors in Task Force W* about his findings from contacts with Cubans that he had in connection with requests from Robert Kennedy (discussed in detail above). *Of course*, those reports were written and remain in the declassified record. *Of course*, Bobby did not issue "instructions" to withhold Ford's reports on his Cuban contacts—not from his TFW superiors or from anybody else. *Of course*, Halpern and Hersh did not mention Ford's CIA reports—because those reports destroyed their mythical RFK-Mafia plot. But Halpern *knew* about these Ford reports. As I stated above, *Halpern's signature appeared on the most important document of them all!*

Moreover, as I mentioned above, there is another episode to this baleful tale that took place on or about the time of the Church Committee investigation. A crucial 1975 sworn interview and written report for the committee by Ford about his contacts with Cubans for Bobby and other TFW matters has disappeared. Obviously, that did

---

800 Hersh, ***Dark Side of Camelot***, p. 287.
801 Ibid.

not take place on Bobby's instructions—he was assassinated eight years earlier. To repeat, we know about this missing Ford report because it was mentioned in another sworn interview and written report by Ford shortly afterward. The second Ford report stipulated that he had "spent a great deal of time going over all of my meetings with the attorney general" with the committee.[802] Furthermore, Ford said that the details of the second report were the same as the details in the first report.

Thus, Ford was interviewed twice by the committee and *only the second interview survives* today. The truth is that the disappearance of that first Ford report—no matter how it disappeared—is more helpful to *Halpern's fraudulent case* against RFK than the reverse. Why? Because, as Ford testified on *both* occasions, he was "*never* directed to take the initiative in establishing contacts with the underworld." *Two* sworn interviews debunking Halpern is even stronger than one.

The 7 May 1962 Briefing for RFK: Behind His Back and Against His Orders

At 4:00 p.m. on 7 May 1962, CIA Inspector General (IG) Lawrence Houston and CIA Office of Security (OS) Director Sheffield Edwards briefed Attorney General Robert Kennedy on the details of "the CIA's operational involvement with gangster elements."[803] I will discuss this meeting and its ramifications again in Chapter Thirteen. Here, I include it briefly to establish the context for my investigation of Halpern's unwarranted and erroneous account of an RFK-Mafia plot to assassinate Castro.

That extraordinary briefing took place at Robert Kennedy's request. In his interview for the IG ***Report on Plots to Assassinate Fidel Castro***, Edwards reported that he had briefed RFK "all the way."[804] In his deposition for the Church Committee, Houston testified that he and Edwards had described the operation to the attorney general as an assassination attempt:

> Mr. Schwarz: Incidentally, in describing the [Mafia] operation, the document [a later 14 May 1962 memo by Edwards and Houston that RFK asked for] does not refer to it as an assassination. Did you refer to it orally as an assassination attempt?

Mr. Houston: *I'm sure we did* Mr. Schwarz. I cannot state unqualifiedly, but that is what we had in mind, and *that is what we went to tell him about*.[805] [Emphasis added]

---

802   9/19/75, Charles D. Ford, memorandum, Subject: Interview by Senate Committee Investigators; RIF 104-10310-10119.
803   5/23/67, CIA IG Report, p. 62a.
804   Ibid.
805   6/2/75, Houston SSCIA deposition, pp. 14-15.

RFK AND THE CASTRO ASSASSINATION PLOTS—PART II

According to the IG Report, Kennedy stated his view— "reportedly quite strongly"—that he wanted to be told in advance of any future CIA intentions to work with or through U.S. gangster elements.[806] Houston recalled that moment vividly:

> Mr. Houston: There is no question that Mr. Kennedy was *very unhappy* with what we brought forth. And he said in *very specific terms* that if we were going to get involved with Mafia personnel again, he wanted to be informed first.
>
> Senator Mondale: How did he express his displeasure?
>
> Mr. Houston: If you have seen Mr. Kennedy's eyes get steely and his jaw set and his voice low and precise, you get a definite impression of unhappiness.[807] [Emphasis added]

The IG report stated that from accounts of the briefing "it is reasonable to assume" that RFK believed he had received a commitment from the CIA that they would comply with his order to inform him before any future activity with the Mafia took place.[808]

Houston also told the committee that during the briefing Robert Kennedy was told that the Mafia assassination attempt against Castro *had been dropped*:

> Senator Mondale: Would the attorney general have gotten a clear understanding as it appears to be reflected in this memo that this was an attempt that was over?
>
> Mr. Houston: My recollection is that we told him the activity had been terminated as of that time.
>
> Senator Mondale: Now, were you speaking in terms of the attempt through the Mafia?
>
> Mr. Houston: That's correct, sir.
>
> Senator Mondale: Or were you talking in terms of all attempts?
>
> Mr. Houston: I knew of no other.
>
> Senator Mondale: So, he would have had the clear impression that this was the only attempt, that there was none other, and that it had been dropped. That's your opinion?
>
> Mr. Houston: That was certainly my feeling at the time, and I thought that's what we were telling him.[809]

However, we can be *certain* that was a lie. According to the IG report, at the time of the 7 May 1962 briefing for RFK, Harvey had just been introduced—on 8 April—to Chicago mobster Johnny Roselli and Cuban exile leader Manuel Varona, whose team had been given the lethal pills, arms, and related support equipment in late April:

---

806 5/23/67, CIA IG Report, p. 64.
807 6/2/75, Houston SSCIA deposition, p. 14.
808 5/23/67, CIA IG Report, p. 64.
809 Ibid, see p. 13 and p. 15.

INTO THE STORM

The attorney general *was not told* that the gambling syndicate operation had already been reactivated, *nor, as far as we know, was he ever told* that CIA had a continuing involvement with U.S. gangster elements. When the attorney general was briefed on 7 May, *Edwards knew* that Harvey had been introduced to Roselli. He must also have known that his subordinate, James O'Connell, was in Miami [with Harvey] and roughly for what purpose (although he does not now recall this).[810] [Emphasis added]

The Church Committee's ***Interim Report—Alleged Assassination Plots Involving Foreign Leaders***—found "implausible" the above statement by Edwards that he was unaware of the continuing Mafia operation.

Incredibly, Harvey testified that Edwards *not only* knew the Mafia operation was still ongoing *but also* that Edwards told him about the briefing for the attorney general afterward. According to Harvey, Edwards *confirmed* that he had made a false statement in a 14 May memorandum—that he (Harvey) had dropped the operation. Edwards did this, Harvey explained, so that the record would incorrectly show that the Mafia assassination operation had been terminated.[811]

In an interview with Hersh, Halpern speculated that "Bobby Kennedy's primary purpose in dealing with Charles Ford was to do what Bill Harvey was not doing—finding someone to assassinate Fidel Castro."[812] Fate was cruel to Halpern. He did not learn the truth about the CIA-Mafia assassination plot until his RFK charade had become baked into the fabric of the Kennedy assassination coverup. When Halpern died, on 7 March 2005, his undying coat of arms, awarded by the Association of Former Intelligence Officers, was his RFK chimera.

I will have more to say about the treatment of Halpern's claims by Seymour Hersh in Chapter Thirteen.

---

810   5/23/67, CIA IG Report, 65. The IG report went on to say, "although Edwards does not now recall this."
811   6/25/75, Harvey SSCIA deposition, pp. 97-102; RIF 157-10002-10106
812   Ibid.

CHAPTER ELEVEN

VECIANA, THE SECRET YEARS—1961-1962

Chapter Three examined the unfeasibility of Veciana's accounts about his recruitment and handling by Phillips in Cuba. Veciana's original chronology for that period in Cuba—proffered during forty years of depositions and interviews—was from mid-1960 to shortly *after* the Bay of Pigs invasion in 1961. After the death of Gaeton Fonzi in 2012, Veciana *altered* his Phillips Cuban chronology twice, and eventually settled on the scenario described in his 2017 book **Trained to Kill**—from mid-September 1959 to March 1960, one year *before* the Bay of Pigs invasion. Veciana's ignorance about the time period of his own story in relation to the Bay of Pigs is dubious—all by itself.

A close examination of the CIA documentary record about Veciana's activities leads to some surprising observations heretofore *never* considered by researchers of the Kennedy assassination. Ironically, Veciana was *forced* to discard his original chronology in order to hang on to his false allegation that Phillips recruited him in Cuba. Preserving that *false* claim in his *revised* chronology was more important to Veciana than preserving the *true* story of his life that took place during the time of his *original* chronology. In other words, to make his Phillips story workable, Veciana had to replace his true life with a false one. Below we will see the value that Veciana placed on being a "CIA agent" for his claim that he met Phillips with Oswald in Dallas during 1963.

The time has come to see what Veciana's true life looks like, without Phillips in the middle of the story, during Veciana's original chronology—from mid-1960 to early 1961. Veciana's work with the CIA in Cuba *did* take place during his *original* timetable with one important exception—Phillips, who was nowhere near Cuba, was not involved! During that period, an attrition of case officers at the CIA station in Havana was taking

INTO THE STORM

place amid security problems related to the impending break in Cuban-American relations (on 1 January 1961). Veciana *was* drafted for use locally (in Cuba) in mid-1960 and trained in the fall of that year by James Joseph O'Mailia, Jr., a CIA contract agent who had a solid cover as a professor at the University of Villanueva. As discussed in Chapter Three, O'Mailia used the pseudonym Joe Melton.

The reader should note that the events in the last two thirds of this chapter parallel the same time period as the Kennedy Mongoose operation—from late 1961 through October 1962. I will cover Operation Mongoose in Chapter Fourteen. This chapter will begin at the point in time that Veciana *originally* claimed his CIA training ended—late November 1960—in Havana's Edificio LaRampa building. While that training was taking place, great pains were being taken by the CIA at HQS and in Havana to prepare for the impending break in relations between Havana and Washington. Three intrepid CIA case officers were selected to remain in Havana without diplomatic protection to manage the stay-behind nets—Emilio Rodriguez, Tony Sforza, *and* James O'Mailia. Their activities lasted less than ninety days. I reported the details of their impossible mission in Volume II (***Countdown to Darkness***, Chapter Four).

Of those three daring CIA officers, O'Mailia was best suited to train Veciana for use on chores too risky for Sforza and Rodriguez to handle. O'Mailia's training of Veciana did *not* take place in the context of a plan inspired by Phillips. Rather, it took place in the context of plans to use Veciana to facilitate a plot to kill Castro and other psychological warfare operations that have thus far been given very little attention.

Which CIA Plot to Assassinate Castro Before the Bay of Pigs Was Veciana Involved In?

Two CIA-inspired plans to assassinate Castro were in motion as the Bay of Pigs invasion approached. I discussed one of them in Chapter Seven of this volume and in much greater detail in Volume II (Chapters Fifteen and Nineteen)—DDP Richard Bissell's CIA-Mafia assassination plot. The one I am about to discuss here was another CIA plot to assassinate Castro during the runup to the Bay of Pigs fiasco. The CIA sent Juan Pujals Maderos (**AMCOAX-1**, AKA "Chacho") to Cuba to head up a four-man team to blow up major utilities and kill Castro at the Sports Palace.[813] The other three team members were Alfredo Izaguirre Revoi (**AMPUG-1**, AKA "Luis"), Emilio Adolfo Rivero Caro (**AMPANIC-7**, AKA "Brand" and "Pancho"), and Juan Manuel Guillot Castelloro (**AMBRONC-5**, pseudonym Octavio Barroso Gomes).[814]

---

813   8/30/77, Comments on Book V, SSC Final Report, the Investigation of the Assassination of President Kennedy: Performance of the Intelligence Agencies, pp. 26-33. RIF 104-10103-10360.
814   We know that Izaguirre worked for Pujals, see Carl Jenkins 5/24/79 debrief of Reinol Gonzalez y Gonzalez,

VECIANA, THE SECRET YEARS—1961-1962

One of the important questions that arises is this: What measures, if any, were planned to protect the families of a *four-man* team on a sabotage-assassination mission from which they might never return? That is where Veciana proved to be useful. On 7 December 1960, Veciana entered the American Embassy in Havana and called on the CIA chief of station, James Noel. Veciana was accompanied by Felix Fernandez Yarzabal, a former member of the Agrapucion Montecristi group, whose members were wealthy Cuban professionals and businessmen, predominantly lawyers and economists, led by Justo Carrillo Hernandez. Veciana was hoping to arrange for visas to evacuate the families of the sabotage-assassination team. Noel had declined Veciana's request and refused to provide any help:

> Veciana informed Olien [James Noel] that a carefully thought out plot exists to wipe out the prime minister and his top associates. He said the plan is closely held and that only two people outside Cuba and only a handful persons inside Cuba, including *four* chosen to pull off the job were aware of it. Said his people aware of site where prime minister and his advisors meet periodically, have cased the area, have access to it and have worked out the details. Veciana said in order to carry out job, however, group needs (A) visas for immediate members of families of *four men* assigned to job. About ten visas for wives and children. (B) Four Garand [the M1 Garand later became the M14] rifles and adaptors for grenades plus grenades.[815] [Emphasis added]

Noel turned down Veciana cold. In his cable to HQS afterward, Noel reported that he "gave Veciana no encouragement whatsoever."

Veciana had also told Noel that he had previously spoken with a State Department "political officer" about his request. Noel told CIA HQS that a subsequent check with that officer revealed that Veciana had made similar "wild eyed" proposals. Veciana, Noel said, was "sincere but a little wild."[816] The CIA queried Veciana's boss, the wealthy Cuban sugar magnate Julio Lobo. Lobo was an important CIA asset and he vouched for Veciana's bona fides.[817]

What plot was the *four-man* assassination team Veciana referred to involved in? Obviously, it was not Bissell's CIA-Mafia assassination plot. Was it the CIA-backed Pujols team? Or was it yet another CIA-backed assassination team? In my view, a three-team scenario is out of the question. There were already too many complicated logistical, operational and *especially security* considerations associated with the planned invasion

---

p. 3; RIF 104-10217-10336. We also know that Guillot worked for Pujals, see Dominique Pantelone, 8/15/61, MFR, **AMBRONC-5** and **AMJAVA-4** Contact Reports; RIF 104-10193-10180.
815 12/13/60, HAVA 7133; RIF 104-10181-10434.
816 1Ibid.
817 7/11/62, DIR 22544, Martha Tharpe, TFW/PA-PROP; RIF 104-10181-10204.

by the exile brigade. Sending a third team into a situation that already included Varona's Rescate group, with their poison pills, and Pujols' four-man squad, with their guns and grenades running around the safe houses on the island, was about as likely as The Three Stooges starring in a production of Swan Lake.

So, what was really going on in December 1960 and what was Veciana really doing at the CIA station in Havana? According to his own testimony to Senator Schweiker in 1976, Veciana was the chief of sabotage for the Peoples' Revolutionary Movement (MRP) at that time. And, as I discussed in Chapter Three, CIA contract officer James O'Mailia was Veciana's handler. O'Mailia had finished training Veciana sometime in late November 1960 and Veciana was boots on the ground inside the CIA Havana station on 9 December 1960.

I believe the preponderance of evidence suggests Veciana visited the CIA to request help procuring visas for the families of Juan Pujols (**AMCOAX-1**) and his team. Emilio Rivero (**AMPANIC-7**) had returned to Miami for briefings before being sent back into Cuba to carry out the mission with the rest of the team. His debrief by the paramilitary operations section of the Cuban Task force—WH/4/PM/OPS—was handled by John D. Peters. Afterward, Peters wrote this:

> **AMPANIC-7** must resolve his personal problems dealing with his *wife and in-laws,* which has had an adverse effect on him personally since his return and may affect his operations inside Cuba. The next several weeks will, therefore, need to be devoted to re-establish A-7's confidence in our ability to support his efforts in Cuba, once he is sent back, and *working out his family problems to obviate any adverse psychological effect which may be detrimental to his operations in Cuba.*[818] [Emphasis added]

Rather than risk using O'Mailia and the other stay-behind net chiefs—Emilio Rodriguez and Tony Sforza—to personally enter the American Embassy just days before the break in relations, Veciana was chosen to go in and ask for the visas.

The Pujols hit squad was associated with the MRP—a CIA-backed Catholic action group. At the time of Veciana's visit to the Havana CIA Station, their leader was Reinol Gonzalez y Gonzalez (**AMCALL-1,** war name "Antonio"). O'Mailia (codenamed "Pepe') had begun handling Gonzalez for the CIA as early as 1959.[819] By December 1960, several anti-Castro Cuban groups had been integrated into Gonzalez' MRP. During an interview on Cuban television shortly after his arrest in October 1961, Gonzalez stated that the MRP had not received as much CIA assistance as other groups associated with the upcoming Bay of Pigs invasion and therefore "maintained relations mainly" with

---

818 11/26/60, CIA Memo, Preliminary Debriefing Report on AMPANIC-7 Activities in Cuba. RIF 104-10103-10125.
819 5/28/79, CIA MFR, Reinol Gonzalez y Gonzalez interview in Miami; RIF 104-10217-10082, p. 8.

VECIANA, THE SECRET YEARS—1961-1962

the State Department.[820] That may have been why Veciana went first to a State Department representative to seek visas at the embassy.

In the televised interview, Gonzalez explained that when the MRP emerged in October 1960, they had planned to fight in an open war and not by means of sabotage and terrorism. He said the CIA had declined to deliver weapons unless they were sure the weapons were going to groups completely dependent on the Agency. The CIA relied exclusively on the invasion training camps, Gonzales recalled, and were "simply not delivering the weapons to us Cubans." As a result, due to those circumstances, he added, "the MRP simply decided to start acts of sabotage and terrorism."[821]

Having failed to secure help for the MRP from the State Department at the embassy, Veciana had turned to the CIA station. The fact that Noel turned him down so flatly indicates he (Noel) probably had no idea about the assassination squad Veciana was trying to get the visas for. This supports Veciana's claim that this assassination operation was very closely held on the island and restricted to *only two people* in the U.S. It would take time for the CIA officers assigned to the new JMWAVE (formerly JMASH) station in Miami to catch up with the fast-moving—and perilous—events taking place on the ground in Cuba.

The date for the Pujals [**AMCOAX-1**] team's sabotage operation was scheduled for 9 April—just eight days before the invasion. That date might have been selected after the CIA-mob plot (using June Cobb's boss Juan Orta) fell through in late January. The situation for Pujals' squad became increasingly desperate as the Bay of Pigs approached. Unlike Varona's assassination team (that had replaced Orta) in Cuba that had to stand down when the green light from Varona never came, Pujals' team was locked and loaded, ready to strike at Castro—and scared out of their minds.

As the moment of no return drew near, three dramatic messages arrived at HQS from the hit team in Cuba. On 27 March 1961, the first message was sent from **AMBRONC-5**:[822]

> The message requested the Agency's opinion on a proposed sabotage of the electric company in Havana, stating that this would be coordinated "with attempt against Fidel in public appearance (at) Sports Palace." The cable expressed the view that an "attempt against Fidel (is) in accordance with general plan."

There was no answer to this message from HQS. On 29 March, **AMBRONC-5** sent another, more desperate, message:

> Plan [is for] 9 April. Fidel will talk at the [Sports] Palace. Assassination attempt at said place followed by a general shutting off of the main

---

820   11/14/61 JMWAVE Dispatch p. 4.
821   Ibid, p. 3.
822   8/30/77, Comments on Book V, SSC Final Report, pp. 26-27; RIF 104-10103-10360.

electric plants in Havana Veladura. Occupy the public square. Telephone company, Atares [Arsenal] and Minfar [Armed Forces Ministry]. ...We need arms [to] enter Havana. We have sufficient men and courage. *State of mind desperate. Impossible to endure this longer. Every day situation worse.* Daily arrests. We can blow up any electric company at any time. Consider what this represents for us after the action. Answer before 1 April. [Emphasis added]

This message was answered on 30 March. It said, "We agree major effort should be launched [on] Havana on date you selected," and added, "Once uprising commences, we will provide all possible support."

Obviously, HQS had the opportunity to prohibit an assassination attempt; however, no comment about assassinating Castro was made. A third message arrived on 5 April:

Brand [**AMPANIC-7**], Chacho [**AMCOAX-1**] and Luis [**AMPUG-1**] only have arms for fifty men. Blowing up [of] central electric plant and possible attempt on Fidel will be decidedly carried out 9 April. Once this achieved impossible to maintain clandestine organization in Cuba. *Your military aid is decisive. If it does not come that date we are lost.*

Once again, HQS said nothing at all, and left Pujols' team in the lurch. His plan failed, as did the Bay of Pigs invasion twelve days later.

In a 1977 review of the Church Committee Final Report, the CIA stated, "No further reference to this plan has been found. ... We have interviewed a case officer who was responsible for one of them [the four members of the squad]."[823] One such case officer, James S. Pekich, worked in the paramilitary section of the Cuban Task Force (WH/4).[824] He denied that the team had been sent to Cuba with a mission to assassinate Castro. Contrary to Pekich's denial, we know that the assassin on the team was Emilio Adolpho Rivero, AKA "Brand," [**AMPANIC-7**]. Described in CIA documents as a "walk-in" in July 1960, the Agency trained him in the use of a rifle with a telescopic sight at the Warrenton, Virginia firing range that month. Rivero's training was overseen by "Ernest W. Sparks," chief of the paramilitary section of the CIA Cuban task force (C/WH/4/PM).[825] That name was on the daily log for Rivero's check-out with the rifle and scope. Because we know that the C/WH/4/PM was Colonel Jack Hawkins, Ernest Sparks was a files pseudonym used for him.

---

823 Ibid.
824 11/2/60, Memorandum for Record: Preliminary Debriefing Report on Activities in Cuba; RIF 104-10103-10125. Pekich denied sending this team "to conduct an assassination." See 8/10/77, John L. Leader Memo for Record, Interview with Mr. James S. Pekich; RIF 104-10103-10120. Whether Pekich's denial was true, the Church Committee confirmed that the team was sent to assassinate Castro; see n. 1 above.
825 7/18/60, Ernest W. Sparks, C/WH/4/PM, "Daily Log—[WH/4] Paramilitary Section"; RIF 104-10315-10056. See also Pfeiffer, CIA *Official History of the Bay of Pigs*, Volume III, p. 283. 104-10301-10004.

VECIANA, THE SECRET YEARS—1961-1962

After the Bay of Pigs disaster, the motivation within U.S. national security organizations to topple the Castro regime continued to build. The Kennedy brothers paved the way by working to clear the roadblocks in Berlin, Laos, and Vietnam. However, in the meantime, subterranean plans to overthrow and assassinate Castro were hatched and not shared with the White House. With the stay behind net chiefs in hiding or in prison, *only* Veciana's cover continued to hold—but in October 1961, he, too, had to flee.

Operation Patty

The first post-Bay of Pigs invasion American plan to overthrow Castro was Operation Patty. The plan was to assassinate Fidel and Raul Castro and ignite a provocation at Guantanamo, forcing a U.S. invasion. It took place while the Kennedy Administration was still investigating what went wrong with the CIA's Bay of Pigs fiasco. Researcher Bill Simpich has recently done excellent work on the reconstruction of this lost episode in American anti-Castro activities. Operation Patty was a plan to assassinate Fidel and Raul Castro in Havana on the Cuban holiday, 26 July. At the same time, the plan called for engineering a provocation at the American naval base at Guantanamo by shooting both *Americans and Cubans*, in the hopes of igniting a battle that would be the pretext for an American invasion. That false flag concept was the forerunner of the Joint Chiefs' of Staff Operation Northwoods, proposed during Operation Mongoose in 1962.

The activities associated with Operation Patty during May-July 1961 do not appear to have been part of a CIA plan. Simpich has recently investigated this episode further. He argues that Patty looks more like a plan orchestrated by the Office of Naval Intelligence (ONI). A prime mover in this scheme was Spanish-speaking ONI Navy Lieutenant Commander Harold "Hal" Feeney (AKA Finney), the Base Intelligence Officer at the Guantanamo Bay Naval Facility.[826] As Feeney later explained:

> Before the break in diplomatic relations, most of the contacts with the resistance movements in Cuba were made by CIA agents operating out of the embassy and the consulates. After the break it became very difficult to communicate, and urgent that *CIA-trained Cuban exile secret agents be infiltrated to carry out the work*—arranging air drops of weapons, recruiting other agents, gathering intelligence, organizing and training an underground force. Time was growing short. ...At the time, hundreds of native Cubans worked at the Guantanamo Base and

---

[826] 2/10/62, Passavoy (Colonel Wendell G. Johnson) MFR No. 200, U.S. Navy Officer Harold Finney (or Feeney) Visits Dr. Miro 7 February; RIF 104-10233-10432. See also 4/2/62, JMWAVE dispatch UFGA-3694, Possible Use of FPO Shipment of Weapons to Guantanamo Bay Naval Facility; RIF 104-10163-10235.

commuted daily through the main gate, properly identifying themselves in each direction. ...Other than myself, my little team consisted of my assistant, ENS Jack H. Modesett, Jr., USNR, and occasional help from one or two ONI civilian agents who were assigned to do background security investigations. ...*we carefully recruited our own espionage ring.*[827]
[Emphasis added]

ONI arranged for Feeney to brief the CIA and Chief of Naval Operations (CNO) Arleigh Burke. The CIA was ecstatic about the idea and Burke was so enthusiastic that he gave his plane to Feeney to get back to Guantanamo as quickly as possible.

Feeney worked with Francisco Bilbao Alvarez (**AMCRAG-1**),[828] the Revolutionary Recovery Movement (MRR) chief in Oriente Province; also involved with this group was MRR member Alfredo Izaguirre (**AMPUG-1**), who lived at the Guantanamo base. According to Warren Hinckle and William Turner, Izaguirre's leader was a "Navy Lieutenant Commander."[829]

In May 1961, Izaguirre bought his own airline ticket to Washington and secured an audience with an old CIA contact, Paul D. Wiecha, who was working in the Foreign Intelligence (FI) unit of the Cuban task force (WH/4). Izaguirre said that the internal (inside Cuba) section of Revolutionary Unity (UR) had sent him as their emissary, although he himself was not a member of the group. He added that ever since the Bay of Pigs failure the underground in Cuba was "united as never before." However, he warned Wiecha that the UR could not work with the "Consejo"—the Cuban Revolutionary Council (CRC):

> ...the UR realizes that it cannot close its eyes to political reality, and it knows that the president of the U.S. has publicly recognized the Consejo. ...The UR realizes that internal resistance alone cannot topple the Castro government. ...He said he was instructed by the UR to go to the highest level possible in the U.S. to present its operational proposals.

After this meeting, Wiecha let Izaguirre borrow his typewriter to type up a plan to present to "the people with whom he was going to speak."[830]

According to Cuban intelligence chief Fabian Escalante, Izaguirre then met with "Frank Bender" (Gerry Droller). After a chance "to feel him out," Droller told Izaguirre about the Taylor Commission that was heading up JFK's investigation of the Bay of Pigs at that time:

> Days later he [Izaguirre] was taken to the Pentagon, to an office with General Maxwell Taylor's name on it. Inside were several people, in

---

827 CDR Harold Feeney, USN (Ret), "The Night of the White Horse," *Naval Intelligence Professionals* (NIP), Fall 1988.
828 MFF, Cryptonyms, **AMCRAG-1**.
829 Hinckle and Turner, *Deadly Secrets*, p. 114.
830 5/22/61, Robert Wiecha, WH/4/FI, Memo for Record; 104-10266-10174.

addition to the general himself. ... [The other "people" said:] "We agree with your assessment, but the Cubans should get the idea out of their heads that the marines will come in cold to resolve the Cuban problem. It depends on you to create a situation to propitiate direct aid." Later, in the privacy of his hotel room, Izaguirre confided to Frank Bender his impressions of the meeting. "I understand that the U.S. needs a pretext to intervene militarily in Cuba, and I assure you that we won't fail them. The naval base will be attacked, and you can blame Castro for this act."

Escalante added that toward the end of May, Izaguirre returned to Havana with new instructions and a U.S. guarantee to back them up with material and financial resources. According to Escalante, the details of this account were taken from "the Declarations by Alfredo Izaguirre de la Riva to Cuban State Security, July 1961"[831]—after his arrest.

In his work *The Cuban Counterrevolution*, Jesus Arboleya states that Izaguirre met with General Taylor for 45 minutes:

> Taylor explored the situation of counterrevolutionary groups within the country. Taylor gave assurances that the Cuban question would have an *adequate solution* and he would do all in his power to achieve it.[832] [Emphasis added]

Arboleya's account of Izaguirre's meeting in Taylor's office is less detailed than the confession extracted from Izaguirre by Cuban intelligence.

Whether or not all of the details of Izaguirre's confession were accurate, Escalante's account incorrectly, in my view, described Operation Patty as a CIA operation. Simpich suggests that this was an ONI operation. I agree. In any event, at the very least, Izaguirre had returned to Cuba, encouraged by what he had heard in Washington. On 12 July 1961, after meeting with Izaguirre, Pujals traveled from Cuba to Miami to report on the progress of Operation Patty.[833]

On 20 July 1961, a memo from Martha Tharpe in the HQS Cuban task force (WH/4) reported news from Pujals about a meeting among counterrevolutionary groups in Havana to unify the underground. Tharpe noted that the CIA had no knowledge of an alleged CIA "proposition," but conceded that it was conceivable that the underground considered Pujals and Izaguirre as representatives of the CIA.[834] CIA records indicate that Izaguirre was captured the next day—21 July. As a result, Operation Patty fell through.

---

831 Escalante, *The Cuba Project*, pp. 88-89.
832 Jesus Arboleya, *The Cuban Counterrevolution* (Miami: Ohio University, 2000), pp. 94-95.
833 Escalante, *The Cuba Project*, pp. 90-92.
834 7/20/61, DIR 01772, Martha Tharpe, WH/4/PA-PROP; RIF 104-10243-10080.

INTO THE STORM

Operation Liborio

According to Cuban intelligence chief Fabian Escalante, on 22 July 1961, the day after the capture of Izaguirre, at the behest of the CIA Juan Pujals took command of the resistance inside Cuba:

> Izaguirre and his associates were arrested, but the CIA still had one card left, and they decided to play it. CIA officials *Harold Bishop* and Frank Bender [Gerry Droller] met with agent Jose Pujals, who had been in Washington when he was caught unawares by the Operation Patty setback. Pujals was ordered to assume command of the CIA agents on the island... ...he was to coordinate an operation whose codename would be Liborio, which would include assassinating the Cuban leader, launching an extensive sabotage and terrorism campaign, and orchestrating, in conjunction with the Catholic hierarchy, a psychological warfare project designed to discredit the revolution in the eyes of the people.[835] [Emphasis added]

I will return to Pujols'—and a CIA case officer with the pseudonym "Cal Hitch"—involvement in Operation Liborio after addressing the question: Who was the "Harold Bishop" Escalante referred to? Bill Simpich suggests that Harold Bishop might have been Harold Swenson. That case involves four CIA men during a thirty-year time span—and is based on more than the fact that both men had the same first name.

After serving for six years undercover as an attaché in Argentina, Swenson was suddenly sent to CIA HQS on 31 October 1962 to become William Harvey's foreign intelligence chief in Task Force W (C/TFW/FI).[836] That posting took place at the time of Harvey's fatal fight with Robert Kennedy at the height of the Cuban Missile Crisis. After Harvey was banished to Rome in 1963, his deputy, Bruce Cheever, took over as Swenson's immediate supervisor. According to Swenson's CIA Personal History Statement (PHS), John L. Hart replaced Cheever as Swenson's supervisor in February 1965.[837]

On his PHS, Swenson listed "Al Rodriguez" as a professional and social associate. Rodriguez was a pseudonym for Earl Williamson, a ubiquitous CIA staff officer whose checkered career was the subject of several chapters in Volume II (*Countdown to Darkness*). Williamson's career had included an assignment as the deputy to the CIA chief of station in Havana, William Caldwell, during the mid-1950s.[838] A noteworthy detail

---

835   Escalante, *The Cuba Project*, pp. 94-95.
836   10/31/62, Notification of Personnel Action, Harold Swenson; RIF 104-10194-10002.
837   2/22/65, Supplemental Personal History Statement, Harold Francis Swenson; 104-10131-10001.
838   In Volume I (*Where Angels Tread Lightly*, Chapter Four), I reported finding two names for the Havana chief of station in Antonio Varona's CIA 201 file. It indicates that Varona was "first introduced to James R. Palinger and Wallace A. Growery [true name Earl Williamson] by a contact of Palinger in May 1957." These two men were,

VECIANA, THE SECRET YEARS—1961-1962

on Swenson's PHS indicated that William Harvey had known him since 1942.[839] One line of work Swenson and Harvey had in common was running background checks—as did Harvey's Staff D replacement, Ronald A. MacMillan. In 1970, Bill Harvey, William Caldwell, Ronald MacMillan and Harold Swenson *all* ended up working in a "confidential reporting service" named "Bishop's Service."[840]

I have taken time here to mention Simpich's work on the Harold Bishop lead provided by Escalante because of its possible relevance to Veciana's uncertain claim that David Phillips used the name "Maurice Bishop." Simpich rightly points out that *in 1976* Veciana did *not* know the first name of Bishop and that, over the next twelve months, Veciana added "Morris" as the first name and then later changed it to "Maurice."

Now, I return to the involvement of CIA case officer "Cal Hitch" and Juan Pujals in Operation Liborio. We know from CIA records that Cal Hitch was a pseudonym for CIA staff officer Calvin Hicks.[841] Escalante claims, I believe correctly, that Pujals replaced Alfredo Izaguirre as head of the internal resistance while Operation Liborio was in the planning stage.[842] According to Escalante (as discussed above), after meeting in Washington with Jim Bender (Gerry Droller, AKA Frank Bender), Cal Hitch (Calvin Hicks), Harold Bishop (possibly Harold Swenson[843]), and Pujals attended a "conspiracy" session at the Guantanamo Bay Naval Facility.[844]

According to Castro's "black book," at that meeting the conspirators received "a lot of warlike material and equipment for the accomplishment of these plans."[845] Escalante's description of Liborio included the assassination of Castro and an extensive campaign of sabotage and terrorism.[846] Castro claimed "Captain Carl E. Schenweias" was one of the most aggressive organizers at this meeting.[847]

---

respectively, the chief and deputy chief of the CIA Station in Havana. Although the name "Palinger" appears at the bottom of several CIA Havana Station documents at the time, the initials "SPR" are clearly visible at the top of several of them. Those initials very likely stood for Sherwood P. Rochom, whose name also appears in a 1959 PRQ-II as a case officer for Manolo Ray. The identities and pseudonyms for these CIA officers are discussed in Appendix Four (pp. 355-357). Rochom and Palinger were possibly pseudonyms for William Caldwell.

839   Ibid.
840   "More Society Members Serving as Area Representatives for Bishop's Service," *Grapevine*, November 1970.
841   10/9/61, Calvin Hicks memorandum, Contact Between Mr. Hicks (used name Cal Hitch) and Elena Mederos del Gonzales, Between 21 and 23 September 1961; RIF 104-10271-10083.
842   Escalante, *The Cuba Project*, p. 94.
843   Bill Simpich suggests that it would have been easy for Swenson to take some TDY time and come from Argentina to JMWAVE and consult with officers running Cuba operations during 1960-62. 4/23/18, personal communication with Simpich.
844   Castro's Black Book, based on information given to him by Senator McGovern, p. 19; RIF 180-10090-10232.
845   Ibid.
846   Escalante, *The Cuba Project*, pp, 94-95.
847   Castro's Black Book, p. 19. The actual spelling was Carl W. Schoenweiss. In 1961, he was transferred to the Office of Naval Material, where he served until his retirement.

INTO THE STORM

On 29 July 1961, Pujals was again infiltrated into Cuba.[848] As Escalante recalled:
> Pujals arrived in the capitol in late July 1961, after a risky voyage in which the CIA infiltrated him back into the country along the coast north of Havana. A few days later he met with Reinol Gonzalez (**AMCALL-1**), Veciana, and the spy Octavio Barroso, and explained to them the plan as instructed by his CIA controllers. The idea was to ignite Havana—to burn down the big clothing stores and the electrical and transportation facilities—and at the same time to assassinate various leaders of revolutionary organizations. This would provoke public indignation, and surely end in a mass demonstration in front of the Presidential Palace which would be the opportunity to assassinate Fidel.[849]

According to CIA records, in August Pujals and Barroso (**AMBRONC-5**) were arrested by Cuban security forces, who, after having been alerted by Pujals' collaborators of the presence of spies, captured them in Barroso's home.[850]

At the end of September one of the underground members of the MRP sabotage teams, Dalia Jorge Diaz, was caught in the act of planting an incendiary device in the Sears store. Afterward, all of her contacts were arrested while those who were not her contacts were not arrested. The conclusion was unavoidable that she had been working for Cuban intelligence all along. By 4 October, the day to carry out the assassination of Castro by bazooka at the Presidential Palace, many members of the underground had already been rounded up and imprisoned.

On 5 October 1961, Veciana's "Liborio" plot failed.[851] At the time, Veciana was just about the last man standing in what remained of the sabotage operations associated with the People's Revolutionary Movement (MRP) inside of Cuba. The MRP had been the largest and most important CIA-backed underground organization in Cuba and a center piece of the CIA's stay-behind nets after the break in Cuban-American relations in January 1961.

As I pointed out in Chapter Three, October 1961 was the moment that the White House finally returned to the problem of disposing of Castro with the implementation of Operation Mongoose. That was also the point at which Harvey took over the CIA-Mafia plot to kill Castro. Against the backdrop of all that, Veciana, having narrowly escaped arrest in Cuba, stepped off a small boat in Miami and launched Alpha-66.

---

848   8/30/77, Comments on Book V, SSC Final Report, p. 29; RIF 104-10103-10360.
849   Escalante, *The Cuba Project*, p. 95.
850   10/9/61, Calvin Hicks memorandum, Contact Between Mr. Hicks (used name Cal Hitch) and Elena Mederos del Gonzales, between 21 and 23 September 1961; RIF 104-10271-10083.
851   11/23/61, Jay Mallen, *Miami News*, "A Bazooka Didn't Fire in Havana and Castro Talked On"; RIF 104-10276-10157.

VECIANA, THE SECRET YEARS—1961-1962

Veciana, Alpha-66 and the Pentagon—1962

The CIA's plan to use Veciana in a sabotage role was flawed. Veciana—like the rest of the People's Revolutionary Party (MRP)—knew that CIA financing for sabotage operations brought with it complete subordination to the Agency. But the main problem was that the MRP had been crippled by the end of 1961—partly because of the failure of Veciana's operation Liborio. That debacle had led to the arrest of MRP National Coordinator Reynold Gonzalez y Gonzalez (**AMCALL-1**) and many other MRP members inside Cuba. The MRP's leadership was forced to seek asylum in Havana's foreign embassies. WH/4 paramilitary case officer Calvin Hicks had been monitoring—and maintaining contact with—more than two dozen of these conspirators right up to the moment that Operation Liborio collapsed.[852]

Months passed while the CIA came to grips with the extent of the damage suffered by the MRP in Cuba. Well before that, however, the Agency had initiated the procedures for CIA to use Veciana operationally. The processing of Veciana for this mission began normally enough. On 29 December 1961, the CIA JMWAVE station in Miami requested a Provisional Operational Approval (POA) for use of Veciana as an MRP sabotage asset.[853] On the same day, Calvin Hicks relayed the JMWAVE request to the Counterintelligence Operational Approvals Division.[854] On 8 January 1962, the Miami station followed up with a Personal Record Questionnaire (PRQ), Part-1.[855] The PRQ-1 stated that Veciana's alias "Victor" had been used in Havana City in the underground against the Castro regime. At HQS on 10 January, an expedited check on Veciana was sent to the FBI. Finally, on 30 January, HQS informed the JMWAVE Station that Veciana's POA had been approved for use by the MRP and that he had been assigned the CIA cryptonym **AMSHALE-1**.[856]

What was left of Veciana's already minor operational relationship with the CIA fell completely apart during the spring and summer of 1962. What we learn from that development is that Veciana *never* intended to work for the CIA. Beyond finagling funds from the CIA for his own use, Veciana *detested* the CIA. It is also clear that the CIA approved Veciana's POA for use as an MRP sabotage asset *before* they understood that the MRP was not as significant as it had been in the past and that it would *never* recover inside Cuba.[857] Veciana fled first to the U.S., and then settled in Puerto Rico in the

---

852 10/3/61, Hicks MFR, Contact with Justo by "Cal Hitch"; RIF 104-10226-10032. See also 10/9/61, Hicks MFR, Hicks and Elena Mederos del Gonzalez; RIF 104-10271-10083
853 12/29/61, WAVE 0311; RIF 104-10181-10432.
854 See 1/25/62, re Hicks 12/29/61 request; RIF 104-10181-10429. See also 12/29/61, Request for Approval or Investigative Action from Calvin Hicks for Antonio Veciana; RIF 104-10181-10288.
855 1/8/62, WAVE Dispatch UFGA-3001, PRQ-1—Antonio Veciana; RIF 104-10181-10423.
856 1/30/62, DIR 38699, Veciana, 201-312966; RIF 104-10181-10206.
857 CIA Cuban Revolutionary Handbook, p. 390.

spring of 1962, where he created a new anti-Castro organization, Alpha-66. However, Alpha-66 was inept as an action group. After several months, it boasted only one boat and a few weapons and, more importantly, it had no prospect of running raids against Cuba until the fall of 1962—as the height of the Missile Crisis loomed.

As 1961 gave way to 1962, the CIA quickly lost interest in using Veciana. The reasons for that went beyond the decline of the MRP's usefulness in Cuba or the feebleness of Alpha-66's sabotage capabilities. The Kennedy Administration was ramping up Operation Mongoose, a comprehensive government-wide program to overthrow the Castro regime. From the start, the sprawling multi-agency Mongoose program generated security concerns and those concerns escalated as the Missile Crisis approached. Save for one exception during the days just before the thirteen-day climax of the Missile Crisis, the Kennedy brothers were not interested in including Alpha-66 in their plans. The chief of the CIA Mongoose component, William Harvey, found Veciana to be a major nuisance. Harvey broadcasted government-wide alerts of *any* information he received about Veciana's sabotage plans.

However, as we will see in Chapter Fourteen, *dark operations* were being stitched together in opposition to President Kennedy's firm declaration that the U.S. would not go to war in Cuba. The collusion between the Chairman of the Joint Chiefs of Staff, General Lyman L. Lemnitzer, and U.S. Air Force Brigadier General and Assistant to Secretary of Defense Robert McNamara, Edward G. Lansdale, to obtain presidential approval for a false flag pretext (Operation Northwoods) to facilitate a *U.S. invasion of Cuba* fell flat on its face by April 1962. Lansdale would soon find Veciana and his Alpha-66 quite interesting as a potential way to capitalize on the growing Soviet threat in Cuba. Eventually, Veciana let it be known that Alpha-66 planned to assassinate the Soviet Ambassador in Cuba and sink a Soviet ship in Havana's harbor—actions that could potentially stir up a war and *U.S. invasion of Cuba.*

In May and June, Veciana was struggling to build his fledgling Alpha-66 sabotage group. On 23 July 1962, Jay Reeves of the CIA New York Contacts Office interviewed Veciana.[858] The New York office granted Veciana's request for an interview after Julio Lobo alerted the office to the request. Veciana explained that "Alpha," for the letter A, meant it was the first group of its kind, and the number 66 indicated how many founding members belonged to the group. Veciana told Reeves that Alpha-66 intended to *wage war* on Castro's Cuba and that *its first objective was the assassination of Castro.*

Veciana said that Alpha-66 had made several unsuccessful attempts to solicit CIA aid in Miami. He explained that he was still interested in CIA funding and requested a "conversation with someone in the Agency who is sufficiently high-placed to make

---

858   7/26/62, Jay B. L. Reeves to Chief, CIA Contact Division, Subject: Antonio Veciana and Alpha 66; RIF 1993.07.14.17:06:24:150340. See also 5/00/77, CIA Review of Veciana 201 File, NB: the New York Chief was Harry Real, but Reeves did the interview; RIF 104-10102-10176.

VECIANA, THE SECRET YEARS—1961-1962

a commitment." However, Veciana made it clear that he would accept CIA help only if there were no strings attached. That would never happen. By the summer of 1962, the CIA's authorization to use Veciana as an MRP sabotage asset was obsolete. In an 11 July 1962 cable to JMWAVE, TFW officer Martha Tharpe drew attention to the continuing existence of the still open request for Veciana's POA for use in MRP sabotage operations. She asked for a clarification that never came.[859] As the U.S.-Soviet crisis deepened over the summer, events quickly began to unfold that would bring Alpha-66 under the direct control of U.S. Army intelligence and indirectly under the influence of Lansdale's Office of Special Operations in the Pentagon.

By July 1962, the moment of truth—Armageddon—in the escalating Cold War was just three months away. In that month, the CIA station in Miami saw the Missile Crisis coming. In his autobiography, JMWAVE Chief of Station Ted Shackley described the unexpected and disturbing events that came to light in July 1962.[860] From its sources inside of Cuba, the JMWAVE Station detected a secret buildup of Soviet personnel, and this buildup continued in August. Shackley states that the JMWAVE Station knew that the Soviets were moving more of their equipment at night and concluded that they were moving surface-to-air missiles (SAMs).[861]

In August 1962, U.S. intelligence received information from ground observers in Cuba about sightings of Soviet fighters, bombers and SA-2 surface-to-air missile sites at various locations. Director of Central Intelligence (DCI) McCone reasoned that this only made sense "if Moscow intended to use them to shield a base for ballistic missiles aimed at the United States."[862] On 10 August, McCone sent a memo to President Kennedy predicting that the USSR was preparing to introduce ballistic missiles into Cuba.[863]

In the alarming context of this impending crisis, Veciana had become thoroughly disenchanted with President Kennedy. On 8 August 1962, an FBI report from its San Juan, Puerto Rico office called attention to this developing problem.[864] Veciana told a close associate in Puerto Rico (possibly Felix Zabala)—who happened to be an FBI informant—that the U.S. had no intention of liberating Cuba. He said that the U.S. had permitted Castro to take over and had allowed the USSR to set up a base in Cuba without any protest. Accordingly, Veciana revealed this five-step Alpha-66 program:

1) Kill the Russian Ambassador to Cuba.
2) Blow up the Esso Oil Refinery in the Regla section of Havana.

---

859 7/11/62, DIR 22545 (TWF PA-PROP, Tharpe) to JMWAVE, RE use of Veciana for MRP sabotage ops; RIF 104-10181-10203.
860 Ted Shackley, *Spymaster—My Life in the CIA* (Washington D.C., Potomac Books, 2006, paper ed.), p. 60.
861 Ibid, p. 62.
862 Allison, Graham and Phillip Zelikow, *Essence of Decision: Explaining the Cuban Missile Crisis* (New York: Addison Wesley Longman, 1999), p. 80.
863 John T. Correll, "Airpower and the Cuban Missile Crisis," *Air Force Magazine*, 88 (8).
864 8/11/62, FBI SJ to HQS, RE Alpha 66; RIF 104-10102-10073 and 194-10002-10039.

INTO THE STORM

      3) Destroy the power plant in the Tallapiedra suburb of Havana.
      4) Sink a Russian ship in Havana Harbor.
      5) Kill a high-ranking Cuban official.

Veciana predicted that these actions would begin in late July and would be finished by 22 September. As it turned out, *none* of them would begin until early September. And it would be U.S. Army intelligence, not the CIA, that would have a front row seat as Alpha-66 raids took place against Cuban and Soviet shipping.

On 30 August, Veciana complained to his Alpha-66 associates in Puerto Rico that the U.S. Government had intensified efforts to "restrain Cuban exiles" from undertaking paramilitary action against Cuba. Veciana declared that Alpha-66 planned to go ahead anyway. He added that the first attack on Cuba would take place before 22 September. This threat led William Harvey to send a warning on 6 September to *everyone* in Washington: the FBI, State Department, Defense Intelligence Agency, Army Intelligence, Navy Intelligence, and Air Force Intelligence. Harvey stated that the CIA wanted any information that these addressees could develop on Alpha-66.[865] Later on the same day, Harvey sent a follow-up to the same recipients, adding that the Alpha-66 operation was scheduled to take place on 10 September using two small boats. If this operation was successful, Harvey added, Julio Lobo would reportedly commit $250,000 for future Alpha-66 operations.[866]

Obviously, Veciana's intent to attack Cuban and Soviet shipping was well known to Lemnitzer and Lansdale. The question was—could Alpha-66 pull it off?

Operation "Poncew"—Alpha-66 Emerges from the Shadows

In early September 1962, Alpha-66 finally emerged from the shadows—months behind schedule—to begin sabotage operations against Cuba. Ponce was a small town just southwest of San Juan, Puerto Rico. It may have functioned as an Alpha-66 meeting place and might well have been the site where the first raid against Cuba was planned. Details of the raid were widely reported in the media—including the **New York Times**.[867] At 2:50 a.m. on 10 September, a forty-foot gray Alpha-66 launch slipped into the harbor of a small key across from Caibarien, a major Cuban port 210 miles southeast of Havana. The attacking vessel fired more than sixty rounds into the British freighter—the *Newlane*—and a Cuban ship. No casualties were reported. The *Newlane* was loading 31,000 sacks of sugar; the Cuban vessel was a dock boat used to store molasses.

---

865   9/6/62, CIA TFW priority alert, Subject: Alpha-66; RIF 104-10181-10202.
866   Ibid.
867   9/12/62, **New York Times**, AP, "Castro's Foes Raid Ships at Sugar Port."

VECIANA, THE SECRET YEARS—1961-1962

It was probably no coincidence that, at the time of its first raid, Alpha-66 established contact with both the CIA and the U.S. Army through *new* informants. During the first week of September, Veciana designated a U.S. citizen in New York, Robert A. Pratchett, to handle any CIA "coordination" with a designated Alpha-66 member. Superficially, Veciana was still interested in securing CIA "supplies and cash" to get his Alpha-66 harassment projects underway. On 7 September 1962, just days before the first Alpha-66 raid against Cuba, Pratchett began passing information from Alpha-66 to the CIA via Jay Reeves at the Agency's New York Contacts Office.[868] Pratchett indicated that Alpha-66 currently needed $30,000 to match what they had to fully operate.

Whether through Pratchett and Reeves or an FBI source,[869] CIA TFW Chief Harvey quickly learned about the details of Alpha-66's first planned raid against Cuba. On 8 September, Harvey sent another Alpha-66 follow-up alert to the intelligence community.[870] He reported that an Alpha-66 boat sailing under an American flag and equipped with two fifty caliber machine guns had departed from Miami on 7 September to strike Cuba on the night of 8 or 9 September. Veciana was also reportedly looking for a rocket launcher to use on this mission. On 10 September, a new JMWAVE source, **AMSKIN-1**, reported that if there was a delay, the operation would be rescheduled for 11 September.[871]

Reading the incoming intelligence reports on Alpha-66, President Kennedy *immediately became concerned* about what Veciana and his Alpha-66 group were up to. That much was made clear from a 7 September priority cable from CIA TFW Chief Harvey to the CIA stations in Panama City, Panama and San Juan, Puerto Rico.[872] Harvey revealed that President Kennedy was "*concerned*" about the Alpha-66 "case," and instructed the Panama and Puerto Rican stations to "*report all information on Alpha-66 plans and activities.*" At the station's discretion, Harvey suggested that San Juan and Panama City *should contact their local U.S. Army representatives to monitor Alpha-66 plans.* Clearly, Harvey suspected that Veciana was working with the Army. The two CIA stations were asked to add or confirm the information provided by HQS.

Meanwhile, now that Alpha-66 was operational, Veciana sent an *unambiguous signal to the U.S. Army* indicating that he wanted Alpha-66 to work for the U.S. military instead of the CIA. Veciana made this precipitous decision at the time of the first Alpha-66 raid (mentioned above) against Cuba in September 1962—*two months before* Veciana's Interagency Source Register (ISR) transfer to the Army in mid-November 1962. The

---

868 9/7/62, CIA Memo from Chief, New York Office to Chief, Contact Division; RIF 104-10069-10094.
869 One possible candidate for this FBI source in San Juan was Veciana's closest friend, Felix Zabala.
870 9/8/62, CIA, TFW RE Possible Imminent Alpha-66 Strike at Havana; RIF 104-10181-10199.
871 9/10/62, WAVE 8410; RIF 104-10217-10047 (NB: 2017 release).
872 9/7/62, DIR 34963 to PACY and SJAN; RIF 104-10181-10200. Harvey said that a 28 August U.S. Army report from San Juan indicated Alpha-66 was planning an air attack against Cuba sometime during the following week using a Beachhead-18 aircraft from Panama City. However, the cable predicted that the attack "may be imminent."

ISR was a mechanism designed to prevent operational control of a single source by more than one agency at a time.

Veciana designated a U.S. citizen in Miami, Jordan James Pfuntner—who *had already been carded through the ISR as an Army source*—as the Alpha-66 contact with the Army. Pfuntner established contact with an Army Assistant Chief of Staff for Intelligence (ACSI) unit in Puerto Rico—the U.S. Army Operational Survey Detachment (USAOSD)—in early September 1962. During a September meeting in Miami with USAOSD personnel, Pfuntner revealed the following Alpha-66 plans and *enticements for Army support*[873]:

1. Alpha-66 intended to conduct raids against Cuba.
2. Alpha-66 *refused to work with the CIA, but desired to work with the U.S. military.*
3. Alpha-66 *wanted Army support* in the "action phase," i.e., funds, equipment, arms, etc. In return, Alpha-66 would provide *intelligence information, would furnish captured equipment, and could land agents in Cuba.* The group required $100,000 to complete the balance of its program, consisting of four more raids on Cuba.
4. Pfuntner refused to identify any member of the group, or to reveal their plans or modus operandi. [Emphasis added]

To assess Pfuntner's claims, USAOSD asked him to furnish items of Soviet ordnance material and intelligence information on Cuba.

The indelible record of this watershed meeting was written by U.S. Army Colonel Jeff W. Boucher, Chief of the Army's ACSI Collection Division, in a memorandum for General Lansdale. Boucher's memorandum was not declassified until 7 October 1997—nearly two decades *after* Veciana's congressional depositions and interviews with Gaeton Fonzi. Veciana said *nothing* about his memorable proposal to congressional committees, Fonzi, or in his 2017 autobiography, **Trained to Kill**.

At this moment in the impending Missile Crisis, U.S intelligence entered what became known to historians as the "Photo Gap."[874] There was no overhead photography of Cuba available at that time. At this time, on 4 October, the CIA belatedly—but *befittingly*—cancelled Veciana's Provisional Operational Approval (POA) for use as an MRP sabotage asset, for failure to indicate "any further interest" in using Veciana.[875] During the photo gap, CIA memos and cables on Veciana came to a standstill. When

---

873 10/17/62, ACSI-CO 6.201, Col. Boucher to BGen. Lansdale; 198-10004-10015.
874 On 10 September 1962, worried that one of the Cuban or Soviet SAMs in Cuba might shoot down a CIA U-2 and cause an international incident, Secretary of State Dean Rusk and National Security Advisor McGeorge Bundy heavily restricted U-2 flights over Cuban airspace. The result was called the "Photo Gap." Max Holland, "The 'Photo Gap' That Delayed Discovery of Missiles." *Studies in Intelligence*, Vol. 49, No. 4.
875 10/4/62, Instruction Sheet RE C-96796 (Veciana); RIF 104-10181-10278. CI/OA formally notified TFW, ATTN: Calvin Hicks, of the final cancellation on 5 November 1962; RIF 104-10181-10412.

they resumed, it was clear that Veciana was working *exclusively* for the U.S. Army, *not* the CIA. However, it took several weeks longer—until mid-November—for the CIA to agree to an Army request to transfer formal Interagency Source Register (ISR) control of Veciana to the Army.[876] At that time, Veciana was assigned the Army security designation SD-10721.[877]

The Pentagon and the Alpha-66 Raid at *La Isabella*

Meanwhile, on 8 October 1962, Alpha-66 conducted a raid against a Soviet ship at *La Isabella*, in Puerto Plata, Puerto Rico. One of the oldest European settlements in the Americas, *La Isabella* is a westward-facing inlet on the north side of Puerto Rico, which lies along the eastern approaches to Cuba. Veciana publicly reported the raid on the Soviet ship as a success but, in fact, it was a failure.[878] The mine to be used against the Soviet ship was lost when the three frogmen—all from the Second National Front of Escambray (SNFE)—were drawn into the ship and "sucked up" against its side by the strong undercurrents.[879] As a result, the raiding party attacked a beachside camp instead, wounding five Cubans and Soviets. This raid would have important consequences for the Pentagon's use of Alpha-66.

The apocalyptic thirteen-day Cuban Missile Crisis (16-28 October) began with the discovery of Soviet missile bases in Cuba one week after the Alpha-66 raid. It was in this terrifying setting that the Army-Veciana union—a marriage already two months in the making—was consummated. As the climax of the Missile Crisis erupted on 17 October, ACSI Collection Division Chief Colonel Boucher sent a memorandum (described above) to General Lansdale revealing the details of an Army relationship with Veciana that had already been developing for *two months*.[880]

Ostensibly, the subject of Boucher's memorandum was "Cuban Operations," but it reported (as described above) *a request by Veciana* to "work with the U.S. military" *instead* of the CIA. That detail undoubtedly aroused Lansdale's interest. When Veciana told Gaeton Fonzi about his association with the Army (discussed below) in 1992, he only mentioned having been contacted by a man named Patrick Harris in Puerto Rico. As we will see below, *that contact* occurred during a lunch at the Puerto Rican restaurant "Under-the-Trees" *on 1 November 1962*. But Boucher's memo to Lansdale revealed that

---
[876] 11/16/62, ISR Trace Request, confirming ISR transfer of Veciana from CIA to Army on 15 November 1962; RIF 104-10181-10195.
[877] Later, on 30 January 1963, Veciana was assigned the Army ACSI crypt DUP 748.
[878] 10/20, 62, Atlantic Command, U.S. Army Caribbean, Message to ACSI, USAOSD, Subject: Alpha-66; RIF 194-10003-10392; see also Blunt DOD Documents on Veciana, p. 1.
[879] 4/19/66 MAJ John F. McGowan MFR Re Veciana; Blunt DOD Documents on Veciana.
[880] 10/17/62, ACSI-CO 6.201, Col. Boucher to BGen. Lansdale; 198-10004-10015.

INTO THE STORM

Veciana had been in touch—through Jordan Pfuntner—with an Army intelligence unit in Miami (USAOSD) *since 7 September 1962.*

The day before Boucher's memo landed on Lansdale's desk, National Security Advisor McGeorge Bundy showed President Kennedy the U-2 photographs of the Soviet missile sites in Cuba. The Missile Crisis became public when President Kennedy announced the discovery of Soviet missile bases in Cuba during a televised address on 22 October. That same day, Veciana was interviewed by Army Lieutenant Colonel Grover C. King in Puerto Rico.[881] According to King's memo afterward, Veciana *belittled* the Alpha-66 "working agreement" with the CIA and complained that "CIA persons are very nice but constantly asking for information without giving assistance."

Veciana disparaged the Agency's provision of "some form" of food rations. Upset by this paltry assistance, Veciana boasted that before the *La Isabella* raid an Alpha-66 member stole $600 worth of explosives from the CIA to use in the raid. In response to the Agency's attempts to determine Alpha-66's exact plans, Veciana admitted that the "*information given to the CIA had been false.*" During the next two weeks, Army and Navy intelligence officers became interested in *Veciana's offer* to provide access to the frogmen used in the raid for debriefing. The frogmen had potentially important information on *Soviet underwater demolition team (UDT) countermeasures.* Veciana had also offered to provide Soviet equipment from the *La Isabella* raid to the Army.

Boucher told Lansdale that the Office of Naval Intelligence (ONI) wanted to debrief the frogmen and that arrangements were being made to do so in Puerto Rico. Boucher said that Alpha-66 had "excellent potential" to provide military intelligence on Cuba and Soviet ordnance material. Boucher passed the following recommendations to Lansdale that had been *approved by ACSI*:

1. Debrief the Alpha-66 frogmen by USAOSD and ONI representatives.
2. USAOSD explore possibility of purchasing Soviet equipment from Alpha-66.
3. Briefing of General Lansdale on the Alpha-66 proposal to provide intelligence information and material in return for support, pointing out that financing, if any, is the responsibility of the CIA.

The reason for continued CIA financial responsibility was possibly because—from the Army perspective—Veciana had still not been transferred by that time to Army control under the ISR protocol.

The Boucher memo is noteworthy for two reasons. First, Veciana was earnestly working Alpha-66 into a relationship with the Army. Years later, he would first give Gaeton Fonzi, and then the researchers at the 2014 AARC conference in Maryland,

---

881 10/22/62, Veciana interviewed by U.S. Army LTCOL Grover C. King; RIF 194-10003-10394.

VECIANA, THE SECRET YEARS—1961-1962

the distinct impression that it was the Army that had approached him first, not the reverse. I will return to this point below.

The significance of the Boucher memorandum is also underscored by who it was written to—Brigadier General Lansdale. He was head of the Office of Special Operations, a DOD component serving directly under Secretary McNamara, along with the Joint Chiefs of Staff (JCS). Lansdale was also the operations chief of the Kennedy program Operation Mongoose—and, in that capacity, tethered to Attorney General Robert Kennedy. And so, for the officers working in Army intelligence, Lansdale was referred to as "higher levels."[882]

To repeat, the enthusiastic 17 October ACSI-approved measures passed to Lansdale concerning support for Alpha-66 (mentioned above) coincided with the start of the thirteen-day Cuban Missile Crisis. As a result, JFK *immediately* convened a meeting of nine key National Security Council (NSC) members and five other key officials in a group he named the Executive Committee of the NSC (EXCOMM). The impact of these historic events on *any* Lansdale-ACSI interaction with Veciana was evident by Lansdale's marginalia on the bottom of Boucher's memo on Alpha-66. Lansdale wrote, "overtaken by events [the missile bases] per Gilpatric [Deputy Secretary of Defense] said M [McNamara]."

The propinquity of the momentous Missile Crisis to the military's interest in Veciana's promises—at the "highest levels" in the Pentagon—is striking. But just as arresting is the fact that the ACSI proposals for using Veciana were only *superficially* overtaken by events. As we will see in Chapter Fourteen, by this point, Lansdale had already sided with General Lemnitzer in his confrontation with President Kennedy over going to war in Cuba. Using his characteristic skill of subterranean maneuvering, Lansdale acted to keep Veciana's plans to attack Soviet shipping in play. Lansdale worked to screen from view his own oversight of Alpha-66 and to *exclude any CIA control* of the group. As the world waited to see what the United States would do about the Soviet missile bases in Cuba, the Joint Chiefs put intense pressure on the president to bomb the bases. Plans were again readied for a U.S. military invasion of Cuba.

---

882   11/1/62, Colonel Boucher, ACSI Collection Division, "Draft of Contact with Veciana"; ... "so they [Hubbard and King] held discussions with 'higher levels, i.e., General Lansdale.'" DOD Files on Veciana, p. 8 [Blunt, DOD Veciana Files]. Many years ago, British researcher Malcolm Blunt came across 9 pages (page 4 was missing) of important "Department of Defense (DOD) Files"—also referred to as DOD Notes"—on "Antonio Veciana Blanch, #AA90 4916." Blunt shared them with me. At the time, this material was located in NARA's "Reference Copy, JFK Collection, HSCA (RG 233)." So far, my attempts to locate these documents again have been unsuccessful. Researchers can find these documents at my website, jfkjmn.com.

INTO THE STORM

President Kennedy and Antonio Veciana

Recall that well before the photography of Soviet missiles in Cuba were shown to the president, he was already concerned about the activities of Veciana and his Alpha-66 group.

The ebb and flow of White House decision-making during the crucial onset of the thirteen-day Cuban Missile Crisis impacted the Army-Veciana relationship in different ways. Initially, the deteriorating Cuban situation had stimulated Robert Kennedy to temporarily advocate for a full court press of sabotage operations that even included small groups like Alpha-66. At a 4 October 1962 Special Group Augmented (SGA) meeting, RFK reported that the president was "concerned about progress on the Mongoose program and feels that more priority should be given to trying to mount sabotage operations."[883] RFK urged the SGA to unleash "massive" Mongoose activity. And so, on 14 October the SGA decided to "considerably" expand sabotage operations and ordered that "*all efforts should be made to develop new and imaginative approaches with the possibility of getting rid of the Castro regime.*"[884] Such a program was exactly in line with Veciana's stated anti-Castro objectives.

However, the 17 October ACSI memo to Lansdale recommending Army support for Alpha-66 (mentioned above) had run abruptly aground due to the 16-17 October photo reconnaissance revelations about the Soviet missile sites in Cuba. As Lansdale's marginalia on that memo indicated, Secretary of Defense McNamara had thrown ice water on that SGA recommendation in light of the unnerving new photography. For the next eleven days, Kennedy and Khrushchev inched their way toward a possible solution to the impending nuclear crisis. By 26 October, that solution stipulated that the USSR would withdraw its missiles from Cuba in exchange for a *public assurance* that the U.S. would not invade Cuba *and a private promise* that the U.S. would withdraw its Jupiter missiles from Turkey at some point in the future. A 26 October Mongoose memo by Lansdale revealed that plans to sink Cuban-owned shipping in "Cuban or Bloc ports, or on high seas" was in a "pending" status.[885]

On 27 October, RFK offered the above terms to the Soviets. On 28 October, Khrushchev agreed to those terms. On 29 October, it appeared that, for the first time in the crisis, a nuclear conflict might be averted. Then, on 30 October, in a hastily convened meeting of the EXCOMM, President Kennedy ordered a complete stop to all sabotage activities. The president promulgated four directives at the EXCOMM meeting—*the*

---

883   SSCIA Interim Report, p. 147.
884   Ibid.
885   10/26/62, CIA memo, DCI McCone to DDCI Carter, Subject: Operation Mongoose, "Main Points to Consider"; RIF 202-10001-10199.

first three of which pertained to the activities of Alpha-66.[886] First, JFK called on the CIA to do *everything possible* to ensure refugee or émigré provocative actions against Cuba were not undertaken over the next several days. Both the Miami station and the Mongoose Task Force were ordered to exercise *every precaution* to ensure that no unauthorized actions were taken—without discussion or disclosure to the refugee groups. [Underline in original]

Kennedy's second and third directives pertained specifically to Alpha-66. In fact, his second directive singled out Alpha-66 and was adamant about stopping its operations:

CIA should attempt to stop Alpha-66 actions during the next several days. The president was informed by the DCI that we have no contact with or control over Alpha-66. *The DCI was instructed to attempt through every resource available to influence Alpha-66 to stand down operations* during the next several days. [Emphasis added]

The fact that the president so cavalierly brushed aside the CIA's protest—that they had no control over Veciana—is noteworthy. Kennedy's forceful demeanor made it clear that he expected the Agency to *get* control of Alpha-66 quickly. Whether or not the president's unyielding directive was realistic, his message was not lost on those attending the meeting nor those who heard about the order afterward—like Lansdale.

Kennedy's third directive ordered the suspension of *all prior approvals* for sabotage, infiltrations, guerrilla activities, and caching of arms. The fourth directive sharply proscribed any contacts with the press.

After the meeting, DCI McCone, National Security Advisor Bundy and Attorney General Kennedy discussed the previously approved plans for sabotaging Cuban ships and shipping operations in general (discussed above in Lansdale's 26 October memo). All agreed that these operations should be suspended for the next several days. There was still concern that although a solution seemed to be at hand, it would take several more days to be certain whether it would hold.

Harvey Takes a Bullet for Insubordination from Robert Kennedy

Lansdale was immediately informed about the president's decision to halt all Mongoose operations. On 30 October 1962, DCI McCone asked Lansdale to call him on the secure "gray telephone" that morning right after the EXCOMM meeting. In a memorandum for record that same day, Lansdale described the fallout from the orders President Kennedy had given at that meeting.[887]

---

886 10/30/62, McCone Memorandum to General Marshall S. Carter; RIF 104-10306-10020.
887 10/30/62, Lansdale MFR, Subject: Mongoose; RIF 145-10001-10273 (2017 release).

INTO THE STORM

On the telephone, McCone informed Lansdale that the president had decided to "hold back Operation Mongoose" during the negotiations with Khrushchev over the missile bases in Cuba and *had specifically mentioned Alpha-66 sabotage operations* against Cuban shipping:

> Also, during the negotiations re Soviet missile bases in Cuba, there were to be no Mongoose sabotage or similar militant operations. McCone said he had informed [DDCI] General Carter of this, but was letting me know, as chief of operations, to let the operations team know; *he mentioned that Alpha-66 and the [previously] approved sabotage of Cuban shipping were to be held, specifically.*[888] [Emphasis added]

Lansdale told McCone he had just received his [McCone's] memo to Attorney General Bobby Kennedy and Defense Secretary McNamara reporting that the CIA was still waiting for Lansdale's approval to send twenty CIA intelligence collection teams into Cuba by submarine. Lansdale also told McCone he had been ordered two days earlier (28 October) by McGeorge Bundy to hold up these submarine infiltrations. Lansdale said that he assumed McCone had received Bundy's subsequent order to "hold everything."

But the planned submarine insertion of Harvey's CIA intelligence collection teams was still hanging fire. Lansdale told McCone he had also received a phone call from Harvey:

> Harvey had called me Sunday night, asking my permission to discuss *CIA assets* with CINCLANT [Commander in Chief Atlantic Command] and JUWTF [Joint Unconventional Warfare Task Force] for contingency *planning*; I had given Harvey permission to assist in this *planning*, if he felt that the U.S. military needed more *planning* help from CIA.[889] [Emphasis added]

Lansdale's memo was *not sent to anyone*. He was carefully creating a memorandum for record that made a crucial distinction: he had only approved *planning* for the CINCLANT insertion of Harvey's "CIA assets"—*not* the go-ahead to insert them.

Lansdale's memo did not mention any further discussion with Harvey about the insertions because no such discussions had taken place. Lansdale mentioned only that he had spoken with Harvey's deputy, Bruce Cheever, who assured him that he had received orders from DDCI General Carter "that all militant actions under CIA were being held at a stop." In his memo, Lansdale said that he gave "similar orders" to the Defense Department and the Joint Chiefs.[890] But he did *not* mention giving those orders personally to Harvey.

---

888 Ibid.
889 Ibid.
890 Ibid.

And so, the stage was set for a showdown between Harvey and Robert Kennedy. The president had declared *all operations* by the CIA's action arm for Operation Mongoose—Task Force W—*be called to an immediate halt*. The National Security Archive study of the Cuban Missile Crisis described the following insubordination by William Harvey:

> However, during the crisis, Director of Task Force W William Harvey ordered teams of covert operators into Cuba *on his own authority* to support any *conventional U.S. military operation* that might occur.[891] [Emphasis added]

Harvey knew that conventional U.S. military operations in Cuba was what most of the Joint Chiefs wanted to happen.

One of the covert operators affected by Harvey's order was worried about Harvey's decision and sent a warning message about the order to Robert Kennedy. Angered by this news, the Attorney General openly chastised Harvey and instructed DCI McCone to terminate the agent infiltrations. In an affront to Harvey, RFK then ordered that Lansdale—Harvey's enemy—be sent to Miami to *dismantle Harvey's Mongoose operations there*.[892] This was the beginning of the end for William Harvey's relationship with the Kennedys.

Lansdale Dodges a Bullet for *His* Insubordination

The events that took place concerning Alpha-66 during the subsequent days were recorded in an Army memorandum from ACSI's Collection Division[893] and messages between the ACSI USAOSD office in the Pentagon and its field element in Puerto Rico.[894] These communications between Washington and San Juan took place during the tenuous hours during which the implementation of the Kennedy-Khrushchev solution was being closely monitored.

I will return to the records of those frenzied events after a closer examination of what Lansdale was actually up to with Alpha-66. His subterranean activities at this time were also mentioned in Colonel Boucher's 1 November memorandum. There is irony in Robert Kennedy's decision to punish Harvey by removing him from any role in the final dismantling of Mongoose and rewarding Lansdale by sending him to Harvey's fiefdom in Miami to do the honors. Neither Bobby Kennedy nor DCI McCone knew

---

891 Lawrence Chang and Peter Kornbluh, *The Cuban Missile Crisis, 1962* (New York: The New Press, 1992), p. 383.
892 Ibid.
893 11/1/62, Colonel Boucher Draft of Contact with Veciana; Blunt DOD Documents on Veciana.
894 10/22/62 and 11/1/62, Army messages from Puerto Rico to the Commanding Officer, U.S. Army Operational Survey Detachment (USAOSD); see RIF 194-10003-10394 and 194-10003-10393.

INTO THE STORM

about Lansdale's involvement in the Pentagon's continuing cooperation with Alpha-66 *after* the president's order that the group's activities be grounded.

Despite Kennedy's 30 October order, Lansdale's activities with respect to Veciana and Alpha-66 *continued*—during the long days of 1 and 2 November 1962—as the fate of the still vulnerable Kennedy-Khrushchev attempt to pull back from the brink of war hung in the balance. On 1 November 1962, an expanded Pentagon meeting of ACSI and DOD officers took place in the Pentagon to consider *what to do about Alpha-66 operations.* In that meeting, Lansdale once again lived up to his reputation as a "lone wolf and operator." I spent an entire chapter on Lansdale's proclivity toward this kind of behavior in my book, ***JFK and Vietnam*** (see Second Edition, 2017, Chapter Two).

The Army officers at ACSI—and their subordinate Operational Survey Detachment (OSD) in San Juan—were not oblivious to the extreme sensitivity of their association with Alpha-66 operations during the critical moment of Soviet compliance with the agreement to dismantle their missile bases in Cuba. Colonel Boucher realized that mounting the operation being discussed in San Juan on 1 November had significant implications for presidential policy. That operation involved Army and Navy personnel going outside of U.S. territory to visit an Alpha-66 training site and meet with frogmen involved in the attack on the Soviet Ship at *La Isabella*. According to Boucher's 1 November memorandum, the operation was "stymied by the lack of clear policy" on actions against Cuba and the Soviet Union.

The expanded Pentagon meeting included several ACSI and Department of Defense *generals and colonels.* Boucher wrote that the Alpha-66 "matter had been brought to higher levels; i.e. General Lansdale." The question quickly arose about whether the Pentagon's support of Alpha-66 operations should be shared with the CIA. Boucher's memo bluntly stated, "This suggestion was turned down by Lansdale, *who felt that CIA, when informed, then took over operations. Also, (CIA was) in no better position to determine national policy.*" Evidently, Lansdale thought that he was in a *better position.* The memo does show that *Lansdale and Veciana were on the same page with respect to keeping the CIA in the dark* about the Pentagon's plans for the use of Alpha-66 and their exploitation of the group's operations.

Strangely, Boucher's draft memo gives no indication that Lansdale passed along the president's order to suspend Alpha-66 operations. Lansdale's 30 October memo (discussed above)—only two days earlier—makes it crystal clear that he understood the president's orders to stop Alpha-66 activities. On the telephone that same day, McCone had told Lansdale that the president *had specifically ordered Alpha-66 sabotage operations against Cuba be stopped*! I find it difficult to imagine that Colonel Boucher's memo about the 1 November meeting with the generals would not have included the presidential order if Lansdale had—*as he was required to do as the Mongoose operations chief*—relayed the order to the officers present.

VECIANA, THE SECRET YEARS—1961-1962

Boucher's silence on the matter is disturbing. It suggests that Lansdale and others in the Pentagon had a different agenda than the White House and DCI McCone. President Kennedy's firing of General Lemnitzer on 1 October (mentioned in Chapter Fourteen) undoubtedly left a dark cloud hanging over the Pentagon.

Veciana's Big Army Secret

I now return to the unforgettable moment-by-moment action on the Alpha-66 problem that took place on 1 and 2 November 1962. It was still in the early hours of the dismantling of the Soviet missile bases. The Pentagon-Alpha-66 activity that took place during this fragile moment is reported for the first time in this volume. Except for contact with "Patrick Harris," this story is a secret part of Veciana's life that has all but disappeared. The action took place simultaneously along parallel lines. It unfolded in the Pentagon and among the U.S. Army's assets in Puerto Rico. It also unfolded in the hourly—and sometimes moment-by-moment—communications between the Pentagon and Puerto Rico.

What remains of the details of these activities today was captured in just two crucial memoranda. On 1 November in Puerto Rico, Army Lieutenant Colonel Grover C. King wrote a detailed memorandum recapping the messages between ACSI HQS and its Operational Survey Detachment (USAOSD) in the Pentagon, and its field AIS (possibly Army Intelligence Support) element in Puerto Rico.[895] On the same day in the Pentagon, Colonel Jeff W. Boucher, chief of ACSI's Collection Division, wrote a draft memo about the ACSI meeting with several colonels and generals in the Pentagon—including Brigadier General Lansdale—about how to handle the Alpha-66 problem.[896] For reasons that will soon become apparent, I will first take the reader—with minimal commentary by me—through the hectic, moment-by-moment action between the Pentagon and Puerto Rico.

The Army ACSI and other military components in the Pentagon were keen to obtain and exploit as much intelligence as possible from Veciana's raids against Cuban and Soviet shipping. Moreover, they wanted to do that as fast as possible. That had to happen *before* the final negotiations over the Cuban Missile Crisis could preclude the successful acquisition of that intelligence. That concern infused a high degree

---

[895] 10/22/62 and 11/1/62, Army messages from Puerto Rico to the Commanding Officer, U.S. Army Operational Survey Detachment (USAOSD); my examination of an accompanying Army memorandum from Puerto Rico suggests that Lieutenant Colonel Grover C. King was the author of this memo; see RIFs 194-10003-10393 and 194-10003-10394.

[896] 11/1/62, Colonel Boucher Draft of Contact with Veciana; Malcolm Blunt DOD Documents on Veciana.

INTO THE STORM

of urgency into communications between the Pentagon and Puerto Rico and into Army-Veciana activities on the ground in Puerto Rico.

Counterposed to the *frenzied* activities that took place on 1 and 2 November 1962, we have the *nonchalant* scenario that Veciana told Gaeton Fonzi about those activities, two decades later in the mid-1990s. Only by exposure to the sequence of events captured in the contemporary Army memoranda can observers today appreciate the depth of the difference between the events of 1962 and how Veciana described them in 1992.

The final sequence of events in *this episode* of Veciana's life began at approximately 5:17 p.m. EST on 31 October 1962. At that moment, Army ACSI USAOSD in the Pentagon sent the initial message to its unit in Puerto Rico. That USAOSD message was received in San Juan the next morning, 1 November, at 10:30 hours local. The San Juan Commander was Grover C. King. Using the alias "Roberts,"[897] he called a local Army asset, whose Army crypt was DUP 737, and made an appointment to meet at DUP 737's home at 6:30 p.m.

But events were moving very fast, and that plan was rendered obsolete when Roberts received another phone call from the Pentagon at 11:45 a.m. (local), "requesting immediate action" take place on the Alpha-66 plan. Roberts told the caller from the Pentagon that he would call back at 4:00 p.m. to "report on what had been determined." In the interim, Roberts called DUP 737 again and *moved up the time* of their meeting for lunch instead of dinner.

Roberts picked up DUP 737—an as-yet still unidentified Army asset in Puerto Rico—at his office. They departed for lunch in Captain Milford P. Hubbard's vehicle at 12:30 p.m. This was the *only man* that Veciana ever mentioned in connection with his association with the Army. In Army documents, Hubbard is often referred to by the pseudonym "Patrick Harris." The lunch took place at one of the Army's local San Juan haunts, "Under-the-Trees." Hubbard told DUP 737 that it was *extremely important to contact Alpha-66 about the frogmen* who took part in the *La Isabella* raid.

DUP 737 surprised Roberts and Hubbard with the news that Veciana had allegedly been replaced by Leonardo Caballos as head of Alpha-66. DUP 737 added that Alpha-66 had agreed to say that Veciana had resigned instead of being "thrown out."[898] As the ACSI officers at HQS in Washington monitored the initial incoming messages from Puerto Rico, they discovered that Veciana had been working with Eloy Gutierrez Menoyo's Second National Front Escambray (SNFE).[899] They immediately considered using Menoyo in conjunction with Veciana, as Menoyo had been picked up on the Army ISR in 1961.

---

[897] While I cannot be certain about this alias, it is the only identification that fits the detailed unfolding scenario that took place that week and subsequently.
[898] The rift, that had developed because of Veciana's decisions about what to spend money on, did not last long.
[899] This opens the possibility that DUP 737 might have been Menoyo's Army crypt.

VECIANA, THE SECRET YEARS—1961-1962

At 2:30 p.m. (still 1 November), DUP 737 called Roberts to say that Caballos was indisposed but that Veciana had called. DUP 737 told Veciana that "Pat Harris" wanted to talk to him, and Veciana—apparently still in control—provided his phone numbers. The following interaction between Veciana with U.S. Army officers Captain Milford Hubbard (Harris), Colonel Grover King (Roberts), and Ralph DeGagne took place.

At 2:35 p.m., Ralph DeGagne of the 471st INTC Detachment at Fort Brooke, Puerto Rico called Veciana and made an appointment to meet him, along with Harris and Roberts, ten minutes later at the Red Rooster—another favorite Army hangout in San Juan. Veciana joined the three Army officers at the restaurant at 3:15 p.m. After introductions and "small talk," Veciana gave Hubbard (Harris) and King (Roberts)—*just as promised by Pfuntner in September*—rifles and ammunition allegedly taken from the Russians at *La Isabella*. That unforgettable moment—of the payment of that promised tribute of captured Soviet equipment in front of three Army officers—vanished years later when it became inconvenient for the development of Veciana's CIA narrative.

Hubbard, King and Veciana then left the restaurant to talk privately on a side street. Veciana provided the names of two of the *La Isabella* frogmen: Julio Cruz and FNU Castillo, both members of the SNFE. Veciana said they were not on U.S. territory; rather, their base was one and a half days out of Miami by boat. The location of the base on a remote island in the Bahamas would pose a problem for a timely debrief of the frogmen. Harris made an appointment to meet Veciana at 7:30 p.m.

Meanwhile, at 5:40 p.m., Roberts had received a call from Colonel J. E. Boyt, the USAOSD Commander at the Pentagon. Boyt indicated that he had recommended a "go" to the "people upstairs" for the proposed plan to debrief the frogmen. Boyt told Roberts that no decision had been reached yet and that he would call back the next day. Boyt added that consideration was being given to some kind of "financial remuneration" for Alpha-66.

However, events were moving extremely quickly in the Pentagon. At 7:00 p.m. (still 1 November) that evening, Roberts received word that the "go" had been approved. A plan was devised: Roberts would accompany Veciana back to Miami where they would be met by "another man." They would board a boat and depart on a trip to see the frogmen on 6 November.

At 7:30 p.m., Harris met Veciana at the Red Rooster as scheduled. Rather than dining there, they went outside and talked for 30 minutes as they walked on side streets. Veciana asked if the Army wanted to see the frogmen to recruit them for their own use. Harris said no, they only wanted to talk to them. The two men then had dinner at Under-the-Trees. Veciana reportedly "warmed up" to Harris. Crucially, Veciana said *he wanted Harris to see* the training of the Cuban exiles that was taking place "on the island where they were going." I will shortly return to that important remark—about *who wanted whom* to see the exile training camp.

INTO THE STORM

At this point, we need to compare the Army's *contemporary* narrative of events to Veciana's *later* description of them to Gaeton Fonzi. The reason for this is clear: Veciana's later portrayal of his relationship with the Army bears little resemblance to the above story captured in the Army documents.

As discussed above, for the past forty-plus years Veciana has consistently underplayed his relationship with the Army. He did not mention it at all during his HSCA deposition—although I must concede that the committee never asked him about it. In **The Last Investigation**, Gaeton Fonzi described what Veciana told him about the Army:

> From a series of long conversations with Harris, Veciana concluded that Harris was Army Intelligence—especially after he told Veciana that he might be able to provide some support for his anti-Castro activities. But Harris first wanted to make an inspection trip to Alpha-66's operational base in the Bahamas. Veciana eventually came to trust Harris and gave him and a couple of his associates a tour of the base, but Harris never did come through with any aid.[900]

To recapitulate: 1) Veciana claims he was *first approached by the Army*, not the other way around; 2) Specifically, Veciana maintains that *Patrick Harris was the person who approached him*; 3) Veciana claims that Harris offered him a deal: Harris might provide support for Veciana's anti-Castro activities in exchange for being allowed to inspect the Alpha-66 Bahamas base; 4) Veciana claims that he upheld his end of the deal, while Harris did not.

Veciana's account to Fonzi masks the truth about Veciana's campaign of enticements—begun in the first week of September—to secure a relationship working for the Army instead of the CIA. The Army did *not* approach Veciana first; rather, it was Veciana who approached the Army first. To repeat, *Veciana's first message to the Army*, delivered through Pfuntner, was that he wanted his Alpha-66 group "to work with the U.S. military" *instead* of the CIA.[901] A month later, after the Alpha-66 attempt to sink a Soviet ship at *La Isabella*, Veciana offered—through Pfuntner—to make Soviet military equipment and the frogmen used in the raid available to Army intelligence.

Twelve days later, on 20 October in San Juan, Veciana was interviewed by the Army about the raid. The Army interviewer was *not* Captain Hubbard (Harris); rather, it was Colonel King (Roberts). The Army officers in Puerto Rico felt that the Soviet rifles

---

900   Gaeton Fonzi, **The Last Investigation** (New York: Shyhorse, 2013 Edition) p. 136. Fonzi further elaborated: "From a discussion with an Army Intelligence asset I had been sent to interview in New Orleans, I also deduced that the CIA had told the Committee that Veciana and Alpha 66 were monitored not by the Agency but by Army Intelligence. I thought this was a misdirection. I pointed out that Veciana was aware of his contacts with Army Intelligence, that they covered only a limited period of his anti-Castro activities, and that they were separate and distinct from his relationship with Maurice Bishop. Nevertheless, after the CIA denied an interest in Veciana, the Committee staff pursued the Army Intelligence angle up until the end." See pp. 147-148.

901   10/17/62, ACSI-CO 6.201, Col. Boucher to BGen. Lansdale; 198-10004-10015.

VECIANA, THE SECRET YEARS—1961–1962

could have been obtained elsewhere and that there was "no conclusive evidence that the operation at *La Isabella* actually took place!"[902] Nevertheless, Veciana's enticing offer to work with the Army succeeded. ACSI decided to move forward to see if *Veciana could deliver the access to the frogmen that he had promised.*

Contrary to Veciana's 2014 story to the AARC (see below), Captain Hubbard (Harris) was not his first and only contact with the Army. Harris did not enter the story until 1 November 1962—*two months after Veciana's communications with the Army began through Pfuntner.* Therefore, Veciana did not need several conversations with "Harris" (as he had told Fonzi) in November to understand what he already knew—that he had been dealing with the *Army* since the first week in September.

At the 2014 AARC conference in Bethesda, Maryland, Malcolm Blunt asked Veciana about his relationship with the U.S. Army. Veciana downplayed that relationship. He suggested that it was no more than meeting with a man named "Harris" in the Caribbean. The bottom line: Veciana's account in 2014, like his earlier account to Gaeton Fonzi, downplayed his own—crucial—role in establishing his relationship with the Army. The idea of debriefing the frogmen was not something that Hubbard (Harris) came up with during the 1 November dinner at Under-the-Trees. That idea had been in train ever since Veciana first used it on 12 October as a lure (relayed through Pfuntner) to help ingratiate his way into the hands of the U.S. Army. And the thirteen-day Missile Crisis provided the perfect motivation for the Army to take the bait quickly.

I will now return to the remaining minute-by-minute communications between the Army ACSI—in the Pentagon—and their unit in Puerto Rico. The record of that anxious back-and-forth interplay is fascinating. There was not a moment to lose. The situation unfolding on 1 November 1962 raised the possibility of excluding *any* American naval expedition outside of U.S. territorial waters to make contact with anti-Castro exile sabotage operations. On 1 November—the key moment as the U.S. and UN monitored the Soviet dismantling of their missile bases in Cuba—Grover King and Patrick Harris learned this unsettling news from Veciana at 3:15 p.m.:

> The two frogmen *are not* on U.S. territory. They are one and a half days out of Miami by boat. Veciana agreed to take two men in to meet the frogmen but that the outsiders would have to be blindfolded. If we [the Army] could furnish a boat, *we could arrive there sooner because there would be a four-to-six-day delay if he [Veciana] has to arrange for the boat.*[903] [Emphasis added]

---

[902] 10/27/62, CGANTCOMC/USAR CARIB, Fort Brooke, PR to ACSI, DA, WASH DC; Malcolm Blunt DOD Documents on Veciana.
[903] Ibid.

INTO THE STORM

As discussed above, at 5:30 p.m., the USAOSD commander had recommended a "go" to the "people upstairs," anticipating an answer the following day. But he did not have to wait. *The authorization to proceed came just 90 minutes later* at 7:00 p.m. However, President Kennedy had not yet decided that the evidence of the dismantling of Soviet missiles was enough to declare that the crisis was over.

And so, the next day, 2 November, just as Veciana and Harris were about to board the boat and head to the training island in the Bahamas, this *urgent* message from ACSI HQS arrived in San Juan:

> 15:40 hrs: [HQS] called—NO GO!!!!
> SORRY!!!!
> COMMAND DECISION—Neither the Navy Commander, nor us [i.e., the Army], can go outside U.S. territorial waters for this type mission.
> MEND YOUR FENCES—SORRY!!!![904]

This is exactly what ACSI HQS had feared might happen and why there had been such a rush to debrief the frogmen before the president slammed the door shut.

This story has an interesting postscript. As things turned out, the situation changed the next day, on 3 November. President Kennedy told his subordinates that the evidence of the dismantling of Soviet missiles *was* sufficient. USAOSD called San Juan with the good news:

> 12:15 hrs: CO, USAOSD said "GO."
> Authorize pay boat expenses.
> Authorized to meet frogmen and Veciana in Miami.
> Authorized to go back to training area with Veciana. OSD is playing it tight. Will ask Navy Commander if he would want to meet in Miami.[905]

None of the actual high drama that took place in the Pentagon and Puerto Rico during the most intense moments of the Cuban Missile Crisis is reflected in *any* of Veciana's later recapitulations of his relationship with the Army.

According to the Army's records, showing Hubbard (Harris) the Alpha-66 exile training program on the island was Veciana's idea. *He was the one* who "warmed up" to Harris and said that *he wanted Harris to see* the training of Cuban exiles "on the island where they were going to" debrief the frogmen. How important is this distinction between the *contemporary ACSI account* of their involvement with Veciana and *Veciana's later account* to Fonzi? It is very important. The credibility of Veciana's account of his nearly nonexistent relationship with the Army is already hanging by a thread and the contemporary Army records undercut that account.

---

904   Ibid.
905   Ibid.

VECIANA, THE SECRET YEARS—1961-1962

In a nutshell, Veciana buried a dramatic high-level ACSI-DOD rush plan—taking place as the U.S. waited to see if Khrushchev would dismantle the missiles—to get crucial intelligence on UDT countermeasures out of the *La Isabella* frogmen. Instead, Veciana turned that dramatic event into a nonchalant query—unconnected to the global crisis taking place at that time—by a single low-level Army asset in San Juan, Puerto Rico.

How could Veciana not remember giving instructions to Jordan Pfuntner to approach the Army with a landmark entreaty to work for *them—instead of the CIA*—in return for promising to furnish the Army captured Soviet equipment and to land their agents in Cuba? How could Veciana not remember that his conversations with Hubbard (Harris) occurred at the *most critical moments of the Missile Crisis*? How could Veciana not remember the many times that the Army-Navy trip to debrief the frogmen was off and then on again? How could Veciana have forgotten *his meeting with three U.S. Army officers*—Captain Hubbard (Harris), Colonel King (Roberts), and Ralph DeGagne at the Red Rooster on 1 November—the meeting at which Veciana gave Hubbard and Roberts two rifles and ammunition allegedly taken from the Russians at *La Isabella*? And how credible are those forgotten Army memories compared to the hundreds of details Veciana recalls about his alleged work with the CIA?

The years of Veciana's relationship with the Army (1962-1965)—*the Alpha-66 years*—are the most secret period in his life. The reason for that is because Veciana has chosen to keep it that way. He largely avoids the events that took place during his work for the Pentagon. His HSCA deposition avoids them; he only discussed them lightly with Gaeton Fonzi; he downplayed them at the 2014 Bethesda, Maryland symposium; and he *never mentioned the Army at all* in his 2017 autobiography, **Trained to Kill**.

What was Veciana's likely motive in changing the story in this manner? At this point, I can only proffer a guess. By the time Veciana later recounted his story to Fonzi—during the years 1976-1980 and beyond—Veciana was disingenuously establishing his alleged long-term bona fides with an organization he had disliked and distrusted—the CIA. Veciana needed to bury the truth about what happened in Puerto Rico on 1 and 2 November 1962 in order to underpin his fictional long-term work for the CIA—in particular, his association with the Army during the years 1962-1965. That Army relationship was harmful to Veciana's claim that he was working for Dave Phillips before the meeting with Oswald in 1963 and all the way up to his imprisonment in 1974. We now know that the Alpha-66 years were *exclusively* Veciana's years with the Army. That fact destroys his 2 March 1976 claim to the Church Committee (the Schweiker subcommittee) that "*the man behind all of Alpha-66's strategy*" was his CIA case officer—"Maurice Bishop!"[906]

---

906   3/00/79, HSCA document: Anti-Castro Activities and Organizations and LHO in New Orleans; "Antonio Veciana Blanch," Fonzi interview for Schweiker subcommittee of the Church Committee, p. 99; RIF 180-10147-10240.

It is possible that Veciana concocted the story of his work for the CIA in 1963 in an Atlanta prison during the period January 1974 to February 1976. He was serving time due to a—possibly trumped up—conviction for cocaine smuggling. My suspicion—at this point—is that Veciana's twenty-six months in prison might be the key to the entire story of his association with Phillips from 1959 to 1973. Decisions made during his incarceration might explain everything. And, then again, they might not. I have not yet come to any firm conclusion and am in no hurry to do so.

But, at this point, it is only fair to the reader that I report what I discovered in the 14 November 2017 release of JFK documents about Veciana's big Zabala secret—*a true story that he has never shared publicly.*

Veciana's Big Zabala Secret

Let me end this chapter with an escapade that Veciana pulled off after he was released from prison in February 1976. It was an exploit rife with implications for Veciana's claim that he met Oswald with Phillips in Dallas in the fall of 1963. Many years ago, Veciana's big Zabala secret was buried in an FBI report behind the blackened lines of a redactor. Those redactions were not removed until the JFK documents release on 14 November 2017. That secret story is reported—along with its possible implications for Veciana's claim to have been working for his CIA case officer during that Dallas meeting—in this volume for the first time.[907]

Felix Zabala Mas was Veciana's closest friend. Other than his wife and children, there was no one closer to Veciana than Zabala. Veciana was the godfather of Zabala's son. Like Veciana, Zabala had been a banker in Havana and a member of the anti-Castro resistance. He fled to the U.S. and settled in San Juan, Puerto Rico where he became a boxing promoter and a charter member of Veciana's Alpha-66. Zabala was an FBI informant. He told the Bureau that Veciana was "like his own brother," and that they were business partners.[908] When Veciana stayed in Puerto Rico, he lived in Zabala's home.[909]

Zabala was loyal to Veciana through thick and thin. He participated in Veciana's alleged abortive attempt to assassinate Castro in Chile in November 1971. That alleged assassination attempt in Chile took place during Veciana's work for the U.S. Agency for International Development in neighboring La Paz, Bolivia, from 1968 to 30 June

---

[907] 4/9/77, FBI San Juan to Director FBI, RIF 124-90152-10013. See the 11/14/2017 release of this document and compare it to the former, heavily redacted, version.
[908] 4/8/77, FBI, San Juan, Antonio Veciana, Interview with Zabala; RIF 124-10325-10301, p. 43.
[909] 12/31/64, FBI San Juan Teletype to DIR, SUBJ: SNFE, Alpha-66; 124-10280-10046. In this case, Veciana, on a fund-raising trip, was staying at Zabala's home since 10/23/64.

VECIANA, THE SECRET YEARS—1961-1962

1972.[910] On 14 January 1974, Veciana was convicted on three counts related to cocaine trafficking. He was released on probation twenty-six months later in February 1976. Within days after Veciana returned to his home in Florida, Gaeton Fonzi—a staff investigator working for Senator Schweiker of the Church Committee[911] —began making phone calls to Veciana's house.[912]

Fonzi formally interviewed Veciana for the Schweiker subcommittee on 2 March 1976. According to the record of the interview, "Veciana revealed that at one meeting with Bishop in Dallas in late August or September 1963, he saw with him a young man he later recognized as Lee Harvey Oswald." Veciana added that he "had not previously disclosed that information to anyone."[913]

Six months later, in September 1976, Veciana approached Zabala and asked him to participate in an extraordinary plan. According to author Shane O'Sullivan, the purpose of Veciana's plan was to sabotage President Jimmy Carter's "attempts to soften relations with Cuba."[914] However, FBI reporting from San Juan, Puerto Rico, suggests that Veciana's plan was intended to publicly establish credibility for the shiny story he told Fonzi in March 1976 about the alleged meeting with Oswald in Dallas in 1963:

> Veciana approached subject [Zabala] in September of 1976, stating that he *had been* called to testify before a United States congressional committee investigating the assassination of President Kennedy during 1976, and *for an unexplained reason, needed to publicly establish himself as a former CIA operative. Veciana confided that he, [and] a CIA contact with a code name of "Bishop," and Lee Harvey Oswald had a meeting approximately one month prior to the assassination of Kennedy in 1963.* Veciana did not furnish any other information.[915] [Emphasis added]

In Zabala's memory of that approach, the proximity of Veciana's confidential sharing of his alleged 1963 Bishop-Oswald meeting in Dallas to Veciana's need to *publicly establish himself as a former CIA operative* speaks volumes today. It may be a crucial beacon shining light on that singular moment that has captivated researchers of the Kennedy assassination ever since Fonzi reported his 1976 interview with Veciana.

---

910 7/26/73, DEA immediate for John T. Cusack, DEA International Operations Division; RIF 104-10181-10185. NB: There is a mistake on the RIF sheet: the 7/26/63 date is a garble for 7/26/73.

911 3/00/79, HSCA document: Anti-Castro Activities and Organizations and LHO in New Orleans; "Antonio Veciana Blanch," Fonzi interview for Schweiker subcommittee of the Church Committee, p. 99; RIF 180-10147-10240.

912 Veciana, *Trained to Kill*, p. 187.

913 3/00/79, HSCA document: Anti-Castro Activities and Organizations and LHO in New Orleans; "Antonio Veciana Blanch," Fonzi interview for Schweiker subcommittee of the Church Committee, p. 99; RIF 180-10147-10240.

914 Shane O'Sulllivan, *Dirty Tricks—Nixon, Watergate, and the CIA* (New York: Hot Books, Skyhorse Publishing, 2018), p. 360. Washingtonpost.com printed O'Sullivan's story about this on 3 December 2018— "The Cuban spy and Watergate burglar who won a presidential pardon."

915 4/9/77, FBI, San Juan to FBI Director, Felix Zabala Mas—IS-Cuba; RIF 124-90152-10013.

INTO THE STORM

But there is more to the story. Upon confiding the Bishop-Oswald story to Zabala, Veciana then asked Zabala for a very unusual favor. He asked Zabala to use his sister—who was married to Cuban Interior Minister Ramiro Valdez—to place into Castro's hands a letter describing Veciana's involvement in the 1971 plot to assassinate Castro in Chile.

The plan was for Zabala to tell his sister he had recently had "a falling out with Veciana over business matters and was taking this action as revenge." Veciana's real objective was to provoke the hot-headed despot to scream about it on the radio so that everyone in Miami would hear all about it, and thereby, get Fidel Castro *himself* to establish Veciana "as a former CIA agent!"[916]

In *all* of his interviews with Gaeton Fonzi and in his testimony for the Church Committee and House Select Committee on Assassinations, Veciana said *nothing* about Felix Zabala. Veciana's best friend—who had been with him from their days as bankers in Cuba, to the creation of Alpha-66, and through the abortive assassination plot in Chile—was nowhere to be found in Veciana's 2017 autobiography, **Trained to Kill**. Why did Veciana leave him out? Veciana was working with the Army in 1963—not the CIA. Would including Zabala in his book undercut the credibility of Veciana's alleged meeting with Phillips and Oswald in 1963?

I will have much more to say about these events and the rest of Veciana's story in Volumes IV and V.

---

916   Ibid.

CHAPTER TWELVE
KGB-CIA SPY WARS—1962

By the time of Oswald's defection in Moscow—31 October 1959—Pyotr Popov was already under KGB control and being used against the CIA's agents working out of the American Embassy.[917] With Popov safely in a trave, Khrushchev had thoroughly purged the Soviet intelligence services to undo the six years of damage caused by Popov's treason. His new KGB chairman, Aleksandr Shelepin, had already created the newly independent KGB *dezinformatsiya* department ("D") *deep inside of the existing* KGB.[918] Department D was the noxious *active measures* component that Golitsyn warned the Americans about after his defection in December 1961.

By that time, Shelepin and his deception czar, Oleg Gribanov, had not fallen for the Oswald bait in the USSR and, as a result, Oswald had begun planning his return to America. While Angleton's Oswald gambit was falling apart, his wily counterpart, Gribanov, was on a roll. He had learned about Penkovsky's treason as soon as the GRU colonel defected in April 1961. During 1962, Gribanov had Penkovsky cornered in Moscow "like a bear in its den,"[919] while he fed a new poison pill—Yuri Nosenko—to the CIA in Geneva, Switzerland.

Meanwhile, the KGB's brand-new *active measures* capability, known as the "Shelepin Plan," was based on a five-page memorandum authored by Ivan Agayants, the former head of KGB disinformation operations. Shelepin had assigned Agayants as the chief of the new unit—Department D.[920] Agayants was searching for the best candidate to

---

917 Murphy, Kondrashev and Bailey, **Battleground Berlin**, pp. 279-281
918 Bagley, **Spymaster** p. 168.
919 Bagley, "Ghosts of the Spy Wars," p. 9.
920 Bagley, **Spymaster** pp. 166-168.

become his deputy and supervise the implementation of this mission in Europe. Not surprisingly, that man was Sergey Kondrashev.

Two Job Offers for Sergey Kondrashev

During the late summer of 1961, the acting KGB chief in Vienna, Sergey Kondrashev, was hosting an important visitor from Moscow: Ivan Agayants. Agayants was head of the KGB First Chief Directorate (FCD) disinformation operations (Department D), and *also* one of the most *respected* officers in the history of Soviet Intelligence. Agayants explained that his main focus was sowing division in Germany. At that time, the world was in the grip of the Cold War crisis over Berlin, and Agayants wanted a senior colleague with the right background for that region. He had worked with Kondrashev when the latter was deputy chief of the German Department in 1955–1957. Knowing that the end of Sergey's tour in Vienna was approaching, Agayants invited him to Moscow to be his deputy.[921]

Years later, Kondrashev remembered how irresistible that offer was. He knew it was an opportunity to participate directly in support of worldwide Soviet foreign policy. He accepted Agayants' offer with "genuine pleasure."[922] In early 1962, Sergey Kondrashev returned to his new assignment in Moscow.

Before reporting for duty as Agayants' deputy in early March 1962, Kondrashev received an invitation to visit Second Chief Directorate (SCD) Chief Gribanov in his office. Gribanov knew about Kondrashev's nine years of experience in the SCD and that he was about to join Agayants' high-level deception work as his deputy in the FCD. Gribanov came straight to the point:

> He was *in the process, he said, of launching a complex deception operation against the CIA* which he wanted Kondrashev to help him run. If Sergey would come back to the SCD for this purpose, Gribanov would make him *his* deputy, a post carrying with it the rank of a one-star general.
> [Emphasis added]

When Kondrashev visited Agayants to talk over the situation, he recalls sensing that the latter *already* knew about the complex operation Gribanov was preparing:

> "I understand that you're tempted," Agayants said. "But relax. You'll get general's rank soon enough in the FCD. And in this particular case, you wouldn't be doing yourself any good in the long run. Gribanov is

---
[921] Bagley, *Spymaster*, pp. 165-166.
[922] Ibid.

going to screw it up. He's rash and doesn't have time for the detailed preparations that these things need."[923]

Kondrashev followed Agayants' advice and turned down Gribanov's offer. Later, Kondrashev would realize just how risky working for Gribanov would have been. If Gribanov's actions blew up, Kondrashev would share the blame.

Gribanov *did* go ahead with his *poisonous* "complex deception." By coincidence, Kondrashev discovered key details about the deception operation—including who Gribanov was feeding to the CIA as well as the identity of the officer who was managing the operation in the field. This is how Kondrashev found out. In May 1962, he bumped into an old SCD friend, Yuri Ivanovich Guk. Kondrashev knew that Guk was stationed in Switzerland and asked what he was doing in Moscow:

> "Just in to discuss an operation," Guk replied cheerily, "I'm still in Geneva." And he began extolling the pleasures of life in that city and talking about colleagues. Right now, in fact, he was having a lot of fun carousing there with Yuri Nosenko. Sergey knew that name only as a minor SCD headquarters officer. *"What in the world is Nosenko doing in Geneva?"* Guk stiffened at the realization that he had committed an indiscretion. ... *He passed his finger near his lip, shook his head, and said,* "Sorry. I can't talk about it. Forget I mentioned it."[924] [Emphasis added]

Kondrashev knew Guk was a long-time expert in counterintelligence deception and that he was still working in the SCD. Obviously, Guk and Nosenko were part of Gribanov's grandiloquent deception plan. The identity of the officer that Gribanov was sending to participate in a major deception operation against the CIA *had* to be Yuri Nosenko. And the identity of the officer that Gribanov was sending to manage the operation in the field *had* to be Ivan Guk.

The Nosenko Defection—Gribanov's Lethal Poison Plan

Just three months after Gribanov told Kondrashev he was launching a provocation against the CIA in Switzerland, a minor SCD Moscow officer was temporarily assigned as a watchdog for a Soviet delegation to a disarmament conference in Geneva. During the conference, this SCD officer did something that would forever play a central role in the investigation of the assassination of President Kennedy. At the end of May 1962 in Geneva, Yuri Nosenko volunteered to spy for the CIA.

---

923 Ibid, pp. 197-198.
924 Ibid, pp. 198-199.

And, as fate would have it, Pete Bagley was the CIA officer who received Nosenko's offer to "defect in place"—meaning that he would remain based in the Soviet Union. Defecting in place is a far more dangerous and harrowing arrangement than simply hightailing it to safety in America. Two days before Nosenko walked into Pete Bagley's apartment, overlooking the Old Town of Geneva, he made his move. Nosenko approached an American diplomat that he knew had served in Moscow and asked for urgent help to contact the CIA. The American quickly got the message to Bagley's supervisor, and, after escorting Nosenko to Bagley's apartment, he disappeared.[925]

Nosenko brushed aside any introductory pleasantries and said straight away that he had "important things" to tell Bagley and that he urgently needed money:

> "I think you'll help me, because I am here to talk about my real business. I am an officer of the KGB, and I work against your people in Moscow. I am a Major in the Second Chief Directorate," Nosenko said, assuming correctly that I would know it as the KGB's huge counterintelligence and security organization. "I am responsible for the security of our delegation."

Bagley poured Nosenko a *second* glass of whisky while the Russian acknowledged he was doing something dangerous. He needed money quickly. Nosenko lamented that he had been in too many bars, with too many girls, and had drank too much whiskey. Nosenko said he and his drinking partner, Yuri Guk—a long-time friend on an assignment at the Soviet intelligence station in Switzerland—were having *a great time* together.

Now, near the end of his three-month stay in Geneva, Nosenko had to account for his finances. He said he didn't mind speaking with Bagley because "I don't believe in our system anymore." He added, "But it's this damned money problem that drove me here."[926] The amount he needed was eight hundred francs—a curiously small sum for a defection—about $250. Nosenko promised to answer all of Bagley's questions. He also said that he would never go to America because he would not leave his wife and two daughters in Russia.

Nosenko then made a big mistake. He gave up a piece of information that eventually would come back to haunt him. While showing Bagley photographs of his daughters, he said, "Look, I just got these from my wife. *Guk was back in Moscow for a few days* and my wife asked him to bring them to me." Later, Guk's quick trip to Moscow *at this particular moment* would invite suspicion at the CIA.

When Bagley asked Nosenko if he would be missed during the meetings at the conference, he blundered again:

---

925 Bagley, *Spy Wars*, pp. 3-4.
926 Ibid, pp. 4-6.

"No problem," Nosenko replied. "*I don't have any fixed duties in the conference and no one knows or cares when I come and go.* I'm not accountable to anyone." He took a deep gulp of his whiskey and pulled a pack of American cigarettes from his jacket pocket and offered one to me. I declined but picked up a book of matches that lay on the coffee table and lit his. "*I'm not staying with the rest of the delegation.* They're in the Hotel Rex but four of us are in another hotel, *not even close.*" ... "*The only person who really knows how I spend my time is Guk,* but he's my friend, no problem."[927] [Emphasis added]

Not staying with the delegation that he was supposed to be watching was outside of standard KGB protocol. That was one thing. But bragging about it to a CIA case officer was something else—a greenhorn gaffe.

When Bagley asked *who* the three people in the other hotel were, Nosenko made his third mistake during this seemingly casual exchange:

"Yes, but how about those three?" I asked. "Will they notice and report your absences?" "Absolutely not. *The guy sharing my room is just a journalist with nothing to do with the KGB.* Same for the other two." "What's your roommate's name?" "Aleksandr Kislov," he replied.

Nosenko had bluntly lied to Bagley about Kislov's profession. As I pointed out in the Kondrashev section above, Guk worked for the KGB in Gribanov's SCD. And so did Aleksandr Kislov—*in the SCD's deception department!*[928] Whether or not Bagley knew it right away, at HQS that lie would join the many other howlers that Nosenko made during his "defection" in Geneva.

When Bagley asked Nosenko to describe his job in Moscow, Nosenko made his fourth mistake in as many minutes. He replied that, until a few weeks before leaving for Geneva, he had been the number two man in the section operating against the American Embassy in Moscow. Years later, no less than four authoritative KGB officers would state that Nosenko had *never* held that position. They included[929]:

- Anatoliy Golitsyn, who had visited the American Embassy section more than once during this period.
- Roman Markov, a leading member of the section at the time.
- Sergey Kondrashev, a top-level supervisor of KGB operations who had himself held that position earlier.
- Oleg Kalugin, who had headed KGB foreign counterintelligence.

Nosenko then offered Bagley information about the new assignment he had received just three weeks before:

---

927 Ibid, pp. 7-8.
928 Bagley, "Ghosts of the Spy Wars," pp. 30-33.
929 Ibid, p. 30.

> Just now he had become the section chief supervising work against American and British tourists in the USSR. Earlier he had served in both these sections, always working against the Americans. The Second Chief Directorate was trying not just to prevent their spying... but especially to recruit them as spies.[930]

Nosenko's puffed up claim about working as the chief of another section was likely as much of a lie as his supposed supervisory job for the section working against the American Embassy in Moscow. If Nosenko had replied truthfully to the query about his job, it would have revealed the true nature of his mission in Geneva—to deceive the CIA.

Nosenko was one of *several* poison pills working for Gribanov's operational deception section—Department 14. And, as Agayants had warned Kondrashev, Gribanov's grand deception plan was rash and lacked the detailed preparations for it to succeed. The reason Nosenko could not go to America was not because he would be leaving his family behind; rather, it was because his story would have fallen apart. That is exactly what happened to his account when, in desperation after the Kennedy assassination, the KGB ordered Nosenko to America for good. His story immediately fell flat on its face. Apparently, in 1962, no one in Moscow would ever have imagined that Nosenko would have to be sent to America.

So far, I have been discussing the first meeting between Bagley and Nosenko. The most important moment in all of Nosenko's meetings with Bagley and George Kisevalter occurred during that first meeting *before* Kisevalter arrived to join Bagley. After the above banter and several glasses of whiskey, Bagley astutely cut to the chase. He challenged Nosenko to provide *the most important thing* he could tell the CIA.

Nosenko, who had come to Bagley with a script prepared by Gribanov's deception unit in Moscow, became disoriented when confronted by Bagley's challenging test. The answer that rolled off Nosenko's tongue was an odd mixture of his prepared script and some embellishments meant to excite Bagley with his insights and savvy about sensitive KGB secrets:

> *I know the most important American spy the KGB ever recruited in Moscow.* He was a sergeant in your Embassy, a *cipher machine mechanic*. He had the code name "Andrey." I never knew his true name. He got involved with a Russian woman working for us in the Embassy's apartments. The old thing—it usually works—well, you know... ... We took compromising pictures *and he cooperated to get them back and save his marriage.* A tremendously valuable source. In fact, *my boss went himself all the way to the United States* just to reactivate "Andrey" after the rezidentura lost contact with him." [Emphasis added]

---

930   Bagley, *Spy Wars*, p. 7.

Two points need to be emphasized about Nosenko's response. First, during the next meeting in Bagley's apartment—just a few days later with Kisevalter present—Nosenko would *go out of his way* to walk back the importance of Andrey!

Clearly, Nosenko had said something wrong at the first meeting. Apparently, he had gone *off script*. Nosenko off script was like a fish out of water, and proof of Agayants' prediction that Gribanov's grand deception scheme would be flawed by a lack of thorough preparation. But what exactly was off script? And, was Guk involved in an effort to mask a major misstep? I will answer these questions shortly.

The second noteworthy point is what happened when Nosenko said his "boss" had been the chief of KGB operations against the American Embassy in Moscow and had gone to Washington at some point before Nosenko's assignment to Geneva. Bagley was quick enough on his feet to ask the name of the boss who had gone to Washington. "Kovshuk, Vladislav Kovshuk," Nosenko answered.[931] I will also return to this nice nugget shortly.

To help set the scene for this first debrief with Bagley, I want to fast forward to information that Bagley learned from 1) the Golitsyn files during a quick trip to CIA HQS immediately after Nosenko's trip ended in Geneva; and 2) after the end of the Cold War, information Bagley learned from Sergey Kondrashev. At HQS, Bagley discovered the true nature of Kovshuk's 1957 trip to the U.S. Crucially, *both* Yuri Guk and Aleksandr Kislov had accompanied Kovshuk on a sensitive mission to Washington in January 1957. In addition, Bagley also learned that Golitsyn had mentioned a code clerk code-named "Jack." In post-Cold War conversations with Bagley, Kondrashev revealed that during Kovshuk's 1957 trip to Washington he had learned about Popov's defection *and* that the source of that news was a spy "who was never uncovered."[932] Meanwhile, back in 1962, during Nosenko's "defection" in Geneva, none of the details I just mentioned were known to Bagley and Kisevalter. For the moment, they believed that Nosenko was trying to be truthful.

Bagley cabled CIA HQS about Nosenko's defection and the reply came back within hours. The HQS file on Nosenko had no information except for a single Caribbean trip with a Soviet group. "There was nothing on him personally nor had any other KGB defector ever mentioned his name." In early June 1962, only a week after Nosenko first made contact with Bagley, the Geneva disarmament conference ended. During that week, George Kisevalter joined Bagley for four additional meetings with Nosenko that lasted from one to three hours. Oddly, once again his conference security duties were virtually nonexistent.[933]

---

931 Ibid, pp. 7-8.
932 Ibid, p. 94 and p. 208.
933 Bagley, *Spy Wars*, pp. 10-11.

INTO THE STORM

During this second meeting, Nosenko *initially* stayed on script, giving the two CIA men the account contrived by the KGB four years earlier—in December 1958—about how Popov had been "discovered" in Moscow. This is how Nosenko effectively backstopped that "routine surveillance" deception:

> Our guys were routinely tailing George Winters, an attaché at your embassy. Sometime in early 1959 they saw him drop a letter into a street mailbox. It was written in Russian with a false return address and addressed to Popov. That was all we needed—diplomats don't post innocent letters to GRU officers. Popov was put under twenty-four-hour surveillance. Within a few days they followed him to a clandestine meeting with [Russell] Langelle, the American Embassy security officer. They arrested Popov a few days later, interrogated and got his confession, and ran him for a while as a double agent before closing the operation down. Langelle was arrested moments after Popov handed him some reports the KGB had concocted.

Nosenko added that they tried to recruit Langelle, but he refused and "got kicked out on his diplomatic ass." Popov, on the other hand, was tried and shot.[934] What cannot be overemphasized is that—unlike most of his disheveled and disorganized performance—Nosenko had clearly been *very well rehearsed* for this part in the play. His detailed false account about the end of Popov was definitely *on script*. For the moment, this story about the uncovering of Popov would ring true with the CIA.

As I mentioned above, Nosenko had gone *off script* during the first meeting with Bagley. Now, at the second meeting, Nosenko changed his story about Andrey. The change was *drastic*. Nosenko and his manager, Yuri Guk, were desperate to undo the damage caused by that *deviation from his prepared script* at the first meeting. The damage was *so severe* that fully fixing the problem was impossible. Gribanov's plan had been to use the Andrey story as the *excuse* for Kovshuk's trip to Washington—*to hide the fact that Kovshuk's true mission was to contact the KGB mole in the CIA*. Below, I will show that in 1957 Gribanov had carefully choreographed a Kovshuk-Andrey contact in Washington that would come to the attention of the FBI. The purpose of that *contrived contact with Andrey* was to create the peg upon which Kovshuk's Washington mission could be credibly hung.

But Nosenko's boastful response to Bagley's challenge had nearly ruined everything. Nosenko's deviation from his prepared script had come perilously close to exposing the KGB's mole! (More on this below.) And so, by the time of this second meeting, Guk and Nosenko were in full damage control. They came up with an *altered script* in a desperate attempt to fix the problem. In front of Bagley and Kisevalter,

---

934 Ibid, pp. 11-12.

Nosenko declared, "*We never managed to recruit any American code clerk. The closest we ever came was 'Andrey.'*"[935]

This news joggled Kisevalter's memory about the time when the KGB had attempted to recruit a CIA security officer working for the embassy in Moscow, Ellis Smith. Kisevalter asked, "Do you know about the approach to Ed Smith?" Nosenko had prepared for this question. He replied, "We gave him the code name 'Ryzhiy' [Redhead]. ...Yes, we knew. Well, we tried," Nosenko shrugged, "nothing doing. Ryzhiy refused, reported it to the ambassador, and was pulled back to the States. Case closed." [936]

Nosenko's reply worked. Bagley recalled that because Nosenko's answer squared with Kisevalter's memory, "He grew further in our esteem." For the moment, Guk and Nosenko had dodged a bullet. But not for long. And the Ellis Smith case was *far from closed*.

Bagley would eventually decipher Nosenko's adjusted script, "*We never managed to recruit any American code clerk. The closest we ever came was 'Andrey.'*" Nosenko had been *anxious to downplay* his previous description of Andrey as *the most important American spy the KGB ever recruited in Moscow*. Now, the importance of Nosenko's Andrey paled in comparison to the importance of a real American *code clerk*! Moreover, Nosenko now suddenly denied that the KGB had ever recruited an *American code clerk*. But the truth was that the KGB *had* successfully recruited a *very important* American code clerk. Kondrashev had recruited "Jack" in 1949—the same "Jack" that Golitsyn had mentioned to the CIA in 1961.

Below, I will return to the astonishing story of Kondrashev's recruitment of "Jack" and the unprecedented damage he caused to American national security. But the biggest threat caused by Nosenko's off script comments at the first meeting was this boast: "Andrey was *the most important American spy the KGB ever recruited in Moscow*." That boast was missing in the second meeting—and for good reason. It was—with one minor exception—true! I believe that we can now establish, with a high degree of certainty, that the *most important American spy* that the KGB ever recruited *was* in the American Embassy in Moscow at the time of his recruitment. That American spy had been reassigned to the CIA and had become the KGB's mole in the CIA that Popov reported in April 1958. And finally, as Bagley later reported, the CIA security officer at the embassy in Moscow, Edward Ellis Smith, had played a role in the recruitment of that KGB mole.[937] As I mentioned in Chapter Eight, Smith had been sent by the CIA to create dead drops for Popov in Moscow during 1954-1955!

So, Nosenko's drunken boast to Bagley nearly destroyed Gribanov's grand deception plan right out of the gate. The *whole purpose* for the use of the Andrey story had been to protect the KGB mole in the CIA, and Nosenko had inadvertently come close

---

935 Ibid, p. 16.
936 Ibid, pp. 16-17.
937 Ibid, p. 78.

to exposing that mole! Of course, the KGB mole in the CIA was not Andrey. When the FBI caught up with and interviewed Andrey, they knew right away he was no threat and decided to let him retire in peace. The mole in the CIA was never caught.

During the final meeting with Nosenko, communication signals were worked out to ensure that Nosenko could let the CIA know when he would next be in the West. That would not take place until just a few weeks after the assassination of President Kennedy. In the interim, the CIA would discover that Nosenko was not who he had pretended to be at the 1962 disarmament convention in Geneva.

Bagley is Reassigned to CIA HQS

At the time of the Geneva sessions with Nosenko, the CIA station did *not yet* know who "Andrey" was. That was a *puzzle* that Bagley began working on in earnest during a brief visit to HQS after the end of the Geneva conference in early June 1962. At that time, Jack Maury was the chief of the Soviet Russia Division at HQS. His first question about Nosenko to Bagley and Kisevalter was, "Is he for real?" Kisevalter replied that there had been no sign to the contrary, but he wondered, "why in hell did he take that kind of risk for a few hundred bucks?"[938]

Maury advised Bagley to look at the Golitsyn files. When Bagley met with Angleton, he advised the same thing and directed his office manager to show the Golitsyn files to Bagley. As he poured over them in a small counterintelligence meeting room, this item stood out like a sore thumb. Bagley recalls:

> Golitsyn was the *first source* to reveal—five years after the fact—that Vladislav Kovshuk's trip [to Washington] was the same trip that Nosenko had described at our first meeting. Had it been known at the time that the chief of KGB operations against the American Embassy in Moscow had traveled to Washington, the question would have *screamed*—as it still did—"*Why?*" It seemed more than fortuitous that shortly after Golitsyn's revelation, Kovshuk's deputy Nosenko had come and explained that long-ago trip authoritatively, but in a banal, almost benign light. [Emphasis added]

And then one clue led to another. "It was in that tiny room, poring over thick files and busily penciling page after page of notes on a lined yellow pad," Bagley recalled, "that doubts began to arise that had not occurred to me in Geneva." Bagley concluded that the KGB might have sent Nosenko to CIA to divert them from Golitsyn's leads.[939]

---

938   Ibid, p. 19.
939   Ibid, pp. 23-26.

A couple days later, Bagley went back to see Angleton and told him the bad news. Angleton asked Bagley to write down the main points of the problem so that he could carefully study them. That same afternoon, Angleton called Bagley back to his office and said he thought Bagley was on to something. Angleton pointed out that Golitsyn had predicted the KGB would try to divert the Agency from the leads he had given them. Angleton and Bagley agreed that there wasn't enough data to be certain—*yet*. Angleton told Bagley to keep the Nosenko matter quiet for the time being and that he and Bagley could look deeper into the problem when the latter returned to HQS for duty that fall.[940]

Three months later, Bagley and his family returned to Washington. Bagley was assigned to work on the CIA's counterintelligence operations against the KGB and GRU. Nothing more was heard from Nosenko—until right after the assassination of President Kennedy. In the meantime, Bagley began working on putting the pieces of Gribanov's puzzle together. Bagley had a mind like a steel trap. And he would need it.

How Bagley Cracked the Nosenko Case—and Much More

By November 1962, Pete Bagley was settled into his new job as chief of the counterintelligence section of the Soviet Russia Division. Certain that Nosenko had been sent to Geneva to deceive the CIA, Bagley began hunting for any piece of information that would begin to unravel *who* and *what* Nosenko's deceptions had been designed to provide cover for.

Nosenko's bland explanation of Kovshuk's January 1957 mission to Washington still worried Bagley. He remembered that the *initial* piece of that problem was how Nosenko's Andrey account permitted the CIA to breathe *more easily*. Principally, it weakened Golitsyn's alarming identification of Komarov as a pseudonym for Kovshuk.[941] Nosenko had used Kovshuk's true name for his trip to Washington *and* had reported that the purpose of the trip was to reactivate Andrey.

Bagley realized that a sergeant-mechanic working on cipher machines—*but not himself dealing with ciphers*—could *not* endanger American security, as might, for instance, a higher military, diplomatic, or intelligence officer.[942] And so, Nosenko's report that Kovshuk went all the way to Washington to reactivate Andrey was suspicious. It felt like a pacifier.

Coincidentally, one of Bagley's analysts had assembled a dossier of documents describing FBI *surveillance of Komarov* (Kovshuk) during that trip. While reading

---

940 Ibid.
941 Bagley, "Ghosts of the Spy Wars," p. 14, n. 31.
942 Bagley, *Spy Wars*, p. 64.

through that file, Bagley discovered a document containing another significant piece of the Komarov conundrum. The official diplomatic description of Komarov's business was a *permanent assignment* to the Soviet Embassy in Washington. That description was contradicted by Golitsyn, who described the visit as *only a trip*.[943]

A normal assignment to the Washington embassy would have lasted for *two years*. But those FBI documents revealed that Kovshuk had returned to his job in Moscow after only *ten months*. The FBI's information *matched* Nosenko's *quickie scenario*—that his boss had gone all the way to America only to restore contact with a busted sergeant-mechanic. The permanent status of Kovshuk's Washington assignment was obviously a *contrived* cover story to disguise the truth about Kovshuk's short-term mission.

This initial breakthrough led Bagley to think about how such a short-duration trip to Washington might *fit* with Kovshuk's mission in Moscow—penetrating the American Embassy. Then this question quickly came to Bagley: did Kovshuk have *unfinished business* with an American in Washington that his section had *recruited* in the embassy in Moscow? Bagley *did* eventually find—in that same file of FBI documents—a piece of information about Kovshuk's trip that helped answer that question and eventually filled in several pieces of Gribanov's deceptive puzzle.

Kovshuk had *not been alone* on his Washington trip. FBI surveillants had reported that while they were tailing a *known* KGB operative from the Soviet Embassy, Yuri Guk, they spied him in clandestine tactics with *"Komarov"* (Kovshuk) and a *third* Soviet official. The third man was also under cover. To the FBI, he appeared to be little more than a Soviet news correspondent from New York.[944]

Kovshuk's clever use of the pseudonym "Komarov" made him appear as a nondescript diplomat. As a result, the FBI did not, at first, take any special interest in him. After *many* weeks had passed, the FBI observed these three men working together so often that they gave them the moniker *the three musketeers*. The pattern of their activities provided Bagley with the next piece to place into Gribanov's puzzle. The Musketeer's maneuvers suggested they were meeting with a spy. But the trio worked with *such* professional skill that *even with intensified surveillance* the FBI was never able to observe the spy.[945] The trio had made effective use of meeting in movie theaters.

Finally, after combining and analyzing the data obtained from the FBI files and Golitsyn's information, Bagley was *floored* to see the completed picture of the three musketeers. The KGB man the FBI had been tailing was Yuri Guk. He was only *nominally assigned* as a diplomat to the Soviet Embassy. He was a *provocateur* from Gribanov's Second Chief Directorate. And the musketeer posing as the newsman from New York was Aleksandr Kislov, a KGB agent in Gribanov's *deception department*. As the reader will

---

943 Bagley, "Ghosts of the Spy Wars, p. 14, n. 31.
944 Bagley, *Spy Wars*, pp. 65-66.
945 Ibid.

by now recall, both of Kovshuk's cohorts in Washington in 1957 were *Nosenko's cohorts in Geneva* in 1962! Kislov had been Nosenko's roommate.[946]

At this point, Bagley was satisfied that these apparent disparate events in Washington, Moscow, and Geneva were *not* coincidental at all; rather, they were *adjacent pieces of the same puzzle*. In fact, the emerging picture was quite a spectacle. *At the very moment* in Geneva that Nosenko was telling Bagley and Kisevalter about Kovshuk's trip five years earlier, those same two Gribanov deception operatives were now supporting Nosenko's provocation in Geneva. Pretending to have read the KGB file on Kislov, Nosenko now certified that Kislov had no connection at all with the KGB. The unavoidable conclusion was that Gribanov had sent Nosenko to the CIA to divert attention from Golitsyn's legitimate leads.[947]

As former DCI Allen Dulles often reminded his subordinates, once a *single* piece of a black operation is compromised, the *remaining* pieces are more *easily* deciphered. With so many pieces in hand, much of the remaining details of Gribanov's operation were easy pickings for Bagley:

> Nosenko's story of Andrey—his "most important" story—could not be true. The facts of Kovshuk's trip made that clear. It was not to restore an old contact that led the KGB to send one of its key counterintelligence officers away on an ostensibly permanent assignment while holding his job for him back in Moscow.[948]

In sum: in early January 1957, Gribanov's agents had flown to the United States at a two-day interval: Kislov as a journalist to New York, and Kovshuk as a diplomat to Washington. Within weeks, the FBI observed them working together in Washington with a known KGB operative, Yuri Guk.[949]

Bagley's investigation had made steady progress. He had put this much of the puzzle together: In 1962, Gribanov sent Guk and Nosenko to join Kislov in Geneva to 1) backstop the false story of how the KGB learned about Popov's defection in 1957; and 2) disguise Kovshuk's real mission in Washington in 1957. At this point, this question was front and center: what was Kovshuk's mission to Washington about?

The Edward Ellis Smith Affair

As promised in Chapter Eight, I now return to the Ellis Smith affair. By the end of 1962, Bagley was ready to test this working hypothesis for the Kovshuk trip: Its purpose had

---

946 Bagley, "Ghosts of the Spy Wars, p. 33.
947 Bagley, *Spy Wars*, pp. 66-67.
948 Ibid, pp. 67-68.
949 Ibid.

INTO THE STORM

been to *reconnect with an asset that the KGB had recruited in the American Embassy in Moscow that had been reassigned to Washington*—the place where the musketeers had been spotted. So, Bagley asked his counterintelligence section to examine the records on departures of American personnel from the embassy in Moscow *prior* to Kovshuk's 1957 visa request.

Bagley's section produced a list of *everyone* who left the Moscow embassy from August to November 1956. One name on the list immediately jumped off the page— *the man the CIA had sent to Moscow to support the Popov operation.* That was a big BINGO! He was Edward Ellis Smith, the U.S. Embassy security officer. Smith had been one of a *minute* number of CIA officers who were aware of Popov's defection.[950]

Kovshuk had planted an attractive KGB agent as Smith's maid and he carelessly fell straight into a sex trap. In September 1956, the KGB stormed in and caught Smith in the act. Kovshuk confronted him and offered to do nothing if Smith agreed to collaborate with the KGB. Kovshuk did not know about Smith's mission to support Popov and still assumed Smith was the Embassy security officer! Smith vacillated for several days. Fearing that if he refused Kovshuk's offer the KGB might drug and kidnap him, Smith informed the surprised American Ambassador, Charles Bohlen, about his true mission. The CIA recalled Smith to Washington right away where he was evasive during "long harrowing sessions" with an Agency security team led by future Watergate burglar James McCord.[951] As a result, the CIA fired him in October 1956.[952]

After that Ellis Smith breakthrough, the CIA got an *incredibly* lucky break. Until late summer of 1957, Ellis Smith remained in Washington while waiting for a job in California to begin. At that moment, a new key piece of the puzzle fell into Bagley's hands. That piece put Smith in an entirely new light. It was a note written by a CIA operations officer at the time the three musketeers appeared to be meeting with a spy in Washington. The note indicated that during the spring of 1957 the author had fortuitously bumped into Smith on the street. When the operations officer asked Smith how things were going, Smith replied that while waiting to go out to California he was spending a lot of time in Washington's *movie houses*. That was the precise time that the three musketeers were observed operating around Washington's *movie houses*—and, as Golitsyn had heard, learning things that put the KGB onto *the trail of Pyotr Popov.*

Bagley drilled down further for information on Smith by reexamining Nosenko's 1962 trip to Geneva. Nosenko had shown an uncanny awareness of the Ellis Smith case, even alleging his personal participation. It was not difficult for Bagley to discover why that had *not* been possible. It was during the second half of 1956 that Kovshuk had compromised Smith in a honey trap. Nosenko was *unable* to participate in the Ellis

---

950 Bagley, *Spy Wars*, pp. 68-71.
951 Smith, Richard Harris, "The First Moscow Station: An Espionage Footnote to Cold War History," *International Journal of Intelligence and Counterintelligence*, Vol 3, 1989, Issue 3, p. 34.
952 Ibid, pp. 69-70.

affair because a year earlier he, Nosenko, had transferred out of Kovshuk's embassy section to an assignment in a department unrelated to KGB operations against the American Embassy.

Much later, the KGB admitted that they had, in fact, recruited Smith. So Golitsyn had been right after all: Kovshuk's 1957 trip led the KGB onto the defection of Pyotr Popov, and the Nosenko stories about the trip were part of the KGB's strategy to divert American counterintelligence away from Smith's track. At this point, Bagley had come very close to completing the Andrey puzzle.[953]

The picture taking shape began to show the great pains to which the KGB had resorted to protect its real source on Popov's treason—the KGB mole in the CIA—*and* the crucial role of Ellis Smith in providing *access* to the mole. In his book ***Spy Wars***, however, Bagley said that he suspected Smith might have helped the KGB recruit the mole in the CIA.[954] Protecting this information had been the imperative driving the *delay* of Popov's recall from Berlin and keeping his arrest *secret* after his return to Moscow.

As I pointed out in Chapter Eight, keeping Popov's arrest secret gave the KGB time to create a false scenario for how Popov's treason was discovered. The KGB's delicate handling of Popov secured his contrition during the interrogation and enabled the KGB to double him back against the CIA's agents in Moscow.[955] A month before Oswald's October 1959 defection in Moscow, the KGB successfully used Popov to draw a CIA agent out of the Embassy to contact him. That contact was then used as the sole explanation for how "routine surveillance of diplomats" had led to the KGB's discovery of Popov's defection. That *contrived story* was then placed in a note that the KGB forced Popov to give to his CIA contact.

Three years later, Gribanov sent Nosenko to Geneva to tell that *same* contrived story to Pete Bagley.[956] But it took Bagley less than a year to figure that out and *much more* about Gribanov's deception game. Kovshuk did *not* go to Washington for the cipher-machine mechanic. There was a much bigger fish to find. When Andrey was finally identified and interviewed by the FBI, his account made that clear. Angleton and Bagley had locked horns with Shelepin and Gribanov, each side going all out to neutralize the successful penetration by the other. The KGB did not want the CIA to discover *who* had betrayed Popov's treason and *when* that event had occurred. The final piece of the puzzle could now be put into place. Smith's presence in Washington had played a pivotal role in putting the KGB onto *the trail of Pyotr Popov*. But how? For now, the best answer is this: *Smith knew the identity of the KGB mole in the CIA* and had facilitated a secret meeting between the mole and Kovshuk.

---

953 Ibid, p. 71.
954 Ibid, p. 78.
955 Bagley, "Ghosts of the Spy Wars, p. 14.
956 Bagley, ***Spy Wars***, p. 75.

INTO THE STORM

At the moment Gribanov learned of Golitsyn's defection, he understood that Golitsyn might help the CIA discover *when and where* the KGB had learned about Popov's defection. At this point, the CIA was on the verge of discovering that the source of the U-2 leak and the uncovering of Popov was probably a *single KGB mole* in the CIA. The fifteen months between January 1957 and April 1958 separated the uncovering of Popov—and Popov's news about the KGB mole. All of these time and location *data points* were a big deal: Knowing that the true time and location was *Washington in 1957* and that the false time and location was *Moscow in 1959,* would permit Angleton and Bagley to develop a more accurate profile of the KGB mole. This information would also help the CIA identify other false defectors.

Gribanov sent Nosenko to Geneva to sow confusion by loading him up with poisonous but tasty tidbits to disconnect the *time and place* of Popov's uncovering from *the time* and *place* of the U-2 leak. And, as Agayants had warned Kondrashev, Gribanov's plan would be highly risky and not well prepared. Nosenko's missteps had enabled Bagley to put the entire Gribanov puzzle together with one exception: the *name* of the KGB mole in the CIA.

After the Cold War, Sergey Kondrashev, a former colleague of Kovshuk, told Bagley that Kovshuk had gone to Washington to "meet an important agent—*one who was never uncovered.*"[957] Thus, Kondrashev confirmed that Kovshuk *personally* met the KGB mole. In his book *Spy Wars*, Bagley wrote that they never found out *why* the KGB had such a keen operational interest in Ellis Smith. However, Bagley suspected that Smith might have helped the KGB *recruit* the mole in the CIA.[958] If that is true, and I suspect that it was, the recruitment of that mole must have taken place in Moscow when Smith was the security chief at the American Embassy. The mole might have been a CIA officer assigned to the embassy.

I will keep searching for the identity of that elusive mole. I have long wondered if Kondrashev told Bagley who it was and, if so, did Bagley take that secret to his grave?

Before moving on to the conclusion of this chapter, I want to clean up the remaining loose ends of this arcane episode of the KGB-CIA spy wars.

"Andrey"—Part Two

In the fall of 1951, Andrey left his wife and children in the United States and went to work in the American Embassy in Moscow as a cipher-machine mechanic. Andrey's job was to repair and test the *exterior parts* of the machines. Deeper repairs and maintenance

---

957 Bagley, "Ghosts of the Spy Wars, pp. 14-15, n. 31.
958 Bagley, *Spy Wars*, p. 78.

were only performed by *visiting specialists*. Andrey *never* saw the *secret rotors* inside of the sealed housings. Whenever he was admitted to the code room, he was accompanied very closely by a code room official *everywhere* he went—*even* to the toilet.[959]

In 1953, a few months *before* the end of Andrey's Moscow tour of duty, he fell for his pretty housemaid's tempting invitation to visit her small apartment.[960] Hidden cameras installed by the KGB caught Andrey in the act. They soon confronted Andrey and offered to give him the photos and negatives if he would *steal the keys* to the Embassy's codes.[961]

Andrey readily agreed to meet them again. At the second meeting, one of the KGB officers provided him special paper and a flashlight to use on a *list of rotor settings*. But he *never* had an opportunity to carry out the task and returned the blank paper at the next meeting. There were no further meetings during Andrey's remaining months in Moscow. Apparently, the KGB realized that Andrey was an *expendable dud* that would come in handy in the future.

In the U. S., Andrey lived in *constant fear* that the KGB would find him and ask him to commit *espionage*. He happily accepted an offer to transfer to an army recruiting station where *he would not have access* to classified materials. *Four years* later, in October 1957, the KGB contacted him and brought up the subject of his Moscow maid and the pictures. Andrey was met by a short, heavyset Russian who offered to return the compromising pictures in exchange for documents—*documents that the KGB knew would be useless*. Andrey brought a handful of unclassified army recruitment pamphlets to the next meeting. The short man was accompanied by an *older* Russian man, whom Andrey recognized from photographs the FBI had shown him. Not surprisingly, the older man was "*Komarov*"—the *pseudonym* for Vladislav Kovshuk.[962]

Gribanov knew that Andrey's 1957 contact with the KGB in Washington would later provide a suitable peg upon which to *hang a false reason* for Kovshuk's trip and activities with the two other musketeers. Andrey retired from the army in late 1961, six months *before* Nosenko first reported him to the CIA in Geneva. Andrey had no access to classified information and Nosenko's tip surrendering him to the Americans not only cost the KGB *nothing* but also helped to *cover up* Kovshuk's true mission in Washington.

The FBI determined that Andrey could *not* have delivered sensitive information. So, they decided *not* to charge him and to let him live out his retirement without further disturbance. In 1964, Nosenko gave different data on Andrey that finally made it possible for the FBI to identify who this Andrey was: Army Sergeant Dayle W. Smith.[963]

---

959 Ibid, pp. 75-76.
960 Bagley, "Ghosts of the Spy Wars, p. 14, n. 31.
961 Bagley, *Spy Wars*, pp 75-76.
962 Bagley, "Ghosts of the Spy Wars, p. 14, n. 31.
963 Ibid, p. 18.

In his first meeting with Bagley, Nosenko had said that the Andrey he knew—the most important American spy ever recruited in Moscow—had been recruited in 1949. That was a bad mistake—Nosenko did not join the KGB until 1953. Furthermore, that was two years after Sergeant Dayle Smith was recruited by the KGB. The truth was that a *very important* American spy *was* recruited in Moscow in 1949—and he was a valuable code clerk, not a harmless cipher mechanic! Nosenko did not know him personally or have anything to do with him at all. After the Cold War, when Kondrashev told Bagley about the successful recruitment of this *code clerk*, his name was "Jack," *not* "Andrey." Kondrashev had recruited him in 1949!

Jack—The Most Important American Spy?

In 1949, the KGB (at the time it was called the MGB) had recruited an American code clerk in Moscow. That enabled them to *break* America's military ciphers at a critical moment of the Cold War. Only *eight people in the world*—aside from the recruiter himself, Sergey Kondrashev—were aware of these details and the cipher break.[964] When Stalin learned that the U.S. had excluded Korea from its new Pacific defense perimeter, he removed his objection to the North Koreans' long-standing plans to invade the south. This American code clerk may thus have *inadvertently touched off the Korean War*. Until Pete Bagley's 2013 book, **Spymaster**, that traitor's role had remained unknown.[965]

The first hint leaked to the West about the code clerk's recruitment came on the heels of Anatoliy Golitsyn's defection at the end of 1961. Golitsyn had learned about the recruitment of an American code clerk, but only that his code-name was "*Jack*." That code-name *indeed* belonged to Kondrashev's recruit. To throw American investigators off the track opened by Golitsyn, the KGB put to work its time-tested practice of deception. It succeeded, and the Americans failed to pin down the identity of "Jack" or any of the other code clerks Golitsyn had pointed to.[966]

In 1948, Roman Markov reported an observation by surveillants of an American code clerk spending the night with a Russian girl— "Nadya." Markov visited Nadya and told her the affair was known, but far from *discouraging* it, the authorities wanted her to *develop* it. Kondrashev *directed* her relationship with the code clerk, to whom the section now gave the code name "*Jack*." Kondrashev learned that Jack was unscrupulous and greedy for money. He planned to marry Nadya and leave with enough money to enjoy a rich life in America. Kondrashev met Jack at Nadya's apartment two

---

964 Bagley, *Spymaster*, p. 1.
965 Ibid, p. 2.
966 Bagley, "Ghosts of the Spy Wars, p. 18.

or three times a month, and Jack answered all of Kondrashev's questions. Kondrashev began giving Jack envelopes containing five hundred U.S. dollars, the equivalent of about five thousand in today's currency. Soon the envelopes had a thousand dollars inside. Jack brought used parts of cipher machines to the meetings and, eventually, he succeeded in bringing a *cipher key settings schedule*. He did so again whenever the key settings were changed.[967]

"Misha," a *cipher specialist* of the KGB's Eighth Chief Directorate, who was familiar with the codes and ciphers equivalent to America's National Security Agency, began to attend almost every meeting. Misha asked detailed questions and gave Jack concrete assignments. Kondrashev began providing Jack envelopes containing $5,000 at each meeting. By the time Jack was transferred from Moscow in late 1949, he had received $50,000, and a send-off bonus of another $50,000 in cash. The value of that $100,000 at that time would amount to more than *$5 million today!*[968]

But, for the KGB, the value of his services was incalculable. After the cipher-breakers had worked for a time on Jack's materials, they *succeeded in intercepting clear text*. Jack's information enabled them to *assemble a copy of the machine*, and they could *read* American secret communications between Washington *and all the American posts* around the world. This continued throughout the months that the *keys* provided by Jack remained valid.[969] When Jack's new posting came, he left thinking he would meet and marry Nadya in Europe. But the KGB had made sure that he would never get the chance.

Shortly after another brutal purge by Stalin, Kondrashev's bosses were arrested and thrown into prison. As a result, years passed before the KGB could pull itself together enough to even think of reactivating Jack. When an attempt to do so was finally made, it failed. In a talk with Bagley after the Cold War, Kondrashev did not remember—or was unwilling to tell—*why* the attempt failed.[970]

The true identity of "Jack" is still classified. In any event, Jack was *not* the most important spy ever recruited by the KGB in Moscow. That spy was the KGB mole in the CIA.

October 1963—Oswald's Secret Mission in Moscow

We now jump to the *other* side of the galaxy at the *end* of the Kennedy presidency. In late September 1963, Lee Oswald allegedly traveled to Mexico City. After the assassination, John Whitten, the HQS CIA officer in charge of the Mexico desk, wrote a

---

967   Bagley, *Spymaster*, pp. 6-10.
968   Ibid, pp. 10-11.
969   Ibid.
970   Ibid, pp. 14-16.

report about Oswald's visit to Mexico City. Whitten said that when they learned that *Lee Harvey Oswald* had been arrested for the president's murder, "*the effect was electric.*"

For more than the *next half century*, Oswald's fall 1963 Mexico City trip has been the subject of top-secret congressional investigations—and scores of books, including my own. That trip is *not* the subject of this chapter—with *one* exception. As I reported in Volume II (**Countdown to Darkness**, Chapter One), a *surprising* piece of evidence that emerged from Oswald's Mexico trip in 1963 bears *directly* upon the case for a *false* defection during Oswald's Russian trip in 1959. The reader will recall from Chapter Eight of the present volume that in October 1959 Angleton tried to use Oswald as U-2 flypaper in Moscow to entice the KGB to contact its mole in the CIA. On that occasion, Oswald had declared he was prepared to tell the USSR what he had learned about radar and *something special*—a not so subtle allusion to the CIA's U-2 program.[971]

Now, just *seven weeks* before the Kennedy assassination in 1963, Oswald *again* dropped a provocative hint, *this* time in front of Soviet consular officers at their embassy in Mexico City. According to KGB officer Oleg Nechiporenko, who was present when Oswald made the comment, "*He even dropped some hints that he had supposedly carried out a secret mission*" in the Soviet Union.[972] In my view, serious consideration needs to be given to the possibility that Oswald had been instructed to drop this hint to the KGB in Mexico City. I will examine this subject closely in Volume V.

The Impact of the USSR'S Demise on Nosenko's Bona Fides

The false claims by the CIA and KGB of no contact with nor interest in Oswald remained a frozen glacier for the rest of the Cold War. The most recent breakthrough in the case for a false Oswald defection was a revelation in 2012 by the CIA officer who received Nosenko's defection in 1962, Pete Bagley. That happened just two years before Bagley died. I will get to that shortly. However, the first major breakthrough came in the wake of the tumultuous events of August 1991 in the Soviet Union.

The collapse of a hardline coup precipitated the demise of the communist system. This, in turn, led to a brief honeymoon with the West during which many Soviet Central Committee archives—including KGB records on Oswald—were temporarily opened. Amazingly, former KGB officers compared notes with former CIA officers about this and other cases. Startling revelations flowed from a new and lasting friendship between Pete Bagley and Sergey Kondrashev, one the most dominant KGB officers during the Cold War. I will explain more about these matters in a moment.

---

971 11/2/59, Foreign Service Dispatch 234 from Moscow, p. 2; see Newman, **Oswald and the CIA** (2008), p. 6.
972 Oleg Nechiporenko, **Passport to Assassination** (New York: Birch Lane Press, 1993), pp. 76-77.

The Soviet tale of denial of interest in Oswald collapsed with the demise of the USSR. And that event *demolished* the bona fides of Yuri Nosenko as a genuine defector. Sadly, the CIA has so far failed to apologize to the truthful officers whose careers were crushed when the Agency finally made the decision to accept Nosenko as a genuine defector.[973] For forty-six years the controversy over that 18 October 1972 decision by DCI Helms[974] has continued to the present day. The possible role of FBI Director J. Edgar Hoover in Helms' decision has been given scant attention. I will examine the recollections of former CIA and DEA agent Tom Tripodi about this possibility in Volume V or VI.[975]

In early 1964, Nosenko permanently defected to the U.S., loaded up with the false claim that the KGB had never been interested in Oswald. We now know for certain, as Pete Bagley and David Murphy of the Soviet Russia Division deduced in early 1964, that Nosenko's Oswald story was the opposite of the truth. During the years 1962 to November 1963, neither Nosenko nor his Soviet handlers had any idea that the USSR would fall and the unwelcome truth about Nosenko would be exposed by a KGB officer—Oleg Nechiporenko. I first reported Nechiporenko's work on this matter in Volume II (***Countdown to Darkness***, Chapter One). I will briefly mention the highlights of his work here.

Nechiporenko had worked in the KGB's Moscow regional directorate in 1958 and 1959—while Oswald was in Moscow. Nechiporenko assembled and published the *cold hard facts* about Oswald and the KGB from files made available to him *after* the fall of the Soviet Union. The Russian Foreign Intelligence Service, the Russian Ministry of Security, and the Belarus KGB directed him to the *relevant* archival materials.[976] Nechiporenko's book, ***Passport to Assassination***, was published in 1993.

During Oswald's stay in the Soviet Union, he was *twice* covertly interviewed by the KGB in Moscow, and *several* times by the Minsk KGB. His *work associates* at the Minsk Radio factory were *recruited as informants*, his *apartment was bugged*, and *his mail was surreptitiously opened*.[977] Not surprisingly, the CIA mole hunting unit—Special Investigation Group (CI/SIG)—*also* opened Oswald's mail.[978]

Nechiporenko's work *destroyed* the credibility of the KGB's denial after the Kennedy assassination of any previous interest in Oswald. Similarly, the CIA also falsely denied any pre-assassination interest in Oswald. One can understand and even empathize with the dilemma that the KGB and CIA faced. Oswald was the alleged *lone* killer of

---

973 Bagley, "Ghosts of the Spy Wars," p. 1.
974 See 9/23/78, *Washington Post*, "Helms Clashes with Probe Panel."
975 Tom Tripodi, ***Crusade: Undercover Against the Mafia and KGB*** (New York: Brassey's, 1993), pp. 96-103.
976 Nechiporenko, ***Passport to Assassination***, p. viii.
977 Ibid, pp. 32-49, 54-65.
978 Newman, ***Oswald and the CIA*** (2008), pp. 8-9.

the president and, as Whitten recognized, he was *radioactive*.[979] Yet, Whitten, who was initially given the task of authoring a CIA report to be used by the Warren Commission, made the mistake of poking around in the Agency's secret involvement with anti-Castro Cuban groups and plots to assassinate Castro. The CIA had hired the Mafia to murder Castro by poisoning him. That operation, like the other attempts to assassinate Castro, failed.

Angleton *relieved* Whitten from his assignment and withheld the Agency's Cuban operations from the Warren Commission. But Angleton would end up with much more than Whitten to worry about. The counterintelligence chief became consumed with finding Popov's mole.

Kondrashev's Secret Spy Who Was Never Discovered

I want to close this chapter with two seminal historical moments after the end of the Cold War that I reported in Chapter One of Volume II. One of them was the first meeting between two of the Cold War's most important spy chiefs: the CIA's Tennent Bagley and the KGB's Sergey Kondrashev. At a March 1994 gathering of retired spy-service veterans—two from the East and two from the West—Bagley and Kondrashev had their first ever conversation in a quiet corner of a breakfast room.

Within *minutes* into their discussion, old mysteries *rushed* into Bagley's mind. In particular, Bagley was thinking about Vladislav Kovshuk's trip to the United States in January 1957. Bagley decided to take a chance and ask Kondrashev about it. "Tell me, then," Bagley said without preamble or explanation, "there is something that has been bothering me for a long time. Why *ever* did Kovshuk make that trip to Washington?" Kondrashev could have deflected the question or pretended ignorance, but instead he answered *matter-of-factly* and *right away*, "Oh, that was to meet an important agent." After a brief pause, he added, "*One who was never uncovered.*"

Just ten minutes into their acquaintance, the Soviet spymaster had confirmed that Popov's mole in fact existed *and* had never been caught. Bagley recalled:

I nodded. "Yes, I've *long* thought so" (as indeed I had), and then dropped the subject. To dig for the identity of that still-hidden spy would surely force him to pull back. We smiled at each other, knowing how exceptional our exchange had been.[980]

The other seminal moment I am referring to occurred during a meeting between Bagley and British researcher Malcolm Blunt. They had developed a close friendship over the course of many years. Early on, both had set aside their differences; Blunt's

---

979   12/13/63, CIA "Draft Report on Oswald's Stay in Mexico City," by John Whitten, AKA John Scelso; RIF 104-10414-10414. "When the name Lee Oswald was heard, the effect was *electric*."
980   Bagley, ***Spymaster***, see pp. ix-xiii.

belief that there was a conspiracy to kill President Kennedy, and Bagley's belief that Oswald was a "nut" who got lucky.

It was during a meeting in 2012 that the most *telling moment* in their relationship took place. Malcolm Blunt laid out in front of Pete Bagley, *piece by piece*, the documents demonstrating the *capture of the Oswald paper trail* by the Security Office's Security Research Staff after Oswald's defection in 1959. Bagley had not arrived in the Soviet Russia Division until September 1962. As such, Bagley was *not present* for Oswald's 1959 defection in Moscow *and* the subsequent subversion of the dissemination of Oswald's records inside the CIA.

However, Bagley was a quick study. As *soon* as Blunt put the defection records and their original locations in front of Bagley, right *out of the blue* Bagley asked Blunt: "Okay. Was he *witting* or *unwitting*?" Bagley knew Malcolm would have no trouble understanding that he was referring to Oswald. Blunt replied, "You *can't* ask me that question, how would *I* know?"

At this, and raising his voice, Bagley responded, "*No, No, you have to know*! Was he *witting* or *unwitting*?" Challenged in this manner, Malcolm had little choice but to proffer a guess. With some *reluctance* he replied, "*Okay,* unwitting." With even firmer emphasis Bagley countered, "*OH NO—HE HAD TO BE WITTING!*" Malcolm believes that in that *instant* Bagley saw that this high school dropout, a nothing, a nobody, may have indeed been utilized by the Agency. *Lee Harvey Oswald had been a witting false defector.*

Oswald's defection occurred during the middle of this spy wars saga. At the end of that epic, Oswald's activities in Mexico City implicated Castro and the KGB in the Kennedy assassination. Neither Castro nor the KGB *had anything to do* with the assassination of President Kennedy. While that is my considered opinion and the result of 25 years of studying many thousands of formerly classified documents, it is beyond the scope of this chapter. In Volume V, I will deal with this—*still the darkest*—chapter in American history.

I want to close with a final remark about the credibility of Kondrashev's and Bagley's recollections. Pete Bagley was one of the best counterintelligence officers of the Cold War era. He personally handled Nosenko's 1962 defection in Geneva. Afterward, he served as Chief of Counterintelligence in the CIA's Soviet Russia Division and then as the Deputy Chief of that division. Bagley's reaction to the documents that Blunt showed him is one of the reasons I have come to the view that Oswald's 1959 defection in Moscow *was* a CIA provocation.

Kondrashev was the most accomplished Soviet counterintelligence officer of the Cold War. He rose to the position of deputy, and then chief of the First Chief Directorate. Moreover, in that capacity he was also responsible for overseeing disinformation operations abroad—including the grandiose deception plan conceived by the head

INTO THE STORM

of the Second Chief Directorate, Oleg Gribanov. *No one was in a better position than Kondrashev to assess the bona fides of Yuri Nosenko.*

In a moment of passion and pity, Kondrashev looked at Bagley and asked, "How could your service ever have believed in that man?"[981]

---

981 Bagley, *Spymaster*, p. 210.

CHAPTER THIRTEEN

RFK AND THE CASTRO ASSASSINATION PLOTS— PART III

This is the final chapter among four chapters devoted to the long-standing controversy over whether Robert Kennedy was involved in a personal campaign with the Mafia to assassinate Fidel Castro. Up to this point, I have mostly avoided alerting the reader to the timing and extent of Sam Halpern's awareness of the real CIA-Mafia plot to assassinate Castro that took place during the years 1960-1962. So far, I have chosen to introduce the reader to the following three case studies:

- Richard Bissell's alleged White House pressures ploy to create an Executive Action assassination program in the CIA in January 1961 (Chapter Seven).
- Sam Halpern's allegations about RFK's personal campaign to use a CIA case officer for contact with the Mafia to assassinate Fidel Castro during 1962 (Chapter Nine).
- Robert Kennedy's routine requests to the CIA for assistance to investigate appeals for help from anti-Castro Cubans during 1962; and Charles Ford's work for RFK on those projects. (Chapter Ten).

In this progressive exposition of events, Chapters Nine and Ten form two separate overlays of events—real or imagined—during the period from March 1962 to the Missile Crisis in October of that year. The first overlay reflects events from Halpern's perspective and the second reflects events from Kennedy's perspective.

INTO THE STORM

The third and final overlay is the subject of this chapter. One of its principal foci is the true story of the CIA-Mafia plot to assassinate Castro. The exclusion of the third overlay until now was necessary to help demonstrate why combining the first two overlays, by themselves, is impossible. They cannot both be true. The third overlay can help resolve this conflict and remove a pernicious incubus from the still unsolved cold case of the assassination of President Kennedy.

Halpern's Close Reading of the Church Committee's Interim Report

What facts do we know about how closely Sam Halpern studied the publications of the Church Committee? A lot. There is no doubt that Halpern had been reading the Church Committee Interim Report very closely from the moment it was released in November 1975. During his interviews afterward, Halpern began citing details selectively from the Interim Report. Naturally, Halpern was very interested in what the Report had to say about him: "*I'm all over the Church Committee Report.* I'm listed as the 'Executive Officer to' or the 'Executive Assistant to' or whatever phraseology."[982]

Within three years of the Interim Report's publication—during his interviews with Ralph Weber and Mary McAuliffe in 1977 and 1978,[983] respectively—Halpern used numerous passages from the Church Committee's Interim Report to substantiate his viewpoints on more than twenty separate occasions. These are just a few examples:

- Halpern discussed the committee's investigation of the existence of the CIA's **ZR/RIFLE** program and an Agency plot related to that program to use Rolando Cubela (**AMLASH-1**) to poison Castro with Black Leaf-40.
- Halpern complained about how the committee's Interim Report was used to "denigrate the Agency."
- Halpern used the committee's Interim Report to illustrate the mistakes in the books of authors like William F. Buckley.
- When authors that Halpern disliked were used as sources for books, he complained that the Church Committee's Interim Report *should* have been used as the source instead.
- Halpern often referred to the committee's Interim Report to support his views about the CIA and the Mafia.

---

982 10/30/97, Ralph E. Weber Interview with Sam Halpern, p. 86; RIF 104-10324-10002.
983 1/15/88, Halpern interview with Mary S. McAuliffe, RIF 104-10324-10003; and 10/30/97, Ralph E. Weber Interview with Sam Halpern, RIF 104-10324-10002.

- Halpern said that the committee's Interim Report accurately described the Special Group (Augmented) work on Operation Mongoose.
- Halpern used the committee's Interim Report to parody Lansdale's use of fire flares from U.S. submarines to convince the Cuban people that the Second Coming of Christ was imminent— "*this business about the Jesus Christ superstar.*"
- Halpern used the committee's Interim Report to back up *his* version of the alleged chewing out of DDP Bissell by the Kennedy brothers in the fall of 1961.

The above examples demonstrate Halpern's proclivity to appeal to the authority of the Church Committee to establish his own bona fides as an expert on Robert Kennedy's alleged campaign to assassinate Castro. Crucially, his penchant to do this reveals much more than he intended and gives us an important tool for evaluating the prominent points of his appalling RFK-Mafia memorial.

Although Halpern was mostly critical of the Church Committee's investigation, its work also gave him an opportunity to upgrade his inaccurate RFK saga beyond its initial boundaries in 1967—when he had delivered it to CIA Deputy Inspector General Scott Breckinridge. The Church investigation gave Halpern an *unanticipated gift* from DDP Bissell. Bissell's *lie* that right after the inauguration the Kennedy brothers ordered the creation of an executive action program to get rid of Castro—by assassination if necessary—became a new cornerstone in Halpern's campaign of defamation against Bobby Kennedy. Here, I will briefly review that subject.

Revisiting Halpern's Use of Bissell's White House Pressures Ploy

In his 1997 interview with Ralph Weber, Halpern revealed that, by chance, during his early 1975 preparations for the Church Committee investigation he had come across what he referred to as "the original papers about the **ZR/RIFLE** activity." With characteristic sarcasm, Halpern said this is what he discovered:

> ...one of the first things that John Kennedy, John, not Robert, asked Dick Bissell for in January 1961 after he had gotten inaugurated, one of the first things was an assassination capability. Nobody in particular in mind. Just an assassination capability. "Create one please." *And that's when Bissell got ahold of Bill Harvey and **ZR/RIFLE** was created.*
> [Emphasis added]

INTO THE STORM

Halpern also gave Weber what—from our vantage point today—was an important new piece of his Bissell **ZR/RIFLE** stratagem: "I didn't know, I'd never heard of it until after the thing hit in 1975."[984]

In the months immediately prior to the publication of the CIA Inspector General's (IG) ***Report on Plots to Assassinate Fidel Castro***, Deputy IG Scott Breckinridge interviewed Halpern. He revealed his theory of the RFK-Mafia plot *as it stood at that point in time*: Bobby "directed the CIA to provide an operations officer to meet with Mafia figures identified by Kennedy" whom he assumed had "channels into Cuba to protect such remaining assets as they might have there."[985]

From Breckinridge's summary of the account provided by Halpern during those interviews, we can discern that assassination had not yet been included in Halpern's RFK-Mafia myth. The Breckinridge summary did not appear until the 1995 publication of his book, ***CIA and the Cold War***.[986] Moreover, we learned that Breckinridge had *not* revealed the CIA's Executive Action program and the cryptonym eventually used for it—**ZR/RIFLE**—to Halpern. Although Breckinridge found that Halpern's RFK account merited a mention in his 1995 book, that account did *not make the cut* for inclusion in the 1967 IG Report.

And so, in 1975 Halpern discovered a *shiny new detail* to insert into his RFK-Mafia paradigm: *assassination*. The Church Committee conducted a vigorous investigation of the CIA's Executive Action project (**ZR/RIFLE**). In previous chapters I mentioned that the principal feature of this program was the creation of a "standby assassination capability."[987] The committee reported that in early 1961 DDP Bissell instructed William Harvey—then chief of the CIA's Foreign Intelligence (FI) staff—to establish an Executive Action capability in the CIA.

But that capability had already been in existence for six months before JFK was inaugurated. It was an Eisenhower program targeting Castro and other foreign leaders to be assassinated by the Mafia. The plan was put into motion in August 1960, when DDP Bissell asked the Security Office to locate an asset to perform a "gangster-type operation."[988]

While this program was eventually given the CIA cryptonym **ZR/RIFLE**, one should *not conflate*—as many observers have done, *including Sam Halpern*—the date that cryptonym was first used with the date that the assassination program began. The mistake of conflating those two dates resulted in the presence—in many studies and investigations, including the 1967 CIA IG Report—of the incorrect conclusion that the CIA's

---

984 10/30/97, Ralph E. Weber Interview with Sam Halpern, p. 99; RIF 104-10324-10002.
985 Breckinridge, ***CIA and the Cold War***, p. 95.
986 Breckinridge, ***CIA and the Cold War*** (Westport, Connecticut: Praeger, 1993).
987 SSCIA Interim Report, p. 37; see also 00/00/00, CIA blind memorandum, "Highly Sensitive Activities," RIF 104-10310-10259.
988 Church Committee Index card, RE the 23 May 1975 testimony of former CIA Director William Colby.

RFK AND THE CASTRO ASSASSINATION PLOTS—PART III

Executive Action capability was first put into place by the Kennedy Administration. Halpern quickly embraced this misconception.

What Halpern Really Knew Versus What He Said about Bissell's White House Pressures Ploy

While reading the Church Committee's Interim Report in late 1975, Halpern discovered that Bissell's first deposition to the committee contained a fictional account about a White House order to create an Executive Action capability in the CIA. Knowing full well that such an order had never been issued by the Kennedys, nor anyone else in the White House—and that *Bissell had confessed that the Kennedy order never happened*—Halpern nevertheless took the position that the brothers had twice ordered Bissell to create an assassination program. Halpern exploited that false story for the rest of his natural life.

Why did Halpern do this? Because he wanted to use it as evidence that RFK was favorably disposed, if necessary, to the assassination of Castro. Halpern also used this ploy to buttress his claim that RFK directed the CIA to provide an operations officer to meet with Mafia figures capable of arranging an assassination.

As I discussed in Chapter Seven, Bissell's claim that the White House had twice ordered him to create an Executive Action capability was a ploy to get Harvey to arrange Castro's assassination *before* the Bay of Pigs invasion. Yet, on *six* separate occasions during Bissell's 9 June 1975 appearance in the witness seat before the Church Committee, Bissell claimed that he had no memory of receiving any request from the Kennedy White House about establishing a capability for assassination.

In disbelief, Senator Church insisted that what Bissell was saying seemed strange. Church pointed out that Bissell *must have had personal knowledge that such an assassination capability already existed and was underway*. Again, Bissell agreed but reiterated that he had no recollection of having done so. Fed up at that point, Church countered with this: "*I can't understand why you would keep that matter concealed in the face of a direct request by the White House to develop a capability.*" Once again, all that Bissell could do was agree.[989]

From this confrontational exchange, it is obvious that Senator Church *already knew the truth*—that the CIA's Executive Action program began in the summer of 1960, during the party nominating conventions for the presidential election. What Church did *not* know was the reason behind Bissell's story. In Chapter Seven, I argued that Bissell's White House pressures ploy was a desperate ruse to save his Bay of Pigs operation and, crucially, *his anticipated promotion to become the new Director of Central Intelligence.*

---

989   6/9/75, Bissell SSCIA deposition, pp. 48-53. 81; RIF 157-10011-10020.

INTO THE STORM

The details of Bissell's bizarre performance during his *six* sworn depositions before the Church Committee are fulsomely set forth in the committee's various publications of 1975 and 1976. I have already established that we know Halpern carefully studied those reports. Halpern was fully cognizant of Bissell's poor performance during those depositions *and* of the fact that during Bissell's first deposition he had said that the January 1961 activation of the Executive Action program "may have been initiated within the Agency"![990]

And so, what are we to make of Halpern's declaration—that he stuck to doggedly for the remainder of his life—that in January 1961 the president twice ordered Bissell to create an Executive Action capability in the CIA? Halpern was not just wrong. The truth is that *he knew* he was wrong; *he knew* that Bissell's story was a sham; *he knew* the story was concocted to get Harvey to arrange for Castro's assassination; and *he knew* he was perpetrating a lie about the Kennedy brothers. Halpern also understood how valuable that lie was to his allegation that Bobby Kennedy was behind a plot to use the Mafia to assassinate Castro.

Revisiting Bissell's Story about Being Scolded by the Kennedy Brothers in October 1961

Chapter Ten introduced an *alleged* account by DDP Bissell that he had attended a meeting in the Cabinet Room of the White House in mid-October 1961. He said he had been chewed out by President Kennedy and Attorney General Robert Kennedy for doing nothing to get rid of Castro. The source of that allegation was Sam Halpern. In his 18 June 1975 deposition before the Church Committee, Halpern testified that in a later meeting with Bissell he had learned about that dressing down by the Kennedy brothers. According to Halpern, Bissell said he had been chewed out by the Kennedy brothers for, as he put it, sitting on his ass and not doing anything about getting rid of Castro and the Castro regime.[991]

In his 18 June 1975 Church Committee deposition, Halpern testified that Bissell ordered he (Halpern) and his then boss, Goshen Zogbey, to carry out the Kennedys' instructions to "get rid of Castro." When asked if those plans included assassination, Halpern testified, "*The subject never came up per se.*"[992] In a 1988 interview, when Halpern was not under oath, he was more succinct: "It didn't mean assassinate him, per se, it just meant change the government. But if it meant assassination, fine, too."[993] In fact,

---

990 Ibid, p. 53.
991 6/18/75, Halpern SSCIA deposition, pp. 8-9; RIF 157-10002-10087.
992 Ibid.
993 1/15/88, Halpern interview with Mary S. McAuliffe, p. 18; RIF 104-10324-10003.

RFK AND THE CASTRO ASSASSINATION PLOTS—PART III

in 1975 Senator Church told the committee that his interpretation of Halpern's story was "*to use the Mafia for the purpose of assassinations.*"[994]

Under oath, Bissell denied three times remembering *any specific occasion* on which he suffered the above alleged scolding by the Kennedy brothers.[995] There is no record of that White House meeting in the State Department Foreign Relations series. There is no indication of such a meeting in the NARA JFK records collection—other than Halpern's hearsay. There is no independent record in the memoirs of those who knew the president. Citing the Church Committee's Interim Report, Arthur Schlesinger, Jr. mentioned the possibility of such a meeting but added that Bissell had no memory of it. Halpern was aware that Bissell had no memory of this event. Nevertheless, like Bissell's January 1961 White House pressures ploy, the alleged Cabinet Room reproach became a permanent part of Halpern's RFK-Mafia medley.

The more interesting question is this: What was Bissell doing with this sorrowful story? The circumstances of Bissell's life in the fall of 1961 may provide the answer to that question. He was experiencing a torturously slow excommunication from the Kennedy inner circle for his lack of candor and inept handling of the Bay of Pigs invasion. It matters less whether Bissell endured Bobby's disdain in the grandiloquent setting of the Cabinet Room or alone in the unadorned moments of settling his affairs for the last time. As I mentioned in Chapter Nine, Bissell decided to leave DDP Helms with a *live hand grenade*—an assassination plot against Castro on steroids—*still unknown* in the White House.

What Halpern *Knew* about Bissell's Order to Harvey to Take Control of the CIA-Mafia Plot to Assassinate Castro

There is *nothing* in the documentary record and all of the literature on American anti-Castro activities more upsetting to Halpern's RFK-Mafia myth than the history of Harvey's tenure as the administrator of the CIA-Mafia plot to assassinate Castro. Halpern's RFK-Mafia myth cannot coexist with the true CIA-Mafia plot to assassinate Castro. Harvey was also Halpern's direct supervisor. Halpern claims Harvey never told him about the plot. If so, then Halpern had a big surprise when he discovered all of the details of that plot carefully laid out in the Church Committee's 1975 Interim Report (***Alleged Assassination Plots Involving Foreign Leaders***).

By November 1975, Halpern was thoroughly familiar with the CIA's contact with, and use of, the Mafia *before and after* the Bay of Pigs; at what level these Mafia plots were

---

994 6/18/75, Halpern SSCIA deposition, p. 3; RIF 157-10002-10087.
995 7/22/75, Bissell SSCIA deposition, pp. 36-38; RIF 157-10011-10017.

INTO THE STORM

known about and authorized *inside and outside* of the CIA; and, the CIA's activities with respect to the Mafia *preceding and during* Operation Mongoose.

Halpern also knew the details about the following subjects:
- Harvey's passing of poison pills to Roselli
- Details of Harvey's testimony about the Special Group, the Special Group (Augmented), and events surrounding the 10 August 1962 meeting during which Lansdale slipped up by using the term "liquidation" for disposing of Cuban leaders
- Roselli's three depositions to the Church Committee
- Roselli's activities in the provision of "pure intelligence" about what was happening in Cuba
- How the Agency's use of Roselli could lead to embarrassing demands from him in later years
- How and when Harvey brought Helms into the picture about his (Harvey's) recruitment and use of Roselli
- Harvey's testimony about his discussions with Bissell on Mafia figures including Roselli, Giancana, and Maheu
- What the investigations of Giancana and Roselli revealed about their involvement in the CIA's assassination plots to the FBI, Department of Justice, Attorney General Robert Kennedy and the President.

In short, there was very little about the true CIA-Mafia plot that Halpern didn't know. Halpern *knew* that Bissell had instructed Harvey to take over responsibility for Mafia contacts and that (in his 11 June 1975 deposition[996]) Bissell had acknowledged that the purpose of the CIA's contact with the Mafia *was* the assassination of Castro. Halpern, *knew* the details of the CIA assassination operation involving Maheu, Roselli, and Giancana.

Halpern *knew all about* the 7 May 1962, CIA Inspector General (IG) Lawrence Houston and CIA Office of Security (OS) Director Sheffield Edwards briefing of Attorney General Robert Kennedy (see Chapter Ten) that took place at RFK's request. Halpern *knew* how upset Kennedy was when he learned that the CIA had used Giancana and that Bobby had "then issued orders to CIA to never again in the future take such steps without first checking with the Department of Justice."[997] Halpern *knew* about Edwards' memorandum after the briefing stating that RFK had been told that the operation had begun in August 1960 and had ended by May 1961.[998] In other words, Halpern *knew* that Harvey's management of the CIA-Mafia plot continued during 1962 *behind*

---

[996] 6/11/75, Bissell SSCIA deposition, p. 19; RIF 157-10011-10017; see also, SSCIA Interim Report, p. 188.
[997] SSCIA Interim Report, pp. 131-133.
[998] Ibid.

RFK AND THE CASTRO ASSASSINATION PLOTS—PART III

the attorney general's back and *against* his orders. Halpern *knew* that DCI Helms testified that he was unable to explain the "fun and games" going on between the officers involved, and if they intended to create a fiction about whether the Mafia plot was still going on or had been terminated.[999]

One can only imagine what went through Halpern's mind when he read these eye-popping whoppers about Harvey's CIA-Mafia reminiscences *published* in the Church Committee Interim Report. Halpern *knew* that at the time of the 7 May 1962 briefing for RFK, Harvey had just been introduced to Chicago mobster Johnny Roselli and Cuban exile leader Manuel Varona. Halpern *knew* that Harvey had overseen the provision of the lethal pills, arms, and related support equipment to the Mafia. Halpern *knew* that RFK believed he had received a commitment from the CIA that they would comply with his order to inform him before any future activity with the Mafia took place.

We need no imagination to figure out what Halpern did with all of this information about Harvey's trysts with the Mafia and all of the lies to Robert Kennedy. He denied knowing anything about it!

What Halpern *Said* about Harvey's Takeover of the CIA-Mafia Plot to Assassinate Castro

Eleven years after the publication of the 350-page Church Committee Interim Report titled **Alleged Assassination Plots Involving Foreign Leaders**, Ralph Weber interviewed Halpern.[1000] In that 30 October 1987 interview, Halpern was still struggling to reconcile his own RFK-Mafia myth with the truth about Harvey's management of the real CIA-Mafia plot to assassinate Castro. I mentioned this moment briefly in Chapter Nine. Here, I will deal more fully with how Halpern struggled with the truth. About half way through the 200-page transcript of that interview, Weber brought up the subject of assassination. In less than sixty seconds, Halpern mentioned Bill Harvey's use of the Mafia.

Weber asked, "How about the assassination? Did that business surprise you when it came out?" The ambiguity of Weber's question mattered less than Halpern's visceral reaction to the word "assassination." A stream of disorganized discourse erupted as Halpern's awareness descended into a subconscious zone still suffering from the damaging effects of the new experience learned from the Interim Report. With no pause to disentangle new memory from old, he blurted out:

> No, because I was involved with one. Some of the others that I had known about, yeah, sure, *it wasn't in my area. So, I wasn't involved, I didn't*

---
999 Ibid.
1000 10/30/87, Ralph E. Weber Interview with Sam Halpern; RIF 104-10324-10002.

know. The one I was involved in was the one ... against Castro. One of the one's against Castro. *I did not know about the use of the Mafia by Bill Harvey.*[1001] [Emphasis added]

Until a psychiatrist examines Halpern's schizophrenic reply, the following observations will have to suffice. One notices that two separate assassination attempts were entangled in Halpern's answer. His focus jumped back repeatedly to an older memory, apparently threatened by a newer experience.

First, Halpern mentioned the older recollection—the assassination attempt in which he *had* been involved and *had* talked about many times—the 1963 CIA plot using Rolando Cubela [**AMLASH-1**] to assassinate Castro. Yet, in a split second, that older *safe* memory was overwhelmed by awareness of a *disturbing* newer memory of another assassination plot lurking in the depths of Halpern's consciousness.

Halpern was referring to the assassination plot that was bothering him when he blurted out, "*it* wasn't in my area. I wasn't involved." Then, like a butterfly, his awareness jumped back to the first attempt that he *had* been a part of—the 1963 abortive Cubela plot. Then, once again, just as quickly, that disturbing obscure experience resurfaced. As it did so, the cat jumped out of the bag: It was the assassination plot in which *his boss had used the Mafia*. That was the plot that had been bothering him—likely from the moment he first learned about it from the committee's Interim Report.

Halpern's admission that he had *not known* about a CIA-Mafia operation run by his boss, Harvey, took Weber by surprise and triggered this lopsided exchange:

Weber: You didn't know about...

Halpern: No, Bill [Harvey]—you think I was *tight lipped*. He [Harvey] *could run rings around me.*

Weber: I can imagine.

Halpern: He'll teach you lessons in how to keep your mouth shut. Oh brother, that guy was great. *No, but I wasn't the only one personally...*[1002]

[Emphasis added]

In order to answer Weber's question, Halpern had narrowed his focus on Harvey's activities to 1962. Then, an obsequious tribute to Harvey's secrecy skill ended abruptly with the unfinished recollection, "but I wasn't the only one personally..."

Ending that sentence would have required revealing the brand-new information that Halpern was struggling with. The completed thought would have looked something like this: "I wasn't the only one *who didn't know about Harvey's use of the Mafia to assassinate Castro.*" And that was the way he *did* complete that thought several weeks later during his interview with Mary McAuliffe. Undoubtedly, reading the committee's

---

1001 Ibid, p. 98.
1002 Ibid, pp. 98-99.

RFK AND THE CASTRO ASSASSINATION PLOTS—PART III

Interim Report had been a startling and humbling experience for Halpern. Feeling left out of Harvey's big CIA-Mafia secret, Halpern consoled himself with the thought that *he wasn't the only one* left in the dark.

The interview with Weber meandered for nearly *three more pages* of text. They talked about topics Halpern was comfortable with, including the White House pressures ploy to create an assassination capability and the 1963 **AM/LASH** assassination attempt against Castro. Then Weber asked Halpern if the **AM/LASH** attempt had created anxiety over the possibility that the operation might be leaked. Halpern responded with several examples of sensitive covert CIA activities that had been cause for such concern. While talking about that, Halpern returned to his own *personal* anxiety:

> So yes, there was that kind of an anxiety in terms of keeping our hand out of the assassination plots as much as possible. *Having been involved in only one of them, I have no idea, for example, if Bill Harvey was mucking around with Roselli of the Mafia. Bill knew how to keep a secret. And even though I was his Executive, I had no idea and I know his deputy had no idea at all.*[1003] [Emphasis added]

This extraordinary admission by Halpern was very revealing. In the middle of this soliloquy was the crucial kernel of a more worrisome *present* anxiety: "I *have* no idea, for example, if Bill Harvey was mucking around with Roselli of the Mafia."

Halpern was saying that he *still*—in 1987—had no idea about what Harvey had been doing with the Mafia in 1962. That was a rare mistake. He would not make it again. We know, of course, that Halpern *had much more than an idea* about Harvey's big secret. We know that Halpern had—only fifteen months before—read the details of *exactly* how Harvey was mucking around with Roselli and the Mafia. We know Halpern *knew* that in April 1962 Harvey had been in Miami with O'Connell, passing the poison pills and other weapons to Roselli and Varona for use in an assassination attempt against Castro.

What are we to make of these awkward moments during Halpern's interview with Weber? Did he lie when he said he had no idea what Harvey had been doing with the Mafia? Had Halpern repressed this unwelcome information immediately or soon after he read it in the Interim Report? Or, was he simply still struggling with a recent unwelcome discovery? I prefer the latter explanation. But we can only guess what went through Halpern's mind the first time he realized the implications of his extraordinary discovery about his boss. Yet, there is no denying that he confessed that—at some point—he had difficulty understanding the implications of Harvey's role in the CIA-Mafia assassination plot against Castro.

1003 Ibid, p. 101.

INTO THE STORM

My suspicion is that Halpern's discovery about the real CIA-Mafia plot was hard to reconcile with his claim that Robert Kennedy was running a virtually identical operation at the same time. The 1987 interview with Weber provides strong evidence about the timing of Halpern's eureka experience and confirms the thoroughness with which he had immersed himself in the Church Committee's Interim Report in 1976.

I want to stress the importance of the *proximity in time* between the moment Halpern learned about Harvey's management of the CIA-Mafia plot and his struggle to make sense of that information during the interview with Weber. That propinquity *affords us a valuable window* into the evolution of Halpern's RFK-Mafia tale. The disturbing details about the real CIA-Mafia plot were on Halpern's mind during the interview with Weber and were *still* on his mind just seventy-five days later.

On 1 January 1988, Halpern was interviewed by CIA History Staff Deputy Chief Mary S. McAuliffe.[1004] When I mentioned that interview in Chapter Nine, I avoided—as I had for the Weber interview—looking at the McAuliffe interview through the lens of what Halpern had learned from reading the Interim Report. Now, I will examine her interview astride what we know that Halpern learned from that report.

Harvey's use of the Mafia to assassinate Castro came up only once. About half way through the interview, McAuliffe observed that Halpern seemed to recall that most of the assassination attempts had occurred under Desmond Fitzgerald in 1963. Halpern took issue with that characterization:

> Not true, not true. The ones I knew about—there's only one basically, the **AM/LASH** (Cubela) operation. The only one I was directly involved in. ...*Under Harvey*, Harvey being a good old bureau [FBI] man, kept his own counsel, and *all of his dealings with Roselli were unknown to me and unknown to his deputy*.[1005] [Emphasis added]

Inconveniently, at that point a phone call interrupted the interview. Moments later, Halpern picked up where he had left off:

> I was commenting about the fact that under Harvey, his dealings with Roselli *were not known to anybody*. They weren't known to Ted Shackley as Chief of Miami (JMWAVE in Miami, the station). They were *not known to Bruce Cheever*, who was Harvey's deputy. They were *not known to me*, Harvey's Exec. Harvey kept his own counsel. And I guess about *the only one who even knew that Harvey had been in touch with Roselli may have been Sheffield Edwards* [CIA Security Director Sheffield Edwards], but Sheffield would never know the details. *Sheffield maybe put Roselli and Harvey*

1004 1/15/78, Halpern interview with Mary McAuliffe; 104-10324-10003.
1005 Ibid, p. 18.

352

together, or at least his Office of Security did, originally, but Harvey wouldn't tell anybody a bloody thing, I'm sure.[1006] [Emphasis added.

The information about Edwards and the security office's introduction of Harvey to Roselli was accurate. Halpern could only have learned about that from the Church Committee's Interim Report.

Clearly, this soliloquy with McAuliffe confirmed Halpern's earlier account to Weber that he "*had no idea*" about Harvey's control of the CIA-Mafia plot when it was taking place. Taken together, the Weber and McAuliffe interviews firmly establish that Halpern's original 1962 RFK-Mafia myth had been contrived in a state of surreal ignorance. The real CIA-Mafia plot, created all the way back in the summer of 1960, was *still* ongoing in 1962—and Halpern didn't know about it!

I find it ridiculous that Halpern's boss, Harvey, knew nothing about a 1962 Mafia assassination plot against Castro under Bobby's direction. At no time during his three depositions before the Church Committee did Harvey say one word about any RFK-Mafia plot—he hated Bobby and certainly would have mentioned it if it were true. And so, let us imagine a scenario in which both Mafia plots were true. Once again, we encounter ships passing each other unnoticed in the night. Incredibly, Harvey was as ignorant about RFK's Mafia plot as Halpern was about Harvey's Mafia plot. It doesn't take a genius to realize that these two virtually identical Mafia plots cannot both be true. There are not enough Johnny Rosellis to go around.

So, Halpern truthfully told both Weber *and* McAuliffe that back in 1962 he had no idea about Harvey's CIA-Mafia duties. He didn't know about it in 1967 either. He learned about it at the end of 1975. By 1978, Halpern seemed to realize that *still being confused* about Harvey's use of Roselli was not an option. Halpern never mentioned the real CIA-Mafia plot in public again.

The RFK-Ford Highlights from the McAuliffe and Latell-Warner Halpern Interviews

Halpern's struggle with the true CIA-Mafia plot did not result in a scaling back of the parameters of his own RFK-Mafia story. On the contrary, the publication of the Interim Report provided new opportunities for Halpern to further flourish his RFK narrative. In this section, I will review and add to what I discussed in Chapters Nine and Ten about Bobby's alleged use of Charles Ford as his Mafia go-to-guy.

Early in the McAuliffe interview, the subject of Bobby Kennedy's pressures on the officers in Harvey's Task Force W (TFW) came up:

1006 Ibid, pp. 18-19.

INTO THE STORM

> Halpern: Oh yeah. *Bobby was on the phone to case officers on the Task Force*, and later the Task Force became SAS. *And Bobby's secretary*—Angie, or Angela—she *was on the phone relaying orders from Bobby, as well.* To case officers, right down in the—we were in the basement…[1007] [Emphasis added] [Note: the SAS was the CIA Special Affairs Staff, an unrevealing name for the Agency Cuban operations component.]

At this point, Halpern discussed a crucial detail of his RFK story that he had avoided mentioning during the Weber interview—Bobby's alleged *exclusive* use of Charles Ford as a personal case officer to the Mafia:

> I remember *we had to have a case officer* [Ford], for example, whose *sole job* was to carry out Bobby's wishes vis-a-vis the underworld—let me call it the gangster world. This case officer was given… an Italian-sounding name. …And his *sole job in life* was to go to the various people that Bobby sent him to, *all underworld types, all across the United States*, because Bobby had the idea that since the underworld had had lots of connections inside of pre-Castro Cuba, that they must have left their own stay-behinds behind there. And therefore, they knew the place, and had the place pretty well wired for information. Knew how to survive. And why the hell wasn't CIA tapping this resource, this marvelous resource? And we had to tap it.[1008] [Emphasis added]

Halpern described for McAuliffe the office atmosphere that resulted from the "pressure" of Bobby's alleged—almost daily—phone interruptions:

> So, *we assigned one guy full time*, and the telephone calls he got from Bobby, right out in the—we had a big front area, the only way we could devise it: there was the Chief's office, the Deputy Chief's office, my office, and then what they called the "big arena," where we had several secretaries out in a big bullpen kind of thing. We had a couple of phones, the outside lines, out in that bullpen. And Charlie was *always* answering the phone or being called to the phone, *because his boss was calling—namely, Bobby.* And, "OK," Charlie would say, "Guess I got another trip to make."
> And so, the pressure was direct. [Emphasis added]

We should note that Halpern did not *explicitly* state that Ford announced—to everyone in the bullpen or just to him privately—that it was Robert Kennedy who made all of those phone calls. But Halpern certainly implied that somehow, he knew it was "always" Bobby Kennedy.

1007 1/15/88, Halpern interview with Mary S. McAuliffe, pp. 15-17; RIF 104-10324-10003.
1008 Ibid.

RFK AND THE CASTRO ASSASSINATION PLOTS—PART III

Halpern claimed that *he* was the one Ford checked in with—before *every* trip. DCI McCone didn't know. DDP Helms didn't know. Halpern said, "*Charlie would stick his head in to me—he wasn't going to bother Bill Harvey...with all those details.*" Halpern insists that Ford would only tell him, "*I'm off again, Sam*, good-bye."[1009] *Conveniently*, Halpern was the *only* person who knew that Ford was working exclusively for Bobby! How privileged Halpern was! No wonder not a word about RFK's alleged use of Ford as a Mafia contact was mentioned by DCI McCone, DDCI Carter, TFW Chief Harvey or *anyone else* in their depositions, interviews and memoirs.

It must be emphasized that, on occasion, Attorney General Kennedy *did* call Ford. Many other outside calls to Ford would have come from outside contacts involved with Ford's work on several CIA operations involving anti-Castro Cubans—operations *unconnected* to requests for help from Robert Kennedy. Furthermore, the calls that Robert Kennedy *did* make to the TFW office had *nothing* to do with Ford contacts with the Mafia. Neither documents and depositions, nor interviews and memoirs, corroborate Halpern's fairy tales about such underworld activities by Ford.

Ford's sworn interview destroys Halpern's RFK-Mafia myth. I find it strange that McAuliffe did not ask Halpern *who* he discussed these Ford Mafia contacts with and *what* exactly was said. Given the potential historical significance of such sensational claims, failure to follow them up during this interview was a grievous waste of a valuable opportunity.

Another ten years passed before Halpern sat down for a lengthy question and answer session in 1998 with CIA interviewers Brian Latell and Michael Warner.[1010] Interestingly, there was *no* mention of the CIA-Mafia plot—let alone Harvey's use of the Mafia. The McAuliffe interview a decade earlier was the last time Halpern ever mentioned it in an interview. These continuities and discontinuities between Halpern's successive interviews are worth paying attention to. They provide valuable insights into Halpern's developing epic tale of RFK's alleged secret mafia machinations.

Let me recapitulate here. There was continuity between the Weber and McAuliffe interviews about Halpern's *initial ignorance* (i.e. in 1962) with respect to Harvey's use of the Mafia. There was discontinuity between those two interviews with respect to Halpern's *later confusion* (i.e. in 1987) about Harvey's use of the Mafia. Finally, both the *initial ignorance* and *later confusion* about Harvey's use of the Mafia had completely disappeared by the time of the 1998 Latell-Warner interview.

We also need to pay particularly close attention to the sudden appearance of unusual surprises in Halpern's RFK narrative. The most striking example of that phenomenon happened during Halpern's interview with Latell and Warner:

1009 Ibid, p. 18.
1010 4/7/98, CIA Center for the Study of Intelligence, Sam Halpern Interview by Brian Latell and Michael Warner, pp. 23-24; RIF 104-10324-10000.

> The *one thing* that I don't know enough about is *when* we had to assign an officer to Bobby Kennedy, *to be used by Bobby Kennedy to make contact with Mafia types* in this country and in Canada. That Bobby Kennedy would pick and set the appointment time and place and our case officer would then go and meet whoever this person was and come back and report to Bobby Kennedy.[1011] [Emphasis added]

It is astonishing that the date of the birth of RFK's alleged secret back channel to the Mafia had suddenly become—after thirty years—the *one thing* Halpern *didn't know enough about*. It defies logic that the master of uncanny memory himself, Sam Halpern, who claimed to have been right in the middle of the assignment of Ford to RFK, would declare—out of the blue—that he no longer knew *enough* about *when* that decision was first made. Was Halpern's blind spot feigned? Something does not add up.

Halpern's RFK-mob scenario defies logic in other ways as well. According to Halpern's putative RFK-Mafia plot, Bobby was not content with creating the conditions in which the Cubans themselves would decide how to dispose of Castro. Halpern's screenplay featured a *central role* for Bobby Kennedy so twisted that he wanted to secretly use the dark levers of power that he had battled against for many years—organized crime. Halpern emphasized RFK's alleged thinking to Latell and Warner this way:

> The theory behind this apparently was that Bobby had some bright idea that *the Mafia* must have left some kind of stay behind network in Cuba because of all of *their interests* that they had in Cuba when Fidel arrived: in *prostitution, gambling, drug running and whatever else was involved*. He *said* they must have had a good stay-behind network and we could get some decent information to what's going on. [Emphasis added]

Note that here Halpern claims that RFK, in fact, made this statement. Halpern kept to himself the identity of the person or persons to whom RFK made such a statement.

And so, the question remains: With so much information about the inner workings of Bobby Kennedy's mind, *what was it* that Halpern still needed to know more about *when* TFW assigned Ford as RFK's case officer? Brian Latell pressed Halpern for more information about *who*, among senior CIA officers, knew about this "secret" relationship between Bobby Kennedy and Charley Ford. Halpern replied that at the top of the Agency only DDCI Marshall Carter knew about it. Halpern added that he was sure Helms "never knew," and that McCone would only have known if Carter had told him.[1012]

Halpern's description of that peculiar *circle of knowledge* helps us today to investigate and discover the bits of true information that Halpern folded into a narrative that wasn't true. Halpern's description of the circle of knowledge inside the CIA about

---

1011 Ibid, p. 16.
1012 Ibid, pp. 19-20.

RFK AND THE CASTRO ASSASSINATION PLOTS—PART III

RFK's use of Ford was a perfect match with his description of the *line of transmission* inside the Agency for an important *true* RFK request for a CIA case officer:

> … the way the request came was *from Bobby to General Marshall Carter, who was then DDCI, to Bill Harvey, and Bill Harvey to me, to pick a case officer to assign to Bobby*. I sat with Bruce Cheever and then, of course, with Bill himself and *we decided on a guy named Charles Ford, Charley Ford*.[1013]
> [Emphasis added]

Bruce B. Cheever was Harvey's deputy. A marine colonel and a decorated member of the U.S. Marine Corps Reserve, Cheever was recalled from Paris by Harvey. Halpern was Harvey's executive assistant.[1014]

Let me be clear about what Halpern was doing with this peculiar *transmission footprint* inside the CIA. That DDCI (Carter) entry point *had* been used for a *true* RFK request for use of a CIA case officer in an *acknowledged* Cuban anti-Castro operation. Halpern inserted that identical transmission footprint into an *imaginary* RFK request for use of a CIA case officer in a *secret* Mafia operation.

Crucially, Halpern did *not* tell Latell and Warner *when* Kennedy's request led TFW to come to a decision—made by himself, Cheever and Harvey—on Charles Ford as the case officer for RFK. It is not a coincidence that this mysterious missing detail was, in Halpern's words, "the *one thing* that I don't know enough about."

Fortunately for history, the details of the 1962 CIA documents on Robert Kennedy's use of Charles Ford are easy to find. I presented them in Chapter Ten. Those documents establish that the decision to assign Charles Ford *personally* to RFK was made pursuant to an RFK request to General Carter on or about 20 September 1962. Moreover, those same documents prove that Halpern not only knew about the date of that request and Ford's assignment, but also that Halpern was involved in the CIA operation that followed. And, finally, those documents conclusively establish that the operation had *nothing to do with the Mafia*.

All the crucial details in those documents were known to Halpern. His signature can be seen at the bottom of the most important cable—sent to JMWAVE in September 1962—laying out the history of the well-known abortive ELC operation that I presented in detail in Chapter Ten. Halpern chose *not* to share any of those details with Latell and Warner. To have done so would have precluded his use of that peculiar internal *transmission footprint* in his imaginary RFK-Mafia operation. Instead, Halpern hammed up his own role in setting up Ford for that imaginary operation:

> Charley and *I sat* and *we figured out* he's got to have some kind of name to use—*we can't use* Charley Ford. But Charley also had some handkerchiefs

---

1013 Ibid, p. 16.
1014 Stockton, *Flawed Patriot*, p. 123.

and some shirts with CF on it; and rather than risk an exposure of some kind, Charley *and I* sat in *my* office, the ground floor of the building, *and we said,* "How about Charley Rocky Fiscalini?" And ever since then, I always called Charley 'til he died, "Rocky." [Emphasis added]

However, the 1962 CIA documents clearly show that Ford was given the alias Fiscalini six months earlier *in March 1962* for a mission that Halpern had nothing at all to do with. In September 1962, Ford used the alias Don Barton. Halpern's mob movie about Bobby's use of Ford *conflated two separate events* from 1962 and used them as evidence to buttress his false RFK narrative.

As Halpern mused back over the reaction of "people" to his Church Committee testimony, he told Latell and Warner that "people"—Halpern didn't specify who they were—said Ford and RFK *"must have been working on using the Mafia in some kind of assassination plots."*[1015] Latell rightly pointed out that apparently the belief of many scholars that President Kennedy was "fully witting if not involved in assassination plotting against Castro" was based "just on circumstantial evidence." Latell asked Halpern what he thought about that. Of course, Halpern replied that he agreed with their belief:

Yes, I agree with the people who say the same thing because I can't imagine Bobby on his own without telling Brother Jack some of the things he's done and including probably Jack being the inspiration for some of the things that Bobby finally did. I think they were so close together.[1016] [Emphasis added]

And, armed with this foul fiction, Halpern was *Johnny at the rathole*[1017] when Sy Hersh came knocking.

Seymour Hersh Loses His Way in the Dark Labyrinth of JFK Research

Seymour Myron "Sy" Hersh is a controversial political writer of books and articles on national security affairs. His extensive contacts in American national security organizations are responsible for several public revelations about sensitive matters. At the same time, those associations have also rendered his works vulnerable to use as conduits for misinformation—a problem made more difficult by his journalistic style of lax source citation. Like it or not, Hersh's works are part of the landscape on a number of subjects of interest in the body politic, including Vietnam, the Middle East, and the presidency of John Kennedy.

1015 Ibid, p. 18.
1016 Ibid, p. 21.
1017 *Johnny at the rathole* was the moniker that Halpern pinned on Bobby Kennedy.

RFK AND THE CASTRO ASSASSINATION PLOTS—PART III

In my view, *The Dark Side of Camelot* is one of Hersh's poorest performances over the course of his career in journalism. In my current multi-volume series on the Kennedy presidency and assassination, I have found it necessary to address some of Hersh's findings and suppositions. That is the case for this volume. *The Dark Side of Camelot* contains an accounting about a controversial topic discussed in some of the chapters—including this one—of this volume. That topic is an alleged plot by RFK to use the Mafia to assassinate Fidel Castro.

Sy Hersh located and interviewed Sam Halpern for *The Dark Side of Camelot*. By the time Hersh entered the labyrinth of Kennedy research, Halpern's RFK-Mafia montage had already—for more than three decades—seeded the landscape of congressional inquiry and interviews by CIA and quasi-CIA researchers.

Halpern's marquee creation was his mythical RFK-Mafia plot to assassinate Castro. As such, he coveted every opportunity to spread his fictional account to historians, journalists, and documentarians. A golden opportunity in the mid-1990s was presented by *The Dark Side of Camelot*. Halpern was only too happy to add Hersh's journalistic reputation to his vitae by cooperating with Hersh's endeavor to depict the *dark side* of John Kennedy and his brother Robert. The truth is that Halpern couldn't have cared less about the lasting legacy of the many positive political, economic, and social accomplishments of the Kennedy Administration for the United States and the world. Halpern's invective was a projection of his own state of mind: *He* was the person possessed with a fixation.

Hersh Embraces Halpern's JFK Assassination Capabilities Charade

In 1975, the Church Committee investigation exposed the untrue nature of Bissell's White House pressures ploy. By that time, Halpern had seized upon that false story to use as the cornerstone of a much larger false narrative about the Kennedy brothers that has survived to the present day. In 1997, Halpern's account ended up in Hersh's *The Dark Side of Camelot*.

Here, I will begin with the way Hersh presented Halpern's account of Bissell's false claim to Harvey:

> At some point he [Harvey] told a valued colleague, Sam Halpern, the executive officer of Task Force W, what no one in the CIA would ever tell Congress: that Jack Kennedy had *personally authorized Richard Bissell* to set up **ZR/RIFLE** *before* the inauguration. "After the election," Halpern recalled in one of his many interviews for this book, "Kennedy

INTO THE STORM

asked Bissell to create a capacity for political assassination. That's why Harvey set up **ZR/RIFLE**."[1018] [Emphasis added]

The key parties involved in this controversy—Harvey, Bissell, and the president's national security advisor, McGeorge Bundy—had to be deposed multiple times and confer with each other in order to finally establish *who said what to whom*. The result was not good news for Hersh: neither Bissell nor anyone in the White House spoke with JFK about an Executive Action capability or the creation of any assassination capability. This conflicts sharply with Hersh's claim—based on an account from McGeorge Bundy—that "there was *talk of murder in the White House*, and that the men of the CIA had not been on their own in the assassination plotting."[1019] That was a sentence full of dramatic license fit for the movies—but not for the facts that emerged from the investigation.

All of this sworn testimony and information was published in the Church Committee's November 1975 Interim Report, **Alleged Assassination Plots Involving Foreign Leaders**. How Hersh could, in good conscience, cherry-pick his way through all of this evidence and flatly conclude that "Jack Kennedy had *personally authorized Richard Bissell* to set up **ZR/RIFLE**," *should* be beyond belief. But, after my thirty years of exposure to Kennedy research, there is almost nothing I find beyond belief.

Sy Hersh's Strange Embrace of Halpern's RFK-Mafia Myth

Here, I will begin with a short summary of Hersh's version of the alleged RFK-Mafia plot as told in **The Dark Side of Camelot**:

> Bobby Kennedy, increasingly impatient with the lack of progress in Cuba, decided in *the early spring of 1962* to run his *own* operation. He once again moved into the back channel, as he had done with the Soviets, *this time working with the Mafia*. On his orders, an experienced clandestine CIA operative named Charles Ford was assigned as the attorney general's personal agent. *Kennedy's unprecedented request went up the chain of command to General Marshall Carter, the new deputy CIA director, for approval.*[1020] [Emphasis added]

According to Hersh, the pressure from Robert Kennedy to use the Mafia was "further humiliation for the men of Task Force W." Not surprisingly, Hersh's notes gave no clear indication of his source for the humiliation he says CIA officers endured.[1021] However,

---

1018 Hersh, **The Dark Side of Camelot**, p. 192. Note: Most accounts differ with the timing of such a presidential authorization, and instead place it just after Kennedy's inauguration.
1019 Ibid, p. 190.
1020 Hersh, **The Dark Side of Camelot**, p. 286.
1021 Ibid, see Chapter Notes, "Target Castro," p. 468.

RFK AND THE CASTRO ASSASSINATION PLOTS—PART III

we know that Hersh had read the 1993 book ***CIA and the Cold War*** by CIA Deputy Inspector General Scott Breckinridge[1022] and that Hersh interviewed Breckinridge for ***The Dark Side of Camelot***. A close read of the Breckinridge manuscript reveals that he was the likely source for Hersh's allegation about RFK's humiliation of CIA officers in TFW:

> *It was not at all easy or comfortable* for CIA operations officers to carry out unprofessionally conceived clandestine activities run by a young man who spoke for the president as few, if any, could. The attorney general's initiative in involving the syndicate is interesting… …*For some it will suggest the genesis of CIA's decision to approach the syndicate again in its plan against Castro during the Kennedy Administration.*[1023] [Emphasis added]

From this, we can see that Hersh upgraded Breckinridge's "not at all easy or comfortable" characterization to "humiliation." Why was RFK's alleged use of Ford so humiliating? Because Halpern was not privy to several of the Agency operations that Ford was involved in. For many years, Halpern's fertile imagination filled in those blanks with furtive Ford escapades for Bobby.

In addition to the above inset comment, Breckinridge made this authoritative declaration:

> Among the initiatives emanating from Mongoose was one arising from a *theory* entertained by the attorney general that the criminal syndicate, the Mafia, must have channels into Cuba to protect such remaining assets as they might have there. *CIA was directed to provide an operations officer to meet with Mafia figures identified by Kennedy under circumstances over which CIA had no control.*[1024] [Emphasis added]

This alleged RFK-Mafia initiative was one detail in what Breckinridge called a "footnote" on the Cuban affair, as told to him by Goshen Zogbey and Sam Halpern.[1025]

Hersh had in mind that long "Cuban footnote" in Breckinridge's ***CIA and the Cold War*** when he [Hersh] made this comment:

> Scott D. Breckinridge, who was one of the authors of the CIA Inspector General's 1967 report on [Castro] assassination plotting, *cryptically described the Ford assignment.* As part of Mongoose, the CIA "was directed to provide an operations officer to meet with Mafia figures identified by Kennedy under circumstances over which CIA had no control." *Breckinridge acknowledged in an interview for this book that he had been told the story by Halpern, and others, during the 1967 inquiry.*[1026] [Emphasis added]

1022 Breckinridge, ***CIA and the Cold War*** (Westport, Connecticut: Praeger, 1993).
1023 Ibid, p. 95.
1024 Ibid.
1025 Ibid, p. 94.
1026 Hersh, ***The Dark Side of Camelot***, p. 287.

INTO THE STORM

From all of the above, we can discern that on some points the transmission line for the RFK-Mafia plot was from Halpern to Breckinridge (1967) to Hersh (mid-1990s); and on others it was Halpern directly to Hersh—also in the mid-1990s. Crucially, the treatment of the RFK-Mafia myth by Breckinridge and Hersh indicates that this tale goes back at least as far as the spring of 1967.

Hersh's observation that the years prior to the publication of **The Dark Side of Camelot** saw the declassification of thousands of CIA documents was correct—and also relevant to what was missing in Hersh's book. In Chapter Ten, I listed and discussed the extensive release of those CIA documents. They showed what Robert Kennedy was *really* doing with Charles Ford and Harvey's Task Force W during the crucial months of 1962. That was the same period, according to Halpern, during which RFK secretly used Ford to maintain a secret back channel with the Mafia.

When I compared the CIA documentary record of what Bobby Kennedy was *actually* doing against what Halpern claimed RFK was *surreptitiously* doing, Halpern's malicious myth *fell flat on its face.* Halpern's signature on the most detailed account of RFK's work with Ford undermines his phony account of a secret Ford-Mafia back channel for Bobby.

Hersh's account about Charles Ford's activities for Bobby Kennedy is *completely uninformed* by the relevant CIA documentary record. Instead, Hersh relied almost *entirely* on what Halpern told him:

> It was also possible, Halpern said, that *Bobby Kennedy's primary purpose* in dealing with Charles Ford was to do what Bill Harvey was not doing—*find someone to assassinate Fidel Castro.* "*Charlie saw Kennedy in his office and of course talked to him on the phone quite regularly,*" Halpern told me. "*Charlie was a good officer, and Bobby was his case officer. Charlie never reported that kind of information to me. He may never have reported it to anybody.* He was Bobby's man. Nobody's going to touch him.'[1027] [Emphasis added]

The details in this account reflect evidence that Halpern borrowed from a different story—*the true story of Ford's work with Robert Kennedy* preserved in a plentiful collection of CIA documents. *Of course,* Ford saw Kennedy in his office. *Of course,* Ford talked to Kennedy on the phone. They were working—along with General Carter, Harvey *and Halpern*—on the CIA operation to reign in the abortive September 1962 ELC uprising in Santiago Province.

Unlike Halpern's crazy claim that Ford told *no one* about his work for RFK, the truth is that Ford told *everyone about it.* Ford *did* report his activities with Bobby to Halpern. Ford *did* report those activities to Harvey; and Ford *did* write a lengthy memo to Harvey

---

1027 Ibid, p. 286.

RFK AND THE CASTRO ASSASSINATION PLOTS—PART III

about his meeting in Bobby's office and their work on the ELC operation. Halpern himself *did coordinate and sign off on the entire operation* in a crucial cable to JMWAVE.

The Beginning of the End of Halpern's Uncanny Memory

There is no reason to doubt that Hersh clearly understood what Halpern had told him. So, what we have—forever encased in concrete in Hersh's book—is the most damaging debunking of Halpern's RFK-Mafia myth *in Halpern's own words*. It defies logic that Halpern would have *purposely* provided an account so senseless that it collapsed his thirty-year-long sensational claims about Robert Kennedy. Ironically, Hersh did not understand the evolution of Halpern's RFK fiction.

Previously, I mentioned that Halpern eventually became unsure about when Ford's assignment for RFK *began*. The same thing happened for when that assignment *ended*. In his mid-1990s interviews with Hersh, Halpern reported that Ford's assignment for RFK *ended* in November 1963:

> *Ford spent the next eighteen months [after the early spring of 1962], until the assassination of President Kennedy,* making secret trips, at Bobby's direction, to Mafia chieftains in the United States and Canada, while continuing to serve with Harvey and Halpern on Task Force W.[1028]
> [Emphasis added]

In his 1998 interview with Latell and Warner, Halpern *changed his mind* about when Ford's assignment ended. On that occasion, Halpern reported that Ford's assignment for Robert Kennedy *ended* in November 1962: "Charley's activities stopped after the Missile Crisis."[1029]

What caused Halpern *in 1998* to eliminate the final twelve months—November 1962 to November 1963—from his original story about Ford's assignment for RFK? That question is all the more interesting because that was when Halpern *also changed his mind*—in a strange way—about *when* Ford's assignment for RFK *began*. Halpern did not switch the beginning of Ford's assignment to a new date. Instead, Halpern told Latell and Warner that he was no longer certain about *when* Ford's assignment began: "The *one thing* that I don't know enough about is *when* we had to assign an officer to Bobby Kennedy, *to be used by Bobby Kennedy to make contact with Mafia types.*"[1030]

So, suddenly in the same 1998 interview, Halpern cut out the last half of Ford's assignment for RFK *and* pleaded what amounted to a loss of memory about when the

---

1028 Hersh, ***The Dark Side of Camelot***, p. 286.
1029 4/7/98, CIA Center for the Study of Intelligence, Sam Halpern Interview by Brian Latell and Michael Warner, p. 19; RIF 104-10324-10000.
1030 Ibid, p. 16.

INTO THE STORM

assignment began. There were *no longer two parallel Mafia plots* to assassinate Castro. Halpern *told* Hersh that Harvey was *not looking for someone to assassinate Fidel Castro*. Halpern *told* Hersh that Bobby Kennedy's primary purpose in dealing with Charles Ford was to do *what Bill Harvey was not doing*.

Halpern had finally reconciled the true CIA-Mafia plot with his own *skewed memory* of RFK's alleged Mafia plot. Apparently, the celebrated master of uncanny memory was losing *his* memory. Halpern died of dementia in 2005.[1031] Apparently, the symptoms of this cruel disease were already in evidence during Hersh's interviews of Halpern ten years earlier.

To properly vet Halpern's RFK-Ford narrative, we must consult the copious CIA documentary record of Ford's activities. Behind Halpern's false façade of a secret RFK-Mafia back channel, the true facts reveal a very different story. They tell us about Bobby's routine referrals to the CIA of requests for assistance he had received from anti-Castro Cubans. Some were seeking help for Cuban exiles imprisoned in Cuba since their capture in the Bay of Pigs invasion. Others were planning sabotage operations inside Cuba.

Those referrals to the Agency led to Bobby's work with Ford on CIA operations—operations *connected neither* with the Mafia *nor* with assassination plots by the Agency or Bobby. The CIA documents pertaining to those operations and Ford's use by the attorney general are in the National Archives where they have been *in the open* since the mid-1990s. Hersh's book shows no awareness of this rich CIA documentary record. I should add that, curiously, those revealing documents are not found or mentioned in the countless books written on the JFK assassination. They are described and quoted for the first time in this Volume.

The single most devastating document debunking Halpern's RFK-Mafia fabrication is Ford's sworn testimony to the Church Committee.[1032] Ford categorically rejected the claim that he was *ever* directed to establish contacts with Giancana, Roselli, or anyone else in the underworld. Although Hersh mentioned Ford's name several times in connection with Halpern's fabricated RFK story, Hersh never mentioned Ford's sworn testimony.

Roselli's participation in two separate and simultaneous mob plots to kill Castro was an intractable problem. Although that scenario stretched the limits of credibility beyond all reason, by then Halpern was too fully invested in his RFK-Mafia marquee to walk it back. Over the course of the next twenty years, Halpern adjusted what he would continue to say and what he could no longer say. By the time Hersh got in touch with

---

1031 3/12/2005, **Washington Post** obituary on Samuel Halpern.
1032 9/19/75, Charles D. Ford, memorandum, Subject: Interview by Senate Committee Investigators; RIF 104-10310-10119.

RFK AND THE CASTRO ASSASSINATION PLOTS—PART III

Halpern, his memory was confused and fading. It was a cruel end for Halpern and an outcome full of irony for Hersh.

Halpern is dead now. His bumpy ride through the years to protect his legacy RFK marquee is over. That marquee now rests on his AFIO[1033] tombstone, chiseled into Halpern's afterlife in the coverup of the Kennedy Assassination. In the meantime, the battle for the truth in this case has reached a limited hangout: A conspiratorial coverup now in vogue is permitted so long as the Kennedys are to blame.

And, finally, as I mentioned in previous chapters, the truth destroys this malicious piece of handiwork by Halpern and Hersh:

> *Ford, obviously following instructions from Kennedy, relayed nothing to his nominal superiors in Task Force W. "We never got a single solitary piece of [written] information."* Charlie Ford's reports, if they still exist, presumably are among the millions of pages of Robert F. Kennedy papers that *have yet to be released* by the John F. Kennedy Library.[1034]

Unfortunately, Bobby Kennedy did not survive to defend himself against these lies. Those who continue to embrace them today would profit by the following observation by a highly decorated Army officer, Lieutenant General James Gavin: "Let us not lay on the dead the blame for our own failures."[1035]

1033 AFIO—David Phillips' Association of Former Intelligence Officers.
1034 Hersh, **The Dark Side of Camelot**, p. 287.
1035 General James Gavin, "We Can Get out of Vietnam," **Saturday Evening Post**, February 24, 1968. Lieutenant General Gavin was the Commanding General of the 82nd Airborne Division in WWII.

CHAPTER FOURTEEN

INTO THE STORM: MONGOOSE AND NORTHWOODS

Anger is an acid that can do more harm to the vessel in which it is stored than to anything on which it is poured.

—Mark Twain[1036]

Mongoose was poorly conceived and wretchedly executed. It deserved greatly to fail. It was Robert Kennedy's most conspicuous folly.
        —Arthur Schlesinger, Jr., **Robert Kennedy and His Times**

Halpern later acknowledged that he would have considered murdering my father had he confirmed the CIA suspicion that operation Mongoose was just "busy work."
        —Robert F. Kennedy, Jr., **American Values**[1037]

This chapter and the following very short chapter— "Intermission"—are the *beginning* of a journey through the events that really happened in 1962. In the Table of Contents, I refer to those events collectively as a "shipwreck." The intrepid researcher

---
[1036] Also attributed to Lucius Annaeus Seneca the Younger.
[1037] Robert F. Kennedy Jr., *American Values—Lessons I Learned from My Family* (New York: Harper Collins Publishers, 2018), p. 131.

INTO THE STORM

will find any expedition into 1962 blocked by false signposts to roads that lead all journeymen to dead ends. Some of those roadblocks were created in 1961 and 1962, and some were created in the years that followed. In this volume, I have endeavored to explore and expose many of those false paths in Chapters Nine, Ten, Eleven, Twelve and Thirteen in order to clear away the wreckage that obscures our view of the second seminal year of the Kennedy presidency. I will end this volume by *beginning* that journey unshackled by the detritus of deception, and pick up the trail in Volume IV.

The 1962 Kennedy program to topple the Castro regime, Operation Mongoose, was born from the ashes of defeat at the Bay of Pigs. Shortly after that disastrous failure on 22 April 1961, President Kennedy directed retired Army General Maxwell Taylor to chair a "board of inquiry on Cuban operations conducted by the CIA."[1038] In a letter to Taylor that same day, the president instructed Taylor to "take a close look at all our practices in the areas of military, paramilitary, and guerrilla and antiguerrilla activities which fall *short of outright war.*"[1039] The reader must keep that indelible instruction foremost in mind during the examination of Operation Mongoose in the present chapter.

The principal purpose of the Taylor Board of Inquiry was to undertake an assessment of the reasons for the devastating failure of the CIA's Bay of Pigs invasion. The president told Taylor that Attorney General Robert Kennedy was to be his "principal colleague" in that assessment.[1040] Their assessment concluded with this estimate:

> We have been struck with the general feeling that *there can be no long-term living with Castro as a neighbor.* His continued presence within the hemispheric community as a dangerously effective exponent of communism and anti-Americanism constitutes a real menace capable of eventually overthrowing the elected governments in any one or more of weak Latin American Republics.[1041] [Emphasis added]

That dire prophecy was heavily influenced by the president's brother, Robert Kennedy.

On 19 April 1961, as the exile brigade was being cut to pieces on the beachhead, RFK wrote this clarion call to JFK:

> *The time has come for a showdown for in a year or two years the situation will be vastly worse. If we don't want Russia to set up missile bases in Cuba, we had better decide now what we are willing to do to stop it.*[1042] [Emphasis added]

1038 6/13/61, *FRUS*, 1961-1963, Volume X, Cuba, 1961-1962, Document #169, First Meeting of General Maxwell Taylor's Board of Inquiry on Cuban Operations Conducted by the CIA." See also 5/3/61, DIR 37947, Book Message, from **ASCHAM** (Dulles); RIF 104-104-10227-10121.
1039 Ibid, source note.
1040 SSCIA, Interim Report, p. 135.
1041 6/13/61, *FRUS*, Vol. X, Cuba, Document 234, Memorandum No. 4 from the Cuban Study Group to President Kennedy.
1042 4/19/61, *FRUS*, Vol. X, Cuba, Document 157, Memorandum from Attorney General Kennedy to President Kennedy.

The truth was that the Bay of Pigs defeat had been deeply humiliating for the president personally and for the CIA institutionally.

For many of the Pentagon chiefs the defeat in Cuba "broke the dike" of the resentment they felt toward their "no-win" commander-in-chief in the White House. Chairman of the Joint Chiefs of Staff General Lyman Lemnitzer later wrote that the Kennedy Administration was "crippled not only by inexperience but also arrogance arising from failure to recognize its own limitations."[1043] With that censure, Lemnitzer washed his hands of his own responsibility for the arrogant lies he had used in an attempt to manipulate the president into a war in Cuba (see Volume II, *Countdown to Darkness*, Chapter Twenty-Two). In the spring of 1962, Lemnitzer's arrogance would once again be on full display when he attempted to push President Kennedy into war in Cuba *and* Vietnam.

In the months following the Bay of Pigs disaster—and partly because of it—a series of geopolitical aftershocks (see Chapter Four) erupted in Berlin, Congo, Laos, Vietnam, and elsewhere. The Berlin Crisis brought with it the eschatological dimensions of a nuclear Armageddon. President Kennedy understood that the Cuban problem would have to wait until these larger seemingly intractable Cold War challenges had been stabilized.

In this disordered and dangerous context, Lemnitzer was on hand to support the presentation of a plan to the president for a *surprise U.S nuclear attack against the Soviet Union*—exactly the kind of plan that Kennedy did not want. At a White House meeting on 20 July 1961, General Thomas Francis Hickey, Staff Director of the NSC's Net Evaluation Subcommittee, briefed the president on the plan. General Lemnitzer, General Hickey and DCI Dulles told the president that the window of maximum opportunity for a disarming counterforce strike against the USSR's nuclear capability would occur in late 1963— "preceded by a period of heightened tensions."[1044]

I discussed this briefing in Chapter Four and will only briefly recapitulate it here. As James Galbraith explained, the Net Evaluation briefing took place in the context "of an increasing nuclear edge based on a runaway lead in land-based missiles" facing the president in the perilous "nuclear-tinged crisis that erupted over Berlin in July of 1961."[1045] Presidential Special Advisor Arthur Schlesinger, Jr., recalled that Berlin threatened a war that "might destroy civilization," and Kennedy "thought about little

---

1043 2/12/76, Walter S. Poole, JCS, General Lyman L. Lemnitzer Oral History (U.S. Army Center for Military History, Washington, D.C.); cited in Bamford, *Body of Secrets*, p. 81.
1044 7/20/61, Notes on National Security Council Meeting by Colonel Burris. LBJ Library.
1045 James Galbraith, "Did the U.S. Military Plan a Nuclear First Strike for 1963?" *The American Prospect*, Fall 1994, p. 90. On 4 June 1993, the LBJ Library declassified the notes, taken by Vice President Johnson's military aide Colonel Howard Burris, at the 20 July 1961 presentation. The Burris memorandum to LBJ was first published by Dr. James Galbraith of the University of Texas at Austin.

else that summer."[1046] Disgusted, Kennedy "got up and walked right out in the middle of the meeting."[1047] He ordered that the subject of the meeting not be disclosed by anyone attending.[1048]

It is noteworthy that twice during the NSC session, the president obliquely broached a concern that those present could not yet have been aware of: "the president asked for an appraisal of the *trend* in the effectiveness of the attack." Kennedy's next question revealed what was on his mind: "Since the basic assumption of this year's presentation was an attack in late 1963, *the president asked about probable effects in the winter of 1962.*"[1049] Only JFK and RFK knew what that question was about: *how would the strategic balance of power look in late 1962?* Their intention—after dealing with the flash points in Berlin, Laos, and Vietnam—was to reactivate the plan to overthrow Castro. The question was: *what would Khrushchev be able to do about it?*

However, what the Kennedy brothers did not know as they listened to that wretched recommendation of the Net Evaluation Subcommittee was *what the Joint Chiefs*—not Castro and Khrushchev—*would be up to in 1962*. The JCS agenda would be for war. They planned to use the window of American strategic superiority to intervene with U.S. combat forces in Cuba *and* Vietnam.

As Schlesinger observed, the Mongoose plan rightly deserved to fail. And it did. But, not before General Lemnitzer turned it into something outrageous—Operation Northwoods.

Getting Even with Castro

The 1961-1962 period was one of the most dangerous chapters in the history of the Cold War. The Bay of Pigs debacle sparked non-stop xenophobic Cold War sabre rattling over Laos and Berlin. The escalating Cold War had become a runaway train. And, still, the *cancer of Cuba* remained. It was always there, a canker eating away at any remnants of self-confidence and whatever vestiges of an even-tempered psychological outlook remained in the president, and even more so in his brother. The frustration with Castro roiled beneath the surface in the brothers Kennedy, even as they undertook strong measures—quietly but inexorably—to begin the purge in Washington of the officers they held to account for the Bay of Pigs debacle.

The Pentagon chiefs were far from ready to throw in the towel. They still viewed President Kennedy as too inexperienced to handle the constant traps Khrushchev

---

1046 Schlesinger, *A Thousand Days*, p. 391.
1047 Schlesinger, **Robert Kennedy and His Times**, p. 449.
1048 7/20/61, Notes on National Security Council Meeting by Colonel Burris. LBJ Library.
1049 Ibid.

MONGOOSE AND NORTHWOODS

would spring on the Americans. Moreover, the determination of the Kennedy Administration to topple Castro, far from abating as time moved on, evolved instead into a hazardous obsession in the White House. That preoccupation only played into the hands of the interventionists.

Unconcerned with the daunting dangers that lay everywhere on this dark path, JFK and RFK steered headlong into the perilous storm of the Cold War. Their decision produced an ill-fated orphan—Operation Mongoose. Deputy Director of Central Intelligence (DDCI) Marshall Carter privately compared Robert Kennedy's performances at Mongoose meetings to the "gnawing of an enraged rat terrier."[1050] In the end, this path would not just come to be regretted. It would ultimately be deeply lamented. The unforeseen outcome could only be mourned in the darkness and secrecy that enshrouded—then, and even up to the present day—the death of President John Kennedy.

And so, the May 1961 policy assessment of the Bay of Pigs led in November of that year to the tragic decision to implement a *new* covert program to overthrow the Castro regime. President Kennedy wanted all operations to be "kept in a low key" so that nothing "big" could be attributed to the U.S.[1051] At the outset, all concerned paid lip service to the president's rule that "the one thing that was off limits was military invasion." Yet, both the Pentagon *and* the relevant CIA officers were soon unable to comprehend the objective—the creation and sustainment of internal Cuban resistance—without eventual U.S. military intervention. As Schlesinger pointed out, the CIA "was more bent than ever on fighting a war. It proved this by the men to whom it offered command of Task Force W"[1052]—including its chief, William Harvey. I would hasten to add that this resolve was just as applicable—*if not more so*—to the Pentagon.

Through rose-colored glasses the president directed his subordinates to go about overthrowing Castro "short of outright war."[1053] But once the train left the station in early 1962, the Kennedys were dismayed to discover that full U.S. military intervention was being baked into the recommended plan *all over again*. It was as if nothing had been learned from the mistakes of the dreadful experience of early 1961. Possessed by the *rage* born from that experience, the chiefs and certain allies in the CIA resolved to do it again, apparently, they hoped, rightly this time. The Kennedy brothers, too, hoped to get it right this time. Unfortunately, that *hope* was the only difference—and it turned out to be wrong again.

1050 Tim Weiner, *Legacy of Ashes* (New York: Anchor Books, 2008, Paper edition), p. 229.
1051 Schlesinger, *Robert Kennedy and His Times*, p. 477.
1052 Ibid., p. 478.
1053 6/13/61, *FRUS*, 1961-1963, Volume X, Cuba, Document #230, General Taylor Letter to President Kennedy.

INTO THE STORM

What the Kennedys proposed to do no longer meant carrying out a flawed inheritance from the Eisenhower administration. This time the new administration owned the idea *and* the outcome—lock, stock and barrel. And, just as before, the end state—the overthrow of Castro—was plugged into the equation first. Once again, the rest of the equation to bring about the end state was assembled afterward. The history of Operation Mongoose was an excruciating breakdown of the logic of that equation as Kennedy's military bided their time before springing a plan for full-scale war on their commander-in-chief.

Nothing had changed in Cuba that suggested that the same flawed equation could work this time. On the contrary, by the time Mongoose was implemented at the start of 1962 the situation was *far worse* than it had been in the weeks leading up to the Bay of Pigs fiasco. At the outset of the new program, a CIA memorandum warned the Special Group about a systemic *flaw* in Air Force Brigadier General Edward Lansdale's plan for Mongoose:

> The pervasive informant system, efficient propaganda machine, and military and civil suppression are supported by jet fighter, radar, patrol boats, and communications capabilities *far beyond the level of April 1961.*[1054] [Emphasis added]

The CIA predicted that those factors made it unlikely "that we can make the resistance groups self-sustaining as is envisaged in General Lansdale's 'Concept of Operation.'"

Bringing in new people like Lansdale and the CIA's secretive William Harvey to rewrite the same impossible—and now even worse—equation would inevitably degenerate into another exercise in futility. And, as Robert Kennedy had predicted nine months earlier, this time the equation would include Soviet medium-range nuclear-tipped missiles in Cuba aimed at the U.S.

What the Kennedy brothers probably did not know about in January 1962 was an extraordinarily *bad idea* that had surfaced up in the desperate situation of January 1961. During the weeks prior to the Kennedy Inauguration former President Eisenhower and his national security advisor, Gordon Gray, had *suggested the possibility of using the CIA-backed exiles to mount a simulated attack on Guantanamo in order to offer a pretext for overt intervention.*[1055] Eisenhower had told Lemnitzer that he would move against Castro before the inauguration *if* the Cubans gave him a really good excuse and, *if not*, the U.S. "could think of manufacturing something that would be generally acceptable."[1056] In January 1962, Lemnitzer, of course, *did* remember Eisenhower's surprisingly devious

---

1054 1/24/62, CIA Memorandum for the Special Group; RIF 145-10001-10172.
1055 11/3/60, Minutes of Special Group Meeting; RIF 157-10002-10154.
1056 Bissell, *Reflections of a Cold Warrior*, pp. 82-83 and p. 161; see also Stephen E. Ambrose, *Ike's Spies: Eisenhower and the Espionage Establishment* (New York: Doubleday & Company, 1981) p. 609.

suggestion. And this time, Lemnitzer *and* Lansdale were planning to advocate that same false flag proposal again.

Robert Kennedy and the Creation of Operation Mongoose

On 3 November 1961, President Kennedy authorized "the development of a new program designed to undermine the Castro government" codenamed Operation Mongoose.[1057] The president directed his brother Bobby to run the operation. Defense Secretary McNamara said he would make his assistant, General Lansdale, available to RFK, and he assigned Lansdale to make a survey of the Cuban problem and the available U.S. assets to deal with it.[1058]

By this time, the horribly expensive lesson of the Bay of Pigs had already turned the national security apparatus upside down (see Chapter Four). Arthur Schlesinger recalls:

> He [JFK] set quietly to work to make sure that nothing like the Bay of Pigs could happen to him again. The first lesson was never to rely on the experts. He now knew that he would have to broaden the range of his advice, make greater use of generalists in whom he had personal confidence and remake every great decision on his own terms.[1059]

So, the president turned to the people he had personally worked with and trusted the most—the people he had brought in himself. Although Robert Kennedy and Ted Sorensen had not participated in cabinet meetings before the Bay of Pigs, Schlesinger reported that *afterward both were at his right hand at every subsequent moment of crisis for the rest of his presidency*. Kennedy ensured that he had access to the unfettered advice of his own people and gave them license for "impolite inquiry and the rude comment."[1060]

After completing his review of the Bay of Pigs failure, Maxwell Taylor was assigned as the president's advisor on military affairs until he could—after a decent interval—replace General Lemnitzer as Chairman of the Joint Chiefs of Staff. Later, President Kennedy would come to regret this delay in firing Lemnitzer. McGeorge Bundy was moved from the Executive Office Building into the West Wing and given charge of national security affairs. Richard Goodwin was assigned the responsibility for managing the Cuban exiles.

President Kennedy formalized these new structural arrangements in November 1961 at the time Operation Mongoose was created. Consistent with Kennedy's

---

1057 11/3/61, *FRUS*, 1961-1963, Volume X, Cuba, Document #70, Editorial Note.
1058 Ibid.
1059 Schlesinger, *A Thousand Days*, p. 296.
1060 Ibid.

conviction that covert paramilitary operations would no longer be solely under the purview of the CIA, Mongoose involved the coordination of activities between the CIA, Defense Department, and State Department. General Lansdale, head of the Office of Special Operations—and Assistant to the Secretary of Defense—would be charged with the necessary interdepartmental coordination.

For Operation Mongoose, the Special Group (also known as the 5412 Committee) was augmented by Robert Kennedy and General Taylor and thus bore the moniker the Special Group (Augmented). Taylor oversaw the program at the White House, but real power over the management of Mongoose was firmly in the hands of the president's brother, Robert Kennedy. Much to Lansdale's dismay, his daily activities were closely managed by RFK. However, Lansdale would find a way to circumvent Bobby's control.

This passage from Richard Bissell's **Reflections of a Cold Warrior** is an interesting summary of the evolution of Operation Mongoose under the Kennedy brothers:

> From their perspective, Castro won the first round at the Bay of Pigs. He had defeated the Kennedy team; they were bitter, and they could not tolerate his getting away with it. *The president and his brother were ready to avenge their personal embarrassment at any cost.* I don't believe there was any significant policy debate in the executive branch on the desirability of getting rid of Castro. ... Robert Kennedy's involvement in organizing and directing Mongoose became so intense that *he might as well have been the* [CIA] *deputy director of plans for the operation.* ...I never lost sight of *the irony that the same president who had cancelled the air strikes and ruled out open intervention was now having his brother put tremendous pressure on the agency to accomplish even more.*[1061] [Emphasis added]

I find Bissell's recollection accurate with respect to the revenge motive behind Mongoose *and* with respect to the key leadership role Bobby Kennedy played in the unfolding operation. But I disagree with Bissell's implication that *even more than air strikes and open intervention* was what the president was asking his brother to pressure the CIA to accomplish. On the contrary, the president had taken open U.S. intervention off the table. *It was the Pentagon that was emphasizing the eventual necessity for outright war against Castro.*

Bissell, the officer in charge when the Bay of Pigs blew up, was damaged goods. He remained as the nominal DDP for a few weeks into 1962. The new DCI, John McCone, made sure that everyone knew that Richard Helms would be his choice to head the Plans Directorate. His assignment was made official on 17 February 1962. Kennedy's choice of McCone to replace Allen Dulles might have been intended to make the CIA more subservient to presidential authority. If so, it failed to do so.

[1061] Bissell, *Reflections of a Cold Warrior*, p. 201.

MONGOOSE AND NORTHWOODS

On 22 November 1961, DCI John McCone drafted a memorandum recapping a White House meeting held the previous day with President Kennedy, Robert Kennedy, Edward Lansdale, and Richard Goodwin of the White House staff.[1062] The president opened the meeting by explaining that General Lansdale, under the direction of Attorney General Kennedy, had been engaged in a study of possible U.S. actions regarding Cuba. RFK expressed his "grave concern" over Cuba and the need for "immediate dynamic action." He stated that such action would include covert operations, propaganda, and all possible actions to sow dissent in Cuba and discredit the Castro regime.

After the meeting, Lansdale told McCone that he would be going to South Vietnam as a Special Advisor to President Diem. Lansdale added that he would need backup by a "very able officer" on Cuban matters. On 29 November 1961, after a meeting with Robert Kennedy, a McCone memorandum revealed that Lansdale would *not* be going to Vietnam after all. Instead, McCone said, Lansdale would be heading up the new inter-agency group on Cuba. McCone added this revealing comment:

> [Robert] Kennedy resented CIA resistance to this idea, hoped that we would appoint the most able man to the Lansdale committee (not J.C. King) and agreed without reservation that the Lansdale committee must operate under the 5412 [Special Group] Committee.[1063]

The next day, 30 November, in a widely disseminated memorandum, President Kennedy removed all doubt about Lansdale's status as "Chief of Operations" of the new interagency group on Cuba *and* that he was subordinate to Attorney General Kennedy.[1064] RFK's role as Lansdale's boss was only mentioned in the first of the two versions of the president's memorandum. However, there was no doubt in anyone's mind about the fact that RFK was in charge.

And so, when the Special Group met on 1 December 1961, it was no surprise that Robert Kennedy was in charge of matters.[1065] RFK told the group about a series of meetings with President Kennedy and that JFK had decided higher priority should be given to Cuba. In addition, RFK revealed the following:

> General Lansdale had been designated as "Chief of Operations," with authority to call on all appropriate government agencies for assistance, including the assignment of senior representatives from State, Defense and CIA. ... In making this appointment, the need for General Lansdale

---

1062 11/22/61, *FRUS*, 1961-1963, Volume X, Cuba, Document #275, McCone MFR re 11/21/61 meeting on Cuba.
1063 11/22/61, *FRUS*, 1961-1963, Volume X, Cuba, Document #276, McCone MFR re meeting with RFK on Cuba and Lansdale.
1064 11/22/61, *FRUS*, 1961-1963, Volume X, Cuba, Document #278, Memorandum from President Kennedy. There were two versions of this memorandum and in RFK's role as Lansdale's boss was only mentioned in the first version. However, there was no doubt in anyone's mind about the fact that RFK was in charge.
1065 11/22/61, *FRUS*, 1961-1963, Volume X, Cuba, Document #280, Memorandum or the Record on Cuba.

> in the Far East has been recognized but it had been decided that for the time being his responsibility would be Cuba.

The group agreed that Lansdale should develop a long-range program that would be reviewed by the Special Group and presented to higher authority (i.e., the president) for approval.

Lansdale answered to the Special Group to which Taylor had been designated chairman, but no one doubted who the real boss was—Robert Kennedy. Despite his busy schedule, the attorney general regularly checked in on Mongoose meetings:

> … to "needle the bureaucracy." At meeting after meeting, the attorney general stressed that there had to be "maximum effort" and that "there will be no acceptable alibi" for failure. "Let's get the hell on with it," he would say. "The president wants some action, right now."[1066]

From the get-go, Robert Kennedy cracked the whip to get things moving. On 12 January 1962, he met with DCI McCone to ask for his "frank and personal opinion" about Lansdale and the new Cuban program.[1067] That question was really probing for information about the attitude of the CIA officers involved in Mongoose—most notably William Harvey—who would have to work under his (RFK's) direction. McCone answered that this type of operation was "extremely difficult" as it had never been attempted before. McCone added, however, that the Agency was "lending every effort and all-out support."

Lansdale was a snake. Ultimately, his loyalties would be with Lemnitzer, not with the president and his brother. Lansdale was also a control freak. Typically, he would try to get as much control as possible over anything he became a part of. Once coronated as the Mongoose Chief of Operations, he wanted an organizational structure giving him a fiefdom that would include personnel, money and material detailed to him from the Defense and State Departments and the CIA. That idea went over like a lead balloon. Sam Halpern recalled:

> McCone was the first to have said, "Hell no." He said, "That money was appropriated by Congress under my command, my responsibility. It stays with me. We'll work with you and we'll help you, and we'll be part of your team… But I can't relinquish control over men, money, and material appropriated to me. And McNamara said the same thing and Rusk said the same thing—so that they didn't achieve creating a brand-new Agency in effect.[1068]

[1066] Max Boot, *The Road Not Taken: Edward Lansdale and the American Tragedy in Vietnam* (New York: Liveright, 2018), p. 381.

[1067] 1/12/62, *FRUS*, 1961-1963, Volume X, Cuba, Document #287, Memorandum for the Record, McCone meeting with RFK.

[1068] 10/3/87, 10/30/87, Ralph E. Weber Interview with Sam Halpern, pp. 80-81; RIF 104-10324-10002.

CIA DDP Richard Helms remembered that "The notion that the various agencies were simply to detail men, money, and material to Lansdale was dead on arrival."[1069]

After that ignominious start, it was not surprising that Lansdale would cross swords with Harvey. Harvey's fiefdom at the CIA—Task Force W—controlled a significant portion of the operational structure of Mongoose. Harvey would jealously protect it like a bird protecting its nest. He enjoyed telling Lansdale as little as possible about what he was up to. Lansdale, however, knew better than to bite the hand that feeds, and that hand belonged to Bobby Kennedy. The irreverent Harvey was not as good at that. In the end, the attorney general would send Lansdale to dismantle Harvey's part of Mongoose.

The Dysfunctional Mongoose Triumvirate: Robert Kennedy, Edward Lansdale and William Harvey

The Mongoose team that emerged in January 1962 was about as stable as an atom with one proton and five electrons.[1070] In the Kennedy-Lansdale-Harvey threesome the only positive outlook was Kennedy's view of Lansdale, and that was only temporary. Right out of the gate, Lansdale disliked Kennedy and hated Harvey, and Harvey loathed the other two. It is hard to imagine a more dysfunctional triumvirate.

The problem began with the leader of this unlikely trio—the attorney general. Kennedy historian Arthur Schlesinger put it this way: RFK declared that no time, money, effort or manpower would be spared, "but he was never clear how the time, money, etc., were to be used."[1071] Bobby was always dissatisfied with Mongoose: "He wanted it to do more, the terrors of the earth, but what they were he knew not."[1072] This lack of clarity was compounded by the deviousness of Lansdale, whose self-centered egoism was not sufficiently understood by either JFK or RFK—at that point.

The full weight of the pressure Robert Kennedy applied to the administration during Mongoose fell directly on Lansdale. According to Lansdale biographer Max Boot, Lansdale sized up RFK this way:

When he first saw the attorney general at a meeting, Lansdale recalled, he "wondered what the youngster was doing sitting in the meeting talking so much." He didn't connect the man before him "with the pictures

---

[1069] Boot, *The Road Not Taken*, pp. 382-383.
[1070] In this metaphor we have the following: 1 positive charge: RFK View of Lansdale; 5 negative charges: RFK view of Harvey, Lansdale views of RFK and Harvey, and Harvey views of RFK and Lansdale.
[1071] Schlesinger, *Robert Kennedy and His Times*, p. 477.
[1072] Ibid, p. 480.

of him on TV." The mistake was understandable, given that Robert Kennedy was still only thirty-seven years old (to Lansdale's fifty-three).[1073]
Boot claims, I believe correctly, that Lansdale had a practical reason for embracing his new assignment: He wanted to give the Kennedys the very thing they wanted the most—a plan to overthrow Castro— "in the hope that in return they would give him what he wanted most: a return ticket to Saigon.[1074]

That would never happen. And Lansdale abhorred being micromanaged my Robert Kennedy:

> Bobby, Lansdale said, "was the most interested of anyone in the room of what I would say on things and would plague me with many questions." It was hardly surprising that Lansdale chafed under this constant harassment. His friend Rufus Phillips recalled, "While Ed respected the president, he didn't like Bobby worth a damn."[1075]

To comply with his mandate to manage interdepartmental cooperation for Mongoose, Lansdale had no choice but to depend on uninterested liaison officers from those departments.

Many of those liaison officers were skeptical about the CIA, the operation in general, and Lansdale in particular. Lansdale recalled that "It was the most frustrating damn thing I've ever tackled." Lansdale's decrees led CIA operatives to mock him behind his back as "the FM," short for field marshal.[1076] Within the CIA, DDP Bissell initially selected Howard Hunt as the Agency's Mongoose representative. Hunt declined because he felt there was no serious interest in overthrowing Castro.[1077] So, Bissell had chosen the legendary gun-toting Bill Harvey instead. Schlesinger recalls Harvey's eccentric behavior:

> "If you ever know as many secrets as I do," he [Harvey] would say mysteriously, "then you'll know why I carry a gun." Far from wanting the independent Cuban movement envisaged by Lansdale, Harvey was determined to reduce his Cuban operatives to abject dependence. "Your CO [case officer] was like your priest," one of Harvey's Cubans said later. … "You learned to tell him everything, your complete life."[1078]

It was an unlikely threesome. Robert Kennedy found Harvey detestable: Too much "Gunsmoke stance." Schlesinger stated that Lansdale "came to cross purposes with

---

1073 Boot, *The Road Not Taken*, p. 382.
1074 Ibid.
1075 Ibid.
1076 Ibid, pp. 382-383.
1077 Schlesinger, *Robert Kennedy and His Times*, p. 478.
1078 Ibid, pp. 478-479.

CIA and they didn't like his interferences." Lansdale thought Harvey was intensely secretive and effectively paranoid.[1079]

Harvey "writhed under the irksome goading" of Lansdale; and Lansdale hated Harvey. Harvey biographer Bayard Stockton explained:

> To Harvey, Lansdale was worse than wacky. He was a security risk. "Harvey seldom really talked to me," Lansdale said. "He would never initiate conversations. It was very hard to get information from him…. I'd ask for a full explanation, and I'd get one sentence back…. It used to burn me up…. If I was talking to Harvey, and he got a phone call, he'd start talking code. After a while, I caught on and realized he was talking about me. The son of a bitch."[1080]

Years later, Harvey's wife Clara Grace commented, "Fifth Avenue cowboys, that's the way Bill used to describe the Bobby Kennedy group. It hurt me when they made all those derogatory statements about Bill and his backwoods upbringing."[1081]

An aside is appropriate here in view of the deep dislike that both Lansdale and Harvey had for Robert Kennedy. According to Halpern's *uncanny memory*, the central period of Robert Kennedy's use of TFW Special Assistant Charles Ford as a Mafia contact took place during Operation Mongoose. If there was any truth to Halpern's allegations about Bobby's exclusive use of Ford in a secret plot to assassinate Castro, why didn't Harvey or Lansdale—in their depositions and interviews for the rest of their lives—ever say anything about it? The odds of both men—especially Harvey—failing to notice RFK in such an ineffaceable plot is about as likely as a couple of flies that can't smell a cow pie.

As Mongoose unfolded in January 1962, it was astonishing that anything substantial got done at all. The spectacle of the Cuban triumvirate made it easier for Lemnitzer and his team to stay under the radar while the Kennedy Mongoose program took its first awkward steps back into the fault zone that had spawned so much Cold War instability after April 1961. For the moment, Lemnitzer was content to complain about Kennedy's reluctance to put American combat forces in Vietnam. On Cuba, the chiefs remained inconspicuous while turf tussles ran their course in the National Security Council, Special Group and Caribbean Survey Group.

Initially, Bobby's job was to galvanize the Cuban policy apparatus behind Lansdale's guidance and mission hand-outs. However, by the end of February it became apparent to RFK that Lansdale's guidance was coming less from presidential direction than from the Pentagon. Increasingly, it became necessary to reign in Lansdale. At CIA, the Cuban policy apparatus was broken. Harvey cut Helms in on the continuing plot

---
1079 Ibid, 479-480.
1080 Bayard Stockton, *Flawed Patriot*, p. 119.
1081 Ibid, p. 120.

to use the Mafia to assassinate Castro; and together they decided to cut out the new DCI, John McCone.[1082]

RFK: "We Can't Sit on Our Asses"

On 18 January 1962, Operation Mongoose Chief of Operations General Lansdale authored a massive memorandum titled "The Cuban Project." He defined the objective of Mongoose this way: "To help the Cubans overthrow the communist regime from within Cuba and institute a new government with which the United States can live in peace."[1083] Lansdale laid out the "Concept of Operations" for the political actions, economic warfare and psychological operations to generate a revolt in Cuba. This plan had to have the sympathetic support of the majority of Cuban people, Lansdale said, and that fact had to be made known to the outside world. The U.S. he added, would then give support to the Cuban people's revolt, "including military support as necessary." That last sentence was a red flag.

Lansdale outlined an "Estimate of the Situation" and a twelve-part summary of operations—including a 32-Task "Target Schedule"—in support of the "Initial Phase" of Mongoose. At CIA, Harvey was working on Cover and Deception (C&D) plans to fracture the communist regime in Cuba *and* ginning up an operations schedule for initiating Lansdale's required popular movement within Cuba. Neither objective stood a snowball's chance in hell of succeeding.

On 19 January 1962, Lansdale authored the minutes of a Special Group (Augmented) meeting in RFK's office.[1084] Besides Robert Kennedy and Lansdale, those present included Craig, Hand and Patchell from the Pentagon; and Helms and Wilson from the CIA. The State Department representatives did not bother to show up for the meeting. Irritated, Lansdale complained that Mongoose was in *slow motion*:

> We must get things off dead center. … It is high time the U.S. Government gave this project and the tasks involved a fair trial. It is high time the United States gets busy. …Lansdale expressed his concern regarding the absence of a State [Department] representative in the meeting. He does not feel that State realizes the importance of this project. State should give this project more emphasis.

1082 6/13/75, Helms SSCIA Deposition, pp. 90-91: Senator Hart of Michigan: "There is a note in the Inspector General's file there, phase II, that 'Harvey added that when he briefed Helms on Roselli he obtained Helms' approval not to brief the director.'" RIF 157-10014-10075. Also see 7/11/75, Harvey SSCIA Deposition, p. 66, RIF 157-10011-10053.
1083 1/18/62, General E. G. Lansdale, "The Cuba Project," RIF 145-10001-10182.
1084 1/19/62, Lansdale Minutes of Meeting in Robert Kennedy's office; RIF 178-10002-10479.

The attorney general stated that money was no object to get things moving. "We must cause Castro trouble that is meaningful."[1085] RFK then summarized how the situation had developed. Following the Bay of Pigs fiasco, he said, the U.S. "had to lie low for obvious reasons." Refugee reports during this interim period revealed that the Cuban military was getting stronger day by day. That was true. Kennedy warned that Castro's control was drawing tighter and that "Time, effort, manpower and dollars are not to be spared." RFK added, "The president has indicated that Castro cannot be tolerated and the final chapter to this has not been written."[1086] That chapter, however, would prove to be less tolerable than Castro.

Robert Kennedy then counseled those attending this meeting that he would be watching their "conduct" and that he expected them to take Lansdale's "guidance" to heart:

> The group will be required to make periodic reports to the 5412 Group. If it does not go, you members of the Caribbean Survey Group are responsible. *Imagination, ideas and thoughts are to be forwarded to General Lansdale.* These are important to the project. *Members of this group must not wait and react only to Lansdale's guidance; they must produce ideas and thoughts of their own. The big bird is on your shoulders, you members of the group.* There is no question but that you must see that absolutely nothing stands in the way. We must do this job now. *We cannot stand by and sit on our asses.* We must get going now. [Emphasis added]

Lansdale was pleased with the attorney general's admonishment of the Special Group (Augmented—SGA). After summarizing the above lecture in his memorandum, Lansdale concluded that Robert Kennedy's remarks left no doubt in his mind that "the Caribbean Survey Group has the full backing of the president of the United States."[1087]

Others were not so sure about how much of Lansdale's vision for Mongoose was shared by the "big bird" in the White House. For example, Schlesinger noted that the SGA had directed Lansdale to focus on *principled* activities and making intelligence collection the "immediate priority objective" of U.S. activities in the months ahead. Schlesinger said that the SGA was willing to go no further than "concurrent sabotage" activities—providing that they were "inconspicuous" and on a scale "short of those reasonably calculated to inspire a revolt." The SGA, Schlesinger said, insisted that all "sensitive" operations such as sabotage would have to be presented in more detail on a case by case basis."[1088] As we shall see, what Lansdale actually proposed was anything but principled.

1085 Ibid.
1086 Ibid.
1087 Ibid.
1088 Schlesinger, *Robert Kennedy and His Times*, p. 477.

INTO THE STORM

Lansdale's "Sensitive" Task 33

As I mentioned above, on 18 January Lansdale put together a comprehensive "program review" of thirty-two tasks to be implemented by the various departments and agencies of the government. These tasks were divided into the following categories: a) Intelligence; b) Political; c) Economic; d) Psychological; and e) Military Action. The next day, Lansdale transmitted a copy of this plan to the attorney general and an additional copy for the president. Lansdale included a handwritten note to Robert Kennedy stating, "my review does not include the sensitive work I have referred to you; I felt you preferred informing the president privately."[1089] The handwritten note concerned Task 33. At the time, the note was for limited distribution—only to Bobby and the president. Originally released with redactions, this document was eventually released in the clear in 2017.[1090]

During his 8 July 1975 Church Committee deposition, Lansdale was asked to explain the meaning of his handwritten note:

> General Lansdale: As far as I can recollect, and to the best of my knowledge now, that concerned the BW (biological warfare) operation on incapacitating sugar workers.

Mr. Schwarz: Now, assassinations would have been a sensitive matter.

> General Lansdale: But this was not assassination. I am positive that I never took up assassination with either the attorney general or the president.[1091]

The idea of using "non-lethal" biological warfare agents to incapacitate large numbers of workers in Cuban cane fields was Lansdale's idea; he tasked the CIA to study the idea and submit a report by 15 February. The study revealed that "the idea was infeasible, and it was cancelled."[1092]

The biological warfare plan was only one part—33b—of an *unbelievable* four-part Task 33. Tasks 33a, 33c and 33d were far more sensitive than the BW component. They were the specific steps of a highly classified Pentagon plan for a *false "Cuban" attack on the U.S base at Guantanamo to justify a U.S. military invasion of Cuba*. I will discuss that Pentagon plan in detail below. At this point, at the end of January, 33a, 33c and 33d *appeared* only as ideas submitted by the man chosen by the Kennedys to be the Mongoose Chief of Operations.

1089 7/8/75, Lansdale, SSCIA deposition, p. 30; RIF 157-10005-10236.
1090 1/19/62, Lansdale memo Cuba Project, Task 33; RIF 202-10001-10184. The 2017 released version is in the clear; RIF 202-10001-10183. NB: There is no list indicating who was privy to this sensitive memo; our only information about it comes from Lansdale's 7/8/75 SSCIA deposition.
1091 7/8/75, Lansdale, SSCIA deposition, pp. 30-31; RIF 157-10005-10236. Note: the transcriber mistakenly used the digraph PW which would mean psychological warfare, when BW was what Lansdale said.
1092 Ibid, pp. 27-29.

Task 33a was a plan for a joint Pentagon-CIA plot to create fake photographs to convince Cuban intelligence collectors that the U.S. was planning an invasion. This, it was hoped, would stimulate the Cubans to put their militia and sugar cane workers on a general alert.[1093] Task 33c called for the Pentagon to devise a Cover and Deception (C&D) plan to conduct a military exercise in a manner to convince the Cubans that an American invasion of Cuba was imminent. Lansdale explained, "*The C&D theme would be that this is a cover for an invasion, with a plan for a "provocation" which would justify a U.S. response.* The overt story makes it readily explainable as a normal U.S. military activity." Task 33d was another C&D plan to be devised by the Pentagon. The idea was to create a *false Cuban attack against the American naval base at Guantanamo.*

By March, it would become obvious that Lansdale's Task 33 recommendations in January were nearly an exact match for the outrageous plan that JCS Chairman Lemnitzer would propose to the president—Operation Northwoods. *From the very beginning, Lemnitzer had been using the Kennedys' point man—General Lansdale—to turn Operation Mongoose into Operation Northwoods.*

Putting "American Genius to Work" on Operation Mongoose

Meanwhile, in late January 1962 Lansdale was riding high. On 20 January, Lansdale flaunted his success in a finger-waving memo to the Caribbean Survey Group[1094]:

> At yesterday's meeting, the attorney general *underscored with emphasis* that it is your responsibility to develop and apply the maximum effort of your department (agency) to win the goal of the Cuba Project. As *he so adequately tasked us, there will be no acceptable alibi.*

Lansdale warned the group against entertaining any ideas that the "vital national security and foreign policy goal" for Cuba could not be achieved. He declared:

> It is our job to *put American genius to work* on this project, quickly and effectively. This demands a change in business-as-usual and a hard facing of *the fact that we are in a combat situation—where we have been given full command.* [Emphasis added]

However, the "genius" behind the proposals that followed left a great deal to be desired—especially if the genius was General Lemnitzer.

Beside Lansdale's incipient Northwoods Task 33 that the Caribbean Survey Group was *not* privy to, some of Lansdale's other ideas for putting American genius to work in

---

1093 1/19/62, Lansdale memo Cuba Project, Task 33; RIF 202-10001-10184. The 2017 released version is in the clear; RIF 202-10001-10183. NB: There is no list indicating who was privy to this sensitive memo; our only information about it comes from Lansdale's 7/8/75 SSCIA deposition.
1094 1/20/62, Lansdale Memo for Members of the Caribbean Survey Group; RIF 145-10001-10146.

INTO THE STORM

Cuba included "gangster elements" to attack police officials; defections "from the top echelon of the communist gang"; even spreading word that Castro was the anti-Christ and that the Second Coming was imminent. It was to be an "elimination by illumination" event verified by star shells sent up from an American submarine off the Cuban coast—to mimic the glittery spectacle of the Second Coming.[1095]

In his biography of Lansdale, Max Boot describes a "deluge" of far-fetched ideas by the Pentagon's General Craig—Lemnitzer's chief of covert action—and others presented for consideration:[1096]

- Operation Bounty: "a system of financial rewards commensurate with position and stature, for killing or delivering alive known communists." The proposed bounty system was $100,000 for Cuban government officials, $97,000 for foreign communists, $45,000 for Soviet Bloc leaders.
- Operation Free Ride: creating unrest and dissension in Cuba by airdropping valid one-way airline tickets good for passage to Mexico City and Caracas.
- Fake photos: disillusioning the Cuban population with fake photographic images of an obese Castro or Castro in sexual situations "with two beauties" in a lavishly furnished room in Castro's residence, replete with a table overflowing with delectable Cuban food with an underlying caption in Spanish that read "My ration is different."
- Toilet paper: in response to a shortage of toilet paper and female sanitary napkins in Cuba the CIA would air-drop toilet paper "with pictures on alternate sheets of Fidel Castro and Nikita Khrushchev to drive Castro mad."

Lansdale biographer Max Boot rightly pointed out that Lansdale recognized all of these internal shenanigans to stimulate the internal resistance movement were merely designed to legitimate an "American military intervention." Moreover, Boot correctly observed, "President Kennedy was no more willing in early 1962 than he had been a year earlier, during the Bay of Pigs invasion, to wage open war against Castro."[1097]

U.S. military intervention in Cuba was contrary to the specific instructions of the president. Obviously, using a pretext to justify such intervention would have been even more anathema to presidential policy. There were no enemy combatants to poison with biological warfare—only peasants working in the sugar fields. America

---

1095 Schlesinger, *Robert Kennedy and His Times*, p. 477.
1096 Boot, *The Road Not Taken*, pp. 386-387.
1097 Boot, *The Road Not Taken*, p. 384 and 388.

was *not* at war with Cuba despite Sam Halpern's later insistence that we *were* at war with Cuba:

> The Kennedy boys were in charge. And *they were running the war*. And *we were fighting a war* against Cuba, undeclared or otherwise, but *we were fighting a war*. I said if *we* were sending people in to create sabotage activities inside Cuba, *we* were blowing things up, people got killed on both sides, on their side and our side.[1098] [Emphasis added]

For decades after the Kennedy assassination, Halpern made a sport of showcasing the "stupidity" that his colleagues in Task Force W were getting "from the president and his brother."[1099]

Clearly, Cuba and America were *not* at war. However, Lansdale, like Halpern, knew less about true combat than propaganda and both of them liked to think they were playing soldier. Crucially, the Joint Chiefs were waiting on Lansdale before springing their plan for a *real* war in Cuba on the Kennedy brothers. The brothers, however, were not blind to what was coming. They could see that Mongoose was spiraling out of control. And, by late February, the Kennedys realized that Lansdale had become a stalking horse for Lemnitzer.

The 26 February Special Group Meeting: A Lansdale Reset and a Two-Track Paper on Assumptions about Intervention

On 26 February 1962, the Special Group (Augmented—SGA) held an historic meeting. The decisions reached reflected the reaction of the Kennedy brothers to Lansdale's incipient false flag Northwoods-style intervention. A decision on U.S. intervention was deferred. An order was given that Lansdale's reference to a presidential memorandum in the first two lines of his 20 February paper "will be deleted." Lansdale's 20 February paper had said that an early decision was required on whether the U.S. would, if necessary, promptly respond with military force to aid a Cuban revolt.[1100] The president's 30 November memorandum had said *nothing* about U.S. military intervention.

The 26 February SGA order to delete the offending sentences in Lansdale's 20 February report speaks volumes about the wariness of the Kennedy brothers to the track Lansdale was taking. Thomas Parrott's minutes from the 26 February SGA meeting revealed that Lansdale's wings had been clipped. His mission for the next ninety days had been reset and sharply circumscribed.[1101] Parrott's notes also revealed that a

---

1098 10/30/87, Halpern interview with Weber, p. 82; RIF 104-10324-10002.
1099 Weber, *Spymasters*, pp. 123-124.
1100 2/20/62, Lansdale memorandum, "The Cuba Project"; RIF 145-10001-10003.
1101 2/26/62, Minutes of the Special Group Meeting; RIF 104-10001-10272.

INTO THE STORM

decision had been reached to draft a *two-track* paper. Close analysis of the language used suggests that this paper was meant to deal with Lansdale's proposal for a pretext-based U.S. intervention in Cuba.

The two-track paper was to be "for higher authority," i.e., the president, and would include two *assumptions*:

> These are (1) the U.S. will make maximum use of Cuban resources but recognizes that final success will require decisive U.S. military intervention; and (2) the development of Cuban resources will be for the purpose of facilitating and supporting this intervention and to provide a preparation and supporting justification for it.

Parrott's notes also made crystal clear that the paper would *not* ask the president to "make a policy decision at this time, but simply to note the assumptions."

A decision was also reached ordering Lansdale to "recast" his plan. He was directed to write *one* paper on "short-range actions" for the months of March through May. These actions were to be limited to "short-range actions" such as "the acquisition of hard intelligence." He was directed to write another paper that would include "those actions which would have the effect of committing the U.S. to a greater or lesser degree of intervention."

A lot more than meets the eye was involved in the Kennedy brothers' handling of Lansdale's 20 February paper and the decisions of the 26 February SGA meeting. I will return to these matters in Chapter Fifteen.

A quick aside is in order here. As the reader will recall from Chapter Nine, in his mid-1990s interviews with Sy Hersh, Sam Halpern anchored the start of RFK's alleged *eighteen-month-long* campaign with the Mafia to arrange the assassination of Fidel in "the early spring of 1962."[1102] And, as discussed at length in Chapters Ten and Thirteen, we know that Halpern *knew* the truth that it was his boss, William Harvey, who was the person directing those assassination arrangements. Crucially, the CIA-Mafia plot to assassinate Castro was assigned to Harvey at the time that General Lemnitzer's Operation Northwoods reared its ugly head.

Operation Northwoods

On 13 March 1962, the Joint Chiefs of Staff (JCS) sent a Top Secret, Special Handling, NOFORN (no foreign dissemination) memorandum to Secretary of Defense McNamara under the title "Justification for U.S. Military Intervention in Cuba."[1103] The chiefs named this plan Operation Northwoods. They said they were responding to *a*

1102 Hersh, *The Dark Side of Camelot*, p. 286.
1103 3/13/62, "Northwoods" documents; RIF 202-10002-10104. NB: On 18 November 1997, the Assassination Records Review Board (ARRB) released an unredacted version of these documents.

MONGOOSE AND NORTHWOODS

request from Lansdale for a brief but precise description of *pretexts* which would provide justification for U.S. military intervention in Cuba—Lansdale's Task 33. On 14 March, the JCS approved the recommendations set forth in the 9 March 1962 report by the Caribbean Survey Group for intervention in Cuba.[1104]

In responding to Lansdale's request, the Chiefs' 9 March report recognized that any pretext for U.S military intervention in Cuba would require a "political decision," meaning an approval by the president. Operation Northwoods was engineered so that a U.S. invasion of Cuba would result from heightened U.S.-Cuban tensions concocted so that the U.S. was *apparently* "suffering justifiable grievances." Furthermore, according to the chiefs' scheme, world opinion would favor U.S. intervention as these grievances produced an "international image of the Cuban government as rash and irresponsible, and an alarming threat to the peace of the Western Hemisphere." The chiefs recommended that "all projects" associated with their plan should take place in "the next few months."[1105] Finally, the chiefs wanted responsibility for both the overt and covert operations associated with Northwoods to be assigned to themselves.[1106]

To bring this about, Lemnitzer's plan called for the fabrication of a series of well-coordinated incidents to take place in and around Guantanamo to "camouflage the ultimate objective" of U.S. military intervention.[1107] To "establish a credible [Cuban] attack," the chiefs' proposed the creation of the following incidents: (1) Start many rumors; (2) Land friendly Cubans in uniform "over-the-fence" to stage attack on the base; (3) Capture Cuban (friendly) saboteurs inside the base; (4) Start riots near the base main gate (friendly Cubans); (5) Blow up ammunition inside the base; start fires; (6) Burn aircraft on air base (sabotage); (7) Lob mortar shells from outside into base. Some damage to installations; (8) Capture assault teams approaching from the sea or vicinity of Guantanamo City; (9) Capture militia group which storms the base; (10) Sabotage ship in harbor; large fires – naphthalene; (11) Sink ship near harbor entrance.[1108]

The chiefs said that the U.S. would "respond" to this fake Cuban attack by commencing large-scale offensive military operations. A "Remember the Maine" incident would be arranged by blowing up a U.S. ship in Guantanamo Bay and blaming Cuba for it. "Casualty lists in the U.S. newspapers," the chiefs' added, "would cause a helpful wave of national indignation."[1109] This would have been an attempt to recreate the infamous incident in February 1898 when the U.S. engineered an explosion aboard

---
1104 3/14/62, "Justification for U.S. Military Intervention in Cuba"; RIF 202-10002-10104.
1105 3/9/62, Califano Papers, Operation Northwoods, "Cuba Project," pp. 1-2; RIF 198-10004-10020.
1106 Ibid, p. 4.
1107 Ibid, p. 5.
1108 Ibid, pp. 7-8.
1109 Ibid, p. 8.

INTO THE STORM

the battleship Maine in Havana Harbor killing 266 U.S. sailors. The incident sparked the Spanish-American War with Cuba. More than one million men, incited by the alleged attack, volunteered for duty. Lemnitzer also wanted to attack U.S. cities and blame Cuba for it:

> We could develop a communist Cuban terror campaign *in the Miami area, in other Florida cities and even in Washington*. The Terror campaign could be pointed at the Cuban refugees seeking haven in the United States. We could sink a boatload of Cubans en route to Florida (*real or simulated*). We could foster attempts on lives of Cuban refugees in the United States *even to the extent of wounding in instances to be widely publicized*. Exploding a few plastic bombs in carefully chosen spots; the arrest of Cuban agents and the release of prepared documents substantiating Cuban involvement also would be helpful in projecting the idea of an irresponsible government.

The Founding Fathers of the American Republic would have been outraged. They probably turned over in their graves at the moral depravity of General Lemnitzer and those chiefs who agreed with his Northwoods recommendations.

The senseless sacrifice of innocent U.S. and Cuban citizens to trick America into a war with Cuba was a recommendation that was dead on arrival in the White House. What could Lemnitzer have possibly been thinking? In April 1961, Lemnitzer had believed that President Kennedy would change his mind and send American military forces into Cuba once the Cuban exile brigade was being cut to pieces on the beachhead. And Lemnitzer had been wrong about that. Kennedy did not fall for such degenerate subterfuges then or in 1962. By what twisted logic did Lemnitzer think he could get JFK to go along with his sordid plan this time? Didn't Lemnitzer realize he would live in infamy for proposing crimes against humanity?

I will leave those questions and many more on the table for Volume IV. I will end this volume with the Kennedy brothers' ship sailing headlong into the storm. As spring turned into summer in 1962, apocalyptic winds were once again fanning the embers of war.

CHAPTER FIFTEEN

INTERMISSION: THE WINDS OF WAR

At the precise moment President Kennedy launched Operation Mongoose—on 3 November 1961—official Washington was already in an uproar over the report General Taylor had made that same day recommending that 8,000 U.S. combat troops be deployed in South Vietnam (see *JFK and Vietnam*, 2017 edition, Chapter Seven). Taylor had just returned from a mission to Vietnam for which the president had instructed him *not* to come back with a recommendation for U.S. military intervention. Kennedy was so shocked by Taylor's recommendation that he tried, unsuccessfully, to suppress it by recalling copies of the final report.[1110] Taylor's recommendation to send combat troops was a very closely held secret.

The fact that the president tried to suppress a recommendation to send combat troops to Vietnam on the same day that he launched Operation Mongoose tells us a lot about how he would react to a similar recommendation to send American combat troops into Cuba. No record of the 3 November meeting that launched Mongoose has ever been found.[1111] However, the decisions reached that day were summarized in a 30 November 1961 memorandum from the president to his senior cabinet members, as well as General Taylor and General Lansdale. Kennedy told his subordinates to "go ahead" with the project to "overthrow" the Castro regime.[1112]

1110 Halberstam, *The Best and the Brightest*, p. 169.
1111 11/3/61, *FRUS*, Vol. X, Cuba, Document 270, Editorial Note.
1112 11/30/61, *FRUS*, Vol. X, Cuba, Document 278, Memorandum from President Kennedy.

INTO THE STORM

Lansdale made use of that presidential memorandum in a report he authored on 20 February 1962.[1113] But Lansdale's report was remanded six days later by the Special Group (Augmented—SGA) because he had asked if the president would approve U.S. military intervention in Cuba. I mentioned that key SGA meeting in Chapter Fourteen and promised to revisit it here. Before I do that, I want to draw the reader's attention to the fact that eight days before the president gave the "go ahead" for Mongoose on 30 November 1961, he had overruled a recommendation by Secretary McNamara, Secretary Rusk, the Joint Chiefs and General Taylor, for U.S. military intervention in Vietnam. Etched in stone in NSAM-111 on 22 November 1961, that was the defining decision on Vietnam during Kennedy's presidency. It was promulgated two years to the day before his assassination.

The Battle Between General Lemnitzer and President Kennedy Over War in Vietnam

The key NSC meeting leading up to President Kennedy's decision against intervention in Vietnam occurred on November 15, 1961. During that meeting, a caustic and revealing exchange took place between JCS Chairman General Lemnitzer and the president. When Kennedy asked for the justification for sending U.S. combat troops to Vietnam, this heated moment took place:

> Lemnitzer replied that the world would be divided in the area of Southeast Asia on the sea, in the air and in communications. He said communist conquest would deal a severe blow to freedom and extend communism to a great portion of the world. The president asked *how he could justify the proposed courses of action in Vietnam while at the same time ignoring Cuba.* General Lemnitzer hastened to add that *the JCS feel that even at this point the United States should go into Cuba.*[1114]

This passage was a dramatic illustration of the degree to which the president had become isolated from the cold warriors demanding full U.S. intervention in Vietnam *and* Cuba. It foreshadowed the uncompromising conflict that erupted three months later over Lemnitzer's proposal for full U.S. military intervention in Cuba.

In the days immediately after Thanksgiving—26-29 November—Kennedy purged the Vietnam hawks in the State Department (see **JFK and Vietnam**, 2017 edition, Chapter Seven). At the same time, as I mentioned before, when the president fired DCI Allen Dulles and replaced him with John McCone, he warned the new DCI, "We

---

1113   2/20/62, Lansdale report on "The Cuba Project"; RIF 145-10001-10003.
1114   Notes on National Security Council Meeting 15, November 1961, LBJ Library, VP Security File, Box 4.

want to welcome you here and to say that you are now living on the bull's-eye, and I welcome you to that spot."[1115]

The lesson from the president's climactic Vietnam decision was this: *Kennedy turned down combat troops, not when the decision was clouded by ambiguities and contradictions in the reports from the battlefield, but when the battle was unequivocally desperate, when all concerned agreed that Vietnam's fate hung in the balance, and when his principal advisors told him that vital U.S. interests in the region and the world were at stake.*

But the chiefs in the Pentagon remained frustrated with the president's decision. Air Force Chief of Staff General LeMay was particularly dismayed. He later claimed that none of the Joint Chiefs at the time believed the president's Vietnam program was "anything except some diplomatic fiddling around" with a little more aid.[1116] On 13 January 1962, General Lemnitzer authored his most strongly worded warning yet that his recommendation to send U.S. military combat forces to Vietnam had to be considered again, and asked Defense Secretary McNamara to send it on to the president.[1117] McNamara did this, along with his own comment that he did not endorse it.[1118]

In an emphatic and foreboding lecture to the president, Lemnitzer said that failure to heed his recommendation would lead to "communist domination of all of the Southeast Asian mainland." Singapore and Malaysia would be lost as the Indonesian archipelago came under "Soviet domination." Control of the eastern access to the Indian Ocean would be lost and India would be "outflanked." Australia and New Zealand would be threatened, and the American bases in the Philippines and Japan would be lost.

Given Kennedy's repeated refusals to intervene in Vietnam, Lemnitzer's memo bordered on insubordination. His the-sky-is-falling memorandum rebuked the president for his "failure" to send in U.S. combat troops. Lemnitzer added impudently that this "will merely extend the date when such action must be taken and will make our ultimate task proportionately more difficult." The message to Kennedy was clear: We told you a year ago to send combat troops, but you didn't listen. If you fail to listen when your program falls apart, we'll do it anyway.

And, as we know from the subsequent history of events, they *did* do it anyway.

The Battle Between General Lemnitzer and President Kennedy Over War in Cuba

---

1115 Kennedy, remarks at the swearing in of John McCone, CIA, November 29, 1961, **Public Papers**, 1961, p. 490.
1116 LeMay, interview with Belden, March 29, 1972, in *Air Force History*, p. 91.
1117 *PP*, DOD ed., Book 12, pp. 448-54.
1118 Ibid., p. 447.

INTO THE STORM

The battle over U.S. intervention in Vietnam was the context for Lansdale's 28 January 1962 submission of his "sensitive" Task 33 false-flag operation to create a pretext for U.S. intervention in Cuba. As I mentioned in Chapter Fourteen, Lansdale took a surprising step forward on the path to U.S. intervention in his 20 February report titled "The Cuba Project."[1119] Lansdale's report began with this sentence:

> In keeping with the spirit of the presidential memorandum of 30 November 1961, the U.S. will *help the people of Cuba overthrow the communist regime* from within Cuba and institute a new government with which the U.S. can live in peace. [Emphasis added]

That statement was essentially true. The president's memorandum was simpler: "We will use our available assets to go ahead with the discussed project in order to *help Cuba overthrow the communist regime.*"[1120]

But Lansdale's report ended with a question that was completely at odds with presidential policy:

> *If* the conditions and assets permitting a revolt are achieved in Cuba, and *if* U.S. help is required to sustain this condition, *will the U.S. respond promptly with military force to aid the Cuban revolt?* ...An early decision is required. [Emphasis added]

Of course, Lansdale knew that the president had barred U.S. military intervention from being considered in the Mongoose operation. So, why had Lansdale become the stalking horse for a proposal specifically opposed by the president? There can only be one answer: just as Lansdale had cast his lot with the chiefs on intervention in Vietnam back in the spring of 1961, now he was once again casting his lot with them on intervention—this time in Cuba. While the president would keep Lansdale around for a while longer, that episode effectively ended his usefulness to the Kennedy brothers. Lansdale's embrace of U.S. military intervention in Cuba ensured that he would never be rewarded with his coveted prize—an assignment to Vietnam as a special U.S. advisor to President Diem.

As I mentioned in Chapter Fourteen, the Kennedy brothers had seen the false-flag pretext for U.S. military intervention in Lansdale's 18 January memorandum. Two days later, Lansdale's 20 February report went even further by asking if the president would agree to U.S. intervention to save a Cuban revolt. It is likely the Kennedys understood that Lemnitzer was behind Lansdale's switch to an intervention track. And so, the brothers conducted countermeasures by using a key 26 February SGA meeting to 1) restrict Lansdale's future mission to "short-range actions" to acquire "hard intelligence" about Cuba, and 2) order the deletion of Lansdale's reference to the president's

---

[1119] 2/20/62, Lansdale Report, "The Cuba Project"; RIF 145-10001-10003.
[1120] 11/30/61, **FRUS**, Vol. X, Cuba, Document 278, Memorandum from President Kennedy.

INTERMISSION: THE WINDS OF WAR

memorandum in his (Lansdale's) 20 February paper. The message was unmistakable: Lansdale's question about intervening militarily to save a Cuban revolt was decidedly *not* "in keeping with the spirit" of the president's memorandum.

The Kennedy brothers knew that clipping Lansdale's wings was only the beginning of the battle that was about to unfold. If the false-flag pretext was only Lansdale's idea, then there was nothing more to worry about. But the brothers intended to force the real snake in the grass out into the open. And General Lemnitzer had no qualms about stepping to the front of the line.

Not surprisingly, Lemnitzer had *already* swung into action in the Pentagon. A later (13 March 1962) memorandum traced the evolution of the activity Lemnitzer assigned to his Joint Staff.[1121] By the time of Lansdale's 18 January false-flag pretext proposal, Lemnitzer had already placed his chief of covert action, General Craig, in charge of a working group of five officers—from the Joint Staff's J-5 plans and policy component—on a full-time basis. After Lansdale's 18 January recommendation, Lemnitzer enlarged Craig's working group by "the addition of full-time representatives of the Joint Staff's J-1 (manpower and personnel), J-2 (intelligence), J-3 (operations), J-4 (logistics), and representatives from the Defense Intelligence Agency (DIA). Lemnitzer was ahead of his skis at this point.

While neither of the Kennedy brothers was physically present at the crucial 26 February SGA meeting, their interests were well represented. The presence of the president's security advisor, McGeorge Bundy, and Defense Secretary McNamara, along with his deputy, Roswell Gilpatrick, was sufficient to apply the brakes on Lansdale's future duties. Lansdale was there to witness the first step on his journey toward impotence. That surprise undoubtedly pleased William Harvey—who was also a witness to Lansdale's falling star—but he was hardly oblivious to the worrisome implications. Little did Harvey suspect at the time that Lansdale's last act, at the height of the Cuban Missile Crisis, would be to dismantle his own (Harvey's) CIA fiefdom on the orders of Robert Kennedy.

In Chapter Fourteen I mentioned that there was a lot more than met the eye taking place during that seminal February SGA meeting. The unseen hand of the Kennedy brothers was responsible for the use of a bureaucratic *trick* the president had fashioned after the Bay of Pigs failure. The participants at the SGA meeting were informed about

---

1121 3/13/62, DOD/JCS memorandum, "Consolidated Status Report" for the Special Group (Augmented). Note: This important memorandum may never see the light of day. I discovered extracts from it in the Church Committee Index Card collection that I copied at NARA at a very early date after the passage of the JFK Assassination Records Collection Act was passed in 1992. I have made back-up copies for safe keeping of these valuable records (in secure locations) which contain more than a thousand index cards on important meetings of the Special Group and the National Security Council. When the current Trump administration has finished whatever they decide to do pursuant to mandated full release of JFK records, we will take action to approach NARA and the JFK Presidential Library to ensure that what I have copied from this SSCIA Index Card collection will be available to researchers.

several "papers for higher authority" that had to be drafted "before the coming weekend"—i.e. in four days. There were two key papers. The first paper was to plan for the maximum use of Cuban resources, while recognizing that *final success will require decisive U.S. military intervention*. The second paper was to plan for the development of Cuban resources to *facilitate, support, and justify that intervention.*

On the surface, the guidance for these two "papers" appeared to be an approval for what Lansdale (on behalf of Lemnitzer) had proposed on 18 January and 20 February. But those instructions were a bureaucratic *sleight of hand.* Officials who had experience trying to convince President Kennedy to approve something he did not support were used to being told to go write a paper and get back to him. In this case, only *one* paper was drafted afterward, and it was written on 5 March by General Taylor with slight revisions by McGeorge Bundy and DCI McCone. The first two lines were identical, word-for-word, with the language used in the guidance from the 26 February SGA meeting.[1122]

The formula used at that meeting on behalf of the Kennedys was not a direct affront to Lemnitzer's plans for war in Cuba. But the reprimand of Lansdale put the ball firmly in Lemnitzer's court. He understood what he had to do. And so, Lemnitzer put his Operation Northwoods on the table two weeks later, on 13 March. In Chapter Fourteen, I discussed the morally depraved details of Lemnitzer's plan—sinking an American ship, attacking Miami, Washington and other American cities, and blaming it all on Cuba.

Three days later, Kennedy and Lemnitzer met face-to face with, perhaps, a half dozen other officers. It is very difficult to find a formal memo of the discussion in that meeting. We do have a brief handwritten note authored by Deputy Under Secretary of State U. Alexis Johnson who witnessed the event:

> The president also *expressed skepticism that,* in so far as can now be foreseen, *circumstances will arise that would justify and make desirable the use of American forces for overt military action.* It was clearly understood no decision was expressed or implied approving the use of such forces although contingency planning would proceed.[1123] [Emphasis added]

However, as this volume went to press, I discovered a memorandum indicating that a blunt rebuke of Lemnitzer by JFK took place. I will discuss that memo further in Volume IV.

Here, as a career U.S. Army officer, I am compelled to speak my mind. I speak for myself and will leave other officers of the American Armed Forces to their own counsel in this matter. General Lemnitzer betrayed his country and his oath of office to protect

---

1122 2/26/62, 11/30/61, ***FRUS***, Vol. X, Cuba, Document 314, Guidelines for Operation Mongoose.
1123 Ibid.

INTERMISSION: THE WINDS OF WAR

and defend its constitution. U.S. Army Major General Joseph Alexander McChristian, perhaps the finest Army intelligence officer ever to wear the uniform, was once asked what it means to lie about the enemy in a time of war. He spoke for what is in my heart when he replied, "*It jeopardizes not only the lives of the soldiers on the battlefield, but also the future liberty of your people at home.*"[1124]

****

As the moment of maximum danger in the Cuban Missile Crisis approached, the president finally got around to firing Lemnitzer. On 1 October 1962, Kennedy installed General Maxwell Taylor as the new Chairman of the Joint Chiefs of Staff. The choice of Taylor, as events turned out, was a very bad mistake. Taylor would end up working secretly with other senior officers to subvert President Kennedy's order to begin the withdrawal of U.S. military advisors from Vietnam.

The ship of the brothers Kennedy was sailing headlong into the winds of war. Though they might still stop it in Cuba, war was coming nonetheless. The miraculous conclusion of the Cuban Missile Crisis would be short-lived. It was only an intermission—much like the passing eye of a huge hurricane.

At the moment, for me—save for the steadily building hatred for the Kennedy brothers and the metamorphosing CIA plots to assassinate Castro—what lies on the other side of that intermission is mostly dark. But a saying John Kennedy was wont to quote comes to mind:

Except the Lord keep the city, the watchman waketh in vain. [Psalm 127:1]
—Remarks prepared [undelivered] for speech at the Trade Mart
Dallas, Texas, 22 November 1963

1124 See Newman, *JFK and Vietnam*, 2017 Edition, p. xxiv.

APPENDIX

GARY THOMAS ROWE FBI INFORMANT IN THE ALABAMA KKK

This Appendix is an extract from a July 1979 study of Gary Thomas Rowe, Jr., by the Office of Professional Responsibility, Office of the Attorney General, United States Department of Justice. This extract is relevant to Chapter Six of this volume, which covers the Freedom Rides that took place during the summer of 1961.

****

Introduction

From 1960 to 1965, Gary Thomas Rowe, Jr. was a paid FBI informant within the ranks of the Ku Klux Klan in the Birmingham, Alabama, area. During this period, there was considerable racial violence in Birmingham and the rest of the state. Federal law enforcement authorities believed that the Klan was responsible for much of this violence.

On April 13, 1960, an informant file was opened on Rowe in the FBI field office in Birmingham, and on June 23, 1960, Rowe was initiated into the Eastview Klavern 13 of the Alabama Knights, Knights of the Ku Klux Klan, Inc. Rowe reported to the FBI on Klan members and activities from this time until April 1965, when Rowe's service as an informant became public knowledge after the fatal shooting of Mrs. Viola Liuzzo.

In July 1978, reports by the ***New York Times*** and ABC television suggested that Rowe had participated in violent crimes with other Klansmen while an informant for the FBI and that the FBI was aware of his participation. The most serious of these allegations was that Rowe had fired the shot which killed Mrs. Liuzzo. On July 12, 1978, Senators Kennedy and Abourezk sent a letter to the Department stating that the Senate Judiciary Committee was interested in receiving a full report on these allegations. In September 1978, Rowe was indicted by an Alabama grand jury for the 1965 murder of Viola Liuzzo.

In October 1978, Attorney General Bell created a Task Force to investigate the Rowe matter. The Task Force investigation focused on three issues: (1) whether the FBI's supervision of Rowe as an informant was adequate; (2) whether there was any evidence to support the allegation that Rowe was responsible for the death of Mrs. Liuzzo; and (3) whether federal prosecutors had reason to doubt Rowe's reliability and credibility as a principal witness in the federal civil rights case arising out of the Liuzzo shooting.

In the course of its investigation, the Task Force reviewed hundreds of volumes of FBI files, files from the Civil Rights Division, trial transcripts, and documents provided by the Senate Select Committee on Intelligence. The Task Force also conducted 64 interviews, including interviews of Rowe and each of the agents who was responsible for supervising him.

The following is a summary of the results of the Task Force's investigation.

I. Rowe's Activities as an FBI Informant

The Task Force's examination of the FBI's handling of Rowe as an informant centered on the extent of Rowe's participation in Klan violence and whether the FBI had knowledge of such participation. Since 1976, there have been Attorney General guidelines dealing with informant participation in violence and other criminal activity. However, at the time Rowe was an informant, there were no such specific written guidelines. Nonetheless, persons who occupied supervisory positions in the FBI during the time Rowe was an informant told the Task Force that it was established FBI policy that informants were to be told orally not to engage in violence and that agents were informed of this policy in the course of their training. The agents, in turn, were to instruct informants to avoid violence and to warn them that the FBI would not condone any criminal acts on their part.

During the time that Rowe was an informant, there is no question but that the Klan and many of its members were deeply involved in racial violence. FBI Headquarters was stressing the importance of the development of informants within the Klan during this time. Two of Rowe's handling agents expressed in their Task Force interviews doubts that Rowe could have penetrated the higher levels of the Klan organization, been present at and reported on Klan violence, and maintained his credibility within the

GARY THOMAS ROWE FBI INFORMANT IN THE ALABAMA KKK

Klan without some limited and occasional participation with Klan members in racial harassment and brawls.

One of these handling agents stated that he repeatedly warned Rowe not to become involved in any violence and that if Rowe did become involved, he would be disowned by the FBI and treated as an ordinary criminal. However, in 1975 before the Senate Select Committee and in his 1979 interview with the Task Force, Rowe stated that during this early period he was actively involved in violent incidents, including beatings relating to the integration of Birmingham department stores and buses, and that he so advised the FBI. FBI records from this period identify only two such incidents, and in both cases, these written reports characterize Rowe's involvement as quite limited.

One of these two incidents is that concerning violence at the Trailways bus station in 1961, which is discussed in detail below. The other involved an attempted Klan attack on an elderly white couple who were raising a black child. Rowe told the Task Force that during this incident he had tried to throw a sheet over the man's head, but FBI documents from the time reveal no such active involvement by Rowe. These reports indicate that Rowe was simply present, that he could not avoid going, and that after the incident his handling agent again warned him to avoid being present at such violent incidents.

Rowe did report to the FBI Klan plans to attack persons attempting to integrate stores and buses, but there was no evidence discovered that would substantiate Rowe's current claims that he participated in such attacks. Instead, FBI files indicate that the plans were never carried out, and that in one instance Rowe actually discouraged the use of violence at a meeting in which these plans were discussed.

In sum, with the exception of the Trailways bus station incident discussed below, the Task Force found no evidence to corroborate Rowe's recent claims that he actively participated in acts of criminal violence for the Klan in this early period and reported them to his handling agent. Additionally, records from that time indicate that agents did warn Rowe not to engage in violence.

The Trailways Bus Station Incident

The Task Force conducted an extensive investigation of Rowe's role in the violence which occurred at the Trailways bus station in Birmingham when CORE Freedom Riders arrived on May 14, 1961. The evidence examined by the Task Force supports Rowe's recent claims that he was more deeply involved in the violence than FBI files of the period would indicate. Furthermore, the investigation suggests that one of Rowe's handling agents may have or should have been aware in 1961 that Rowe may have been an active participant in the violence of the day.

On May 12, 1961, Rowe reported to his handling agent Klan plans to attack the CORE Freedom Riders when they arrived at the bus station on the 14th. The FBI in turn related this information to local authorities. Rowe also reported that he was set to act as one of five "squad leaders" at the depot. The "squad leaders" were not to participate in the planned violence at the station but were to follow the CORE leaders and attack them later. The information Rowe provided was transmitted to FBI headquarters.

On the 14th, a brawl broke out as the CORE group approached a "white only" waiting room at the station. Several people were injured in the melee. The beating of one victim who was not a member of the CORE group, George Webb, was photographed by Tom Langston of the Birmingham *Post-Herald* and published on the front page of that newspaper. The FBI's copy of the photograph, which was used extensively in the FBI's investigations of the Trailways bus incident, bears notations on the back indicating that it was Rowe who identified three of the men in the picture. In addition, a May 1961 FBI memorandum establishes that one of Rowe's handling agents had discussed the photograph with Rowe. When interviewed by the Task Force, Rowe was able to identify the large man in the photograph with his back to the camera and holding the victim as Rowe.

Rowe's appearance in the *Post-Herald* photograph, and statements of witnesses in the incident in reference to the photograph, link Rowe not only to the beating of Webb but also to the subsequent beating of the photographer, Langston, and the harassment of another reporter named Bud Gordon. Another reporter at the scene, Clancy Lake, was also harassed, and several days after the incident Rowe told his handling agent that he had smashed the window of Lake's car.

A May 16th field office teletype to FBI Headquarters reported that the field office was intensively investigating the incident and had interviewed Rowe about it. Rowe had advised that he was not personally involved in the violence at the station, that he peacefully obtained film from a photographer (Gordon), and that he had participated in the Lake incident, but had not struck Lake. Furthermore, a memorandum written the next day indicates that when Rowe advised his handling agent about the Trailways plans before the incident, his handling agent specifically told him not to attend that or any other scene of violence. When Rowe told the agent that he had been ordered to go and that no excuse would be accepted, his agent then reminded him not to get involved in any violence.

Thus, while the *Post-Herald* photograph linked Rowe to the Webb and Langston beatings and a memorandum by Rowe's handling agent establishes that he discussed the photograph with Rowe soon after the incident, there is no FBI record of Rowe having been identified as one of the men in the photograph or as a possible participant in the Webb and Langston beatings. To the contrary, at the time Rowe down played his role and documents indicate that the FBI believed his accounts.

SELECTED ACRONYMS

AARC: Assassination Archives and Research Center
ACSI, Assistant Chief of Staff (Intelligence)
ACSI/USAOSD): ACSI Army Operational Survey Detachment
AFIO: Association of Former Intelligence Officers
BOB: Berlin Operations Base (CIA)
CEA: Council of Economic Advisers
CI: Counterintellligence (CIA)
CI/SIG: CI/Special Investigations Group (CIA mole hunting component)
CIA, Central Intelligence Agency
CINCLANT, Commander in Chief, Atlantic
CINCPAC: Commander-in-Chief Pacific
C&D: Cover and Deception (Department of Defense)
CNO: Chief of Naval Operations
COG: Cuban Operations Group (CIA)
COINTELPRO: Counterintelligence Program (FBI)
COPS: Chief of Operations (CIA)
CORE: Congress of Racial Equality
COS: Chief of Station (CIA)
CRC: Cuban Revolutionary Council (Cuban anti-Castro group)
DA/OP: Directorate of Administration/Office of Personnel
DCI: Director of Central Intelligence
D/DCI: Deputy Director of Central Intelligence
DCOS: Deputy Chief of Station (CIA)
DCSOPS, Deputy Chief of Staff for Operations, United States Army

DDP: Deputy Director of Plans (covert operations)
DDS/IS: Deputy Director of Security, Investigations and Support (CIA)
DDS/PS: Deputy Director of Security, Personnel & Support (CIA)
DIA: Defense Intelligence Agency
DIER: Cuban Army Intelligence (G-2)
DO/IMS/OG: Directorate of Operations Information Management Staff/Operations Group
DOD: Department of Defense
DOJ: Department of Justice
DRE: Cuban Student Directorate, formed in Miami JMWAVE Station in 1960
EE(D): East European Division (CIA)
ELC: Ejercito Libertador de Cuba (Cuban anti-Castro group)
EXCOMM: Executive Committee (President Kennedy group, Cuban Missile Crisis)
FBI Federal Bureau of Investigation
FBN: Federal Bureau of Narcotics
FCD: KGB First Chief Directorate
FEU: Federation of University Students (Cuba)
FI: Foreign Intelligence (CIA)
GDR: German Democratic Republic (East Germany)
GRU: Soviet military intelligence
GSFG: Group of Soviet Forces Germany
HSCA: House Select Committee on Assassinations
ICC: Interstate Commerce Commission
IG: Inspector General's Office (CIA)
IR: Interim Report (SSCIA)
JCS, Joint Chiefs of Staff
JMWAVE: CIA Station in Miami
KGB: Committee for State Security (Soviet Union)
KKK: Ku Klux Klan
LAD: Latin American Division (CIA)
MDC, Movimiento Democrático Cristiano, Christian Democratic Movement
MFR: Memorandum for Record
MRC, Movimiento de Resistencia Cívica, Civic Resistance Movement
MRP: People's Revolutionary Movement, formed by Manuel Ray
MRR: Movement of Revolutionary Rescue, formed by Artime and Sergio Sanjenis
NACC: National Association of Cattlemen of Cuba
NATO: North Atlantic Treaty Organization
NIE: National Intelligence Estimate
NSA: National Security Agency

SELECTED ACRONYMS

NSAM: National Security Action Memorandum
NSC: National Security Council (U.S.)
OA: Operational Approval (CIA)
OAS: Organization of American States
OLC: Office of Legislative Counsel
ONI: Office of Naval Intelligence
OPC: Office of Policy Coordination (U.S., pre-CIA)
Opergruppa: Strategic Intelligence Operational Group (Soviet Union/GRU)
OS: Office of Security (CIA)
OSS: Office of Strategic Services (forerunner of the CIA)
PCS/LOC: Policy Coordination Staff/Liaison and Oversight Control
POA: Provisional Operational Approval (CIA)
PP: Psychological and Paramilitary Operations Staff (CIA)
PRQ: Personal Record Questionnaire (CIA)
SAC: Special Agent-in-Charge (FBI)
SAS: Special Affairs Staff (CIA Cuban operations)
SCLC: Southern Christian Leadership Conference
SEATO: Southeast Asia Treaty Organization
SCD: KGB Second Chief Directorate
SFNE: Frente Nacional del Escambray, "Second Front"
SG: Special Group (NSC, AKA "5412 Committee)
SGA: Special Group Augmented (NSC)
SNCC: Student Nonviolent Coordinating Committee
SNIE: Special National Intelligence Estimate
SO: Security Office (CIA)
SSCIA: Senate Select Committee on Intelligence Activities (Also "SSC"), AKA Church Committee
SRD: Soviet Russia Division (CIA)
TFW: Task Force W (CIA, Cuban operations)
UR: Revolutionary Unity (Cuban anti-Castro group)
USN: United States Navy
WHD: Western Hemisphere Division (CIA)
WH/4: Western Hemisphere Division/Branch 4 (CIA, Cuban operations)

BIBLIOGRAPHY

Arboleya, Jesus, *The Cuban Counterrevolution* (Miami: Ohio University, 2000)
Allison, Graham and Phillip Zelikow, *Essence of Decision: Explaining the Cuban Missile Crisis* (New York: Addison Wesley Longman, 1999)
Ambrose, Steven, *Ike's Spies: Eisenhower and the Espionage Establishment* (New York: Doubleday & Company, 1981)
Arsenault, Raymond, *Freedom Riders* (New York: Oxford University Press, 2006)
Bagley, Tennent H., *Spy Wars—Moles, Mysteries, and Deadly Games* (New Haven: Yale University Press, 2007)
____*Spymaster—Startling Cold War Revelations of a Soviet KGB Chief* (New York: Skyhorse Publishing, 2013)
____"Ghosts of the Spy Wars, A Personal Reminder to Interested Parties," *Journal of Intelligence and Counterintelligence*, Volume 28, No. 1, Spring 2017
Bamford, James, *Body of Secrets—Anatomy of the Ultra-Secret National Security Agency* (New York: Anchor Books, 2002)
Beschloss, Michael, *The Crisis Years: Kennedy and Khrushchev, 1960-1963* (New York: Edward Burlingame Books, 1991)
Bissell, Richard, *Reflections of a Cold Warrior* (New Haven: Yale University Press, 1996)
Boot, Max, *The Road Not Taken: Edward Lansdale and the American Tragedy in Vietnam* (New York: Liveright, 2018)
Bowles, Chester, *Promises to Keep* (New York: Harper and Row, 1971)
Branch, Taylor, *Parting the Waters: America in the King Years 1954-63* (New York: Simon & Schuster, 1988)
Breckinridge, Scott, *CIA and the Cold War* (Westport, Connecticut: Praeger, 1993)

Bundy, McGeorge, *Danger and Survival: Choices About the Bomb in the First Fifty Years* (New York: Schwartz & Wilkinson, 1990)

Burns, James MacGregor, *John Kennedy: A Political Profile* (New York: Harcourt, Brace & Company, 1960)

Carl, Leo D., **CIA Insider's Dictionary of U.S. and Foreign Intelligence, Counterintelligence and Tradecraft** (Washington, D.C.: NIBC Press, 1996)

Carson, Clayborne, Senior Editor, **The Papers of Martin Luther King, Jr.**, vol. IV, Volume editors: S. Carson, A. Clay, V. Shadron and K. Taylor, (Berkeley - Los Angeles: University of California Press, 2000)

Chang, Lawrence and Peter Kornbluh, **The Cuban Missile Crisis, 1962** (New York: The New Press, 1992)

Crankshaw, Edward, ***Khrushchev Remembers*** (New York: Little, Brown and Company: 1970)

Dallek, Robert, *An Unfinished Life, John F. Kennedy, 1917-1963* (New York: Little, Brown and Company, 2003)

Epstein, Edward J., *Deception—The Once and Future Cold War* (New York: G. P. Putnam, 1989)

Escalante, Fabian, *The Secret War: CIA Covert Operations Against Cuba, 1959-62* (New York: Ocean Press, 1995)

____*The Cuba Project* (New York: Ocean Press, 2004)

Fonzi, Gaeton, ***The Last Investigation*** (New York: Skyhorse, 2013 Edition)

Garrow, David, ***Bearing the Cross*** (New York: Open Road Media, 2015)

Galbraith, John Kenneth, ***Ambassador's Journal*** (New York: Paragon House, 1969 ed.)

____*A Journey Through Economic Time—A Firsthand View* (New York: Houghton Mifflin, 1994)

Galbraith, James, "Did the U.S. Military Plan a Nuclear First Strike for 1963?" *The American Prospect*, Fall 1994, pp. 88-96.

Golitsyn, Anatoliy, ***New Lies for Old*** (San Pedro California: GSG & Associates, 1984)

Grimes, Sandra, and Jeanne Vertefeuille, ***Circle of Treason*** (Annapolis: Naval Institute Press, 2012)

Halberstam, David, ***The Best and the Brightest***, (New York: Fawcett, 1973)

Helms, Richard, with William Hood, *A Look over my Shoulder—A Life in the Central Intelligence* Agency (New York: Random House, 2003)

Hersh, Seymour, ***The Dark Side of Camelot*** (New York: Little, Brown and Company, 1997 ed.)

Holland, Max, "The 'Photo Gap' That Delayed Discovery of Missiles," *Studies in Intelligence*, Vol. 49, No. 4.

Hood William, *Mole—The True Story of the First Russian Spy to Become and American Counterspy* (London: Endeavor Press, 1982)

BIBLIOGRAPHY

Hunt, E. Howard, *Give Us This Day—the Inside Story of the Bay of Pigs Invasion* (New Rochelle, N.Y.: Arlington House, 1973)

Johnson, U. Alexis, *Right Hand of Power* (New York: Prentice-Hall, 1984)

Kalugin, Oleg, *Spymaster* (New York: Basic Books, 2009)

Kempe, Frederick, *Berlin 1961—Kennedy, Khrushchev, and the Most Dangerous Place on Earth* (New York: G.P. Putnam's Sons, 2011)

Kennedy, John F., *The Strategy of Peace* (New York: Harper & Brothers, 1960)

Kennedy Robert F. Jr., *American Values—Lessons I Learned from My Family* (New York: Harper Collins Publishers, 2018)

King, Martin Luther Jr., Clayborne Carson, Editor, *The Autobiography of Martin Luther King, Jr.* (New York: Grand Central Publishing, 1976)

Kinzer, Stephen, *The Brothers—John Foster Dulles, Allen Dulles, and Their Secret World War* (New York: St. Martin's Press, trade paper edition, 2013)

Koehler, John O., *Stasi: The Untold Story of The East German Secret Police* (Boulder: Westview Press, 1999)

Lewis, John in Fred Hampton, *Voices of Freedom* (New York: Bantam Books, 1990)

Maheu, Robert, *Next to Hughes* (New York: Harper Collins, 1992)

Mahoney, Richard D, *JFK: Ordeal in Africa* (New York: Oxford University Press, 1983)

____*The Kennedy Brothers—The Rise and Fall of Jack and Bobby* (New York: Arcade Publishing, 2011 edition)

Murphy David E., Sergei Kondrashev and George Bailey, *Battleground Berlin* (New Haven: Yale University Press, 1997)

Nechiporenko, Oleg, *Passport to Assassination* (New York: Birch Lane Press, 1993)

Newman, John, *Oswald and the CIA* (New York: Skyhorse, 2008)

____*JFK and Vietnam: Deception, Intrigue and the Struggle for Power* (Amazon: Create Space, 2017 Edition)

____*Where Angels Tread Lightly—The Assassination of President Kennedy, Volume I* (Amazon: Create Space, 2017 Edition)

____*Countdown to Darkness—The Assassination of President Kennedy, Volume II* (Amazon: Create Space, 2017)

Niebuhr, Reinhold, *Moral Man and Immoral Society* (New York: Charles Scribner's Sons, 1932),

Nixon, Richard M. *Six Crises* (New York: Doubleday & Company, Inc., 1962)

O'Sulllivan, Shane, *Dirty Tricks—Nixon, Watergate, and the CIA* (New York: Hot Books, Skyhorse Publishing, 2018)

Penkovsky, Oleg, *The Penkovsky Papers* (New York: Doubleday, 1965)

Phillips, David Atlee *The Night Watch: Twenty Five Years of Peculiar Service* (New York: Atheneum, 1977)

____*Secret Wars Diary—My Adventures in Combat, Espionage Operations and Covert Action* (Bethesda MD: Stone Tail Press, 1989)

Prouty, Fletcher, **The Secret Team** (Englewood Cliffs, NJ: Prentice-Hall, 1973)

Rathbone, John, **The Sugar King of Havana** (New York: Penguin Press, 2010)

Reibling Mark, **Wedge: The Secret War Between the FBI and CIA** (New York: Knopf, 1994)

Rusk, Dean, **As I Saw It** (New York: Penguin, 1991 ed.)

Russell, Middleton, "The Civil Rights Issue and Presidential Voting Among Southern Negroes and Whites," Social Forces, 40: 209–215, March 1962

Schlesinger, Arthur Jr., **A Thousand Days: John F. Kennedy in the White House** (New York: Houghton Mifflin, 2002 ed.)

____**RFK and his Times** (New York: Houghton Mifflin, 2002 Ed.)

Scott, Peter Dale, **Oswald, Mexico, and Deep Politics: Revelations from CIA Records on the Assassination of JFK** (New York: Skyhorse Publishing, 2013)

____**Dallas 63—the First Deep State Revolt Against the White House** (Forbidden Bookshelf, Kindle, 2016)

____ **Deep Politics II: Essays on Oswald, Mexico, and Cuba** (Skokie, Illinois: Green Archive Publications, 1995)

Ted Shackley, **Spymaster—My Life in the CIA** (Washington D.C., Potomac Books, 2006, paper ed.)

Smith, Richard Harris, "The First Moscow Station: An Espionage Footnote to Cold War History," **Journal of Intelligence and Counterintelligence**, 1989, Volume 3, Number 3, pp. 333-346.

Sorensen, Theodore, **Kennedy** (New York: Harper & Row, 1965)

Stevenson, Charles, **The End of Nowhere: American Policy toward Laos since 1954** (Boston: Beacon, 1972)

Stockton, Bayard, **Flawed Patriot: The Rise and Fall of CIA Legend Bill Harvey** (Washington D.C.: Potomac Books, 2006)

Summers, Anthony, **Conspiracy** (New York: Paragon House, 1989)

____**Not in Your Lifetime** (New York: Open Road, 2013 Edition)

Talbot, David, **The Devil's Chessboard—Allen Dulles, the CIA, and the Rise of America's Secret Government** (New York: Harper Collins, 2015)

Taylor, Frederick, **The Berlin Wall: August 13, 1961 - November 9, 1989** (New York: Harper Collins, 2007)

Taylor, Maxwell, **Swords and Plowshares**, (Boston: De Capo Press, 1990)

Thomas, Evan, **The Very Best Men** (New York: Simon and Schuster, 1995)

Thomas, Hugh, **Cuba—The Pursuit of Freedom** (New York: Harper & Row, 1971)

Richard C. Thornton, "Soviet Strategy and the Vietnam War," **Asian Affairs**, No. 4, March-April 1974, pp. 205-228.

BIBLIOGRAPHY

Veciana, Antonio, *Trained to Kill—The Inside Story of CIA Plots Against Castro, Kennedy, and Che* (Skyhorse: New York, 2017)
Weber, Ralph, *Spymasters: Ten CIA Officers in their Own Words* (Lanham MD: Rowman & Littlefield Publishers, 1999)
Weiner, Tim, *Legacy of Ashes* (New York: Anchor Books, 2008, Paper edition)
West, Nigel, *Historical Dictionary of Cold War Counterintelligence* (Lanham MD: Scarecrow Press, 2007)
White, Theodore H., *The Making of the President, 1960* (New York: Harper Collins, 1961)
____*The Making of the President, 1964* (New York: Harper Collins, 1965)
Zinn, Howard, *SNCC—The New Abolitionists* (New York: Haymarket Books, 2013 edition)
Zubok, Vladislav and Constantine Pleshakov, *Inside the Kremlin's Cold War—From Stalin to Khrushchev* (Cambridge: Harvard University Press, 1996)

Reports, Government, and Miscellaneous Sources
The CIA Inspector General's (IG) *Report on Plots to Assassinate Fidel Castro*, 5/23/67, RIF 104-10213-10101.
6/24/66, Howard J. Osborne, Director of Security, Memorandum for the Deputy Director of Central Intelligence; RIF 104-10122-10218.
Alleged Assassination Plots Involving Foreign Leaders, United States Senate, Interim Report of the Select Committee to Study Governmental Operations (Washington DC: US Government Printing Office, 1975)
Jack B. Pfeiffer, the *CIA Official History of the Bay of Pigs Operations*, Volume III, p. 42; RIF 104-10301-10004.
Alleged Assassination Plots Involving Foreign Leaders, United States Senate, Interim Report of the Select Committee to Study Governmental Operations (Washington DC: US Government Printing Office, 1975)
The United States Navy and the Vietnam Conflict (Washington, D.C.: U.S. Government Printing Office, 1986)
FRUS (Foreign Relations of the United States), Department of State (Washington, D.C.: U.S. Government Printing Office)
PP (Pentagon Papers), Senator Gravel Edition (Five Volumes), 1975
PP (Pentagon Papers), Department of Defense Edition (Four Volumes), 1971
MFF (Mary Ferrell Foundation) web site

INDEX

Agayants, Ivan, (KGB): 218, 317-323, 332

Alpha-66: 92, 292-310, 312-314, 316

Angleton, James Jesus, (CIA C/CI): 75 n., 80, 197, 201, 213-215, 317, 326-327, 331-332, 336, 338

Grau Alsina, Maria Leopoldina: 186

Bagley, Tennent "Pete," (CIA SRD): vi, 197-206, 208-210 n., 213, 216-221, 223, 317-318 n., 320-340

Bannerman, Robert L. (CIA C/SO): 75, 79

Batista, Fulgencio: 78 n., 262, 273

Bender, Frank; pseudonym, see Gerry Droller

Betancourt, Ernesto: 259, 261-266, 268 n., 269, 272

Biniaris, Gordon' pseudonym, see James Joseph O'Mailia

Bissell, Richard, (CIA, DDP): 121-122, 179, 182-195, 225, 228, 230, 232, 236, 240-242, 246-249, 253, 257, 282-283, 341, 343-348, 359-360, 372 n., 374, 378

Blake, George: 209-210, 216

Blakey, G. Robert, (Chief Counsel HSCA): 86 n., 87

Blunt, Malcolm: vi, 299 n., 301 n., 305 n., 307 n., 311, 338-339

Booth, Amos; pseudonym, see Pete Bagley

Bowles, Chester (State Dept.): 94-95, 98 n., 100, 192

Breckinridge, Scott, (CIA): 86 n., 229-233, 251, 253-254, 343-344, 361-362

Bundy, McGeorge, (NS Advisor): 49, 101, 103, 106, 110, 113 n., 133-134, 140-141, 189-190, 298 n., 300, 303-304, 360, 373, 393-394

Burke, Arleigh (Admiral, CNO): 40, 97-103, 133, 288

Cabell, Charles P., General (CIA D/DCI): 183, 236, 240

Caro, Emilio Adolfo Rivero: 282

Carter, Marshall, General, (CIA DDCI): 240, 261, 263, 266 n., 268-269, 273, 302- 303 n., 304, 355-357, 360, 362, 371

Caso, Alberto Cruz: 186

Castro, Fidel: 2-5, 28, 68-74, 76-79, 83-88, 90-92, 94-97, 104, 107, 116, 118, 122 n., 129, 150, 179, 181-187, 189-195, 225-232, 235, 237, 240-243, 246-247, 249-251, 253-254, 257-258, 262, 266-268, 270-271, 273, 275-276, 278-280, 282, 284-289, 291-296 n., 302, 310-311, 313-316, 338-339, 341-362, 368, 370-375, 378-381, 383-384, 386, 389, 395, 401-403

Castro, Raul: 266, 287

411

INTO THE STORM

Charron, Lawrence R.; pseudonym, see Henry Hecksher

Cheever, Bruce B., (CIA): 240, 268, 272, 275, 290, 304, 352, 357

Choaden, Michael; pseudonym, see Dave Phillips

Church Committee: 91, 95, 182-184-185 n., 187-189, 194-195, 229, 232-237, 239, 243-246, 248-249, 251-254, 258-259, 261, 269-271, 275-278, 280, 286, 313, 315-316, 342-349, 352-353, 358-360, 364, 382, 393 n., 403

Church, Frank, Senator: 189, 194-195, 233-234, 243-246, 248, 250, 269-270, 345, 347

Colby, William, (DCI): 184, 187, 233, 253, 270, 344 n.

Cordova, Juan Orta: 185

Cubela, Rolando; **AMLASH-1:** 253, 342, 350, 352

Curbelo, Rodolfo Leon: 186

Dale, Alan: v

Decker, George, General (Army COS): 98-100

DeGagne, Ralph: 309, 313

Dillon, Douglas: 35 n., 41-43, 45, 61-63

Domnin, Gregory; pseudonym, see George Kisevalter

Droller, Gerry, (CIA): 288, 290-291

Drain, Richard, (CIA WH/4): 241

Dulles, Allen, (DCI): 77 n., 105-107, 121-122, 134, 179, 184-185, 187, 192-193, 236, 240, 329, 368 n., 369, 374, 390

Edwards, Sheffield, (CIA Director of Security): 184, 187-188, 240, 243, 278, 280, 348, 352-353

Eisenhower Dwight D., (President): 2, 9, 16, 31, 39, 42-43, 50, 59, 61, 69, 96, 99, 103, 105, 111, 120, 151, 344, 371-372

Escalante, Fabian: 66 n., 67, 69, 289-292

Esterline, Jacob D., (CIA WH/4): 121, 192, 240

Eugenio: See Emilio Rodriguez:

Farmer, James L., (CORE): 147, 152-153 n., 154-156, 160, 165, 171-175, 177-178

Ferrell, Mary, (MFF): vi, 90 n.

Fiscalini, Charles (Rocky); pseudonym, see Charles D. Ford

Fitzgerald, Desmond, (CIA SAS): 352

Fonzi, Gaeton: 65-66, 68-70, 82-86, 90-91, 281, 298-300, 308, 310-313, 315-316

Ford, Charles D., (CIA): 229, 231, 237, 239, 243, 251, 254, 258-261, 263-265, 267-271, 275, 280, 341, 353-354, 357, 360, 362, 364, 379

Galbraith, James: 106-107, 369

Galbraith, John Kenneth: 35, 41-42, 44, 48-50, 62

Giancana, Sam: 185

Golitsyn, Anatoliy, (KGB defector): 221-223, 317, 321, 323, 325-332, 334

Gonzalez, Reinol, Gonzalez: 89-90, 282 n., 284, 292

Gonzalez, Eduardo, Perez (AKA Eddie Bayo): 264-266

Gottlieb, Sidney, (CIA): 184 n.

Gray, Gordon, (National Security Advisor): 372

Gribanov, Oleg Mikhailovich, (KGB): 198, 201, 211-213, 215-221, 223, 317-319, 321-325, 327-329, 331-333, 340

Guevara, Che: 68, 76, 266, 274

Guk, Ivan, (KGB): 319-321, 323-325, 328-329

Halpern, Samuel, (CIA): 2, 179-195, 225-255, 257-280, 341-365

Hardway, Dan, (HSCA): vi

Harriman, Averell, (Ambassador): 42, 98 n.

INDEX

Harris, Patrick, pseudonym, See Milford Hubbard: 299, 307-313
Harvey, Jay: v
Harvey, William K., (FI/D): 92, 121-122, 131, 183-184, 188-194, 208-215, 227-254, 257-280, 290-305, 343-364, 372-393, 408
Hawkins, Jack, Colonel, (USMC): 121, 192, 286
Hecksher, Henry, (CIA): 75-76
Helms, Richard, (DCI): 229-259, 264, 268, 374-380, 406
Hersh, Seymour: 229-235, 260-263, 276-280, 358-365
Hicks, Calvin (CIA): 291-293, 298 n.
Hitch, Cal, pseudonym, See Calvin Hicks: 290-293, 269-272, 275, 337, 348-349, 355-356
Hood, William (CIA): 198-212, 406
Hoover, J. Edgar, (FBI Director): 95-96, 150-153, 160-161, 185, 212, 226 n., 337
Houston, Lawrence, (CIA IG): 243, 278-279
Hubbard, Milford, Captain, U.S. Army; pseudonym, see Patrick Harris: 301 n., 308-313
Hunt, E. Howard, (CIA): 378, 407
Izaguirre, Alfredo, Revoi: 282, 288-291
Johnson, Lyndon B., (President): 5, 94, 100 n., 109, 117
Johnson, U. Alexis: 98, 113, 407
Kennedy, John F., (President): iv, 9-33, 35-64, 93-116, 117-146, 147-178, 179-195, 225-255, 257-280, 296-316, 341-365, 367-388, 389-395
Kennedy, Robert F., (Attorney General): iii, vii, 9-33, 95, 141, 147-178, 179-195, 225-255, 257-280, 305-307, 341-365, 367-388, 389-395
King, J. C., (CIA C/WHD): 187, 375, 407
King, Martin Luther, Jr.: 3, 9-33, 147-178
Kisevalter, George, (CIA): 199-219, 323-329
Komarov (Kovshuk): 327-328, 209, 333
Kondrashev, Sergey, (KGB): 120-124 n., 138, 198-202, 211-225, 332-340, 407
Kostikov, Valery, (KGB): 5
Kovshuk, Vladislav, (KGB); pseudonym, see Komarov: 200, 209, 213, 218, 223, 323-333, 338
Khrushchev, Nikita, (Premier): 3-4, 94-97, 105-108, 113, 117-146, 162-163, 170, 207, 216-217, 302-306, 313, 317, 370, 384, 406, 409
Langelle, Russell, (CIA): 217, 324
Lansdale, Edward, General: 111, 114, 245, 255, 269, 319, 320, 322, 324-334, 338, 379, 406-422, 425, 428-430, 441
LeMay, Curtis, General, (Air Force COS): 98-101, 105, 149, 427
Lemnitzer, Lyman L., General (Chairman JCS): 98-100, 105-6, 108-9, 113, 117-9, 145-6, 319, 322, 324, 328, 333, 402-3, 406-7, 410, 414, 418-20, 422-24, 426-31
Lesar, Jim: (FOIA attorney, president, AARC): ii
Lobo, Julio: 61, 73-6, 82, 91, 307, 319, 322
Maheu, Robert: 198, 380,
Malone, Michael P.: 69, 70, 72
Maury, Jack, (SRD): 355
McCone, John, (DCI): 253-5, 258, 262, 275, 320-1, 329-33, 387, 389, 408-11, 414, 426, 427, 430
McGuire, Phyllis: 198, 199
McNamara, Robert S., (Secretary of Defense): 41, 94-95, 98-100, 105, 114-116, 119, 133-134, 138-141, 294, 301-302, 304, 373, 376, 386, 390-391, 393
Mikoyan, Anastas I.: 130-1
MRP, People's Revolutionary Party: 89-90, 284-285, 292-295, 298, 402
Murphy, David, (CIA SRD): 137, 145, 212-3, 216, 225-7, 230, 232, 234, 345, 368, 442

413

INTO THE STORM

Nechiporenko, Oleg, (KGB): 167, 368-9, 442
Niebuhr, Reinhold: 4-7, 12
Nixon, Richard M., (Vice President): 1-2, 9-12, 17, 21-3, 25-7, 37, 250, 343, 443
Noel, James, (CIA, Havana Station Chief): 68, 73, 306-8
Nosenko, Yuri (KGB defector): 347-62, 364, 367-8, 371
Olien, Woodward C.; pseudonym, see James Noel: 306
Operation Liborio: 290-292
Operation Mongoose: 230-233, 238, 282, 287, 294, 302-306, 361, 367-388
Operation Northwoods: 367-388
Operation Patty: 92, 287-289
Operation Poncew: 296-299
Operation Switchback: 111 n.
Osborne, Howard, (CIA): 201, 444
Oswald, Lee Harvey: 211-2, 215, 230-1, 241, 243, 304, 342-5, 361, 366-71, 442, 443
Parrott, Thomas, (CIA): 259, 421
Patterson, John, (Governor of Alabama): 164, 166, 172, 174-6, 181, 183-4, 187-90
Penkovsky, Oleg, (GRU): 235, 237-8, 310, 345, 443-4
Pfeiffer, Jack: (CIA): 126, 260
Phillips, David, (CIA WH/4): vii, xi, 61-8, 70-1, 72-84, 86-91, 245, 272, 283, 304-5, 315, 341-2, 344, 398, 412, 443-5
Polyakov, Dmitry, (KGB): 227-30, 235-9
Popov, Pyotr, (GRU): 212-226, 239, 244, 345, 352-4, 359-62, 370
Rayburn, Sam, (House Speaker):
Rionda, Czarnikow: 69
Rivero, Emilio Adolpho: 306-7, 310
Rodriguez, Emilio Americo (CIA): 78-9, 92, 106, 305, 308, 315
Roman, Jane (CIA CI/LIA): 294
Rostow, Walt: 34, 99, 103, 112, 115-7, 127-8
Roselli, Johnny: 262, 274-5, 296, 302, 379, 380, 383-5, 398, 414
Rowe, Gary Thomas, Jr.: 158, 161, 168-71
Rusk, Dean, (Secretary of State): 35, 99-102, 108, 117-8, 137, 140-1, 145-6, 148, 206, 324, 411, 426, 443
Russell, Dick: 61, 64-5
San Martin, Ramon Grau, (Cuban President): 200
Schlesinger, Arthur, Jr.: 2, 18, 20n, 34, 35n, 35-7, 38n, 39n, 41-2,43n, 51, 56-7, 59-60, 98-99, 100n, 105-9, 108, 110, 131, 132, 136, 140, 141n, 147, 148, 156, 157n, 159, 168, 171, 172n, 269, 378, 400,
Scott, Peter Dale: ii, 443
Sforza, Tony, (CIA): 92, 106, 305, 308
Shackley, Ted: 320, 385, 443
Shelepin, Aleksandr, (Chairman, KGB): "Shelepin Plan,": 122, 129, 234-5, 239, 345, 361
Shoup, David, General, (USMC Commandant): 100, 101, 198
Shriver, Sargent:19-27, 36
Shuttlesworth, Fred: 163, 170, 173, 175, 182, 184, 185
Silver, Arnold, (CIA): 184 n.
Smith, Dayle W.: 333-334
Smith, Edward Ellis: 208, 325, 329-332
Sorensen, Theodore: 26 ,39-40, 102, 135
Stevenson, Adlai, (UN Ambassador): 32, 41, 98, 102 n.
Summers, Anthony: 65, 80-3

INDEX

Taylor, Maxwell, General, (JCS Chairman): 103, 109-111, 113-114, 116, 136 n. -137 n., 141, 143 n.-145, 240 n., 262, 266, 288-289, 368, 371 n., 373-374, 376, 389-390, 394-395

Tharpe, Martha, (CIA WH/4): 307, 314, 320

Teeter, Christine (McGuire): 198

Teeter, John: 199

Thomas, Evan: 259, 261, 443

Todd, Peter; pseudonym, see William Hood: 213, 218, 224

Trafficante, Santo: 199-200

Trujillo, Raphael: 70

Varona, Manuel Antonio: 199-200, 207, 302, 307, 309, 315, 380, 383

Veciana, Antonio (Blanch): 65-92, 281-316

Weber, Ralph: 245-6, 250-3, 264-5, 268, 271-5, 373-5, 381-5, 444

White, Theodore: 2, 26, 41

Whitten, John, (CIA WH/4): 366, 369

Wofford, Harris: 9-11, 16-7, 18-27, 171-2

Zabala, Felix: 63, 321-2, 341-4

If we are going to make America great again, we need to start by understanding our own history. John Newman is uniquely qualified, as a distinguished historian and a highly experienced intelligence analyst, to illuminate that history. His research is an order of magnitude ahead of all others in the field. This book is the deepest dive yet into the secret story of the Kennedy years and the dark forces that led up to his assassination. *Into the Storm* is epic and cinematic in its sweep and scope.

—Eric Hamburg, Producer of *Nixon* film, and former aide to Senator John Kerry and Representative Lee Hamilton.

Dr. Newman's review and analysis of the now available documents is insightful and well-documented, shedding new light as well as testing things we thought we knew about the history of early 1960's America. Every serious student of this era should carefully consider this work. I highly recommend it.

—Dan Hardway, former HSCA investigator.

By centering his third book—*Into the Storm*—on the repeated misstatements of three men—Yuri Nosenko, Antonio Veciana, and Sam Halpern—Newman puts the roles of David Phillips, Bobby Kennedy, and the U.S. intelligence community into sharp focus. Now our work can continue on sure footing.

—Bill Simpich, author of *State Secret*

Into the Storm turns so-called "settled history" inside out. Major Newman once again challenges the prevailing orthodoxy and forces us to question, with much greater focus, "facts" previously taken for granted.

—Malcolm Blunt, British Researcher

Printed in Great Britain
by Amazon